Mary Jewry

Warnes Every-Day Cookery

Containing one thousand eight hundred and fifty-eight distinct receipts

Mary Jewry

Warnes Every-Day Cookery
Containing one thousand eight hundred and fifty-eight distinct receipts

ISBN/EAN: 9783744794053

Printed in Europe, USA, Canada, Australia, Japan

Cover: Foto ©Lupo / pixelio.de

More available books at **www.hansebooks.com**

PHILLIPS,

PRIZE MEDAL, By Appointment to H.R.H. PRIZE MEDAL.

The Prince  of Wales.

International Exhibition, 1862. ESTABLISHED 1760. International Exhibition, 1862.

358 & 359, OXFORD STREET, W.

NEXT TO THE PANTHEON,

AND

155, NEW BOND STREET, W.

CHINA AND GLASS MANUFACTURERS,

AND IMPORTERS OF FOREIGN CHINA & GLASS.

Messrs. W. P. AND G. PHILLIPS *respectfully solicit the favour of an inspection of their extensive stock of*

CHINA DINNER SERVICES,	from 14 to 60 Guineas.		
STONE	do.	,, 63s. to 18	,,
DESSERT	do.	,, 42s. to 50	,,
BREAKFAST	do.	,, 42s. to 10	,,
TEA	do.	,, 30s. to 10	,,
TOILETTE	do.	,, 10s. 6d. to 63s.	
RICHLY CUT TABLE GLASS,	in every variety.		
ENGRAVED	do.	of the most recherche designs.	

Ornamental Goods of all descriptions suitable for Wedding or Birthday Presents.

INDIAN ORDERS EXECUTED WITH DESPATCH.
NUMEROUS DESIGNS ALWAYS ON VIEW FOR FINISHING SERVICES TO ORDER, WITH CRESTS, MONOGRAMS, ETC.
Samples of any of the above sent carriage free.

DR. J. COLLIS BROWNE'S CHLORODYNE
IS THE ORIGINAL AND ONLY GENUINE.

The Public are CAUTIONED against the unfounded statements frequently made, "that the composition of CHLORODYNE is known to Chemists and the Medical Profession." The fact is, CHLORODYNE was Discovered and Invented by Dr. J. COLLIS BROWNE (ex-Army Medical Staff), and so named by him, and it has baffled all attempts at Analysis by the first Chemists of the day. The method and secret of the preparation have never been published. It is obvious, therefore, that anything sold under the name, save Dr. J. COLLIS BROWNE'S CHLORODYNE, is a spurious imitation.

CAUTION.—Vice-Chancellor Sir W. P. Wood stated that Dr. J. COLLIS BROWNE was, undoubtedly, the Inventor of CHLORODYNE.

CHLORODYNE is admitted by the Profession to be the most wonderful and valuable remedy ever discovered.

CHLORODYNE is the best remedy known for Coughs, Consumption, Bronchitis, Asthma.

CHLORODYNE effectually checks and arrests those too often fatal diseases—Diphtheria, Fever, Croup, Ague.

CHLORODYNE acts like a charm in Diarrhœa, and is the only specific in Cholera and Dysentery.

CHLORODYNE effectually cuts short all attacks of Epilepsy, Hysteria, Palpitation, and Spasms.

CHLORODYNE is the only palliative in Neuralgia, Rheumatism, Gout, Cancer, Toothache Meningitis, &c.

J. C. Baker, Esq., M.D., Bideford.—"It is, without doubt, the most valuable and certain Anodyne we have."

Dr. M'Millman, of New Galloway, Scotland.—"I consider it the most valuable medicine known."

*** Earl Russell communicated to the College of Physicians that he had received a despatch from Her Majesty's Consul at Manilla, to the effect that Cholera had been raging fearfully, and that the ONLY remedy of any service was CHLORODYNE.—See *Lancet*, Dec. 1, 1864.

Sold in Bottles at 1s. 1½d., 2s. 9d., and 4s. 6d. each. None is genuine without the words "Dr. J. COLLIS BROWNE'S CHLORODYNE" on the Government Stamp. Overwhelming Medical Testimony accompanies each Bottle.

Sole Manufacturer—J. T. DAVENPORT, 33, Gt. Russell Street, Bloomsbury, London.

NOTICE.—ALL BOXES issued by the Proprietors have the Government Stamp pasted over each box, instead of being on the outside wrapper as heretofore; and on each respective box and on the outside wrapper are printed the NAME and the TRADE MARK of the Firm, thus:

Are WARRANTED not to contain a single particle of MERCURY or any other MINERAL SUBSTANCE, but to consist entirely of Medicinal Matters, PURELY VEGETABLE.

For nearly Forty Years they have proved their value in thousands of instances in diseases of the Head, Chest, Bowels, Liver, and Kidneys; and in all Skin Complaints are one of the

BEST MEDICINES KNOWN.

Sold in boxes, price 7½d., 1s. 1½d., and 2s. 9d. each, by G. WHELPTON & Son, 3, Crane Court, Fleet Street, London; and by all Chemists and Medicine Vendors at Home and Abroad. Sent free on receipt of 8, 14, or 33 stamps.

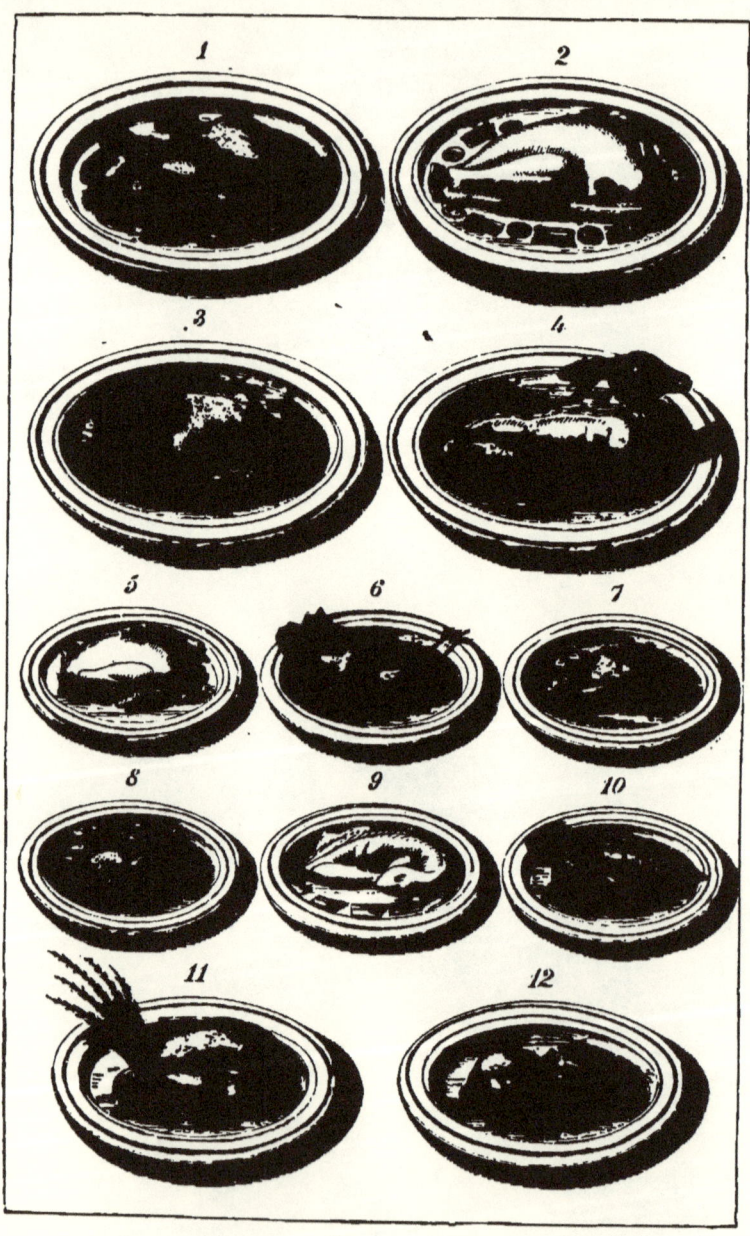

1. Roast Turkey.
2. Boiled Turkey.
3. Roast Goose.
4. Hare.
5. Boiled Fowl.
6. Roast Fowl.
7. Roast Duck.
8. Roast Pigeon.
9. Boiled Rabbit.
10. Roast Rabbit.
11. Roast Pheasant.
12. Partridges.

PREFACE.

The receipts in the "Every-day Cookery Book" are chiefly intended for persons of moderate income; though amongst them will be found some few which are expensive and elaborate.

The instructions in cookery are given in very full detail for the convenience of inexperienced housekeepers and cooks. For the same reason the nearest possible approximation to the time required for cooking the various dishes has been given; while the coloured plates will educate the eye of the cook, and enable her to judge how her preparations should look.

That the book may answer the purpose for which it is intended is the earnest hope of the Editor.

CONTENTS.

	PAGE		PAGE
The mistress of a family	1	Lamb	120
Allowance of food for one person weekly	1	Veal	123
		Pork	128
How to market	3	Venison	134
To choose poultry and game	8	Poultry	135
To choose fish	8	Made dishes and entrées	149
To choose eggs	8	Curries and Indian dishes	160
To choose vegetables	9	Meat pies and puddings	163
To choose apples	9	Vegetables—vegetable purées, salads, and salad mixtures	171
The store room	9		
Keeping accounts	10	Curing bacon, hams, &c.	188
Ordering dinner	11	Potting, collaring, &c.	188
Cook's calendar	13	To make pastes and pastry	196
Kitchen utensils	17	Mincemeat for mincepies	205
Plain directions for—		Baked and boiled puddings	206
Boiling	30	Pancakes and fritters	239
Boning	32	Flummery, blancmange, syllabubs, &c.	244
Braising	33	Soufflés and omelets	249
Broiling	31	Creams	253
Frying	32	Jellies and sweet dishes	260
Glazing	32	Second course dishes, relishes, &c.	273
Larding	32	Ices	276
Roasting	29	Biscuits and cakes	278
Sautéing	33	Dessert dishes	298
Steaming	34	Preserves and pickles	301
Stewing	31	Butter and cheese	318
A vocabulary of cooking terms	34	Wines, syrups, punch, cups, and brewing	322
Carving	35		
Bread, and breakfast dishes	42	Cooking for the sick	329
Fish	51	Luncheons, dinners, &c.	334
Soups	77	Useful receipts for housekeepers and servants	343
Sauces and gravies	91		
Forcemeats, garnishing, flavouring, &c.	99	Duties of household servants	346
Beef	104	Servants' characters	356
Mutton	114	Index	357

ILLUSTRATIONS.

	PAGE		PAGE
Aitchbone of beef	124	Jelly of two colours	228
Artichokes	184	Jerusalem artichokes	184
Asparagus	184		
		Kippered salmon	168
Beetroot	184		
Blancmange	288	Lobster	74
" rice	228	Lobster salad	168
Birds' nests	48		
Boiled fowl	144	Mackerel	74
" rabbit	144	Mayonaise of salmon	168
" turkey	144	Meringues	288
Brawn	48	Milan soufflé	288
		Minced veal	168
Calf's head	124		
Cauliflowers	184	Open jelly with whipped cream	288
Chantilly basket	228	Oranges and jelly	228
Chine of pork	124		
Cod's head	74	Partridges	144
Crab	74	Pears and rice	228
Crimped skate	74	Plover's eggs in a basket	48
Curried eggs	168	Plum-pudding	228
Custard with jelly	288	Pigeon pie	168
		Prawns	74
Eggs à la bonne femme	48		
Egg toast	48	Queen Mab's pudding	228
Fillet of veal	124	Rissoles	168
Fricandeau of veal	124	Roast duck	144
		" fowl	144
Grated ham and toast	48	" goose	144
		" pheasant	144
Haddock	74	" pig	144
Ham	124	" pigeon	144
Hare	144	" rabbit	144
Huîtres au lit	48	" turkey	144

Illustrations.

	PAGE		PAGE
Salmon	74	Twelfth cake	288
Scalloped oysters	74		
Sirloin of beef	128	Veal cake	168
Spinach and eggs	184	Vegetable marrow	184
		Vol-au-vent	168
Tartlets	288		
Toad in a hole	168	Wedding-cake	288
Trifle	228	Whiting	74
Turbot	74		

THE
EVERY-DAY COOKERY.

THE MISTRESS OF A FAMILY.

THE mistress of a family commands daily a small realm of which she is queen. Let her rule with justice, meekness, and quietness. The most self-governed person will always govern best, and we should have fewer bad servants if they were all under the firm and patient training of an employer who understood what their duties really were, and required the best fulfilment of them, compatible with the frailty of human nature.

Good temper, patience, and a knowledge of domestic matters, come first therefore in the list of requirements for a model housewife.

After these, we shall name *early rising*, which is very important.

A lady will find it best to give her servants orders for the day, *before breakfast*, if convenient, and, to do this well, she may judge of what is required. Her cook should have a book-slate and pencil, and enter the orders for dinner on one leaf of it, that there may be no mistakes made in them. On the other leaf she should be ordered to enter daily the amount of milk, bread, &c., bought on the previous day, which the mistress should then transfer to her commonplace book, to be entered in the account-book at the end of the week.

She should pay all her bills, *if possible*, every week. If some few remain to be paid quarterly, she should not on that account delay to examine them weekly, and to make up the week's accounts. She will then be sure of her expenditure.

She must take care that the butcher always brings a ticket of weight with the meat; and have those weight tickets brought to her weekly in order that she may compare them with the entries in her book. All meat brought into the house should be weighed to see if the ticket is correct, and for this purpose a pair of scales should be kept in the kitchen; groceries, &c., should also be tested as to weight on receipt of them.

She should ascertain the price of every article of food in her neighbourhood; as prices differ with localities, and that which might be economical food in one place is frequently the reverse in another. In order to learn the prices, she must not disdain to market for herself, if she is her own housekeeper. She will thus be able by personal observation to learn which are the best shops for different articles, and what are the fair rates of payment for them. It is also essential that a housekeeper should know the average weekly consumption for food of each person in an ordinary family, that she may be able to check waste and provide provisions for any period she may desire. For this purpose we subjoin a list of the usual allowances, which will of course vary very much from differing circumstances; but it will give a general idea on the subject, which personal experience will modify :—

Food for one Person Weekly.

Tea, two ounces.
Coffee, a quarter of a pound (if for breakfast only).
Cocoa paste, a quarter of a pound, for breakfasts.
Sugar, half a pound.
Cheese, half a pound.
Butter, half a pound.
Milk, one quart; varying with the taste of the family.
Bread, eight pounds for a woman, sixteen pounds for a man or boy.
Meat, six pounds.
Beer, one gallon for a woman, seven quarts for a man.
Potatoes, three and a half pounds.

Of course this estimate of quantities must be modified greatly by the habits and tastes of the family, and by the fact of residence either in the town or country.

A large supply of vegetables, fish, or puddings will greatly reduce the scale of meat; and making tea and coffee for numbers will reduce the amount of those articles. We merely give this general *idea* of quantity to guide, in a measure, the inexperienced housewife. We should have been thankful for such knowledge ourselves, as without it one invariably buys more than is actually needed for the consumption of the household.

With regard to meat, an allowance must be made for its waste in cooking (of which a table is given in this work), and also for the weight of bone found in every joint, except buttock of beef.

Having advanced thus far in our knowledge of housekeeping, the next step is how *to choose* meat,

An ox is divided by the butcher into the following joints:—*London style.*

1. Sirloin.
2. Top, or aitch-bone.
3. Rump.
4. Buttock, or round.
5. Mouse buttock.
6. Veiny piece.
7. Thick flank.
8. Thin flank.
9. Leg.
10. Forerib (5 ribs).
11. Middle rib (4 ribs).
12. Chuck rib (3 ribs).
13. Shoulder, or leg-of-mutton piece.
14. Brisket.
15. Clod.
16. Sticking.
17. Shin.
18. Cheeks or Head.

HOW TO MARKET.

We advise our lady housekeepers to market for themselves; but as some skill is required in a purchaser (if this duty is to be performed to advantage), we will endeavour to give directions by which inexperienced housewives may be enabled to choose good articles.

First in the list comes butcher's meat; of which beef is considered the best by the generality of English people. An ox should be kept five or six years before it is killed; it is then in its prime. *Ox-beef* is the best. It is a fine grained meat; the lean of a bright red colour, intermingled with grains of fat, when it is well fed and good. The fat should be white, not yellow, and the

A CALF is cut into the following joints:—

1. Loin, best end.
2. Loin, chump end.
3. Fillet.
4. Hind knuckle.
5. Fore knuckle.
6. Neck, best end.
7. Neck, scrag end.
8. Blade bone.
9. Breast, best end.
10. Breast, brisket end.
11. Head.

suet also white and firm. Beef should never be lean; it is tough and bad unless there is a good quantity of fat. Heifer-beef is paler than ox-beef, and closer grained; the fat whiter, and the bones, of course, smaller. Bull-beef is only described to be avoided. It is dark-coloured and coarse-grained; has very little fat, and a strong meaty smell about it.

Of these joints choose the rib or sirloin for roasting. If you purchase ribs of beef, let them be the middle ribs. You may have one, two, three, or four ribs, as you will; but one rib is too thin to be economical, as it dries up in cooking. If, however, your family be small, a single rib, with the bones taken out, rolled and stuffed, will make a nice little roast. If you buy a sirloin, take care to have it cut from the chump end, which has a good under cut or fillet, as then, in addition to a roast joint, you will have another dish—*i.e., fillets-de-bœuf*, one of the best dishes ever served.

The rump is preferred to the sirloin by

A SHEEP is thus divided:—

1. Leg.
2. Chump end of loin.
3. Best end of loin.
4. Neck, best end.
5. Neck, scrag end.
6. Shoulder. 7. Breast.

A saddle is the two loins undivided. A chine is the two sides of the neck undivided.

Hints to Housekeepers. 5

epicures; but it is too large to serve whole. A sufficiently large joint is cut from the chump end to roast.

For the servants' hall, or as a dinner for a large family where economy is essential, the buttock of beef is excellent, and very profitable. It is cheaper than the other roasting portions of the ox, has no bones, and affords quantities of rich gravy. But it should be hung for sometime until quite tender. The round, aitch-bone, and silver-side are usually salted and boiled. The neck is used for making soup or gravy—ask for it as "gravy beef;" the thin flank is the part to be collared. A "rumpsteak" is to be ordered for frying, &c. A "beefsteak" does for stewing, puddings, pies, &c. The inferior and cheaper parts of beef make excellent *bouilli*—a dish for which you will find directions in the body of the book.

VEAL should be small and pink, and the kidney well covered with fat. The calf should not be older than eight or ten weeks when it is killed, or the flesh will be coarse. If veal is large it should be cheaper, as it is less delicate. The flesh should be dry, closely grained, and pinky; if it is moist and clammy it is stale, and not fit for cooking.

The fillet, loin, shoulder, and best end of the neck, are the roasting joints. The breast is sometimes roasted in very small families, but it is usually stewed, as is also the knuckle; or the knuckle may be boiled, and served with parsley and butter. A calf's head is a delicacy. Calf's feet are

1. Leg. | 2. Loin. | 3. Shoulder. | 4. Breast. | 5. Ribs.
3, 4, 5, together, Fore-quarter.

also valuable boiled, stewed, or used for jelly. Veal makes the best stock for rich soups and gravies. It is a most useful meat for made dishes of all kinds, on account of its delicate flavour.

MUTTON.—Wether mutton is the best. It may be known by its having a knob of fat on the upper part of the leg. It should be dark-coloured, and have plenty of fat. The colour is important, as it is a proof of age, and the older mutton is the better it is. It should, properly, be the flesh of a sheep four or five years old, to be in perfection, but such meat is rarely to be bought at a butcher's; one tastes it only at the houses of country gentlemen who kill their own animals.

All the joints of a sheep may be roasted. The saddle is the best. The haunch is next best to the saddle; it is the leg and loin undivided. The leg and neck are frequently boiled. The leg and loin, separated, are the best joints after the haunch. Chops are cut from the loin; cutlets from the thick end of the loin, best end of the neck, or middle of the leg. The leg is sometimes cured and smoked as a ham. The breast of mutton is often salted and boiled. The scrag end of mutton is very good stewed with rice.

LAMB should be small; of a pale-coloured

A DEER is cut up in four portions.

1. Haunch.
2. Neck.
3. Shoulder.
4. Breast.

Hints to Housekeepers.

red, and fat. Lamb is generally roasted. The leg of "house-lamb" (which is in season just before Christmas), is sometimes boiled and served with white sauce.

VENISON is not very often bought, but when it is you can tell as to its being "high" or not, by running a skewer into the shoulder, and observing the scent on it when withdrawn. The fat should be thick and clean. If the cleft of the haunch is smooth and close, the animal is young.

PORK. — Buy pork of a respectable butcher; or get it from some place where you know it has been carefully fed; from a dairy farm is the best place, or from a miller's, or even from some country neighbour, as diseased or bad pork is very dangerous food. The fat of pork should be firm, and the lean white, and finely grained. The rind or skin thin and smooth. If the flesh feels clammy to the touch, the pork is bad. If the fat has kernels in it, the pig has been measly, and the meat should not be eaten. Pork should be perfectly sweet to be good, therefore do not hang it long.

BACON.—If bacon is good the rind is

The PIG is divided thus :—

thin, the fat firm and pinkish, the lean tender and adhering to the bone. Rusty bacon has yellow streaks in it.

HAMS are tried by sticking a knife or skewer into them up to the knuckle; if when drawn out it has a nice smell, the ham is good. A bad scent will be perceived if it is tainted.

The roasting joints of pork are the spare rib, loin, and leg; the other joints are salted; the leg may also be cured and boiled. The sides or flitches are made into bacon. The leg makes a ham.

Meat should be wiped with a dry, clean cloth as soon as it comes from the butcher's; flyblows should be cut out, and in loins, the long pipe that runs by the bone should be taken out, as it soon taints; the kernels also should be removed from beef. Never receive *bruised* joints. If you wish to keep your meat hanging longer than ordinary, dredge it well with pepper. Powdered charcoal dusted over it will also prevent its tainting, nay, will absolutely remove the taint from meat already gone. We have seen a pair of fowls quite green from unavoidably long keeping, made fresh and sweet as ever by being sprinkled with powdered charcoal for an hour before dressing. In hot summers it is very advisable to keep a lump of charcoal in the larder. Meat becomes more digestible and tender by hanging, but lamb and veal cannot be kept so well as beef and mutton. Remember that the best, and therefore the dearest joints are the most economical in the end, because they contain more solid meat than the others; but very large joints are not economical for a small family; nor are they as wholesome as our old-fashioned English prejudices once deemed them.

Poultry and Game, to Choose.

TURKEY.—The cock bird, when young, has a smooth black leg with a short spur. The eyes are bright and full, and the feet supple, when fresh; the absence of these signs denotes age and staleness; the hen may be judged by the same rules.

FOWLS.—The young cock has a smooth leg and a short spur; when fresh, the vent is close and dark. Hens, when young, have smooth legs and combs; when old, these will be rough; a good capon has a thick belly and large rump, a poll comb, and a swelling breast.

GEESE.—In young geese the feet and bills will be yellow, and free from hair. When fresh, the feet are pliable; they are stiff when stale.

DUCKS may be selected by the same rules.

PIGEONS, when fresh, have supple feet, and the vent will be firm; if discoloured they are stale.

PLOVERS, when fat, have hard vents; but like almost all other birds, may be chosen by the above rules.

HARES.—When a hare is young and fresh, the cleft in the lip is narrow, the body stiff, and the claws are smooth and sharp; old and stale hares will be the opposite of this. Rabbits the same. In order to ascertain whether a hare is young or old, turn the claws sideways; if they crack it is young. The ears also should be tender and capable of bending easily.

PARTRIDGES.—Yellow legs and a dark bill are signs by which a young bird may be known; a rigid vent when fresh. When this part is green the bird is stale.

PHEASANTS may be chosen as above; the young birds are known by the short or round spur, which in the old is long and pointed.

MOOR GAME.—Grouse, Woodcocks, Snipes, Quails, Ortolans, &c., may be chosen by the rules above given.

Choose white legged fowls for boiling, and dark for roasting.

To Choose Fish.

The eyes of fish, if fresh, are bright, the gills of a fine clear red, the body stiff, and the smell not unpleasant. Chloride of soda will restore fish that is not extremely fresh, but it is never so good as when it has not been kept.

A turbot should be thick; the under side of a pale yellowish white, the colour of rich cream.

The salmon and the cod should have a small head, very thick shoulders, and a small tail. The flesh of the salmon should be of a bright red colour, the scales very bright.

Do not buy herrings, mackerel, or whitings unless *quite* fresh, and do not attempt to keep them even till the next day. Cod may be kept twenty-four hours. Soles the same.

Eels should be bought alive. Crabs and lobsters should be heavy and very stiff: if they feel limp they are stale. They are often bought alive. Oysters, if fresh, will close forcibly on the knife when opened. If the shell gapes in the least degree, the oyster is losing its freshness. When the fish is dead the shell remains open. Small "natives" are the best oysters for eating; for sauces or other culinary purposes the larger kinds are good enough.

To Choose Eggs.

Shake the eggs; if they are bad they will

Hints to Housekeepers.

rattle. But we think the best plan is to put them in a basin of water, and see if they lie on their side, down in it. If the egg turns upon its end, it is bad; if it lies obliquely, it is only *not quite fresh*, but may do for puddings, &c.

M. Soyer tells us that the "safest way is to hold them up to the light, forming a focus with your hand; should the shell be covered with small dark spots they are very doubtful." . . . "If, however, in looking at them you see no transparency in the shells, you may be sure they are rotten and only fit to be thrown away. The most precise way is to look at them by the light of a candle; if quite fresh there are no spots upon the shells, and they have a brilliant light yellow tint."

Eggs to be preserved for use should be *quite* fresh from the nest.

To Choose Vegetables.

Take care that they are fresh-looking and crisp.

POTATOES.—*We* think the best are the walnut-leaf kidney for summer and the regents for winter use. But tastes differ so much with regard to potatoes, that we can only advise buying them of the best and most respectable dealers.

To Choose Apples.

In choosing apples, be guided by the weight; the heaviest are the best, and those should always be selected which, on being pressed by the thumb, yield to it with a slight crackling noise. Prefer large apples to small, for waste is saved in peeling and coring them.

Apples should be kept on dry straw in a dry place, and pears hung up by the stalk.

The Store-Room.

Every lady should have a small closet for her stores if she has not a regular storeroom. Groceries should always be bought in quantities, if possible; thus the turn of the scale and the weight of paper, &c., is saved. At certain seasons of the year some articles may be bought cheaper than at others. Advantage should be taken of any fall in the market.

A book should be kept in the store-room to enter the date when each store is bought, and at what price.

The store-room should be very dry, and furnished with drawers, shelves, and nails, with a few little nets suspended from them for hanging lemons in. It should contain also earthenware jars for sugars, and tins for keeping tea, coffee, and biscuits. The large or small tins in which biscuits are sold should be retained for these uses. Jams, pickles, and preserves should be kept in the coolest part of the room or closet. Coffee should not be bought in large quantities, because it soon loses its flavour; unless, indeed, it is roasted at home, which is a very economical plan for large families. It can be bought very cheaply unroasted; if purchased by the twenty-eight pounds it can be had at one shilling per pound; and there is a roaster (peculiar to Ireland) which is turned over the fire like a mop, that any one can use with ease, to prepare it whenever required.

Loaf sugar should be *very* white, close, heavy, and glittering; it is economy to buy the best, as the more refined the sugar is, the less the quantity required for sweetening.

Moist or brown sugar should have a crystalline, sparkling look, and should not be too powdery or sandlike.

Tallow candles should be bought in large quantities, if possible; and purchased in the winter, as they keep best when made in cold weather. They should be kept several months in a cool place before they are used. Soap should be bought by the hundredweight for cheapness, and kept long before it is used. It should be cut in pieces fit for use, and then put in a drawer to dry and harden slowly, without being exposed to the air; for if it were to dry quickly it would be likely to break when used. Mottled soap is the most economical; the best yellow soap melts much more rapidly in water. Soft soap for washing linen is a saving of half the quantity; therefore it is economical, though dearer in price than hard soap. Soda, by softening the water, saves soap.

Starch should be left in a warm, dry place. Sugar, sweetmeats, and salt, must all be kept *very dry.*

Rice, tapioca, sago, &c., should be kept close covered, or they will get insects in them; it is better *not* to have large supplies of these articles.

Buy lemons in June or July when they are freshly imported, and hang them in separate nets, for if they touch they will spoil.

Onions, shallots, and garlic should be hung in ropes from a ceiling in an out-house (*not* in the store-room); and parsley, basil, savory, knotted marjoram, and thyme should be dried and hung up in paper bags, each bag containing only one description of herb. They should be dried in the wind, and not in the sun, and when ordered in a receipt should be cautiously used, as a preponderance of one flavour in any seasoning spoils it.

When oranges or lemons are squeezed for

juice, chop down the peel, put it in small pots and tie it down for use.

Vegetables will keep best on a stone floor, out of the air.

Eggs may be preserved by brushing them all over the shell with a thin solution of gum and laying them in bran. Some persons brush them over with oil; in fact, anything which will render the shell impervious to the air suffices for the purpose of preserving them. Some friends of the author wash them with a solution of two quarts of quick-lime, half a pound of saltpetre, and an ounce of cream of tartar; but this is troublesome, and not so good as a more simple plan.

Suet may be kept for a twelvemonth, thus: choose the firmest and most free from skin or veins, remove all trace of these, put the suet in a saucepan at some distance from the fire, and let it melt gradually; when melted, pour it into a pan of cold spring water; when hard, wipe it dry, fold it in white paper, put it into a linen bag, and keep it in a dry cool place; when used it must be scraped; it will make an excellent pie-crust, either with or without butter.

The trouble of housekeeping is much diminished by having a fixed day for giving out to the cook the tea, sugar, coffee, plums, &c., which are likely to be required during the coming week; weighing out the quantities in proportion to the number of the family. Every week she should account for these quantities, bringing back whatever may chance to remain over and above her use.

The spice-box in the kitchen should be occasionally replenished from the store-room.

Keeping Accounts.

So many good Housekeeper's books are now published that much need not be said as to the mode of entry. But we think daily expenses are too minute in small families to be entered under all the various headings in most of the books with printed lists. The housewife is advised to keep a tiny MS. book and pencil in her pocket, and enter *at the moment* everything she buys or receives in the course of the day. This little record may be examined once a week, and its contents (so far as they relate to housekeeping) entered in the family account-book. The cook should produce her slate to check the lady's accounts, and the amount should be carefully added up.

We prefer ourselves a plain-ruled account-book *without* printed items. Then on one side, the left, we enter whatever money we receive during the week; on the opposite page the outlay we have made, which, when added up, can be subtracted at the bottom of the left page from the money received; a weekly check is thus placed on the expenditure, which is continually compared with the means of payment.

It is well to have a fixed sum for house-keeping, which may not be exceeded. If any amount may be *left*, it is a good reserve fund for extra expenses, or for charity.

Ready reckoners * will be found of great use both to save time, and also to help those who are slow at figures. One of them should always be kept lying next to or on the housekeeper's book.

Butcher's bills require careful weekly supervision, even when not paid till the quarter has elapsed, as errors in weight, even of ounces, or of price, as of farthings,† come to a considerable item in the course of the year. The memoranda of weight should be also compared with the book. One morning every week will suffice for these accounts, and, if faithfully carried out, the practice will be attended with a constant improvement in economy and good housekeeping.

Do not allow dripping or bones to become a perquisite of the cook. Dripping is most useful in a moderate family. It is an excellent medium for frying; it will make good family pie-crust, and supply the place of suet in a dumpling. Bones are absolutely necessary for making gravies and stock for soup.

Take care that butter is kept in a cool place and covered from the air. In summer get some saltpetre, dissolve it in cold water, and *stand* the butter crock in it, so that the saltpetre water may reach well up the sides. Cover it over with a wet cloth, the ends of which resting in the saltpetre water will keep it constantly moist. This is nearly as good as icing the butter.

Milk should be kept in scrupulously clean vessels, and stale and fresh milk should never be mixed, or the good will be spoiled.

Set apart from your income yearly a small sum to be invested in replacing worn household linen. Buy occasionally a tablecloth, a pair of sheets, &c., &c. You will feel these purchases much less than having to supply a whole stock of linen at once.

House linen should be looked over every six weeks or quarter, and carefully repaired. We like lavender-bags among the linen, to give it a fresh, agreeable smell; but some persons assert that they bring moth.

If you observe iron-moulds on the linen, speak at once to the laundress on the sub-

* See Warne's "Model Ready Reckoner."
† "My Market Table."

ject. It is possible she throws the washing cloths on a *brick floor*, which will cause iron-mould as soon as rusty iron does.

Ordering Dinner.

When economy is to be considered, ordering dinner requires some foresight and ingenuity in making one day tell into the next. Many very small families will have a large sirloin of beef on Sunday, say, and go on eating it cold and badly hashed day after day till it is gone. Now this need not be. Let the housewife choose the very same joint with a good undercut, and we will see how many different fresh dinners may be made from it in our bill of fare for a week.

1st. Let the cook turn back the fat and cut out the undercut, as it is called, leaving a little fat on it, and replacing the upper fat so as not to disfigure the joint. Cut off the flap (which will enable you to carve the joint more easily), and put it in pickle. Now cut the under part into *fillets-de-bœuf*, dress them according to our recipe, and you will have a delicious dish, No. 1.

The joint roasted, No. 2.

Cold, and a few slices of the least dressed parts cut up for beef olives, No. 3.

The flap-end nicely salted, boiled with a garnish of carrots, &c., No. 4.

But as we all object to dinners of "*toujours perdrix*," we advise the housewife to alternate these dishes thus :—

First dinner, Saturday—Fillets-de-bœuf, potatoes mashed in dish, also served fried in curled ribbons.

Sunday.—Roast beef, Yorkshire pudding, boiled potatoes or Brussels sprouts.

Monday—Roast loin of mutton, potatoes.

Tuesday—Cold beef and beef olives, potatoes, salad, stewed fruit or pudding.

Wednesday—Hashed mutton, or curry, vegetables.

Thursday—Rumpsteak, greens, potatoes.

Friday—Soup, any remains of cold meat curried, (or a little veal cutlet to make up), vegetables, &c.

Or if the inevitable leg of mutton be ordered (and it is unquestionably a good joint), it may be divided : the knuckle part boiled, the other end stewed with green peas ; but it does *not* roast well cut in halves, it is always spoilt as to flavour and juiciness.

We are writing now for those who are compelled to be economical. Therefore we may observe that the bones of the sirloin with a small addition of meat should be put into the stock-pot, and thus a nice soup may be obtained according to our recipes.

And do not let the housewife (hampered by small means) be frightened at the name of a sauce. Some of the best and most appetizing are really not expensive, if carefully made, and they will often suffice to turn a "scrap dinner" into quite a *recherché* little repast.

Ingenuity, care, and taste will do much to remedy the want of means. But if the wife has not a first-rate cook, let her try to dress any especial dish herself. Cultivated intellect will help her much more than she would suppose in mastering difficulties never overcome by an ordinary servant. It is said that cooks, as well as poets, must be to the manner born ; but we think the inspiration of affection may supply the birthright of talent, and the desire to add to home-happiness be strong enough to help the unsteady and unpractised hand. "Where there is a will there is a way."

If means are abundant, there is no sort of excuse for an ill-kept table ; then the wife (still studying the matter) may fearlessly exert her taste and vary the home fare with equal delicacy and address. She may have her "*fillets-de-bœuf*" still, for they are "a dainty dish to set before the queen," but she may retain the rolled flap on the joint, and eat boiled beef in its best form, the round or silver-side. She may vary meat with poultry, add game to her second course, and should never be without good soup. Still there should be no waste ; economy should be practised *for the sake of the poor,* who should be in every rich wife's thoughts.

We will give a nice and economical bill of fare here for a week, for six or eight persons, for the wife who can command a liberal sum for her table :—

SUMMER.

Sunday—Julienne soup, a sirloin of beef, half a calf's head, greens, potatoes, and cauliflower ; *pudding*, either baked tapioca, gooseberry pudding, or ramekins.

Monday—Middle slice of salmon, cold beef, hashed calf's head, asparagus, potatoes, salad ; *pudding*, apple or cold tapioca.

Tuesday—Salmon pudding, or *boudin de saumon* (from the remains of day before) leg of lamb, green peas, potatoes ; *pudding* boiled custards, or fruit tart (say currant and raspberry).

Wednesday.—Green pea soup, boiled chicken, cold lamb ; potatoes, salad ; *pudding*, Brazenose College pudding, or open jam tart (apricot).

Thursday.—Soles, fillet of veal, or bacon, asparagus, potatoes ; *pudding*, queen Mab's, or German pudding.

Friday.—Small turbot, rolled loin of mutton, minced veal, potatoes, early carrots ; *pudding*, slices of German pudding fried, or black currant pudding.

Saturday.—Curried turbot. rolled mutton (cold), roast duck,* green peas, potatoes ; *pudding*, cherry tart, boiled or baked custard.

This bill of fare may be varied weekly a multitude of ways, and let the house-wife remember that *variety* has an especial charm for the appetite.

To the wife who has to provide on *very* slender means we will now resume addressing ourselves.

Take care that your table-linen is spotlessly pure and white, the cloth well pressed, and that you have table napkins and finger glasses for dessert. These little elegancies cost next to nothing, and add immensely to the air of comfort and refinement which your table should possess. In summer, manage, if possible, to have a centre ornament of flowers, if only a cheap vase. In winter, the lamp will supply its place. Let the plate be well cleaned, the glasses *very* clear—in short, exquisite cleanliness, and everything which can charm the eye, will help you to make a poorer dinner more welcome than a sumptuous one would be with these delicacies omitted. You will find the style of your table one of those unconscious home-influences which will form the taste and tone of your children's minds, and greatly act on their manner. If you have not a very good cook, study the art a little yourself. Practise on one dish rather more frequently than on others, till you can do it to perfection.

A *well-dressed* mutton chop, an inexpensive yet appetizing pudding, will be a good dinner in themselves. *Whatever* you have, let it be *well-dressed*, and you have the essential principle of a first-rate dinner.

Dinner parties in the present day are rendered much less expensive affairs than they used to be, by the fashion of serving them in the Russian style. But this mode requires a sufficient number of servants for waiters, and a good carver ; also the table should be elegantly ornamented with fruit, flowers, &c. No one should attempt to give such dinners, who has not means to render them perfect. In fact, large formal dinner parties should not be given *at all* unless the host and hostess have good means. Evening parties are all that should be expected from people who are not rich, and they will be, in many instances, much better liked by the guests.

At the same time we would not suggest anything like inhospitality. A few friends —*really friends*—may meet round the home table with probably twice the pleasure of the regular diners-out ; and the house-wife should take care that these gatherings are made pleasant and easy by her previous care. She should not attempt anything beyond her means, nor try any dishes which she is not sure of making successfully. If she is careful (as she ought to be) to make her parlour-maid wait properly, and lay the table nicely, *every day*, she will be sure of her performance of the daily routine correctly, and the guests will be spared the anxious glances, divided attention, frowns, and signals of the hostess at the head of the table momentarily expecting catastrophes, and looking wretched, like a skeleton at an Egyptian feast. Let us advise her to have an ordinary but VERY good soup, very hot ; well-dressed fish ; *few* made dishes—two will be enough, handed round before the top and bottom dish are uncovered, and let them be very nicely made or not made at all. The joint and poultry should be plain but well dressed ; plates hot ; salt, water, and bread, within reach of each guest. The tiny sixpenny glass salt-cellars sold now are very useful ; one is placed between every two persons. A water caraffe covered with its glass should stand close by the plates of two guests, *i. e.*, one at each corner of the table, and one in the middle of each side will be essential. We are speaking only of a small friendly dinner, but these are *essential* comforts, and save waiting if they are ready at hand.

Any lady may venture to give a *little* dinner party in a *modified* Russian style, *i.e.*, put an épergne of flowers in the middle of the table ; arrange on each side of it a semicircle of dishes of fruits and sweetmeats, every two fruit dishes, divided by small glass plates, containing on one side preserved ginger, on the other, damson cheese, or any other sweetmeat. At the top and bottom of the table, soup and fish. When they are removed, the joints and poultry. The two side dishes on the sideboard are handed before the removes are uncovered. This will save the delay of spreading the dessert after the dinner is over. The cloth may be swiftly brushed, the fruit dishes drawn forward, and two centre ones placed on the table. In this form you will require fewer, *i. e.*, only two entrées or side dishes, and time will also be saved—a great object when there is only a single waiter.

The regular dinner *à la Russe* is served

---

* Ducks are a second course dish at first-rate dinners.

thus:—Either a silver or glass plateau runs down the centre of the table, or a handsome centre-piece of plate is placed in the middle of it, such as a silver tree, with figures or animals at the foot of it; or a raised centre dessert dish, containing fruit, flowers, &c. &c. (*See* engravings of Desserts towards the end of the volume.) Round this centre are small glass dishes of preserves; outside, alternate dishes of fruit, and vases of flowers with occasional bottles of sherry, and caraffes of water with their several tumblers on them, a finger glass holding a wine glass to each plate. In short, the table is made to look as handsome as possible with glass, plate, &c. &c. In each plate is a "carte" of the dinner.

The dishes are brought in and placed on the sideboard or on a side table. The soup is handed round, then the fish; then the side dishes or entrées. Next the removes, as turkey, roast saddle of mutton, &c. &c., ready carved, of course, and on the plate. Then comes the second course, *i.e.*, game, or duck, or artichokes, puddings, jelly, cream, tarts, &c.; next, cheese, maccaroni, celery, &c.

The butler goes round with the wine as usual—sherry, Champagne, hock, &c. &c.—between the courses.

Then the servants place the dessert plates, &c., and retire.

A much less number of dishes is required for this style of dinner, than were needed when it was usual to place them on the table. Dinner is more rapidly served; and each dish is handed *hot*, and at the moment i should be eaten.

THE COOK'S CALENDAR.

January.

Meat.
Beef
Doe venison
House lamb
Mutton
Pork
Veal

Poultry and Game.
Capons
Chickens
Ducks
Fowls
Geese
Grouse
Larks
Moor game
Partridges
Pheasants
Pullets
Snipes
Tame Pigeons
Turkeys, hen
Widgeons
Wild ducks
Woodcocks

Fish.
Barbel
Brill
Carp
Cod
Crabs
Crayfish
Dace
Eels
Flounders
Herrings
Lampreys

Ling
Lobsters
Mussels
Oysters
Perch
Pike
Plaice
Prawns
Salmon trout
Shrimps
Skate
Smelt
Soles
Sprats
Sturgeon
Thornback
Turbot

Vegetables.
Beet
Brocoli
Brussels sprouts
Cabbage
Cardoons
Carrots
Celery
Chervil
Colewort
Cresses
Endive
Garlic
Kale, Scotch
Leeks
Lettuces
Onions
Potatoes
Salsify
Savoys
Sorrel
Tarragon
Turnips
Winter spinach

Forced Vegetables.
Asparagus
Cucumber
Jerusalem artichokes
Mushrooms

Fruit.
Almonds
Apples, *i.e.*:
French pippin
Golden pippin
Golden russet
Kentish pippin
Nonpareil.
Winter pearmain
Pears:
Bergamot d'Holland
Bon Chrétien
Chaumontelle
Colmar
Chestnuts
Grapes
Medlars
Nuts
Oranges
Walnuts

Especially in Season.

Fish.
Haddocks
Tench
Whiting.

Poultry and Game.
Hares
Rabbits.

February.

Meat.
Beef
House lamb
Mutton
Pork
Veal

Poultry and Game.
Capons
Chickens
Ducklings
Fowl (wild)
Green geese
Hares
Partridges
Pheasants
Pullets
Poults
Rabbits (tame)
Snipes
Turkeys
Woodcocks

Fish.
Barbel
Brill
Carp
Cockles
Cod
Crab
Crayfish
Dace
Eels
Flounders
Haddocks
Herrings
Lampreys
Ling
Lobsters

Mussels
Oysters
Perch
Pike
Plaice
Prawns
Salmon
Shrimps
Skate
Smelt
Soles
Sturgeon
Tench
Thornback
Turbot
Whiting

Vegetables.
Beet
Brocoli
Cabbage
Cardoons
Carrots
Celery
Chervil
Cresses
Endive
Garlic
Leeks
Lettuces
Mushrooms
Onions
Parsnips
Potatoes
Salsify
Shallots
Sorrel
Spinach
Sprouts
Tarragon

Turnips
Winter savory

Forced Vegetables.
Asparagus
Cucumbers
Jerusalem artichokes

Fruit.
Apples:
French pippin
Golden pippin
Golden russet
Holland pippin
Kentish pippin
Nonpareil
Wheeler's russet
Winter Pearmain
Pears:
Bergamot de Pasque
Winter Bon Chrétien
Chestnuts
Oranges

Especially in Season.

Poultry.
Ducklings
Green geese
Turkey poults

March.

Meat.
Beef
House lamb
Mutton
Pork
Veal

Poultry and Game.
Capons
Chickens
Ducklings
Fowls
Green geese
Grouse
Leverets
Moor game
Pigeons
Snipes
Tame rabbits
Turkeys
Woodcocks

Fish.
Brill
Carp
Cockles
Cod
Conger eels
Crabs
Dory
Eels
Flounders
Lobsters
Ling
Mackerel
Mullet
Mussels
Oysters
Perch
Pike
Plaice
Prawns
Salmon
Salmon trout
Shrimps
Skate
Smelts
Soles
Sturgeon
Turbot
Tench
Whiting

Vegetables.
Artichokes (Jerusalem)
Beet
Brocoli
Brussels sprouts
Cabbage
Cardoons
Carrots
Celery
Chervil
Cresses
Endive
Garlic
Sea and Scotch kale
Lettuces
Mushrooms
Onions
Parsnips
Potatoes
Spinach
Turnips
Turnip tops

Forced Vegetables.
Asparagus
Beans
Cucumber
Rhubarb

Fruit.
Apples:
 French pippin
 Golden russet
 Holland pippin
 John apple
 Kentish pippin
 Nonpareil
 Norfolk biffin
 Wheeler's russet
Pears:
 Bergamot
 Chaumontelle
 St. Martial
 Winter Bon Chrétien
Chestnuts
Oranges

Forced Fruit.
Strawberries

Especially in Season.
Fish.
Mackerel
Mullet
Pears, cont.
Bon Chrétien
Carmelite
St. Martial
A few strawberries (if early).
Walnuts

April.

Meat.
Beef
Grass lamb
House lamb
Mutton
Pork
Veal

Poultry and Game.
Chickens
Ducklings
Fowls
Green geese
Leverets
Pigeons
Pullets
Rabbits
Turkey poults
Wood pigeons

Fish.
Brill
Carp
Chub
Cockles
Cod
Conger eel
Crabs
Dory
Eels
Flounders
Halibut
Herrings
Lobsters
Ling
Mackerel
Mullets
Mussels
Oysters
Perch
Pike
Plaice
Salmon
Shrimps
Skate
Smelts
Soles
Sturgeon
Tench
Trout
Turbot
Whitings

Vegetables.
Asparagus
Beans
Brocoli
Chervil
Cucumbers
Endive
Fennel
Lettuce
Onions
Parsley
Peas
Radishes
Rhubarb
Sea kale
Sorrel
Spinach
Small salad
Turnips
Turnip tops

Fruit.
Apples:
 Golden russet
 John apple.
 Nonpareil
 Wheeler's russet
Nuts
Oranges
Pears:
 Bergamot

May.

Meat.
Beef
Grass lamb
House lamb
Mutton
Pork
Veal

Poultry and Game.
Chickens
Ducklings
Fowls
Green geese
Leverets
Pigeons
Pullets
Rabbits
Wood pigeons

Fish.
Brill
Carp
Chub
Cod
Conger eels
Crayfish
Dace
Dories
Eels
Flounders
Gurnet
Haddocks
Halibut
Herrings
Ling
Lobsters
Mackerel
Mullet
Perch
Pike
Plaice
Prawns
Salmon
Shrimps
Skate
Smelts
Soles
Sturgeon
Tench
Trout
Turbot
Whitings

Vegetables.
Artichokes
Asparagus
Beans, kidney
Cabbage
Carrots
Cauliflowers
Chervil
Cucumbers
Lettuce
Onions
Peas
Potatoes, new
Radishes
Rhubarb
Salad of all kinds
Seakale
Sorrel
Spinach
Turnips

June.

Meat.
Beef
Grass lamb
House lamb
Mutton
Veal
Pork

Poultry and Game.
Chickens
Ducklings
Fowls
Green geese
Leverets
Pigeons
Plovers
Pullets
Rabbits
Turkey poults

Forced Fruit. Crabs
Apricots   Lobsters
Cherries   Prawns
Strawberries Salmon
            Skate
Especially in Season. Tench
Grass lamb Asparagus
            Cucumbers

Forced Vegetables.
Artichokes
Asparagus
Kidney beans

Fruit.
Apples:
 Golden russet
 John apple
 May duke
 Winter russet
Cherries
Currants
Gooseberries
Melons
Pears:
 L'Amozette
 Scarlet Strawberry
 Winter green

Forced Fruit.
Apricots
Cherries
Nutmeg-peaches
Strawberries

Especially in Season.
Crabs
Lobster
Prawns
Salmon
Skate

Wheatears
Wood pigeons

Fish.
Carp
Cod
Conger eels
Crabs
Crayfish
Dace
Dory
Eels
Flounders
Gurnets
Haddock
Herrings
Lobsters
Mackerel
Mullet
Perch
Pike

Plaice
Prawns
Lobster
Salmon trout
Skate
Smelts
Soles
Sturgeon
Tench
Trout
Turbot
Whitebait
Whitings

Vegetables.
Artichokes
Asparagus
Beans:
 French
 Kidney
 Windsor

June—continued.

Cabbages
Carrots
Cauliflowers
Chervil
Cucumbers
Endive
Leeks
Lettuces
Onions
Parsley
Peas
Potatoes, new
Radishes
Salads
Spinach
Turnips
Vegetable marrow

Fruit.

Apples:
  John apple
  Golden russet.

Apples, *cont.*
  Stone pippin
Cherries:
  Bigaroon
  Blackheart
  Duke
Currants
Gooseberries
Melons
Pears:
  Winter green
Strawberries

Forced Fruit.

Grapes
Nectarine
Peaches
Pines

Herbs for Drying.

Burnet

Mint
Orange Thyme.
Tarragon

For Pickling.

Garlic

Especially in Season.

Grass lamb
Crabs
Lobsters
Prawns
Salmon
Salmon trout
Skate
Whitebait
Vegetable marrow

July.

Meat.
Beef
Buck venison
Grass lamb
Mutton
Veal

Poultry and Game.
Chickens
Ducks
Fowls
Green geese
Leverets
Pigeons
Plovers
Tame rabbits
Turkey poults
Wheatears
Wild rabbits

Fish.
Barbel
Bill
Carp
Cod
Conger eels
Crabs
Crayfish
Dace
Dory
Eels
Flounders
Gurnet
Haddocks
Herrings
Ling
Lobsters
Mackerel
Mullet
Perch
Pike

Plaice
Salmon
Skate
Soles
Tench
Thornback
Trout

Vegetables.
Artichokes
Asparagus
Beans of all kinds
Carrots
Cauliflowers
Celery
Chervil
Cucumbers
Endive
Lettuces
Mushrooms
Peas
Potatoes
Radishes
Salad
Salsify
Sorrel
Spinach
Turnips

Fruit.
Apples
  Codling
  Jenneting
  Margaret
  Summer pearmain
  Summer pippin
Apricots
Cherries
Currants
Damsons
Gooseberries

Melons
Nectarines
Peaches
Pears:—
  Catherine
  Green Chisel
  Jargonelle
  Musk
Oranges
Pineapples
Plums
Raspberries
Strawberries

For Pickling.

French beans
Red cabbage
Cauliflowers
Garlic
Gherkins
Nasturtiums
Onions

For Drying.

Knotted Marjoram
Mushrooms
Winter Savory

Especially in Season.

Grass lamb
Crabs
Dace
Lobsters
Mackerel
Prawns
Chickens
Green geese
Plovers
Wild pigeons
Damsons

August.

Meat.
Beef
Buck venison
Grass lamb
Mutton
Veal

Poultry and Game.
Chickens
Ducks
Fowls
Green geese
Grouse
Leverets
Moor game
Pigeons
Plovers
Rabbits
Turkeys
Turkey poults
Wheatears
Wild ducks
Wild pigeons
Wild rabbits

Fish.
Barbel
Brill
Carp
Cod
Conger eel
Crabs
Crayfish
Dace
Eels
Flounders
Gurnets
Haddocks
Herrings
Lobsters
Mackerel
Mullet
Oysters

Perch
Pike
Plaice
Salmon
Skate
Soles
Tench
Turbot
Whitings

Vegetables.
Artichokes
Beans of all kinds
Carrots
Cauliflowers
Celery
Cucumber
Endive
Leeks
Lettuces
Mushrooms
Onions
Peas
Potatoes
Radishes
Salads of all kinds
Salsify
Scarlet runners
Shallots
Spinach
Turnips

Fruit.
Apples
  Codling
  Summer pippin
Cherries
Currants
Damsons
Figs
Filberts

Gooseberries
Grapes
Melons
Mulberries
Nectarines
Peaches
Pears:—
  Jargonelle
  Summer Bon Chrétien
  Windsor
Plums:—
  Greengages
  Orleans
Raspberries
Alpine Strawberries

For Drying.

Basil
Sage
Thyme

For Pickling.

Red cabbage
Capsicums
Chillies
Tomatoes
Walnuts

Especially in Season.

Dace
Mackerel
Perch
Pike
Prawns
Turbot
Grouse, from the 12th inst.
Figs
Filberts
Mulberries
Greengages

September.

Meat.
Beef
Buck venison
Mutton
Pork
Veal

Poultry and Game.
Chickens
Ducks
Fowls
Green geese
Grouse
Hares
Larks
Leverets
Moor game
Partridges
Pigeons
Plovers
Rabbits
Teal

Turkeys
Turkey poults
Wheatears
Wild ducks
Wild pigeons
Wild rabbits

Fish.
Barbel
Brill
Carp
Cockles
Cod
Conger eels
Crabs
Dace
Eels
Flounders
Gurnets
Haddock
Hake
Herrings
Lobsters

Mullet
Mussels
Oysters
Perch
Pike
Plaice
Prawns
Shrimps
Soles
Tench
Turbot
Whitings

Vegetables.
Artichokes
Jerusalem ditto
Beans: French and Scarlet
Cabbages
Carrots
Cauliflowers
Celery
Cucumbers

September—*Continued.*

Endive	Morella cherries	Quinces
Leeks	Damsons	Walnuts
Lettuces	Figs	
Mushrooms	Filberts	*Especially in Season.*
Onions	Grapes :—	
Parsnips	Muscadine	
Peas	Frontignac	Dace
Potatoes	Red and black	Oysters
Radishes	Hamburgh	Perch
Salad	Malmsey	Pike
Shallots	Hazel nuts	Grouse
Turnips	Medlars	Hares
Fruit.	Peaches	Moor game
	Pears :—	Partridges
Apples :—	Bergamot	Wild ducks
White Caville	Brown beurré	Grapes
Pearmain	Pineapples	Pineapples
Golden rennet	Plums	

October.

Meat.
Beef
Doe venison
Mutton
Pork
Veal

Poultry and Game.
Chickens
Dotterels
Ducks
Fowls
Green geese
Grouse
Hares
Larks
Moor game
Partridges
Pheasants
Pigeons
Rabbits
Snipes
Teal
Turkeys
Wheatears
Widgeon
Wild ducks
,, pigeons
,, rabbits
Woodcocks

Fish.
Barbel
Brill
Carp
Cockles
Cod
Conger eels
Crabs
Dace
Dory
Eels
Gudgeon
Haddocks
Hake
Halibut
Herrings
Lobsters
Mussels
Oysters
Perch
Pike
Prawns
Salmon trout
Shrimps
Smelts
Soles
Tench
Turbot
Whiting

Vegetables.
Artichokes
Jerusalem ditto
Brocoli
Cabbages
Cauliflower
Celery
Endive
Leeks
Onions
Parsnips
Peas
Potatoes
Radishes
Salad
Savoys
Shallots
Tomatoes
Truffles
Turnips
Winter Spinach

Fruit.
Almonds
Apples :—
  Pearmain
  Golden pippin
  Golden rennet
  Royal russet
  Black and white bullace
Damsons
Figs, late
Filberts
Grapes
Hazel nuts
Medlars
Old Newington peaches
October peaches
Pears :—
  Bergamot
  Beurré
  Chaumontelle
  Bon Chrétien
  Swan's Egg
Quinces
Services
Walnuts

Especially in Season.
Hake
John Dory
Pike
Pheasants
Partridges
Widgeon
Brocoli
Tomatoes
Truffles
Hazel nuts
Grapes
Medlars

November.

Meat.
Beef
Doe venison
House lamb
Mutton
Pork
Veal

Poultry and Game.
Chickens
Dotterels
Ducks
Fowls
Geese
Grouse
Hares
Larks
Moor game
Partridges
Pheasants
Pigeons
Rabbits
Snipes
Teal
Turkeys
Wheatears
Widgeon
Wild ducks
Woodcocks

Fish.
Barbel
Brill
Carp
Cockles
Cod
Crab
Dace
Dory
Eels
Gudgeon
Gurnets
Haddock
Hake
Halibut
Herrings
Ling
Lobsters
Mussels
Oysters
Perch
Pike
Plaice
Prawns

Meat.
Beef
Doe venison
House lamb
Mutton
Pork
Veal

Poultry and Game.
Capons
Chickens
Dotterel
Ducks
Fowls
Geese
Grouse
Guinea fowl
Hares
Larks
Moor game
Partridges
Peafowl
Pheasants
Pigeons
Rabbits
Snipes
Teal
Turkeys
Wheatears

Fish.
Salmon
Shrimps
Skate
Smelts
Soles
Sprats
Tench
Turbot
Whiting

Vegetables.
Artichokes (Jerusalem)
Brocoli
Cabbages
Chard Beets
Cardoons
Carrots
Celery
Chervil
Colewort
Endive
Herbs of all kinds
Leeks
Lettuces
Onions
Parsnips
Potatoes
Salad
Savoys
Shallots
Tomatoes
Turnips
Winter Spinach

Fruit.
Almonds

December.

Widgeon
Wild ducks
Woodcocks

Fish.
Barbel
Brill
Carp
Cockles
Cod
Crabs
Dory
Eels
Gudgeon
Gurnets
Haddocks
Hake
Halibut
Herrings
Ling
Lobsters
Mussels
Oysters
Perch
Pike
Plaice
Salmon
Shrimps
Skate
Smelts
Soles
Sprats
Sturgeon
Tench
Turbot
Whiting

Vegetables.
Artichokes (Jerusalem)
Beets
Brocoli, white and purple
Cabbages
Cardoons
Carrots
Celery
Endive
Forced Asparagus
Herbs
Leeks
Onions
Potatoes
Scorzonera
Shallots
Spinach (winter)
Truffles
Turnips

Apples :
  Golden pippin
  Holland do.
  Kentish do.
  Nonpareil
  Winter pearmain
  Wheeler's russet
Bullaces
Chestnuts
Grapes
Hazel nuts
Medlars
Pears :
  Bergamot
  Berry de Chaumontelle
  Colmar
  Spanish Bon Chrétien
Services
Walnuts

Especially in Season.
Dace
Dory
Hake
Pike
Sprats
Geese
Grouse
Hares
Snipes
Teal
Woodcocks
Chestnuts

Kitchen Utensils.

December—Continued.

Fruit.	Apples cont.	
Almonds	Winter pear-main	Medlars
Apples:		Hazel nuts
Golden pippin	Golden russet	Oranges
Nonpareil	Chestnuts	Pears:
		Bergamot

Pears cont.	Especially in Season.	
Beurré d'hiver		Skate
Colmar		Turbot
Holland	Cod	Capons
St. Germains	Dory	Guineafowl
Walnuts	Hake	Peafowl
	Ling	Turkey

KITCHEN UTENSILS.

The young and inexperienced housekeeper will, we believe, be glad of some guidance in the selection of the utensils needed in her kitchen, so that she may not be at the mercy of those who desire more than is really required, or who are ignorant of the necessity and use of many articles of the first importance in the art. With a view to helping our readers to decide in this matter for themselves, we offer them here three lists of the articles absolutely essential in the kitchen. The first list is for a first-rate kitchen, the second for a medium one, the third for the cottage home. Of course any one of the three lists may be added to, as required; but they will be a guide in the matter as they now stand.

Modern science has greatly aided the cook in the implements of her art, and in order to be able to recommend the newest and best cooking utensils we have solicited and received the aid of some of the first manufacturing and furnishing ironmongers in London.

The more expensive list will seldom be required by persons of moderate income, but they may select from it with profit some one or two articles, such as the Bain Marie pan, Sauté pan, &c., which will add immensely to the cook's resources, and enable her to keep her dinner hot, or perform certain delicate culinary performances much more certainly than she could without them.

We believe that the subject is worthy of the housekeeper's attention, as, though some cooks are so ingenious and fertile in expedients that they will make few utensils suffice, still there are others who would *well* fulfil the duties of their position if supplied with all the mechanical aids they have a right to expect, but who fail utterly without them; and it is surely unfair to expect a cook to prepare a good dinner without allowing her the needful implements.

Some of the recent inventions, as Carson's Patent Salting Apparatus, Kent's Patent Soup Strainer, and the Patent Mincing Machine, will be found to afford an immense saving of labour and time; while the worst cook amongst "general servants" can scarcely achieve the feat of spoiling the joint, if it be cooked in Captain Warren's Everybody's Pot.

We have not given an engraving of every separate article named in the lists; some few are too well known to require illustration. All that are new or least known in ordinary kitchens have been presented to the eye pictorially as well as verbally, and will, we hope, suffice for the full information of the inexperienced housekeeper.

Kitchen Utensils absolutely required by a good Cook:

Set of 6 wrought-iron saucepans.
1 wrought-iron stock-pot.
1 Bain-marie pan.
1 wrought-iron teakettle.
1 oval boiler.
1 digester, 1 saucepan digester, 1 stewpan digester.
6 enamelled stewpans.
1 Sauté pan, 1 French do.
1 potato steamer.
1 salamander and stand.
1 oval frying pan.
1 round do.
1 fluted gridiron.
1 bachelor's frying-pan.
1 omelet pan.
1 omelet soufflé pan.
1 braising pan.
1 preserving pan and spoon.
1 flour dredger.
1 sugar do.
1 brass bottle jack.
1 dripping pan and stand.
1 basting ladle.
1 wooden meat screen.
1 coffee mill.
1 meat chopper.
Meat saw.
1 colander.
Pestle and mortar.
2 gravy strainers.
1 bread grater.
2 sets of skewers.
1 fish slice.
1 egg slice and ladle.
1 pair of steak tongs.
1 egg whisk.
1 beef fork.
1 French cook's knife.
1 steak beater.
Fish kettle.
Mackerel saucepan.
Turbot kettle.
Salmon and jack kettle.
1 pair of fish scissors.
Double hanging gridiron.
Sliding toaster and trivet.

Toasting fork.
Carson's patent salting apparatus.
Kent's patent soup strainer.
Mincing machine.
Weighing machine.
Spice box.
Herb stand.
Box of paste cutters.
12 patty pans.
3 tart pans.
3 Dariol moulds.

Marble slab for making paste.
Rolling pin—American, with revolving handle.
1 paste jigger.
"Piston" freezing machine.
1 cheese toaster.
3 larding pins.
2 cook's knives.
1 mushroom mould.
1 star fritter mould.
1 scroll fritter mould.

1 vegetable cutter, or "the French vegetable cutter."
1 vegetable mould.
3 pudding moulds.
6 jelly moulds.
3 cake moulds.
2 wooden spoons, and mashed potato fork.
Ice closet.
Sugar spinners.
Sugar moulds.

The cost of the above would be £38 10s.

Medium Set.

1 teakettle.
1 toasting fork.
1 bread grater.
1 wooden meat screen and bottle jack.
1 dripping pan and stand.
1 meat chopper.
1 colander.
3 block-tin saucepans.
5 iron saucepans.
1 do. and steamer.
1 large boiling pot.
4 enamelled stewpans.

1 butter saucepan.
1 stock pot.
1 fish and egg slice.
2 fish kettles.
1 flour dredge, and pepper and salt do.
2 frying-pans.
1 omelet pan.
1 double hanging gridiron.
1 salamander.
2 sets of skewers.
1 pair of steak tongs.
1 box of larding pins.

2 pudding moulds.
2 jelly do.
1 rolling pin.
1 paste board.
1 paste jigger.
12 patty pans.
2 tart pans.
1 pan for Yorkshire pudding.
Warren's Everybody's Cooking pot.
Warren's Everybody's curry pot.
1 spice box.

The cost of the above would be £10 15s.

Small Cottage Set.

Slack's patent digester.
1 teakettle.
1 toasting fork.
1 bread grater.
1 tin meat screen and bottle jack.
1 set of skewers.
1 meat chopper.
1 block tin butter saucepan.

1 colander.
2 iron saucepans.
2 iron stewpans.
1 enamelled saucepan.
1 iron boiling pot.
1 fish slice.
1 fish kettle.
1 flour dredge.
2 frying pans.

1 gridiron (hanging).
Salt and pepper dredgers.
1 rolling pin.
1 pasteboard.
12 patty pans.
1 pan for Yorkshire pudding.
1 pair of scales.
1 spice box.

The cost of the above would be £4 5s.

Saucepan.   Braising-pan.   Stewpan.

Kitchen Utensils.

Saucepans of several sizes are required for every kitchen. The cook should be careful to keep them always clean and fresh. The moment she has ceased using one she should pour boiling water into it to wash it, and she should *never* put one away dirty.

Preserving Pan, for making jams, jellies, marmalades, &c.   Bain-marie Pan and Pots, for keeping sauces and entrées hot, &c.   Stock-pot.

Braising Pan.—The food to be braised is put into the lower part of the pan. The lid is covered well with red-hot ashes or charcoal. Full directions for braising are given farther on. The stewpan is a valuable utensil; it will in case of need serve as a braising-pan, if the lid be made to go a little into the edge of the pan as some are made.

Stock Pot.—The stock pot receives in it bones, trimmings of meat, remains of cold game, &c., &c., in short everything available for ordinary or good soup. It is to be wished that every English artizan's wife possessed one; it is the *pot-au-feu* of the French workman, who thus obtains nourishing soup and well-dressed meat at the same time.

Saucepan Digester.   Digester.   Stewpan Digester.

Slack's Patent "Digester" cannot be too warmly recommended to those who have need to practise economy. The mode of using it is simple and easy. Care must be taken in filling a digester to leave room enough for the steam to pass off through the valve at the top of the cover. This may be done by filling the digester only three parts full of water and bruised bones or meat, which it is to be noticed are all to be put in together. It must then be placed near a slow fire, so as only to simmer (more heat injures the quality), and this it must do for the space of eight or ten hours. After this has been done, the soup is to be strained through a hair sieve or colander, in order to separate any bits of bones. The soup is then to be put into the digester again, and afterwards whatever vegetables, spices, &c., are thought necessary are added, the whole is to be well boiled together for an hour or two, and it will be then fit for immediate use. In putting on the lid of the digester, take care that a mark, thus (X) on the lid, is opposite to a similar one on the digester. The digester may also be obtained to contain from four quarts to ten gallons. The saucepan and stewpan digesters hold from one to eight quarts.

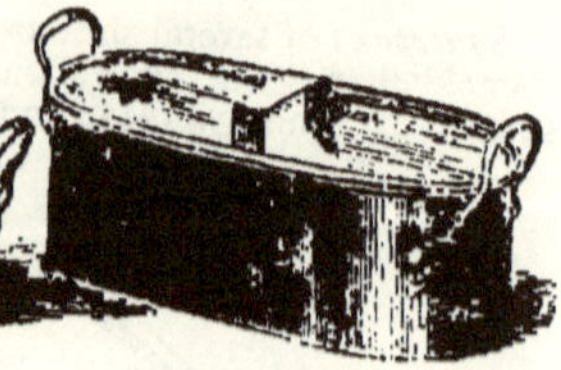

Kitchen Utensils.

Salmon or Jack Kettle.   **Turbot Kettle.**   **Fish Kettle.**

Saucepan, with loose Earthen Lining, for boiling milk, custards, &c.; without burning.

Bottle Jack and Screen, for roasting without a spit and wooden screen.

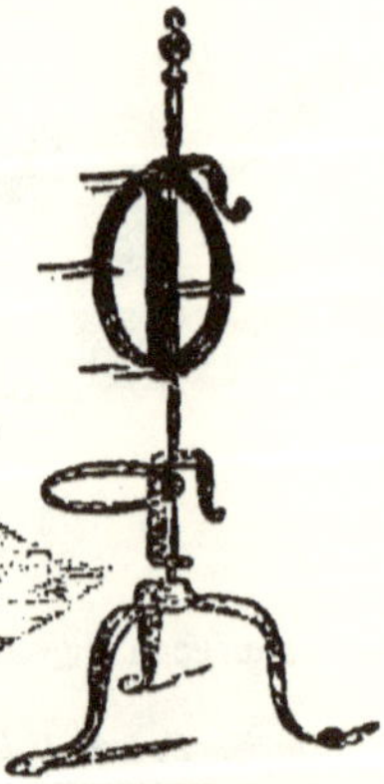

Saucepan, with Lip, for melted butter, gravy, &c.

Double Hanging Gridiron.   Dripping-pan and Ladle.

Toaster and Trivet.

Wire basket, for frying vegetables.   Meat Chopper, for chopping and disjointing bones.   Gravy Strainer.

There is a new and better Gravy Strainer recently invented, in the form of a jelly bag, perforated at the sides, which is more convenient, we think, than the ordinary one.

Captain Warren's Everybody's Cooking Pot.

This new and admirable utensil we have tested ourselves, and can warmly recommend to the housekeeper. Meat is cooked in it by means of *heat only*, without being touched by any liquid, save its own juices, or even wetted by steam. The joint is put, *without water*, into the *inner* saucepan, B. This is put over the lower saucepan, A, which is filled with boiling water, the steam from which ascends round the sides of the inner pot and passes into the *lid*, which is also thus filled with steam. The meat remains cooking in its own juices alone for the period named in the following table :

Captain Warren's Curry Pot.

Time for Dressing Meat by Warren's Everybody's Cooking Pot.

	H.	M.
A leg of mutton, 10lbs.	3	0
Beef, 10lbs.	3	30
Goose	2	30
Turkey	3	0
Ham, 20lbs.	9	0
Hare	2	0
Rabbit	1	30

Another and upper portion of the cooking pot will at the same time dress vegetables, &c., over the meat. They have, of course, to be put in some time after the joint. The meat, thus dressed, is taken out (in spite of an inferior cook) succulent, and scarcely at all reduced in weight; as it wastes two ounces *less* in dressing than by the ordinary system of boiling. The flavour is much better than when the meat is boiled, as it cannot, of course, absorb any water. For sick cookery this pot is admirable, as overboiling, scorching, or smoking, are impossible; and the meat is very digestible and nourishing from the juices being retained, and the fibre made tender. It makes nourishing soup at a temperature of 210 degrees, which Baron Liebig says should never be exceeded. The "Pot" may be used for either boiling or roasting. For the use of the "Cooking Pot," the inventor gives the following directions:—The water in the saucepan or pot should be high enough to touch the bottom of the enclosed pot. Meat to be dressed must be placed in the inner pot, B, *without* water, and the cover put on, with the *pipe* inserted in the tube; or if C be used, then the steam tube at the bottom must be carefully inserted in the tube of B. After bringing the water to the boil, the saucepan must be placed at the side of the fire, near enough to *keep it boiling*. The pot, when not in use, to be kept perfectly dry and uncovered. Meat may be kept for two hours in this pot, at the side of the fire, without being spoiled.

Salt beef, dressed in Captain Warren's Cooking Pot, requires one-third longer to do than fresh, and to be cooked with sufficient *water in the inner vessel* to cover it. The liquor in which it has been boiled will make superior stock for soup.

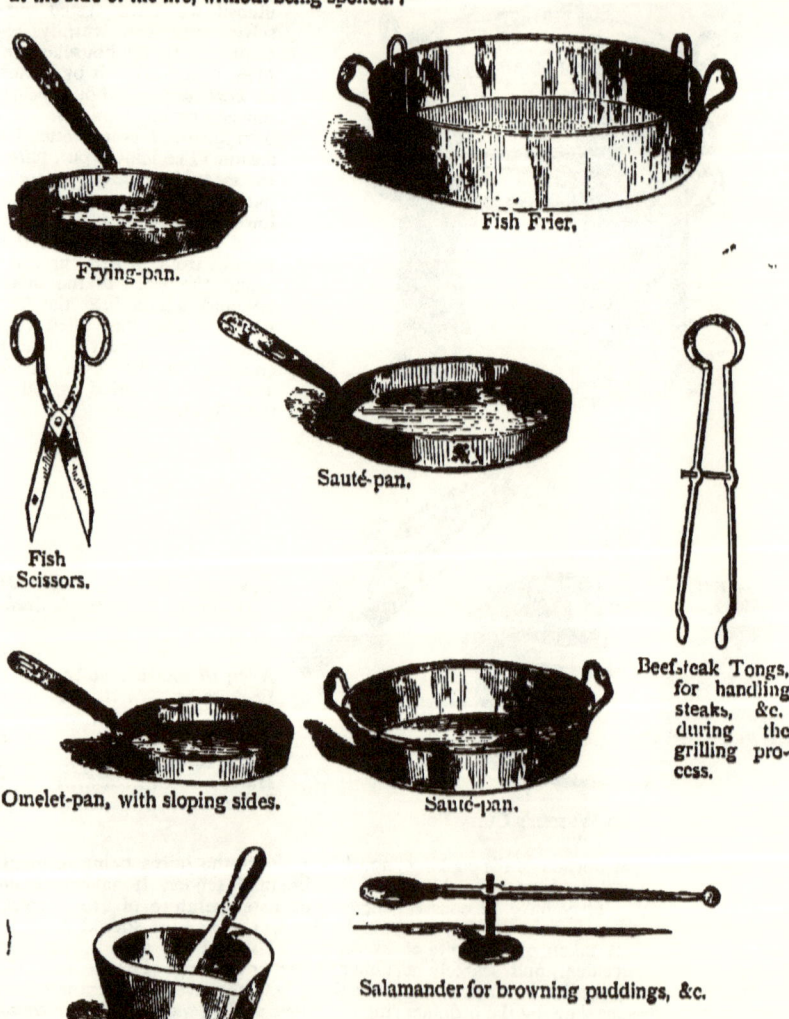

Frying-pan.

Fish Frier.

Fish Scissors.

Sauté-pan.

Omelet-pan, with sloping sides.

Sauté-pan.

Beefsteak Tongs, for handling steaks, &c. during the grilling process.

Pestle and Mortar.

Salamander for browning puddings, &c.

Kitchen Utensils.

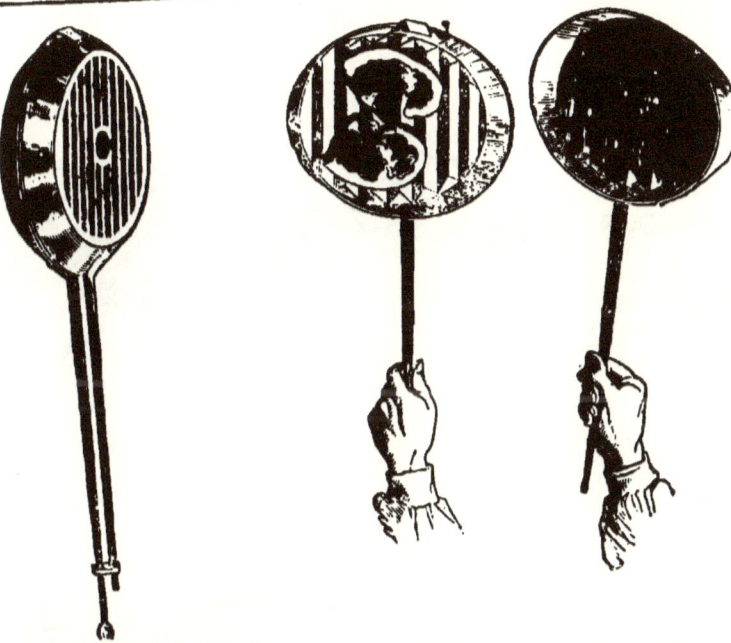

Captain Warren's Bachelor's Frying-pan, closed.

Bachelor's Frying-pan, open.

This frying-pan, invented by Captain Warren, is, we think, preferable to the ordinary frying-pan. It retains the heat better from being fluted instead of plain, and renders it unnecessary to touch the steak with the beef tongs. It shuts (as shown in the engraving) over the steak or chop, and can be turned over from one side to the other, as the cook pleases, till the meat is dressed.

Trussing Needle, for trussing poultry.

Paste Jigger.

Egg Whisk for beating eggs.

Meat Saw, for sawing bones in parts of meat where the chopper cannot be used.

Larding needle, made with split ends, like a cleft stick, to receive strips of fat bacon, which by its means are grafted into the flesh of turkeys, poultry, &c.

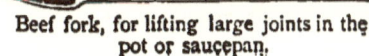

Beef fork, for lifting large joints in the pot or saucepan.

Kitchen Utensils.

Carson's Patent Salting Apparatus, for salting joints of meat in a few minutes. Kent's Patent Soup Strainer. Patent Mincing Machine

Kent's Patent Strainer will be found most useful for procuring the transparency so much required by fashion in modern soups.

The Patent Mincing Machine will greatly economize the cook's time.

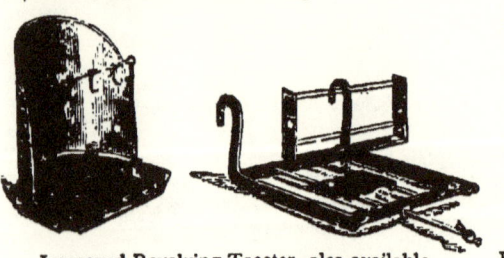

Improved Revolving Toaster, also available as a hanging Trivet, for Kettle Saucepan, or Plate.

Egg Poacher, with a loose inside frame, and ladles to hold the eggs.

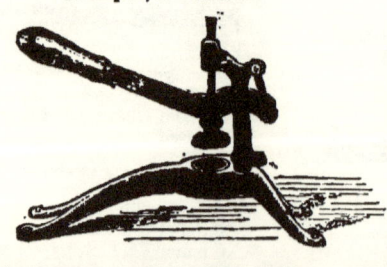

French Vegetable Cutters for cutting carrots and turnips in various shapes, for soups, haricots, garnishing, &c.

When you use this machine, lay the disc or plate you have selected in the place prepared for it in the machine, with the sharp or cutting side upwards. Cut the vegetables into thin slices; lay a slice on the disc and press down the handle of the machine, which will force the vegetable on the disc. Then lay a second slice on the disc, pressing down the handle as before, and the slice first laid on will be forced through, cut into small pieces of the required shape. This may be repeated as often as necessary till the quantity is sufficient; the pieces remaining in the disc should be pushed out with a fork.

Kitchen Utensils.

Scales.—As one of the great elements of success in cooking is precision in the proportions of ingredients, the cook should never be without a good pair of scales, and she should keep them in thorough order. In delicate dishes an unequal proportion of an article inserted only to impart a certain flavour, will ruin the dish. The necessity as well as use of scales is therefore obvious.

Scales and Weights.

Ordinary Jelly Moulds.

Jelly Bag, used for Straining Jelly.

The newest and most fashionable moulds now are the two following shapes, in which an opaque interior is seen through the outer jelly, which is transparent.

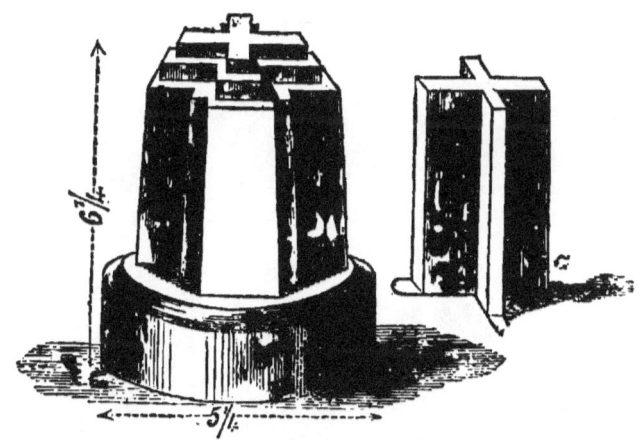

Alexandra Jelly Mould.

Directions for using the Alexandra Jelly Mould.—Place the mould in ice, then whip a little jelly till it becomes white, and fill the small cross on the top of the mould; when set, fill the second cross with a little pink jel'y, then place the lining in the centre of the mould, and fill the outside space with very clear pink jelly up to the level of the plain band of the mould, allow this to set and then pour a little warm water into the lining; it will then draw out easily, leaving a hollow space the form of a cross; this should be filled with white whipped jelly or blancmange. When set, fill up the circular band of the mould with clear gold jelly, and when the whole is turned out it will present a very beautiful representation of the Danish Cross in proper colours, upon a golden base.

Kitchen Utensils.

Brunswick Star Jelly Mould.

Directions for using the Brunswick Star Jelly Mould.—Place the mould in ice, then colour a little clear jelly with cochineal, with which fill the circle at the top of the mould; when set, fill the smaller star with clear jelly, in which a little silver leaf has been broken; when this is set, fill the second or larger star with red jelly, then place the lining in the centre of the mould, and fill the outside space with clear jelly up to the level of the hollow on the plain band of the mould; allow this to set firmly, and then pour a little warm water into the lining, which may then be drawn out easily, leaving a hollow space. This should be filled with white whipped jelly or blancmange, which will form the interior star. When firmly set, fill up the circular band of the mould with red jelly, and when turned out it will present a very beautiful appearance, the main body of the jelly being surmounted by a Brunswick Star.

PIE AND PUDDING MOULDS.

Vegetable Mould.   Raised Pie Mould.   Plain Oval Pudding Mould.   Melon-shpe Pudding Mould.

Cake Moulds.

We give these few specimens of the moulds required in large kitchens for pies, puddings, cakes, &c. A very great choice in such matters is afforded at the great ironmongers shops in the present day.

Gas Cooking Apparatus.

For boiling water. For boiling or stewing at top, and frying or toasting underneath.

Gas Cooking.

Gas cooking finds favour in many kitchens on account of the great economy of fuel obtained by it. In small kitchens, in the heat of summer, the stove here represented will (in cases of early dinner) allow the cook or general servant to let her fire go out and enjoy a cool apartment. The stove should be placed, if possible, in the back kitchen or scullery.

Gas Cooking Stove.

"The Cottager's Stove."
WHICH REQUIRES NO BRICKWORK TO FIX IT.

A a Tin Kettle, holding seven quarts.
B an Iron Cover, which forms an additional oven on the top of the hot plate.
C Toaster.   D Saucepan to fit the top.

Directions.—When coal is used, the front and bottom gratings will be required.

When wood is used these may be removed.

To improve the Draught, if necessary.— Carry the flue-pipe a few feet up the chimney, or enclose the fireplace with an iron plate, in which cut out a round hole for the pipe to pass through.

To use the Stove in the open air, it will be necessary to have about ten feet of perpendicular pipe, to ensure a proper draught.

Economy in the use of fuel is not to be neglected by the housekeeper. Cinders should be carefully sifted. The grate (if the ordinary one alone be possessed) should be screwed in as soon as the fire for cooking is no longer required. The fire *at the back* of the open range may then be made of small coals, wetted and left to cake. Cinders may be used for ironing stoves, and for heating ovens.

The Cottager's Stove will be found an economical assistant to the common open range in small kitchens.

Soyer's Patent Culinary Utensils.

It would be unjust to the memory of a great cook if we omitted from our list the culinary utensils invented by the late M. Soyer, to whom our gratitude as a nation is due. They consist of the Baking Stewing Pan, the Improved Baking Dish, the Vegetable Drainer, and the Portfolio Mea' Screen.

Baking Stewing Pan.—By this pan all the nutriment and flavour of the various ingredients are preserved. It has great advantages over the old method of boiling or stewing—namely, that it gives hardly any trouble; and, in addition to its retaining all the nutriment, it cooks in one-third less time than by the ordinary mode.

Improved Baking Dish.—The late M. Soyer thus described this invention in the "Shilling Cookery for the People"; "I have attached a moveable false grating of wire, to the middle of which is fixed a trivet, three inches in height. I put the pudding at the bottom of the dish, then put in the grating, on which I place the potatoes; then on the trivet I put the meat. By this means the surplus fat, which would otherwise fall in the pudding and prevent its setting, descends on the potatoes, making them delicate and crisp. This is applicable to any joint, and the meat being more elevated than usual when placed in the oven, causes it to partake more of the flavour of a roast joint than it does when put immediately over the pudding or potatoes; the vapour arising from which soddens the meat, instead of leaving it brown and well carbonized,

Vegetable Drainer.—This is a saucepan fitted with a perforated pan and a vegetable drainer, and is one of the most economical cooking utensils ever put before the public; it ought to have a place in every kitchen.

Portfolio Meat Screen.—The portfolio meat screen may be folded up when not required, and put away in a dresser drawer till wanted.

Ventilating Kitchener.

This new range is made from three feet to five feet wide; it has a wrought-iron roaster on one side of the fire, with moveable shelves, double dripping-pan and meat-stand, thoroughly ventilated by means of air-tubes and valves (by closing which the roaster becomes an excellent oven). Strong wrought-iron side boiler, on the other side of the fire, with steam pipe and brass tap. Gridiron for broiling. Ash-pan, hook, key, and raker; dampers, register door, &c.

The top consists of a hot plate, on which boiling, stewing, &c., may be done without injuring and soiling the vessels in use, and which may also be used as an ironing stove.

The advantages offered by this stove are that it requires no brickwork to fix it; it roasts, bakes, boils, and steams with one fire, and supplies a bath if required; it carries off the heat and smell of the kitchen; and it can be fixed in its place in a few hours, after the fireplace is cleared out and prepared for it, by local workmen if preferred. It can be removed, in the event of a change of residence, being quite detached and independent. It is not more expensive than the ordinary kitcheners; whilst the cost of fixing it is much less.

Plain Directions for Roasting, &c.

How to Roast.—Roasting meat, though one of the commonest modes of dressing it, is by no means an easy task. Roast meat is too often sent to table nearly raw, or dried up till there is scarcely any gravy in it. Now *good* roasting consists in dressing the joint thoroughly, and yet retaining its juices in it.

The cook should prepare her fire some little time before she puts the meat down. The grate should be let out sufficiently wide to take in the whole size of the joint, with a margin to spare on each side, and the fire should be *so* good as not to require making up during the time the joint is roasting. It should be sufficiently large to be of an equal strength all the time the meat is dressing, aided by a large coal put on the top of it occasionally. A great deal of the success in roasting will depend on the heat and goodness of the fire.

Begin roasting by placing the meat at some distance from the fire (about twelve inches), and baste it from the first. When it is half done, move it gradually nearer to the fire for it to be well browned. If the meat were to be put close to the fire at first, it would dry up, and the outside would be dressed before the heat had penetrated the mass; the juices being thus shut in, the joint would be under-dressed. Some persons prefer meat roasted *very* slowly. That method is expensive, because it requires a large fire to be kept up for a length of time; and also, unless done by a cook who understands her business well, and who makes a fire fit for it, the meat is apt to get sodden. We need scarcely say that the meat screen should be placed behind it from the first of its being put down.

Cover the fat of veal or lamb with a piece of paper tied on with twine.

Baste the meat very frequently, for the more it is basted the better it will eat. When it is nearly done, the paper over the fat may be removed, and the joint lightly dredged with flour, in order to give it a savoury brown appearance called frothing. Sprinkle a *very* little salt on it also, but not till it is just ready to dish up, as salt draws out the gravy.

The usual time allowed for roasting is a quarter of an hour or twenty minutes for each pound of meat. But this rule does not always answer. Meat fresh killed takes longer to roast than when it has been kept long; and in warm weather it takes less time than in cold. Brown meats require less time than white meats do. In frosty weather it is better to lay the joint before the fire to thaw before it is put on the spit, as, if frozen, it will be impossible to calculate the time required for dressing it, and in fact it will never be dressed through. The cook should always be careful that the spit, and also the hook used in the bottle-jack, be wiped before they are used. She should also be careful how she hangs the meat, so as to avoid disfiguring it by running the spit through the prime parts.

Cradle spits are much the best for large kitchens; for small families, the bottle-jack in a tinned screen does very well, or, better still, the improved spring-jack and roaster.

Let the butcher chop the joints of necks and loins of mutton and lamb before they are dressed, or they cannot be well separated by the carver when they are sent to table.

When the roast meat has been taken up, the fat which has dripped from it into the pan should be poured into a basin, previously dipped in cold water. It must be left till the next day, when beneath the fat at the top will be found a fine meat jelly fit for gravies, &c. The cake of dripping should be melted and strained into cold water, from which it can be removed in cakes for future use.

Veal, pork, and lamb should be thoroughly done, not retaining any red gravy; at the same time, care should be taken not to dry them up, or roast them till the flesh parts from the bones.

Mutton does not take quite the length of time to roast that beef does.

A very economical way of making gravy is to skim the fat from the dripping in the pan under the meat, and pour two or three spoonfuls of hot water into it; stir it, and pour it over the meat through a sieve.

How to Boil.

Joints to be boiled should be washed extremely clean and skewered into good shape, then they should be put in the saucepan and covered well with *cold* water. They must be set over a moderate fire and let boil *slowly*. Just before the water reaches boiling point the scum will rise to the top, and must be carefully skimmed off; if not done at the moment of ebullition it will fall back on the joint boiling and disfigure it. The pot will require skimming every time the scum rises. The saucepan must be kept covered all the time, however, the lid being only removed for the cook to skim the pot.

Gentle simmering, not fast boiling, is most desirable for meat, as by quick boiling the outside is hardened before the joint is done, and the meat becomes hard and tough, from the chemical reasons already given.

Salted meat requires longer boiling than fresh meat; when smoked and dried it takes longer still. Pickled or salted meat should be soaked before boiling in cold water, for a longer or shorter time as its saltness and size may require. Take care that the joint, if large, does not adhere to the bottom of the pot. To prevent this possibility cooks sometimes put a few wooden skewers at the bottom under it.

The time allowed for boiling is from a quarter of an hour to twenty minutes for each pound, supposing of course that the fire is kept up to an equal temperature all the time. Quick boiling is very much to be avoided, but the pot should never be allowed *to stop simmering.*

First-rate cooks preserve the whiteness of their boiled meats, and save them from insipidity, by *not* boiling them in water, but using instead a sort of broth called *poêle*, or another called *blanc.* But these preparations are very expensive, and are not required for ordinary use ; however, we give them amongst the sauces in case they should be needed. For people who cannot afford expensive cooking, a well-floured cloth wrapped round the meat to be boiled will make it white ; but the cloth must be kept very clean, and should be boiled in pure water after each time it is used ; moreover, it must not be suffered to get damp, or it will give a musty flavour to the meat.

How to Broil.

Many kinds of fish, steaks, chops, and cutlets are far better broiled than fried ; but much care, niceness, and skill are required to broil properly. First, the fire should be perfectly free from smoke, though brisk, and giving out a good heat ; secondly, the gridiron should be scrupulously clean, well heated, and rubbed over with mutton suet before the meat is put on it. If the fire be too fierce, the meat will be hardened and scorched ; if it be too dead, the gravy will escape and the meat will be flabby. The gridiron should be held slopingly over the fire in order that the fat may run off to the back of the grate, for if it dropped on the coals it would create a blaze, and blacken and smoke the meat. If by chance a blaze should spring up during the time the steak, &c., is broiling, the gridiron must be caught off the fire and held on one side till the blaze is gone ; a little salt thrown on the fire will make it clear again. Fish should be wrapped in a piece of well-buttered letter-paper before they are placed on the gridiron, to keep them from smoke, and prevent their becoming too dry ; the gridiron may be rubbed with a little chalk first. Cutlets which are covered with egg and bread-crumbs, must be dipped in a little clarified butter before they are put on the gridiron. The best way however, is to season the cutlet with pepper, and brush it over with a little butter before it is broiled. Steaks and chops should be turned often in order that they may be done in every part, but the fork used for this purpose should never be stuck into the lean of the steak, as it would let the gravy escape ; it must be put into the outer skin or fat. All kitchens ought to be provided with steak-tongs for this purpose.

Birds when cut asunder and broiled, must be laid with the *inside* first to the fire.

Most people prefer broiled mutton chops or beefsteaks rather lightly dressed, but lamb and pork chops should be thoroughly cooked. Everything broiled should be served the moment it is done, very hot. The dish should be kept ready to receive it in front of the fire.

When fish are broiled without paper, great care should be taken to have the gridiron very hot before they are put on it, and to rub the bars with grease. To preserve the skin of the fish entire when broiled, it should (after being washed and cleansed) be rubbed well with vinegar, dried in a cloth, and floured. The flour will keep it from adhering to the bars. A cinder or charcoal fire is best for broiling fish. While you are broiling slices of cold meat, put into a hot dish a piece of butter the size of a walnut and a teaspoonful of ketchup—melt them together, and lay the meat from the gridiron on the gravy made by these ingredients, as soon as it is done.

How to Stew.

Stewing is a wholesome, excellent, and economical mode of cooking. Very little fuel is used for it, and meat so prepared is both digestible and delicious. But *boiling* is not *stewing*, and we warn our readers that all we have said in praise of it may be reversed if they let the stewpan do more than simmer very gently. Stewing is best done over a regular stove ; but when a cook can command only an old-fashioned kitchen range she must place her stew-pan on a trivet high above the fire, and constantly watch it, and move it nearer to, or further from the fire. Stewing must of course always be done over a slow fire, and the stew-pan lid should shut quite closely. It should be kept at a gentle simmer, without letting it boil, and it must stew for several hours, according to the weight of the meat, which is not considered done until it is quite tender. Sometimes the cook stews the meat in a jar, placed in a stew-pan full of water, and thus extracts the pure gravy unmixed with water. We have also a recipe for stewing meat and vegetables together, without water being put in the jar with them, thus making an excellent soup from the union of the pieces of the meat and the water contained in the vegetables.

How to Fry.

Cooks should always have two frying-pans, and a third, not much bigger than a large plate, for omelets, fritters, &c., if they have no sauté-pan. The pan must be kept delicately clean and nice; the butter, dripping, lard, or oil in which the fish, meat, &c., is fried must always be *boiling hot* before the meat is put into the pan. The rule is that a sufficient quantity of fat must be heated thus in the pan to *cover* the steak, chop, or whatever is to be fried—frying being actually boiling in fat instead of water. Mutton chops do not require any fat in the pan with them: they have enough in themselves, but they must be often turned and moved about to prevent them from burning. Of course we speak only of chops cooked quite plain, *i.e.*, without being egged and bread-crumbed. Cut and skin the chop nicely, and season it with a little pepper before putting it in the pan.

Lamb cutlets, and lamb chops, must be egged and bread-crumbed twice, in order to look well.

Steaks should be cut three quarters of an inch thick for frying, and should be peppered, but not have salt put on them before they are dressed, as it makes them hard. When done, a little salt is sprinkled lightly over them.

Cutlets, *à la maintenon*, and mullet are fried in buttered paper covers.

The first process in frying is to put enough dripping or butter in your pan, to cover the chop or steak when the butter is melted. Then the fat must be made to *boil* in the pan, and when at its greatest heat the substance to be fried must be plunged into it. The pan must then be lifted from the fire for a minute or two, to prevent the outside from getting black before the inside is dressed.

Fish must be well dried before frying, in a cloth well sprinkled with flour; or first they may be wiped well, thoroughly dried and dredged with flour. Then an egg is well brushed over them, and finely-grated bread, or biscuit, is sprinkled over them. The fat should be *quite* at boiling-point (when it will no longer hiss or bubble) before the fish is put in, and it should be well covered by the liquid butter, or oil, the latter is much the best for frying fish in, but of course it is expensive. Hog's lard and dripping are also used in economical kitchens. The frying-pan should never be left for a moment till the fish is done.

In kitchens where strict economy is demanded, it is usual when liver and bacon are to dressed to fry the bacon *first*, which will leave enough fat in the pan for the liver to be put in without either butter or dripping, but this mode, though economical, is very coarse, and we do not recommend it. The liver will be more delicate if it be fried *before* the bacon.

To Glaze.

Glazing is done by boiling down good rich beef stock till it is reduced to the consistence of a thin, bright brown paste. Of course, all fat and sediment must first be removed from the stock before it is boiled down for glaze. It should be done over a quick fire, boiled fast till well reduced, then changed into a smaller stew-pan, and should continue boiling till it is made. It must be kept in a jar well covered, and when required for use should be put into a stew-pan and let stand in boiling water till the jelly is melted. It must be brushed over the tongue, chicken, or beef with a glazing brush once or twice till the operation is finished.

Boning, Larding, and Braising.

The three most difficult operations to achieve well in cookery are boning, larding, and braising. Boning is so little understood by inferior cooks that it is best, if your servant is not first-rate, to have it done by the poulterer with whom you deal. Nevertheless, it is an art which tends so much to economy, that it would quite repay the mistress of a family to pay for a few lessons for her domestic from a good poulterer or cook. The bones of poultry and hares are most useful for making gravies, and hares are more easily carved, and look better when boned. Any butcher will bone joints when required. Although we cannot hope that our readers will be able to achieve the boning of a fowl, &c., from any verbal discription, we, nevertheless, give a few directions on the subject, from an excellent recipe of Miss Acton's for the performance of the operation. Turkeys, fowls, hares, &c., are boned, as well as joints.

To bone a Turkey or Fowl.—Miss Acton's.

"Cut through the skin down the centre of the back, and raise the flesh carefully on either side with the point of a sharp knife until the sockets of the wings and thighs are reached. Till a little practice has been gained, it will, perhaps, be better to bone these joints before proceeding further; but after they are once detached from it, the whole of the body may easily be separated from the flesh, and taken out entire. Only the neckbones and merrythought will then remain to be removed. The bird thus prepared may either be restored to its original form, by filling the legs and wings with forcemeat, and the body with the livers of two or three fowls, mixed with alternate layers of parboiled tongue, freed from the rind, fine sausage meat, or veal forcemeat, or thin slices of the nicest bacon, or aught else of good flavour, which will give a marbled appearance to the fowl when it is carved, and then be sewn up and trussed as usual; or the legs and wings may be drawn inside the body, and the bird being first flattened on a table, may be covered with sausage meat and the various other ingredients we have named, so placed that it shall be of equal thickness in every part, then tightly rolled, bound firmly together with a fillet of broad tape, wrapped in a thin pudding cloth closely tied at both ends, and dressed."

Larding.

The cook should be provided with larding needles of various sizes.

Cut small smooth strips of the length required, off the firmest part of a piece of bacon fat. Put these bits of bacon fat into a larding needle (*see* page 23), they are called lardoons. Pierce the skin and a very little of the flesh of the meat, fowl, sweetbread, &c., you may wish to lard with it, leaving the bacon in, and the two ends of equal length outwards. These punctures for lardoons are made in rows at any distance from each other the cook pleases. The flavour of larding may be obtained by raising the skin of the meat, and laying a slice of fat bacon beneath it; this mode is not ornamental, but gives an excellent flavour to the flesh, even better than when larded with the needles. It requires a little practice to lard neatly, but as it is really an easy operation, any cook may learn to do it with care. Cut the bacon in slices, lay them one on the other, and cut strips through them the size you require, in order that they may be all of the same size.

Lardoons (as these pieces of bacon are called) should be two inches in length, and one-eighth of an inch in width, for larding poultry, game, and fricandeaux; for fillets of beef and loin of veal they should be rather thicker. We owe, besides many another invaluable lesson, the following admirable description of larding to Soyer:—
"Have the fricandeau trimmed; lay it lengthwise upon a clean napkin across your hand, forming a kind of bridge with your thumb at the part you are about to commence at. Then with the point of the larding needle make three distinct lines across, half an inch apart; run the needle into the third line at the further side of the fricandeau, and bring it out at the first, placing one of the lardoons in it; draw the needle through, leaving out a quarter of an inch of the bacon at each line; proceed thus to the end of the row. Then make another line half an inch distant; stick in another row of lardoons, bringing them out at the second line, leaving the ends of the bacon out all the same length. Make the next row again at the same distance, bringing the ends out between the lardoons of the first row, proceeding in this manner until the whole surface is larded in chequered rows. Everything else is larded in a similar way, and in the case of poultry, hold the breast over a charcoal fire for one minute, or dip it into boiling water, in order to make the flesh firm."

Braising.

Braising is a mode of cooking by the action of heat *above*, as well as *below*, the article cooked. A braising-pan has a deep cover (*see* engraving at Kitchen Utensils) on which live charcoal is placed. The pan is air-tight, and as all evaporation is thus precluded, the food braised imbibes whatever flavour the cook may wish to give it; in order to effect which, she must place in the pan with it whatever vegetables, &c., her recipe may direct. The ingredients should be very well proportioned, and the stewing should go on very slowly.

We will give here one recipe for a braise, as an example of what is meant,

A fowl braised.—Peel and wash a large Portugal onion, and one large turnip: cut them in thin slices, with a little celery, a few sprigs of parsley, and a bay leaf. Lay a few slices of fat bacon at the bottom of the pan, place the bird trussed for boiling on it, cover the breast with slices of fat bacon. Lay the vegetables round it with a few bones or trimmings of fresh meat. Add a pint and a half of stock, and seasoning to your taste. Cover the pot closely, set it over a slow stove, put live charcoal at the top, and let it cook slowly.

When it is done keep the meat hot while you strain the gravy and take off the fat, which you can do quicker by plunging the basin partly into cold water; this will make the fat coagulate. Boil it up very quickly again till it thickens. Some cooks let the gravy adhere to the meat; this is done by boiling it down till it is reduced just to the quantity required for the purpose.

Sauté-ing.

To "Sauté" anything means to dress it quickly, in a small pan, with a *very little* butter, oil, lard, or dripping, doing one side at a time. Two spoonfuls of oil will be enough to *sauté* a small chicken in.

The art of sauté-ing well consists in doing it quickly, to keep the gravy and succulence in the meat. It is an economical mode of dressing small things of every kind of food. It is, you see, very different from frying, which is really boiling in hot fat, and requires a far greater quantity of the butter, oil, &c., for its performance.

Steaming.

Steaming is an admirable mode of dressing bacon and hams. It preserves the flavour in them, and quite saves waste. Any one who has once eaten steamed bacon will never again, we think, order it to be boiled, so tender and succulent will it be found.

In "Kitchen Utensils," page 21, will be found the engraving and description of a new steam saucepan, which promises to be a great addition to the kitchen.

In it the meat or fowl is cooked without being touched by either water or steam. It appears to us to be a cheap and easy mode of *braising* in a new form. It is styled "Everybody's Cooking Pot." The novelty of the process consists in cooking without the viands coming into actual contact with water or steam; the meat, kept from water entirely, is cooked in an inner cylinder, the outer one containing the water being kept at boiling-point. The food thus prepared is cooked in its own vapour, and none of its nutritious properties wasted. The well known fact, that meat cooked by the ordinary methods of roasting or boiling, loses a large portion both in bulk and weight, as well as some very important chemical qualities, is of itself sufficient to stamp with the seal of approbation any invention that avoids these evils. We have proved, by personally trying it, that meat, fish, and poultry, when cooked in this pot, retain those nourishing juices which, if cooked in the ordinary method, would have been thrown off in vapour, but by this mode become condensed and are returned in moisture at a temperature sufficient to cook in the most perfect manner. To the poor as well as the rich, this invention will therefore prove a great boon.

A Vocabulary of Cooking Terms.

A Bouquet of Herbs—Parsley, thyme, and green onions, tied together.

Allemande—Reduced white velouté sauce, thickened with cream and yolks of eggs, seasoned with nutmeg and lemon-juice.

Angelica—A plant preserved in syrup, and used for decorating pastry, &c.

Aspic Jelly—A transparent jelly made from meat, and used for garnishing, &c.

Au-bleu—Fish dressed so as to present a bluish appearance.

Baba—Very light plum-cake.

Bain-marie—A square tin cooking utensil, with a loose bottom. A kind of very shallow cistern, to be placed on a hot hearth. It contains hot water in which vessels containing soup, sauces, &c., are placed, that they may be kept warm without being longer subject to the action of the fire, which would reduce or thicken them.

Bard—A substitute for larding, when the assistance of fat is needed in dressing any substance—*i. e.*, *bard* is a thin slice of bacon fat which is put over the breasts of birds, back of hare, &c.

Béchamel—French white sauce.

Beignet—A fritter.

Bisque—A shell-fish soup.

Blanc—A white broth used instead of water for boiling chickens, &c., to make them white in appearance.

Blanch—To put the substance to be done into cold water, boil it, strain it, and plunge it into cold water. Also to remove the outside skin of almonds.

Blanquettes—Thin slices of white meat warmed in white sauce, thickened with the yolk of eggs.

Boudin—An *entrée* prepared with quenelle forcemeat.

Bouilli—A stew of beef, served with sauce.

Bouillon—Broth.

Braise—A compound used for giving flavour to braised meats, and for keeping poultry, &c., white, while braising.

Braising—A mode of stewing with bacon.

Brioche—A spongy cake resembling Bath buns.

Callipash—The glutinous meat of the upper shell of the turtle.

Calipee—The glutinous meat of the under shell of the same creature.

Caramel—Sugar boiled till the water is all evaporated; used for ornamentation.

Cassarole—A stew-pan.

Cassarole—A rice crust made in the shape of a pie.

Chartreuse of Vegetables—A preparation of vegetables arranged in a plain mould, the interior garnished with game, fillets, tendons, &c.

Compote—Stewed fruit and syrup; or stewed pigeons, &c.
Consommé—A strong gravy left from stewing meat.
Coulis—A rich brown gravy.
Croquantes—Bright mixtures of fruit and boiled sugar.
Croquettes—A savoury mince of fish, meat, &c., formed into shapes of various kinds and fried.
Croustade—A kind of patty.
Croûton—A sippet of bread used for garnishing hashes.
Daubes—Meat or fowl stewed in sauce.
Desosser—To bone.
En papillote (in a paper)—Putting a cutlet into an oiled or buttered paper.
Entrée—A side dish for the first course.
Entremet—A corner dish for second course.
Escalopes—Collops.
Espagnole—A brown sauce, the foundation of most other sauces.
Faggot—A tiny bunch of parsley, thyme, and a bayleaf, tied together.
Farce—Forcemeat or stuffing.
Flancs—Side dishes.
Foncer—To lay ham, veal, or bacon, at the bottom of the saucepan, under meat.
Fricandeau—A made dish of boned and larded veal.
Galette—A peculiar French cake.
Gâteau—A cake.
Glaze—Stock boiled down to a thin paste.
Godiveaux—Different kinds of forcemeat.
Jardinière—A preparation of vegetables stewed down in their own sauce.
Lardoon—The piece of bacon used in larding.
Leason—A mixture of egg and cream.
Lit—A layer.
Luting—A paste to fasten the lids on pie-pans for preserving game.
Maigre—Dishes for fast-days made without flesh.

Marinade—A liquor for boiling or stewing fish or meat in.
Matelote—A rich stew made of fish and wine.
Mayonnaise—Cold salad dressing.
Mignonnette Pepper—Pepper-corns ground coarsely.
Miroton—Pieces of meat not larger than a crown piece made into a ragoût.
Nougat—A mixture of almonds and sugar.
Nouilles—A kind of vermicelli.
Paner—To put breadcrumbs.
Poêlle—A kind of broth made of veal, bacon, &c., used to boil fowls in.
Pot-au-feu—The stock-pot.
Profiterolles—A light kind of pastry creamed inside.
Purée—A thick soup.
Quenelles—Forcemeat of meat, fish, &c., formed into balls, and fried.
Ragoût—A very rich sauce or made dish.
Rissoles—Balls of minced meat covered with egg and breadcrumbs, and fried.
Roux—A thickening made of butter and flour.
Salmis—A hash of half-roasted game.
Sauce Piquante—An acid sauce.
Sauter—A mode of frying.
Seasoning—Three bay leaves, six cloves, a blade or two of mace, pepper, and salt.
Soufflé—The very lightest of puddings; a "puffed up" pudding is the meaning of the word.
Stock—The essence extracted from meat. It is the foundation of soups of all kinds.
Tamis or Tammy—A very fine strainer of woollen canvas.
Tourte—A tart baked in a shallow tin.
Turbans and Mazarines—Ornamental *entrées* of forced meat, and fillets of poultry, game, or fish.
Velouté—A white sauce.
Vol-au-vent—Very light puff paste formed into cups, and filled with ragoût or mince.

CARVING.

One of the most important acquisitions in the routine of daily life is the ability to carve, not only well, but elegantly. It is true that the present fashion of Russian dinners is fast banishing the necessity for promiscuous carving from the richly-served boards of the wealthy; but in the circles of middle life, where it is not adopted, the necessity of skill in the use of a carving-knife is sufficiently obvious.

Ladies ought especially to make carving a study; at their own houses, and at the family dinner, they should be enabled to perform the task allotted to them with sufficient skill to prevent remark, or the calling forth of eager proffers of assistance from good-natured visitors near, who probably would far rather not be so employed.

Carving presents no real difficulties; it simply requires knowledge. All displays of exertion or violence are in very bad taste; for if they are not an evidence of the want of ability on the part of the carver, they present a very strong testimony of the toughness of a joint, or the more than full age of a bird: in both cases they should be avoided. A good knife of moderate size, sufficient length of handle, and great sharpness is requisite; the carving-knife for a lady should be light, and smaller than that used by gentlemen. Fowls are very easily carved; and of joints, such as loins, breasts, fore-quarters, &c., the butcher should have strict injunctions to separate the joints.

The dish upon which the article to be carved is placed should be conveniently near to the carver, so that he may have full control over it; for if it is placed far off, nothing can prevent an ungracefulness of appearance, and a difficulty in performing that which if it were in its proper place could be achieved with ease.

In helping fish, nicety and care must be exercised; lightness of hand and dexterity of management are necessary, and can only be acquired by practice. The flakes which, in fish like salmon and cod, are large, should not be broken in helping, for the beauty of the fish is then destroyed, and it becomes less inviting to the appetite.

In the following directions, accompanied by diagrams, we have endeavoured to be as explicit as possible; but practice alone will enable any person to carve with skill and facility.

RIBS OF BEEF.—There are two modes of carving this joint; the first, which is now becoming common, and is easy to an amateur carver, is to cut across the bone, commencing in the centre, and helping fat from A, as marked in the engraving of the sirloin, or it should be carved in slices from A to B, commencing either in the centre of the joint or at the sides. Occasionally the bones are removed, and the meat formed into a fillet; it should then be carved as a round of beef.

AN AITCH-BONE OF BEEF.—This is a simple joint to carve, but the slices from it must be cut quite even, and of a very moderate thickness. When the joint is boiled, before cutting it, remove a slice from the whole of the upper part, of sufficient thickness (say a quarter of an inch) to arrive at the juicy part of the meat at once. Carve from A to B; let the slices be moderately thin—not too thin—help fat with the lean in one piece, and give a little additional fat which you will find below C; the solid fat is at A, and must be cut in slices horizontally. The round of beef is carved in the same manner.

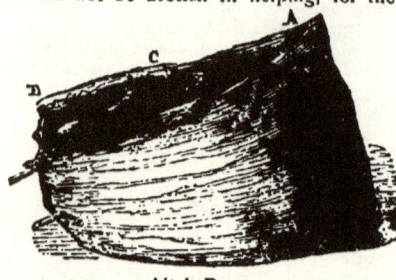

Aitch-Bone.

THE SIRLOIN OF BEEF.—The under part should be first carved, as indicated in the engraving across the bone. In carving the upper part the same directions should be followed as for the ribs, carving either side, or in the centre, from A to B, and helping the fat from D.

FILLET OF VEAL.—Cut a slice off the whole of the upper part in the same way as from a round of beef, this being, if well roasted, of a nice brown, should be helped in small pieces with the slices you cut for each person. The stuffing is skewered in the flap, and where the bone comes out there is some placed; help this with the meat, with a piece of the fat.

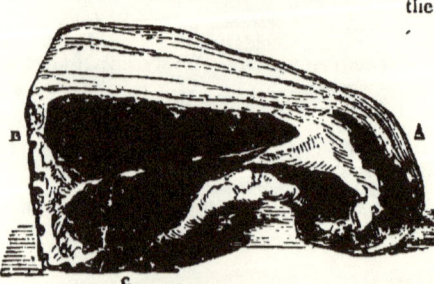

Sirloin of Beef.

NECK OF VEAL.—Were you to attempt to carve each chop, and serve it, you would not only place a gigantic piece upon the plate of the person you intended to help, but you would waste much time, and should the vertebræ not have been jointed by the butcher, you would find yourself in the position of the ungraceful carver, being compelled to exercise a degree of strength which should never be suffered to appear; very possibly, too, splashing gravy in a manner not contemplated by the

Fillet of Veal.

person unfortunately near enough to receive it. Cut diagonally from B to A, and help in slices of moderate thickness; you can then cut from C to D in order to separate the small bones, divide and serve them, having first inquired if they are liked.

LOIN OF VEAL.—This joint is sent to table served as a sirloin of beef. Having turned it over, cut out the kidney and the fat, return it to its proper position, and carve it, as in the neck of veal, from B to A; help with it a slice of kidney and fat. The kidney is usually placed upon a dry toast when removed from the joint.

SHOULDER OF VEAL is sent to table with the underpart placed uppermost. Help it as a shoulder of mutton, beginning at the knuckle end.

THE BREAST OF VEAL.—Separate the ribs from the brisket, cutting from A to B; these small bones are the sweetest, and are mostly preferred; you will cut them as at D D D, and serve. The long ribs are divided as at C C C; and having ascertained the preference of the person, help accordingly; at good tables the scrag is not served, but is found, when properly cooked, a very good stew.

CALF'S HEAD.—There is much more meat to be obtained from a calf's head by carving it one way than another. Carve from A to B, cutting quite down to the bone. At the fleshy part of the neck end you will find the throat sweetbread, of which you can help a slice with the other part; you will remove the eye with the point of the knife and divide it in halves, helping those to it who profess a preference for it; there are some gelatinous pieces around it which are palatable. Remove the jawbone, and then you will meet with some fine-flavoured lean; the palate, which is under the head, is by some thought a dainty, and should be proffered when carving.

A SHOULDER OF MUTTON.—This is a joint upon which a great diversity of opinion exists, many professing a species of horror at its insipidity; others finding much delicacy of flavour in certain parts. In good mutton there is no doubt but that, if pro-

Neck of Veal.

Breast of Veal.

Half of Calf's Head.

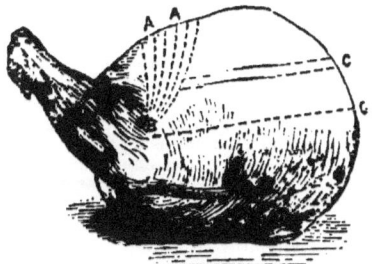

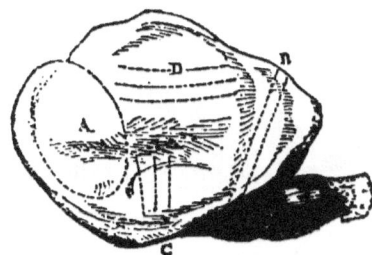

A Shoulder of Mutton.

perly managed, it is an excellent joint, and if judiciously carved, will give satisfaction to all who partake of it. It should be served and eaten very hot. It is sent to table lying on the dish as shown in the annexed engraving. Commence carving from A to B, taking out moderately thin slices in the shape of a wedge; some nice pieces may then be helped from the blade-bone, from C to B, cutting on both sides of the bone. Cut the fat from D, carving it in thin slices. Some of the most delicate parts, however, lie on the under part of the shoulder; take off thin pieces horizontally from B to C, and from A; some tender slices are to be met with at D, but they must be cut through as indicated.

The shoulder of mutton is essentially a joint of tit-bits, and therefore, when carving it, the tastes of those at table should be consulted. It is a very insipid joint when cold, and should therefore be hashed if sent to table a second time.

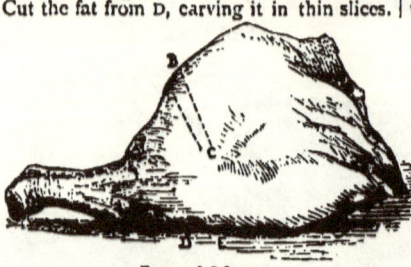

Leg of Mutton.

LEG OF MUTTON.—The under or thickest part of the leg should be placed uppermost, and carved in slices moderately thin, from B to C. Many persons have a taste for the knuckle, and this question should be asked, and, if preferred, it should be sent to the guest. When cold, the back of the leg should be placed uppermost, and thus carved. If the cramp bone is requested, (some persons regard it as a dainty) insert your knife at D, passing it round to E, and you will remove it.

SADDLE OF MUTTON.—The tail end is divided in the engraving, and the kidneys skewered under each division; this is a matter of taste, and is not always done. Carve from A to B in thin slices, help fat from C to D. You may help from the vertebræ on both sides of the loin, and then carve crosswise as marked in the engraving, which gives you both fat and lean; help a slice of kidney to those who desire it.

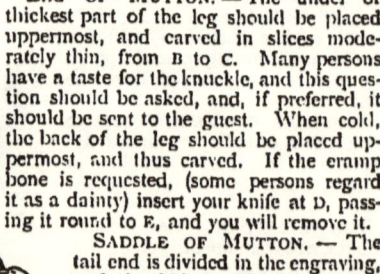

Saddle of Mutton.

THE LOIN OF MUTTON, if small, should be carved in chops, beginning with the outer chop; if large, carve slices the whole length. A neat way is to run the knife along the chine bone, and under the meat along the ribs; it may then be cut in slices as shown in the engraving of the saddle of mutton. By this process fat and lean are served together; your knife should be very sharp, and it should be done cleverly.

NECK OF MUTTON, if the scrag and chine bone are removed, is carved in the direction of the bones.

THE SCRAG OF MUTTON should be separated from the ribs of the neck, and when roasted the bones sent with the meat.

HAUNCH OF MUTTON is carved as haunch of venison.

FORE QUARTER OF LAMB.—Place your fork near the knuckle, and cut from A to C, to B, and on to D; pass your knife under, lifting with your fork at the same time. The juice of half a lemon or Seville orange which has been sprinkled with salt and pepper, is then squeezed under the shoulder, and a slice of fresh butter placed there also, the parts are re-united until the butter is melted, and the shoulder is then placed upon a separate dish; separate the neck from the ribs, from E to D, and then help the breast, G, or the neck, F, according to the taste of your guest.

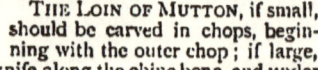

Fore Quarter of Lamb.

HAUNCH OF VENISON.—Have the dish placed before you so that the loin is nearest to you, and the knuckle farthest; then cut from A to B, sufficiently near the knuckle to prevent the escape of any gravy; then make your first cut from A to C, with a slanting cut, and then let each succeeding slice be sloping, so that all the gravy may be retained in the hollow thus formed; the fat will be found at the left side, and must be served with the meat.

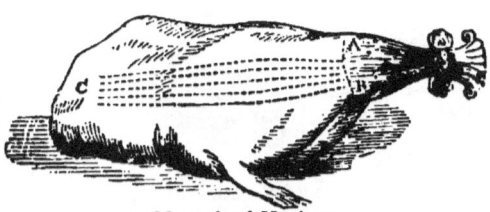

Haunch of Venison.

KID, if kept until the age at which lambs are killed, is served and carved in the same manner; if killed at a month or five weeks, it is roasted whole, and carved in the kitchen.

PORK.—The leg when sent to table should be placed with the back uppermost and the crackling be removed; if sufficiently roasted this may be done with ease. The meat should be cut in thin slices across the leg, the crackling being served with it or not, according to taste. The loins are cut into the pieces scored by the butcher.

Ham is served as placed in the engraving, and should come to table ornamented. Carve from A to B, cutting thin slices slantingly, to give a wedge-like appearance. Those who prefer the hock carve at D, in the same direction as from A to B, then carve from D to C, in thin slices, as indicated in the diagram.

BOILED TONGUE.—Carve across the tongue, but do not cut through; keep the slices rather thin, and help the fat and kernels from underneath.

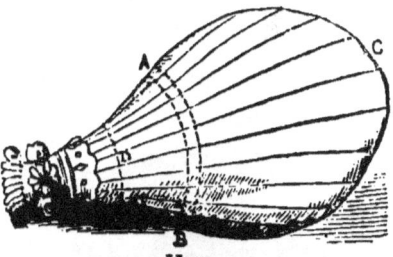

Ham.

ROAST PIG.—The cook should send a roast pig to table as displayed here, garnished with head and ears; carve the joints in the direction shown by the lines in the diagram, then divide the ribs; serve with plenty of sauce. Should one of the joints be too much, it may be separated. Bread sauce and stuffing should accompany it. An ear and the jaw are favourite parts with many people.

HARE.—Cut slices from B to A of moderate thickness. When the hare is young you can, after removing the shoulders and legs, cut across the back, and divide it into several pieces. This is not practicable with a full grown hare, unless it is boned. The shoulders and legs are easily removed by placing the knife between them, and turning them back; the joint will disclose itself, and can then be separated. The head should not be removed until the last; divide it from the neck, remove the lower jaw, then cut through the division which appears from the nose to the top of the skull, and lay it open. The stuffing should be given with whatever portion may be helped.

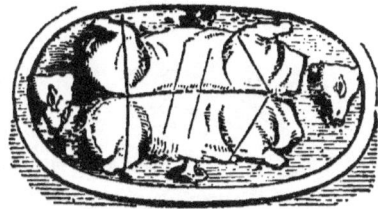

Roast Pig.

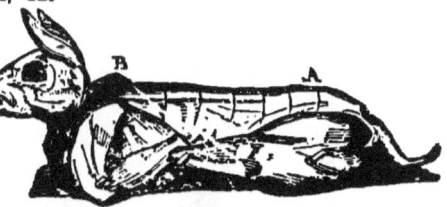

Hare.

ROAST RABBITS are carved in the same manner.

BOILED RABBIT.—Remove the legs and shoulders, they very easily separate. Divide the back into two parts, and by holding the fork firmly in the back, and passing the knife underneath, near the middle, and bending it back, this is accomplished readily.

Boiled Rabbit.

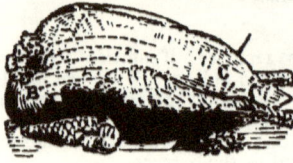

Roast Turkey.

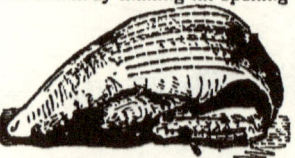

Boiled Turkey.

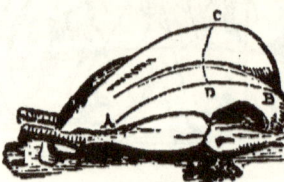

Roast Fowl.

The most tender part is on the loins; the meat there is of a very delicate flavour. Liver should be helped with it.

POULTRY.—Poultry requires skilful carving. The requisites are grace of manner, ease in the performance, a perfect knowledge of the position of the joints, and the most complete mode of dissecting, so as to obtain the largest quantity of meat. In no case is this ability more demanded than in carving a roast turkey. Unless this is done well, there is not only much waste, but the appearance of the turkey is spoiled. You will commence by carving slices from each side of the breast, in the same direction as the lines marked in the engraving, cutting from A to B. Then remove the legs, dividing the thighs from the drumsticks, and here an instrument termed a disjointer will be found serviceable, for unless the turkey be very young, and the union of the joints very accurately taken, carving becomes difficult. The disjointer effects the separation at once, and it possesses also the advantage of enabling the carver to divide a thigh into two, thus permitting a less bulky portion to be served. The pinions and that portion of the body removed with it are always a delicacy, and care should be taken to carve them nicely. The joint of the pinion will be found at B. The stuffing, if it be of truffles, you will obtain by making an opening at C. Ordinary forcemeat is found in helping the breast.

BOILED TURKEY is trussed in a different fashion to the roast, but the direction given for carving the former applies to the latter. The legs in the boiled turkey being drawn into the body may cause some little difficulty at first in their separation, but a little practice will soon surmount it.

ROAST FOWL.—This operation is a nice and skilful one to perform; it requires both observation and practice. Insert the knife between the legs and the side, press back the leg with the blade of the knife, and the joint will come apart if judiciously managed, it will require but a nick where the joints unite. Remove the wing from D to B, cut through and lay it back as with the leg, separating the joint with the edge of the knife, remove the merrythought and neck bones next; this you will accomplish by inserting the knife and forcing it under the bones; raise it and it will readily separate from the breast. You will divide the breast from the body by cutting through the small ribs down to the vent, turn the back uppermost, now put the knife into about the centre between the neck and rump, raise

Boiled fowl (breast).

Boiled Fowl (back).

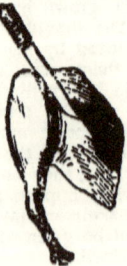

the lower part firmly yet gently, it will easily separate, turn the neck or rump from you, take off the side bones, and the fowl is carved.

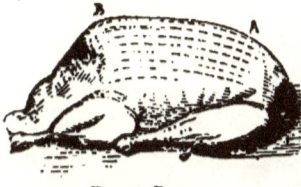

Roast Goose.

In separating the thigh from the drum-stick, you must insert the knife exactly at the joint, as we have indicated in the engraving; this, however, will be found to require practice, for the joint must be accurately hit, or else much difficulty will be experienced in getting the parts asunder. There is no difference in carving roast and boiled fowls, if full grown; but in a very young fowl when roasted, the breast is served whole. The wings and breast are preferred, but the leg of a young fowl is an excellent part. Capons when very fine and roasted should have slices carved from the breast, like a turkey.

Pheasant.

GEESE.—Follow with your knife the lines marked in the engraving, A to B, and cut slices; then remove the wing, and if the party be large, the legs must also be removed, and here the *disjointer* will again prove serviceable. The stuffing will be obtained by making an insertion at the apron, C.

PHEASANT.—Clear the leg by inserting the edge of the knife between it and the body, then take off the wings, B to A, but do not remove much of the breast with them, you are thus enabled to obtain some nice slices; the pheasant is then carved as a fowl. The breast is first in estimation, then the wings, and after these the merrythought; lovers of game prefer a leg.

PARTRIDGE.—Separate the legs, and then divide the bird into three parts, leaving each leg and wing together. The breast is then divided from the back, and helped whole, the latter being helped with any of the other parts. When the party consists of gentlemen only, the bird is divided in halves by cutting lengthwise right through from the centre.

Pigeon (breast).

Partridge.

QUAILS, LANDRAIL, WHEATEARS, LARKS, and all small birds are served whole.

WILD DUCKS AND WIDGEON.—The breast of these fowls being the best portion, is carved in slices, which are removed, and a glass of old port wine is poured in: the half of a lemon seasoned with Cayenne and salt should then be squeezed in, the slices relaid in their places, and then served, the joints being removed the same as in other fowls.

Pigeon (back).

PIGEON.—Like woodcock, these birds are cut in halves, through the breast and back, and the half is sent to the person helped.

FISH.

Fish should never be touched with a steel knife. Fish slices, or a silver fish knife and fork, are used for carving it. It requires more care than knowledge to help fish—the principal thing is to avoid breaking the flakes. In carving a piece of salmon as here engraved, cut thin slices, as from A to B, and help with it pieces of the belly in the direction marked from C to D; the best flavoured is the upper or thick part.

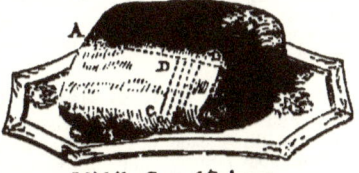

TURBOT.—Cut flat pieces as marked in the engraving without moving the bone; the fin, which is esteemed a delicacy, is always served with it.

Middle Cut of Salmon.

All flat-fish, such as plaice, brill, Johndory, &c., are carved in the same manner; soles are cut either into halves, or, if very large, are divided into three, cutting them across right through. Flounders are served whole.

COD'S HEAD AND SHOULDERS.—Carry the knife from A to B, and then along the line to C, help slices accompanied by some of the sound, which is to be found lining the back,

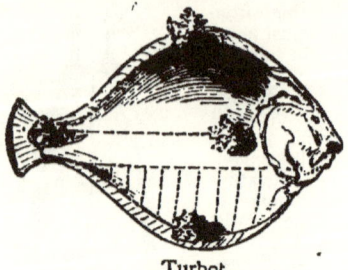

Turbot.

Cod's Head.

and which you may obtain by passing the knife under the backbone at C; send also a piece of liver.

MACKEREL.—Mackerel should always be sent to table head to tail. Divide the meat from the bone by cutting down the back lengthwise; the upper part is the best. All small fish, such as pilchards, herrings, smelts, &c., are served whole. WHITINGS when fried have the tail curled as in the engraving. They are helped whole. PIKE are served in many ways. When baked, the back and belly should be slit up, by this means fewer bones will be given.

A Dish of Mackerel.

Fried Whiting.

and each slice gently drawn downwards;
Remember that constant practice is required to make a good carver. With it and a little care and observation, it will become easy and even pleasant to you to carve; and will greatly add to the comfort and nicety of the home dinner-table.

BREAKFAST RECIPES.

To Roast Coffee.

1. Have either a Patent Roaster, or the Irish mop roaster. To every three pounds of coffee you put in the roaster add a piece of good fresh butter, a little larger than a marble, and two tea-spoonfuls of powdered sugar; then roast the berries. This little addition develops the aroma of the berry. Many people prefer having chicory added to their coffee—the proportion is about a quarter of a pound of chicory to a pound of coffee.

Excellent Coffee for Three Breakfast Cups.

2. Four tablespoonfuls of roasted coffee berries; three teacupfuls of boiling water.
Take four tablespoonfuls of roasted coffee berries and put them in the oven till well warmed through; then grind them. Put the coffee in the pot, which should have a piece of tin over the middle strainer to prevent the coffee from filling up the holes; pour in three teacupfuls of boiling water. The breakfast-cup should be filled up with boiling milk.

Soyer's Mode.

3. Soyer's mode of making coffee was to warm the powder over the fire first, then to pour the boiling water over it; cover it closely for five minutes, strain it and boil it up again for use. This is a good way, but the easier plan is to make it in the percolator; *first* warming the powder in a covered cup before it is put into the coffee-pot to be made.
French coffee is made by adding a pint of *made* coffee to a pint of boiling milk, and warming both together, but not letting them boil too long.

Chocolate.

Time, a quarter of an hour.

4. One cake of chocolate; one pint of water.

Cut a cake of chocolate in very small pieces; boil a pint of water. When it is at boiling point, add the chocolate; mill it off the fire until quite melted. Then place it on a gentle fire till it boils. Pour it into a basin, and it will keep for eight or ten days, or more, When it is required, put a spoonful or two into fresh milk, boil it with sugar, and mix it well. Mill it to a fine froth and serve.

Cocoa Nibs. (Dr. Todd.)

Time, five hours.

5. A quarter of a pound of cocoa nibs; three quarts of water.

A quarter of a pound of cocoa nibs to three quarts of water, to be boiled down to two quarts and a half. The nibs to be strained after five hours' boiling. If they are allowed to remain in the cocoa, it becomes bitter and unpalatable.

Cocoa-Paste or Powder.

Time, two or three minutes.

6. One and a half teaspoonful of cocoa; one cup of boiling milk; a very little sugar.

Put the cocoa in a breakfast-cup, add by degrees a little boiling milk, mix it slowly to a paste, then fill the cup with milk and add the sugar; or

One and a half teaspoonful of cocoa; three quarters of a cupful of boiling water; sugar to taste; quarter of a cupful of milk.

Bread and Milk.

Time, eight minutes.

7. Two or three ounces of bread; half a pint of milk.

Cut the bread into small dice; put them into a breakfast cup or basin; boil the milk; and when boiling, pour it over the bread. Cover the cup over for about five minutes. Add the sugar to taste.

Oatmeal Porridge.

Time, half an hour.

8 Two ounces of oatmeal; one pint of water; half a pint of cold milk.

Put a pint of warm water into a stewpan over the fire and as it boils dredge in the oatmeal with your left hand, and stir with the right. When it is made, turn it into a soup-plate, adding a little salt or a little sugar, according to taste. Send it to table with a jug of hot milk, which should be added to it by degrees for eating.

To Toast Muffins.

9. Pull open the sides of the muffin exactly in the centre, about half an inch in; put the toasting-fork in it and toast it carefully. When it is done, and it should only be *lightly* toasted, pull it apart, lay a little butter on each side, and close the muffin. Put it on a hot plate and cut it in four. If more than one are required, lay them on the first done, but do not send in a great pile of muffins, as they are better served *hot*. A hot-water plate with a cover,—a regular muffin plate,—should be used, and *two* at the most only be sent in at a time.

Crumpets.

10. Do not open crumpets; toast them carefully and very quickly; butter them on both sides, and serve them separately on a hot-water plate, if you have one; if not, send them in hot and hot, as they are not nice lukewarm. *Never* put one crumpet on the top of the other, as the under one would become heavy.

Bread.

Everybody is, I believe, of opinion that home-made bread is cheaper, sweeter, and more wholesome than that bought at the baker's, *unless* it is badly made. Heavy, close, bitter bread is only too well known in many households where it is home-made; this is not economical, as it cannot nourish the eaters as good bread does, and it is, generally speaking, wasted. Let us see if it is not possible to teach how to make bread of all kinds, which shall be good, light, sweet, and appetizing. The oven plays an important part in this manufacture.

A brick oven heated with wood is the right one for economy. It is possible to bake bread in the iron oven attached to a range, but the author, from personal experience, can assure her readers that home-made bread thus baked is more expensive than bakers', on account of the quantity of fuel it takes to heat the oven for bread-baking, and the necessity of making it up in small loaves, which are not economical.

The brick oven is heated by faggot wood; after it is cleared out, the door should be shut very closely for half an hour before you put in your loaves. The oven will then be thoroughly heated, and the heat will last for some time.

A brick oven for baking bread should be as hot as you can bear to hold your hand in (without touching the bricks of course) whilst counting twenty; this is an established rule in most farmhouses.

Bread is longer baking in an iron oven than in a brick one. Next to the oven in importance comes the yeast. We have used, and like, both German and patent yeast, but as many persons prefer their own, and it is always well for the house to be independent of external helps in this matter, we give receipts for making yeast, for the goodness of which we can answer.

FLOUR should be purchased of a miller; it will be less likely to be adulterated than if it passed through a second hand. The best flour is generally used in gentlemen's kitchens; nevertheless, we know several county families (and one nobleman's family) famous for excellent household bread, in which the "best seconds" are always used. There is no doubt that more nutrition is contained in brown bread than in white, and that the *whiter* the bread the less is the nourishment derived from it. Brown bread is excellent for weak digestions, and for many other reasons should be eaten alternately with white bread in all families; moreover, it is less adulterated than the very white bread when purchased from the baker's.

The flour of "hard wheat," as it is called, is the most nutritious; it is not so white as that procured from soft wheat, but has more gluten in it.

Flour when kept in store should be placed in a warm dry room, as, if at all damp, it will make the bread or cakes for which it is used heavy. It is safest to put the quantity of flour you are about to make into bread before the fire in a large dish or pan for an hour or two, in order to have it warm and dry for use.

Great cleanliness is required for making bread—a clean trough or brown earthenware pan; *very* clean hands and arms, and nice fresh yeast. The fresher the yeast, the less you will require of it.

Never leave the dough half made, nor allow it to get cold before it is finished; if you do, it will be heavy. Too small a proportion of yeast will make the dough heavy.

If the sponge or the dough be permitted to overwork itself it will become sour in warm weather. Do not put it *too* near the fire, but keep it warm at a gentle and equal degree of heat.

Bread baked in tins will be lighter than when made into ordinary loaves, and is best for toast or sandwiches.

Too little water will spoil the bread; too much will make it too slack. If by accident the latter fault is perceptible, make the bread up in tins, and it will not much matter.

The proportions given in the numerous recipes contained in this book, may of course be modified according to the quantity of bread required.

How to make your own Yeast.

Time to boil, half an hour; to make, four days.

11. Two ounces of the best hops; four quarts of water; one pound of flour; three pounds of good potatoes.

Monday morning boil two ounces of the best hops in four quarts of water for half an hour; strain it, and let the liquor cool down to new milk warmth; then put in a small handful of salt and half a pound of brown sugar; beat up one pound of the best flour with some of the liquor, and then mix all well together. On Wednesday add three pounds of potatoes, boiled and then mashed, to stand till Thursday; then strain it, and put it into seltzer-water bottles, and it is ready for use.

N.B.—It must be stirred frequently while it is making, and kept near the fire. Before using, shake the bottle well up. It will keep in a cool place for two months, and is best at the latter part of the time. The beauty of this yeast is, that it ferments spontaneously, not requiring the aid of other yeast; and, if care be taken, it will ferment well in the earthen bowl in which it is made.

To make Bread.

Time, one hour to bake loaves of two pounds weight each.

12. Seven pounds of flour; two quarts of warm water; a large tablespoonful of salt; half a gill of yeast.

Put the flour into a deep pan, heap it round the sides, leaving a hollow in the centre; put into it a quart of warm water, a large spoonful of salt, and half a gill of yeast; have ready three pints more of warm water, and with as much of it as may be necessary, make the whole into a rather soft dough, kneading it well with both hands. When it is smooth and shining, strew a little flour on it; lay a thickly folded cloth over it, and set it in a warm place by the fire for four or five hours; then knead it again for a quarter of an hour; cover it over, and set it to rise again; divide it into two or four loaves, and bake in a quick oven. It will take one hour to bake it if divided into loaves weighing two pounds each, and two hours if the loaves weigh four pounds each. This bread need only rise once, and if made of the best superfine flour will be beautifully white and light.

In cold weather bread should be mixed in a warm room, and not allowed to become cold while rising.

If there is any difficulty as to its rising, set the bowl or pan over boiling water.

It is best to mix the bread at night, and cover it close, in a warm room should the weather be cold, till the morning.

Of course, if the family be large, the quantities may be increased or doubled in proportion.

American Mode.

Time to bake, one hour to a loaf of two pounds weight.

13. Two quarterns of flour; four tablespoonfuls of fresh yeast; one tablespoonful of salt; one pint of water.

Mix four tablespoonfuls of good fresh yeast with a pint of lukewarm water; stir the salt well into the flour; make a hole with your hand in the centre, and pour the yeast into it, and stir it thoroughly until you have made it into a rather thin batter; dredge some flour over it; cover the pan with a thick cloth, and set it near the fire for an hour; then add a quart of water just warm, and knead the whole well together until it passes clean through your hand; then let it stand, not too near the fire, for another hour; divide it into loaves, and bake it.

German Yeast Bread.

Time, one and a half to two hours.

14. Two quarterns of flour; one tablespoonful of salt; two ounces of dried German yeast; a cupful of water; a pint and a half of warm water.

Dissolve the yeast in a small cupful of cold water, and then add it to a pint and a half of warm water. Put the flour well mixed with the salt into a deep bread pan; make a hole in the middle of the flour, and pour in the water and yeast; knead it up quickly, and let it stand near the fire covered over with a thick cloth for one hour; then divide it into loaves, and bake them according to their size. You may make up a much larger quantity of flour, and bake the loaves two or three at a time, if care is taken not to keep the dough too warm.

Potato Bread.

Time, to bake, one and a half to two hours.

15. Two and a half pounds of mealy potatoes; seven pounds of flour; a quarter of a pint of yeast; two ounces of salt.

Boil two pounds and a half of nice mealy potatoes till floury; rub and mash them smooth; then mix them with sufficient cold water to let them pass through a coarse sieve, and any lump that remains must be again mashed and pressed through. Mix this paste with the yeast, and then add it to the flour. Set it to rise, well knead it, and make it into a stiff tough dough.

To make Brown Bread.

Time, one or two hours, according to weight.

16. Three parts of second flour; the fourth part of rye; a little milk; and the right proportion of water.

Take three parts of second flour, and the fourth of rye, lay it one night in a cool place, and the next morning work it up with a little milk added to the water. Set it at a proper distance from the fire to rise, and then make into loaves and bake.

Rice Bread.

Time, one and a half to two hours.

17. Half a pound of rice; three pints of water; six pounds of flour.

Boil half a pound of rice in three pints of water till the whole is quite thick; with this, and yeast, and six pounds of flour make the dough. This will make as much as eight pounds of flour without the rice.

American Recipe for Light Breakfast Bread.

Time, to bake, half an hour.

18. One quart of milk (it may be skimmed); three-quarters of a pint of flour; one teacupful of hop-yeast; half a tablespoonful of salt; a small piece of butter.

Heat one-third of the quart of milk and scald it with half a pint of flour. If you use skimmed milk, add a small piece of butter.

When the batter thus made is cool, add the remainder of the milk, a teacupful of hop-yeast, half a tablespoonful of salt, with flour enough to make it quite stiff. Knead it on a paste-board till it is very fine and smooth. Leave it to rise all night.

This will make two small loaves and half a dozen biscuits.

French Rolls.

Time, half an hour.

19. One pound of flour; one egg; one ounce of butter; one spoonful of yeast; a little salt, and some milk.

Well beat the butter into the flour, adding a little salt; beat an egg, and stir it into the flour with the yeast, and a sufficient quantity of milk to make the dough rather stiff. Beat it well without kneading it; set it to rise, and bake it on tins. This quantity will make about six rolls, and when done rasp them before serving. Rolls (or any sort of bread) may be made new by dipping into water, and putting them into the oven to warm for a short time.

Tea Cakes or Loaves.
Time, half or three-quarters of an hour.

20. One egg; two ounces of butter; half a pound of flour; two or three knobs of sugar.
Rub the butter into the flour, add the sugar pounded, and mix it with one beaten egg.
It will make two small loaves for tea or breakfast.

Water Cakes.
21.—Take one pound of fine flour and a piece of butter the size of a nut, rub it well into the flour, mix it with cold water, and one pinch of salt. Roll it out very thin, cut it into cakes, and bake them in a quick oven.

American Muffins.
Time, till the outside blisters.

22. One pint of warm milk; half a teaspoonful of melted butter; half a gill of yeast; a teaspoonful of salt; a bit of saleratus the size of a pea; and sufficient flour to make a thick batter; two eggs.
Mix with a pint of warm milk two well-beaten eggs, the melted butter, salt, and the saleratus dissolved in a little hot water; then stir into it sufficient wheat flour to make a thick batter; set it in a warm place to rise, for three hours in warm weather, or longer in the winter; put a gridle over the fire; when it is hot, rub it over with some butter, grease the inside of the rings, set them on it and half fill them with the batter, or they may be done without rings. When one side is done turn the other; bake them a light colour. When they are done, *break* them open, put a bit of butter into each, and set them before the fire until served. They must never be cut. If cold they must be picked open, toasted on each side lightly, and butter put into them.

Crumpets.
Time, five minutes after the top has blistered.

23. One and a half ounce of German yeast, or half a gill of common yeast; a quart of warm milk; a cupful of melted butter; a little salt.
Make the milk warm, and stir it into the yeast with a little salt. Add a sufficient quantity of flour to make it into a batter. Set it to rise for half an hour; then add a cupful of melted butter. Stir it well in, and pour it into iron rings previously placed on a hot plate, and bake them very lightly on both sides. When required, toast them on each side, taking care they do not burn; butter them nicely, cut them across, and put them upon a hot plate; serving them quickly, hot and hot.

Devilled Biscuits.
24. Get some *very* thin plain biscuits, pour over them a little clarified butter, and let them stand for a short time; then dredge over them on each side a little pepper, salt, and Cayenne; press it lightly over with a knife, and toast them on a gridiron over a clear fire.
A thin layer of sardines, salmon, or anchovies may be placed on the biscuits, and browned with a salamander, or in the oven, and will make a delicious relish; but they are extremely nice without, served plain.

Fadge—Irish Receipt.
Time, one hour.

25. Half a pint of new milk; three ounces of butter; one pound of wheaten meal flour; a little salt.
Take half a pint of new milk, put three ounces of butter into it, and melt it on the fire in the milk, shaking it continually *one way*, in order that it may not burn. Put one pound of wheaten flour into a bowl and a little salt. Make a hole in the middle of the flour and pour the milk into it, stirring it well as you do so. Put it on the pasteboard, flour a roller, and roll it out to about three quarters of an inch thick. Cut it out into cakes, and lay them on a gridle, turning them often to prevent them from burning.

Sir Tatton Sykes' Water Cakes.
Time, fifteen minutes.

26. One pound of flour; a piece of butter the size of a nut; a quarter of a pint of cold water; one pinch of salt.

To Boil Eggs for Breakfast.
Time, three minutes, or very soft, two minutes and a half.

27. Fill a pint saucepan with water, set it over the fire and let it boil. Then, as it boils, put in with a spoon two or three fresh eggs. Take care not to crack the shells, or to boil them too fast. Serve them in eggcups on a stand.
N.B.—Do not use a fresh egg till it has been laid ten hours. The albumen, or white, will not be set before that time has elapsed.

Poached Eggs.
Time, two minutes.

28. One pint of water; one tablespoonful of vinegar; one saltspoonful of salt: as many eggs as required.

Put the vinegar and salt into the water, let it boil, then break the eggs carefully into it, let them boil gently three minutes. Take them out with a slice, let them drain, and put them on a slice or round of thin buttered toast. If the yolk separates from the white, the egg is not fresh. The egg may also be done in a regular egg-poacher.

Eggs and Bacon.
Time, three to four minutes.

29. Six eggs; a quarter of a pound of dripping or butter; some slices of ham or bacon.

Break five or six fresh eggs into cups, and slip them into a delicately clean frying-pan of boiling dripping or butter. When the whites are set, take them up with a slice, trim off the rough edges, and drain them from the grease. Then place them in the centre of the dish, and the slices of fried bacon round the edge, or the eggs may be served on the bacon, whichever you prefer.

Baked Eggs.
Time, five minutes.

30. A piece of butter; five eggs; pepper and salt.

Well butter a dish, and break five eggs very carefully on it; put on the top of each a little pepper and salt and a bit of butter, and put them into a slow oven until well set. Serve them up hot.

Devilled Eggs.
Time to boil, from ten to twelve minutes.

31. Four eggs; half a teaspoonful of salt; one full teaspoonful of anchovy sauce; a little Cayenne.

Boil four eggs; lay them in fresh water until they are cold. Cut them in halves; flatten the ends a little to make them stand upright. Take out the yolks and mix them with the anchovy, Cayenne, and salt. Replace the mixture in the eggs, and place them in a round dish, with small salad round; either mustard and cress, or lettuces chopped very fine.

Eggs à la Bonne Femme.
Time, ten minutes.

32. Three eggs; two or three slices of beetroot; a slice or two of cold chicken, or any cold meat; three heads of coss lettuce.

Boil three fresh eggs for ten minutes, roll them to break their shells on the table; shell them, cut them in halves, and just cut off the point of the white so that they may stand well. Take out the yolks and fill the white cup, thus; two with beetroot (already boiled) cut into tiny dice; two with cold chicken or meat cut into dice; two with tiny dice of the yolks, piled up in them. Cut up some coss lettuce very nicely; lay it on the dish, and place the eggs on it.

Brawn.
Oxford brawn is considered the best to purchase. The following recipes, especially the first, will be found excellent for family use.

Brawn.
Time, three nights; six hours to boil, three hours to get cold.

33. Pickled porker's head; two tongues; two feet, and two extra ears; four fried sausages; some slices of boiled ox tongue; dried sage, pepper and salt, one teaspoonful of each for seasoning; three tablespoonfuls of salt to cover the head.

Cut the porker's head in half, and soak one night; cover it with salt for one night, boil slowly six hours. Let it get cold. Take out the bones. Boil the two tongues, feet, and ears one hour and a half; remove the bones and gristle. Cut all the meat into small pieces; season with sage, pepper, and salt, well mixed. Cut the sausages into slices. Place slices of ox tongue, which should be of a nice red colour, in a pattern round the mould or tin; put in the meat, and press it firmly down with a weight on the top. Let it stand one night.

The tongues may be put in whole, if preferred, about the middle of the mould.

Plovers' Eggs.
Time, two minutes.

34. Plovers' eggs must be boiled hard and served either hot or cold. For breakfast, line a little basket with moss and lay them in it. If you have no basket, serve them on a folded tablenapkin, or shell them and pour Béchamel sauce over them.

You may manufacture a satisfactory basket for plovers' eggs, by lining one of the round baskets in which strawberries are sold with moss, both outside and inside, and bending a twig or wire over it for a handle. This basket of eggs is a great ornament to a breakfast table.

Ham Toast.
Time, two minutes.

35. Slices of toasted bread; two eggs; one ounce of butter; some cold ham or tongue, grated.

Cut some thin slices from a stale loaf, toast them as for breakfast, and then cut them into square pieces. Put the yolks and whites of two beaten eggs into a stewpan with an ounce of butter; stir them two minutes over the fire; spread them over the toast, and lay over them a sufficient quantity of cold ham or tongue, grated or minced, to cover the eggs; serve it up very hot.

Plain Grated Ham and Toast.
Time, about four minutes,

36. Five ounces of grated ham; five square pieces of toast.
Toast and nicely butter two or three slices of bread, cut them in five squares. Heap in a little pile on each of them, one ounce of finely grated ham.

Birds' Nests.
Time, fifteen minutes, ten minutes to boil eggs.

37. Four eggs; half a pint of rich brown gravy; a quarter of a pound of forcemeat—for which you will require about one ounce of beef suet, chopped *very fine;* one ounce of bread crumbs; half an ounce of chopped parsley; powdered thyme and marjoram; a little grated rind of a lemon and half its juice; one egg to bind it.
Make your forcemeat by chopping up the beef suet very fine; grating the bread, chopping the parsley, and mixing the whole; grate in a little lemon peel, season it with pepper and salt. (Soyer was wont to say that seasoning could not be sufficiently accurate unless it was *sprinkled* from the cook's fingers.) Beat the yolk of an egg and bind the forcemeat with it; let four eggs boil for ten minutes. Warm half a pint of rich brown gravy. When the eggs are boiled hard take them from their shells, and brush them over *thickly* with the forcemeat. Put a little butter in a stew-pan; fry them a light brown, dish them up, cut them in halves (first cut off also the top of the white that they may stand), and serve them hot with rich brown gravy poured over them.

Huitres au Lit.
Time, ten minutes.

38. Eight oysters; four thin slices of fat bacon; a round of toasted bread.
Take two oysters from their shells and roll them in a *thin broad* slice of fat bacon; fasten them with a small silver skewer (or steel one), and toast the tiny roll before the fire in a Dutch oven. Make four of these rolls, roast them at the same time, and serve them hot on a round of nicely toasted bread. *See* engraving.

Egg Toast.
Time, five minutes.

39. Four ounces of clarified butter; four eggs well beaten; one table-spoonful of anchovy paste; one round of toast.
Put the yolks of four eggs and the whites of two with four ounces of clarified butter; beat them well together, then stir it over the fire in the same direction till mixed. Make a round of thin delicate toast, spread anchovy paste over it, then put on the mixture with a fork. Cut the toast into pieces and serve very hot.

Kegeree for Breakfast.
Time, six minutes, fifteen after the rice is boiled.

40. One teaspoonful of rice; four hard boiled eggs; any white fish previously boiled; a lump of *fresh butter*, pepper and salt.
Boil a cupful of rice very tender, boil four eggs very hard, and when cold chop them small; take the remains of any white fish that has been previously boiled, mince it fine, and mix all well together, and put the mixture into a stewpan with a lump of fresh butter; stew it till thoroughly hot, stirring it constantly to prevent its burning; season it with pepper and salt, and serve it up very hot. Take care not to make it too moist. Cold salmon answers very well for this dish; but haddock, turbot, soles, or pike are generally preferred.

Omelet.
Time, eleven minutes.

41. Four eggs; two dessertspoonfuls of milk; two ounces of butter; a sprig of parsley, and a few chives.
Beat four whole eggs with two dessert-spoonfuls of milk, a sprig of parsley, chives, and a seasoning of pepper and salt. Put the butter into an omelet-pan, and set it over the fire for five or six minutes, beating the herbs and eggs all the time; then pour them into the pan, and let them stand for a few minutes over the fire, but taking care to separate the omelet gently from the bottom of the pan, and shaking it to prevent its burning; fry it for about five minutes on one side, and serve it doubled over.

Ham or Tongue Omelet.
Time, four or six minutes.

42. Five ounces of butter; six eggs; a little pepper and salt; three dessertspoonfuls of grated ham or tongue.
Grate a little ready dressed ham or tongue very fine, and fry it for two or three minutes

1. Eggs a la bonne femme.
2. Grated Ham and Toast.
3. Huitres au lit.
4. Brawn.
5. Birds' Nests.
6. Egg Toast.
7. Plovers' Eggs in a Basket

In a piece of butter; put the yolks of six and the whites of three eggs into a plate, season with a little pepper and salt, and beat it well till very light and smooth; stir in the grated ham or tongue. Put some butter into an omelet-pan, and when it just begins to bubble, whisk up the mixture, and pour it into the pan, stir it with a spoon one way until it thickens and becomes warm, and then fold the edges of the omelet over in an oval form. Brown it nicely, and serve as quickly as possible, as the lightness of an omelet is spoilt unless it is served immediately. It may be browned on the top with a salamander.

Pigs' Kidneys

Time, fifteen minutes.

43. Pigs' kidneys are prepared exactly as sheep's kidneys are; they are nearly divided, fastened flat open with a tiny skewer, and broiled over a clear fire. They are served quite plain, or with maître d'hôtel sauce, if preferred.

Pigs' Feet and Ears.

Time, to boil, one hour and a half; to broil, ten minutes.

44. Two onions; one teaspoonful of made mustard; two ounces of butter; one teaspoonful of flour.

When you have cleaned and prepared the feet and ears, boil them; then split the feet in halves, egg and bread-crumb them, and broil them. Cut the ears into fillets, put them into a stew-pan with two sliced onions, two ounces of butter, and a teaspoonful of flour. When they are browned, take them up, add a teaspoonful of made mustard to the *purée*, and lay them on a hot dish. Put the feet on the top of them, and serve.

Or Fried in Batter.

Time, twenty minutes.

45. One egg; one tablespoonful of flour; one and a half gill of milk; a pinch of salt; a little lard for the pan.

Clean the feet and ears carefully; boil them gently, then take them up and lay them aside for the morning. Make a nice batter of an egg, a tablespoonful of flour, a gill and a half of milk, and a pinch of salt. Split the feet in halves, and dip them and the ears into the batter. Fry them a nice brown, and serve on a table-napkin.

Pigs' Feet Soused.

Time, one hour and a half.

46. Two feet; one teaspoonful of salt; three-quarters of a pint of vinegar; a quarter of a pint of the water in which they are boiled; six pepper corns; a little allspice; four cloves; a little mace.

Scald the feet and scrape them clean; if the covering of the toes will not come off without, singe them in hot embers, until they are loose; then take them off. Some persons put the feet in weak lime-water to whiten them. Having scraped them clean and white, wash them and put them into a pot of warm, but not boiling water, with a little salt. Let them boil gently till by turning a fork in the flesh it will easily break, and the bones are all loosened. Take off the scum as it rises. When they are done take them out of the water and lay them in vinegar enough to cover them, adding to it a quarter of a pint of the water in which they were boiled. Add whole pepper and spice with cloves and mace. Put them in a jar, and cover them closely.

Soused feet may be eaten cold from the vinegar, split in two from top to toe; or they may be split in two, dipped in flour, and fried in hot lard; or they may be broiled and buttered.

But, in the latter case, they should be nicely browned

Anchovy Toast.

47. Six or eight anchovies; one and a half ounce of butter; slices of toast.

Bone and skin six or seven anchovies. After washing them very clean pound them in a mortar with an ounce and a half of butter, and then rub them through a sieve; take some thin slices of bread, and cut them out with a tin cutter, into squares or rounds; fry them brown in a little butter, and spread over them (when cold) the anchovy mixture. Wash some anchovies, cut them in four, and put a piece on the top of each slice of toast; serve on a napkin garnished with crisped parsley.

Madras Anchovy Toast.

48. A piece of butter the size of an apple; yolks of two eggs; Cayenne pepper to taste; half a teaspoonful of white wine, or a teaspoonful of anchovy paste.

Put a piece of butter upon a very hot plate; add the well-beaten yolks of two eggs; Cayenne pepper to taste; half a teaspoonful of white wine, or a teaspoonful of anchovy paste; mix well, soak hot toast in it, and serve very hot. The toast should not be cut too thin.

This is the receipt by which the officers of the Madras army prepare their celebrated anchovy toast.

To Broil Sheep's Kidneys.

Time, eight to ten minutes.

49. Take a sharp knife and cut each kidney open, lengthwise, down to the root, but do not separate them; skin them, and put a very small skewer under the white part of each, to keep them flat. Make the gridiron warm, and rub it over with butter; place the kidneys with the inside downwards, and broil them over a clear fire. When sufficiently done on one side, turn them on the other; remove the skewers, season them with a little pepper and salt, put a piece of butter in the centre of each, and serve them with a small piece of well buttered toast, cut into squares, under each. They must be sent to table as hot as possible.

Mr. Dodd's Relish.

Altogether about two hours.

50. One kidney; one large onion; salt; pepper; one ounce of butter.

Take a large onion, parboil and drain it; cut out a piece from the flat side like a lid; scoop out as much of the inside as will suffice to leave a hollow big enough to hold a sheep's kidney; then cut the kidney in quarters, without quite separating it; put in some butter, pepper, and salt; close it, and place it in the scooped-out onion. Put the lid on again, and lay the onion in a dish with a little butter. Bake in the oven. Brown it, before serving, in the Dutch oven before the fire.

Broiled Mushrooms.

Time, eight minutes.

51. Sufficient flap mushrooms for a dish; pepper and salt; a piece of butter.

Wipe the mushrooms very clean with a piece of flannel, and salt; peel the tops, and cut the stalks partly off. Put them over a very clear fire, and broil them lightly on both sides. When done, arrange them on a dish; dust a little pepper and salt over them, and put a piece of butter on each mushroom. Place them before the fire for a few minutes to melt the butter, and serve them up quickly.

Devilled Chicken.

Time, ten or twelve minutes.

52. A cold fowl, or part of one; three tablespoonfuls of mustard; two saltspoonfuls of salt; one teaspoonful of pepper; half a saltspoonful of Cayenne pepper.

Take off the wings and legs of the fowl; make incisions in them, and fill these cuts with made mustard. Season them highly with salt, white and Cayenne pepper. Grill them over a clear fire, and serve them very dry on a hot table-napkin.

Oyster Loaves (America).

Time, to stew the oysters, five to six minutes.

53. Four small round breakfast rolls; two dozen of oysters and their liquor; four ounces of butter; one large teaspoonful of salt; half a teaspoonful of pepper; one teaspoonful of essence of anchovies; half a teaspoonful of pounded mace.

Have ready four small round breakfast loaves; take a circular piece neatly out of the top of each, and carefully scoop out the crumb. Put two dozen oysters into a stewpan with their liquor, four ounces of butter, one teaspoonful of salt, half a teaspoonful of pepper, one teaspoonful of essence of anchovies, and *half* the crumbs from the loaves. Let them gently simmer for five or six minutes; stir in a tablespoonful of cream, and fill directly the holes in the loaves. Fit in the tops again, and put them into an oven to crisp. To be served on a napkin.

The small rolls may in like manner be filled with nicely minced veal, or remains of game or cold chicken.

Cold turbot minced in a little cream is also nice when thus dressed and served up.

To Cook Kippered Salmon for Breakfast.

Time, about five minutes to broil the salmon.

54. Half to three-quarters of a pound of kippered salmon; a little pepper.

Have ready a well-heated gridiron, the bars of which should be greased, and a nice clear fire. Cut the salmon into narrow bars of convenient size, wrap them in buttered writing-paper, and broil, turning them once or twice. Serve on a very hot dish, laying the pieces across each other.

Kippered Salmon Toasted.

Time, ten minutes.

55. The salmon; boiling water; one ounce of butter.

Toast the salmon; place it in a basin with the outside downwards; pour boiling water over it; if salt be objected to, repeat the process. Place it on a dish the right side upwards, and spread butter on it before the fire.

Finnan Haddocks.

Time, about ten minutes.

56. These fish, which are much esteemed, are dressed open on account of one side being thicker than the other. They are

generally bought prepared for cooking, and only require a little soaking before they are put on the gridiron. When done, lay the fish on a hot dish, and put a little cold fresh butter on it.

To Cook Red Herrings and Bloaters.
Time, five minutes.

57. Scrape them and wipe them nicely; cut them from head to tail: lay them open; broil them on a greased gridiron for about six minutes, turning them as required. When they are done, lay them open on a hot dish, and put a little butter on them.

Herrings *too* dry may be rendered fit for use by soaking them for half an hour or so in warm water.

To Broil Black Puddings.
Time, five minutes.

58. Make little diagonal cuts in the skin of the black pudding with a knife. Broil it over a brisk fire, turning it often. Serve it *very* hot.

Sausages.
Time, twenty minutes.

Cambridge sausages are thought the best for breakfast. But we advise our readers, *if possible*, to make their sausage meat at home, as they may then be sure of the materials of which they are made. If they cannot be home-made they should be purchased at a *very* respectable shop, so that no doubts may be entertained of them. Prick the sausages with a large needle or fine skewer all over, this will prevent the skin from cracking, broil them over a gentle fire for about twenty minutes. Serve very hot on toast. We prefer putting them into hot water for one minute before dressing, to extract the oil from the skin. Directions for making sausage meat will be found under the head of PORK.

FISH.

FISH is a delicious adjunct to the dinner-table, and in some families may suffice for a good dinner by itself; but it requires nice and careful dressing. What can be more unappetizing than a fish brought to table broken all to pieces, as we have seen it, or not half done—salmon red with blood—cod nearly raw—or mackerel not properly cleaned? It is a wicked waste of the provision God has made for his creatures to thus spoil it, when a little attention and study may preserve it for us.

And first, let great care be taken to well clean the fish before it is dressed. It is better to let the fishmonger clean it for you; but if you are compelled to do it yourself, take care that you slit it *low* enough, so as not to leave any blood, &c., on the back-bone. We have been obliged to send fish from our own table untasted in consequence of a careless cook neglecting this part of her duty.

In almost all kinds of fish the portions to be removed are the gills, the alimentary organs, and the settlement of slime and other impurities inside and outside the fish. Dexterity must be used to cleanse the inside thoroughly without making too large an incision, which disfigures the fish when it comes to table, and may make it, if it is for boiling, watery. The sound, which adheres to the bone, must be left undisturbed, but cleansed; the hard and soft roe must also be left in their places; and care must be taken not to injure the liver, but, with most fish, to replace it. Especial care must be taken not to break the gall, as that renders the fish very bitter.

As a medium in which to fry, there is nothing better than pure oil, but it is expensive, because the fish must have abundance in the pan or it will not turn out well, and wear the bright gold hue that should characterize fried fish.

If it be found inconvenient to use oil, plenty of good dripping or lard will do as well. Butter is apt to burn fish black, and make them soft.

It is utterly useless, however, to provide fine oil or clear fat for frying, if the pan be soiled or smoked, for that will spoil the colour and the flavour too of the fish, be it dressed as carefully as it can be in other respects. Fish-kettles, with plates, of convenient sizes, and kept scrupulously clean, are likewise necessary; also a gridiron for broiling. These utensils are requisite for the methods of dressing fish which are generally most popular.

For fricassees and stews, good stewpans of different sizes will be needed; stewpans lined with enamel are best, and if they are of first-rate quality, and cleaned with care, they will last a great number of years. Stewpans are most convenient made of an oblong shape, and with the handle set on at one end. These are much more convenient to handle when full, than those with the handles on the broad side; and they are likewise more easy to place on the fire or stove, from standing on any narrow space at liberty, instead of requiring a good width of fire. Placed on the wide way, one stewpan will occupy a range of medium size; whereas those which can be placed the narrow way can stand several side by side on the same space. Engravings of the fish-kettles now used are given in Kitchen Utensils.

Apparatuses for cooking *au gratin* should have a place in every kitchen. The principle of cooking *au gratin* is to place fire both above and below the food to be so dressed, which of course effectually keeps in the juices of the viands, and their full flavour. The utensil used for the purpose in France is a *four de campagne*, a kind of long-handled chafing-dish with a flat bottom—for holding hot charcoal. The thing which has to be dressed *au gratin* is put in a deep dish which will stand fire, and in which also it is served; this is placed on a stove where the under side of the fish or meat in it will cook slowly, and the *four de campagne* is placed on the top of the dish, when the heat from the hot charcoal at the same time cooks the upper surface of the fish. The manner in which the steam is kept in renders the flavour excellent.

Boiled fish should always be washed and rubbed carefully with a little vinegar, before they are put into the water, except salmon and trout.

Put the fish into cold water, in which you have thrown a good quantity of coarse salt (about four ounces to one gallon of water). Allow for time of cooking about ten minutes for each pound of fish; but when a fish weighs a good many pounds, allow six minutes a pound for the whole—*i.e.*, a fish of ten pounds may be dressed in an hour; or you may *try* if it be done by passing a knife next to the bone. If the fish parts easily from it, it is done; if it adheres *at all* to the bone, it is not done. Under-dressed fish is very unwholesome.

Take the fish from the water the moment it is done, or it will become woolly. If it is dressed before you are ready to serve it, take it out of the water, set the drainer across the kettle, and lay a folded napkin over the fish.

Supposing you chance not to have a fish-kettle, and yet wish to dress fish by boiling, you may manage thus: put the fish in a circle on a dinner-plate, and tie a napkin over it; then put it in a large saucepan. When it has boiled long enough, take it up carefully *by the cloth*, drain off all the water, and slide the fish on a white napkin neatly folded on a dish. Garnish and serve.

Fresh-water fish have often a muddy taste and smell, which may be got rid of by soaking them in strong salt and water before they are cooked.

Salt fish should be soaked in water before boiling according to the time it has been in salt. When it is hard and dry, it will require thirty-six hours soaking before it is dressed, and the water must be changed three or four times. When fish is not very salt, twenty-four hours, or even one night, will suffice.

Crimped fish must be put into *boiling* water, and when it has been placed on the fire and re-boils, pour in a teacupful of cold water to check it, and let it simmer a few minutes. Salmon is put into warm water to be dressed.

Cod, whiting, and haddock are better if kept a day before boiling; just putting a little salt on them the night before dressing. But some great cooks have advocated dressing cod *quite* fresh; from our own experience we prefer it kept for twelve hours.*

To Fry Fish.

59. Cleanse them thoroughly, dry them on a folded cloth, dredge flour lightly over them; brush them with a well-beaten egg, then dip them in fine bread-crumbs.

Have ready enough fine oil, or melted lard or beef dripping (clarified), to entirely cover the fish. Place the frying-pan over a clear fire. Let the lard reach boiling-point, and then immerse the fish in it. You may try whether the fat is hot enough by letting a drop of cold water fall into it from the end of your spoon. If the hot fat spits it is ready for use. Then fry, turning the fish (when one side is browned) to the other. When it is done lay it on a cloth, or on white blotting-paper, to drain off all the fat; or put it on a reversed sieve for a little while. Serve it extremely dry on a white cloth or embossed fish paper.

To Broil Fish.

60. A clear fire is required. Rub the bars of your gridiron with dripping or a piece of beef suet, to prevent the fish from sticking to it. Put a good piece of butter into a dish, work into it enough salt and pepper to season the fish. Lay the fish on it when it is broiled, and with a knife blade put the butter over every part. Serve very hot.

Batter for Frying Fish.

61. One egg; a little flour; pepper and salt; mace and nutmeg; butter or oil.

* For a great variety of modes of dressing fish, see Warne's "Fish, and How to Dress Them," by E. Watts.

Beat up an egg until it thoroughly froths, and then beat in flour enough to make the batter very thick, so that a sufficiency of it will adhere to the fish dipped into it before frying. To make the dish savoury, season the batter with pepper, salt, and add mace and nutmeg in powder, if the flavour of spice is liked. Dip the fish into this batter, and put each piece as dipped into the boiling butter or oil.

Boiled Turbot.

Turbot is the finest of the flat fish. It is very expensive, but can sometimes be bought cheap, if it happens to be disfigured by having red spots on the under side. But these can be removed by rubbing salt and lemon on them; and in the new way of sending up turbot with the dark side garnished, they would not matter in the least degree.

It has been celebrated from the days of ancient Greece and Rome. Its usual weight is from five to twenty pounds. A good fish should be thick; the flesh is firm, and the fish stiff when it is fresh.

In season from March till August.

Time, one hour, for ten pounds, more or less according to weight.

62. Empty the fish, wash the inside, rub a little salt over the outside to help remove the slime. Put it in water to cleanse it, change the water several times. Pour plenty of cold spring water into a fish-kettle, add to each gallon of water four ounces of salt, and a quarter of an ounce, *or less*, of saltpetre. Let this dissolve while you prepare your turbot. Make an incision in the skin of the back nearly to the bone, to prevent the skin of the white side from cracking. Do not cut off the fins, these are considered a delicacy. Place the turbot on the fish plate, and put it into the water, which should quite cover it. Let it boil slowly and skim the water very carefully. Then let it simmer gently for about half an hour if it is of great size, according to the proportionate weight.

When it is done lift up the fish plate and let it drain; keep it very hot while you garnish it with lobster coral (which must be rubbed through a fine hair sieve); then slide it gently on a hot dish, on which a folded damask napkin or an ornamental fish paper has been placed previously.

It is usual to serve the under or *white* part of the turbot uppermost, and certainly the contrast of the pure white skin with the lobster coral ornamentation on it, makes it the most inviting-looking fish served. But epicures have lately preferred it served with the dark side or back upwards, on account of some supposed superiority of the flesh of the fish on that side. It is given in our engraving in the newest mode of serving it; but not being an epicure ourselves, we prefer the old and more picturesque fashion. Garnish with sprigs of curled parsley and slices of lemon alternately.

Sauce.—Lobster, shrimp, or anchovy, in a tureen.

Twice-laid Turbot.

Time, twenty minutes.

63. The remains of a turbot boiled the day previously; two tablespoonfuls of flour; one quart of milk; a small bunch of parsley; a bay-leaf and a little thyme; a spoonful of salt, and a saltspoon (not quite full) of pepper; a quarter of a pound of fresh butter.

Pick the fish from its bones and warm it gently in salt and water. While it is doing make a sauce of the ingredients given above by mixing the flour and milk very smoothly, adding the herbs and seasoning, and stirring it over the fire till it is tolerably thick. Then lift it to the side of the fire, stir in a quarter of a pound of butter, and pass it through a sieve. Cover the bottom of the dish with this simple white sauce, lay on it some of your fish, sprinkling it with white pepper and salt, then put more sauce, then more fish, till the whole is used up. Sprinkle breadcrumbs over it, and bake it in a hot oven for twenty minutes. Brown it, and serve it in the same dish.

Fillets of Turbot.

Time, six minutes to each pound of fish.

64. One small turbot; one lemon; a little pepper and salt, and a large lump of butter.

Divide a small turbot down the middle of the back, next separate it from the fins, and raise the fish clean from the bones with a sharp knife; divide it into oblong pieces, and put them in a stewpan with a large lump of butter; the juice of a strained lemon, and a little pepper and salt. Set them over the fire, and turn the fillets to admit of their being thoroughly dressed and browned on both sides. When done, drain them, and dish them in a similar way to cutlets, cover them with either lobster, shrimp, or maître d'hôtel sauce.

To Dress a very Small Turbot.

65. One small turbot; two ounces of grated cheese; half a pint of white sauce, or butter melted in milk; some breadcrumbs.

Boil a very small turbot; pull it to pieces,

and mix with it the grated cheese, and white sauce or butter. Put the mixture into a dish, sprinkle breadcrumbs well over the top, and brown with a salamander, or before the fire in a Dutch oven.

Cold Turbot.

66. Three heads of coss lettuce; two eggs; two anchovies; a teaspoonful of capers; two or three gherkins.
The cold turbot which remains from a dinner does very well for a salad. Divide it into pieces of convenient size, and arrange them in a mould in the middle of the dish; put lettuce, and hard-boiled eggs cut in quarters round; strew over all slices of anchovy, capers, and gherkins. Then pour over without disarrangement some salad mixture. Cold turbot is excellent *en Mayonnaise*, or dressed after any of the receipts given for cold cod.

Water Souchy.

67. Two quarts of water; one bouquet of parsley.
Plaice, flounders, or any freshwater-fish, are good for a souchy. Boil the fish; stand aside the handsomest looking, and boil down one or two to rags in the liquor, of which there should be about two quarts; boil in it also a bouquet of parsley. Pulp the fish which is boiled down, and chop the parsley fine. Return them to the liquor, heat the fish in it, and serve it in a deep dish accompanied by thin slices of brown bread and butter.

THE BRILL.

A large brill is with difficulty to be distinguished from a small turbot when very well cooked. It is longer and not so round. In season from August to April.

Brill.

Time, ten to twenty minutes.

68. One brill; four ounces of salt to each gallon of water; a tablespoonful of vinegar.
Thoroughly clean and remove the scales from a fine fresh brill; do not cut off the fins, but rub it over with the juice of a lemon and a little salt; set it in a fish-kettle with sufficient cold water, a handful of salt, and a tablespoonful of vinegar to cover it; let it gradually boil, and then simmer for ten or twenty minutes, according to the size of the fish. Skim it well, as great care is required to preserve the beauty of its colour. Serve it on a napkin, and garnish with lemon, curled parsley, and horseradish; send it to table with lobster-sauce in a tureen.

JOHN DORY.

A fish much esteemed by epicures, and, unlike all other table-fish, extremely ugly. It should be quite a foot long, and about four or five pounds in weight, and eaten very fresh. The thickest fish are the best.

To Boil the John Dory.

Time, three-quarters of an hour.

69. Four ounces of salt; one gallon of water.
Prepare the fish as you do a turbot. Put it into a fish-kettle with sufficient water to cover it, with the salt in proportion to the quantity of water; bring it to the boil, and let it simmer gradually for about three-quarters of an hour—more or less according to the size of your fish. Serve it in a neatly-folded napkin, and garnish with curled parsley and slices of lemon alternately. Lobster-sauce, shrimp-sauce, or plain melted butter can be sent to table in a tureen.

FRESHWATER BREAM.

A flat fish, very delicate, but seldom sent to table.

To Bake Sea Bream.

Time, forty minutes.

70. One sea bream; some veal-stuffing; a quarter of a pound of butter; a little pepper, salt, and Cayenne.
Thoroughly wash and wipe the bream in a cloth, but none of the scales must be removed. Rub over and inside a little pepper, salt, and Cayenne; stuff it with veal stuffing, sew it up, and place it in a baking-dish with pieces of butter over it. Put it in a moderate oven for about forty minutes, and serve; or it may be broiled, and served with white sauce.

SALMON.

Salmon is the king of fish, and is welcome at every table.
Salmon, like all other fish, should be stiff, and red in the gills; the flesh should be of a bright full colour, and the scales bright and silvery. Good judges prefer those which are small in the head, and thick in the neck. Before dressing the fish, scale it carefully, and cleanse it thoroughly. For the last named process, scrape away the blood and impurities with a knife, using washing as little as possible.
It is the present fashion to dress salmon as fresh as possible; but it is not really hurt, nay, is far more wholesome, if kept two or three days before it is cooked. Most probably this is the case with the fish we buy at the fishmonger's. Salmon, when out of

season, has scarlet, purple, and blue spots on its sides; when in season, the salmon should be a silvery, pinkish grey.

Boiled Salmon.

Time, according to weight.

71. One salmon; four ounces of salt to one gallon of water.

Salmon is put into warm water instead of cold, in order to preserve its colour and set the curd. It should be thoroughly well dressed to be wholesome.

Scale it; empty and wash it with the greatest care. Do not leave any blood in the inside that you can remove.

Boil the salt rapidly in the fish-kettle for a minute or two, taking off the scum as it rises; put in the salmon, first trussing it in the shape of the letter S, and let it boil gently till it is thoroughly done. Take it from the water on the fish-plate, let it drain, put it on a hot folded fish-napkin, and garnish with slices of lemon. Sauce: shrimp or lobster.

Send up dressed cucumber with salmon.

Middle Slice of Salmon.

Time, ten minutes to the pound.

72. Middle piece or slice.

Boil slowly in salt and water. Salmon should be put into warm water, which makes it eat firmer. Boil gently. Serve on a napkin. Sauce: lobster, shrimp, or plain melted butter and parsley.

Boudin de Saumon—Salmon Pudding.

Time, one hour.

73. One slice of salmon; an equal weight of butter; two eggs, or according to the weight of the slice—enough to prevent it from breaking; one salt-spoonful of Cayenne; one of salt.

Take a slice of salmon of the weight you require, pound it well in a mortar, and pass it through a sieve; make it up into a ball. Pound up with it again *an equal weight of* butter. Mix with the *panade* sufficient eggs to prevent it from breaking; season with salt and Cayenne. Put it into a pudding-mould, and steam it for an hour. Make a good Béchamel sauce, add a little essence of anchovies, and serve round it.

Broiled Salmon.

Time, ten to fifteen minutes.

74. Slices from the middle of a salmon; one tablespoonful of flour; a sheet or two of oiled letter-paper; a little Cayenne pepper.

Cut slices of an inch or an inch and a half thick from the middle of a large salmon; dust a little Cayenne pepper over them; wrap them in oiled or buttered paper, and broil them over a clear fire, first rubbing the bars of the gridiron with suet.

Broiled salmon is extremely rich, and really requires no sauce; nevertheless, one especially intended for it will be found amidst the sauces.

The slices may also be simply dried in a cloth, floured, and broiled over a clear fire; but they require the *greatest* care then to prevent them from burning. The gridiron is always rubbed with suet first.

Grilled Salmon Cutlets.

Time, eight to ten minutes.

75. Two or three slices of salmon; some caper, tomato, or brown butter sauce; a little pepper and salt.

Cut two or three slices of salmon about an inch thick; rub a little oil or butter over them, and a dust of pepper and salt. Put them on a gridiron over a very clear fire; turn them occasionally until done, rubbing a little butter over them each time they are turned. When quite dressed, place them on a hot dish, and pour over them caper, tomato, or brown butter sauce.

Fillets of Salmon.

Time, fifteen minutes.

76. Some fillets of salmon; egg; and bread-crumbs.

Cut about a pound and a half or two pounds of salmon, into small fillets, removing them from the bone with a sharp knife; carefully take away all the skin; dip each fillet into a well beaten egg, then into bread-crumbs, and fry them a light colour in some boiling dripping or lard. Dish them up, and pour over them some Indian sauce.

Fried Salmon.

Time, twenty minutes.

77. Half a pint of salad oil; one egg.

Cut slices of salmon, sprinkle them with salt, and let them lie for a quarter of an hour; flour them, brush them over with yolk of egg, well beaten up, and fry them in boiling salad oil. The salmon is nice either hot or cold, and will keep good for many days.

Cold Salmon.

Salmon is too good a fish, and too well appreciated in most houses, for that which is left after the first meal at which a fine one makes its appearance, to receive no further consideration. Perhaps there is no better way of eating cold salmon than simply with a little salt and Cayenne, and well cut brown or white bread and butter. It makes a *recherché* dish for breakfast, luncheon, or croquet teas.

Home-made Pickled Salmon.

Time, about ten minutes; one day to pickle.

78. Equal parts of vinegar, and the liquor the fish was boiled in; one teaspoonful of pepper; one saltspoonful of salt; a little allspice.

Place the remains of cold salmon in a dish. Boil up together the vinegar, the liquor, and seasoning; then let it get cool. Pour it over the fish; keep it for a day.

Send it to table garnished with fresh fennel.

THE COD.

There is not a more useful, nourishing, or wholesome fish brought to our market than the cod. It is in the greatest perfection from October to Christmas. It may be bought nearly all the year round, but from February to July it is not so good as at other times. The ling is even larger than the cod, but inferior to it in quality. The hake is a capital fish, it frequents our south-western coast; it should be all day sprinkled with salt before it is eaten; and it will turn out good dressed in any way that does well for cod; but the head is less available as food than that of the cod; being long and lean. Haddock and whiting are excellent fish; they cannot be eaten too fresh.

Cod should have a small head and a thick neck. It is better dressed in slices than boiled whole. It should possess a flavour of oysters. It should be put into cold water when cooked.

Cod's Head and Shoulders.

Time, half an hour or more.

79. Cod's head and shoulders; four ounces of salt to each gallon of water; a little horseradish.

Rub a little salt down the bone and the thick part of the fish, and tie a fold or two of wide tape round it, to prevent its breaking. Lay it in a fish-kettle with sufficient cold water to cover it, with salt in the above proportion; add three spoonfuls of vinegar, and a little horseradish. Let the water be brought just to the point of boiling; then draw the fish-kettle to the side of the fire, to simmer gently till the fish is done; which can be ascertained by trying it with a fish slice, to see if the meat can be separated easily from the bone: skim it well and carefully. When done, drain it and slip it off the fish strainer on a napkin neatly folded in a dish. Garnish with double parsley, lemon, and the roe and liver of the cod.

Browned Cod's Head.

Time, according to size, half an hour more or less.

80. Cod's head; butter; flour; breadcrumbs.

Boil the head, and take it up; take off the skin; set it before a brisk fire; dredge it with flour, and baste it with butter. When it begins to froth, sprinkle fine bread-crumbs over it; and continue basting it until it is well frothed, and of a fine light brown, and serve it. Garnish with slices of lemon, and sauce to taste.

It is a great mistake to use small fried fish as a garnish to boiled fish, as the appearance, and flavour too, of the one must be spoiled by the steam from the other.

Crimped Cod.

Time, fifteen minutes.

81. One pound and a half of crimped cod, and a large handful of salt.

Take a pound and a half of crimped cod, cut it into slices, put it into a fish-kettle of boiling water, with a large handful of salt, and let it boil over a slow fire very gently for rather more than a quarter of an hour. Boil the liver, cut it into slices, and add it as a garnish to the cod, with tufts of double parsley. Serve it with oyster sauce in a tureen.

Picked Cod.

Time, fifteen minutes.

82. About one pound and a half of dressed cod; a little oyster and egg sauce; two hard-boiled eggs; and four parsnips, or some mashed potatoes.

Pick about a pound and a half of dressed cod-fish into flakes, and put it in layers, with a little oyster and egg sauce alternately, in a stew-pan. Make it thoroughly hot. When it is done, pile it in the centre of a dish, and serve with mashed potatoes in a wall round it, browned with a salamander; or garnish it with slices of hard-boiled eggs, and parsnips cut into shapes.

SALT FISH.

Salt fish with a black skin are best. Follow the instructions given previously as to soaking it all night in water.

Salt Fish.

Time, one hour.

83. Put the cod in water the night before it is wanted, and let it soak all night; boil

it; lay it in a dish; separate the flakes; pour egg sauce over it, and sent it up hot.

If it be preferred, instead of the egg sauce, boil parsnips quite tender, mash them with butter, cream or milk, and spread them round the salt fish.

If the cod be very dry, soak it for several hours, lay it out to dry in a cold place, and then soak it again for a number of hours. This double soaking is said to soften the driest fish.

Salt Fish the Second Day.
Time, twenty minutes.

84. The remains of salt fish previously dressed; same quantity of mashed potatoes and parsnips; a quarter of a pound of butter; a *little* Cayenne; one egg.

Pick the remains of the fish into small flakes; butter the bottom of a pie-dish, place it in alternate layers with the mashed parsnips and potatoes; sprinkle a little Cayenne in the dish. Bake for about twenty minutes in the oven; turn it out on a dish; garnish with a hard-boiled egg cut in slices, and pour over it a little melted butter, or instead of the sliced egg, use egg sauce.

Cod Sounds Boiled.
Time, to boil, half an hour.

85. Cod sounds; half a pint of milk.

Soak the cod sounds in warm water half an hour, then scrape and clean them; boil them in milk and water until tender; when done, serve them in a napkin with egg sauce. The salt must not be soaked out of the sounds, unless for fricassee.

A Recherche Dish of Cod Sounds.
Time, one hour.

86. Cod sounds; forcemeat of oysters; bread-crumbs; butter; yolk of egg; and pepper, salt, and nutmeg; lardoons of pork or bacon; butter, and flour.

Boil some cod sounds until they are tender, but not too much done; turn them out and let them stand until they are cold. Make forcemeat of chopped oysters, bread-crumbs, butter, yolk of egg, and seasoning of pepper, salt, and grated nutmeg. Fill the sounds with the forcemeat, roll them up and skewer them, and lard down each side of each roll with pork or bacon; dredge them with flour; put them into a Dutch oven before the fire; baste them with butter until they are nicely browned, and serve them with oyster sauce over them.

Broiled Cod Sounds.
Time, three-quarters of an hour.

87. Lay the cod sounds for a few minutes in hot water, rub them with a little salt, clean them until they look white, and give them a gentle boil. Take them up, dry them, flour them, sprinkle salt and pepper over them, and broil them. Serve them with melted butter and mustard, or whatever sauce may be preferred.

To Broil Cod Sounds.
Time, three-quarters of an hour.

88. Two cod sounds; half a pint of brown gravy; a teaspoonful of soy; a little pepper, salt, and mustard.

Scald the sounds in hot water, rub them well with salt, pull off the skin, and put them to simmer till tender; take them out of the pan, flour, and broil them a nice brown. While this is being done, season half a pint of brown gravy with pepper, salt, a teaspoonful of soy, and a very little mustard. Boil it with a piece of butter rolled in flour, pour it over the sounds, and serve hot.

To Bake a Cod.
Time, one hour and ten minutes.

89. A small codfish; a bunch of sweet herbs; a quart of water; some bread-crumbs; a pint of shrimps; three dozen oysters; two tablespoonfuls of Harvey sauce; one ounce of essence of anchovies; three ounces of butter, and a little pepper and salt.

Well butter a dish, lay in the cod with a quart of water, a bunch of sweet herbs, and some pepper and salt; dredge the fish with a little flour, put over it the grated crumbs, and about two ounces of butter cut into small pieces. Put it into the oven and bake it for an hour, or until sufficiently done. Then take the cod carefully out; strain the gravy through a sieve, thicken it with an ounce of butter and a spoonful of flour; add a pint of picked shrimps, three dozen oysters, two tablespoonfuls of sauce, and a little essence of anchovies. Let it boil once, pour it round the cod, and garnish with lemon and parsley.

Cold Cod.
There are many ways of utilizing any remains of fine cod that there may be after the day it is cooked. Divided into flakes, and nicely seasoned with pepper, salt, and fragrant herbs, it will make a good Mayonnaise for supper or luncheon. Similarly divided into flakes, and mixed into a good salad, it is no bad substitute for lobster salad, and it makes capital rissoles. For another rifacimento separate the flakes of the cold fish, stir it into rich new milk, cream, or thin rich melted butter, arrange it in a pie-dish, spread mashed potatoes

over it, and put it in an oven until the top is nicely browned.

Cold cod's head and shoulders may be made very nice and *appétissant*. Place it in a deep dish, the chief bones of the head in the middle, and the flakes of flesh there may be, round. Take the liquor under the fish-plate, in the dish in which the fish has been served, and add to it liquor from the fish-kettle to make enough. Flavour this with ketchup, lemon pickle, Harvey's or other sauce, tomatoes, or any flavouring that may be preferred. Thicken it a little, cover it down close with a dish or close-fitting cover, and put it in the oven for half or three-quarters of an hour, according to the size of the dish and the heat of the oven.

HAKE.

A common west-country fish, much eaten on the coast of Devonshire.

It cannot be cooked too fresh, though some persons keep it in salt for twelve hours before they dress it.

It should be stuffed and baked as haddock. It is sometimes sold by the itinerant fishmongers round London as "White Salmon!"

Baked Hake.

Time, varying with size.

In season from May to August.

90. Be very careful in cleaning your hake, then stuff it with veal stuffing, sew it up with packthread, egg and bread-crumb it over, set it in a baking dish, and put it into a hot oven. Let it bake till the fish parts easily from the bones. It is impossible to fix a time, unless the size of the fish were stated.

Hake Cutlets.

91. Cutlets of hake; egg; bread-crumbs.

Cut a moderate-sized hake into cutlets, lengthwise, about the size of ordinary veal cutlets, dry them well in a cloth, egg them, cover them with bread-crumbs, and fry a light brown; then serve on a hot napkin, and garnish with fried parsley.

WHITING.

Whiting should not be too large. They are in season all the year round.

Fried Whiting.

Time to fry, ten minutes.

92. Egg; bread-crumbs; and a little flour.

Clean the whitings, take off the skin, turn them round, and fasten the tail into the mouth; dry them in flour, brush them over with an egg well beaten, roll them in bread-crumbs, and fry them in hot lard, and serve them on a napkin, garnished with fried parsley.

Whitings Filleted.

Time, ten minutes.

93. Six whitings; half a pint of oyster sauce; two eggs; and bread-crumbs.

Fillet as many whitings as you may require, divide each fillet; flour, and brush it over with egg; dip it into bread-crumbs, and fry it a light brown in hot fat or with butter. Dish them up as cutlets of soles, with a good thick oyster sauce in the centre of the dish; or on a napkin garnished with fried parsley. Serve with them piquante or maître d'hôtel sauce, separately.

To Boil Whiting.

Time, ten minutes for large fish.

94. Four or six whitings; three ounces of salt to each gallon of water.

Thoroughly cleanse the fish, and lay them in the fish-kettle, with sufficient water to cover them. Bring them slowly to a boil, and simmer for five or six minutes or for a longer time should your fish be large. Dish them on a folded napkin, and garnish with bunches of double parsley. Serve with anchovy sauce, or plain melted butter.

MULLET.

Red mullet is a very delicate fish, and has been justly called the woodcock of the seas. They are in season when the roe is just forming. Red mullet are better than grey; they should be *very* red, rather short and firm to the touch. Take care how you clean them. It is sufficient to scrape them lightly and pull out the gills, with them all the inside necessary to be removed will come also. They are not fully emptied.

Red Mullets in Papers.

Time, twenty-five minutes.

95. Two mullets; one ounce of butter; one teaspoonful of Harvey sauce; one glass of wine; four truffles; six mushrooms; a little parsley; a little shallot; one teaspoonful of lemon juice; a little flour; three eggs; one spoonful of cream; a little nutmeg.

Place the mullets in a sauté-pan with the butter, sauce, and wine. Bake them in the oven slowly for ten minutes. Take the fish out of the pan; strain off their liquor; add to it the truffles, mushrooms, parsley, shallot, nutmeg, lemon juice, and flour; stir all together over the fire for six or eight minutes, then add a *liaison* of three well-beaten yolks of eggs and a spoonful of cream.

Take two sheets of letter paper, oil them well, lay the mullets on them, and spread an equal proportion of sauce over each. Then fold the papers over them and roll the edges together to fasten them.

Broil the mullets over a slow fire, sufficiently to brown them on both sides, and warm them through, but be careful not to burn the paper. When done, serve them on a napkin.

To Dress Mullets.

Time, twenty-five minutes.

96. Three red mullets; four spoonfuls of anchovy sauce; a little pepper and salt; one tablespoonful of chopped shallot; one of chopped parsley; one spoonful of chopped mushrooms; four tablespoonfuls of claret; a piece of glaze the size of a walnut.

Take three red mullets, place them in a tin in the oven, with four spoonfuls of anchovy sauce, a little pepper and salt.

Put into a deep sauté-pan a tablespoonful of chopped shallot, the same of parsley, the same of chopped mushrooms, four tablespoonfuls of claret, a piece of glaze the size of a walnut. Stew them well together. When the fish is baked, pour this sauce over them.

Red Mullet Baked.

Time, twenty-five minutes.

97. Two mullets; some essence of anchovies; a glass of port, or white wine; a piece of butter; a little flour, and the juice of half a lemon.

Fold each mullet in oiled, or well-buttered paper, tie the ends, pass the string over them, and bake in a small dish in a moderate oven. Make a sauce of the liquor that comes from the fish, with a piece of butter, a little flour, a teaspoonful of essence of anchovies, a glass of port, or sherry, and the juice of half a lemon. Boil it and serve it in a sauceboat, and the fish in their paper cases.

To Stew Red Mullet.

Time, twenty to thirty minutes.

98. Three mullets; one carrot; one turnip; one or two bay leaves; half a blade of mace; a bunch of thyme and parsley; half a lemon; a glass of sherry, and two of hock.

Stew two or three mullets for about twenty or thirty minutes over a moderate fire, with two glassfuls of hock, one of sherry, a carrot and a turnip cut into slices, half a blade of mace, one large bay leaf, a bunch of thyme and parsley, and half a lemon sliced, with pepper and salt to your taste. When done, lay them in a hot dish, strain the sauce, thicken it with a piece of butter rolled in flour, pour it over the fish. Serve them up very hot.

GREY MULLET.

Time, a quarter to three-quarters of an hour.

99. This is a fish of a very different flavour and character to the preceding. It may be boiled, broiled, roasted, or baked; when small it may be cooked in the usual fashion of dressing such fish as whitings, &c.; if large, it may be cooked as cod or salmon.

TROUT.

There are three kinds of trout: the common trout, the white, and the salt water or sea trout. White trout is never very large; sea trout is less, and has an excellent flavour. It is as beautiful a fish as the red mullet. Clean them as you do salmon.

In season, May to September.

Trout Boiled.

Time, twenty to thirty minutes.

100. The fish; one wineglassful of vinegar, water, salt, and a piece of horseradish.

Rub and wipe the fish very dry, put them into a fish-kettle of boiling water with a wineglassful of vinegar, two tablespoonfuls of salt, and a piece of horseradish. Boil them slowly for twenty minutes or half an hour, taking care that the skin is not broken, and serve them on a napkin with anchovy sauce or plain melted butter.

To Fry Trout.

Time, twenty minutes.

101. One or two trout; one egg; breadcrumbs; one lemon.

Thoroughly clean and remove the gills, brush them over with the yolk of a well beaten egg, dip them into bread-crumbs, and fry them in hot fat until of a fine brown. Serve with anchovy sauce, and garnish with sliced lemon.

To Broil Trout.

Time, fifteen minutes.

102. The trout; a quarter of a pound of butter; some salt; one anchovy; one tablespoonful of capers; half a spoonful of vinegar; pepper, salt, nutmeg, and a little flour.

When you have thoroughly cleaned your fish, wipe it dry in a cloth, and tie it round with thread to preserve its shape entire. Then melt the butter with one tablespoonful of salt, and pour it over the trout till it is perfectly covered; let it remain for two or three minutes, take it out, and put it on a gridiron over a clear fire, that it may do gradually. When done, lay it in a dish, and pour over it the sauce previously made, with an anchovy washed, boned, and cut up very small, a large spoonful of chopped capers, a little pepper, salt, and nutmeg, half a spoonful of vinegar, and some melted butter. Boil it up for a few minutes and pour it over your fish.

STURGEON

Sturgeon is so rare and expensive a fish that it seems useless to give directions for dressing it in an ordinary Cookery Book; but as no cook can foresee what may fall into her hands to dress, we will not leave her the helpless possessor of a sturgeon—the Queen's very own fish. For every sturgeon caught in the English rivers is Her Majesty's born vassal, and belongs to her, except those which swim in the Thames below Temple Bar, which belong to the civic chief, the Lord Mayor.

The sturgeon is as large as a shark, but has no teeth. It is a very delicious fish, and may be cooked like veal.

To Roast Sturgeon.

Time, three-quarters of an hour to one hour.

103. The tail end of a sturgeon; some veal stuffing; a glass of white wine; juice of a lemon; a cupful of beef gravy.

Take the tail end of a fine sturgeon, skin and bone it; wash it clean, and fill the part from which the bone has been removed with veal stuffing, roll it in buttered paper, and tie it round to resemble a fillet of veal. Roast it in a Dutch oven before the fire, baste it constantly with butter, place it on a hot dish, and serve it with a cupful of rich beef gravy, a little lemon juice, and a wine-glass of white wine, previously made hot. Pour the sauce round the sturgeon.

Sturgeon Cutlets.

Time, ten to fifteen minutes.

104. One egg; a few bread-crumbs; pepper; salt; thyme and parsley.

Cut some thin slices from a sturgeon, wash, and dry them in a cloth, dredge them with flour, and brush over them the yolk of a well beaten egg; cover them with bread-crumbs, pepper, salt, and a little thyme and parsley chopped very fine; fry them a nice brown, and serve them with piquante sauce.

Russian Sauce for Sturgeon.

Time, ten minutes.

105. One glass of white wine; two anchovies; a piece of onion; a piece of lemon peel; a quarter of a pint of good broth; a little cream; butter and flour.

Put a glass of white wine into a stewpan, with two anchovies chopped up, a piece of onion, and of lemon peel, with a cupful of good broth. Thicken it with a piece of butter rolled in flour. Stir in two or three spoonfuls of cream, and either pour the sauce over the fish or serve it in a tureen.

Stewed Sturgeon.

Time, altogether, about an hour.

106. A nice piece of sturgeon; a little vinegar; flour; some good broth; two spoonfuls of cream, or a piece of butter rolled in flour; one tablespoonful of Harvey's sauce; a glass of wine.

Cut a piece of sturgeon into nice sized pieces, dip them into vinegar, dry them, flour them, and broil them over a clear fire. Flour them again, arrange them in a stewpan of appropriate size, and put in enough good broth to cover them. Let them stew until they are done and the gravy diminished. Thicken the gravy with cream, or a piece of butter rolled in flour; stir in a tablespoonful of Harvey's sauce, and a glass of wine. Serve it in the gravy, garnished with slices of lemon, and with capers strewed over it.

HALIBUT.

Halibut is a flat fish of enormous size, being sometimes five or six feet long, and weighing from four to five hundred pounds. Being so large, it is of course sold in pieces. A fine piece can be boiled like cod or any other fish, and served with any sauce usually eaten with boiled fish. Nicely cut collops can be covered with egg and bread-crumbs and fried.

Stewed Halibut's Head.

Time one hour and a half.

107. Halibut; half a pint of beer; two or three anchovies; one onion stuck with cloves; a sprig of parsley; pepper and salt; one ounce and a half of butter rolled in flour.

Put into a stewpan which will hold the head, half a pint of beer, some anchovies, an onion stuck with cloves and a bunch of parsley; season it with pepper and salt;

...ld water enough to cover the fish; let it ...ew for an hour, and strain it. Put the ...ead into this liquor; let it stew until tender; ...icken the liquor with butter and flour; ...avour it with fish sauce, and serve it with ...rcemeat balls, made with some of the fish, ...read-crumbs, sweet herbs, pepper, salt, ...d dripping.

Halibut Collops.
Time, forty minutes.

108. A piece of halibut; one onion; a little celery; a bunch of sweet herbs; pepper and salt; a little mace; a spoonful of lemon juice; one of sauce.

Cut a piece of halibut into nice-shaped collops. With the bones and odd bits, an onion in quarters, a bit of celery, a bunch of sweet herbs, and seasoning of pepper and salt, make some good broth; strain it and thicken it. Fry the collops, stew them in the liquor for half an hour, and flavour it with a little mace, a spoonful of whatever fish sauce may be preferred, and a spoonful of lemon juice.

THE BASSE.

The basse is a fish of a beautiful silvery appearance, which is very popular in some localities. It has been called the white salmon, a fish that it rather resembles in form, and in the firmness of the flesh. It is not very abundant in the London fish-shops. In the Channel Islands it is often plentiful in its season, but never, I believe, very cheap, and it abounds along our South coast, in St. George's and the Bristol Channel, and on different parts of the Irish coast.

It is frequently eaten simply boiled, and the remarks made on boiling salmon will apply equally well to it, proportioning the time allowed to the size of the fish. Fish weighing as much as fifteen pounds have occasionally been caught, but they are usually much smaller. Basse cut in slices may be boiled, fried, or fricasseed, following the plan given for dressing salmon in these various ways. It may be collared like salmon, or, if small, cut open and fried, with bread-crumbs, seasoning, and minced herbs, following the directions given hereafter for frying mackerel.

They are good dressed *au court bouillon d'eau*, with a little white wine. They are served on a napkin.

Basse Dressed en Casserole.
Time, six minutes to the pound.

109. Basse: a piece of butter rolled in flour; a few sweet herbs; pepper, salt, and grated nutmeg; juice of half a lemon.

After the fish is properly cleaned and prepared, fill the inside with butter well worked up with flour, sweet herbs minced fine, and seasoned with, pepper, salt, and grated nutmeg. Stew it with just liquid enough to prevent its burning, and squeeze lemon juice over it when it is taken up.

WHITEBAIT.
Time, one minute.

In season, May, June, and July.

110. Wash and drain them in a colander, flour them well, and sift fine bread crumbs over them; fry them in hot lard. As soon as they rise, take them out; that will be in about one minute.

If you possess a wire basket, it is better to cook them in it instead of the pan.

Serve them very hot, on a fish cloth, sprinkling first a little salt over them.

GRAYLING.

In season, July and August.

Grayling may be either baked or broiled. If small, they should be cut at the back, rubbed with butter, and a little pepper and salt dusted over them, then placed on a gridiron over a clear fire for four or five minutes to broil, and served on a dish, head and tail together, with the juice of a lemon squeezed over them.

To Fry Graylings.
Time, five minutes.

111. Scale, gut, and well wash them, dust some flour over them, lay them separately on a board before the fire; fry them of a delicate brown in fresh dripping.

Serve garnished with crimped parsley. Sauce: plain melted butter.

CARP.

Carp should be of a medium size, with a soft roe. The gills, if fresh, will be very hard to pull out. Take off the scales, and lay the fish for an hour before you dress it in water, to get rid of the blood, then dry it on a cloth.

Baked Carp.
Time, one hour and a quarter.

In season from March to October.

112. One large carp; forcemeat; egg; bread-crumbs; a little butter, one pint of stock; half a pint of port wine; two onions; two bay leaves; a bunch of herbs six anchovies; one teaspoonful of mustard one of soy; a little salt; Cayenne; and a piece of butter.

Clean and scale a large carp; put a stuffing as for soles, dressed in the Portuguese way, and sew it up; brush it over with the yolk of an egg, and cover it with breadcrumbs, then drop some oiled butter over it. Place the carp in a deep earthen dish, with a pint of stock, two onions sliced, two bay-leaves, a bunch of herbs, half a pint of port wine and six anchovies; cover the pan, and bake it one hour. Put a good-sized piece of butter into a stewpan with a dust of flour; when melted, pour in the strained liquor from the carp, with a teaspoonful of mustard, one of soy, and a little salt and Cayenne; boil it up again, and serve the fish on a dish, garnished with slices of lemon and bunches of parsley, and the sauce in a boat.

Fried Carp.

Time, twenty minutes or longer, according to size.

113. Carp; slices of bread; a lemon.

Clean and dry the fish, flour them well, put them in the pan, and fry them of a light brown; lay them on a cloth to drain, and fry some three-cornered pieces of bread and the roes. Serve the carp with the roes on each side of the dish; garnish it with the fried bread and lemon in slices, and make anchovy sauce, with the juice of a lemon added, to eat with it.

Carp au Bleu.

Time, one hour or more.

114. Carp: half a bottle of vinegar; port wine; three onions; two carrots; a sprig or two of parsley; two or three laurel or bay leaves; a bunch of thyme; three cloves; pepper and salt.

Clean the carp well, but in doing so make as small an opening as possible; tie up the head, place the fish in a fish kettle of the right size, and pour over it half a bottle of boiling vinegar, and add enough port wine for the carp to be covered with the liquid. Put in three onions in slices, two carrots, a sprig of parsley, a bunch of thyme, two or three laurel or bay-leaves, three cloves, pepper, and salt; put it over a slow fire, and let it simmer gently for about an hour (more or less, according to the size of the carp); take it from the fire, let it get cold in the liquor, and serve it upon a folded napkin.

Any fish can be dressed au bleu from the same receipt.

Carpe Frite.

Time, twelve or fifteen minutes.

115. A small soft-roed carp; lemon juice; flour.

Choose a small soft-roed carp, open it down the back, press it open very flat, and take out the roe. Flour both the fish and the roe well, put them in a very hot frying-pan, and fry them of a fine colour. Serve them with lemon juice squeezed over them.

To Boil Carp.

Time, thirty minutes.

116. Scale and remove the gills from the carp, and rub some salt down the backbone, then lay it for half an hour in strong salt and water, which will thoroughly cleanse it; dry it, and place it in a fish-kettle of boiling-water, with a tablespoonful of salt. Boil it for thirty minutes, or less time should it be small; boil the roe with it, and when done serve it on a napkin. Garnish with parsley and slices of lemon. Plain melted butter and fish sauces must be served with it.

Stewed Carp.

Time, one hour and a quarter.

117. A carp; equal parts of port wine and water; a tablespoonful of lemon pickle; one of browning; one teaspoonful of mushroom powder; one onion; six cloves; one stick of horseradish; some Cayenne; a large lump of butter; a little flour; juice of one lemon.

Having scaled, cleaned, and taken out the gills, wash it thoroughly, by soaking it in spring water for half an hour, and dry it in a cloth; dredge over it a little flour, and fry it a light brown. Then put it into a stewpan with half a pint of port wine, and the same of water (or more if desired); a tablespoonful of lemon pickle, another of browning, a teaspoonful of mushroom powder, an onion stuck with six cloves, a stick of horse-radish, and a little Cayenne pepper. Cover your stewpan closely, that the steam may not escape, and let it stew gently over a slow fire until the gravy is reduced to just enough to cover the fish. Then take it out, and put it into the dish it is to be served in. Set the gravy again on the fire, and thicken it with a lump of butter rolled in flour; boil it up, and then strain it over your fish, and garnish with sippets.

Just before you send it to table, squeeze into the sauce the juice of a lemon.

Fried Tench.

Time, varying with size—about twenty minutes.

118. Two tench; a little salt; lemon juice; butter; and flour.

Clean two fine tench by throwing them into boiling water just long enough to enable you to raise the skin. Remove the gills and fins, gut them, and clean them thoroughly. Cut them down the back, and take out the bones, sprinkle a little salt over them, flour them, squeeze some lemon juice over them; fry them in butter, and serve them upon a napkin.

To Stew Tench Brown.

Time, one hour and a half.

119. Tench; water and red wine in equal parts; one tablespoonful of lemon pickle; the same of browning; the same of walnut ketchup; a little mushroom powder; Cayenne pepper to taste; an onion stuck with cloves; a bit of horse-radish.

Clean and dry the fish: place them before the fire for a few minutes, dredge them with flour, and brown them in a frying-pan. Put them in a stewpan, cover them with red wine and water in equal parts; add the lemon pickle, browning, walnut ketchup, mushroom powder, Cayenne pepper to taste, an onion stuck with cloves, and a piece of horse-radish.

Cover the stewpan close to keep in the steam, and let the fish stew gently over a slow fire until the liquor is reduced to barely enough to cover the fish in the dish. Take out the fish, keep them hot, thicken the gravy with a lump of butter rolled in flour, boil it up, strain it over the fish, garnish with pickled mushrooms and scraped horse-radish.

Either of these receipts for stewing tench (*i.e.*, brown and white) will do also for carp, observing always to save and add the blood. Garnish with fried oysters, sippets of toasted bread, slices of lemon, or scraped horse-radish, according to taste; or with the roe (alternate pieces boiled and fried) placed round the dish; serve very hot.

Tanches sur le Gril, or aux Fines Herbes.

Time, according to size.

120. Three or four tench; a little oil; a sprig of parsley and thyme; one onion; one shallot; pepper and salt.

Clean the slime from three or four tench, plunge them for a minute into boiling water, and scale them, beginning at the head, and taking care not to injure the skin, and gut them. Lay them on a dish, cover them with oil, parsley, thyme, onion, and shallot minced fine, salt, and pepper. Fold them in two thicknesses of paper dipped in the oil, &c., in which the fish have been lying, and broil them. When they are done, take off the writing paper, pour over them *sauce piquante*, or caper sauce, and serve them.

This is a famous receipt at Brussels.

PLAICE.

Plaice are rather common fish, and lack the delicacy and flavour of the other piscatory delicacies of our table; but *filleted* they are very nice, and supply the place of better very well, if carefully dressed.

In season from May to January.

To Fillet Plaice.

Time, about twelve minutes.

121. Skin them, lay them flat on the table, and cut right down the backbone, then raise the fillet from head to tail. Having quite removed the fillets from the bones, cut them nicely in pieces, and fry them in two ounces of dripping or lard, with a little pepper and salt, and the juice of half a lemon.

Drain them on a cloth to absorb the grease, and serve them upon a hot white table-napkin.

To Boil Plaice or Flounders.

Time, six to seven minutes.

Flounders are in season from September to November.

122. A quarter of a pound of salt to a gallon of water, and a very little saltpetre.

Well clean and empty your fish, draw a sharp knife down the thickest part of the middle of the back, nearly through to the bone; lay them in a fish-kettle of cold water, with salt in the above proportion, with a small piece of saltpetre; let them simmer for six or seven minutes after the water begins to boil, or longer should your fish be very large, taking great care they are not broken. Serve them (with plain melted butter) on a folded napkin.

To Fry Plaice or Flounders.

Time, five minutes.

123. Two tablespoonfuls of vinegar; an egg; bread crumbs; fried parsley; and some anchovy sauce.

Sprinkle the plaice or flounders with salt, and let them lie for twenty-four hours, then wash them and wipe them dry; brush them over with egg, and cover them with bread-crumbs; make some lard or dripping mixed with two tablespoonfuls of vinegar boiling hot in a frying-pan; lay the fish in, and fry them a nice brown colour, drain them from the fat on a cloth, and serve them on a folded napkin, garnished with fried parsley. Anchovy sauce.

SMELTS.

A delicate little fish which has a singular perfume of violets or syringa. It requires great care in cleaning. Pull the gills out, and the inside will come with them. Wipe and dry them gently.

In season from October to May.

To Fry Smelts.
Time, three or four minutes.

124. Seven smelts; two eggs; bread-crumbs; a little flour, and a piece of butter. Smelts should not be washed more than is necessary to just clean them; cut off the fins, dry them in a cloth, and dredge a little flour over them, melt half an ounce of butter and beat into it the yolks of two eggs. Dip the smelts into it, then into bread-crumbs finely grated, and plunge them into a frying-pan of boiling fat; let them fry gently, and a few minutes will make them of a bright yellow brown. Be careful not to take off the light roughness of the crumbs, or their beauty will be lost. When done, dish them up on a napkin, garnish with fried parsley, and serve anchovy or shrimp sauce with them separately.

Fried Smelts, French Way.
Time, three or four minutes.

125. Smelts; a little flour; milk; crisped parsley.

After the smelts are prepared and dried dip them into milk, dredge them with flour, and fry them until they are of a fine colour, and serve them with crisped parsley.

SPRATS.
Time, two or three minutes.

126. Well clean a number of sprats, fasten them in rows by a skewer run through their gills, place them on a close-barred gridiron, broil them a nice brown and serve them hot and hot.

SOLES.
Soles are either white soles or black soles, according to the colour of their back. Middle sized soles are of the best flavour. When they have roes they should be only used for fillets, because they have then very little flavour. A large fine roe is not so great a recommendation to a sole as inexperienced housewives believe.

In season from April to December.

Filleted Soles.
Time, ten minutes.

127. Two soles; two eggs; and bread-crumbs.

Take two soles, divide them from the backbone, and remove the head, fins, and tail. Sprinkle the inside with salt, roll them up from the tail end upwards, and fasten them with very small skewers. If small or middling sized soles, put half a fish in each roll. Dip them into the yolk of one well beaten egg, and then into bread-crumbs: then into the eggs a second time, and again sprinkle them with crumbs; fry them in hot lard or in clarified butter.

Instead of rolling the fish they may be cut into pieces, and arranged in the form of a pyramid in the centre of a dish, and garnished with parsley and slices of lemon.

Cutlets of Soles.
Time, ten minutes.

128. Two soles; one egg; bread-crumbs, and parsley.

Cut two soles into narrow pieces, crosswise, dredge a little flour over them, dip each piece in an egg well beaten, and then into bread-crumbs; fry them a nice brown in hot fat; drain, and serve them with fried parsley in the centre, with the slices of sole raised round it.

Boiled Soles.
Time, eight to ten minutes.

129. Two soles; a large handful of salt in one gallon of water.

Well wash and clean the soles, cut off the fins, and put them into a fish-kettle with salt and water. Let them boil slowly, and then simmer until done, which must be according to the weight of the fish, a large one requiring about ten minutes, a medium size eight. When done serve them on a napkin, with the white side uppermost. Garnish with slices of lemon and parsley. Anchovy or shrimp sauce are usually sent to table with boiled soles, but may be varied at pleasure.

Fried Soles.
Time, eight minutes.

130. Two soles; one egg; a few bread-crumbs.

Remove the skin from the dark side of the soles, clean them, and wipe them dry, and dredge a little flour over them; brush them over with the yolk of a well-beaten egg, dip them into bread-crumbs, and fry them of a light brown, in sufficient boiling fat for them to swim in. When done, lay them on a cloth to absorb the grease; dish them on a napkin neatly folded, and garnish with fried parsley. Plain melted butter or shrimp sauce may be sent to table with them.

Fillets de Soles au Gratin.
Time, according to size, about twenty minutes.

131. Fillets of soles; veal stuffing; a piece of bread; bread-crumbs.

Divide each side of a fine sole in four

fillets; spread veal stuffing on each piece, and roll it up; spread a layer of the same stuffing over the bottom of a dish, three-quarters of an inch in thickness; arrange the rolled fillets on it in the form of a crown; fill up the interstices with the stuffing; and place a piece of crumb of bread in the centre; cover the fillets with bread-crumbs, and cook *au gratin*, or put the fish into an oven, or in a Dutch oven before the fire; and when the sole is cooked enough, and the outside is a nice brown, serve it in the same dish.

EELS.

It is one of the most painful tasks of the cook to kill and skin an eel, and it is effected with some difficulty. By striking the head very hard it may be stunned, however, and will then probably feel less pain. We believe that there is also a mode of killing them by cutting through the vertebræ near the head.

Take a cloth in your hand; hold the eel by the head; cut the skin round the neck, and turn it a little way down; then pull the head one way and the skin the other, and it will come off; open the fish, take out the inside, being careful not to break the gall, and cut off the back bristles.

Eels are in season all the year round.

Eels Spitchcocked.

Time, half an hour, or till the skin turns up.

132. Two or three eels; some chopped parsley; pepper; salt; a little sage; juice of half a lemon; eggs, and bread-crumbs; a little mace; and a little warmed butter.

Skin two or three large eels, open them on the belly side, and clean them thoroughly; remove the backbone; and cut them into pieces, three or four inches long; strew over them, on both sides, some chopped parsley, a very little sage, pepper, salt, a little mace pounded fine, a little warmed butter, and the juice of nearly half a lemon; dip each piece carefully in egg and bread-crumbs; fry them in a pan of boiling fat, and serve them on a hot dish, in a circular form, with piquante sauce (or any other you like) in the centre.

Stewed Eels.

Time, three-quarters of an hour.

133. One gill of port wine; half a pint of stock; two blades of mace; two bay-leaves; a few allspice; two cloves; half a lemon; one onion; a bunch of thyme and parsley; and some pepper and salt; a teaspoonful of anchovy sauce, and one of ketchup.

Take one or two large eels, skin and cut them into pieces about three or four inches in length; put them into a stewpan with some stock, half a pint of port wine, two blades of mace, some allspice, two cloves, a bunch of herbs, a very small onion, half a lemon cut into slices, and some pepper and salt to your taste. Simmer over a slow fire for about three-quarters of an hour, or until the eels are done. Strain and thicken the gravy with a piece of butter, and a dust of flour, and stir in a teaspoonful of anchovy sauce, and one of ketchup. Serve the eels with their sauce over them.

Baked Eels.

Time, three-quarters of an hour.

134. Four large eels; some veal stock; a bunch of savoury herbs; a sprig of parsley; two glasses of port wine; juice of a small lemon; salt and Cayenne; one teaspoonful of Worcestershire sauce.

Skin, empty, and thoroughly wash the eels, cut off the heads, and divide the fish into rather short pieces, wipe them very dry, dip each piece into a seasoning of Cayenne, salt, minced parsley, and a little powdered savoury herbs; pour them into a deep dish, cover them with veal stock, put a thick paper or cover over the dish, and set it in the oven until the eels are tender.

Skim off the fat, take the pieces of fish carefully out on a hot dish to keep warm, and stir into the gravy the wine, strained lemon juice, and sauce; make it just boil up, and pour it over the fish. Garnish with sliced lemon.

Boiled Eels.

Time, half an hour

135. Some small eels, and a little parsley and butter.

The small eels are the best; do them in sufficient water to cover them, add a bunch of parsley, when tender they are done. Serve them up in a shallow tureen, with parsley and butter sauce poured over them.

Fried Eels.

Time, eighteen or twenty minutes.

136. One large eel, or two small ones; one egg, and a few bread-crumbs.

Prepare and wash the eels, wipe them thoroughly dry, and dredge over them a very little flour; if large, cut them into pieces of about four inches long, brush them over with egg, dip them into bread-crumbs, and fry them in hot fat. If small, they should be curled round and fried, being first dipped into egg and bread-crumbs. Serve them up garnished with fried parsley.

Baked Eels—Stuffed.

Time, about three-quarters of an hour.

137. Eels; a forcemeat of shrimps or oysters; a slice of bread crumbled; peel of half a lemon; yolk of one egg; pepper; salt, and nutmeg; two ounces of butter; a little flour; one teaspoonful of lemon pickle; one tablespoonful of walnut ketchup; a glass of white wine; one anchovy; two teaspoonfuls of browning; a little lemon juice.

Cut off the heads of the eels, and clean them very well; make a forcemeat with shrimps or oysters chopped, a good slice of bread crumbled, a little lemon peel shred fine, the yolk of an egg, salt, pepper, and nutmeg. Stuff the eels with this, sew them up, and turn them round in a dish. Put butter and flour over them, pour a little water into the dish, and bake them in a moderate oven. When done enough, take the gravy from under them, skim off the fat, strain it, and add to it one teaspoonful of lemon pickle, the walnut ketchup, one anchovy, two spoonfuls of browning, and a squeeze of lemon juice. Let it boil ten minutes, thicken it with butter and flour, if necessary, and serve it garnished with slices of lemon and crimped parsley.

LAMPREYS.

Rich but very *ugly* fish, unlikely to fall into the hands of an ordinary cook. They are a very ancient delicacy, and are remarkable as having tempted our first great Plantagenet King to his death by eating too much of them. The city of Gloucester still presents the Queen with a lamprey-pie every Christmas.

To Stew Lamprey as at Worcester.

Time, one hour and twenty minutes.

138. A small quantity of mace; cloves; nutmeg; pepper and allspice, and an equal quantity of beef gravy, Madeira or sherry; two anchovies; a spoonful of made mustard; juice of a lemon; a little butter, and flour.

Thoroughly cleanse, and remove the cartilage which runs down the back of the fish, season it with pepper, mace, allspice, and cloves, and place it in a closely covered stewpan with equal quantities of good beef gravy and sherry, sufficient to cover it. When tender, take out the lamprey, and keep it hot. Boil the gravy it was stewed in with two anchovies chopped up very fine, and a lump of butter rolled in a little flour. Strain it through a hair sieve, and squeeze in the juice of a lemon, and a teaspoonful of made mustard. Serve it with sippets and horse-radish.

Note.—Cider will answer in the place of the wine for common purposes.

GARFISH.

The garfish, called "long noses" in some localities, are little appreciated by some on account of their green bones; but they are said to be very nice when well cooked. They may be boiled and eaten with shrimp sauce, or boiled or fried. They may also be cooked according to the Worcester receipts for stewing lampreys, using good but not sweet home-made wine instead of Madeira; and any of the French receipts for dressing eels may be used for the garfish. Perhaps they are best of all dressed by means of the bain-marie jar.

139. Cut them in pieces and lay them in a dish, and put over them either vinegar, wine, or oil, with minced sweet herbs, pepper, and salt, and any flavouring that may be liked; when they have lain an hour or two remove them, and the marinade in which they lie, to the bain-marie jar; add a little to the liquor if it be thought that more gravy will be needed, fasten the lid down with a cloth, put the jar in a saucepan of water, and let the fish cook until it is done enough.

THE CONGER.

The conger may with justice consider himself an ill-used fish, since, by many, he is condemned untried, and loaded with hard names, which are quite undeserved; whereas a good conger eel, well cooked, is more wholesome, more nutritious, and nicer than more *recherché* and more lauded viands. In addition to being very nice, and more wholesome than most other kinds of fish, it has the merit of great abundance in our seas; and if the supply of our markets with it were encouraged by the free use of it by buyers (which it is not, on account of the unfounded prejudice against it), we might have in it a fish as solid and as nutritious as butcher's meat, at from 2d. to 4d. a pound in our dearest markets, This noble fish is fully deserving of free use, and protection of the immature fish, as a thing of real importance; the best substitute for meat that our seas give us. Let all who are anxious to aid the country's need, by lessening the consumption of meat in times of scarcity, give the conger a fair trial. At a time when meat may reach famine prices, do not let us allow tons of nutritious fish to be slighted, or worse, wasted. In the ways of dressing it we have great variety, as well as other gastronomic merits, and different parts of the fish are adapted for different purposes. The head and tail are the best for soup, because the rich gelatinous picking about the first gives thickness to the soup, and the tail is too bony to be as appropriate as the centre cuts to dress other ways. The portions next to the head offer good cuts (the number dependent on the length and size of the fish) for stuffing, and either boiling or baking. The fat adhering to the bone (I believe, in truth, the roe of the fish), is very rich, yet delicate, and should on no account be removed when the fish is cleaned. In taking this out some London fishmongers commit a great mistake. Still further on in the conger, may be cut compact slices and collops for frying, stewing, or fricasseeing, and for making into pies. A long piece, boned, cut from near the head to within half a foot of the tail, one side, or both, according to the size of the fish, is good for collaring, and the end near the tail may be salted for breakfast.

Boiled Conger.
Time, half an hour.

140. White conger eel ; bread-crumbs ; peel of half a lemon ; a sprig of parsley ; lemon thyme ; winter savory ; sweet marjoram ; a piece of butter or dripping ; pepper ; salt ; nutmeg, and a spoonful of suet.

Cut a piece about a foot long from the head end of a fine conger, make a stuffing of the bread-crumbs, minced parsley, lemon thyme, winter savory, and sweet marjoram minced fine ; a little chopped suet, grated lemon peel, and butter or dripping ; season it with pepper, salt, and nutmeg ; stuff the fish, and sew it up. Put it into warm water, let it simmer until it is cooked enough, and serve it with any sauce usually eaten with boiled fish.

A thick piece will take half an hour after it simmers. It may be boiled without the stuffing, if it be preferred.

Stewed Conger.
Time, according to size.

141. A conger eel : a bunch of sweet herbs ; one onion ; pepper, salt, and mace ; water or broth ; a little flour.

Cut the conger into pieces as for frying, dry and flour the pieces, and brown them in a frying-pan. Put them into a stew-pan with a bunch of sweet herbs, an onion cut in quarters, seasoning of pepper and salt, and of spice, if it be liked, and enough water, or broth, nearly to cover the fish. Let it stew gently until it is cooked enough, thicken the gravy with flour just enough to take off the richness that may have risen to the top, and serve the conger with the gravy round it.

The gravy may be flavoured with tomatoes, chutney, or any other sauce. The stewed conger is nice with oysters ; open them, and save the liquor, mix it with a little flour, use it to thicken the gravy, as much as necessary, let it just boil up, and put in the oysters long enough for them to get hot.

Baked Conger.
Time, one hour, less in a quick oven.

142. Take such a piece of fine conger as would be chosen for boiling : make a stuffing, and stuff it as mentioned for boiled conger. Put it into a pie dish or a baking dish, with a pint of water, lay pieces of butter over the fish, flour it well, and put it into a moderate oven ; baste it often with the liquor while it is cooking, and when it is almost done thicken the liquor with flour, just enough to correct any little richness that may float on the top of it ; not more. Baked conger may be varied in many ways. It is very nice with potatoes baked under it: but as there must be liquor in the dish with which to baste the fish, to prevent the skin from getting dry and hard, they will not brown on the outside. The gravy may be thickened with tomatoes, or with tomato sauce, and this is particularly nice. It may be taken from the liquor, and eaten with dressed cucumber and early potatoes. It may be flavoured with or eaten with any sauce that is nice, and it will be excellent any way. A good flavouring for a change, is a tablespoonful of lemon pickle, the same of walnut ketchup, and a dessert spoonful of soy.

Fried Conger.
Time, twenty to twenty-five minutes, or longer.

143. Conger ; egg ; bread-crumbs.

Cut the conger into slices an inch and a half or two inches thick, or a little thicker, according to the size of the fish. This is the best way to cut conger for frying, and most other purposes for which it may require similar subdivision ; because by it the solid back of the fish and the richer under part go together, which they do not when collops are cut longitudinally. Cover the fish with egg and bread-crumbs, and fry it in plenty of fat, made to boil before the fish is put in. Take care that the frying-pan is perfectly clean, and that the fish is fried to a bright colour. Serve it with lemon to squeeze over it, plain melted butter, oyster sauce, shrimp sauce, or any sauce preferred.

PERCH.

It is so difficult to scale perch that some people have them boiled with the scales on, as they come off easily afterwards.

Clean it carefully. A perch weighs, when fine, from three to four pounds.

To Boil Perch.

Time, half an hour, if large.

In season from September to November.

144. Cut off the spines from the back, scrape off the scales with an oyster knife, and thoroughly clean and wash them. Then boil them in cold water very carefully, as they are a most delicate fish.

Fried Perch.

Time, twelve minutes.

145. Some bread-crumbs, and egg.

Thoroughly clean and scale the perch, brush them over with a well beaten egg, dip them into bread-crumbs, and fry them a nice brown in boiling fat. Serve them with anchovy sauce or melted butter.

Fish Scallop.

Time, twenty minutes.

146. Cold fish; a teacupful of milk or cream; a large teaspoonful of anchovy sauce; a little pepper and salt; a little made mustard; a lump of butter; some bread-crumbs.

Pick any cold fish from the bones, mix with it a teacupful of milk or cream, a large teaspoonful of anchovy sauce, a little pepper and salt, and a saltspoonful of made mustard. Put it into a stewpan over a moderate fire for two or three minutes, stirring it all the time, then put it into scallop shells or a dish, strew some grated bread thickly over it, and a few thin pieces of butter; brown it in a Dutch oven before the fire, and serve it very hot.

To Fry Perch Plain.

Time, twelve minutes.

147. When the perch are scaled, gutted, and washed, dry them well with a cloth, and lay them out singly before the fire for a few minutes. Flour them well, and fry them a fine brown in plenty of good dripping. Serve them with melted butter and crisped parsley.

PIKE.

This voracious river fish depends greatly upon the manner in which it is dressed. We have eaten excellent "Jacks," as they are called in the midland counties, and others quite undeserving of approbation. It *ought* always to be baked or roasted, and not boiled; but as some families dress it in the latter manner, we give directions for it. The fins are usually cut off it, and it must be very carefully scraped and cleaned.

In season from September to March.

To Boil Pike.

Time, half an hour to one hour.

148. Pike; twelve oysters; half of a French roll; two eggs; lemon; sweet herbs; pepper; salt; nutmeg; a lump of butter; a wineglass of vinegar.

When you have taken out the gills, cleaned and thoroughly washed the fish, make a forcemeat of a dozen chopped oysters, the crumb of half, or a whole French roll, a little lemon peel shred fine, a lump of butter, a few sweet herbs, the yolks of two well beaten eggs, seasoned to your taste with pepper, salt, and nutmeg. Mix all together and stuff the fish; sew it up, and fasten it with the tail in the mouth with a small skewer. Put it into a fish-kettle of boiling water with a wineglassful of vinegar and a tablespoonful of salt. If it is of a middling size, it will be done in about half an hour; or, if large, one hour. Serve it up with melted butter and a lemon, or with anchovy sauce. Garnish with pickled barberries.

To Bake Pike.

Time, one hour.

149. A large pike; some forcemeat; two or three anchovies; half the peel of a lemon; one glass of wine; one tablespoonful of sauce; a spoonful of capers.

Scale and wash a large pike, fill it well with stuffing made as for veal, skewer the tail in the mouth, and place it in a deep dish. Season it with salt. Put a good sized piece of butter over it, and bake it for one hour. When done, add to it about half a pint or more of the gravy, two or three small anchovies chopped very fine, the rind of half a lemon, grated, a spoonful of capers, a large spoonful of sauce, either Worcester or Reading, a glass of wine, and a little butter rolled in flour to thicken it. Serve the fish on a dish, and the sauce in a boat.

Stewed Pike.

Time, three-quarters of an hour.

150. Pike; two ounces of butter; a little flour; one pint of red wine; a bunch of sweet herbs; four cloves; twelve young

onions; pepper and salt; two anchovies; one spoonful of capers.

Brown butter and flour in the bottom of a stewpan; and mix into it a pint of red wine; add a bunch of sweet herbs, the cloves, and a dozen young onions boiled tender, and sufficient seasoning of pepper and salt. Cut the pike in pieces, put it in, and let it stew gently until it is cooked enough. Take it out, and keep it hot. Add to the sauce two anchovies chopped up, and a spoonful of capers minced. Let it boil up for a minute or two, pour it over the fish, and lay sippets of toasted bread round the dish.

Roasted Pike, or Mackerel.

Time, half an hour.

151. Pike; bread-crumbs; four anchovies; one pint of oysters or shrimps; a sprig of parsley; one onion; pepper and salt; nutmeg; cloves, and mace; half a pound of butter.

Clean the fish well; make stuffing with bread-crumbs, oysters, or shrimps, chopped parsley, onions, and the seasoning and spices. Mix all well together with half a pound of butter, stuff the fish, and put some of the stuffing over the outside. Put the pike in a cradle, and roast it, basting it unceasingly all the time it is cooking.

MACKEREL

requires to be eaten quite fresh; it will not, in fact, keep at all. Some people call it the "pig of the sea," as it is scaleless, and, like pork, disagrees with some eaters.

Mackerel Boiled.

Time, fifteen to twenty minutes.

152. Cut the fish open sufficiently to empty the inside, remove the roes, and thoroughly wash them and the mackerel. Put them into a fish-kettle of cold water with a large tablespoonful of salt, bring them gradually to a boil, and simmer for about twenty minutes if the fish is large, if small, fifteen minutes will be sufficient, or even less time; but they must be taken carefully out when the eyes are starting. Remove the scum as it rises, and when done, serve them on a napkin, and send fennel sauce, plain melted butter, or gooseberry sauce to table with them.

Mackerel a la Maitre d'Hotel.

Time, twenty minutes.

153. One mackerel; three spoonfuls of *maitre d'hôtel* sauce, or juice of half a lemon, and a little salt, Cayenne, and two spoonfuls of clarified butter.

Make a deep incision on either side of the backbone of a fine mackerel, after thoroughly cleansing and drying it in a cloth, and put in a little salt, Cayenne, and a spoonful of clarified butter. Lay it on a well-heated gridiron rubbed over with butter or suet, and when of a nice brown colour, turn the back to the fire, taking care that the fish does not stick to the gridiron. When done, put into the incision of the back two spoonfuls of *maitre d'hôtel* batter, previously putting your mackerel on a hot dish without a napkin, then spread three more spoonfuls of butter over it, place it in the oven for a few minutes, and serve it very hot.

Fillets of Mackerel Stewed.

Time, fifteen to twenty minutes.

154. Two mackerels; one lemon; two ounces of butter; nearly half a pint of port wine; two teaspoonfuls of soy, and a little salt, Cayenne, and pounded mace.

Raise and divide each fillet from the mackerel into two, and lay them in a stewpan with two ounces of butter previously melted with a little flour, Cayenne, salt, and the rind of half a lemon. Shake the stewpan over a moderate fire for a few minutes, turning the fillets. Then pour in slowly nearly half a pint of port wine, with the two spoonfuls of soy and the mace, boil up and pour over the fish.

HADDOCKS.

The haddock is a delicate fish with a fine flavour. This fish has a superstition attached to it. On each side of the body near the gills it has a dark spot, fabled to be the impression made by the finger and thumb of St. Peter when taking the tribute money from its mouth.

It is in season from August to February.

To Boil Haddocks.

Time, a quarter to half an hour, according to size.

155. Two haddocks; enough water to cover them; a quarter of a pound of salt to each gallon of water.

Clean the fish, and wash them thoroughly, they will require scraping first, then put them in the fish-kettle; simmer them gently. Serve with a garnish of sliced lemon and parsley.

Sauce: melted butter, or anchovy.

Fried Haddock.

Time, a quarter of an hour or eighteen minutes.

156. Haddock; egg; bread-crumbs; a

sprig of parsley; a little lemon thyme; a few chives; pepper and salt.

Haddocks of medium size are very nice cut open, covered with egg, bread-crumbs, chives, parsley, and a little lemon thyme minced very fine, salt and pepper, and fried.

Baked Haddock.
Time, from half an hour to an hour.

157. One haddock; some veal stuffing; bread-crumbs; and one egg.

Thoroughly clean and dry the haddock, fill the inside with veal stuffing, sew it up, and curl the tail into its mouth. Brush it over with egg, and strew bread-crumbs over it. Set it in a warm oven to bake for about half an hour, but if a Dublin Bay haddock, it will require double that time. Serve it on a dish without a napkin, with any sauce you please, anchovy, melted butter, &c.

To Broil Haddock.
Time, fifteen minutes.

158. Thoroughly clean and dry them in a cloth, rub them over with a little vinegar, and dredge them with flour. Rub some grease on the bars of the gridiron, put it over a clear fire, and when it is *hot*, place your fish on it; turn them two or three times, and broil them a nice brown colour. Serve them with shrimp sauce, or plain melted butter.

Or.
Time, half an hour.

159. Clean and dry the haddock, and put it into a Dutch oven before a very quick fire; as soon as the skin rises take it from the fire, brush it over with the yolk of a well-beaten egg. Strew bread-crumbs thickly over it, and dredge it with flour. Rub some butter over a gridiron, lay the fish carefully on it, and each time turned, lay a small slice of butter over it. Serve with shrimp sauce, or melted butter.

To Dry Haddock.
Time to dry, two or three days.

160. One haddock of three pounds weight; egg; and bread-crumbs.

Choose the fish from two to three pounds in weight, take out the gills and the inside, and well clean the blood from the backbone. Dry them in a cloth, and put some salt into the bodies and eyes. Lay them on a board for a night, then hang them up in a dry place, and after two or three days they will be fit for use; skin and brush them over with egg, and strew bread-crumbs over them. Lay them before the fire, and baste them with butter. Serve with egg sauce.

SKATE.

Cut off the fin part, put it into fresh water, and it will curl up.

In season from August to April.

To Crimp Skate.
Time to soak, one hour.

161. Have the skate alive; skin, and wash it very clean, cut it in long slips the whole length of the fish, about an inch broad, roll it over your finger, and throw it into spring water; cut the middle part of the fish in any form you like, wash it well, and put it into spring water for one hour, then wash it very clean, and put it to drain for use.

To Boil Crimped Skate.
Time, fifteen to twenty minutes.

162. Clean, skin, and cut the fish into slices, roll them over your finger, and fasten them round with a thin string. Put them into a stewpan with a large quantity of salt in the water; boil them for about fifteen or twenty minutes, and hold them over the stewpan to drain; remove the string, and serve them on a folded napkin placed in a hot dish. Shrimp or lobster sauce may be served with it.

To Fry Skate.

163. Brush it over with the yolk of a well-beaten egg, and cover it with bread-crumbs, fry it a nice brown, and serve it on a hot table-napkin, with anchovy or shrimp sauce.

SHELL-FISH—LOBSTER.
To Choose Lobsters.

164. The heaviest are the best, and very often a good small-sized lobster will weigh heavier than a large one.

The male is the best for boiling, the flesh is firmer, the shell of a brighter red. You may easily distinguish the hen lobster by its broader tail, and the two uppermost fins within the tail being less stiff and hard than those of the male lobster. Hen lobsters are best for sauce or salad, on account of their coral.

To Boil a Lobster.
Time, half an hour.

165. Boiling a lobster may be made a horrible operation if the advice we are about to give is not attended to; and its cries in dying are said to be most pain-

ful. Happily it is possible to kill it immediately.

It is done thus :—

Put into a large kettle water enough to cover the lobster, with a quarter of a pound of salt to every gallon of water.

When it boils fast put in the lobster, *head first;* this is a little difficult to achieve, as the lobster is not easy to hold thus over the hot steam, but we are sure any humane cook will do it. If the head goes in first it is killed instantly. Boil it briskly for half an hour, then take it from the hot water with the tongs, and lay it to drain. Wipe off all the scum from it ; tie a little piece of butter in a cloth and rub it over with it.

A lobster weighing a pound takes one hour to boil, others in like proportion, more or less.

To Dress Lobsters.

166. When sent to table, separate the body from the tail, remove the large claws, and crack them at each joint carefully, and split the tail down the middle with a sharp knife ; place the body upright in the centre of a dish on a napkin, and arrange the tail and claws on each side. Garnish it with double parsley.

Scalloped Lobster.

Time, fifteen minutes.

167. One or two lobsters ; a little pepper, salt, Cayenne, and a tablespoonful of white sauce, or thin melted butter, and bread-crumbs.

Pick out all the meat from one large, or two middling-sized lobsters, and pound it in a mortar with a little pepper, salt, Cayenne, and a spoonful or more of white sauce, or thin melted butter, sufficient to moisten it. Split the empty shells of the tails and the bodies, and fill each of them neatly with the pounded lobster, cover them with grated bread, and put them into an oven. Serve on a folded napkin with fried parsley. Six or seven divided shells will be sufficient for a dish.

Broiled Lobsters—An American Receipt.

Time, fifteen or twenty minutes.

168. After having boiled the lobster, split it from head to tail. Take out the uneatable part called the "lady," lay it open, put pieces of butter over the meat, sprinkle it with pepper, and set the shells on a gridiron over bright coals until nicely heated through. Serve in the shells.

Buttered Lobster—American also.

Time, twenty minutes.

169. One lobster ; one wineglassful of vinegar ; quarter of a pound of fresh butter, one saltspoonful of Cayenne pepper ; one saltspoonful of made mustard , three heads of lettuce ; one hard-boiled egg.

Boil a lobster, take the meat from the shell and mince or chop it fine. put the coral and green inside—but leave out the "lady" —to a wineglass of vinegar, or hot water, add a quarter of a pound of fresh butter ; add the Cayenne pepper and mustard, and put it with the lobster into a stewpan over a gentle fire. Stir it until it is thoroughly heated through.

Cut the heads of lettuce, nicely wash them, put them at the sides of a salad bowl, lay the hot lobster in the middle, garnish with the hard-boiled egg cut in circles, and serve it hot.

To Stew Lobsters.

Time, twenty minutes.

170. One large, or two small hen lobsters ; one pint of water ; one blade of mace ; some white pepper corns ; some melted butter ; a glass of white wine ; juice of half a lemon.

Pick the meat from one large, or two small lobsters in large pieces ; boil the shells in a pint of water with a blade of mace and some whole pepper corns ; when all the strength is extracted from the shells and spice, strain the liquor, mix the coral and the rich part of the lobster with a few spoonfuls of melted butter, a wineglass of white wine, and the juice of half a lemon strained. Put in the picked lobster, boil it up, and serve.

Lobster Cutlets.

Time, eight minutes to fry.

171. One large hen lobster ; two small ones ; two ounces of fresh butter ; pepper and salt ; one blade of mace ; nutmeg, and Cayenne pepper ; a dessertspoonful of anchovy sauce ; yolks of four eggs ; white of one ; bread-crumbs. For the sauce—the coral of the lobster ; a spoonful of anchovy sauce ; a small cupful of melted butter.

Pick the meat from a fine hen lobster, and two small ones, and pound it in a mortar with a part of the coral, and a seasoning of pepper and salt, a blade of pounded mace, a little nutmeg and Cayenne pepper. Add the yolks of two well-beaten eggs, the white of one, and a spoonful of anchovy sauce ; mix the above ingredients thoroughly together, and roll it out as you would paste with a little flour, nearly two inches thick.

Cut it into cutlets, brush them over with the yolk of egg, dip them into bread-crumbs, and fry a nice brown in butter. Make a sauce with a cupful of melted butter, a spoonful of anchovy sauce, and the remainder of the coral. Pour it into the centre of a hot dish, and arrange the lobster cutlets round it, as you would cutlets of meat ; place between each the horns of the lobster cut into short lengths.

Lobster Balls.

Time, eight or ten minutes to fry.

172. A fine hen lobster ; two eggs ; bread-crumbs ; two ounces of butter ; pepper ; salt, and a very little Cayenne pepper.

Take the meat from a fine hen lobster, and pound it in a mortar with the coral and spawn. Mix with it not quite an equal quantity of bread-crumbs, seasoned with pepper and salt, and a *very* little Cayenne ; bind the whole with two ounces of fresh butter warmed, roll the mixture into balls the size of a large duck's egg, brush them over with beaten egg, cover them with bread-crumbs, and fry them lightly. Serve them hot (after draining the grease from them) on a napkin.

To Choose Crabs.

173. The heaviest crabs are usually considered the best, although those of a middling size are the sweetest, when perfectly fresh and in perfection, the shell, whether alive or dead, should be of a bright red colour, and the joints of the legs stiff. Crabs are stale when the eyes look dull. They are boiled in the same manner as lobsters, but require a much longer time, and are usually eaten cold.

To Dress Boiled Crabs.

174. Empty the large shell ; mix the flesh with a *very* little oil, vinegar, salt, white pepper, and Cayenne to your taste, replace the meat in the large shell, and place it in the dish with the claws.

Buttered Crab.

Time, one hour.

175. One large crab ; bread-crumbs ; a little parsley ; three ounces of butter ; pepper, salt, and Cayenne to taste ; juice of a lemon.

Boil the crab, pick the meat out of the shell, cut it into small pieces, and mix all well together with bread-crumbs, and a little minced parsley, equal to a third of the crab in quantity. Mix in pieces of butter here and there ; season it with pepper, salt, and Cayenne to taste, pack it into the shell and squeeze over it the juice of a lemon, or drop in a spoonful of lemon pickle, or vinegar. Cover the top with a thick layer of bread-crumbs, put small pieces of butter over it, and bake either in a moderate oven or before the fire.

To Stew Crab.

Time, a quarter of an hour.

176. One large crab ; some bread-crumbs ; pepper ; salt ; a piece of butter ; the juice of a lemon.

Pick all the meat from a good-sized crab ; cut it into very small pieces, mix it with rather more than a quarter its weight in bread-crumbs, season it with pepper and salt, return it to the shell with sufficient butter to moisten it, squeeze in the juice of a lemon, and put a thick layer of bread-crumbs on the top, with small pieces of butter laid over them. Place the shells in the oven, or in a Dutch oven before the fire, to brown the crumbs. Serve on a napkin, garnished with parsley and slices of lemon.

To Boil and Serve Crayfish.

Time, a quarter of an hour.

177. Crayfish ; salt ; boiling-water ; one tablespoonful of vinegar ; parsley.

Throw your crayfish into a stewpan of boiling salt and water with a tablespoonful of vinegar ; boil them quickly a quarter of an hour, and then drain them dry. When cold, place a few sprigs of double parsley in the centre of your dish, and arrange your crayfish all round as close as you can, with the tails outside, and at the top of the parsley put a few in any form you please, garnishing the edge of the dish with the same in small sprigs.

OYSTERS.

They must be fresh and fat to be good.
In season from August till May.
They are excellent eaten cold, opened and laid on a dish, and served with thin slices of brown bread and butter, or alone.

Oysters for Keeping and Opening.

178. Take the oysters from the barrel, and put them in a clean milk-pan covered with pure water moderately salted and changed every day. Keep them in a cool place.

In opening them, try and avoid cutting them by keeping the point of the knife close to the shell.

Modes of Dressing Oysters.

To Feed Oysters.

179. Wash them perfectly clean in a pan of water, then lay them bottom downwards in a deep pan, and pour over them water with a large quantity of salt. Change the water every day. The salt should be previously dissolved in the water, allowing about five or six ounces to each gallon of water. You may fatten them by putting oatmeal into the water every day.

Oysters Stewed.

Time, ten or twelve minutes in all.

180. A pint and a half of oysters; two ounces and a half of butter; a dessertspoonful of flour; a quarter of a pint of cream; and a little mace and Cayenne.

Open a pint and a half of oysters and wash them in their own liquor, then strain the liquor into a small stewpan; add a little mace and Cayenne, two ounces and a half of butter, and a large teaspoonful of flour. Boil it for three or four minutes, then take out the mace, and stir in a quarter of a pint of cream; throw in the oysters, previously bearded, shake them round, and let them stew at the side of the fire for four or five minutes, but do not let them boil. Garnish with sippets fried lightly.

Scalloped Oysters.

Time, a quarter of an hour.

181. Three dozen oysters; grated bread-crumbs about a large teacupful; two ounces of fresh butter; pepper.

Butter some scallop shells, or if you have not any, a small tart dish. Strew in a layer of grated bread, then put some thin slices of butter, then oysters enough to fill your shells or dish. Cover them thickly with bread-crumbs; again add slices of butter. Pepper the whole well, add a little of the liquor kept from the oysters. Put butter over the whole surface, and bake in a quick oven.

Serve them in their shells or in the dish.

Brown them with a salamander. If you have not one, make the kitchen shovel red-hot, and hold it over closely enough to brown your scallops.

French Scalloped Oysters.

182. Oysters; an ounce and a half of butter; a sprig of parsley; pepper; a little lemon juice.

Throw the oysters into boiling water over the fire, and let them just bubble up, not boil. Roll them in butter with minced parsley, pepper, and lemon juice. Make some of the deep shells quite clean, arrange the oysters three or four in each, put them on the gridiron, and the moment the liquor bubbles at the side, take them up and serve them.

Another way is to open some large oysters in the deep shells, put over each a little *maître d'hôtel* sauce cold, place them on the gridiron, and serve them the moment the liquor boils.

To Stew Oysters Plain.

Time, three or four minutes.

183. Three dozen oysters; thin melted butter; a blade of mace; twenty pepper corns.

Open the oysters, cut off the beards, and wash them in their own liquor to remove the grit. Strain it into a small stewpan, add a little thin melted butter to thicken it, a blade of mace, and twenty pepper corns tied up in muslin. Let the oysters simmer in this sauce for about three or four minutes, taking care they do not boil. Serve with sippets of bread.

Fried Oysters, to Garnish Boiled Fish.

Time, five minutes.

184. Half a pint of oysters; half a pint of milk; two eggs; a little flour; pepper; salt; nutmeg; bread-crumbs.

Open and remove the beards from half a pint of oysters, scald them in their own liquor, and drain them on a fine sieve. Then dip them into a batter made with half a pint of milk, two eggs, some grated bread-crumbs, pepper, salt, and nutmeg. Put them one at a time into a pan of boiling fat, and fry them a light brown. Take them out carefully with a skewer, or one prong of a fork, and serve them as a garnish for boiled fish.

Oyster Fritters.

Time, five or six minutes.

185. Some good-sized oysters; four whole eggs; a tablespoonful of milk; salt and pepper; bread-crumbs.

Beard some good-sized oysters, make a thick omelet batter with four eggs and a tablespoonful of milk, dip each oyster into the batter, and then into grated bread, fry them a nice colour, and use them to garnish fried fish.

Oysters in Marinade.

Time, six minutes.

186. Oysters; pepper; salt; grated nutmeg; lemon juice; batter.

Put the oysters (out of their shells) in cold water over the fire, and when it boils take them out and throw them into cold water, and then lay them out upon a cloth to dry. Spread them on a dish, sprinkle them with pepper, salt, and a little grated nutmeg, squeeze lemon juice over them, let them lie a little time, dip them in batter, and fry them.

Scallop Fish, or St. James's Cockle.
Time, half an hour.

187. Scallops; bread-crumbs; pepper; salt; a sprig of minced parsley; flour; a spoonful of lemon pickle.

Open the scallops with a knife, and take them out as you would oysters; cover them with beaten egg and bread-crumbs, well seasoned with pepper, salt, and minced parsley, and fry them nicely. Put them to keep hot, dredge flour into the frying-pan to take up the grease, mix in water enough for gravy, season with pepper and salt, thicken it, if required, make the scallops hot in it, and serve them with the gravy together. Lemon pickle may be added.

They may also be floured and fried; and then stewed.

Scalloped Scallops
Time, nine minutes.

188. Bread-crumbs; a piece of butter; pepper and salt.

Take them out of their shells, cut off their beards, and divide each into three or four pieces. Fry some bread-crumbs with butter, pepper, and salt, until they are brown; put in the scallops, and fry them and the bread-crumbs for three minutes, shaking the pan all the time. Pack them nicely in the shells, brown the tops, and serve them.

Baked Scallops.
Time, half an hour.

189. Scallops; bread-crumbs; pepper and salt; thin slices of butter.

Take the scallops from their shells, and beard them. Season fine bread-crumbs with pepper and salt, and lay them a quarter of an inch thick at the bottom of a dish; spread the scallops over, cover them with bread-crumbs, put thin slices of butter over the surface, and bake them in a moderate oven. They will take from twenty minutes to half an hour.

To Boil and Serve Prawns.
Time, ten minutes.

190. Prawns; strong salt and water; one large China orange, or a lemon; sprigs of double parsley.

Boil your prawns for ten minutes in a stewpan of boiling salt and water, and then drain them dry. Put a large China orange, or lemon into the centre of a dish, and stick the prawns thickly over it, commencing at the bottom, with their backs upwards. At the top place three with the backs down, and a sprig of double parsley arranged between them and at the edge of your dish.

To Boil Cockles and Periwinkles.
191. Put them in a stewpan, with only a small quantity of water, to prevent the pan from burning; when the cockle-shells open the fish will be done.

To Pickle Cockles.
192. Equal quantities of vinegar and wine; with the liquor from the cockles: one blade of mace; and some salt.

Wash your cockles clean, and put them in a stewpan, cover them close; set them over the fire and shake them till the shells open, then take them out; let the liquor settle till it is clear; then add an equal quantity of wine and vinegar, a little salt, and a blade of mace. Boil this pickle and pour it over your cockles; put them in jars or bottles, and cover them close.

MUSSELS AND COCKLES.

Clean the shells well with repeated washings, but do not keep them longer than necessary in water, as it is not their nature to remain immersed, and stew them with a small quantity of boiling-water. The saucepan should be covered, and shaken continually while they cook, that they may be done equally; when the shells open they are done. Mussels and cockles must always be boiled in this way (to facilitate getting them out of the shells) before dressing them other ways, as it would be too troublesome to free them from the shells, small as they are, with the knife as we do oysters. In boiling mussels put a silver spoon in with them, and if it turns black do not eat them. Eat boiled mussels very hot, and take care to pick out the beards.

To Stew Mussels.
Time, ten minutes.

193. One pint of mussels; half a pint of liquor; one blade of mace; a small piece of butter rolled in flour.

Clean the shells thoroughly with repeated washings, and cook them until they open, as mentioned above. Pick them out of the shells, and as you do so save the liquor that runs from them, and pick out from each one

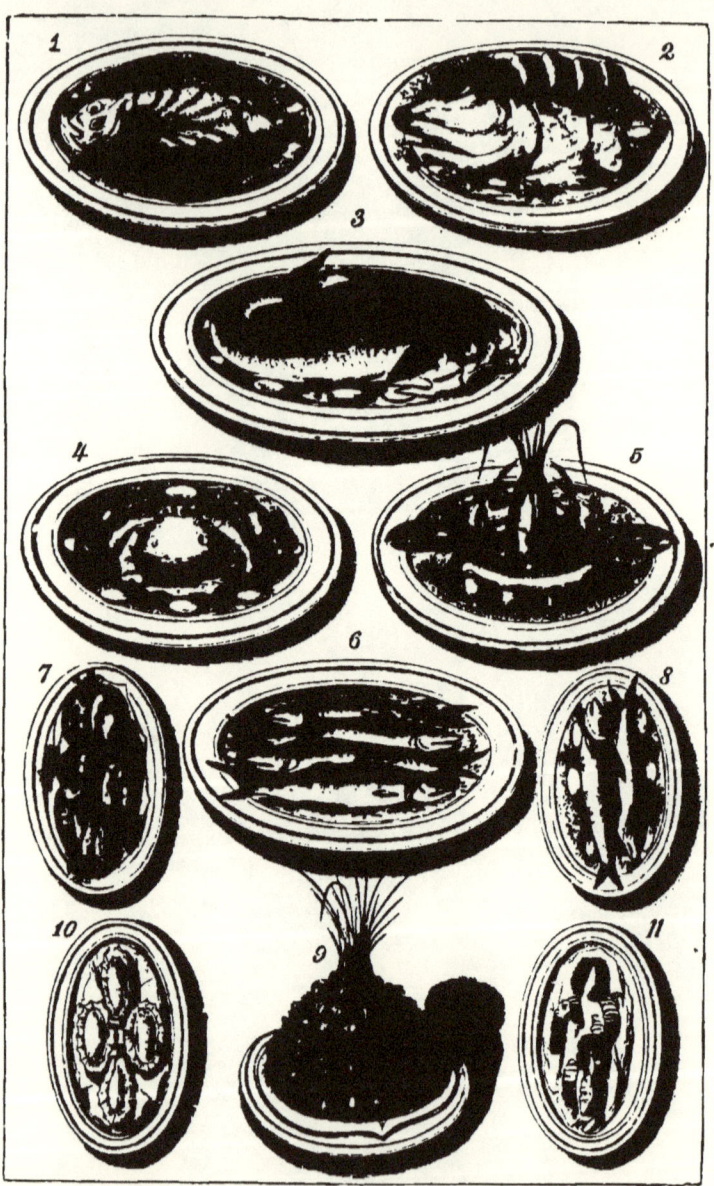

1. Turbot.
2. Cod's Head.
3. Salmon.
4. Crab.
5. Lobster.
6. Mackerel.
7. Whiting.
8. Haddock.
9. Prawns.
10. Scalloped Oysters.
11. Crimped Skate.

the little hairy appendage to be found at the root of the little member shaped like a tongue. To the mussels, thus prepared, put half a pint of the liquor saved, and if there is not enough of it, eke out the quantity with a little of the liquor in which they were boiled, poured off clear. Put in a blade of mace, thicken it with a piece of butter rolled in flour, let them stew gently for a few minutes, and serve them on toast.

HERRINGS.

194. Herrings are the most important of our British fish, forming one of the sources of our wealth, and feeding great numbers of our people.

Still we seldom see them on a gentleman's table; fashion perhaps, or the absurdity of a dislike for that which is abundant and common, preventing us from using them as much as we do other fish. We have heard assigned as another reason that the great number of small bones which they contain render them dangerous food for children or old people.

The herring is a very rich and wholesome fish, however, and we recommend all good housewives to give it a place at their table.

To Boil Herrings.

Time, twenty minutes.

In season from May to October.

195. Some scraped horseradish; vinegar, and salt.

Clean and wash the fish; dry them in a cloth, and rub over them a little vinegar and salt. Skewer them with their tails in their mouths, lay them on a strainer in a stewpan, and when the water boils put them in, and let them continue simmering slowly for about twenty minutes. When they are done, drain and place them in the dish with the heads turned into the centre, garnish with scraped horseradish, and serve with parsley and butter sauce.

To Bake Herrings.

Time, one hour.

196. Two herrings; a large spoonful of pepper; twelve cloves; a teaspoonful of salt; two bay-leaves, and some vinegar.

Clean and wash your herrings, lay them on a dish or board, and rub well over and into them a spoonful of pepper, one of salt, and twelve cloves pounded. Lay them in an earthen pan, cover them with vinegar, add two or three bay-leaves, and tie them over with a thick paper. Put them into a moderate oven, and bake them for an hour. To be eaten cold.

To Smoke Herrings.

Time, twenty-four hours.

197. Herrings and some sawdust.

Clean and lay some fresh herrings in salt and a little saltpetre for *one* night; then run a stick through their eyes, and hang them in a row. Put some sawdust into an old cask, and in the midst of it a *heater red hot*; hang the stick on which you have threaded the fish over the smoke, and let them remain for twenty-four hours.

Fried Herrings.

Time, six or eight minutes.

198. Clean and scale the fish, and dry them thoroughly in a cloth. When they are quite dry, fry them to a bright colour. The herring, being so rich a fish, should be fried with less butter than fish of most kinds, and well drained and dried afterwards. A nice sauce to eat with herrings is sugar, mustard, and a little salt and vinegar. Some serve melted butter, but herrings are too rich to eat with a rich sauce. Crisp parsley may be used as a garnish. Fry sprats in the same way; they require no sauce, unless it may be a little lemon pickle or ketchup.

Broiled Herrings.

Time, six or eight minutes.

199. Herrings; a spoonful of flour; a quarter of a pint of table beer or ale; a slice of onion; six ounces of whole peppers; one ounce of butter; a spoonful of mustard.

Clean and dry the fish, cut off their heads, flour them and broil them. Break up the heads and boil them for a quarter of an hour in a little table beer or ale, with a little whole pepper and a slice of onion; strain off the liquor, thicken it with butter and flour, beat mustard up with it, and serve it in a tureen to eat with the herrings.

Home-salted Herrings.

200. Have the fish as fresh out of the sea as possible, clean and scale them with wiping, but do not wash them. Pepper them slightly, and sprinkle them well over with salt. They are very nice for breakfast fried. If they are to be eaten the next morning they should be turned after lying in the salt twelve hours; if they are for the morning after, turn them when they have lain twenty-four hours.

GURNETS.

There are several kinds of this fish, the grey, red, streaked yellow, and sappharine; of these the last is the best, but they are all very nice flavoured.

Baked Gurnets.

Time, thirty or forty minutes.

201. Two gurnets; two or three slices of bacon; one onion; half a pint of melted butter; two tablespoonfuls of Harvey sauce. Stuff the gurnets with veal stuffing, sew them up with packthread, and put the tail round the fish's mouth, as you do the whiting or haddock. Put them in a baking dish, cover them with thin slices of bacon, and bake in a hot oven for about half an hour, or longer if they are large fish.

When done, put them on a dish, and serve with sauce over them, made of the onion, melted butter, and Harvey sauce.

Boiled Gurnets.

Time, two hours.

202. Thoroughly clean your fish, and boil them in a fish-kettle of *very* strong salt and water, serve them on a napkin, and send anchovy sauce, or plain melted butter to table with them.

Fish Cake of Cold Fish.

Time, two hours.

203. The remains of cold fish; cod; soles; turbot, &c.; a bunch of sweet herbs; bread-crumbs; cold potatoes; a sprig of parsley; one or two eggs; pepper and salt; quite half a pint of water.

Pick the meat from the fish with two forks, and mince it very fine; mix it well with equal quantities of bread-crumbs and cold mashed potatoes, and season it highly with pepper and salt. Put the bones, heads, and trimmings of the fish into a stewpan, with the sweet herbs, parsley, and a little pepper and salt; pour over it about a pint of water, and let it simmer slowly for an hour and three-quarters, or longer, if not done enough. Make the minced fish, bread, and potatoes into a cake, binding it with the white of a beaten egg; brush it over with the yolk, strew it well with bread-crumbs, and fry it lightly. Pour over it the strained gravy, and set it over a gentle fire to stew slowly for nearly twenty minutes, stirring it occasionally. Garnish it with slices of lemon.

To Dress Cold Fish.

204. Some cold fish; fowl; game, &c.; some lettuce; a cucumber; beetroot, and hard-boiled eggs.

Place at the bottom of a dish a layer of cut lettuce, place over it some cold picked fish, and any cold picked fowl, game, &c, Then another layer of lettuce, encircled with hard-boiled eggs cut into quarters, then more lettuce, encircled with thin slices of cucumber and of beetroot.

Pour over the whole any delicate sauce you may have.

Rissoles of Cooked Fish.

Time, a quarter of an hour.

205. Any cooked rich light fish; an equal quantity of bread-crumbs; a piece of butter; one onion; a small bunch of sweet herbs; pepper, salt, and one or two eggs; a little lemon pickle.

Herrings and similar rich fish are especially good for the purpose, and even cold salt fish will do, on account of its savouriness. Pick all the meat from the bones, pound it in a mortar, or pull it to pieces with a silver fork; mix it well with an equal quantity of bread-crumbs, and some butter, season it with an onion chopped very fine, and a sprig of parsley and sweet herbs minced, with pepper and salt. Mix with it sufficient beaten egg to bind it, make it up into flat and rather small cakes, and fry the rissoles with butter or dripping. When they are dished, dredge into the frying-pan flour enough to absorb the grease; stir in a very little water, add pepper and salt, with a little lemon pickle, or any other flavouring that is liked, pour the gravy round the rissoles, and serve them very hot.

DRESSED FISH.

After turbot, salmon, or any other fish has been dressed, take it from the bone in small pieces.

Time, twenty minutes.

206. To one pound of fish, half a pint of cream; one dessertspoonful of mustard; one tablespoonful of essence of anchovies; one tablespoonful of ketchup; a little pepper; two ounces of butter; one ounce of flour; a few bread-crumbs.

Take the fish from the bones in small pieces; mix them with half a pint of cream, one tablespoonful of essence of anchovies, one tablespoonful of ketchup, with a little pepper and salt. Rub one ounce of flour into two ounces of butter, then put it into a stew-pan, and make it quite hot. Put it into the dish it is to be served in; strew bread-crumbs over it, and brown with a salamander.

La Bouillabaisse.

Time, fifteen to twenty minutes.

207. Several different kinds of fish; one onion; a piece of garlic; a sprig of pars-

ley; a piece of Seville orange peel; pepper; salt; spice; a pinch of saffron; and a little oil.

This French dish should be made of several different kinds of fish, and the more variety the better; pilchards, mackerel, and other rich fish being excluded. The best kinds are haddocks, gurnet, whiting, and fish of that description, with any small fish there may be at hand. Place in a stewpan an onion cut into five or six pieces, a piece of garlic, some parsley minced fine, a piece of Seville orange peel, pepper, salt, spice, and a pinch of saffron, and water barely enough to cover the fish, and afterwards to be put into it with a very little oil; the oil and the saffron are to be measured according to taste. Let this mixture cook well, cut the fish in pieces, put it in the stewpan, stir all well together, and put it over a *fierce* fire. The name *bouillabaise* indicates that the cooking should be very quick; the sooner, therefore, it comes to a boil, and the faster it boils the better. It should cook enough in about a quarter of an hour, but some kinds of fish render it necessary to allow five or six minutes longer. The indispensable ingredients in a *bouillabaisse* are, onion, garlic, pepper, salt, spice, parsley, orange peel, saffron, and oil; the quantity, of course, must depend on the quantity of fish to be dressed. Fennel, sage, or a bay-leaf may be added at the option of the cook. If there is liver to the fish, it should be put in only long enough to cook.

Pickled Ormers.

Time, four hours.

208. Ormers; three bay-leaves; a few white peppers; slices of whole ginger; salt, and vinegar.

After your ormers are well cleaned, beat them till quite tender, put them in a stewpan, cover them well with water, allowing for the boiling. Put in three bay-leaves, a few white peppers, and some whole ginger sliced. Boil gently for four hours, or till tender, then add the salt and vinegar to your taste. If meant to keep long, add more vinegar than for present use; or take the whole of the water in which they have boiled away, wash the stewpan, put them in again and cover them with vinegar, leaving them to boil only a few minutes.

SOUPS.

The cook who would succeed in sending good soup to table must take care that she has strong and excellent stock ready for it, and the economical housewife will soon find that stock does not *always* require meat to be bought for its production.

The water in which mutton has been boiled, the liquor left from dressing a calf's head, the bones taken from rolled ribs of beef, or from any boned joint, hare, or poultry, will make excellent stock for a family soup. Fish bones will also produce a good jelly for it. The trimmings of large joints or cutlets, the shanks of mutton, the shank of a ham, the large bone of the sirloin of beef, will all add to the stock-pot, and supply a good foundation for her soup. Ox-cheek carefully managed, and sheep's head and trotters, also make excellent stock with a flavouring of ham or anchovy for the soup.

Soup should never be made with hard water, unless it is of green-peas, in which case the water *must* be hard to preserve their colour.

The rule as to quantity is: a quart of water to a pound of meat without bone; but whenever this quantity of water is diminished, the soup is increased in strength and richness.

Meat should be put into the soup-kettle with *very* little water at first, and with a piece of butter to keep it from burning. It should be let stew *very* slowly till the essence of the meat is extracted. Very long, very slow stewing, is the certain way to procure good soup.

"The more haste the worse speed" is the proverb of the soup-kettle.

Skim the soup frequently also, and do not let it cool until it is quite made. Let the meat of which your soup is made be freshly killed, and very lean, every particle of fat should be removed from it. Onions should be put in the soup soon after it is begun to be made; herbs, carrots, and celery three hours afterwards; turnips, or any delicate vegetable, just before the soup is finished. When celery is out of season, the *seeds* of the plant, tied up in a piece of clean muslin, will give the flavour equally well.

To Colour Soups.

A piece of bread toasted *very* brown may be simmered in the soup for a short time before it is done, and will give it a brown colour. The ordinary colouring, however, is done, by putting a little burnt brown sugar into it. The sugar should be put into a saucepan with a piece of butter the size of a walnut, and a glass of ketchup; it should be melted together, and then put into the soup-kettle. Further directions are given in "Soups." For those who do not dislike them, burnt onions are an improvement, both as to colour and flavour.

Colouring to be kept for use is made thus: a gill of water, a quarter of a pound of lump sugar, and half an ounce of roll butter, should be set over the fire in the smallest frying-pan, and stirred till it is of a bright brown colour; add to it half a pint of water, boil and skim it, let it get cold, and then bottle and cork it down for future use.

The flavouring of soups must in a great measure depend on the cook; her taste, therefore, should be discriminating and delicate. She should be careful in the use of ketchups and sauces, though they are both useful and important. Cow-heel, calfs-feet, and ox-tail soups, all require flavouring, and will bear a *little* sauce or ketchup, but it should never be overdone.

Clear soups have been the fashion of late years: *purées,* such as pea-soup, &c., being not so often seen, except at *old-fashioned* people's tables. To clarify soup break an egg, and throw the white and the shell together into a basin, but take care not to let a particle of the yolk go in.

Beat the white *well* to a stiff froth, and mix it by degrees, and very completely with the soup, which should then be put on the fire and stirred till it again boils. Take it off the moment it boils, cover it close, and let it stand for a quarter of an hour; then strain it off. When a soup is clarified it will bear a stronger flavouring, as it loses a portion of its own in the process. Forcemeat balls and whole eggs are sometimes put into soups, but they are not as fashionable as they used to be.

Summary of Directions for Making Soups.

Take care that the soup-kettle or stewpan is perfectly clean and free from any grease or sand. An iron soup-pot should be washed the moment you have finished using it, with a piece of soda the size of a small nutmeg, dissolved in hot water, to remove all greasiness or taste of onion. A teaspoonful of potash will answer the same purpose.

Remember that *slow* boiling is necessary to make good soup.

Do not uncover the soup-kettle more frequently than necessary for skimming it clean; but if your soup is too weak, do not cover the pot in boiling, as the water will evaporate in steam and leave your liquor stronger. Skim frequently; it is important that every portion of scum should be removed from the soup. Pour in occasionally a little cold water, which will cause the albumen to rise in abundant scum, or if you put in the required quantity of salt with the meat it will cause the scum to rise; but the cup of fresh water is much the better mode of helping the soup to clear itself.

Always stir your soup with a wooden spoon.

Let the soup be quite free from scum before the vegetables are put in.

Do not drown your meat in water, but draw the juices out slowly by putting it into the stewpan with only a *very* little water and a piece of butter, to keep it from burning, and then add the given quantity of water to it.

It will take six or eight hours to extract the essence from a few pounds of beef.

It is better to make your soup the day before it is required, because then the fat will cake at the top of it and can be easily taken off, and you can judge of the goodness of your soup by the consistency and firmness of the jelly.

The water in which meat or fowls have been boiled will make good broth, but for soup add a little gravy beef to it.

Vegetables to be added to soup should be well cleaned, washed, and picked.

It is very difficult to give a perfect measurement of seasoning, as the tastes of people differ considerably with regard to it, and the cook must conform to that which suits the palates of her employers; but, in a rough way, it is usual to add about a teaspoonful of salt to a pound of meat, and pepper according to taste, some naturally insipid broths and soups requiring more; very savoury soups less.

It is better to season too little than too highly.

Put fresh meat into *cold* water to stew for soup. If you make soup of already cooked meat, pour hot, but not boiling water over it.

Time and attention are required to achieve a good soup.

Stock.

Make your dark stock of beef; mutton gives a peculiar and tallowy taste unless it has been previously roasted; then it may help, but it will not do to *make* stock alone.

Let your meat be fresh and lean; cut it in tiny pieces. Draw the juices of the meat out before you add the water, by putting it in a stewpan with half a pint of water (or less) and a quarter of a pound of butter, and letting it stew till a glaze is formed on the pan; then set it aside and let it simmer for six or seven hours very slowly. The albumen will then rise and bring with it all the impurities of the meat. This is called the scum. By skimming it off carefully, the soup is cleared. Keep your fire of an equal temperature, and beware of letting the stock boil fast; if it does the scum will dissolve and part will sink to the bottom, and render it difficult for you to clarify your stock. Add cold water, if necessary, to make the stock clear. When the stock is clear of the albumen let it boil, and put in the broken bones in a bag, and the gristly part of cold meat, trimmings, &c., &c.; for, from the bones, as has been already said, you will get gelatine, the nutritious part of the stock. They should be well broken up; the smaller the better, so as to present the larger amount of surface.

Add flavouring and vegetables, and then let the stock simmer again.

Six or eight hours will make it fit for use; to preserve its flavour it will be well then to remove it from the fire; but do not let it *cool* till it is quite made.

Let it stand during the night; the next day take off the fat, and put it by in a stone jar for use.

If your stock is made in an uncovered stewpan it will be all the stronger, for water evaporates, and consequently there will be the less of it left with the juices of the meat.

Brown stock may be made from ox-cheek, shin of beef, ox-tail, brisket or flank of beef.

General Stock-pot.

209. Stock, in its composition, is not confined to fresh meat only, any meat or bones are useful; pieces of beef, from any part from which gravy can be extracted; bones, skin, brisket, or tops of ribs, ox-cheek, pieces of mutton, bacon, ham, and trimmings of turkeys, fowls, veal, &c.; and also of hare and pheasant, if they are old and fit for no other purpose; in fact, anything that will become a jelly, will assist in making stock; to this medley of ingredients add carrots cut into slices, herbs, onions, pepper, salt, spice, &c.; and when all have stewed until the stock is of a rich consistency, take it from the fire and pour it out to cool. When cold, all the fat must be taken off, and it must be poured clear from the sediment. When the soup is required to be very rich, the jelly from a cow-heel, or a lump of butter rolled in flour, must be added to the stock.

The stock-pot should never be suffered to be empty, as almost any meats (save salt meats) or fowls make stock; the remnants should never be thrown anywhere but into the stock-pot, and should too much stock be already in your possession, boil it down to a glaze; waste is thus avoided.

Cheap Stock.

Time, six hours.

210. Three or four quarts of the liquor in which mutton or beef has been boiled; any bones of dressed meat; trimmings of poultry; meat, &c.; two large onions; five cloves; pepper and salt to taste; one turnip; two carrots; a head of celery; a bunch of savoury herbs; a sprig of parsley; two blades of mace.

Put any bones of roast beef, trimmings of meat and poultry into a stew-pan; add a head of celery cut into pieces, two onions stuck with cloves, a turnip, carrot, savoury herbs, with a sprig of parsley, two blades of mace, a few pepper corns, and a little pepper and salt; pour in four quarts of the liquor in which any meat has been boiled; set it over a slow fire, and let it simmer gently for quite six hours. Remove all the scum the moment it rises, and continue to do so until the stock is clear; then strain it through a fine hair sieve, and it will be fit for use.

Bone Stock for Soup.

Time, two to three hours.

211. Bones of any meat which has been dressed, as sirloin bone; leg of mutton bone, &c., &c.; two scraped carrots; one stick of celery; enough cold water to cover the bones, or enough of the liquor left from braising meat to cover them; one spoonful of salt.

Break the bones into very small pieces, put them into a stew-pan with the carrots and celery; cover them with cold water, or cold braise liquor; and let it boil quickly till the scum rises; skim it off and throw in some cold water, when the scum will rise again. This must be done two or three times, till the stock is quite clear; then draw the pan from the fire and let it stew for two hours, till all the goodness is extracted from the bones. Strain it off and let it stand all night. The next day take off the grease very carefully, not leaving the least atom on it, and lift it from the sediment at the bottom of the pan. It will then be fit for use.

Browning for Soups.

212. Three tablespoonfuls of sugar; about a pint of boiling water.

Put three tablespoonfuls of brown sugar into a frying-pan; set it on the fire to brown, stirring it with a wooden spoon, that it may not burn. When sufficiently dark-coloured, stir into it about a pint of boiling water; when it is thoroughly incorporated, put it into a bottle; and when cold, cork it closely over; and use a tablespoonful or more, as may be required, to give a colour to your soup.

A burnt onion or two can be made use of for the purpose of browning, and are often considered far better than the above receipt.

Or onions, after the outer skin has been taken off, dried in a slow oven until a dark brown, and pressed flat like biffins, are very useful to keep by you, as with care they can be preserved good for some time.

To Clarify Stock or Soups

213. The whites of two eggs to about four quarts of stock or soup; two pints and a half of cold water.

Whisk the whites of two very fresh eggs with half a pint of water for ten minutes; then pour in very gently the four quarts of boiling stock or soup; whisking it all the time. Place the stew-pan over the fire; skim it clear; and when on the point of boiling whisk it all well together; then draw it to the side, and let it settle till the whites of the eggs become separated. Strain it through a fine cloth placed over a sieve, and it will be clear and good.

Beef Soup.

Time, eight hours.

214. Five pounds of shin of beef; a quart of water to each pound of meat; one head of celery; one onion; four small, or three large carrots; two turnips; a bunch of sweet herbs; pepper and salt.

Cut off the meat from a shin of beef, and put the bone into a stew-pan with five quarts of water, and let it boil slowly for four hours. Then strain it into a large basin, and when cold, remove the cake of fat. Cut the meat into small pieces, and put them into a stew-pan with the strained gravy, the bunch of herbs, tied together, a large head of celery, one onion, the four carrots, and two turnips, all cut up small. Let them simmer slowly for four hours, seasoning them with pepper and salt to your taste, and adding a spoonful of browning.

When done, take out the bunch of thyme, and it will be ready to serve.

Soupe et Bouilli.

Time, eight hours.

215. Two pounds and a half of brisket of beef; two pounds of the leg of mutton; piece of beef; one gallon of water; one onion; two carrots; two turnips; one leek; one head of celery; three cloves; a little whole pepper; one French roll; one head of endive.

Take about two pounds and a half of brisket of beef, roll it up tight, and fasten it with a piece of tape. Put it into a stew-pan with two pounds of the leg of mutton, piece of beef, and a gallon of water; let it boil slowly, skim it well, and put in an onion stuck with cloves, two carrots, two turnips, a leek, a head of celery cut into slices, with some whole pepper. Cover the stew-pan close, and stew the whole *very slowly* for seven hours. About an hour before it is served, strain the soup quite clear from the meat. Have ready a few boiled carrots cut into wheels, some turnips cut into balls, the endive, and a little celery cut into pieces. Put these into a tureen with a roll, dried after removing the crumb. Pour the soup over these boiling hot, add a little salt and Cayenne, remove the tape from the beef, and serve it on a separate dish.

Plain Soup.

Time, eight hours and a half.

216. Two pounds of bones; half a pound of calf's liver, and a small piece of lean ham or mutton; two turnips; two carrots; a burnt onion; two bay-leaves; a sprig of thyme; four cloves; two ounces of rice; pepper and salt.

Put two pounds of bones into a stew-pan with half a pound of calf's liver, and a small piece of ham or mutton. Add a little pepper and salt, two turnips, two carrots, a burnt onion, the bay-leaves, thyme, cloves, and rice; pour in a quart of water, and let it simmer for half an hour, then add six pints of hot water, or the liquor in which mutton has been boiled, and let it stew gently for eight hours. Skim it frequently, and when done strain it through a sieve, and serve; half a head of celery cut into pieces, boiled with it improves the broth, and a few slips may be served with it.

Very Cheap Soup.

Time, four hours.

217. One pound and a half of lean beef;

six quarts of water; three onions; six turnips; thyme; parsley; pepper and salt; a half pound of rice; one pound of potatoes; one handful of oatmeal.

Cut the beef into small pieces, and put them into a stew-pan with the water, onions, and the turnips; add a bunch of thyme and parsley, a seasoning of pepper and salt, half a pound of Patna rice, a pound of potatoes peeled and cut in quarters, and a handful of oatmeal. Let all stew for four hours, and serve.

Cottage Soup—a very Cheap Soup.

Time, four hours.

218. Two ounces of dripping; half a pound of any solid fresh meat in dice one inch square; a quarter of a pound of onions; a quarter of a pound of turnips; two pounds of leeks; three ounces of celery; half a pound of rice; three ounces of salt; a quarter of an ounce of brown sugar; six quarts of water.

Put the meat, sugar, dripping, and onions into an iron saucepan; stir them till lightly browned; add turnips, celery, leeks. Stir ten minutes. Mix well with it a quart of cold water and rice. Add five quarts of hot water, and salt to your taste. Stir occasionally till it boils. If to be kept, stir gently till the soup is nearly cold. Let it simmer three hours.

Cottage Soup Baked.

Time, three or four hours.

219. A pound of meat; two onions; two carrots; two ounces of rice; a pint of whole peas; pepper and salt; a gallon of water.

Cut the meat into slices, put one or two at the bottom of an earthen jar or pan, lay on it the onions sliced, then put meat again, then the carrots sliced. Soak the pint of peas all the previous night, put them in with one gallon of water. Tie the jar down, and put it in a hot oven for three or four hours.

Poor Man's Soup.

Time, one hour and ten minutes.

220. Two quarts of water; four spoonfuls of beef dripping; an ounce and a half of butter; a pint basinful of raw potatoes; a young cabbage; a little salt.

Put two quarts of water in a stew-pan, and when boiling throw in four spoonfuls of beef dripping and an ounce and a half of butter, a pint basinful of raw potatoes sliced, and let them boil one hour. Pick a young cabbage, leaf by leaf, or the heart of a white cabbage, but do not chop it small, throw it in and let it boil ten minutes, or till the cabbage be done to taste, though when boiled fast and green it eats much better. Season it with a little salt, and throw it over thin slices of bread in a tureen.

A French Receipt.
Pot au Feu.

Time, three hours.

221. Three quarts of water; four pounds of meat; two teaspoonfuls of salt; three small carrots; three middling-sized onions (one being stuck with two cloves); a head of celery; a bunch of thyme; a bay-leaf, and a little parsley, tied together; two turnips; a burnt onion, or a little browning.

Put the meat into a stock-pot full of water, set it over a slow fire, and let it gently boil, carefully taking off the scum that will rise to the top. Pour in a teacupful of cold water to help the scum to rise. When no more scum rises, it is time to put in the vegetables, which you should have ready washed and prepared. Cut the carrots in slices, stick the onions with cloves, cut the turnips each in four pieces. Put them into the pot, and let them boil gently for two hours. If the water boils away too much, add a little *hot* water in addition. A few bones improve the soup very much.

It is not necessary to keep the pot very closely covered. It is better to raise the lid a little; it facilitates the operation.

Cocoa Nut Soup.

Time, one hour and a quarter.

222. Three ounces of grated cocoa nut; three pints of veal stock; some cold stock; a little corn or rice flour; half a pint of cream; salt to taste.

Put the cocoa nut (omitting the dark rind) to the veal stock; boil it gently for one hour, then mix with it a little cold stock, and sufficient corn or rice flour to make the soup sufficiently thick; season to taste, add the cream, and simmer all for a quarter of an hour. Nutmeg or mace may be added if liked.

Chicken Broth.

Time, one hour.

223. A full-grown chicken; three pints of water or weak broth; half a teacupful of pearl barley or rice; pepper and salt.

Cut up a chicken, put to it the cold water, or weak broth, a tablespoonful of salt, half a teacupful of pearl barley (or rice if preferred); cover it close and let it simmer for an hour, skim it clear, and add pepper to your taste. The chicken may be placed on a dish with pieces of butter over it, a dust of pepper, and served with mashed potatoes.

Calf's Head Soup.
Time, two hours and a half.

224. Half a calf's head; three quarts of water that meat has been boiled in; a bunch of sweet herbs; two blades of mace; one onion; six ounces of rice flour; three spoonfuls of ketchup; six cloves, and a little pepper and salt.

After thoroughly cleaning half a calf's head, rub over it a little salt, and put it to soak in cold water for about six hours. Then put it into a stew-pan with the three quarts of liquor, one onion stuck with cloves, and a bunch of sweet herbs. Boil and skim it well for an hour and a half, take out the meat, and strain the soup through a sieve. Mix a little flour with three spoonfuls of ketchup, stir it into the soup, and let it simmer for a few minutes. Then cut the head into square pieces, put it to the soup, and let it simmer again until quite tender. Add pepper, salt, pounded mace, and the juice of a lemon. Serve with forcemeat balls in the tureen.

Calf's Feet Soup.
Time, two hours and a half.

225. Four calf's feet; a bunch of thyme and parsley; two shallots; half a blade of mace; a little salt; one head of celery; one onion stuck with three cloves; yolks of three eggs; two tablespoonfuls of cream; a glass of white wine.

Divide four calf's feet, and put them into a stew-pan with a bunch of herbs, two shallots, one onion stuck with three cloves, a head of celery cut into pieces, half a blade of mace, and a little pepper and salt; pour over them rather more than two quarts of weak stock, and boil them slowly for about two hours. Then strain the soup into another stew-pan, thicken it with a piece of butter rolled in flour; boil it up again, skim off all the grease, and strain it again through a fine sieve; add it to the feet cut into small pieces, and a few forcemeat balls. When ready to serve, stir into it the yolks of three or four well beaten eggs, and two tablespoonfuls of cream; stir it over a clear fire for a few minutes, and serve up very hot.

Curry Soup.
Time, six hours.

226. One ox-cheek; four onions; one bunch of pot-herbs; half a pound of rice; one teaspoonful of curry powder; a little pepper and salt; three quarts of water.

Cut the meat from an ox-cheek, and soak it for two hours; then put it in a stew-pan with four onions cut in slices, and the savoury herbs; add three quarts of water, stew it slowly, and remove the scum frequently. Then strain it; add to it half a pound of soaked rice, the teaspoonful of curry powder, pepper and salt to your taste, and stew it again for four hours.

Best Manner of Making Clear Soups.
Time, eight hours.

227. Seven or eight pounds of shin of beef; a slice of ham; one dozen onions; six cloves; two blades of mace; a little whole pepper; two or three turnips; two or three carrots; two heads of celery; a few leeks; one onion; a bunch of parsley and thyme; six bay-leaves; white of an egg; a few leaves of lettuce; tarragon, and chervil; season to taste.

Grease the bottom of a stewpan or stock-pot slightly with butter; slice a large onion *thin*, cut the meat off the shin in small pieces, put them in the stock-pot, and set them over a quick fire to draw down. Put in the bones; add boiling water, allowing a pint to each pound of meat; when it boils up remove it to the side. Let it simmer ten minutes; skim off all the fat quite clean, then add one dozen onions. sticking two cloves in three of them, two blades of mace, a little whole pepper, two or three carrots, and the same of turnips, a bunch of thyme and parsley, and six bay-leaves tied up in a bunch, and boil it slowly for eight hours.

Then strain it through a sieve into a large pan. The next day take off the fat, wipe off all remaining grease with a napkin wrung out of hot water; boil it ten minutes, and pour it into small basins. Before using it, put it into a stewpan; add a slice of lean ham chopped fine, carrot, turnip, and celery also chopped fine, and boil it twenty minutes. Strain it through a sieve into a basin, and let it stand till quite cold, then put it into a stewpan; add the white of one egg well whipped. When it boils, draw it to the side; let it simmer ten minutes, then strain it through a napkin before sending up. Boil in the soup a few leaves of lettuce, tarragon, and chervil, and season to taste.

Cock-a-Leekie.
Time, three or four hours.

228. One fowl; three bunches of winter

leeks; pepper and salt; and five quarts of medium stock.

Well wash the leeks, take off part of the heads and the roots, scald them in boiling water for five or six minutes, and then cut them into small pieces. Put a fowl trussed as for boiling into a stewpan, with the pieces of leek, a little pepper and salt, and nearly five quarts of stock; let the whole simmer very slowly at the corner of the fire for three or four hours, keeping it well skimmed. When ready to serve, take out the fowl, cut it into neat pieces, place them in a tureen, and pour the leeks and the broth over them (the leeks being made into a purée), as the soup should be very thick of leeks.

This soup is greatly improved by warming it up a second time. It will keep for some little time good.

Hotch-Potch.

Time, after it is made, a quarter of an hour.

229. One pint of peas; three pounds of the lean end of a loin of mutton; one gallon of water; four carrots; four turnips; pepper and salt; one onion; one head of celery.

Put a pint of peas into a stewpan with a quart of water, and boil them until they will pulp through a sieve. Then take the lean end of a loin of mutton, cut it into chops, put it into a stewpan with a gallon of water, the carrots and turnips cut into small pieces, and a seasoning of pepper and salt. Boil it until all the vegetables are *quite* tender, put in the pulped peas and a head of celery, and an onion sliced; let it boil fifteen minutes, and serve.

Kidney Soup.

Time, six hours.

230. One bullock's kidney; three sticks of celery; three or four turnips; three or four carrots; a bunch of sweet herbs; pepper and salt; a spoonful of mushroom ketchup; the liquor in which a leg of mutton has been boiled.

Add to the liquor from a boiled leg of mutton a bullock's kidney, put it over the fire, and when half done take out the kidney, and cut it into pieces the size of dice. Add three sticks of celery, three or four turnips, and the same of carrots, all cut small, and a bunch of sweet herbs tied together. Season to your taste with pepper and salt. Let it boil slowly for five or six hours, adding the ketchup. When done take out the herbs and serve the vegetables in the soup. It is always better (as all soups are) made the day before it is wanted.

Mutton Soup.

Time, thirteen hours.

231. Seven pounds of neck of mutton; seven pints of water; a bunch of sweet herbs; one onion; three turnips; three carrots; a little pepper and salt; and three dessertspoonfuls of arrowroot.

Put seven pounds of neck of mutton into a stewpan with seven pints of water, a large bunch of sweet herbs, an onion, three turnips, three carrots, and a little pepper and salt. Let it remain at the side of the fire for at least ten hours, stirring it frequently. Put it by until the following day, then place it over the fire until it boils, when it must be put on the side of the stove to simmer slowly for three hours. When done, take out the meat, which must be served on a separate dish, garnished with carrots and turnips. Strain the soup through a hair sieve, and when cold take off the fat, and add a little pepper, salt, and three dessertspoonfuls of arrowroot mixed smooth, and stirred gradually in to thicken it.

Scotch Barley Broth.

Time, three hours and a half.

232. Knuckle of veal; three-quarters of a pound of Scotch barley; seven onions; two heads of celery; two turnips; and enough water to cover the meat.

Throw the barley into some clean water; when thoroughly cleansed place it with a knuckle of veal in a stewpan; *cover* it with water; let it boil very slowly; add the onions; and simmer it slowly for two hours, skimming it well; then add the celery and the turnips cut in slices, or any shape you please; add as much salt as required; and let it simmer for an hour and a half, skimming it constantly; then serve. If it is intended to serve the veal with it, take two pints of the broth, put it in a stewpan over a clear fire, add two spoonfuls of flour, stirring the broth as you shake it in until it boils; then add a little pepper and Cayenne, and a glass of port wine; boil for ten minutes, and strain it over the veal in a hot dish.

Scotch Mutton Broth.

Time, three hours and a half.

233. Six pounds of neck of mutton; three quarts of water; five carrots; five turnips; two onions; four tablespoonfuls of Scotch barley; and a little salt.

Soak a neck of mutton in water for an hour, cut off the scrag, and put it into a stewpan with three quarts of water. As soon as it boils skim it well, and then simmer it for an hour and a half. Cut the best end of the mutton into cutlets, dividing it with two bones in each. Take off nearly all the fat before you put it into the broth; skim it the moment the meat boils, and every ten minutes afterwards: add five carrots, five turnips, and two onions, all cut into two or three pieces; and put them into the soup soon enough to be thoroughly done; stir in four tablespoonfuls of Scotch barley well washed in cold water; add salt to your taste; and let all stew together for three hours; about half an hour before sending to table put in a little chopped parsley, and serve all together.

Mock Turtle Soup.

Time, twelve hours and a half.

234. Ten pounds of the shin of beef; a bunch of sweet herbs; two onions; half a calf's head; a very little flour; a little pounded mace and cloves; two spoonfuls of mushroom ketchup; pepper and salt; a glass of sherry; and some egg-balls.

Take about ten pounds of the shin of beef, cut it into small pieces, and fry the lean part a light brown; put the rest of the beef into a stewpan with boiling-water, and stew it for eight hours, with a bunch of sweet herbs, and two onions. When cold, take off the fat. Then get half a calf's head with the skin *on*, half boil it, and cut it into small square pieces, put it into the soup, and let it stew all together till *quite tender*. Thicken it with a very little flour, add the mace, cloves, mushroom ketchup, and a little soy. Season it with pepper and salt to your taste. Put in a few egg-balls, and a wine glass of sherry.

A Flavouring to make Soup taste like Turtle.

Time, one week.

235. An ounce and a half of shallot wine; an ounce and a half of essence of anchovies; a quarter of a pint of basil wine; two ounces of mushroom ketchup; half a teaspoonful of curry powder; half an ounce of thin lemon peel; half a drachm of citric acid.

Pour one ounce and a half of shallot wine into the same quantity of essence of anchovies; add a quarter of a pint of basil wine, half that quantity of mushroom ketchup, and stir in about half a teaspoonful of curry powder; also add half an ounce of thin lemon peel, half a drachm of citric acid, and let it remain for a week. It will be found, when added to soup, to give the flavour of turtle.

Mulligatawny Soup

Time, two hours.

236. One rabbit, or one fowl; a slice of garlic; three pints o[f] tablespoonfuls of curry powder of powdered almonds; a lit[tle] mango juice; a good lump o[f] salt to taste.

Cut up a rabbit or fowl into and brown them in a frying-pan them into a stew-pan with the a slice of garlic, and three pi into which you have previous currie powder; let all simmer hours, then add the almonds lemon or mango juice, with a li and salt to taste. Serve very h up a large dish of boiled rice w rice may be put into the soup i

Ox-Head Soup.

Time, four or five ho[urs]

237. One ox-head; one hea two carrots; two onions; one t black pepper corns; twenty-fiv[e] a teaspoonful of salt; a bun herbs; a bay-leaf; a little brow[n] of white wine; and five quart[s]

After the head has been soak[ed] three hours, the bones must be the whole well washed in warm put it into a stewpan with fi cold water, cover it closely ov boils, which should be slowly, Put in a head of celery cut int[o] carrots, two onions, one turnip corns, and allspice, with a bu[n] herbs. Cover it over, and set a slow fire, taking care to remo and let it stew gently for thr until reduced to four quarts. head and put it on a dish. St through a fine sieve, and set it The next day cut the meat fro into small pieces, drain off the after removing the fat, put it w[i] into a stewpan, and let it simm half an hour, when it will be re The oftener this soup is warmo it becomes. Before sending it a glass of white wine.

Ox-Tail Soup.

Time, four hours and a

238. Two ox-tails; a quarter of lean ham; a head and a ha two carrots; two turnips; two bunch of savoury herbs; five c spoonful of pepper corns; o[n]

Curry Soup, Veal Broth, and White Soup. 85

a wine glass of ketchup, and one of port wine, with three quarts of water.

Cut up two ox-tails, separating them at the joints; put them into a stewpan with about an ounce and a half of butter, a head of celery, two onions, two turnips, and two carrots cut into slices, and a quarter of a pound of lean ham, cut very thin; the pepper corns and savoury herbs, and about half a pint of cold water. Stir it over a quick fire for a short time to extract the flavour of the herbs, or until the pan is covered with a glaze. Then pour in three quarts of water, skim it well and simmer slowly for four hours, or until the tails are tender. Take them out, strain the soup, stir in a little flour to thicken it, add a glass of port wine, the ketchup, and half a head of celery (previously boiled and cut into small pieces). Put the pieces of tail into the stewpan with the strained soup. Boil it up for a few minutes, and serve.

This soup can be served clear, by omitting the flour and adding to it carrots and turnips cut into fancy shapes, with a head of celery in slices. These may be boiled in a little of the soup, and put into the tureen before sending it to table.

Curry Soup.

Time, nearly two hours.

239. One fowl; three or four onions; two ounces of butter; a little flour; one large tablespoonful of curry powder; three tablespoonfuls of gravy soup; one tablespoonful of tamarinds.

Mince small three or four onions according to their size, put them into a saucepan with two ounces of butter; dredge in some flour, and fry them of a light brown, taking care not to burn them; rub in by degrees a large tablespoonful of curry powder till it is quite a paste, gradually stir in three tablespoonfuls of gravy soup, mixing it well together; boil it gently until it is well flavoured with the curry powder, strain it into another saucepan, and add a fowl skinned and cut into small pieces, stew it slowly for an hour, take out half a pint of the soup and stew in it a large tablespoonful of tamarinds, until you can easily take away the stones; strain, and stir into the soup; boil all together for a quarter of an hour. Serve rice with it.

Veal Broth.

Time, two hours and three-quarters.

240. Four pounds of the scrag of veal; three quarts of water; one onion; one turnip; half a pound of rice; three blades of mace, and a little salt.

Cut four pounds of scrag of veal into small pieces, and put them into a stewpan. Pour over them three quarts of water, and set it over the fire. When the scum rises, skim it off. Add one onion, one turnip, three blades of mace, and a little salt. Let it all stew slowly for two hours. Then strain it through a sieve, and put in a quarter of a pound of rice boiled very tender. Boil it again for ten minutes, and serve it.

Cheap White Soup.

Time, one hour.

241. Remains of cold veal, game, poultry, or rabbit · one quart of stock made of bones.

Chop up any remains you may have of cold veal, chicken, game, or rabbit roasted dry. Grate them, beat them in a mortar, and rub them through a tammy or sieve. Then add to the panada a quart of stock, put it into a stewpan, and pay great attention to skimming it.

An Excellent White Soup.

Time, five hours and a half.

242. Two pounds of scrag of mutton; a knuckle of veal after removing some collops; two shank bones of mutton; a quarter of a pound of lean bacon; a bunch of sweet herbs; the peel of a lemon; two onions; four blades of mace; two teaspoonfuls of white pepper; seven pints of water; two ounces of vermicelli; a quarter of a pound of sweet almonds; a slice of cold veal or chicken; a slice of bread; one pint of cream; and a pint of white stock.

Take two pounds of scrag of mutton, a knuckle of veal after cutting off sufficient meat for collops, two shank *bones* of mutton, and a quarter of a pound of lean bacon with a bunch of sweet herbs, the peel of half a lemon, two onions, three blades of mace, and some white pepper; boil all in seven pints of water till the meat falls to pieces. Skim it well; set it by to cool until the next day; then take off the fat, remove the jelly from the sediment, and put it into a stewpan. Have ready the thickening, which is to be made of half a pound of sweet almonds blanched and pounded in a mortar, with a spoonful of water to prevent them from oiling; a large slice of cold veal or chicken minced, and well beaten with a slice of stale bread; all added to a pint of cream, half the rind of a lemon, and a blade of mace finely powdered. Boil it a few minutes, and pour in a pint of stock; strain and rub it through a coarse sieve; add it to the rest, with two ounces of vermicelli, and boil all together for half an hour.

Wrexham Soup.

Time, six or seven hours.

243. One pound of lean beef, and every description of vegetables in season; no water.

Cut a pound of gravy beef into very small pieces; put them into a half gallon jar; fill it up with every description of vegetables, even lettuces. Tie the jar over with a bladder, and put it over the fire in a deep saucepan of boiling water, or in the oven, which is far better, for at least six hours.

This generally makes sufficient soup for four persons. A little pepper and salt must be added.

Soup in Haste.

Time, half an hour.

244. One pound of cold cooked meat; two ounces of butter; one tablespoonful of flour; one quart of water; a few slices of browned bread.

Chop your meat *very* fine, and put a pound of it into a stewpan with two ounces of butter, and pepper and salt to taste. Dredge over it an even tablespoonful of flour; then add a quart or more of boiling water, cover it close, and set it over a moderate fire for half an hour. Strain it through a loose cloth; toast some thin slices of bread delicately brown, cut them in small squares or diamonds, put them into a tureen, and pour the soup over them. Macaroni or vermicelli boiled tender may be put to the soup ten or twelve minutes before serving.

Baked Soup.

Time, four hours.

245. One pound and a half of meat; any trimmings from joints; one onion; two carrots; two ounces and a half of Patna rice; one pint of split peas; eight pints of water.

Cut the beef or mutton, and the vegetables in pieces, season them with a little pepper and salt, and put them into a jar with a pint of peas and the Patna rice. Pour in four quarts of water, cover the jar very closely, and set it in the oven to bake. When done, strain it through a sieve, and erve it up very hot.

Vermicelli Soup.

Time, three hours and a half.

246. Four pounds of knuckle of veal; about one pound and a half of scrag of mutton; five or six slices of ham; four ounces of butter; three blades of mace; two carrots; one onion; four cloves; four heads of celery; a bunch of sweet herbs; one anchovy; four ounces of vermicelli; a little pepper, salt, Cayenne; a French roll, and four quarts of water.

Cut about four pounds of knuckle of veal, one pound and a half of the scrag of mutton, and a few slices of ham, into small pieces; put them into a stewpan with one onion stuck with cloves, and four ounces of butter; then add the carrots, mace, bunch of sweet herbs, one anchovy, and the celery. Mix all together, cover it close, and set it over the fire till all the gravy has been extracted from the meat; pour the liquor into a basin, let the meat brown in the pan, and add to it four quarts of water; boil it slowly till it is reduced to three pints, strain it, and stir in the gravy drawn from the meat. Set it over the fire, add the vermicelli, one head of celery cut small, a little Cayenne, and salt; boil it up for ten minutes. Lay the roll in the tureen, pour the soup over it, and strew some vermicelli on the top.

Vermicelli can also be made by boiling one quart of clear stock, adding two ounces of vermicelli to it while boiling, first cutting the vermicelli into short lengths, and boiling it again for ten minutes.

Macaroni Soup.

Time, three-quarters of an hour.

247. Four ounces of macaroni; one large onion; five cloves; one ounce of butter; and two quarts of clear gravy soup.

Put into a stewpan of boiling water four ounces of macaroni, one ounce of butter, and an onion stuck with five cloves. When the macaroni has become quite tender, drain it very dry, and pour on it two quarts of clear gravy soup. Let it simmer for ten minutes, taking care that the macaroni does not burst or become a pulp; it will then be ready to serve. It should be sent to table with grated Parmesan cheese.

Macaroni is a great improvement to white soup, or to clear gravy soup, but it must be previously boiled for twenty minutes in water.

Soup (Liebig).

Time, ten minutes.

248. One pound of gravy beef; one pint of water; one carrot; one turnip; one onion; one clove.

Take a pound of gravy beef without bone, mince it very fine, and pour on it a pint of water in which a turnip, carrot, onion, and a clove have been boiled. Let it simmer by the side of the fire ten minutes, and it is fit for use. When strained off, it will make two small basins of soup. Stir before using.

Pepperpot.

Time, three hours and a half.

249. Four pounds of gravy beef; six quarts of water; a bouquet of savoury herbs; two small crabs or lobsters; a large bunch of spinach; half a pound of cold bacon; a few suet dumplings, (made of flour, beef-suet, and yolk of one egg); one pound of asparagus tops; Cayenne pepper; pepper and salt to taste; juice of a lemon.

Put four pounds of gravy beef into six quarts of water, with the bouquet of savoury herbs; let it simmer well till all the goodness is extracted, skimming it well. Let it stand till cold, that all the fat may be taken off it. Put it into a stewpan and heat it. When hot, add the flesh of two middling-sized crabs or lobsters, nicely cut up, spinach well boiled and chopped fine, half a pound of cold bacon or pickled pork, dressed previously and cut into small pieces, a few small dumplings, made very light with flour, beef-suet, yolk of egg, and a little water. Add one pound of asparagus tops, season to your taste with Cayenne, salt, pepper, and juice of a lemon; stew for about half an hour, stirring it constantly.

Hare Soup.

Time, eight hours.

250. One hare; a pound and a half of gravy beef; one pound of bones; a slice of lean bacon; a bunch of sweet herbs; one onion; a spoonful of soy; a little Cayenne, salt, and two quarts of water.

Cut an old hare into pieces, and put it into a large jar with a pound and a half of gravy beef, a pound of bones well cleaned, a slice of lean bacon, one onion, and a bunch of sweet herbs. Pour over it two quarts of water, and cover the jar well over with bladder and paper; set it in a kettle of boiling water, and let it simmer till the hare is stewed to rags. Strain off the gravy, add an anchovy cut into small pieces, a spoonful of soy, with a little Cayenne and salt. Serve a few forcemeat balls in the tureen.

Brown Rabbit Soup.

Time, five hours and a half.

251. Two large rabbits; two onions; four carrots; a bunch of parsley; forty pepper corns; a little salt and pounded mace; three quarts of water.

Cut two old rabbits into joints, dredge them with a little flour, and fry them lightly with two onions cut into slices. Put them into a large stewpan, and pour gradually over them three quarts of hot water, add a little salt and pounded mace, the pepper corns, bunch of parsley, and the carrots cut into slices, boil the whole slowly for five hours and a half. Skim it well, strain off the soup, and set it to cool, that the fat may be thoroughly taken off. Put it again into a stewpan, make it hot, and serve with sippets of fried bread.

Giblet Soup.

Time, three hours.

252. The giblets; a pint and a half of water; one onion; three or four cloves; a small piece of toasted bread; a bunch of sweet herbs, pepper-corns and salt.

Crack the bones, put one pint and a half of water to them, an onion stuck with cloves, a small piece of toasted bread, a bunch of sweet herbs, some pepper corns and salt. Let all simmer *very gently* till the giblets are *quite tender*. When cold, take off all the fat. If you wish it to be rich, add two pounds of shin of beef.

VEGETABLE SOUPS.

The vegetables should be nicely prepared for these soups.

Cut carrots in thin rounds with the edges notched; grated, they give an amber colour to soup.

Wash parsley carefully and cut it small. Cut turnips in thin slices, and then divide the round in four. Cut leeks in slices. Cut celery in half-inch lengths, the delicate green leaves impart a fine flavour to the soup. Take the skins from tomatoes and squeeze out some of the seeds. Add a lump of sugar to soups of vegetables or roots, to soften them and improve the flavour.

Vegetable Soup.

Time, four hours and a half.

253. Three onions; six potatoes; six carrots; four turnips; half a pound of butter; four quarts of water; one head of celery; a spoonful of ketchup; a bunch of sweet herbs.

Peel and slice six potatoes, five carrots, three turnips, and three onions; fry them in half a pound of butter, and pour over them two quarts of boiling water. Put half a head of celery, a bunch of sweet herbs, a little pepper and salt, and a crust of bread toasted *very* brown to the above, and let it stew slowly for four hours, then strain it through a coarse cloth or sieve; put it into the stewpan with the remaining half head of celery, one carrot and turnip cut prettily into shapes, and stew them tender in the soup. Add a spoonful of ketchup and serve.

Vegetable Mulligatawny.

254. A quarter of a pound of butter; two or three small vegetable marrows; two large onions; three or four apples; two or three tomatoes; one cucumber; one tablespoonful and a half of curry powder; salt to taste; some good stock; a squeezed lemon.

Put the butter into a fryingpan, slightly brown it; add the marrows cut up and freed from seeds; two large onions; three or four apples peeled and cored; the tomatoes if in season; and the cucumber cut up, taking care not to put any of the seeds in. Stew these gently until tender, then add the curry powder; salt to taste. Let this simmer a quarter of an hour longer, adding sufficient good stock to cover them. Reduce it all to a pulp and press it through a sieve; put the liquid into a fresh stewpan; take as much stock as will make it the required thickness. Add a squeezed lemon if baked, and serve the soup as hot as possible.

Green Pea Soup Maigre.

Time, two hours.

255. One quart of old green peas; one pint of young peas; two quarts of water; two lettuces; one onion; a sprig of mint; three ounces of butter; a handful of spinach; and a little pepper and salt.

Boil in two quarts of water one quart of old green peas, and a large sprig of green mint, until they will pulp through a sieve. Put to the liquor that stewed them a pint of young peas, the hearts of two lettuces, a handful of spinach cut small, one onion, and three ounces of butter, melted with just enough flour to keep it from boiling, then add all together, and boil the soup for half an hour. Serve with fried bread.

Pea Soup without Meat.

Time, three hours.

256. One pint of split peas; three quarts of spring water; six large onions; outside sticks of two heads of celery; one bunch of sweet herbs; two carrots; a little dried mint; a handful of spinach; a few bones, or tiny pieces of bacon, flavour it nicely; pepper and salt to your taste.

Boil all these vegetables together till they are quite soft and tender; strain them through a hair sieve, pressing the carrot pulp through it. Then boil the soup well for an hour with the best part of the celery, and a teaspoonful of pepper, add a little dried mint and fried bread, with a little spinach. A few roast beef bones, or a slice of bacon, will be an improvement.

Simple Pea Soup.

Time, four hours.

257. One quart of split peas; four quarts of water; a quarter of a pound of lean bacon; some roast-beef bones; two heads of celery; three turnips; a little pepper, salt, and Cayenne.

Put a quart of split peas into four quarts of water, with a quarter of a pound of lean ham, and some ribs of beef bones; add a head of celery cut small, with three turnips. Let it boil gently till reduced to two quarts, and then rub it through a fine colander with a wooden spoon. Mix a spoonful of flour and water well together, and boil it in the soup with another head of celery sliced thin, and a little pepper, salt, and Cayenne to your taste. Cut a slice of bread into dice, fry them a light brown, and put them into the tureen; pour in the soup, and serve with dried mint.

Winter Pea Soup—Plain for Family Use.

Time, four hours and three-quarters.

258. One pint of split peas; three quarts of water; a pound and a half of beef; one handful of spinach; one slice of ham or bacon; a few cloves; a little mace; half a bunch of mint; one lump of sugar; one saltspoonful of pepper; same of salt, or to your taste.

Boil one pint of split peas in three quarts of water till quite soft. Then stew in the soup a pound and a half of beef and a slice of bacon, with the handful of spinach, the cloves and mace. Let it stew for two hours, then rub it through a sieve, then stew in it half a bunch of mint and a little spinach cut in shreds, with pepper and salt to your taste, and a lump of sugar.

Serve with fried bread cut into dice, on a separate dish.

Common Carrot Soup.

Time, four hours and a half.

259. Thirteen ounces of scraped carrot to a quart of gravy.

Boil as many red carrots in water as you require until tender; then cut up the red part and pound it very fine. Weigh it, and to every twelve or thirteen ounces of pounded carrot add a quart of gravy soup, or rich stock, mixed gradually with it; season with a little salt and Cayenne; strain it through a sieve, and serve it very hot with fried bread cut into dice in a separate dish.

Purée of Carrots.
Time, two hours and a half.

260. Seven or eight carrots; one onion; one turnip; two or three slices of lean ham or bacon; a bunch of parsley; two bay leaves; two dessertspoonfuls of flour; a quarter of a pound of butter; one pint of water; five pints of stock, and one teaspoonful of powdered white sugar.

Scrape and cut into very thin slices all the red part of seven or eight carrots, slice a small onion and a turnip; put them into a stewpan with a bunch of parsley, a couple of bayleaves, and fry them in about a quarter of a pound of butter, then add the scraped carrots with a pint of water, and let all stew until tender; pour in the stock with a little salt, and two dessertspoonfuls of flour. Stir it over the fire, and let it boil for about twenty minutes; strain through a sieve, give it a boil again for ten or twelve minutes, and serve with croûtons of fried bread in the tureen.

Celery Soup.
Time, about one hour.

261. Ten heads of celery; rather more than half a pint of good stock; five pints of water; one pint of cream; a little salt and sugar.

After cutting your celery into pieces of about an inch long, put it into a stewpan of boiling water, seasoned with a little salt and sugar; put it over a clear fire, and when very tender take out the celery and pulp it through a sieve; add it to the stock, and let it stew slowly for nearly three quarters of an hour; then stir in a pint of nice fresh cream, make it very hot, but do not let it boil, and serve it in a tureen.

Brown Onion Soup.
Time, three hours.

262. Six large Spanish onions; five quarts of water; a little pepper and salt; a penny roll; yolks of two eggs; two spoonfuls of vinegar.

Skin and cut in thin rings six large Spanish onions, fry them in a little butter till they are of a nice brown colour and very tender; then lay them on a hair sieve to drain from the butter. Put them into a stewpan with five quarts of water, boil them for one hour, and stir them often; then add pepper and salt to your taste. Rub the crumb of a penny roll through a colander, put it to the soup, stirring it well to keep it smooth as you do so. Boil it two hours more. Ten minutes before you serve it, beat the yolks of two eggs with two spoonfuls of vinegar and a little of the soup; pour it in by degrees, and keep stirring it all the time one way. It will then be ready to serve.

This soup will keep three or four days.

Vegetable Marrow Soup.
Time, one hour.

263. Six small or four large vegetable marrows; half a pint of cream; one quart of white stock; pepper and salt.

Pare six small or four large vegetable marrows, cut them into slices, and put them into a stewpan. Pour over them about two pints of boiling veal stock, and let them simmer until they will press through a sieve; then put the purée into a stewpan with a pint more stock. Add a seasoning of pepper and salt; make it very hot, and just before it is served pour in half a pint of boiling cream.

Palestine Soup.
Time, one hour and a half.

264. Six pounds of Jerusalem artichokes, three turnips; one head of celery; one onion; half a pint of cream; a lump of sugar; salt and Cayenne to your taste; sufficient white stock to cover the artichokes.

Pare and cut into pieces six pounds of Jerusalem artichokes, three turnips, one onion, and a head of celery; put them into a stewpan with sufficient white stock to cover them, and let them boil gently for an hour until they are quite tender; then rub them through a sieve; if the *purée* be too thick, thin it with a little fresh milk; boil all together again; season it with a spoonful of sugar, pepper, salt, and Cayenne to your taste. Send it up very hot, with some fried bread served separately, cut into very small dice.

Jardiniere Soup—A Summer Soup.
Time, one hour and a half.

265. Two quarts of clear stock seasoned to taste; four small carrots; four small turnips; equal quantity of button onions; a head of celery; eight lettuce leaves; a little tarragon and chervil; one lump of sugar.

Cut the vegetables in the French vegetable cutter of any pattern you please, or shape them with the ordinary vegetable scoop as you like best in the form of peas, olives, &c.; add the leaves and onions, put them in a soup-kettle, fill it up with two quarts (or more as required) of *clear* stock, let it boil gently till the vegetables are done, add a lump of sugar, as is best in all vegetable soups, and serve this soup very hot.

Leek Soup—Scotch Receipt.
Time, three hours.

266. Three or four dozen leeks; four quarts of beef stock; one teaspoonful of pepper; two teaspoonfuls of salt; one small fowl.

Carefully wash the leeks, and then cut them into pieces about an inch long, strain them through a colander; put them into the beef stock, seasoning it according to taste. Let it boil gently, adding a fowl in time for it to be well boiled.

Stock for Brown or White Fish Soups.
Time, two hours.

267. Two pounds of English eels; four flounders and trimmings of filleted fish, or a pound and a half of skate; a blade of mace; a little pepper and salt; one onion; a bunch of sweet herbs; two parsley roots; one head of celery; four cloves, and two quarts of water.

Take two pounds of eels, four flounders, and any trimmings of fish, or from filleted fish, or a pound and a half of skate, clean them thoroughly, and cut them into pieces; cover them with about two quarts of water; season with a blade of mace, a little pepper and salt, one onion stuck with four cloves, a head of celery cut into pieces, and two parsley roots. Let all simmer together for two hours, skim the liquor carefully, and strain it off for use. If for brown fish soup, first fry the fish and vegetables brown in butter, and then do as above directed.

Fish-stock will not keep more than two or three days, therefore a small quantity only should be made, as required.

Fish soups are very economical, as the cheaper kinds of fish can be used for them.

Conger Soup.

268. Head and tail of a large conger eel; three quarts of water; a quarter of a pound of butter; one leek; the blossoms and leaves of four or five marigolds; half a pint of green peas, or asparagus, or cabbage; half a teacupful of parsley, bunch of thyme; two tablespoonfuls of flour or arrowroot; one pint of milk; a little salt.

Put the head and tail of a large conger eel in a stewpan, with three quarts of water, and let them simmer two hours and a half or more, till it breaks to pieces when tried with a fork. Strain through a china colander, and pour back the liquor into the stewpan with a quarter of a pound of butter. When boiling, throw in rather more than a pint basinful of the following herbs and vegetables, cut up small: one leek, a few green leaves of marigold, the green ends of asparagus, or green peas when asparagus cannot be procured, or, what is by many preferred, the white heart of a cabbage cut up, half a teacupful of chopped parsley, and a bunch of thyme. Mix two heaped tablespoonfuls of flour in a pint of milk, the plucked blossoms of four or five marigolds, and when the vegetables are done, throw it into the stewpan, taking care to stir till it comes to a boil; then let it simmer eight or ten minutes, to take off the rawness of the flour, the lid of the stewpan being off, or it would boil over. Some, who prefer the parsley green, do not throw it in till after the milk boils. Season with salt before dishing up, as the salt is apt to curdle the milk if added before. Have ready thin slices of bread in your tureen, and pour the soup over.

Lobster Soup (American).
Time, one hour and a quarter.

269. One lobster; two or three plain biscuits; one quart of milk; one quart of water; one tablespoonful of salt; one teaspoonful of pepper; a quarter of a pound of fresh butter.

Pick the meat of a lobster already boiled from its shell, and cut it into *small* pieces; roll the biscuits to a powder. Put a quart of milk and a quart of water into a stewpan, with a tablespoonful of salt, and a teaspoonful of pepper. When the milk and water are boiling hot, add the lobster and pounded biscuit, mixed, to the soup with a quarter of a pound of fresh butter. Let it boil closely covered for half an hour. Pour it into a tureen and serve.

Oyster Soup.
Time, two hours.

270. Eighteen shallots; one sprig of thyme; two bay-leaves; half a pound of fresh butter; six ounces of flour; one quart of fish gravy or veal gravy; four dozen oysters; half a pint of cream.

Take eighteen shallots cut small, a sprig of thyme, and two bay-leaves: stew them till they are a little brown, in half a pound of fresh butter. Add six ounces of flour, stir well together for a few minutes, add the veal or fish gravy (made from fish bones), the beards and juice of two dozen oysters. Let all simmer gently together for two hours. Skim off all the fat, add half a pint of cream, and then pass it through a tammy. Blanch two dozen more oysters, beard them, keep them in their own gravy until wanted; put them in the soup a second before sending up.

The Young Fisherman's Soup.

Time, two hours.

271. One pound (each) of any freshwater fish, of different kinds; one tomato; two carrots; one leek; two onions; a bunch of sweet herbs; one teaspoonful of Chili vinegar; one teaspoonful of soy; enough water to cover the fish; two turnips; one head of celery; pepper and salt to taste.
Take a pound (each) of all the fish you have caught in your day's fishing, such as carp, dace, roach, perch, pike, and tench, wash them in salt and water; then put them in a stewpan with a tomato, two carrots, one leek, two fried onions, and a bunch of sweet herbs; put as much water to them as will cover them, and let them stew till the whole is reduced to a pulp, which will be in about three quarters of an hour. Strain off the liquor, and let it boil for another hour. Have ready two turnips and a head of celery, cut into small pieces and previously boiled; add them to the fish soup, with the Chili vinegar and soy, pepper and salt to taste.

Haddock Soup.

Time, one hour.

272. One haddock; one pint of picked shrimps; one egg; half a pint of cream; one French roll; one tablespoonful of salt; one teaspoonful of pepper; a pinch of Cayenne; a blade of mace; a piece of butter the size of a walnut; a tablespoonful of flour.
Separate all the meat from the bones of a fine fresh haddock, and pound it in a mortar with a pint of picked shrimps; chop a little bunch of parsley very fine, and add it to the fish with the crumb of a French roll steeped in half a pint of cream. Beat one egg well and mix it with the above ingredients, which must then be put into two quarts of good warm broth, and seasoned with the pepper, salt, Cayenne, and mace; let it boil closely covered for half an hour, and then pulp it through a sieve; thicken the soup with a little piece of butter rolled in flour; warm it up and serve.

Eel Soup.

Time, one hour and ten minutes.

273. Three pounds of eels; two quarts of water; a crust of bread; three blades of mace; thirty whole peppers; one onion; three ounces of butter; a bunch of sweet herbs; one carrot; a quarter of a pint of cream; three dessertspoonfuls of flour; and a little salt.
Take three pounds of eels, cut them into slices, and stew them for ten minutes over a slow fire in three ounces of butter; then pour over them two quarts of water, put in a crust of bread, an onion cut into slices, three blades of mace, thirty whole peppers, one carrot, a bunch of sweet herbs, and a little salt; cover the stewpan closely and simmer till the eels are tender, but not broken. Mix three dessertspoonfuls of flour with a quarter of a pint of cream rubbed smooth, add to it the soup, which must be previously strained, and the slices of eel taken carefully out; boil it up and pour it over the sliced eels in your tureen. Toast a slice of bread, cut it into dice, and place it at the bottom of the tureen.

SAUCES AND GRAVIES.

FISH SAUCES.

A well made sauce is, perhaps, one of the best testimonies of the skill of the cook, and is a very essential part of a good dinner. A badly made sauce will spoil the food with which it is served, and is a sure sign of inefficiency and ignorance in both the cook and her mistress.

Sauces are expensive, and a housewife who studies economy, and has only small means, will not use as many nor as varied forms, perhaps, of the same sauce, as the cook in a wealthy family; but it *is* economical to be able to serve up a sauce which, at a trifling expense, will greatly improve a dinner made, perhaps, from cold remains, and for fish, sauce of some kind is absolutely required.

The sauce peculiar to the English housekeeper is Melted Butter; and yet, common as it is, we scarcely ever find it well made. Now, every lady should know experimentally how to make it, that she may direct her cook. She should also know experimentally how to make Bread Sauce and common White and Brown Sauce, on which most other sauces are founded. Take care that your sauces are delicately flavoured; if your cook is not *first-rate*, taste them yourself. This is quite possible, even immediately before you receive your guests or sit down to your family dinner, as sauces must be made before the fish is dressed, and kept warm till required in a bain-marie—or, if your kitchen does not possess that most useful utensil, the saucepan in which they have been made should be placed in a large stewpan of boiling water near the fire.

The thickest saucepans should be used for this operation, and only wooden spoons should be used for stirring. Remember, also, that your saucepan must be exquisitely clean and fresh if you would have your sauce a success, *especially* when it is melted butter. Let your fire be clear and not too fierce.

RECEIPTS FOR MELTING BUTTER.

The Author's Way.

Time, two or three minutes.

274. Two ounces of butter; a little flour; and about two tablespoonfuls of water.

Put about two ounces or two ounces and a half of butter into a very clean saucepan, with two tablespoonfuls of water, dredge in a little flour, and shake it over a clear fire, *one way*, until it boils. Then pour it into your tureen, and serve as directed.

Melted Butter.

Time, one minute.

275. One teaspoonful of flour; four ounces of fresh butter; three tablespoonfuls of hot water.

Mix the flour and butter *well* together in a basin, till *quite* smoothly incorporated with each other; then put the paste into a butter saucepan with two or three tablespoonfuls of *hot* water. Shake it round always in the same direction, or it will become oily. Boil it quickly for one minute.

French Melted Butter.

Time, three minutes.

276. Four ounces of fresh butter; half a pint of water; yolks of two eggs; squeeze of a lemon.

Beat the yolks of two very fresh eggs well, then melt the butter; boil it and pour it instantly on the beaten eggs, stirring them quickly round while you pour in the butter. Put the mixture into the saucepan again, and shake it over the fire for a minute, but *do not let it boil;* then squeeze a little lemon juice into it, taking care no pips from the fruit fall into your sauce, as they give a bitter flavour.

Common Egg Sauce.

Time, twenty minutes.

277. Two eggs; a quarter of a pint of melted butter.

Boil the eggs for twenty minutes, then take them out of the egg saucepan and put them in cold water to get cool, shell them, and cut them into very small dice, put the minced egg into a very hot sauce tureen, and pour over them a quarter of a pint of boiling melted butter. Stir the sauce round to mix the eggs with it.

Fennel Sauce.

Time, ten minutes.

278. Half a pint of melted butter; a small bunch of fennel leaves; a little salt.

Strip the leaves of the fennel from their stems, wash it very carefully, and boil it quickly (with a little salt in the water) till it is quite tender; squeeze it till all the water is expressed from it; mince it very fine, and mix it with hot melted butter.

Parsley Sauce.

Time, six or seven minutes.

279. Half a pint of melted butter; a bunch of parsley (about a small handful).

Wash the parsley thoroughly, boil it for six or seven minutes till tender, then press the water well out of it; chop it very fine; make half or a quarter of a pint of melted butter as required (the less butter the less parsley, of course), mix it gradually with the hot melted butter.

Green Gooseberry Sauce for Boiled Mackerel.

Time, a quarter of an hour.

280. Half a pint of green gooseberries; two tablespoonfuls of green sorrel; a small

piece of butter; one ounce of sugar; a little pepper, salt, and nutmeg.

Wash some green sorrel, and press out the juice through a cloth; boil half a pint of green gooseberries, drain them from the water, and rub them through a sieve. Put the sorrel juice into a stewpan, allowing about a wineglassful of it to the pulp of the gooseberries; add a small piece of butter, a lump of sugar, pepper, salt, and nutmeg. Make the sauce very hot, and serve it up in a tureen.

French Marinade for Flavouring Fish before cooking.

281. Pepper and salt; three cloves; three slices of onion; a sprig of sweet basil; a teaspoonful of lemon juice or vinegar.

A good French marinade for flavouring fish before cooking is to sprinkle over the fish, laid out on a dish, the pepper, salt, spice in fine powder, three cloves, the slices of onion, the basil minced fine, and a teaspoonful of lemon juice, or a little vinegar. After a few hours the fish may be taken from this marinade, and either fried, boiled, or stewed. The marinade may be used in the cooking, or for sauce at pleasure.

A marinade of oil and sweet herbs minced fine is excellent for fish before frying or broiling. When taken from the marinade, it can be either floured or covered with breadcrumbs and beaten egg. A squeeze of lemon juice or similar pleasant acid, so perceptible in French cookery, is well worth our imitation.

French White Caper Sauce.

Time, four minutes.

282. A piece of butter the size of an egg; a little flour; a teacupful of broth; salt; white pepper; a spoonful of capers; one onion, or a scallion.

To make the French white caper sauce, rub down a piece of butter, as large as an egg, in flour, put it in a saucepan over the fire, mix in carefully a teacupful of broth, with salt, white pepper, and the capers. Put in also an onion or a scallion or two; let it thicken, stirring it over the fire. Take out the onions or scallions, and serve the sauce, either poured over the turbot or other fish, or in a tureen.

Lobster Sauce.

Time, ten minutes.

283. One hen lobster with coral; two-thirds of its weight of good cream; one-third of fresh butter.

Cut the flesh in small pieces, mix it up with two-thirds of good cream and one-third of fresh butter.

No stock, fish-sauces, anchovies, or essences to be used.

Oyster Sauce.

Time, five minutes.

284. One dozen of oysters; half a teacupful of good gravy; half a pint of melted butter.

Stew the beards of the oysters in their own juice with half a teacupful of good clear gravy; strain it off, add it to the melted butter—which should be ready—put in the oysters, and let them simmer gently for three minutes.

Oyster Sauce for a large party.

Time, ten minutes.

285. Two dozen oysters; two ounces of butter; one ounce and a half of flour; one pint of milk; one saltspoon of salt; quarter of a saltspoon of Cayenne; one clove; four pepper corns.

Mix the butter and flour in your stewpan; beard the oysters, and put them into a little saucepan; add their beards and liquor to the flour and butter, mixing the whole liquor with a pint of milk, the salt, Cayenne, and pepper corns. Boil it ten minutes, stirring it all the time; add a tablespoonful of Harvey sauce; strain the liquor over the oysters; make the whole hot, but do not let it boil. Some people add the juice of half a lemon, but we prefer it without.

Shrimp Sauce.

Time, five or six minutes.

286. Half a pint of picked shrimps; a gill of gravy, or water; half a pound of butter; a little flour; one spoonful of anchovy liquor; one of ketchup; half a lemon.

Take half a pint of picked shrimps and wash them clean; put them into a stewpan with a gill of gravy or water, half a pound of butter, and a little nut of butter mixed with a little flour, a spoonful of anchovy liquor, one of ketchup, and half a lemon; boil it till the butter is melted and it is thick and smooth; take out the lemon and squeeze the juice of the other half in; stir it well, and serve in a tureen.

Cockle Sauce.

Time, ten minutes.

287. One hundred cockles; half a pound of butter; half of the liquor from the cockles;

two spoonfuls of anchovy liquor; one of ketchup; a piece of butter; and flour.

Wash a hundred cockles very clean, put them into a large saucepan, cover them close, stew them gently till they open, strain the liquor through a sieve; wash the cockles clean in cold water, and put them into a stewpan, pour half the liquor in on them with half a pound of butter, and a little flour, two spoonfuls of anchovy liquor, and one of ketchup. Boil the sauce gently till the butter is melted, and it is thick and smooth, then serve it in a tureen.

Sauce for any Freshwater Fish.

Time, five minutes.

288. Four small anchovies; one onion; two spoonfuls of vinegar; two wineglasses of white wine; a quarter of a pint of melted butter or cream.

Chop the onion and anchovies very fine, and put them into the stewpan with the vinegar and white wine; boil it up for a few minutes, and then stir in a quarter of a pint of melted butter or cream.

Dutch Sauce for Fish.

Time, till it thickens.

289. Four eggs; two ounces of butter; one teaspoonful of Chili or tarragon vinegar; two tablespoonfuls of cream; pepper, salt, and nutmeg.

Put the yolks of the eggs well beaten into a stewpan with the cream, a large piece of butter, a teaspoonful of Chili or tarragon vinegar, and a little pepper, salt, and nutmeg. Set it over a *very* moderate fire until it has a thick creamy appearance, stirring it constantly, and taking great care it does not curdle, which it will do if allowed to boil.

Horseradish Sauce for Fish.

Time, five minutes.

290. A large teaspoonful of grated horseradish; two of the essence of anchovies; one ounce and a half of butter; one onion; a spoonful of lemon pickle.

Boil an onion in a little fish gravy until it will pulp through a sieve, then add the essence of anchovies and the grated horseradish; thicken it with an ounce and a half of butter, and stir it over the fire until it boils. Mix in lemon pickle and serve it.

Anchovy Sauce for Fish.

Time, four minutes.

291. Three dessertspoonfuls of anchovy essence; half a pint of melted butter; seasoning to your taste.

Stir three dessertspoonfuls of anchovy essence into half a pint of good melted butter, add a seasoning to your taste, and boil it up for a minute or two. Use plenty of Cayenne and a little mace in this sauce.

MADE GRAVIES AND SAUCES.

Plain joints roasted make their own gravy, except perhaps lamb. Made gravies and sauces are necessary for more elaborate, and less homely cooking.

Two kinds of gravies are *made—i.e.*, brown and white. We shall give receipts first for these, which are required for making nearly all the other more complicated gravies and sauces, premising that beef is the foundation of brown or savoury gravies, and veal or fowls that of the white and more delicate gravy; but as you may not always possess gravy beef at the time you want to make your gravy, it will be as well to tell you that *any kind* of stock will do; the trimmings of beef, veal, or mutton, and the bones of cold joints of meat, or uncooked bones, will all afford materials for it.

Place these, whatever they may be, in a stewpan, lay the beef at the bottom, then the mutton, with a slice or two of bacon or ham, and any bones you have, broken up small; add a few slices of carrot, an onion, a blade of mace, two or three cloves, a little black and white pepper, a bunch of sweet herbs, and lay over them any small pieces of veal you may have. Cover the stewpan close, and set it over a slow fire for six or seven minutes, shaking the pan often. Then dredge in a little flour, and pour in water till the whole is rather more than covered. Cover the stewpan close, and let it simmer for several hours until your gravy be rich and good; then season it to your taste with a little salt, and strain it off, and you will have a gravy that will answer for ordinary purposes. Or you can make a good gravy from a melt, a kidney, the skirts of beef, the knuckle of dressed mutton, or any other meat cut into small pieces, and fried a nice brown, with onions, a bunch of sweet herbs, and spices. The water in which meat has been boiled, used instead of pure water, improves and adds to the richness of gravy. A cowheel, also, will yield a good gravy stock. Soak it for about twelve hours in cold water, and then boil it for about two hours and a half or three hours. When strained and quite cold, take the fat off with great care.

Truffles and morels thicken and improve the flavour of gravies or soups; about half an ounce of either being simmered in a pint of water, and added to the gravy. But in all cases the proportions used, and their quality, should be attended to, as the flavour of any gravy or sauce should be adapted skilfully to the dishes for which it is required.

White meats, and all *white* made dishes, require a smooth, delicately flavoured gravy or sauce; brown made dishes, a more piquant and savoury one.

Do not let any separate flavour predominate in your gravy; the different materials should harmonise completely with each other, and blend into one perfect whole.

Some cooks make their gravy by first boiling a rich, but small quantity of stock to a glaze, and then pouring slowly over it a sufficient quantity of boiling stock or broth for the gravy. Flavour it with a few sweet herbs, mushrooms, &c., &c.

Both Tarragon and knotted marjoram greatly improve the flavour of gravies.

Directions for making colouring for soup have already been given; the same may be used for gravies.

Glaze.

Time, till it becomes a jelly.

292. Boil some very strong clear gravy or jelly over a quick fire to the thickness of cream, stirring it *constantly* until it will adhere like jelly to the spoon. It must then be immediately poured out of the stewpan; the greatest care is required during the time of thickening to prevent it from burning. When required for use, dissolve it by placing the jar (or whatever it may be kept in) in boiling water, and brushing it over the meat two or three times, when it will form a clear varnish. Any kind of very rich stock can be boiled down to a glaze. To be used for hams, tongues, &c.

To Brown Flour.

Time, five minutes.

293. Put some flour in a pan or dish, and set it in the oven or over the fire. Stir it about that it may not burn; but let it brown well. Keep it in a dredging-box for browning ordinary gravies.

A Cheap Gravy.

Time, half an hour.

294. Three-quarters of a pound of shin or gravy beef; a slice of onion; one carrot; a few savoury herbs; a little Cayenne and salt; a quarter of a pound of butter; one pint of water.

Put the piece of butter into a small stewpan, with the carrot and onion cut into slices, and the meat into dice. Stir it over a quick fire until it is lightly browned; then add the herbs and the water, and let it all simmer slowly. Skim it clean, add a spoonful of mushroom ketchup or Worcestershire sauce, strain it through a sieve, and it will be fit for use.

Kidney Gravy.

Time, one hour and three quarters.

295. Four kidneys; two ounces and a half of butter; a few sweet herbs; a little salt and Cayenne; one tablespoonful of ketchup; half an onion: one pint of water.

Slice four kidneys, cut them into pieces, and dredge them with flour; put them into a stewpan with two ounces and a half of butter, a few sweet herbs, and half an onion. Shake these over the fire for six or eight minutes, and then add about a pint of water. Let it simmer for an hour and three-quarter; skimming it carefully; strain the gravy, and set it by for use.

This gravy can be made from one beef kidney instead of four sheep's kidneys.

Gravy for Hashes, &c.

Time, two hours and a quarter.

296. The bones and cuttings from any cooked joint; a little salt and pepper; twelve whole allspice; a bunch of sweet herbs; a piece of butter; one small onion; half a head of celery; water; and two tablespoonfuls of ketchup.

Break the bones, and put them into a stewpan, with any spare cuttings of meat you may have; add a little pepper, salt, and twelve allspice, half a head of celery, and a bunch of sweet herbs, and simmer it for about two hours, with sufficient water to cover it. Cut a small onion into slices, fry it in a piece of butter, and boil it up with the gravy for fifteen or twenty minutes. Strain it into another stewpan, with two tablespoonfuls of walnut ketchup, and a piece of butter rolled in flour, boil it up, and it will be ready for your meat.

Jugged Gravy.

Time, eight hours.

297. Two pounds of shin of beef; three slices of lean ham; two shallots; half a head of celery; one blade of mace; a bunch of sweet herbs; one carrot; a little salt and whole pepper; one quart of water; one tablespoonful of ketchup; one of soy.

Cut two pounds of shin of beef, and three slices of ham or bacon, into small pieces; put them into a stone jar, with alternate layers of shallot, celery, and carrot, cut into slices; seasoning of salt, pepper, and a bunch of sweet herbs, chopped up. Pour in a quart of water, tie the jar closely down to prevent the steam from escaping, and set in a moderate oven for eight hours; then strain the gravy. Stir in a tablespoonful of ketchup, and one of soy, or a glass of port wine, and when cold take off the fat carefully from the top.

Gravy for a Goose or Ducks.

Time, three hours.

298. One set of giblets; half a pound of beef; three sage leaves; one onion; some whole pepper and salt: a glass of port wine; three pints of water.

Put one set of giblets and half a pound of lean beef into a stewpan, with three sage leaves, one onion, some whole pepper, salt, and three pints of water, and boil it for three hours; then add a glass of port wine, with a spoonful of flour mixed smooth to thicken it, and boil it again for two or three minutes.

Gravy for a Hare or Goose.

Time, one hour.

299. One melt, or one pound of gravy beef; two small onions; half a head of celery; a bunch of sweet herbs; some white and black pepper corns; one ounce of butter; one glass of port wine; a spoonful of soy; a spoonful of Harvey sauce; one pint of water.

Cut a melt, or a pound of gravy beef, into very small pieces, and put it into a stewpan with a pint of water, two small onions, a bunch of sweet herbs, half a head of celery cut into small pieces a few bread-crumbs, and some pepper corns. Let it simmer slowly after it has once boiled. When done strain it, and add a little butter rolled in flour to thicken it, a spoonful of soy, one of Harvey sauce, and a glass of port wine.

White Sauce.

Time, fifteen minutes.

300. Half a pint of cream; a quarter of a pound of butter; four anchovies; two cloves; half a pint of water; one blade of mace; fifteen pepper corns; salt.

Boil in half a pint of water two cloves, a blade of mace, and the pepper corns, then strain it into a stewpan; add four anchovies chopped fine, a quarter of a pound of butter, a little flour, and half a pint of cream; boil it up for three or four minutes, stirring it all the time.

Bread Sauce for Roast Turkey, or Fowl.

Time, one hour and a half.

301. One pint of milk; breakfastcupful of stale bread; one onion; a little mace, Cayenne, and salt; one ounce of butter.

Peel and slice an onion, and simmer it in a pint of new milk until tender, break the bread into pieces and put it into a small stewpan. Strain the hot milk over it, cover it close, and let it soak for an hour. Then beat it up smooth with a fork, add the pounded mace, Cayenne, salt, and an ounce of butter; boil it up, and serve it in a tureen. The onion must be taken out before the milk is poured over the bread.

Apple Sauce.

Time, twenty minutes.

302. Eight apples; a small piece of butter, and sugar.

Pare, core, and cut into slices eight good boiling apples; put them into a saucepan with sufficient water to moisten and prevent them from burning, boil them until sufficiently tender to pulp. Then beat them up smoothly with a piece of butter, and put sugar to your taste.

Chestnut Sauce for Turkey or Fowls.

Time, one hour and thirty-five minutes.

303. Half a pint of veal stock; half a pound of chestnuts; peel of half a lemon; a cupful of cream or milk; a very little Cayenne, and salt.

Remove the dark shell of the chestnuts, and scald them until the inner skin can be easily taken off. Then put them into a stewpan with the stock, the lemon peel cut very thin, and a very little Cayenne pepper and salt. Let it simmer until the chestnuts are quite soft. Rub or press it through a sieve, add the seasoning and cream, and let it simmer for a few minutes, stirring it constantly, but taking care it does not boil.

White Celery Sauce.

Time, half an hour.

304. Four small, or two large heads of celery; half a pint of white gravy; half a pint of cream; a little flour, salt, and nutmeg.

Wash the celery clean, and boil it in two quarts of water and a little salt; when tender drain it on a sieve, and cut it in pieces about an inch long.

In the meantime, boil the gravy with a lump of butter rolled in flour till it is thick and smooth, grate in a little nutmeg, add it to the celery, and boil it up for a few minutes, then add the cream; just warm it again, serve it in a tureen, or pour it over boiled fowls or turkeys. The cream may be omitted from this sauce for a plain family dinner, and the celery, &c., may be reduced.

Common Onion Sauce.
Time, nearly half an hour.

305. Four or six nice white onions, according to size; half a pint of hot milk; one ounce of butter; saltspoonful of salt, and pepper to your taste.

Peel the onions and boil them till they are tender, press the water from them, and chop them very fine. Make half a pint of milk hot, pulp the onions into it, add a little piece of butter, a saltspoonful of salt, and pepper to your taste.

Sauce Maître d'Hôtel.

306. Two large spoonfuls of glaze; one shallot or small onion stewed in the stock, and taken out whole; strain, and add two large spoonfuls of cream, a little chopped sorrel; thicken with a teaspoonful of flour. Serve hot, with or over veal cutlets, fowls and rabbits. Leaving out the cream and sorrel, and adding a glass of port wine and a blade of mace, makes a good sauce for wild duck, and for hare with the liver chopped fine and added to it.

Maître d'Hôtel Sauce.
Time, one minute to simmer.

307. Half a pint of melted butter; one teaspoonful of chopped parsley; one lemon; Cayenne and salt to taste.

Melt the butter, add to it the strained juice of a lemon, the parsley and seasoning, and let it just boil.

Maître d'Hôtel Butter.
Time, eight minutes.

308. Half a pound of butter; two lemons; two sprigs of parsley; pepper, and salt.

Mix half a pound of butter very smooth with the juice of two lemons, minced parsley, and a little pepper and salt. Stir it all well together, and set it in a cold place.

White Sauce for Fowls.
Time, ten minutes.

309. One tablespoonful of cream; one lemon; half a pint of milk; a little salt and Cayenne; a dozen oysters.

Mix a tablespoonful of cream (or if you have not any, two well-beaten yolks of eggs) with half a pint of milk, add a little pepper and salt, and a dozen oysters. Boil it till the oysters are tender, then take it up and squeeze in the juice of half a lemon.

Horseradish Sauce for Boiled Mutton or Roast Beef.
Time, two or three minutes.

310. A wine-glass of good cream; a teaspoonful of mustard; a stick of horseradish; half a tumbler of vinegar; a little salt.

Mix a stick of grated horseradish with a wine-glass of cream, a teaspoonful of mustard, and a pinch of salt, then stir in half a tumbler of the best vinegar, and a pinch of salt. Bruise them with a spoon, and when thoroughly mixed together, serve in a tureen.

Mint Sauce for Roast Lamb.

311. Two tablespoonfuls of green mint; one tablespoonful of pounded sugar; and a quarter of a pint of vinegar.

Pick and wash the green mint very clean, chop it fine, mix the sugar and vinegar in a sauce tureen, put in the mint, and let it stand.

Mushroom Sauce for Chickens, &c.
Time, a quarter of an hour.

312. One pint of young mushrooms; one blade of mace; a little nutmeg and salt; one ounce and a half of butter; one pint of cream; a little flour.

Rub off the tender skin from about a pint of young mushrooms, with a little salt; then put them into a stewpan with a blade of mace, a little grated nutmeg, an ounce and a half of butter rolled in a teaspoonful of flour, and a pint of good cream. Put it over a clear fire, and boil it up till sufficiently thick, stirring it all the time; then pour it round boiled fowls or rabbits.

Tomato Sauce—No. 1.
Time, one hour and a half.

313. To every pound of tomatoes, one quart of Chili vinegar, or common vinegar mixed with Cayenne; a quarter of an ounce of white pepper; one ounce of garlic; one ounce of shallot; half an ounce of coarse salt; juice of three lemons.

Take some tomatoes when quite ripe, skin and rub them through a coarse sieve; to every pound of tomatoes put one quart of common vinegar, mixed with Cayenne pepper, or a quart of Chili vinegar, a quarter of an ounce of white pepper, one ounce of garlic, one ounce of shallot sliced, and half an ounce of coarse salt; if the Chili vinegar is not strong enough, half an ounce of pepper may be added; boil the ingredients till quite tender. And to every pound of tomatoes add the juice of three lemons; boil the whole again till it becomes the thickness of cream. When the pepper is added it must be sifted fine. When cold, put it into bottles for use.

When capsicums are to be had, a good number boiled in the vinegar will answer the purpose of Chili vinegar.

Sauce Tartare.

314. Yolks of two eggs; half a dessertspoonful of vinegar; two dessertspoonfuls of oil; a pinch of salt; a pinch of parsley; a teaspoonful of mustard; a little Cayenne pepper.

Put into a very small saucepan the yolks of two eggs, a dessertspoonful of the best vinegar, and a little salt; whip up this mixture with a whisk as quickly as possible. When the whole forms a sort of cream, add the oil and mustard, which must be well mixed previously; a pinch of parsley minced very fine, and a little Cayenne. The oil should be put in drop by drop, to mix perfectly.

To Improve the Flavour of Gravies.

Time, one hour.

315. Three ounces of lean ham or bacon; a good lump of butter; one blade of mace; three cloves; one shallot or small onion; a bit of parsley root; a pint and a half of beef stock or broth.

Cut the ham or bacon into very small pieces, and put them into a stewpan with about two ounces of butter at the bottom, a blade of mace, three cloves, a shallot, or onion, and a piece of parsley root; shake it over the fire occasionally for half an hour, until the bottom of the pan has a dark glaze, then pour in a pint and a half of beef broth, or stock, and boil all together for about another half hour, shaking the pan often, when it will be converted into an excellent gravy, and strain it off for use.

Savoury Jelly to put into Cold Pies.

Time, two or three hours.

316. Two pounds of knuckle of veal or mutton; two slices of ham; a bunch of sweet herbs; two blades of mace; one onion; peel of half a lemon; two eggs; some whole pepper; a little black pepper; three quarts of water; whites of two eggs; salt.

Make this jelly of a small bare knuckle of veal, or shoulder, or a piece of scrag of mutton; put the meat into a stewpan, that shuts very closely, with two slices of ham, a bunch of sweet herbs, two blades of mace, one onion, the peel of half a lemon, a teaspoonful of Jamaica pepper bruised, the same of whole pepper, and three pints of water. As soon as it boils skim it clean, and let it simmer slowly till quite strong and rich; strain it, and when cold take off the fat with a spoon, then lay over it a clean piece of blotting paper to remove every particle of grease. When cold, boil it a few minutes with the whites of two well-beaten eggs, (but do not add the sediment), and strain it through a sieve, with a napkin in it, which has been dipped in boiling water. If the pie be of fowl, or rabbit, the carcases, necks and heads, added to a small piece of meat or a cow heel, or shanks of mutton will be better suited than the jelly of meat alone.

Aspic Jelly for Garnishing.

Time, three-quarters of an hour.

317. One pint and a half of white stock; one ounce of isinglass; two eggs; two tablespoonfuls of tarragon vinegar; one wineglassful of sherry; one bay-leaf; a cupful of water.

Melt the stock, which should be a firm jelly when cold, then when boiling dissolve the isinglass in it, and set it aside to cool. Mix and whisk together the whites of the two eggs *with their shells*, the tarragon vinegar, the wine, and a cupful of water (nearly, but not quite half a pint). Whisk them all into the stock, and stir it till it boils for about a quarter of an hour. Take it off the fire, let it stand to settle, and pour it through a jelly bag into a basin or plain mould which you have first dipped in cold water. Let it stand all night to get cold, and the next day you may turn it out of the mould, by dipping the bottom of it in cold water (as for sweet jelly); then cut it into small cubes for garnishing your pie, meat cake, or ham.

Arrowroot Sauce for Plum Puddings.

Time, fifteen minutes.

318. One dessertspoonful of arrowroot; two of sifted sugar; a glass of white wine; juice of half a lemon; half a pint of water.

Rub very smoothly a dessertspoonful of arrowroot in a little water, or in a glass of white wine, squeeze in the juice of half a lemon, add the pounded sugar, and pour gradually in half a pint of water. Stir it very quickly over a clear fire until it boils. Serve it with plum pudding.

This sauce may be flavoured with anything you prefer.

Sauce for Cabinet or Souffle Pudding.

Time, ten minutes.

319. Yolks of four eggs; a glass of white wine; a lemon; sugar to your taste.

Put the yolks of three or four eggs into a large basin, and whisk them for two minutes; then add the wine, and lemon juice strained and the rind grated. Put the basin into a stewpan of boiling water over a clear bright fire, and whisk it all together until it is a creamy froth. Then pour it over the pudding.

Almond Sauce for Puddings.
Time, fifteen minutes.

320. An ounce and a half of sweet almonds; seven bitter almonds; two teaspoonfuls of orange flower-water; yolks of two or three eggs; three tablespoonfuls of cream; five lumps of sugar, or to your taste.

Blanch and pound the bitter and sweet almonds in a mortar with the orange-flower water until they are a pulp; then put them into a delicately clean saucepan with the cream, the yolks of the eggs well beaten, and sugar to your taste. Whisk it over a moderate fire until it is smooth and frothy, and serve it up with puddings.

White Wine Sauce.
Time, five minutes.

321. Half a pint of melted butter; four tablespoonfuls of white wine; the peel of half a lemon; sugar to your taste.

Add to half a pint of good melted butter four spoonfuls of white wine, the grated rind of half a lemon, and the sugar pounded and sifted. Let it boil, and serve with plum, bread, or boiled batter pudding, &c.

Sauce for Polka Pudding.
Time, five minutes.

322. Three ounces of fresh butter; one cupful of powdered sugar; three glasses of sherry.

Beat the three ounces of butter with the sugar to a cream; add to it three glasses of sherry; mix it well. Boil it, stirring it incessantly in one direction till it is done.

Serve it boiling hot. The pudding is served *quite cold* with hot plates.

Clarified Butter.
Time, two or three minutes.

323. Melt some butter in a tin saucepan over a slow fire; when it begins to simmer take off the scum, and let it stand at the side of the fire for the buttermilk to sink to the bottom; then strain it through a very fine hair sieve. It will keep good for some time, if it is potted in jars and kept in a *cool* storeroom.

When clarified butter is melted again for use, it must be skimmed and strained from the sediment it will leave.

To Use Dried Mushrooms.
Time, ten minutes to a quarter of an hour.

324. Simmer them in gravy; they will swell to nearly their original size.

How to use Glaze.

325. Glaze is merely very strong gravy, boiled quickly down till it is of the consistency of liquid jelly. When it is of this thickness it must be poured out of the stewpan at once, or it will of course burn.

When you require to use it, stand the jar in which you keep the glaze or jelly in a pan of boiling water, and thus melt it gently. Lay it on the meat or cutlets with a paste brush. It soon becomes firm. When one layer is dry put on another, till it forms a clear varnish. A ham will take three layers to look *very* nice.

A glaze pot and brush are to be found in most well-furnished kitchens, but any lady may make a little glaze for herself if she requires it, and a preserve jar will hold it; a pan of boiling water will dissolve it.

FORCEMEATS, GARNISHING, FLAVOURING, &c.

MAKING forcemeat is an essential part of good cookery. It depends very greatly, as sauces do, on a delicate taste in the cook, who should so harmonize the ingredients that no one flavour may predominate over the other.

A selection can be made from the following list of meat, herbs, and spice, for any particular forcemeat or stuffing that may be required, taking care that no particular flavour predominates, as thyme and lemon peel frequently overcome all others, and entirely destroy the effect of the whole. It must always be firm enough to cut with a knife, but not dry.

Bacon or butter must take the place of suet, when the forcemeat is required to be eaten cold, and if required very light, the bread should be soaked, and well beaten up when the water has been thoroughly pressed from it, and used instead of breadcrumbs.

7—2

Herbs,—Parsley, thyme, tarragon, savory, knotted marjoram, basil.
Ham or bacon, suet, oysters, anchovy, bread-crumbs, soaked bread.
Spice. — Pepper, salt, nutmeg, cloves, mace, garlic, shallots, chives.
Eggs.—The whites and yolks.

Bread Panada for Forcemeat, Quenelles, &c.

326, One pound of bread; an ounce of butter or a little milk; a little salt.
Take the crumb of a new loaf, soak it in water, and then press it dry; mix it with the butter and a little salt; stir it over the fire with a wooden spoon until it forms a smooth tough paste, and ceases to adhere to the stewpan. Put the panada to cool on a clean plate, and it will then be fit for use.

A common Forcemeat for Veal or Hare.

327. Six ounces of bread-crumbs; the rind of half a lemon; one tablespoonful of minced savoury herbs; three ounces of suet, or butter; two eggs; pepper and salt; and nutmeg.
Mix with the bread-crumbs the peel of the lemon minced very fine; a tablespoonful of chopped savoury herbs, or dried ones if not able to procure them green; three ounces of finely chopped beef suet, or of butter broken into small pieces; season it with pepper, salt, and nutmeg, and bind it with two well-beaten eggs.

Sage and Onion Stuffing for Geese, Ducks, or Pork.

328. Three onions; five ounces of bread-crumbs; eight sage leaves; one ounce of butter; pepper; salt; one egg.
Wash, peel, and boil the onions in two waters to extract the strong flavour, and scald the sage leaves for a few minutes. Chop the onions and leaves very fine, mix them with the bread-crumbs, seasoned with pepper and salt, a piece of butter broken into pieces, and the yolk of one egg.

Forcemeat for Savoury Pies.

329. Half a pound of veal; half a pound of fat ham or bacon; a very few savoury herbs; two eggs; pepper; salt; nutmeg; and Cayenne; a little lemon peel; a sprig of parsley; three mushrooms.
Mince very fine half a pound of fat bacon or ham and the veal, add to them the minced herbs, lemon peel, and the seasoning of pepper, salt, nutmeg, Cayenne, and the mushrooms chopped very fine. Pound it all well together in a mortar after it has been well mixed together, and then bind it with two well-beaten eggs; stir the whole well together, and use it as directed for savoury pies.

Oyster Forcemeat.

330. Half a pint of oysters; five ounces of bread-crumbs; one ounce of butter; the peel of half a lemon; a sprig of parsley; salt; nutmeg; a very little Cayenne; and one egg.
Take off the beards from half a pint of oysters, wash them well in their own liquor, and mince them very fine; mix with them the peel of half a lemon chopped small, a sprig of parsley, a seasoning of salt, nutmeg, and a *very* little Cayenne, and about an ounce of butter in small pieces. Stir into these ingredients five ounces of bread-crumbs, and when thoroughly mixed together, bind it with the yolk of an egg and part of the oyster liquor.

Forcemeat for Haddock or Carp.

331. Two ounces of suet; two ounces of butter; two ounces of bacon; one dessertspoonful of savoury herbs; a very small sprig of parsley; half a pound of bread-crumbs; two or three eggs; pepper; salt, and nutmeg; twelve oysters.
Chop the suet *very* fine, and mix it with some lean and fat of bacon or ham minced up with the savoury herbs and parsley. Beard and chop up twelve oysters; mix them with the bread-crumbs and the butter; add it to all the other ingredients, and rub all smoothly together with the well-beaten eggs.

Egg Balls for Made Dishes or Soup.

Time, twenty minutes to boil the eggs.

332. Twelve eggs; a little flour and salt.
Pound the hard-boiled yolks of eight eggs in a mortar until very smooth; then mix with them the yolks of four raw eggs, a little salt, and a dust or so of flour to make them bind. Roll them into small balls, boil them in water, and then add them to any made dishes or soups that they may be required for.

Forcemeat Balls.

Time, six or seven minutes.

333. Half a pound of bread-crumbs; a bunch of sweet herbs; a little salt; and eggs.

Grate half a pound of stale bread, and mix it with the sweet herbs chopped very fine, a little salt, and two hard-boiled eggs minced up; add a sufficient number of eggs to bind it together; roll it into balls, and drop them into the soup when boiling, about six or seven minutes before serving.

Onions for Garnishing.
Time, one hour.

334. Twelve onions; two or three ounces of butter, in slices; half an ounce of sugar; a little salt; one glass of stock.

Pick a dozen large onions carefully, without breaking the skins; lightly take off the stem part. Lay a few slices of butter at the bottom of a stewpan; place the onions in it; add half an ounce of powdered white sugar; one saltspoonful and a half of salt; and a gill of stock. Stew the onions over a slow fire, and reduce the sauce to a glaze. When the onions are done, and of a good colour, they are used for putting round beef, &c.

Mix the sauce remaining at the bottom of the stewpan with a little stock, and add it to the gravy.

Green Pea Garnish.
Time, twenty minutes.

335. One pint of young peas; two tablespoonfuls of white sauce; one ounce of butter; half a teaspoonful of powdered sugar; a little salt; one small onion; a sprig of parsley; two eggs.

Put the peas in a stewpan with the above ingredients; moisten them with boiling water. Boil for twenty minutes. Add two tablespoonfuls of liaison, stir it quickly together, and serve under and round fricandeau of veal, &c.

Croutons.
Time, five minutes.

336. Two rounds of a half-quartern loaf; two ounces of butter.

Cut the bread in thin slices, then shape them as you please in lozenges, crescents, stars, or larger rounds. Fry them in boiling butter a nice brown. When fried, take them out, and drain them on a cloth.

TRUFFLES.

The truffle is a species of mushroom fungus without roots. It is found in Hampshire, Wiltshire, and Kent, and is of a good size in our own country, though not so large as the Italian truffle is. In the New Forest, truffles are frequently rooted up from beneath the giant oak-trees which "came in with the Conqueror," by the hogs, who (true epicures) are extravagantly fond of them. In France they form an article of considerable traffic, and have often been purchased at fabulous prices for the royal table. They are very expensive, and chiefly used for garnishings and seasoning.

Good truffles have a pleasant flavour, and are light and elastic. Bad truffles have a musty smell. They ought to be eaten quite fresh, as their flavour is a good deal injured by drying for keeping.

To Prepare Truffles au Naturel.
Time, one hour.

337. Wash them several times in lukewarm water and brush them carefully all the time to remove every particle of earth or grit from them. Then wrap each truffle in buttered paper, and bake them in a hot oven —or (better still) roast them in hot ashes for an hour. Take off the paper, wipe the truffles, and serve them on a hot table-napkin, or use them for garnishing.

Season for Drying Herbs for Flavouring.

Basil is fit for drying about the middle of August.
Chervil in May, June, and July.
Elder-flowers, May, June, and July.
Fennel, May, June, and July.
Knotted marjoram, July.
Lemon thyme, July and August.
Mint, the end of June and July.
Orange thyme, June and July.
Parsley, May, June, July.
Sage, August and September.
Summer Savory, end of July and August.
Tarragon, June, July, and August.
Thyme, end of July and August.
Winter Savoury, end of July and August.

They must be gathered on a dry day, and cleaned and dried immediately by the heat of a stove or Dutch oven, the leaves picked off, sifted, and bottled.

Crisped Parsley.

338. Pick some handsome sprigs of curled parsley, wash them well, dip them into cold water, throw them into a pan of boiling fat, and take them out as soon as they are crisp.

It should be done after the fish, &c., it is to go with is ready, and drained from the grease before the fire for a minute or two after it is done.

A far better plan is to spread the parsley, after it is picked and washed, in a Dutch oven, or on a sheet of paper, at a moderate distance from the fire, and keep turning it till it is quite crisp; lay little pieces of butter on it, but not enough to make it greasy. This is a much better plan than that of frying.

To Prepare Potatoes for Garnishing.

Time, half an hour to three quarters.

339. Twelve potatoes; two ounces and a half of butter; one teaspoonful of salt; a quarter of a teaspoonful of pepper; two dessertspoonfuls of chopped parsley; a pinch of grated nutmeg; two eggs; half a gill of milk; one ounce of bread-crumbs.

Boil and mash a dozen potatoes, putting to them about two ounces and a half of butter, a little pepper, salt, and grated nutmeg. Mix them well up, add one egg and half a gill of milk. Let the mash get cold, then roll it up in balls of any size and form you please, as eggs, as pears, as round pellets; egg and bread-crumb them twice, and fry them lightly.

Glaze.

340. A little cowheel jelly, a quarter of small cupful of isinglass, boil it one hour.

Put in a pan over the fire one ounce of butter, add a quarter of a pound of moist sugar, and keep the two latter ingredients over the fire until quite brown, then mix them with the above, and keep the whole simmering until it will glaze.

Fried Bread for Borders.

341. Cut some thin slices of bread, and stamp them out in any form you please. Fry them in boiling fat, one half a pale colour, the other half a fine dark brown, and when quite crisp brush one side with the white of an egg, beaten with a dust of flour, and arrange them round the edge of your dish, alternately dark and light.

Fried Bread-crumbs.

Time, two minutes.

342. Cut some bread rather thin, put it in a moderate oven until very crisp without being burnt, and then roll it very fine. Put the crumbs into a very clean frying-pan of boiling clarified dripping, or butter, and fry them as quickly as possible. When done lift them out with a slice, and set them to dry before the fire, and thoroughly drain from any grease or moisture.

STORE SAUCES—Receipt 1.

Walnut Ketchup.

Time, to boil, half an hour.

343. One hundred and twenty green walnuts; two pints and a half of vinegar; three-quarters of a pound of salt; one ounce and a quarter of whole peppers; forty cloves; half an ounce of sliced nutmeg; half an ounce of ginger.

Bruise to a mass one hundred and twenty green walnuts—gathered when a pin could pierce one—put to it the salt and a quart of vinegar; stir them every day for a fortnight, then strain and squeeze the liquor from them through a cloth, and set it aside; put to the husks half a pint of vinegar, and let it stand all night, then strain and squeeze them as before; put the liquor from them to that which was put aside, add to it the peppers, cloves, ginger, and sliced nutmeg, and boil it closely covered; then strain it, and when cold bottle it for use. Secure the bottles with new corks, and dip them in melted resin.

Mushroom Ketchup.

344. Be careful in selecting and testing the mushrooms you intend to use. The *true* mushroom has the under side flesh-coloured or pink when very young, and as it grows old it becomes dark-brown or blackish. It has a very pleasant smell, which the toadstool has not.

Let the mushrooms you use for ketchup be full grown mushroom flaps, and take care that they are gathered *in dry weather*, or the ketchup will not keep long.

Time, three hours and a half.

To each peck of mushrooms half a pound of salt.

Put a layer of mushrooms in a deep pan, sprinkle salt over them, cover the salt with another layer of mushrooms, and so on till all are laid in the dish. Let them remain a few hours, then break them in pieces.

Let the pan stand in a cool place for three days. Every morning stir and mash them up to extract their juice.

Measure the quantity of juice, and to each quart allow half an ounce of allspice, half an ounce of ginger, two blades of mace pounded, a quarter of an ounce of Cayenne. Put the whole into a stone jar, cover it very closely, set it in a saucepan of boiling water over the fire, and let it boil for three hours. Then take it up, pour it into a clean stewpan, and let it simmer by the side of the fire for half an hour. Pour it into a jug. Let it stand twelve or more hours in a cool place. Pour it into another jug and strain it off for bottling. Pour it through a strainer into the bottles, add to each quart of liquor thirty drops of brandy. Cork the bottles very closely.

Hot Vinegar.

345. Chop fine two cloves of garlic, put this into a bottle, with a pint of vinegar, a tablespoonful of Worcester sauce, a teaspoonful of salt, an ounce of ground white pepper, and half an ounce of Cayenne. Shake it up well, then let it remain for a

month. Strain it through fine muslin, and bottle it in small bottles, which should be well corked down.

Devil Hot.

346. To three quarts of the best vinegar put eight ounces of salt, two ounces of ginger, half an ounce of mace, quarter of a pound of shallots, one ounce of white pepper, one ounce of mustard seed, half a tablespoonful of good Cayenne pepper. Boil it all together, and when cold put it into a jar.

Gather any fruit or vegetables you like, wipe them, and put them into the pickle. Secure the jar by tying leather and a bladder over it.

Lemon Vinegar.
Time, nine weeks.

347. Two dozen and a half of lemons; four ounces of garlic; one handful of horse-radish; one gallon of vinegar; one ounce of mace; half an ounce of cloves; one ounce of nutmeg; half an ounce of Cayenne; half a pint of mustard seed.

Grate off the outer rinds of the lemons with a piece of glass, cut them across but do not quite separate them; work in as much salt as you can with the fingers; spread them on a large pewter dish, and cover them quite over with salt; then put them into a cool oven three or four times, until the juice is dried into the peels; they must be hard but not burned. Then put to them the garlic peeled, the horseradish sliced, and again place them in the oven till there is no moisture left. As the salt dissolves work in more. Put the vinegar into a stewpan with the cloves pounded, the mace beaten fine, the nutmeg cut into slices, and the Cayenne and mustard slightly bruised, and tied in a muslin bag. Boil all these ingredients with the vinegar, and pour it boiling hot on the lemons. The jar must be well closed, and let stand by the fire for six days, shaking it well every day. Then tie it down and let it stand for three months to take off the bitterness. When it is bottled, the pickle must be put into a hair or lawn sieve two or three times, till it is as fine as possible. After the lemon pickle is cleared off, add about one quart of boiled vinegar to the remaining ingredients, and after it has stood for some time it is excellent for hashes, &c., &c.

This pickle may be put into white sauce, one spoonful being sufficient; two spoonfuls for brown sauce. It is also good for fish, fowls, or any made dish, care always being taken to put it in before the sauce is mixed with cream, or the acid may curdle it.

Chetney Sauce.
Time, four or five weeks.

348. Quarter of a pound of raisins; quarter of a pound of apples; quarter of a pound of moist sugar; quarter of a pound of tomatoes; two ounces of tamarinds; one tablespoonful of salt; ditto of Cayenne, teaspoonful of pounded ginger; two large onions; a little lemon peel; one pint of lemon juice; one quart of vinegar.

Stone and cut up into rather large pieces a quarter of a pound of pudding raisins; add to these a quarter of a pound of apples chopped in small pieces, the same quantity of moist sugar and chopped tomatoes, from which you have taken the seeds, two ounces of tamarinds, a tablespoonful of salt, ditto of Cayenne, a teaspoonful of ground ginger, two large onions chopped fine, very little chopped lemon peel, a pint of lemon juice, and one quart of vinegar; mix all these ingredients well together, then put them into a jar, well covered. Stir the mixture every day for four or five weeks, and if at the end of that time it is too thin, pour enough of the liquid away to make it of a proper thickness, but not dry, bottle the chetney in bottles or jars for use.

Reading Sauce.
Time, three hours.

349. Two pints and a half of walnut pickle; one quart of water; half an ounce of ginger; half an ounce of pepper; one ounce and a half of shallots; one ounce of mustard seed; half an ounce of Cayenne pepper; one anchovy; a dried bay-leaf; three-quarters of a pint of Indian soy.

Put the walnut pickle into a store jar with the shallots (first bruised in a mortar), place the jar in the oven till the liquor is reduced to two pints; then bruise the anchovy, mustard seed, ginger, and pepper, and put all into another jar with the Cayenne and the quart of water; put this jar before the fire, and let it boil for rather more than an hour, that the flavour of all may be extracted. Then mix the contents of the two jars together, stirring them well as you do so. When thoroughly mixed boil them slowly for half an hour, then cover them down closely, and let them stand in a cool place for twenty-four hours. Add the bay-leaves, and let it remain for a week, closed down; then strain it through a thick flannel bag, and put it into bottles, corking it down.

Jipper's Sauce.
Time, a few minutes.

350. Juice of four lemons; a few pieces of lemon peel; a little tamarind juice; a

small quantity of salt; half a teaspoonful of Cayenne.

Simmer the above for a few minutes, and then turn it into a basin; strain through a fine strainer. When cold, bottle it into small bottles, which cork well and keep in a dry place, free from damp.

Nasturtiums used as Capers.

351. Besides being great ornaments to our flower gardens, nasturtiums supply us with a useful adjunct to frugal tables. They save the expense of capers.

Gather the seeds ("cheeses" country children call them) of the nasturtiums, and keep them for a few days on a paper tray; then put them into empty pickle bottles, pour boiling vinegar over them, and leave them to cool. When cold, cover them closely down.

They will be fit to eat the next summer in lieu of capers, with boiled mutton.

The Epicure's Sauce.
Time, two or three weeks.

352. One capsicum; two shallots; one or two birds'-eye chilies; two tablespoonfuls of port wine; six tablespoonfuls of mushroom ketchup; half a teaspoonful of Cayenne, and the same of whole pepper; half a pint of vinegar.

Put all into a bottle, which keep in a warm place for two or three weeks. Then strain, and add half a pint of vinegar.

Carrack.
Time, one month.

353. Eight pickled walnuts; one head of garlic; half a tumblerful of walnut vinegar, soy, and mushroom ketchup; one tablespoonful of Harvey sauce; one quart of vinegar.

Chop eight pickled walnuts and one head of garlic, put these into a large jar; add walnut vinegar, soy, and mushroom ketchup, of each half a tumblerful, a tablespoonful of Harvey sauce, and one quart of vinegar; put the jar in a dry place, and shake it every day for a month; a few spoonfuls of mango pickle is a great improvement.

Walnut Vinegar for Sauces, &c.
Time, a little more than a month.

354. Put some green walnut-shells into salt and water, sufficiently strong to bear an egg. At the end of ten or fourteen days drain them from the brine and lay them in the sun for nine days, then put them into a stone jar, cover them with boiling vinegar, and at the end of a week pour it off; boil it again, pour it over the walnut-shells, and tie them closely over for use.

Horseradish Vinegar.
Time, twelve days.

355. Six ounces of young horseradish; three pints of vinegar.

Scrape the horseradish, and pour over it the boiling vinegar, cover it closely over, and let it stand for ten or twelve days; then pour off the vinegar and bottle it up for use. It may remain some considerable time before it is poured from the horseradish, but if required may be used in ten or twelve days.

Chili Vinegar.
Time, three weeks.

356. Forty-eight chilies; one pint of vinegar.

Chop and pound in a mortar four dozen fresh chilies, and put them into a bottle with a pint of strong vinegar, shake the bottle every day, and in three weeks it will be ready for use.

Lemon Flavouring.
Time, one month.

357. Fill some bottles with the rinds of some fine fresh lemons, cut as thin as possible; add the kernels of some peaches or plums, blanched, and fill up the bottles with brandy; let it stand for nearly a month, then strain it off, put it into bottles, and cork them well down.

Cayenne Vinegar.

358. Put half an ounce of Cayenne pepper into a bottle with a pint of white wine vinegar; cork it tightly, and shake it well for a few days; it will be soon ready for use.

Eschalot Vinegar.

359. Put into a quart bottle nearly full of vinegar, five ounces of eschalots which have been well bruised, and add half a teaspoonful of Cayenne pepper, cork the bottle well, shake it up, and then leave it for a fortnight; at the end of this time, strain it through fine muslin, and bottle it again.

BEEF.

To Dress Beef.
Have a *good* fire.
Do not place the meat too near it at first.
Baste it often.
In frosty weather thaw it before putting it down.

Time to roast brown meats, a quarter of an hour to each pound.

White meats, a quarter of an hour to each pound, and twenty minutes over; in cold weather perhaps a *little* longer; in warm weather not *quite* so long.

Time to boil, about the same time reckoned from the moment the pot *boils*.

Stewing should be a very slow process. Time generally given in the receipts.

Care and attention required for *all* methods.

Beef is in season all the year; but salt beef is best in winter.

To make Tough Meat Tender.

360. Soak it in vinegar and water; if a very large piece, for about twelve hours.

For twenty pounds of beef use six quarts of water to one pint and a half of vinegar, and soak it for six or seven hours.

Sirloin of Beef.

Time, a quarter of an hour to each pound of meat.

361. Make up a good fire; spit or hang the joint evenly, at about twelve inches from it. Put a little clarified dripping in the dripping-pan, and baste the joint well as soon as it is put down to dress; baste again every quarter of an hour till about twenty minutes before it is done; then stir the fire and make it clear; sprinkle a little salt, and dredge a little flour over the meat, turn it again till it is brown and frothed. Take it from the spit, put it on a hot dish, and pour over it some good made gravy, or mix the gravy left at the bottom of the dripping-pan with a little hot water and pour it over it. Garnish with fine scrapings of horseradish in little heaps. Serve Yorkshire pudding with it on a separate dish. Sauce: horseradish.

Roast Ribs of Beef.

Time, a quarter of an hour to the pound.

362. The chine-bone and the upper part of three rib-bones should be taken off, and the flap-ends fastened under with very small skewers. The joint is roasted and served as the sirloin.

Ribs of Beef Rolled.

Time, twenty minutes to the pound, or fifteen minutes, and half an hour over.

363. Order the butcher to take out the bones of the joint. Roll it into a round, and fasten it with skewers and a broad piece of tape in the shape of a round. Place it at the distance of twelve inches before a large fire till it is partly dressed; then move it gradually forward towards the fire. Put some clarified dripping in the pan, baste it the moment the dripping melts, and do the same every quarter of an hour. Just before it is done—*i. e.*, about twenty minutes before you remove it from the spit, dredge it with flour and baste it with a little butter. Remove the tape and skewer, and fasten it with a silver skewer instead. Serve with good gravy over it.

Horseradish sauce.

To Boil Beef.

Reckon the time from the water coming to a boil.

364. Keep the pot boiling, but let it boil *very slowly*. If you let the pot cease boiling, you will be deceived in your time; therefore watch that it does not stop, and keep up a sufficiently good fire. Just before the pot boils the scum rises. Be sure to skim it off carefully, or it will fall back and adhere to the meat, and disfigure it sadly. When you have well skimmed the pot, put in a little cold water, which will cause the scum to rise again. The more carefully you skim, the cleaner and nicer the meat boiled will look.

Put your meat into cold water. Liebig, the great German chemist, advises us to plunge the joint into boiling water, but the great cook, Francatelli, and others of the same high standing, recommend cold; and our own experience and practice are in accordance with the cook rather than the chemist. Put a quart of cold water to every pound of meat. Allow twenty minutes to the pound from the time the pot boils and the scum rises.

It is more profitable to boil than to roast meat.

Aitchbone of Beef.

Time, twenty minutes to the pound.

365. Three-quarters of a pound of salt; one ounce of moist sugar; aitchbone weighing ten pounds; two gallons and a half of water.

Dry the salt, and rub it with the sugar in a mortar, then rub it well into the aitchbone of beef. Turn the joint and rub in some pickle every day for four or five days. Wash it well before you boil it. Put it into a large boiling pot, so as to let it be well surrounded and covered with cold water in the above proportion, set the pot on one side of the fire to boil gently; if it boils fast at first nothing can prevent the meat from becoming hard and tough. The slower it boils the tenderer it will be and the better it will cook.

The soft fat which lies on the back of an aitchbone of beef is delicious when hot, the hard fat is best cold.

Save the liquor in which this joint is boiled for pea-soup.

Garnish with slices of turnip and carrot.

Silverside of Beef Boiled.

Time, a quarter of an hour to each pound.

366. Ten or twelve pounds of the silverside of beef; three gallons of water.

After the beef has been in the pickle for about nine or ten days, take it out and wash it in water, skewer it up in a round form, and bind it with a piece of tape. Put it into a large stewpan of water, and when it boils remove the scum very carefully, or it will sink and spoil the appearance of the meat. Then draw the saucepan to one side of the fire, and let it simmer slowly until done. When ready to serve, draw out the skewers and replace them with a silver one. Pour over it a little of the liquor in which it has been boiled, and garnish with boiled carrots and parsnips.

When taken from the water, trim off any soiled part from the beef before sending it to table.

Tom Thumb Round of Beef.

Time, nearly three hours.

367. Nine or ten pounds of rib of beef; two gallons and a half of water.

Select a fine rib of beef, from nine to ten pounds; have the bone removed, it will make a gravy for anything you may require; rub a little salt over the inside of the rib, roll it like a fillet of veal, and bind it round with a tape or a few wooden skewers; place it in sufficient pickle to cover it, and let it remain in it five or six days, turning it every morning. When it is required, place it in a stewpan of very hot water (to prevent the gravy from being drawn out), and let it only *simmer*, not *boil*, according to the size of the joint, allowing the full time for each pound of meat. When done, remove the skewers and replace them with a silver or plated one.

Beef Bouilli.

Time, a quarter of an hour to each pound of meat, and another extra twenty minutes.

368. Round or part of a round of beef or brisket, pieces of any meat you have, such as trimmings of beef, veal, or lamb, or giblets of poultry. Enough water to well cover the meat; salt and pepper to taste; two carrots sliced; one onion; one bunch of parsley; one teacupful of butter; one teacupful of browned flour; one wineglass of wine or one of mushroom ketchup.

Take the bone out of a round of beef or part of one, tie in a neat shape with a strong cord, put it into a stewpan; add to it any remains of meat or giblets which you have. Cover it with water, set it over a slow fire, and as it boils skim it carefully; add the carrots, onion, and parsley; then put in the flour and butter. Cover it for twenty minutes. Take up the meat, strain the gravy and add the wine or ketchup to it. Pour it over the meat.

If you stew the bone which has been taken out with the meat, the gravy will be all the better.

A Beef Stew.

Time, two hours and twenty minutes.

369. Two or three pounds of the rump of beef; one quart of broth; pepper and salt; the peel of one large lemon, and the juice; two tablespoonfuls of Harvey sauce; one spoonful of flour; a little ketchup; one glass of white wine.

Cut away all the skin and fat from two or three pounds of the rump of beef, and divide it into pieces about two or three inches square; put it into a stewpan, and pour on it a quart of broth; then let it boil, and sprinkle in pepper and salt to taste. When it has boiled very gently, or simmered two hours, shred finely the peel of a large lemon, and add it to the gravy. In twenty minutes pour in a flavouring, composed of two spoonfuls of Harvey sauce, the juice of the lemon, the flour, and a little ketchup. Add at pleasure a glass of sherry, a quarter of an hour after flavouring it, and serve.

Stewed Shin of Beef—A Family Dish.

Time, four hours and a quarter.

370. A shin of beef; one bunch of sweet herbs; one large onion; one head of celery; twelve black pepper corns; twelve allspice; three carrots; two turnips; twelve small button onions.

Saw the bone into three or four pieces; put them into a stewpan, and *just* cover them with cold water. When the pot simmers, skim it clean; and then add the sweet herbs, onion, celery, peppers and allspice. Stew it very gently over a slow fire till the meat is tender. Then peel the carrots and turnips and cut them into shapes; boil them with the button onions till tender. The turnips and onions will take a quarter of an hour to boil, the carrots *half* an hour. Drain them carefully. Put the meat when done on a dish, and keep it warm while you prepare some gravy thus: (*i.e.*)

Take a teacupful of the liquor in which the meat has been stewed, and mix with it three tablespoonfuls of flour; add more liquor till you have a pint and a half of gravy. Season with pepper, salt, and a wineglass of mushroom ketchup. Boil it up, skim off the fat, and strain it through a sieve. Pour it over the meat and lay the vegetables round it.

To Dress the Inside of a Sirloin.
Time, one hour.

371. The inside of a sirloin; a pint and a half of good gravy; one tablespoonful of ketchup; half a blade of mace; pepper and salt.

Cut the inside from a sirloin of beef, and put it into a stewpan with a pint and a half of good gravy, a tablespoonful of ketchup, and a little mace, pepper, and salt. Let it stew slowly for about an hour, and serve with piquante or horseradish sauce.

A la Mode Beef.
Time, five hours and a half.

372. Six or seven pounds of buttock of beef; two ounces of beef dripping; two large onions; six black peppers; sixteen allspice; three bay-leaves; one gallon of water.

Put the beef dripping and onions into a large deep stewpan over the fire. As soon as it is hot, cut the meat into pieces of about three ounces each, dredge these pieces well with flour, put them into the stewpan and stir them continually with a wooden spoon. When the beef has been in ten minutes, dredge in some more flour till it is well thickened; then add *gradually* to it (stirring it all the time, a gallon of boiling water; add the allspice, peppers, and bay-leaves. Place the stewpan at the side of the fire and let it simmer very slowly till done.

Beef Olives.
Time, to stew, one hour and a half.

373. A pound and a half of rump steak; three yolks of eggs; a little beaten mace; pepper and salt; a teacupful of bread-crumbs; two ounces of marrow or suet; a sprig of parsley; the rind of half a lemon; one pint of brown gravy; a tablespoonful of ketchup; one of browning; a teaspoonful of lemon pickle; a piece of butter rolled in flour; eight forcemeat balls.

Cut the steak into slices of about half an inch thick and six or seven inches long, rub them over with the yolk of a beaten egg, and strew thickly over them some bread-crumbs, the marrow or suet chopped fine, then the parsley minced, the grated rind of half a large lemon, a little beaten mace, and some pepper and salt, all mixed well together. Roll each olive round, fasten it with a small skewer, and brown them lightly before the fire in a Dutch oven. Then put them into a stewpan with the gravy, ketchup, browning, and lemon pickle, thicken it with a piece of butter rolled in flour, and serve the olives in the gravy. Garnish with forcemeat balls.

Breslau of Beef.
Time, half an hour.

374. Half a pound of under-dressed roast beef; three ounces of bread-crumbs; two tablespoonfuls of minced parsley and thyme; three ounces of butter; half a cupful of gravy; three eggs; half a teaspoonful of salt; a little grated nutmeg; one teaspoonful of grated lemon peel; pepper and Cayenne to taste.

Trim the brown edges from the beef, shred it very small, and mix it with fine bread-crumbs, minced parsley and thyme, the grated lemon peel, and butter broken into very small pieces; pour on the mince a cupful of gravy (or, if you have it, a cupful of cream); add the three eggs *thoroughly beaten*. Season it well with pepper, Cayenne, salt, and nutmeg, if to your taste. Butter some coffee cups or the tin cups sold for poaching eggs in, put the Breslau into them, bake it for half an hour and serve. Garnish with egg balls, sauce Espagnole, or good gravy.

Fillets de Bœuf.
Time, eight minutes.

375. Under cut of sirloin of beef; one lemon; two ounces of butter; and a little good gravy.

Cut the *undercut* of a sirloin of beef into small slices; fry them for eight minutes in two ounces of butter. Warm the gravy and squeeze half a lemon into it, seasoning it to your taste. Put a mould of mashed potatoes into the centre of a very hot dish. Stand the *fillets* or slices of beef round it, leaning them against the side of the potatoes. Pour round them the gravy as prepared. This dish must be served as hot as possible.

We must beg our lady readers who are obliged to keep house economically, not to be frightened at the idea of having fillets de bœuf (which are seldom seen in middle-class houses), at their table. A little ordinary care, attention, and practice, will enable a tolerable cook to do them well, and they are especially nice dishes. Moreover, they give two fresh dishes from one joint. Use the under-cut of the sirloin, we will say, for example, on the Saturday for fillets de bœuf, and you have your sirloin still ready for the spit on Sunday. It is true that in order to have them you must order a tolerably large joint, but in a large family a good-sized joint is economical, because it wastes less by drying up in cooking. For small families a small dish of fillets de bœuf may be made from a joint weighing ten pounds or even less.

Fillets de Bœuf a la St. Aubyn.

Time to fry, eight minutes.

376. Inside of a sirloin of beef; a quarter of a pint of best olive oil; three ounces of butter; a bouquet of parsley; chervil and lemon thyme; half of a shallot; fifteen drops of vinegar.

Cut out the inside of a sirloin of beef, beat it well to make it tender, cut it in slices, trimming them neatly; lay them in the oil and let them soak for ten minutes, then fry them in butter. Slice some potatoes and fry them in plenty of lard. Chop up as finely as possible the sweet herbs with the shallot and the vinegar, put them in the centre of a hot dish, and lay the fillets and slices of potatoes round them. This dish is especially appetizing.

Beef Cakes.

Time, ten minutes.

377. Any remains of under-dressed beef; salt and pepper to taste; a few sprigs of parsley; one egg; mashed potatoes equal to one-third of the quantity of meat.

Mince the meat very fine. Boil and mash potatoes equal to one-third the quantity of your meat, mix them nicely with it; season with the pepper and salt; mince up and add the parsley to it. Then beat up the yolk of one egg, mix it with the mince to bind it. Wash your hands and flour them. Make the mince into cakes about the size round of the top of a teacup and half an inch thick, flour them, and fry them a nice brown in hot beef dripping or lard. Serve on a cloth with a garnish of fried parsley.

Beef Palates.

Time, three hours to boil.

Beef palates are not often seen at the tables of the middle classes, but they would be a great addition to the ordinary fare. They are not expensive at all, and four are enough for a dish.

378. Four palates; one pint and a half of white stock.

Soak them for four or five hours, to make them disgorge, in a pan of lukewarm water. Then put them into a stewpan with clean water and set them over the fire. While the palates are hard, take them out, dip them into cold water and scrape off the skin; if it will not come off easily replace them in the stewpan till it will, scrape them till they are white and clear looking; then boil them in white stock till they are perfectly tender. Take them up, press them flat between two plates, and let them get cold. Cut them into square pieces and stew them in curry sauce, or according to the following receipt:—

To Stew Beef Palates.

Time, four hours and a half.

379. Four palates; one pint of veal gravy; one tablespoonful of wine; one of ketchup; one of browning; one onion stuck with cloves; and a slice of lemon; with forcemeat balls.

Wash four palates and make them disgorge as directed before. Take off the skin. Boil them until quite tender, and cut them into pieces half an inch broad and three inches long. Put them into a stewpan with a pint of veal gravy, one tablespoonful of white wine, the same of ketchup and of browning, one onion stuck with cloves, and a slice of lemon; thicken the gravy with a little butter rolled in flour. Stew for four hours and a half, put the palates on a hot dish, pour the gravy over them. Garnish with forcemeat balls.

To Broil Beef Palates.

Time to simmer, one hour; to broil, five minutes.

380. Three beef palates; pepper and salt; one shallot; one clove; a bunch of thyme and parsley; yolk of one or two eggs; a few bread-crumbs; a pint and a half of milk.

Wash and soak three palates, and boil them until tender, removing the skin. Then put them into a stewpan with a pint and a half of new milk, a little pepper and salt, one clove, a shallot, a bunch of thyme and parsley, and a piece of butter rolled in flour. Let the whole simmer slowly for one hour, then take them out, brush the palates over with the yolk of a beaten egg, dip them into bread-crumbs, and broil them lightly. Place them on a hot dish, and serve them with piquante or any sharp sauce.

Bullock's Heart Stewed.—American Receipt.

Time, according to size, from two to three hours to stew.

381. One heart; forcemeat of one egg; two ounces of bread-crumbs; one sprig of thyme; one sprig of parsley; a small piece of lemon peel; six ounces of butter; one tablespoonful of flour; one of fine pepper; one of salt; one cup of wine; three pints of hot water.

Soak the heart for two hours in warm water; take the strings from the inside, and fill it with the forcemeat, which is made of the bread-crumbs, the thyme and parsley finely chopped, two ounces of butter, the minced peel of the lemon, and the yolk of an egg to bind it together, seasoned with pepper and salt. Put the heart into a stewpan with three pints of hot water, cover it and let it stew slowly until it is tender; skim it clean; then if the water is not nearly boiled away, take out all *above* half a pint; add a quarter of a pound of butter cut in small pieces, one tablespoonful of flour, a teaspoonful of pepper, the same of salt. Cover the stewpan and set it over a moderate fire. When the lower side begins to brown, turn the other and brown it also. Take it up, add a glass of wine to the gravy, and let it boil up once; stir it smooth, and pour it over the heart through a fine sieve.

Instead of wine, tomato sauce may be used in the gravy, or you may squeeze the juice of half a lemon into the gravy, if you have neither wine nor sauce.

To Dress a Bullock's Heart.—English Fashion.

Time, two hours.

382. One heart; veal stuffing; half a pint of rich gravy.

Soak a bullock's heart for three hours in warm water; remove the lobes, and stuff the inside with veal forcemeat; sew it securely in; fasten some white paper over the heart, and roast it for two hours before a strong fire, keeping it basted *frequently*. Just before serving, remove the paper, baste, and froth it up, and serve with a rich gravy poured round it, and currant jelly separately.

Boiled Marrow Bones.—Served on a Napkin, or on Toast.

Time, two hours.

383. Saw the bones any size you may prefer. Cover the ends with a common paste of flour and water, tie a cloth over them, and place them in a small stewpan, with sufficient boiling water to cover them. When sufficiently boiled, serve them upright on a napkin; or when boiled, take out the marrow, and spread it on toasted bread cut into small square slices; season it with a little pepper and salt, and send it to table quickly.

Cow Heel.

Time, ten minutes.

384. Cow heel; yolk of egg; bread-crumbs; a sprig of parsley; Cayenne; pepper and salt; a piece of butter.

Having thoroughly washed, cleaned, and scalded it, cut the heel into pieces about two inches long and one inch wide; dip them into the yolk of a beaten egg; cover them with fine bread-crumbs mixed with chopped parsley, Cayenne, and a little pepper and salt; fry them in boiling butter, and arrange them neatly on a hot dish.

Beef Fritters.

Time, ten to twelve minutes.

385. Some cold roast beef; ten ounces of flour; two ounces of butter; a cupful of water; whites of two eggs.

Mix to a smooth batter ten ounces of flour with a teacupful of water; warm the butter and stir it into the flour, with the whites of two eggs whisked to a stiff froth. Shred the beef as thin and small as possible; season it to your taste, and add it to the batter. Mix all well together, and drop it into a pan of boiling lard or beef dripping. Fry the fritters on both sides a nice brown, and when done, drain them from the fat, and serve them on a folded napkin.

Ox-Tongue.

Time, one hour to warm; two hours and a half, if large, to simmer.

386. Choose a plump tongue with a smooth skin, which denotes the youth of the animal.

If it has been salted and dried, soak it before you boil it for twenty hours in plenty of water. If it is a green one fresh from the pickle, soak it only three or four hours. Put it into cold water, let it gradually *warm* for one hour; then let it slowly simmer for two hours and a half. Plunge it into cold water, in order to remove the furred skin. Bend it into a nice shape with a strong fork; then trim and glaze it if it is to be served as a cold tongue, and ornament the root with a frill of cut paper or vegetable flowers; when hot garnish with aspic jelly. If it is to be served hot, as an *entrée*, it must be wrapped in a greased paper and warmed again in hot water, after removing the coating; serve, when thus garnished, with macaroni or tomato sauce.

To Roast a Fresh Tongue.

Time, to boil, two hours and a half; to roast, half an hour.

387. The tongue; twenty-four cloves; a quarter of a pound of butter; about six ounces of bread-crumbs; two eggs.

Soak the tongue till it has thoroughly disgorged in lukewarm water, for about ten or twelve hours. Trim and scape it, stick it over with the cloves, and boil it slowly for two or (if large) three hours. Then take it up and brush it over with the yolks of the eggs, sprinkle it with bread-crumbs. Run a long iron skewer through it and roast it of a nice brown, basting it constantly with butter. Put it on a hot dish, and pour round it half a pint of good gravy, with a glass of wine. Serve it with red currant jelly.

To Boil Reindeer Tongues.

Time, two hours to simmer.

388. The proper way to prepare reindeer tongues for boiling, is to soak them in a pan of cold water for three hours, and then expose them to the air; this must be repeated three times. Then scrape them very clean, put them into a stewpan of cold water, and bring them gradually to a boil. Let them simmer slowly, skimming them carefully all the time. Serve them on a table-napkin.

Ox-check Cheese.—A Homely American Receipt.

Time, four hours.

389. Half an ox-head; one teaspoonful of fine salt; half a teaspoonful of pepper; one tablespoonful of powdered thyme; enough water to cover the head.

Split an ox-head in two, take out the eyes, crack the side bones, and lay it in water for one whole night. Then put it in a saucepan with sufficient water to cover it. Let it boil very gently, skimming it carefully. When the meat loosens from the bones take it from the water with a skimmer, and put it into a bowl. Take out every particle of bone, chop the meat very fine, and season it with a teaspoonful of salt, and half a teaspoonful of pepper; add a tablespoonful of powdered thyme. Tie it in a cloth and press it with a weight. When cold, it may be cut in slices for dinner or supper. The gravy remaining will make a rich broth if a few vegetables be stewed in it.

Pressed Beef.

Time, five hours.

390. Ten or eleven pounds of the flank; two pounds of salt; half a pound of moist sugar; a quarter of an ounce of saltpetre.

Take about ten or eleven pounds of the thin flank, and rub well into every part two pounds of salt, and half a pound of moist sugar mixed with the saltpetre dissolved, repeat the rubbing with the pickle every day for a week; and then roll it round and bind it with a wide piece of tape. Have ready a stewpan of scalding water, put in the beef, and when it simmers allow five hours for ten pounds of meat. When sufficiently done, drain off the water in which it was boiled, and pour cold spring water over it for six or eight minutes, drain it on a sieve reversed, and then place it on a board with a weight on it to press the meat well. Then remove the tapes, trim it neatly, and serve it when required.

Beef to Eat Cold.

Time, to pickle, twelve days; to stew, seven or eight hours; to press, twelve hours.

391. Six or seven pounds of the brisket of beef; one ounce of bay salt; half an ounce of sal prunella; two ounces of coarse brown sugar; half a teaspoonful of mixed spices.

Take six or seven pounds of the brisket of beef, put it into a small earthen pan, and rub it well with common salt for four days, turning and rubbing it every morning. Then salt it with the above ingredients, mixed and pounded; let it remain for eight days, rubbing and turning it daily, that it may imbibe the pickle. Before setting it on the fire to stew, strew over it and insert between the flaps half a teaspoonful of mixed spice. Put it in a cloth, and boil it gently for six or seven hours. Then take out the bone, wrap it tightly in a cloth, and put it between two boards with a heavy weight placed upon it for twelve hours. This beef, when cold, is very good for breakfast or luncheon.

Collared Beef.

Time, half an hour to the pound.

392. Six and a half or seven pounds of the thin end of the flank of beef; pickle made of one ounce of saltpetre; six of salt; a little coarse sugar (about two ounces); three ounces of powdered herbs.

Let the beef remain in this pickle for ten days, turning and rubbing it daily. Bone it and remove the skin, gristle, &c. Sprinkle it with powdered herbs, and season it highly with salt and pepper. Roll it up in the shape of a brawn, or fillet of veal, and bind it firmly with a broad tape; wrap a cloth round it, and boil it gently. When it is done, put it under a heavy weight (without loosening it from the bandage) and let it remain till cold.

Spiced Beef—Modes of Dressing Beefsteaks.

Spiced Beef.

Time, according to weight.

393. The thin part of the ribs of beef; half an ounce of cloves; half an ounce of mace; half an ounce of black pepper; half an ounce of Jamaica pepper; and some chopped parsley.

Take the thin part of a piece of beef, after the rib piece (called the flap) has been cut off, if any of the ends of the bones are left, take them out. Rub it well with salt, and let it lay in pickle two days; then take the above quantities of spice and a little chopped parsley, and spread the whole equally over the beef; roll it up neatly and tie it very tight. Set it in a stewpan over a moderate fire, and let it stew slowly till quite tender. Then press it well, and when cold it will be fit to serve. The spices are to be laid on whole.

Beef Liver for Gravy.

Time, twenty-four hours.

394. The liver must be first hung up to drain; after that salt it well and leave it twenty-four hours in a dish. Then hang it up to drain, and when it has ceased dripping hang it in a dry place for use. It is excellent for gravy to cutlets and all made dishes.

Broiled Steak.

Time, eight to ten minutes.

395. Rumpsteak; one ounce of butter; one tablespoonful of mushroom ketchup; pepper and salt.

Rumpsteak is best for broiling and frying; beefsteak for stewing.

Take care that the butcher cuts the steak the right thickness—*i.e.*, about three-quarters or half an inch. Divide it in halves. Place the gridiron over a clear fire, and rub the bars with suet to prevent the meat from adhering to them. Place the two steaks on it and broil them, turning them frequently with the steak tongs, or if with a fork, *carefully* pricking it through the fat. If the steak itself is pricked, the gravy will run out and it will harden. Have ready a hot dish on which you have placed a lump of butter the size of a large walnut, a tablespoonful of mushroom ketchup, and a little salt and pepper. Lay the steaks (rubbing them lightly over with butter) on the dish, and serve as quickly as possible.

An Indian Mode of Dressing Beefsteaks.

Time, twenty minutes.

396. One pint of water; one onion; one spoonful of walnut ketchup; pepper and salt; butter to fry the steak; a little flour and butter for thickening.

Fry a tender rumpsteak in butter to a good brown, then pour in the water on it, add the onion sliced, the ketchup and seasoning. Cover it closely with a dish, and let it stew gently. When tender, thicken the gravy with a piece of butter rolled in flour.

Rumpsteak Fried.

Time, twenty minutes.

397. Broiling is the best mode of cooking steaks and chops; if, however, you prefer a steak fried, do not cut it quite as thick as for broiling, and leave a little fat on it.

Put some clarified dripping in the pan and let it boil; Then lay the steak in the boiling fat and fry it, moving the pan about to prevent it from burning; when one side is well done, turn it on the other with your meat-tongs—if you do not possess a pair, turn it with a fork, but take care not to stick the fork into the juicy part of the stake, put it in the fat or in the edge of the meat. When the steak is done, lay it on a hot dish, with a little made gravy, or a lump of butter and a tablespoonful of ketchup. Season with pepper and salt. Tomato sauce is sometimes eaten with beefsteak.

Fried Onions and Rumpsteak.

Time, twenty minutes.

398. A rumpsteak; three onions; a good-sized piece of butter; and a little salt.

Fry a rumpsteak a nice brown, and put it into a hot dish with a good-sized piece of butter on the top; or pour the fat from the pan, put in a little water, shake it about, let it just boil, and pour it over the steak. Have ready the onions, cut into thin rings, and again divided across; fry them lightly, and when done drain them on a colander before the fire, stirring in a little salt. Serve them in a separate dish, as the flavour of onions is often disliked.

Steak Stewed in a Plain Way.

Time, forty minutes altogether.

399. Half a pint of water; one onion; a spoonful of walnut ketchup; a little caper liquor; a piece of butter rolled in flour; and some pepper and salt.

Fry the steaks in butter a good brown, then put in a stewpan half a pint of water, one onion sliced, a tablespoonful of walnut ketchup, a little caper liquor, pepper and salt. Cover the pan close, and let them stew slowly. Thicken the gravy with a piece of butter rolled in flour, and serve them on a hot dish.

Beefsteaks and Oysters Stewed.

Time, one hour and twenty minutes.

400. A pound and a half of beefsteaks; two ounces of butter; half a pint of water; a dozen and a half of oysters; five dessertspoonfuls of port wine; pepper and salt.

Put into a stewpan a pound and a half of beefsteak, with two ounces of butter and a little water; when the meat is a nice brown, pour in half a pint of water, a little pepper and salt, and the liquor strained from the oysters. Set the pan over a moderate fire, and let the meat stew gently; then add five dessertspoonfuls of port wine, a piece of butter rolled in flour, and the oysters. Stew it all together till the oysters are done, and serve it up very hot.

Broiled Steak with Oyster Sauce.

Time, half an hour.

401. A pound and a half of beefsteak; two dozen oysters; a little mace; peel of half a lemon; a little butter rolled in flour; pepper; salt; and a tablespoonful of cream.

Strain the liquor from the oysters, and throw them into cold water. Simmer the liquor with a little mace, and the peel of half a lemon; then put the oysters in. Stew them a few minutes; add a little cream if you have it, and a piece of butter rolled in flour. Let it boil up once; have a pound and a half of rumpsteak seasoned and broiled, put it in the dish, and pour the oyster sauce over it the moment it is ready to serve.

Fritters of Beef.

Time, eight minutes to fry.

402. Some slices from the under-cut of the sirloin; two or three eggs; a small teaspoonful of white pepper; the same of allspice in powder; a little nutmeg; and sufficient flour and water to make a stiff batter.

Cut some thin slices of beef from the under-cut of the sirloin, and dip each slice into a stiff batter, made of eggs, flour, water, and a seasoning of pepper, allspice, and nutmeg. Have ready a pan of boiling lard or butter, and when the slices are well covered with the batter, put them in and fry them a nice brown. Serve them very hot with mashed potatoes.

Bubble and Squeak.

Time, twenty minutes.

403. About one pound of slices of cold boiled beef; one pound of chopped potato; one pound of chopped-up cabbage—both previously boiled; pepper; salt; and a little butter.

Chop up and fry the cold potatoes and cabbage with a little pepper, salt, and a good large piece of butter. Set it aside to keep hot. Lightly fry some slices of cold boiled beef; put them in a hot dish, with alternate layers of vegetable, piling it higher in the middle.

Savoury Minced Collops.

Time, ten minutes.

404. A pound and a quarter of rumpsteak; a bunch of savoury herbs; a quarter of a teaspoonful of salt; a little pepper; two ounces of butter; a tablespoonful of flour; and a tablespoonful of ketchup, or lemon juice.

Put two ounces of butter and a tablespoonful of flour into a stewpan, and when it becomes of a light brown colour, add a tablespoonful of finely-chopped savoury herbs, and a little pepper and salt. Stir these over a slow fire until they are well browned; mince the steak very fine, and stir it into the herbs and browning; then add nearly half a pint of boiling water, and stew all together very slowly for ten or twelve minutes; then add the ketchup, and serve them very hot.

To Fry Beef Kidney.

Time, ten or twelve minutes.

405. One kidney; three ounces of butter; half a pint of gravy; one tablespoonful of piquante sauce; one lump of sugar.

Take a beef kidney, cut it into slices not too thick, and let them soak in warm water for two hours and a half, changing the water twice to thoroughly cleanse the kidney. Dredge a *very* little flour over these slices, and fry them a nice brown, in about three ounces of butter, seasoning them previously with pepper and salt. Arrange them in a circle, slightly leaning over each other round the dish. Stir a tablespoonful of piquante sauce into half a pint (or rather less) of good gravy, with one lump of sugar in it, and pour it into the *centre* of the dish.

Stewed Beef Kidney.

Time, half an hour.

406. A beef kidney; pepper and salt.

Cut the kidney into slices, and season it highly with pepper and salt, and fry it a light brown; then pour a little warm water into the pan, dredge in some flour, put in the slices of kidney, and let it stew very gently.

Rissoles of Beef Kidney.

Time, half an hour.

407. A beef kidney; a little salt; Cayenne

and nutmeg; a sprig of parsley; one shallot; juice of half a lemon; half a pint of gravy; a glass of white wine; one ounce of butter.

After removing all the fat and skin from the kidney, cut it into moderately thin slices, and sprinkle over it the shallot and parsley chopped very fine, and seasoned highly with salt, nutmeg, and a little Cayenne pepper. Fry the slices over a brisk fire until they are nicely browned on both sides; then mix a glass of white wine with about half a pint of good gravy, and pour it gradually into the pan; boil it up, and then stir in the lemon juice and an ounce of fresh butter. Serve it on a hot dish, garnished with fried bread cut into small square pieces.

Minced Beef.
Time, twenty minutes.

408. One pound and a half of beef; six ounces of bacon; two small onions; a little pepper and nutmeg; one ounce and a half of butter rolled in flour; a spoonful of browning; a few poached or hard-boiled eggs.

Mince about a pound and a half of beef with the bacon and onions, seasoning it highly with pepper and nutmeg. Take a sufficient quantity of stock made from bones, and any trimmings, a piece of butter rolled in flour, and a little browning; make it hot and strain it over the mince; put the whole into a stewpan, let it simmer for a few minutes, and serve it on a hot dish with sippets of toasted bread, and a poached or hard-boiled egg divided and placed on each sippet arranged round the edge of the dish.

It is also served surrounded by a wall of mashed potatoes, with two poached eggs lying on the top of it.

Hashed Beef—Plain.
Time, twenty-five minutes.

409. Some slices of cold roast beef; two tablespoonfuls of Worcestershire sauce; one of mushroom ketchup; and the gravy from the meat or from the bones boiled down; pepper and salt.

Put the gravy saved from the meat (with a little water if not sufficient), or the bones of the cold joint boiled down to a gravy, into a stewpan with two tablespoonfuls of Worcestershire sauce, one of mushroom ketchup, some pepper, salt, and a little butter rolled in flour to thicken it; let it simmer gently for about a quarter of an hour, take it from the fire, and when cold remove the fat. Cut the meat into slices, dredge them with flour, and lay them in the stewpan with the gravy, let it simmer slowly for ten minutes until hot, taking care it does not boil, or the meat will be hard. Garnish it with sippets of toasted bread.

Beef Hash—Rich.
Time, half an hour.

410. Some slices of cold beef; half a pint of stock or broth; pepper and salt; two dessertspoonfuls of lemon pickle; one of mushroom ketchup; four of port wine or claret; two ounces of butter; a quarter of a pint of silver or button onions.

Peel a quarter of a pint of silver or button onions, dredge them well with flour, and fry them in two ounces of butter a fine brown, seasoning them with pepper and salt. Then put them into a stewpan and pour over them the butter in which they were fried, half a pint of stock or broth, the lemon pickle, mushroom ketchup, and wine; set it over a clear fire until the onions are sufficiently done, and then pour it over the slices of beef, and let it stand for half an hour; then put it at the side of the fire until very hot, but do not allow it to boil, or it will harden the meat. Serve it up with the gravy poured over it, and garnished with fried croûtons.

Cold Beef Stewed with Green Peas.
Time, two hours and three-quarters.

411. One gallon and a half of green peas; one cabbage-lettuce; one teaspoonful of mustard; two tablespoonfuls of Worcestershire sauce; rather more than half a pint of stock or weak broth; one small onion; pepper and salt; cold roast beef.

Cut the heart of a cabbage-lettuce into slices, and put it into a stewpan with the green peas and stock; let it simmer slowly for an hour and a quarter; then add some slices of cold roast beef, seasoned highly with pepper and salt, and a small onion sliced and lightly browned, place it again over the fire and let it simmer for an hour and a half. Stir in a piece of butter rolled in flour, the spoonful of mustard, and the sauce. Boil it up and serve it.

Tripe.
Time, two hours and a half to three hours.

412. Two pounds of tripe; equal parts of milk and water; four large onions.

Take two pounds of fresh tripe, cleaned and dressed by the tripe-dresser, cut away the coarsest fat, and boil it in equal parts of milk and water. Boil in the same water which boils the tripe four large onions; the onions should be put on the fire at least half an hour before the tripe is put into the stewpan, and then made into a rich onion sauce, which serve with the tripe.

Tripe may also be cleaned, dried, cut into pieces, fried in batter, and served with melted butter.

Tripe Roasted.

Time, two hours and a half.

413. Some pieces of tripe; some forcemeat; a little flour; some butter.

Cut the tripe into good-sized pieces, and spread some forcemeat over them, roll them up securely, and tie them upon a small spit, or roast them in a cradle spit; flour and baste them with butter, and serve them up garnished with lemon in slices, and melted butter.

A Pickle for Beef, &c.

414. Six ounces of bay-salt; three ounces of saltpetre; four pounds of brown sugar; one pound of common salt; one teaspoonful of black pepper.

Mix all the above ingredients together and rub them over the beef, pork, or hams; rub and turn them every day.

To Pickle Tongues.

Time, fourteen days.

415. Two ounces of saltpetre; one pound of salt; half a pound of coarse sugar.

Procure two fine tongues and wipe them very dry, then rub into them the above proportions of salt, saltpetre and coarse sugar, and let them remain in the pan for a fortnight, turning them every morning.

Or:—

Time, three weeks to smoke; ten to fourteen days to pickle.

416. A teaspoonful of pepper; a quarter of a pound of coarse sugar; two ounces and a half of juniper berries; one ounce of saltpetre; seven ounces of common salt.

Procure a fine large tongue, from seven to eight pounds weight, and rub well into it the common salt, saltpetre, juniper berries, sugar, and pepper, all pounded and well mixed together. Let it remain for ten days or a fortnight, turning it every day, then drain it dry, tie a paper over it, and send it to smoke for three weeks; or it may be boiled from the pickle without being smoked, in which case it should be placed to soak in cold water for a few hours; then put into a stewpan well covered with water and boiled slowly for four hours, or more if large, if small, three hours and a half, skimming it well when it comes to the boil, and letting it simmer gently till tender.

MUTTON.

Mutton is in season all the year, but is not quite so tender and eatable during the early summer when lamb is in season.

Roast Haunch of Mutton.

Time, a quarter of an hour to each pound of meat.

417. Take a fine haunch of Southdown, Welsh, or Devonshire mutton, hang it up for ten days or a fortnight, trim off the skin which covers the fat, remove the shank bone, and cover it with two or three sheets of buttered paper, place it on a spit, or in a cradle spit; set it at about fifteen inches from the fire, and roast it for two hours very slowly to warm it through, basting it with dripping every five minutes. Draw it gradually nearer and nearer to the fire to brown, but take care it does not burn. Sprinkle it with a little fine salt, dredge it over with flour and baste with a little butter, which will give it a fine frothy appearance. Put a glass of port wine into some good brown gravy, and pour over it. Serve it with red currant jelly sauce.

Saddle of Mutton.

Time, a quarter of an hour to a pound.

418. Take off the skin, cover the fat with a sheet of well-greased paper, and roast it as directed for a haunch; just before it is finished cooking remove the paper, sprinkle the joint with salt, dredge it well over with flour, and drop warmed butter over it. Serve it with good gravy, or empty the contents of the dripping-pan into a basin, from which remove the fat, add a little warm water and use this natural gravy. Red currant jelly as sauce.

Leg of Mutton Roasted.

Time, half an hour to the pound, slow method; a quarter of an hour or twenty minutes, ordinary time.

419. A leg of mutton intended for roasting can be kept much longer than for boiling, but it must be wiped very dry, and dusted with flour and pepper.

Cut off the knuckle, remove the thick skin, and trim off the piece of flank. Put a little salt and water into the dripping-pan, and baste the joint for a short time with it, then use the gravy from the meat itself, basting it every ten minutes. Serve it with gravy poured round it, and currant jelly, separately.

The wether leg of mutton is the best for roasting.

A leg of mutton, if too large, can be divided, and the knuckle boiled; and by placing a paste of flour and water over the part cut to keep in the gravy, it can be roasted, by which means two dinners can be had from the one joint.

Roast Shoulder of Mutton.

Time, a quarter of an hour to each pound.

420. A shoulder of mutton should not be basted in roasting, but simply rubbed with a little butter.

Put the spit in close to the shank bone, and run it along the blade bone. Roast this joint at a sharp, brisk fire. It should be well hung; and served with onion sauce.

Roast Loin of Mutton.

Time, a quarter of an hour to the pound.

421. This joint is not economical on account of the weight of fat attached to it; but it is very useful in small families, as it is a joint that can be cut so as not to leave too much cold meat. London butchers generally remove the fat, ready for dressing. Roast it at a bright fire, and baste carefully about every quarter of an hour. Brown and froth it as before directed, for leg, &c.

To Roll a Loin of Mutton.

Time, a quarter of an hour to each pound.

422. A loin of mutton; veal stuffing; a glass of port wine; and a tablespoonful of ketchup.

Hang a loin of mutton till tender, take out the bone, and lay over the meat a stuffing made as for veal; roll it up tightly, fasten it with small skewers to keep it in shape, and tie it round with a string. Roast it before a brisk fire, allowing a quarter of an hour, or twenty minutes, for each pound of meat. Make a gravy of the bones, adding to it a glass of port wine, a tablespoonful of ketchup and a little salt. When the meat is done, pour the gravy made from the bones, mixed with the gravy from the meat, over it, and serve with currant jelly, *separately*.

A Mode of Dressing Fillet of Mutton.

Time, two hours.

423. Take off the chump end of a loin of mutton, and cover it with two sheets of buttered paper as for venison; roast it for two hours, but do not allow it to become the least brown. Have ready some French beans, boiled tender, and well drained from the water on a sieve; while the mutton is being glazed, warm them up in the gravy, put them on a dish, and serve the meat on them.

To Roast a Neck of Mutton.

Time, one hour.

424. Take four pounds of the middle or the best end of a neck of mutton, trim off part of the fat, cut the bones short, and see that it is *thoroughly* jointed. Place it at some distance from a nice brisk fire, dredge it with flour, and baste it frequently. Just before it is done, set it nearer to the fire, and dust a little salt over it. Pour off the dripping, and put a little boiling water into the pan. Dish up the joint, and strain the gravy over it. Serve it with currant jelly, separately.

Mutton Kebbobed.

Time, according to the weight.

425. Loin of mutton; a *small* nutmeg, pepper, and salt; some bread crumbs; a bunch of sweet herbs; yolks of three eggs; half a pint of gravy; two spoonfuls of ketchup; a teaspoonful of flour; two ounces of butter.

Take all the fat out of a loin of mutton, and off the outside also if too fat, and remove the skin. Joint it at every bone. Mix half a *small* nutmeg grated with a little pepper and salt, bread-crumbs, and minced herbs. Dip the steaks into the yolks of three eggs, and sprinkle the above mixture all over them. Then place the steaks together as they were before they were cut asunder, tie them, and fasten them on a small spit. Roast them at a quick fire, set a dish under, and baste them with a good piece of butter and the liquor that comes from the meat; and throw some more of the seasoning over. When done enough, take it up, and lay it in a dish; have half a pint of good gravy ready besides that in the dish, and put into it two spoonfuls of ketchup, and rub down a teaspoonful of flour with it. Let this boil, and pour it over the mutton, but first skim off the fat well. Mind to keep the meat hot till the gravy is quite ready.

Boiled Leg of Mutton.

Time, quarter of an hour to the pound.

426. Cut off the shank bone, trim the knuckle, and wash and wipe it very clean. Then put it into a saucepan with enough cold water for it to swim in, set it over a

good fire. As the scum rises, skim it off carefully. Boil the joint for two hours and a half, or according to its weight. When the joint is taken up, put a frill of cut paper round the shank bone. Mash some turnips with a little piece of butter and cream, and form them into the shape of eggs, and garnish the edge of the dish alternately with the turnip balls and with carrots cut into circular forms. Serve caper sauce in a tureen.

To Boil a Shoulder of Mutton with Oysters.

Time, two days *to salt*; twenty minutes to each pound of meat to stew.

427. Shoulder of mutton; one teaspoonful of pepper; one blade of mace pounded; twenty-four oysters; one onion; six peppercorns; one pint of gravy; a small piece of butter; one teaspoonful of flour.

Hang the mutton till it is tender, salt it well for two days, bone it and sprinkle it with the pepper and mace. Lay eighteen oysters over the inside of the joint, roll it up tightly, and tie it strongly together.

Put it in a stewpan with just enough water to cover it, with an onion and a few pepper corns. Shut the cover very closely over it. Stew the remaining oysters in a pint of good gravy, which should be thickened with a little flour and butter.

Take up the meat when it is done, remove the tape, and pour the gravy over the meat.

Boiled Neck of Mutton.

Time, three quarters of an hour to every two pounds.

428. Take about four pounds of the best end or middle of a neck of mutton, see that it is thoroughly jointed, and put it into a stewpan with sufficient cold water to cover it. When it boils, skim it carefully, and throw in a very little salt. Then draw the stewpan to the side, and let it simmer gently until the meat is well done, allowing about an hour and a half for every four pounds, from the time it begins to simmer. When served, pour a little caper sauce over it, and garnish with boiled turnips.

Boiled Breast of Mutton and Caper Sauce.

Time, about two hours.

429. Breast of mutton; three dessertspoonfuls of savoury herbs; a sprig of parsley; four tablespoonfuls of bread-crumbs; pepper and salt.

Trim off the greater part of the fat, bone the joint. Mince some savoury herbs, and two sprigs of parsley, mix them with the bread-crumbs, and a seasoning of pepper and salt to taste. Put a layer over the boned meat, roll it round, and tie it securely. Boil it *very* slowly for nearly two hours, remove the string, and pour over it a little well-made caper sauce, the remainder of which must be served separately.

BAKING

Is not a good or economical way of cooking joints of mutton, but it is sometimes done on account of its convenience.

A joint to be baked is put on a trivet or stand in a baking dish, sometimes with potatoes under it, which are so savoury thus dressed that they partly reconcile us to the sodden taste of meat dressed in a common oven. A shoulder of mutton is, we believe, the only one thus dressed. To do it nicely, cover it with two sheets of buttered paper—or they may be greased with dripping—to keep it from being dried up. Put potatoes under it with a little water or gravy over them, and a little salt. The meat should be occasionally basted while baking.

Breast of Mutton Grilled.

Time, one hour and a half.

430. A breast of mutton; yolk of one egg; some bread-crumbs; a bunch of sweet herbs; a sprig of parsley; one onion; four pickled cucumbers; a tablespoonful of capers; half a pint of gravy; a piece of butter rolled in flour.

Half boil a breast of mutton, score it, and season it with pepper and salt, rub it over with the yolk of an egg, and sprinkle it with bread-crumbs and sweet herbs chopped fine. Put it over a clear fire, and broil it gently till it is of a fine brown colour, or set it before the fire in a Dutch oven and do the same; chop a sprig of parsley, an onion, four pickled cucumbers, and a spoonful of capers, boil them five minutes in half a pint of gravy, thicken it with a piece of butter rolled in flour, lay the mutton on a hot dish and pour the sauce over it.

Stewed Loin of Mutton.

Time, two hours and three-quarters.

431. A loin of mutton; one ounce and a half of butter; one shallot; a bunch of sweet herbs; four dessertspoonfuls of the best vinegar; rather more than a pint of water; and a glass and a half of port wine.

Cut out the bone, take off the skin carefully, and roll the mutton, securing it with skewers. Put it into a stewpan with a bunch of sweet herbs, one shallot cut in two, an ounce and a half of butter, four dessertspoonfuls of vinegar, and rather more than a pint of water; stew it slowly for nearly three hours, strain the gravy through a hair sieve, add a glass and a half of port wine, and pour it over the meat. Serve it with sweet sauce.

To Stew a Neck of Mutton.

Time, two and a half to three hours.

432. Four or five pounds of neck of mutton; rather more than a pint of water; a little Cayenne; pepper and salt; two sprigs of parsley.

Trim the fat from a neck of mutton, and put the latter into a stewpan with a little pepper and salt, and rather more than a pint of water; let it simmer very gently. About twenty minutes before it is served, take nearly all the broth from the meat, and when it is cold skim off the fat, add a little Cayenne pepper, and two sprigs of chopped parsley to the broth, let it boil for twenty minutes, thicken the gravy with a little butter rolled in flour, and pour it over the meat when sent to table.

The exact quantities of water and seasoning must be regulated by the size of the joint, as some necks of mutton weigh six or seven pounds, in which case an extra half hour must be allowed for it to simmer.

Breast of Mutton and Green Peas.

Time, two hours and a half.

433. A breast of mutton; one quart of green peas; a bunch of sweet herbs; pepper and salt to taste; one shallot or onion.

Select a breast of mutton not too fat, and cut it into small square pieces; dredge it with flour, and fry it a fine brown in butter; then add the herbs and shallot or onion cut into thin slices; *just* cover the whole with water, and set it over a slow fire to stew until the meat is perfectly tender. Take out the meat, skim off all the fat from the gravy, and strain it over the meat into the stewpan, and make the whole very hot. Just before serving add a quart of young green peas, previously boiled, or add them with the strained gravy, and let the whole boil gently until the peas are done.

Mutton Cutlets with Tomato Sauce.

Time, twelve minutes.

434. Some cutlets from the neck of mutton; two ounces of butter; a little pepper and salt.

Trim the neck of mutton before you cut off the cutlets (*i. e.*, cut off from the joint the scrag and three inches of the rib bone); then take off the cutlets, shape them by chopping off the thick part of the chine-bone, beat them flat to about a quarter of an inch in thickness with a chopper, cut off an inch of fat from the top of the rib bone. Season them with pepper and salt. Beat up the yolk of an egg, dip a brush in it and pass it lightly over the cutlet, and then dip it in bread-crumbs. Melt two ounces of butter in an omelet-pan and put the cutlets in it; set it over a gentle clear fire for five minutes, turn them, do them for five minutes longer, lay them on a clean cloth, then put them in a dish in a circle, one leaning over the other, with purée of good tomato sauce in the centre.

Mutton Cutlets.

Time, to stew, seven minutes; to broil, ten minutes.

435. One pound and a half of chops from the loin; a sprig of thyme and parsley; yolk of one or two eggs; bread-crumbs; salt and Cayenne pepper to taste; two ounces of butter; juice of a small lemon.

Cut about a pound and a half of cutlets from a loin of mutton, take off about an inch from the top of each bone, and from the thickest end; melt two ounces of butter in a stewpan, season the cutlets, put them in, and let them stew for a short time without allowing them to gain any colour. Mince a little thyme and parsley fine, and bind it with the yolk of one or two eggs. When the cutlets are nearly cold spread the minced herbs over them, and sprinkle each cutlet thickly with grated bread, and a very little Cayenne pepper. Put them carefully on a gridiron over a clear brisk fire, and broil them a fine brown. Serve them on a hot dish, and squeeze over them the juice of a small lemon.

Or—With Purée of Potatoes.

436. Some mutton cutlets; a little butter; one egg; some bread-crumbs; half a gill of cream; a large piece of butter; pepper and salt; a little grated nutmeg; seven potatoes.

Cut and trim neatly some cutlets from the best end of a loin, or neck of mutton, dip each into some clarified or warm butter, then into the yolk of a well-beaten egg, and strew bread-crumbs thickly over them, smooth them with a knife, and fry them in boiling fat. Have ready seven boiled potatoes, rub them through a wire sieve; mix them with half a gill of cream and about two ounces of butter, a little pepper, salt, and nutmeg, with a piece of glaze the size of a walnut. Stir the purée over the fire until quite hot, place it in the centre of the dish, and stand the cutlets up round it, trimming each bone round the top with a frill of cut paper, either white, or white and pink, alternately.

Mutton Cutlets à la Maintenon.

Time, fifteen minutes.

437. Some cutlets from the neck or loin; a bunch of thyme and parsley; some bread-crumbs; pepper and salt.

Cut about a pound and a half of the neck or loin of mutton into delicate cutlets, and chop each bone short; trim them neatly, and put them into a stewpan with a piece of butter, and a little thyme and parsley chopped fine; season with pepper and salt; fry them lightly and then take them out to cool, after which take some fresh chopped parsley and some bread-crumbs; spread them evenly over the cutlets with a knife, wrap them in buttered papers, and broil them over a clear fire. Serve them up in the papers with sauce piquante in a tureen.

These cutlets are said to have been invented by Madame de Maintenon in order to tempt the waning appetite of Louis XIV. The fat of the dressed meat is absorbed in the papillotes.

Mutton Chops Broiled.

Time, ten minutes.

438. Cut some chops from the best end of the loin or neck, but the loin is preferable, trim them neatly, removing the skin and fat, leaving only enough of the latter to make them palatable; let the fire be very clear before placing the chops on the gridiron, turn them frequently, taking care that the fork is not put into the lean part of the chops; season them with pepper and salt. When just finished cooking, put a piece of fresh butter over each chop, and send them to table on a hot dish, or you may rub maître-d'hôtel butter over each chop when broiled; or serve with any sauce you like over them. In that case the chops become an *entrée*.

To Stew Mutton Chops.

Time, three-quarters of an hour.

439. One pound of chops; cold water enough to cover them, and half a pint over; one onion.

Put a pound of chops into a stewpan, with enough cold water to cover them, and half a pint over, and an onion; when the water is coming to a boil, skim it, cover the pan close, and set it to simmer gently over a very slow fire till the chops are tender; *if they* have been kept a *proper time*, they will take about three-quarters of an hour. Send up turnips, which may be boiled along with the chops, in a deep dish, with the broth they were stewed in.

Haricot of Mutton.

Time, nearly one hour.

440. Two pounds of loin of mutton; two onions; half a pint of gravy; one glass of port wine; two dessertspoonfuls of mushroom ketchup; two turnips, two carrots; half a head of celery; a large piece of butter; a little flour; pepper and salt.

Divide the chops of a loin of mutton, and take off the superfluous fat, cut two onions into rings, and fry them with the meat a nice brown in a good-sized piece of butter; thicken a half-pint of gravy with a little flour, and pour it over the chops. Set them at the side of the fire to stew slowly for three-quarters of an hour, or rather more. Parboil two carrots, two turnips, and half a head of celery, cut the former into shapes and the celery into slices, and add them to the meat about twenty minutes before serving. Pour in a glass of port wine, two spoonfuls of ketchup, and, after boiling it once up, serve it hot.

Minced Mutton.

Time, half an hour.

441. One pound and a half of meat; half a pint of good brown gravy; pepper and salt; six or seven eggs.

Take a pound and a half of dressed mutton, and mince it as fine as possible, season it highly with pepper and salt, warm half a pint of good brown gravy, or gravy made from the bones, make the mince very hot in it, and send it to table with a border of poached eggs.

Irish Stew.

Time, about two hours.

442. Two pounds and a half of chops; eight potatoes; four small onions; nearly a quart of water.

Take about two pounds and a half of chops from a loin of mutton, place them in a stewpan with alternate layers of sliced potatoes and layers of chops, add four small onions, and pour in nearly a quart of cold water; cover the stewpan closely, and let it stew gently until the potatoes are ready to mash, and the greater part of the gravy is absorbed; then place it in a dish, and serve it up very hot.

Hashed Mutton.

Time, one hour and twenty minutes.

443. Some cold mutton; one pint and a half of water; fourteen pepper corns; four allspice; a bunch of savoury herbs; half a head of celery; a large piece of butter; a spoonful of browning.

Take some cold leg or shoulder of mutton, or any cold mutton that you chance to have, and with a sharp knife cut it into thin slices. Put the bones into a stewpan with half a head of celery cut into slices, a bunch of savoury herbs, a few pepper corns, four allspice, and a pint and a half of water; set it over the fire, and let it simmer gently for about an hour. Cut the onion into rings, fry them a nice brown, and put them into the stewpan with the bones and herbs. Let all simmer together for ten or twelve minutes, then strain it through a hair sieve, and when cold take off the fat. Put the slices of meat dredged with flour into the stewpan, add the gravy with a spoonful of browning, and two of walnut ketchup; make it very hot, but do not let it boil. Serve it with sippets of toasted bread round the dish.

Haggis.

Time, two hours.

444. The heart, tongue, and part of the liver of a sheep; rather more than half the weight in bacon, one French roll; rind of a lemon; two eggs; a glass of wine; two anchovies; pepper and salt.

Mince the heart, tongue, and part of the liver of a sheep with rather more than half the weight in fat bacon, add to it the crumb of a French roll, grated, two anchovies chopped very fine, the rind of a lemon, grated, a little pepper and salt, a glass of wine, and two eggs well beaten; stir it thoroughly together, put it into a well-buttered mould, boil it for two hours, place it on a dish, and serve.

Sheep's Head.

Time, two hours.

445. One head; two onions; two carrots; two turnips; a piece of celery; five cloves; a sprig or two of thyme; one bay-leaf; two tablespoonfuls of salt; a quarter of an ounce of pepper; three quarts of water.

Put the head into a gallon of water, and let it soak for two hours or more; wash it thoroughly, saw it in two from the top. Take out the brain, cut away part of the uncovered part of the skull and the ends of the jaws; wash it well. Put in a stewpan two onions, two carrots, a stick of celery, or a little celery-seed tied up in muslin, five cloves, a bouquet of thyme with a bay-leaf, one ounce of salt, a quarter of an ounce of pepper, and three quarts of water. Let it simmer very gently. Take out the vegetables and bunch of herbs. Skim off the fat. Lay the head on a dish. Have the brain ready boiled (it will take ten minutes to do), chop it up fine. Warm it in parsley and butter, put it under the head and serve.

Sheep's Trotters—Very Simple.

Time, three hours.

446. Four trotters; one tablespoonful of flour; a saltspoonful of salt.

Perfectly cleanse and blanch the trotters, taking care to remove the little tuft of hair which is found in the fourche of the foot. Beat up a spoonful of flour and a little salt in the water you use for cooking them in, and let them stew till the bones come out easily.

Or—

You may stew them in white sauce for five or six hours.

Or—

They may be stewed for the same time with white sauce, and served garnished with mushrooms.

Mutton Ham.

Time, twenty-six days to dry, salt, and smoke.

447. A leg of mutton weighing twelve or fourteen pounds; half a pound of bay salt; ten ounces of common salt; one ounce and a half of saltpetre; half a pound of coarse sugar.

Cut the leg of mutton into the form of a ham, and let it hang two days.

Make a powder of half a pound of bay salt, half a pound of common salt, one ounce and a half or two ounces of saltpetre, and half a pound of coarse brown sugar. Mix it well together in a stewpan to make it quite hot, then rub it thoroughly into the ham. Turn it in the pickle every morning for four days, then put two ounces more of common salt to it. Turn it every day for twelve days more; then take it out, dry it, and hang it in wood smoke for a week.

Or—

Time, fourteen days to pickle.

448. One ounce of saltpetre; one pound of common salt; one pound of coarse sugar.

Cut a hind-quarter of mutton like a ham, and rub it well with an ounce of saltpetre, a

120 *Lamb—Roast Fore-Quarter—Roast Leg—Roast Loin.*

pound of coarse sugar, and the same of common salt well mixed together. Lay it in a ham-pan with the skin downwards, and baste it every day for a fortnight, then roll it in sawdust, and hang it in wood smoke for fourteen days. Boil it, and hang it in a dry place, cut it out in slices, and broil them as required. Or boil the ham in cold water over a quick fire for twenty minutes. When done, let it remain in the water until quite cold.

LAMB.

House lamb is in season in December. Grass lamb comes in at Easter. Lamb should be *very* well dressed. It is *best* when only two months old. The fore-quarter should be dressed very fresh; the hind-quarter should hang.

Roast Fore-Quarter of Lamb.

Time, for ten pounds, two hours and a half.

449. Cut off the scrag from the shoulder, saw off the shank bone, and also the chine bone along the fillet of the leg, and joint it thoroughly; partially saw the rib bones, and break the bone of the shoulder, twist it round, and fasten it with a skewer from beneath the breast. Cover the lamb with buttered paper, and spit it evenly, roast it before a quick fire according to the weight. Just before removing it from the spit, dredge it with flour and a little salt, and baste it with butter to make it froth up. Twist a cut paper round the shank bone, place it on a hot dish, and pour round it a little gravy made in the dripping-pan. Serve it with mint sauce in a tureen. A cut lemon, some Cayenne, and a piece of fresh butter should always be ready for use when the shoulder is separated from the ribs, to be laid between it and them.

Boned Quarter of Lamb.

Time, a quarter of an hour to each pound.

450. One pound of forcemeat; melted butter.

Bone a quarter of lamb, fill it with force-meat, roll it round, and tie it with a piece of string, cover it with a buttered paper, and roast it. Serve it with melted butter.

Roast Target of Lamb.

Time, one hour and a quarter, or according to weight.

451. A little butter, flour, and salt.

A target is only the breast and neck joints not separated. The flap bones must be taken from the neck, the chine bone sawed off, and the ribs well chopped. Cover it with buttered paper, place it in an even position on the spit, and roast it before a bright fire for an hour and a quarter. Just before it is taken up, dredge it with a little salt and flour, and baste it well with butter to make it look brown, and froth it up. Then dish it up, and place the gravy made in the dripping-pan round it. Serve it with mint sauce in a tureen.

Roast Leg of Lamb.

Time, one hour and three-quarters for six pounds.

452. Procure a fine fresh leg of lamb, and place it some distance from the fire, basting it frequently a short time before it is done, move it nearer, dredge it with flour and a little salt, and baste it with dissolved butter, to give it a nice frothy appearance. Then empty the dripping-pan of its contents, pour in a cupful of *hot* water, stir it well round, and pour the gravy over the meat, through a fine sieve. Serve with mint sauce and a salad.

Roast Shoulder of Lamb.

Time, one hour and a quarter.

453. Place the joint at a moderate distance from a nice clear fire, and keep it constantly basted, to prevent the skin from becoming burnt. When done, dish it up; and serve it with gravy made in the dripping-pan and poured round it. Send up mint sauce in a tureen.

Roast Loin of Lamb.

Time, a quarter of an hour to each pound.

454. The loin is seldom roasted, on account of its small weight, but for families of two ladies or a single person it will be found very delicate. Care must be taken that it does not burn in roasting. It is best to cover it with a buttered paper and remove it a few minutes before serving, to baste and froth it. Mint sauce.

Saddle of Lamb.

Time, a quarter of an hour to the pound; one hour and a half to two hours.

455. Cover the joint with buttered paper

to prevent the fat catching, and roast it at a brisk fire; constantly basting it at first with a *very* little butter, then with its own dripping. Sauce: brown cucumber.

To Broil a Breast of Lamb—American Receipt.

Time, according to weight.

456. Two ounces of butter; one teaspoonful of salt; half a teaspoonful of pepper.

Make a clear bright fire. When the gridiron is hot, rub it over with a little suet. Lay the meat on it with the inside to the fire first, let it broil gently. When it is nearly cooked through, turn it to the other side. Let it brown nicely. Put about two ounces of butter on a hot dish, work into it a teaspoonful of salt, and half the quantity of pepper, lay it on the meat, turn it once or twice and serve hot.

The shoulder may be broiled in the same manner. The fire must not be scorching hot. Mint sauce in a tureen.

Breast of Lamb à la Milanaise.

Time, two hours.

457. Breast of lamb; two ounces of macaroni; one lemon; half a pint of stock; one onion.

Place a layer of thin slices of bacon in a braising-pan, lay the joint of lamb on them, peel a lemon, cut it in slices, and lay them on the breast; cover it with a few more slices of bacon, add one onion and half a pint of stock, put it on a hot hearth with hot charcoal on the lid of the braising-pan, and let it simmer very slowly. Glaze it when it is done, have ready some dressed macaroni, lay it on the dish, put the breast of lamb on it, and pour over it a rich gravy.

Lamb Stewed with Peas.

Time, one hour.

458. The scrag, or breast of lamb; one quart of green peas; salt; quarter of a pound of butter; a dessertspoonful of flour; one blade of mace; and a little pepper.

Cut the scrag or breast of lamb into pieces, and put it in a stewpan with water enough to cover it; cover the pan close and let it simmer or stew for fifteen or twenty minutes; take off the scum, then add the salt and a quart of shelled green peas; cover the stewpan and let them stew for half an hour; work a small spoonful of flour into a quarter of a pound of butter, and stir it into the stew, add the pepper and blade of mace, let it simmer for ten minutes, and serve.

To Prepare the Brains of a Lamb's Head for Serving under it.

Time, ten minutes.

459. One cupful of vinegar; half a pint of water; one tablespoonful of chopped parsley; salt; and half a lemon.

Boil the brains for ten minutes in a little vinegar and water, with a little salt; cut them into mince, add to them the yolk of an egg, mix them with a little milk, two dessertspoonfuls of chopped parsley, and the juice of half a lemon.

The liver may be blanched and minced up in the same manner if it is liked.

Pluck may be prepared by first scalding it, then letting it get cold, and stewing it in gravy seasoned with an onion, sweet herbs, pepper, salt, and a little nutmeg.

Lamb's Head and Pluck.

Time, one hour and a quarter to boil.

460. A lamb's head; egg; bread-crumbs; a bunch of sweet herbs; a little stock; a piece of lemon peel; pepper, salt, and nutmeg.

Soak the head in water for two hours, then boil it until nearly done, take it out, and brush it over with the yolk of a well-beaten egg, cover it thickly with bread-crumbs; again add the egg, and repeat the bread-crumbs, season it with pepper and salt, and put it into a moderate oven till sufficiently brown. In the meantime, after scalding the pluck and setting it to cool, mince it up fine, mix in the brains and season them with pepper, salt, and grated nutmeg; put them into a stewpan with a piece of lemon peel cut thin, a bunch of sweet herbs minced up, and a little stock. When done, add the yolk of an egg beaten up with a tablespoonful of cream, put the mince into the dish, and serve the lamb's head on it.

Lamb's Head, Liver, and Heart.

Time, one hour and a half.

461. A lamb's head; one lamb's liver; one lamb's heart; yolks of two eggs; a bunch of sweet herbs; bread-crumbs; one ounce of butter; three-quarters of a pint of gravy; one spoonful of lemon pickle, or the juice of a lemon; seasoning.

Thoroughly clean a lamb's head, and parboil it, then brush it over with the yolks of the eggs well beaten; chop a few sweet herbs very fine, mix them with bread-crumbs and a little warmed butter, and spread the mixture thickly over the head, then put it into a Dutch oven before a bright and clear fire to finish dressing. Mince the liver and the heart very small, and let them stew until done, pour in three-quarters of a pint of good gravy, with a spoonful of lemon pickle, or the juice of a lemon, make the brains into small cakes with a little milk and seasoning, and fry them brown. Place the head in the centre of the dish on the minced liver and heart, and garnish with brain cakes, forcemeat balls, and a lemon cut into slices and placed at the edge of the dish.

Lamb's Fry.

Time, altogether twenty minutes.

462. One pound of lamb's fry; one egg; one ounce of bread-crumbs; a sprig of parsley; pepper and salt.

Take a pound of lamb's fry, and boil it for about a quarter of an hour; then drain it dry. Brush it over with the yolk of a beaten egg, and then cover it with bread-crumbs, seasoned with minced parsley, pepper, and salt. Fry it till it is a nice colour—*i.e.*, for about five minutes—and serve it on a folded napkin with fried parsley.

Cold lamb is so excellent that it is often preferred to hot-dressed joints. It is quite a mistake to prepare it by any of the modes of dressing up cold meat. It should be eaten with mint sauce and a nicely-made salad.

Lamb Cutlets and Green Peas.

Time, eight or ten minutes.

463. Two, or two and a half pounds of the best end of a neck of lamb; bread-crumbs; two eggs; pepper and salt; two ounces of butter; half a peck of green peas.

Take the cutlets from the best end of the neck; chop off the thick part of the chine bone, and trim the cutlets neatly by taking off the skin and the greater part of the fat, scraping the upper part of the bones perfectly clean. Brush each cutlet over with well-beaten yolk of egg, and then sprinkle them with fine bread-crumbs, seasoned with pepper and salt. After this dip them separately into a little clarified butter. Sprinkle more crumbs over them and fry them, turning them occasionally. Have ready half a peck of green peas, nicely boiled, and arranged in a pyramid or raised form in the centre of a hot dish. Lay the cutlets before the fire to drain, and then place them round the green peas.

Lamb Cutlets à la Royal.

Time, ten or twelve minutes.

464. A loin of lamb; pepper; salt; nutmeg; one egg; one ounce of bread-crumbs; a sprig of parsley; a dessertspoonful of flour; a cupful of boiling water; one lemon; a piece of butter.

Cut a sufficient number of cutlets from a loin of lamb; season them with pepper, salt, and grated nutmeg. Dip each cutlet into the yolk of a well-beaten egg, strew bread-crumbs over each, and fry them all nicely in butter, or in beef dripping. When done, arrange them in the form of a crown on the dish; make a sauce of two ounces of butter placed in the pan seasoned with a little pepper and a sprig of chopped parsley, or a lemon sliced thin and just browned; dredge into the sauce a dessertspoonful of flour, and stir it smooth; put in a cupful of boiling water, and stir it well together over the fire for a few minutes; pour this sauce inside the crown of cutlets, and serve. Or, when the cutlets are fried, drain them; place them on a dish in a crown; glaze them, and serve with stewed peas or spinach in the centre, instead of the above sauce.

Lamb Chops.

Time, eight to ten minutes.

465. Chops from the loin; pepper and salt; a mould of mashed potatoes.

Cut the chops from a loin of lamb; let them be about three-quarters of an inch thick. Broil them over a clear fire. When they are done, season them with pepper and salt. Have ready a mould of nicely mashed potatoes in a hot dish; place the chops leaning against them, and serve very hot. Or they may be served garnished only with fried parsley.

VEAL.

Veal should be obtained from a calf of about two or three months old, if it is required nice and delicate. Bull-calf veal is best for cooking in joints; cow-calf veal for made dishes.

The failing of this meat is its tendency to turn; should it show symptoms of doing so, put it into scalding water, and let it boil for seven minutes with some pieces of charcoal or sprinkled with charcoal powder. Take it out of the pot, plunge it in cold water, and put it into the coolest spot you can find.

The skirt should always be removed from the breast, and the pipe from the loin in hot weather, as soon as it comes from the butcher's.

Veal supplies numerous *entrées* or made dishes.

The fillet derives much of its pleasant flavour from being stuffed; veal in itself being nearly tasteless. The stuffing should be placed in the hollow place from whence the bone is extracted, and the joint should be roasted a beautiful brown; it should be cooked gradually, as the meat being solid, will require to be thoroughly done through, without burning the outside; like pork, it is rather indigestible. Boiled bacon or ham should accompany it to table, with the addition of a lemon cut in halves and handed to the guests.

In roasting veal, care must be taken that it is not at first placed too near the fire; the fat of a loin, one of the most delicate joints of veal, should be covered with greased paper; a fillet also should have on the caul until nearly done enough; when almost done, dredge with flour, and produce a fine froth. In grand kitchens, or where cream is abundant, cooks occasionally baste veal with it for about fifteen or twenty minutes before serving.

To Roast a Fillet of Veal.

Time, four hours for twelve pounds.

466. Veal; half a pint of melted butter; a lemon; half a pound of forcemeat.

Take out the bone of the joint, and with a sharp knife make a deep incision between the fillet and the udder. Fill it with the forcemeat or veal stuffing. Bind the veal up in a round form, and fasten it securely with skewers and twine. Run the spit as nearly through the middle as you can; cover the veal with buttered paper, and put it at some distance from the fire at first, advancing it as it becomes dressed. Baste it well, and just before it is done, take off the paper, dredge a little flour over it, and baste it well with butter to give it a fine frothy appearance. Remove the skewers, and replace them with a silver one; pour over the fillet some melted butter, with the juice of half a lemon and a little of the brown gravy from the meat. Garnish with slices of cut lemon, and serve with either boiled ham, bacon, or pickled pork.

Fricandeau of Veal.

Time, two hours and a half or three hours.

457. Three or four pounds of the fillet of veal; a few slices of bacon; a bunch of savoury herbs; two blades of mace; two bay-leaves; five allspice; one head of celery; one carrot; one turnip; lardoons; pepper to taste; one pint of gravy or stock.

Cut a thick handsome slice from a fillet of veal, trim it neatly round, and lard it thickly* with fat bacon. Cut the carrot, turnip, and celery into slices, and put them into a stewpan with a bunch of savoury herbs, two blades of mace, five allspice, and two bay-leaves, with some slices of bacon at the top. Lay the fricandeau over the bacon with the larded side uppermost, dust a little salt over it, and pour round it a pint of good gravy or broth. Place it over the fire, and let it boil, then let it simmer *very* gently for two hours and a half or three hours over a slow fire, basting it frequently with the gravy. Take out the fricandeau when done; skim off the fat, strain the gravy, and boil it quickly to a strong glaze, cover the fricandeau with it, and serve it up very hot, upon a purée of green peas. Be careful that the gravy does not touch the fricandeau, but that it only covers the bacon and other ingredients at the bottom of the dish.

Fricandeaux of Veal.

Time, two hours to two hours and a half.

468. Some slices of veal; a quart of good gravy; a slice of lemon; a spoonful of anchovy; two dessertspoonfuls of lemon pickle; two of browning; a little Cayenne pepper; a few shreds of bacon.

Cut some steaks from the thick part of a fillet of veal about half an inch thick and six or seven inches long, lard them neatly

---

* In this and all receipts in which lardoons are used, our readers are referred to the instructions on "Larding" given in the Introduction.

with shreds of fat bacon, and dredge them with flour. Brown them in a Dutch oven before the fire, and then put them into a stewpan with the gravy, and let them stew half an hour. Add a slice of lemon, a little anchovy, lemon pickle, browning, and Cayenne pepper. When the fricandeaux are tender take them up, strain and skim the gravy, boil it to a glaze, and pour it over the fricandeaux, or thicken it with a piece of butter rolled in flour. Serve them with sorrel sauce, and garnish with forcemeat balls, or the yolks of hard-boiled eggs.

CALF'S HEAD.

A calf's head may be bought ready for cooking from the butcher's, but as it is as well to give directions for the cook in all possible circumstances, we will say here that if she has a calf's head to prepare *with the hair on it*, she must have ready a pan of scalding water to remove it. She will find the hair easier to get off if she powders it with resin after letting it soak a little while in warm water. She must then plunge it into the scalding water, holding it by the ear, and carefully scrape off all the hair. Many cooks use scalding water only, but M. Soyer (whose name is a perfect authority) recommends the resin, and it certainly facilitates the operation, though it is not indispensable. Then take out the eyes, saw the head in halves lengthways through the skull. Take the brain and tongue out. Half a calf's head is generally enough to serve at one time, but a whole head is a very handsome dish. Break the jawbone, remove the gums containing the teeth, and then lay the head in a large panful of warm water to disgorge.

Calf's Head Boiled.

Time, to soak, one hour and a half; to simmer, one hour and a half.

469. Half a calf's head; half a pint of melted butter with parsley; one lemon; a pinch of pepper and salt.

Soak the half calf's head in cold water for an hour and a half, then for ten minutes in hot water before it is dressed.

Put it into a saucepan with plenty of cold water (enough for the head to swim), and let it boil gently. When the scum rises skim it *very* carefully. After the head boils, let it simmer gently an hour and a half. Serve it with melted butter and parsley over it, and garnish with slices of lemon and tiny heaps of fried parsley. Ham should be served with calf's head, or slices of bacon.

Or: a Savoury Calf's Head.

470. When the head is boiled, score it on the surface, beat up the yolk of an egg, and rub it over the cheek with a feather. Powder it with some finely-powdered lemon thyme and parsley, pepper and salt, and bread-crumbs. Brown it with a salamander or in a Dutch oven, and when it begins to dry, sprinkle a little melted butter over it. Garnish with rashers of bacon curled round it.

Save some of the liquor in which the calf's head is boiled for a hash the next day.

Calf's Brains and Tongue.

Time, to boil ten or fifteen minutes.

471. A little parsley and thyme; one bay-leaf; a little pepper and salt; two tablespoonfuls of melted butter or cream; juice of a quarter of a lemon; a pinch of Cayenne.

Separate the two lobes of the brain with a knife, soak them in cold water with a little salt in it for an hour; then pour away the cold water and cover them with hot water; clean and skin them. Boil them then very gently in half a pint of water, take off the scum carefully as it rises. Take them up, drain and chop them, and put them to warm in a stewpan with the herbs chopped, the melted butter or cream, and the seasoning. Squeeze a *little* lemon juice over them; stir them well together. Boil the tongue; skin it; take off the roots; lay it in the middle of the dish, and serve the brains round it.

Hashed Calf's Head.

Time, one hour and a half.

472. Half a calf's head; a bunch of savoury herbs; two blades of mace; a little Cayenne; pepper and salt; one lemon; a gill and a half of sherry, or any white wine; two dessertspoonfuls of mushroom ketchup; one onion; one carrot; one quart of broth, or the liquor in which it was boiled.

Cut the meat from the remains of a boiled calf's head, into small round pieces of about two inches across. Put a quart of broth or the liquor in which the head was boiled into a stewpan with a carrot, one *small* onion, two blades of mace, and a bunch of savoury herbs, and boil it until reduced to nearly half the quantity; then strain it through a hair sieve, and add a glass and a half of white wine, the juice of a lemon, two dessert-spoonfuls of mushroom ketchup, and a piece of butter rolled in flour. Lay in the slices of head, and when gradually well heated, let it just boil up. Then serve it on

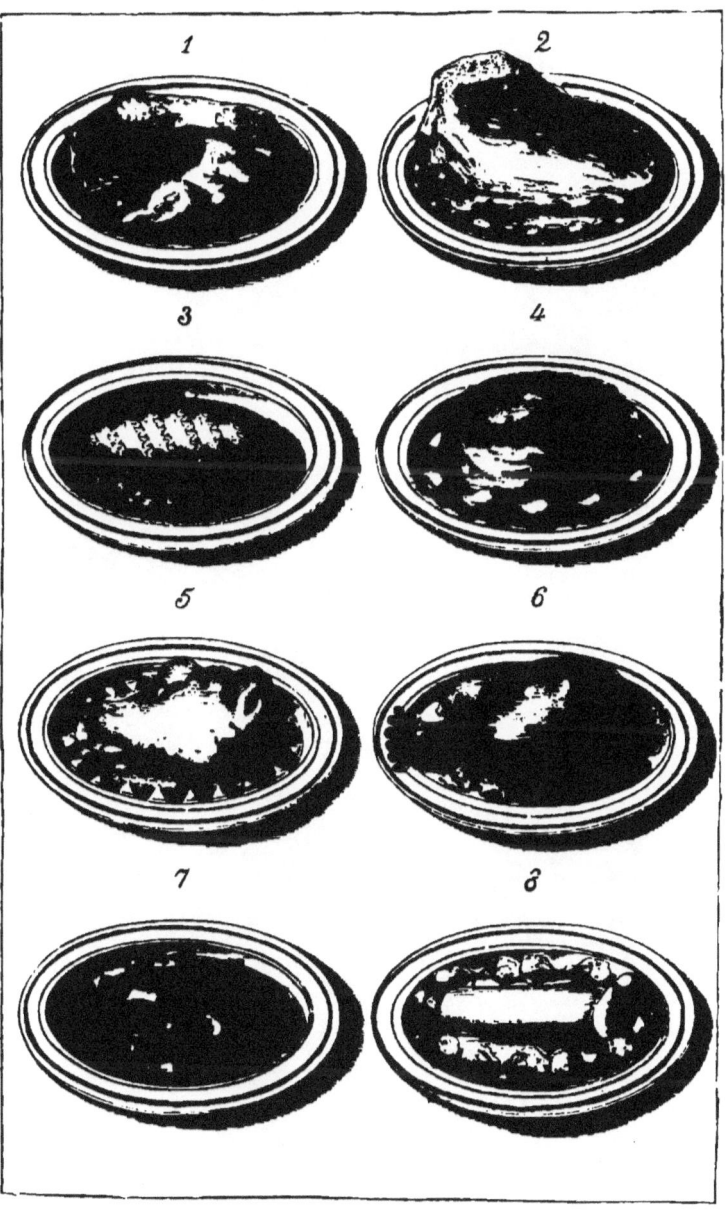

1. Sirloin of Beef.
2. Aitchbone of Beef.
3. Fricaudeau of Veal.
4. Fillet of Veal.
5. Calf's Head.
6. Ham.
7. Roast Pig.
8. Chine of Pork.

a hot dish, with rolled bacon and forcemeat balls as a garnish.

Fricassee of Calf's Head.
Time, one hour and a half.

473. The remains of a boiled calf's head; a bunch of savoury herbs; two dessertspoonfuls of lemon juice; one onion; one blade of mace; pepper and salt; two eggs; a piece of butter and flour; and a quart of the liquor in which the head was boiled.

Cut the meat from the head into nice thin pieces, and put the bones into a stewpan, with nearly a quart of the water in which the head was boiled, a bunch of savoury herbs, a blade of mace, the onion browned, and a little pepper and salt. Let it simmer for nearly an hour, then strain it into another stewpan, put in the slices of head, thicken the gravy with a little butter and flour, and bring it nearly to a boil. When done, take out the meat, and stir gradually in two dessertspoonfuls of lemon juice, and the yolks of two well-beaten eggs, but do not let it boil, or it will curdle; pour it over the meat. Serve it up very hot, with forcemeat balls for a garnish.

Calf's Head Cheese.
Time, three hours and a half.

474. One calf's head; one tablespoonful of salt; one tablespoonful of pepper; one tablespoonful of sweet herbs.

Boil a calf's head in water enough to cover it until the meat leaves the bones, then lift it out with a slice, take out the bones, and chop the meat very small; season it with the salt, pepper, and sweet herbs chopped very fine. Lay a cloth in a colander, put the minced meat and the seasoning (well stirred together) into it, fold the cloth over it, put a trencher on the cloth, and on that a good weight. When cold, it can be served in thin slices or for sandwiches, seasoning each slice with made mustard.

Calf's Head à la Maître d'Hôtel.
Time, one hour and three-quarters.

475. Remains of a cold calf's head; three-quarters of a pint of maître-d'hôtel sauce.

Remove the bones from the head, and cut it into thin slices. When the sauce is sufficiently thick to cover the meat nicely, lay the slices in it; warm it gradually, and as soon as it boils up place it on one side to simmer for a few minutes.

Collared Calf's Head.
Time, six hours altogether.

476. A calf's head; a few thick slices of ham; three tablespoonfuls of minced parsley; three blades of pounded mace; half a teaspoonful of grated nutmeg; one teaspoonful of white pepper; six eggs.

Scald the head and scrape off the hair, clean it, nicely divide it, and take out the brains; boil it for two hours, or till the meat leaves the bones, which must be taken out. Then flatten the head on the table, cover it with a thick layer of parsley, a layer of slices of ham, the yolks of the eggs boiled hard and cut into thin rings; between each layer put a seasoning of the pepper and spices. Roll the head in a cloth *very* tightly, boil it for four hours at least, then take it up and put it under a heavy weight. Let it remain till cold. Remove the cloth, &c., and serve.

Roast Loin of Veal—Plain.
Time, three hours.

477. Take about seven pounds of the kidney end of a loin of veal, fasten the flap over the kidney with a small skewer, run the spit through the thick end lengthways, cover the veal with buttered paper, and place it before a good fire to roast. Just before serving, remove the paper, and froth it up by dredging it with a little flour, and basting it with butter. Pour melted butter over it when placed on the dish, and serve. The kidney and fat may be sent to table separately on a toast if preferred, but it is not very usual to do so.

Roast Loin of Veal Stuffed.
Time, nearly three hours and a half.

478. Seven or eight pounds of veal; half a pound of forcemeat; one pint of butter; and two spoonfuls of ketchup.

Take about seven or eight pounds of the best end of a loin of veal, have the bones well separated, make an incision in the flap and fill it with veal stuffing. Roll in and skewer the flap to make it a good shape, tie round it sheets of paper well buttered, and roast it before a moderate fire, keep it well basted, and just before serving take off the paper, dredge it with flour, baste it with butter, and let it get a nice brown colour. Put it on a hot dish and pour over it some melted butter, with two spoonfuls of mushroom ketchup added to it; or put some melted butter into the dripping-pan, after it has been emptied of its contents, and pour it over the meat. Garnish with slices of lemon and forcemeat balls, and serve either ham, tongue, or boiled bacon with it.

Modes of Dressing Veal.

To Roast a Breast of Veal.
Time, one hour and a quarter.

479 Take off the tendons from a breast of veal, skewer the sweetbread to the joint, and cover it with buttered paper, place it to roast for an hour and a quarter, or according to its weight. Serve it with melted butter and gravy, and sliced lemon. It can be roasted without the sweetbread, which as well as the tendons will serve for an *entrée*.

Stewed Knuckle of Veal and Rice.
Time, three hours.

480. Six pounds of knuckle of veal; two blades of mace; half a pound of rice; a little salt; one onion.
Take off some cutlets or collops before you dress the meat, so as to have the knuckle small; break the shank bone, wash it well, and put it into a stewpan with sufficient water to cover it, bring it gradually to a boil, put in a little salt, and skim it well; let it simmer gently for nearly three-quarters of an hour, then add half a pound of rice, the onion, and the blades of mace, and stew all together for more than two hours. Take up the meat, and pour over it the rice, &c. Serve it with parsley and butter sauce, and boiled bacon in a separate dish. Garnish with vegetables.

Knuckle of Veal Boiled.
Time, twenty minutes to each pound.

481. A knuckle of veal; a dessertspoonful of salt; parsley and butter.
Put a knuckle of veal into a stewpan, and pour over it sufficient water to cover it; let it simmer slowly, and when it reaches the boiling point throw in a dessertspoonful of salt; keep it well skimmed, and let it boil until tender, then serve it with parsley and butter, and a salted pig's cheek.
Three-quarters of a pound of rice may also be boiled with it. Serve with green peas or stewed cucumber.

Stewed Veal and Green Peas.
Time, two hours and twenty minutes.

482. Veal; a bunch of savoury herbs; a blade and a half of mace; two cloves; peel of half a lemon; four allspice; a piece of butter; a teaspoonful of flour; four onions; one glass of sherry; three dessertspoonfuls of tomato sauce; juice of half a lemon; three dessertspoonfuls of ketchup; one quart of green peas; forcemeat balls.
Half roast a breast of veal, and then put it into a stewpan with a bunch of savoury herbs, a blade and a half of mace pounded, cloves, and allspice, four young onions, the peel of half a lemon, and the pepper and salt. Just cover the whole with boiling water, and let it simmer slowly for quite two hours, covered closely over. Strain the gravy through a sieve, and add a glass of sherry or white wine of any sort, the tomato sauce, lemon juice, and ketchup; thicken it with a piece of butter rolled in flour, and let it simmer slowly for a quarter of an hour, skimming it well. Serve it on a hot dish, and surround it with a border of green peas, previously boiled. Garnish with forcemeat balls or bacon.

Veal Cutlets.
Time, twelve to fifteen minutes.

483. A veal cutlet; one bunch of sweet herbs; bread-crumbs; nutmeg; peel of half a lemon; yolks of two eggs; one ounce of butter; a little flour and water.
Let the cutlet be about half an inch thick, and cut it into pieces the size and shape of a crown piece. Chop the herbs very fine; mix them well with the bread-crumbs. Brush the cutlets over with yolk of egg, then cover them with the bread-crumbs and chopped herbs; fry them lightly in butter, turning them when required. Take them out when done.
Mix about an ounce of fresh butter with the grated peel of half a lemon, a little nutmeg, and flour; pour a little water into the frying-pan, and stir the butter, flour, and grated lemon peel into it; then put the cutlets into this gravy to heat. Serve them piled in the centre of the dish with thin rolls of bacon as a garnish.

A Savoury Dish of Veal—Baked.
Time, half an hour.

484. Some thin slices off a fillet of veal; yolks of two eggs; a little veal forcemeat; some bread-crumbs; one pint of brown gravy or broth; a few pickled mushrooms.
Cut some thin slices off a fillet of veal, hack them with the back of a knife, rub them over with the yolks of eggs, lay some veal forcemeat over them, roll each slice up tight, tie them round with thread, brush them over with the beaten yolks of the eggs, and sprinkle bread-crumbs thickly over them, butter a dish and put them in, and bake them for half an hour in a quick oven. Take a pint of brown gravy or broth, with a few pickled mushrooms, boil it up, put the meat into a dish with fried forcemeat balls laid round it, and pour the gravy and mushrooms over it.

Cold Veal.

Time, about twenty minutes.

485. Some slices of cold veal; a few sweet herbs; a sprig of parsley; peel of a lemon; bread-crumbs; pepper, salt, and nutmeg; a piece of butter; a spoonful of ketchup; juice of a small lemon.

Cut the veal into thin pieces, any length you please; have ready some bread-crumbs, a sprig of parsley, a few sweet herbs, and the peel of a lemon, all minced fine, season it with pepper, salt, and grated nutmeg; brush the slices of meat with the yolk of egg, mix the herbs, spice, &c., together and sprinkle it thickly over the meat. Melt a piece of butter in a pan, put in the veal and fry it a nice brown on both sides, when done put it on a hot dish. In the meantime, make a little gravy of the bones, shake some flour into the pan, put into the gravy a spoonful of ketchup and the juice of a small lemon, stir it round, boil it up, and strain it over the veal; put a few pickled mushrooms over it, and garnish with slices of lemon.

Scallops of Cold Veal.

Time, fifteen minutes.

486. Sufficient minced veal to fill the scallop shells; one saltspoonful of pepper and salt; a little nutmeg; two ounces of bread-crumbs; two ounces of butter, a few spoonfuls of cream.

Mince some cold roast veal very fine, season it with a little pepper, salt, and grated nutmeg, stir in a few spoonfuls of cream to moisten it thoroughly, and place it over a slow fire for a few minutes, taking care to keep it constantly stirred, then fill the scallop shells, strew bread-crumbs over them, lay a knob or two of butter on the top of each, and brown them before the fire in a Dutch oven.

Calf's Liver and Bacon.

Time, quarter of an hour.

487. Two pounds and a half of calf's liver; one pound of bacon; juice of one lemon; two ounces of butter; a little flour; pepper and salt.

Soak the liver in cold water for half an hour, then dry it in a cloth, and cut it into thin narrow slices; take about a pound of bacon, or as much as you may require, and cut an equal number of thin slices as you have of liver; fry the bacon *lightly*, take it out and keep it hot; then fry the liver in the same pan, seasoning it with pepper and salt, and dredging over it a little flour. When it is a nice brown, arrange it round the dish with a roll of bacon between each slice. Pour off the fat from the pan, put in about two ounces of butter well rubbed in flour to thicken the gravy. Squeeze in the juice of a lemon, and add a cupful of hot water, boil it, and pour it into the centre of the dish. Serve it garnished with forcemeat balls or slices of lemon.

PORK.

Very great care should be used in purchasing pork, as of late years pigs have been subject to much disease, and the flesh of the animal then becomes perfectly poisonous. If possible, learn where and how the pork you eat is fattened.

A pig is one of the most profitable animals to keep, and will well repay any care and attention bestowed on it. Every part of it is used and is good for food. It should be kept scrupulously clean, the sty carefully cleaned out very often, and the pig washed and scrubbed itself. Its food should be always cooked for it. Skim milk, potatoes, and meat are its best food.

A pig should only be six months old for boiling or roasting, larger and older, of course, for salting. A pig should be short-legged and thick-necked, and have a small head.

A pig should not be suffered to touch food for twenty-four hours before it is killed. Ham, bacon, pickled pork, &c., &c., are indispensable in an English kitchen, but fresh pork is seldom served in joints at the tables of the upper classes. For family use, however, and where people keep their own pigs, the leg and loin of pork are often seen. As many persons are unable to digest fresh pork, it is seldom or never part of the bill of fare for a dinner party.

Modern taste is adverse to the old savoury stuffing of sage and onions, but *this* also is admissible at the family repast if liked.

The skin of young porkers is kept on when it is cooked, and is called "crackling," being very crisp and brown, and making a crackling noise when cut.

Pork must be very much more dressed than all other meats, except veal. It should, therefore, be placed on the spit at a considerable distance from the fire, and thus let get well warmed through before the skin begins to get dry and brown.

Sucking Pig—to Scald it.

488. A sucking pig should be dressed the day after it is killed, if possible, and should not be more than three weeks or a month old. The pig is generally sent from the butcher's prepared for the spit, but in case our readers should ever have occasion to scald and clean it for themselves, we will give a few directions:—Make ready a large pan of scalding water. While the water is boiling, put the pig into cold water for ten minutes; plunge it into the boiling water (holding it by the head), and shake it about till the hairs begin to loosen in the water. Take it out dry it, and with a coarse cloth rub the hairs backwards till they are all removed. When it is clean, cut it open, take out the entrails, and wash it thoroughly in a large pan of cold water. Dry it in a cloth; remove the feet on the first joint, leaving a little skin to pull over the bone. Fold it in a very wet cloth until you are ready to put it on the spit.

To make Sage and Onion Stuffing for Roast Pig or Roast Pork.

Time, twenty-five to thirty minutes.

489. Two large onions; double the quantity of bread-crumbs; three teaspoonfuls of chopped sage; two ounces of butter; half a saltspoonful of pepper; one saltspoonful of salt; one egg.

Boil the onions (unless they are Portugal onions) in two or three waters to take off the strong taste in them; then drain them, chop them up fine, and mix them with double their quantity of bread-crumbs, three very full teaspoonfuls of minced sage, two ounces of butter, a good half saltspoonful of pepper, and double the quantity of salt. Mix the whole with the well beaten yolk of an egg to bind it.

N.B.—Persons who prefer a strong stuffing can use half the quantity of bread-crumbs, and chop the onions raw.

To Roast the Pig.

Time, one hour and a half to two hours.

490. Half a pint of melted butter; two ounces of fresh butter; three-quarters of a pint or one pint of sage and onion forcemeat.

When the pig is well cleaned, make a forcemeat according to previous directions, or a veal stuffing forcemeat if preferred. Sew it up with a strong thread; truss it as a hare is trussed, with its fore-legs skewered back and its hind legs forward. Dry it well and rub it with a little flour. Set it before a clear brisk fire, arrange under it a dripping pan and basins to catch the gravy. Baste it with a little pure olive oil, or with its own gravy, rubbing it occasionally (when you do not use oil) with butter. When it is done, cut off the head, split it in halves, divide the pig with a very sharp knife down the centre, lay the backs together, put the ears on each side, and the halves of the head at each end of the dish. Pour a little of the gravy of the pig, mixed with thin melted butter and a squeeze of lemon juice, over it.

Send some of the same gravy and melted butter (seasoned with a little Cayenne) to table in a sauce tureen.

Sauces to be eaten with it—bread sauce, or tomato sauce, or apple sauce, as preferred.

To Bake a Pig.

Time, two hours.

491. Wash the pig very nicely, rub it with butter, and flour it all over. Well butter the dish in which you intend to bake it, and put it into the oven. When sufficiently done, take it out, rub it well over with a buttered cloth, and put it in again to dry. When it is finished cut off the head, and split it open; divide the pig down the back in halves. Lay it in the dish back to back, with one half of the head at each end, and one of the ears on each side. Take off the fat from the dish it was baked in, and you will find some good gravy remaining at the bottom. Add to this a little veal gravy, with a piece of butter rolled in flour, and boil it up, put it into the dish over the pig and serve.

A stuffing of bread-crumbs, chopped sage leaves, pepper and salt, should be put into the inside before it is baked, as is done for roast pig.

CHINE OF PORK.

This joint is usually sent to table with turkey. It should be salted for about sixty or seventy hours previous to cooking, and then be roasted. A chine is as often sent to table boiled as roasted, but the latter is usually preferred. In roasting pork, the skin should be cut lengthways into small strips, but not deep enough to reach the meat.

Chine Roasted.

Time twenty minutes to the pound.

492. Half a pint of pork stuffing; half a pint of apple sauce.

Score the skin deeply, stuff the chine with pork stuffing, and roast it gently by a clear fire.

To Boil a Chine.

Time, a quarter of an hour to the pound, and twenty minutes *over*.

493. Lay it in brine for nine or ten days, turning it every day. When it is ready, put it into a saucepan, and more than cover it with water. Let it boil slowly, skimming it well.

Send it to table when done, garnished with small well trimmed cauliflowers or greens.

How to Stuff a Chine of Bacon.

Time, two or three hours.

494. The chine is to be soaked for a night in cold water, and then to be cut through the meat from the sward to the bones, in spaces of about one half or three quarters of an inch, the nicks made by the cutting to be filled as full as it is possible to get them with the following green herbs: parsley, pot marjoram, a few green onions, a little thyme, a little lettuce, a little mace, or any other savoury herbs. Some people use also primrose and violet leaves. The whole of the herbs to be chopped fine and sprinkled with a little pepper. The chine to be tied in a cloth and steamed.

This is a very favourite dish to eat when cold in the fens and marshes of Lincolnshire at feasts, sheep clippings, and other festivals, when green herbs can be procured. It is a very nice relish for breakfast.

To Roast a Leg of Pork.

Time, twenty minutes to one pound.

495. The leg to be roasted should not weigh more than 'six or seven pounds. Score the rind or skin with a sharp knife all round the joint, place it at some distance from the fire, turn it constantly and baste it well. It will yield sufficient dripping to baste itself without butter. If the crackling and fat are not kept on, the joint will not require so long a time to roast it. Sauce: brown gravy and tomato.

To Roast a Leg of Pork the Old Fashioned Way with Stuffing.

Time, twenty minutes for each pound.

496. Sage and onion stuffing; a piece of butter.

Select a fine small leg of pork, keep the skin on, and score it in regular stripes of a quarter of an inch wide with the point of a sharp knife; cut a slit in the knuckle, raise the skin, put under it some nice sage and onion stuffing, and fasten it in with a small skewer; put it at some distance from the fire, and baste it frequently. Just before it is done, moisten the skin all over with a little butter, dredge it with flour, and place it near the fire to brown and crisp. When done, put it on a hot dish, pour a little gravy made in the dripping pan round it, and serve with apple sauce.

To Roast a Loin of Pork.

Time, two hours and a half.

497. Take a loin of pork of about five pounds, and score it with a very sharp knife at equal distances, place it at a good distance from the fire to prevent the skin from becoming hard, and baste it very frequently all the time. When done make a little gravy in the dripping-pan, pour it round the meat, and serve with apple sauce in a tureen. A loin of pork may be stuffed with sage and onion, or the stuffing baked and served separately, if the flavour be not objected to by the family.

To Roast a Sparerib of Pork.

Time, one hour and three-quarters for six pounds.

498. Score the skin, put the joint down to a bright fire to roast, rub a little flour over it. If the rind is kept on, roast it without a buttered paper over it, but if the skin and fat are removed, cover it with a buttered paper. Keep it frequently basted. About ten minutes before taking it up, strew over it some powdered sage; froth it with a little butter, and serve with gravy strained over it, and apple sauce in a tureen.

Pork Griskin.

Time, a quarter of an hour to each pound.

499. A griskin is usually very hard. It is well before you roast it to put it into as much cold water as will cover it, and let it just boil. Take it off *the moment* it boils. Rub a piece of butter over it and flour it, then set it in a Dutch oven before the fire to roast a nice brown.

To Steam a Ham.

Time, twenty minutes to each pound.

500. If the ham has been hung for some time, put it into cold water, and let it soak all night, or let it lie on a damp stone sprinkled with water for two days to mellow. Wash it well, put it into a steamer—there

9

are proper ones made for the purpose—over a pot of boiling water. Steam it for as long a time as the weight requires, the proportion of time given above.

This is by far the best way of cooking a ham. It prevents waste, and retains the flavour. When it is done, skin it and strew bread-raspings over it as usual. If you preserve the skin as whole as possible and cover the ham when cold with it, it will prevent its becoming dry.

To Boil a Ham.

Time, four or five hours.

501. A blade of mace; a few cloves; a sprig of thyme; and two bay leaves.

Well soak the ham in a large quantity of water for twenty-four hours, then trim and scrape it very clean, put it into a large stewpan with more than sufficient water to cover it; put in a blade of mace, a few cloves, a sprig of thyme, and two bay leaves. Boil it for four or five hours, according to its weight; and when done, let it become cold in the liquor in which it was boiled. Then remove the rind carefully without injuring the fat, press a cloth over it to absorb as much of the grease as possible, and shake some bread-raspings over the fat, or brush it thickly over with glaze. Serve it cold, garnished with parsley, or aspic jelly in the dish. Ornament the knuckle with a paper frill and vegetable flowers.

Or, to Serve Hot.

Time, four hours for ten pounds.

502. Before placing your ham in soak, run a small sharp knife into it close to the bone, and if when withdrawn it has a pleasant smell, the ham is good. Lay it in cold water to soak for twenty-four hours if it has hung long, changing the water twice; but twelve hours is the usual time for a Yorkshire ham.

Before boiling, wash it thoroughly, and trim it neatly, removing any rusty parts. Cover it well with water, bring it gradually to a boil, taking care that it continues to do so (but not too fast), and as the scum rises skim the pot carefully. When it is done draw off the skin, and sift bread-raspings over the ham. Place a frill of paper round the knuckle, and serve.

To Bake a Ham.

Time, four hours.

503. Take a medium-sized ham, and place it to soak for ten or twelve hours. Then cut away the rusty part from underneath, wipe it dry, and cover it rather thickly over with a paste of flour and water. Put it into an earthen dish, and set it in a moderately-heated oven for four hours. When done, take off the crust carefully, and peel off the skin, put a frill of cut paper round the knuckle, and raspings of bread over the fat of the ham, or serve it glazed and garnished with cut vegetables.

Some persons infinitely prefer a baked ham to a boiled one, but we think it better boiled or steamed.

To Boil a Leg of Pork.

Time, a quarter of an hour for each pound, and half an hour over.

504. Procure a nice small compact leg of pork, rub it well with salt, and let it remain for a week in pickle, turning and rubbing the pickle into it once each day. Let it lie for half an hour in cold water before it is dressed to improve the colour; then put it into a large pot, or stewpan, and well cover it with water. Let it boil gradually, and skim it frequently as the scum rises. On no account let it boil fast, or the meat will be hardened, and the knuckle end will be done before the thick part. When done, serve it on a hot dish with a garnish of turnips, or parsnips. A peas-pudding must be served with boiled leg of pork and greens as vegetables. It may be boiled in a cloth dredged over with flour, which gives it a very delicate appearance, but in that case the water in which it was boiled, cannot be used as a stock for pea-soup, and is thus wasted.

To Choose Bacon.

505. Excellent young bacon may be thus known:—the lean will be tender and of a bright colour; the fat firm and white yet bearing a pale rose tinge, and the rind thin. Rusty bacon has yellow streaks in it.

To Boil Bacon.

Time, one hour and a half for two or three pounds.

506. If very salt, soak it in soft water two hours before cooking. Put it into a saucepan with plenty of water, and let it boil gently. If a fine piece of the gammon of bacon, it may, when done, have the skin, as in hams, stripped off, and have finely-powdered bread-raspings strewed over it.

Bacon and Eggs.

Time, three quarters of an hour.

507. A quarter of a pound of streaked bacon; six or seven eggs; two spoonfuls of gravy; a little pepper and salt.

Cut the bacon up in thin slices, put them in a stewpan over a slow fire, and turn them frequently. Then pour off and strain the melted fat of the bacon into a dish, take a very little of it, add to it two spoonfuls of gravy and a little pepper and salt, break over it six or seven eggs. Stew the whole over a slow fire. Brown with a salamander, and serve.

To Steam Bacon.
Time, twenty minutes to the pound.

508. It is a mistake *to boil* bacon. It should be steamed. No waste then takes place as to quantity, and the flavour is quite preserved, while the bacon is much more tender, as it cannot well be spoiled by too quick boiling.

Scrape the outer rind or skin well, wash the bacon, put it in a steamer over a pot of boiling water, and steam it for as long as required by the weight. Serve it with veal or fowls, or by itself with greens.

To Salt Larding Bacon.

509. Bacon to be used for larding should be very firm and fat, and should not be cured with saltpetre, the effect of which is to redden white meats.

Rub the pieces of bacon you wish to keep for larding with fine salt, lay them, well salted, one on the other, put a weight on them, and leave them for six weeks in pickle, then have them smoked quite dry.

Directions for larding are given in this work, but only practice can enable the cook to lard nicely.

Pickled Pork.
Time, three-quarters of an hour to four pounds.

510. The belly part is considered delicate. It should be nicely streaked. Boil it gently. Serve it with greens as a garnish round it.

A Hand of Pork.
Time, one hour.

511. If the pork should be very salt, it will require to be soaked for nearly two hours before boiling. Boil it, and serve with greens, and peas-pudding in a separate dish.

Pigs' Tongues.

512. Partially boil the tongues in order to remove the skin. Pickle them as you do hams (according to previous receipts); lay them one on the top of each other under a heavy weight. Cover the pan in which you place them, and let them remain for a week, then dry them, and put them into sausage skins. Fasten them up at the ends, and smoke them.

Pig's Pettitoes.
Time, forty minutes.

513. Feet, heart, and liver of a pig; a small piece of butter (size of a walnut); half a teaspoonful of pepper; a little salt; one round of toasted bread.

Put them in just sufficient water to cover them, add the heart and liver, boil them ten minutes, then take out the liver and heart, and mince them small, return them to the feet, and stew until quite tender; thicken with flour and butter, season with pepper and salt, and serve up with sippets of plain or toasted bread; make a pyramid of the minced heart and liver, and lay the feet round them. When pettitoes are fried, they should be first boiled, then dipped in butter, and fried a light brown.

Receipts for dressing pigs' feet and ears will be found amongst breakfast dishes.

To Roast a Pig's Head.
Time, to roast, half an hour.

514. Half an ounce of sage; one tablespoonful of salt; one dessertspoonful of pepper.

Boil it till tender enough to take the bones out. Then chop some sage fine, mix it with the pepper and salt, and rub it over the head. Hang it on the spit, and roast it at a good fire. Baste it well. Make a good gravy and pour over it. Apple sauce is eaten with it.

Pig's Head Boiled.
Time, one hour and a half.

515. This is the more profitable dish, though not so pleasant to the palate; it should first be salted, which is usually done by the pork butcher; it should be boiled gently; serve with vegetables.

Pig's Cheek.
Time, three-quarters of an hour.

516. Pig's cheek; one ounce of bread-crumbs. Boil and trim in the shape of ham, and, if very fat, carve it as a cockleshell; glaze it well, or put over it bread-crumbs and brown them.

Soyer's Method of Dressing a Pig's Cheek.
Time, to boil, one hour and a quarter; ten minutes in an oven.

517. One cheek; half a pint of peas; one ounce of butter; a little pepper and salt; four eggs; one ounce of bread-crumbs.

"Procure a pig's cheek nicely pickled; boil well until it feels very tender. Tie half a pint of split peas in a cloth; put them into a stewpan of boiling water. Boil them about half an hour. Take them out, pass through a hair sieve, put them into a stewpan with an ounce of butter, a little pepper and salt and four eggs, stir them over the fire till the eggs are partially set, then spread it over the pig's cheek, egg with a paste-brush; sprinkle bread-crumbs over, place in the oven ten minutes, brown it with a salamander, and serve."

This is an excellent mode of dressing it.

To Make Brawn.

Time, two and a half or three hours.

518. A pig's head of six or seven pounds; one pound and three-quarters of lean beef; four or five cloves; pepper; salt, and Cayenne pepper.

Well clean and wash a pig's head, and put it into a stewpan with about a pound and three-quarters of lean beef. Cover it with cold water, and let it boil until the bones can be removed, skimming it frequently. Then put the meat into a hot pan before the fire, and mince the beef and head as fine as possible, and as quickly, to prevent its getting cold. Season it well with the spice pounded, and mix with the pepper, salt, and Cayenne. Stir all briskly together, and press it into a brawn tin or cake mould with a heavy weight pressed on it. Let it remain for five or six hours, until thoroughly set and quite cold. When required, dip the mould into boiling water, and turn the brawn out on your dish.

Pork Sausages.

Time, ten to twelve minutes to fry.

519. Three pounds of young pork; two pounds and a half of suet; two tablespoonfuls of chopped sage; the peel of one lemon; one tablespoonful of sweet herbs; one nutmeg; one teaspoonful of pepper; one of salt.

Take the pork, free from skin, gristle, and fat, cut it very small, and beat it fine in a mortar; chop the suet and the sage as fine as possible. Spread the pounded meat on a clean pasteboard, and shake the sage over it, the peel of a lemon chopped fine, and the sweet herbs; grate over it one nutmeg, and add the pepper and salt; then strew over it the suet, and mix all thoroughly together. Put it into a jar, and cover it over for use. When required, roll it up with a beaten egg, make it the size of sausages, and fry them in boiling butter or dripping, rolling them about in the pan; when a nice light brown, serve them up hot.

Veal sausages, or veal mixed with pork, can be made in this manner; or skins may be filled with the sausage meat.

Oxford Sausages.

520. One pound of lean veal; one pound of young pork; one pound of beef suet; half a pound of grated bread; peel of half a lemon; one nutmeg grated; six sage leaves; one teaspoonful of pepper; two of salt; a sprig of thyme, savory, and marjoram.

Take a pound of lean veal, and the same quantity of young pork, fat and lean together, free from skin and gristle, and a pound of beef suet; chop all separately as fine as possible, and then mix together; add the grated bread, the peel of half a lemon shred fine, a nutmeg grated, a teaspoonful of pepper, two of salt, and the sage leaves, thyme, savory, and marjoram, all chopped as fine as you can; mix all thoroughly together, and press it down into a prepared skin. When you use them, fry them in fresh butter a fine brown. Serve as hot as possible.

Oxford Sausages without Skins.

521. One pound and a half of pig meat cut from the griskin, without any skin; half a pound of veal; one pound and a half of beef suet; the yolks and whites of five eggs; a dessertspoonful of sifted sage, after being well dried; one teaspoonful of pepper; two teaspoonfuls of salt.

Chop the above ingredients into small pieces and then pound them together till they are short and tender; chop the suet very fine, separately from the rest. When the eggs are well beaten together, and the white specks are taken out, pour them over the pounded meat and chopped suet; well knead it together with the hand, throwing in the sifted sage, pepper, and salt, from a coarse pepper-box gradually, so as to flavour the whole mass. Press the meat, when well mixed, into a wide-mouthed jar; cover it, and keep it from the air in a cold place. Egg and roll the sausages on a floured board, and use little or no grease in frying them, as they contain sufficient without any addition.

The Cambridge Sausage.

Time, nearly one hour.

522. Quarter of a pound of beef; quarter of a pound of veal; half a pound of pork; half a pound of bacon; half a pound of suet; pepper and salt; a few sage leaves; sweet herbs.

Chop the meat into small pieces, and the suet as fine as possible; season it highly with pepper and salt, a few minced sage leaves, and sweet herbs. Take a delicately-clean skin, fill it with the sausage meat, and tie the ends securely. Prick it lightly in several parts, and put it in boiling water to boil for nearly an hour when required.

Sausage Meat (Mixed).
Time, to fry, ten minutes.

523. Three parts of pork to one of beef; four ounces of salt and one of pepper to every ten pounds of sausage meat.
Chop the pork and the beef nicely together, and mix it well up with the seasoning. Put the sausages into muslin bags, tie them close, and hang them in a dry, cool cellar. When the meat is wanted for use, egg it, cut it in slices, flour the outsides of each, and fry them in hot butter. Let them be nicely browned. Serve them round mashed potatoes, or on sliced toast for breakfast.

Bologna Sausage.
Time, to boil, one hour.

524. One pound of beef; one pound of bacon; one pound of pork; one pound of veal; three-quarters of a pound of beef suet; twelve sage leaves; a few sweet herbs; pepper and salt.
Take a pound of bacon, fat and lean together, the same each of beef, pork, and veal, chop all very fine, and mix it with three-quarters of a pound of finely-chopped beef suet, sage leaves, and sweet herbs; season it highly with pepper and salt. Then fill a large skin, and put it into a saucepan of boiling water, pricking the skin for fear of its bursting; let it boil slowly for an hour, and then place it on straw to dry.

Saveloys.
Time, half an hour to bake.

525. Six pounds of pork; one pound of common salt; one ounce of saltpetre; three teaspoonfuls of pepper; twelve sage leaves; one pound of bread-crumbs.
Remove the skin and bone from six pounds of young pork, and salt it with the saltpetre and common salt; let it stand in the pickle for three days, then mince it up very fine, and season it with pepper, and twelve sage leaves chopped as small as possible; add to it the grated bread, and mix it all well together, fill the skins, and bake them in a slow oven for half au hour. They may be eaten hot or cold.

To Fry Sausages.
Time, twelve minutes.

526. Pork sausages; and a piece of butter.

Prick the sausages very lightly with the prong of a fork, and put them into a frying-pan with a piece of butter over a clear fire, shake the pan frequently, and turn the sausages, that they may be browned all over. The time depends on the size of the sausages, as, if very large, a quarter of an hour will be required to cook them. When done, serve them on toasted bread, or arranged round mashed potatoes pressed into a mould, the sausages as a border. If preferred, sausages may be put into a saucepan of boiling water and allowed to simmer slowly for the same time.

Black Puddings.
Time, to soak, one night; to boil, half an hour.

527. Rather more than one quart of blood; one quart of whole groats; crumb of a quartern loaf; two quarts of new milk; a small bunch of winter savory and thyme, about half a teaspoonful of each; two teaspoonfuls of salt; one teaspoonful of pepper; six cloves; half a teaspoonful of allspice; half a nutmeg; a little grated ginger; three pounds of beef suet; six eggs; three ounces of pork fat.
Stir the hot blood with salt till it is quite cold, put a quart of it or rather more to a quart of whole groats, to soak one night. Soak the crumb of a quartern loaf in rather more than two quarts of new milk made hot. Chop fine a little winter savory and thyme; beat up and strain six eggs; chop three pounds of beef suet; mix the suet, the herbs, and the seasoning of pepper, salt, allspice, cloves, ginger, and nutmeg together with the eggs. Then add to it and beat up with it, the groats, and soaked bread, &c. When well mixed, have ready some skin-bags, as for sausages, but much larger (we suppose, of course, that they have been well cleaned and soaked), put the mixture into these bags; but as you do so, add at regular distances pork fat cut into large dice. Tie the skins in links only half-filled, and boil the puddings in a large kettle, pricking them as they swell, or they will burst. When boiled, dry them in clean cloths and hang them up.
To cook them for eating, scald them for a few minutes in water, and cook them in a Dutch oven.

White Puddings.
Time, twenty minutes.

528. One teacupful of rose-water for soaking the skins; half a pound of blanched almonds; one pound of grated bread; two pounds of marrow or suet; one pound of currants; a little beaten cinnamon; six

cloves; half a blade of mace; one quarter of a nutmeg; one quart of cream; six eggs; two ounces of fine white sugar; half a lemon peel; half an ounce of citron sliced.

Take care that the skins are very nicely cleaned, as directed for sausages, only in this instance rinse and soak them also all night in rose-water. Mix half a pound of blanched almonds chopped fine with a pound of grated bread, two pounds of marrow or chopped suet, a pound of currants, some beaten cinnamon, cloves, mace, and nutmeg, a quart of cream, the yolks of six and the whites of two eggs, a little fine white sugar, and some lemon peel and citron sliced. Mix all *well* together and fill the skins with the mixture, not *too* full, however, lest they should burst. Boil these puddings in milk and water carefully for about twenty minutes, prick them with a small fork as they rise, to prevent the skin from cracking. When they are done, lay them on a cloth to dry. This is a nice sweet dish for luncheon.

VENISON.

There are three kinds of venison in Great Britain. The red deer, the fallow deer, and the roebuck, peculiar to Scotland as the red deer now is to Ireland.

The flesh of the fallow deer is the best. Venison should be dark, finely grained, and firm, with a good coating of fat. It requires to be well hung in a cold, dry larder.

Haunch of Venison.

Time, three to four hours.

529. Haunch from twenty to twenty-five pounds.

This joint is trimmed by cutting off part of the knuckle and sawing off the chine bone, then the flap is folded over, and it is covered with a paste made of flour and water. This paste should be about an inch thick. Tie it up in strong and very thick paper, and place it in a cradle spit very close to the fire till the paste is well hardened or crusted, pouring a few ladlefuls of hot dripping over it occasionally to prevent the paper from catching fire. Then move it further from the fire, take care that your fire is a *very* good one, clear and strong. When the venison has roasted for about four hours take it up, remove the paper and paste, and run a thin skewer in to see if it is done enough. If the skewer goes in easily it is dressed, if not put it down again, as it depends greatly on the strength of the fire for so large a joint. When it is dressed, glaze the top and salamander it. Put a frill round the knuckle, and serve very hot with strong gravy. Red currant jelly in a glass dish or a tureen. Vegetables: French beans.

Neck of Venison.

Time, a quarter of an hour for a pound.

530. Cover it with paste and paper as for the haunch, fix it on a spit and roast.

To Hash Venison.

Time, one hour and a half.

531. Some cold roast venison; three tablespoonfuls of port wine; a little mutton broth; half of a shallot; a pinch of Cayenne; one ounce and a half of butter; a spoonful of flour; and salt to taste.

Cut some cold venison into nice slices, and season them lightly with salt; put the bones, trimmings, any cold gravy from the venison, and as much broth as you may require into a stewpan, and let it simmer slowly for quite an hour, then strain it off; stir the butter and flour over the fire until sufficiently brown to colour the gravy, taking care it does not burn. Pour the gravy from the bones, add the port wine, and let it simmer until it boils. Then draw the stewpan to the side of the fire, put in the slices of venison, and when thoroughly *hot* serve it up, with red currant jelly in a glass dish. Garnish with forcemeat balls about the size of a marble.

To Broil Venison Steaks.

Time, to broil, fifteen minutes.

532. Venison steaks; a piece of butter the size of an egg to each pound of meat; pepper; salt; currant jelly; two tablespoonfuls of wine.

Let the gridiron become hot, rub the bars with a piece of beef suet; then lay the steaks on it, having first dipped them in flour or rolled biscuits. Set it over a clear but not fierce fire. When one side is done take the steak carefully up and hold it over the steak dish, so that the blood may fall into it; then turn the other side on the gridiron, and let it broil nicely. Set the steak dish where it will become hot, put on it a piece of butter the size of an egg for each pound of venison, add a saltspoonful of salt, the same of black pepper, and a little currant jelly made liquid with the wine, lay this mixture on the hot steaks, and turn them once or twice in the gravy; or they may be broiled on both sides, well seasoned, and thin slices of lemon laid over them on the dish.

Cutlets of Venison.
Time, twenty minutes.

533. A few lardoons; a sprig of thyme and parsley; two carrots; one onion; a little glaze; one gill of gravy.

Cut the venison into nice shapes, and lard each cutlet, lay them in a stewpan with the herbs and the vegetables sliced. When they are dressed, glaze them and serve with sauce piquante.

POULTRY.

In London poultry is bought ready trussed from the poulterer; nevertheless, it often happens that the cook has turkeys, fowls, &c. &c., sent from the country to pick and prepare herself, and thus a knowledge of trussing is absolutely necessary.

At the head of the several directions or receipts for dressing poultry and game which are here offered, there will, therefore, be found full and ample instructions as to trussing and preparing the birds.

It has been thought more convenient for the reader of this work, to put both trussing and cooking directions on the same page, rather than for her to have the trouble of turning back for the former to another part of the book. The coloured engravings will serve to exemplify the verbal teaching, and render the art of trussing easy to every comprehension.

All poultry should be carefully picked; every plug or stub removed, and the birds carefully singed with a piece of lighted white paper. French cooks hold them over a flame to remove the down, thinking that lighted paper is apt to blacken the skin.

Poultry should be drawn carefully, taking care that the gall bag and the gut joining the gizzard are not broken. The liver and gizzard will be required under the pinions of the bird; but open the gizzard first and remove the contents, and detach the gall bladder from the liver. Fowls should be drawn through the vent.

Take care to roast poultry by a brisk clear fire, a slow fire will spoil them.

The time given with each receipt for dressing the birds, must be always understood with the modifications required by the different sizes of the same.

General Table of Time for Roasting Poultry.

Turkey of ten pounds' weight, stuffed, two hours; larger, two hours and a half; smaller one; one hour and fifteen minutes.

Large fowl, one hour; smaller, three-quarters of an hour.

Chicken, from twenty minutes to half an hour.

Duck, from three-quarters of an hour to one hour.

Ducklings, from twenty-five to thirty-five minutes.

A capon, full size, one hour.

A goose, one hour and three-quarters; small goose, one hour and a half.

Pigeon, from twenty to twenty-five minutes.

To boil, about the same time.

Roast Turkey.

In season from December to February.

Time, according to size, from one hour and fifteen minutes to two hours, or two hours and a half.

534. Half a pint of forcemeat for veal, or sausage meat; a little butter.

To truss the bird: pick the bird carefully, and singe off the down with a piece of lighted white paper; break the leg bones close to the feet; hang it on a hook and draw out the strings from the thigh; cut the neck off close to the back, but leave the crop skin long enough to turn over the back; remove the crop, and with the middle finger loosen the liver and the gut at the throat end. Cut off the vent, remove the gut, take a crooked wire and pull out the gizzard, and the liver will easily follow. But be very careful not to break the gall bladder; if you do it will spoil the flavour of the bird entirely, by giving it a bitter taste, which no after effort of washing, &c. can remove. Do not break the gut joining the gizzard either, lest the inside should become gritty. Wipe the inside *perfectly* clean with a wet cloth, then cut the breast bone through on each side close to the back, and draw the legs close to the crop. Put a cloth on the breast, and beat the breast bone down with a rolling-pin till it lies flat. Scald the feet, peel off the outer skin, and cut away the claws; leave the legs on.

Fill the inside with veal stuffing or sausage meat (*see* Forcemeat), and either sew the skin of the neck over the back with a trussing needle, or fasten it with a very small skewer. Then run a long skewer into the pinion and thigh through the body, passing it through the opposite pinion and thigh. On the other side put a skewer in the small part of the leg, close on the outside of the sidesman, and push it through. Clean the liver and gizzard and tuck them between the pinions, and turn the point of the pinions on the back. . Pass a string over the points of the skewers, and tie it securely at the back to keep the bird neat and firmly trussed. Cover the breast with a sheet of nicely buttered white paper.

Place the bird on the spit or roasting jack, and set it at some distance from the fire, which should be a very good and bright one. Keep the heat well to the breast. Put a quarter of a pound of butter in the dripping-pan, and baste it frequently to prevent it from drying too much. Just before it is finished dressing, remove the paper, dredge it lightly with flour, and baste it with the butter, so as to brown and froth it. Serve it with good brown gravy poured over it, and garnish with small fried sausages or forcemeat balls. Sauce: bread sauce.

Roast Turkey with Chestnuts.

Time, one hour and three-quarters to two hours and a half, according to size.

535. Fifty chestnuts; marrow from marrow bones; a little butter; flour; and salt.

Truss a turkey for roasting. Boil half a hundred of chestnuts till tender; remove the shell; peel them and chop them very fine. Take the marrow of two marrow bones, cut it into pieces and stuff the inside of the turkey with the marrow and chestnuts. Fix a buttered paper over the breast; put it down to a good fire, and baste it constantly all the time it is roasting. Then take off the paper, baste the turkey well with butter, sprinkle a little salt over it, and dredge it with flour to froth it. When done, take it up, pour over it a little chestnut sauce, and serve it with brown gravy separately. It will take a quarter of an hour longer roasting than when dressed without the marrow and chestnuts.

Sauce: bread sauce.

Boiled Turkey.

Hen turkeys are best for boiling; they should hang quite four days before they are dressed.

Time, large turkey, one hour and three-quarters; smaller, one hour and a half.

536. To truss a boiled turkey.

Cut the first joint of the legs off, pass the middle finger into the inside, raise the skin of the legs, and put them under the apron of the bird.

Put a skewer into the joint of the wing and the middle joint of the leg, and run it through the body and the other leg and wing. The liver and gizzard must be put in the pinions. Then turn the small end of the pinion on the back, and tie a packthread over the ends of the legs to keep them in their places. Having trussed the turkey for boiling, put it, wrapped in a clean cloth, into sufficient *hot* water to more than cover it. Bring it gradually to a boil, and carefully remove the scum as it rises, or it will spoil the appearance of the bird. Let it simmer very gently for an hour and a half, or for a longer time if of a large size. When done, serve it on a hot dish, with a little celery sauce, oyster sauce, or with parsley and butter; put a small quantity of either over it, and send the other up in a tureen separately.

Turkey Stewed with Celery.

Time, altogether two hours and a quarter.

537. A turkey; four large heads of celery; a cupful of cream; a piece of butter the size of a walnut well rolled in flour.

Choose a fine hen turkey, stuff it with veal stuffing, and truss it as for boiling. Put it into a large stewpan filled with water, and let it boil until tender. Take up the turkey with sufficient of the water in which it has been boiled to keep it hot. Wash the celery and put it into a stewpan with the other portion of the water in which the turkey was boiled, and let it stew until tender, which will be in about twenty-five minutes. Then take it out, and put in the turkey breast downwards, and let it stew for a quarter of an hour. Place it when done on a hot dish before the fire. Thicken the sauce with a lump of butter rolled in flour and a large cupful of cream. Put in the celery to warm again, and then pour the sauce and the celery over the turkey.

Turkey Hashed.

Time, one hour for the gravy.

538. Cold roast turkey; pepper; salt; half a pint of gravy; a piece of butter the size of a walnut; a little flour; a spoonful of ketchup; peel of half a lemon.

Cut the breast of a cold turkey, or any of the white meat, into thin slices. Cut off the legs, score them, dredge them with pepper and salt, and broil them over a clear fire a nice brown. Put half a pint of gravy into a stewpan with a little piece of butter rolled in flour, a spoonful of ketchup, some pepper and salt, and the peel of half a lemon shred very fine. Put in the turkey, and shake it over a clear fire till it is thoroughly hot, place it in a dish with the broiled legs on the top, and sippets of fried bread round it.

Turkey Poults.
In season from June to October.
Time, one hour.

539. Butter sufficient for basting; a dredging of flour.

To truss:—Take the neck out of the skin —*i.e.*, cut off the neck, but leave the head attached to the body by the neckskin. Draw the bird as you do a turkey. Put a skewer through the joint of the pinion, with the legs up close, run the skewer through the middle of the leg, through the body, and do the same on the other side.

Cut off the under part of the bill, twist the skin of the neck round and round, and tuck the head under the wing with the bill end forward. Another skewer must then be put into the sidesman, and the legs placed between the sidesman and the apron on each side. Pass the skewer through all; cut off the toe-nails. It is optional whether you use the liver and gizzard or not.

Put it down to roast, placing a buttered paper over the breast, and keep it constantly basted to prevent it from becoming dry. Just before it is done, take off the paper, dredge a little flour over it, and baste it with butter to froth it nicely. Serve it with gravy poured over it, and send in some separately in a tureen.

To Broil the Legs of a Turkey.
Time, a quarter of an hour.

540. The legs of a turkey; a little pepper, salt, Cayenne; and a squeeze of a lemon.

Take the legs from a cold roast turkey, make some incisions across them with a sharp knife, and season them with a little pepper, salt, and a pinch of Cayenne. Squeeze over them a little lemon juice, and place them on a gridiron well buttered, over a clear fire. When done a nice brown, put them on a hot dish with a piece of butter on the top of each, and serve them up very hot.

Pulled Turkey.
Time, twenty minutes.

541. Two spoonfuls of white gravy; one of cream; grated nutmeg; salt; butter, and flour.

Pull the meat with a fork from the breast of a cold turkey, and make it *hot* in a stewpan with two spoonfuls of gravy, one of cream, a piece of butter dredged with flour, and a seasoning of salt and nutmeg. Serve up hot.

To Truss a Goose for Roasting.

542. Pick and stub it clean. Cut the feet off at the joint, and the pinion off at the first joint.

Cut off the neck close to the back, leaving the skin of the neck long enough to turn over the back. Pull out the throat and tie a knot at the end. Loosen the liver, &c., at the breast end with the middle finger, and cut it open between the vent and rump. Draw out all the entrails except the soul or soul, wipe out the inside with a clean cloth. Beat the breastbone flat with a rolling-pin, put a skewer into the wing, and draw the legs up close, put a skewer through the middle of the legs and through the body, do the same on the other side. Put another skewer in the small of the leg, tuck it close down to the sidesman, run it through, and do the same on the other side. Cut off the end of the vent, and make a hole large enough for the passage of the rump, as by that means you will better secure the seasoning in its place.

To Roast a Goose.
Time, a large goose, two hours; a smaller one, one hour and a half.

543. Sage and onion stuffing; some good gravy.

After the goose is prepared for roasting, fill it with sage and onion stuffing, and fasten it in securely at both ends by passing the rump through a slit made in the skin, and tying the skin of the neck into the back of the bird. Roast it before a nice brisk fire for an hour and a half if small; one hour and three-quarters or two hours if large. Keep it frequently basted, and when done remove the skewers, place it on a hot dish, and pour a little good gravy round it. Send up some in a tureen. Serve with apple sauce. Make the giblets into a pie.

To Stew Giblets.
Time, one hour and a half.

544. One set of giblets; a bunch of parsley and thyme; a few sage leaves; pepper and salt; one onion; a quart of gravy; a wine-glass of white wine.

Thoroughly clean and wash the giblets,

cut them into pieces, and stew them for an hour and a half in a quart of gravy, adding a bunch of thyme and parsley, an onion, a few sage leaves, and a seasoning of pepper and salt. When done, put them into water, and trim them ready for serving. Strain the gravy through a fine hair sieve, add a glass of white wine, and a piece of butter the size of a walnut rolled in flour. Boil the giblets up in the gravy, and serve them quickly.

To Truss and Roast a Duck.

545. Ducks are trussed in the same manner as geese (*see* p. 137), except that the feet must be left on and turned close to the legs.

To Roast a Duck.

Time, three-quarters of an hour to one hour.

546. A couple of ducks; sage and onion stuffing.

Ducks should always hang for one day, and even longer if the weather be sufficiently cold to allow it. Stuff *one* with sage and onion stuffing, season the inside of the other with pepper and salt. Put them to roast at a clear bright fire, and keep them constantly basted until done. A short time before serving, dredge over them a little flour, and baste them with butter to make them froth and brown. Serve them very hot, and pour round (not over them) a little good brown gravy. Serve a little of the same separately in a tureen.

Green peas should **always** be sent up with roast ducks, if in season.

Stewed Duck.

Time, two hours and a half.

547. A couple of ducks or one duck; forcemeat; three sage leaves; two onions; one lemon; a glass of port wine.

Take a duck, pick, draw, and stuff it with forcemeat, adding three sage leaves chopped fine. Clean and wash the giblets, and put them into sufficient water to cover them. Make from them a gravy for the duck, add two onions chopped very fine, and a seasoning of pepper and salt. Let the gravy simmer until it is strong enough, then put the duck into a stewpan, pour the gravy and onions over it, and stew it slowly for about two hours, adding a glass of port wine just before it is done. Dish it up and squeeze the juice of a lemon over it; pour the gravy round, and serve it with fried bread.

Cold Duck—Stewed with Green Peas.

Time, twenty minutes.

548. Cold roast duck; peel of half a lemon; one quart of young green peas; a large piece of butter rolled in flour; three-quarters of a pint of gravy; pepper, salt, and Cayenne to your taste.

Cut the duck into neat pieces, and season them with a *very little* Cayenne, pepper, and salt, with the peel of half a lemon minced very fine. Put it in a stewpan, pour over it three-quarters of a pint of good gravy, and place it over a clear fire to become very hot, but do not let it boil.

Boil nearly, or quite, a quart of young green peas in boiling water: drain them on a sieve, and stir into them a large piece of butter mixed with a little flour; just warm the stewpan over the fire, pile the peas in the centre of a hot dish, arrange the pieces of duck round them, and serve.

Ragoût of Duck.

Time, to roast, twenty-five minutes; to stew, one hour and a half; and ten minutes for the gravy.

549. A duck; one pint and a half of broth or water; any trimmings of meat; one large onion stuck with six cloves; twelve berries of allspice; two black peppers; peel of half a lemon; two ounces of butter; flour; one glass of port wine; a teaspoonful of salt; juice of half a lemon.

Half roast a duck and divide it into joints, or neatly cut pieces; put it into a stewpan with a pint and a half of broth, or water, with any trimmings of meat; a large onion stuck with cloves, the allspice and black peppers, and the rind of a lemon cut very thin. Bring the pan to a boil, and skim it clean, then let it simmer gently, with the lid closed, for an hour and a half. Take out the pieces of duck and strain the gravy. Put two ounces of butter into a small stewpan, and sufficient flour to make it a rather stiff paste, and stir in the gravy very gradually. Let it boil up; then add the juice of half a lemon, a glass of port wine, and a little salt. Put the duck in a dish, and pour the gravy over it.

Stewed Giblets—Duck.

Time, full three-quarters of an hour.

550. One or two sets of giblets; one pint and a half of water or stock; two or three cloves; twelve pepper-corns; a bunch of savoury herbs; two dessertspoonfuls of mushroom ketchup; one onion; a piece of butter.

Well wash the giblets, divide the pinions, and the neck, head and gizzard; put them into a stewpan with a bunch of savoury herbs, one onion, and the spice; pour over them a pint and a half of water or weak stock, and set the pan over a gentle fire to stew until the giblets are tender; then thicken the gravy with a piece of butter rolled in flour, and just before serving add the white wine; boil it up and pour it over the giblets.

To Truss a Roast Fowl.

551. The fowl must be picked and singed; the neck cut off close to the back. Take out the crop, and with the middle finger loosen the liver and other parts at the breast end; cut off the vent; draw the fowl clean; wash out and wipe the inside quite dry; beat the breastbone flat with a rolling-pin. Put a skewer in the first joint of the pinion and bring the middle of the leg close to it. Put the skewer through the middle of the leg and through the body, and do the same on the other side. Put another skewer in the small of the leg and through the sidesman. Do the same on the other side, and then put another through the skin of the feet, which should have the nails cut off. Clean out and wash the gizzard, remove the gall bag from the liver, and put both liver and gizzard in the pinions.

To Roast a Fowl or Chicken.

Time, one hour for a large one; three-quarters of an hour for a small one; twenty-five minutes for a chicken.

552. One large fowl or two small ones; some brown gravy; butter, and flour.

When the fowls are trussed for roasting, singe them carefully, and wipe them clean; put a piece of buttered paper over the breasts, and roast them at a clear fire, keeping them frequently basted. Just before they are done, remove the paper, dredge them with flour, and baste them with butter warmed in the basting-ladle until they are nicely browned and have a frothy appearance. Then place them on a hot dish, pour a little brown gravy over them, and serve the remainder in a tureen with another of bread sauce.

To Roast a Fowl—Family Receipt.

Time, one hour.

553. A large fowl; two or three table-spoonfuls of bread-crumbs; half a pound of butter; pepper and salt.

Draw and truss a fowl for roasting, put into the inside two or three tablespoonfuls of fine bread-crumbs, seasoned with pepper and salt, and a piece of butter the size of a large walnut. Put the fowl down before a clear fire to roast, basting it *well* with butter; and just before it is done dredge over it a little flour, and baste it with butter to give it a frothy appearance. When done, add a little warm water to the butter in the dripping-pan, or add a little *very thin* melted butter, and strain it over the fowl. Serve with bread sauce in a tureen, or a little made gravy if preferred.

Roast Fowl with Forcemeat.

Time, one hour.

554. A large fowl; some veal stuffing.

Fill the breast of the fowl with a nice veal stuffing, and truss it for roasting, put it down to a clear fire and dredge over it a little flour. If a large fowl it will require about an hour (as above) to roast, but less time if of a medium size. When done, remove the skewers, and serve it with brown gravy and bread sauce.

To Truss Boiled Fowls.

555. For boiling, choose fowls that are *not* blacklegged.

Pick and singe the fowl; cut off the neck close to the back; take out the crop, and with the middle finger loosen the liver and other parts; cut off the vent, draw it clean, and beat the breastbone flat with a rolling-pin.

Cut off the nails of the feet and tuck them down close to the legs. Put your finger into the inside and raise the skin of the fowl, then cut a hole in the top of the skin, and put the legs under. Put a skewer in the first joint of the pinion and bring the middle of the leg close to it; put the skewer through the middle of the leg and through the body; do the same on the other side; open the gizzard, remove the contents, and wash well, remove the gall bladder from the liver. Put the gizzard and liver in the pinions, turn the points of the pinions on the back, and tie a string over the tops of the legs to keep them in their proper places.

To Boil Fowls or Chickens.

Time, one hour for a large fowl; three-quarters of an hour for a medium size; half an hour for a chicken.

556. After the fowls or chickens are trussed for boiling, fold them in a nice white floured cloth, and put them into a stewpan; cover them well with hot water, bring it gradually to a boil, and skim it very carefully as the scum rises; then let them simmer as *slowly as possible*, which will improve their appearance more than fast boiling, causing them to be whiter and plumper. When done, put them on a hot dish, remove the skewers, and pour over them a little parsley and butter. Boiled tongue, ham, or bacon is usually served to eat with them.

Boiled Chickens and Tongue.
Time, half an hour.

557. Draw and truss a couple of young chickens, and boil as before directed. Have a tongue trimmed and glazed, place it in the centre of the dish, and a chicken on each side. Garnish with brocoli. Pour over the *chickens* and the *brocoli*, but not the tongue, a little white sauce; and serve them up hot.

To Stew a Fowl.
Time, one hour and a half.

558. A fowl; one quart of gravy; one head of celery; two or three blades of mace; two ounces of butter; one wineglassful of port wine; one glass of ketchup; pepper and salt to taste.

Put four clean skewers at the bottom of a stewpan, and lay the fowl on them, pour in a quart of gravy, add a head of celery cut into pieces, and two or three blades of mace. Let it stew gently until there remains only sufficient gravy for the sauce; then stir in a large piece of butter rolled in flour, add a glass of port wine, and the same of ketchup; seasoning with pepper and salt to your taste.

When done, lay the fowl on a hot dish, and serve it up very hot, with the sauce poured over it.

La Remoulade.
Time, one hour and a half.

559. Two fowls; two quarts of water; one tablespoonful of oil; one of vinegar; yolks of hard-boiled eggs.

Take two fine fowls, beat one with a rolling-pin to a mummy, and boil it in *two* quarts of water until reduced to *one*, then boil the other fowl in the soup. When cold, cut it up in a salad dish with the oil, vinegar, and yolks of two hard-boiled eggs well mixed. Cover the whole with French beans pickled, and hard-boiled eggs sliced.

Scallops of Chicken.
Time, twenty minutes.

560. A piece of butter the size of half an egg; one dessertspoonful of flour; one teacupful of gravy; salt and pepper; three or four yolks of eggs; some bread-crumbs; some cold chicken.

Make with the piece of butter well mixed with the flour and gravy a nice white sauce, thickened with a liaison of three or four well-beaten yolks of eggs. Cut the remains of the cold fowl into scallops about the size of the top of a wineglass; dip them in the sauce. Have ready some scallop-shells, fill them with the scallops, grate bread-crumbs all over them, put them in a Dutch oven and brown them.

Fricassee of Cold Roast Fowl.
Time, an hour and a quarter.

561. A cold roast fowl; a bunch of savoury herbs; a quarter of a pint of cream; yolks of two eggs; pepper; salt, and pounded mace; peel of half a lemon.

Take a cold roast fowl, or the remains of two, cut them up, put all the trimmings and bones of the legs into a stewpan with the peel of half a lemon, a bunch of savoury herbs, a little pounded mace, pepper and salt, and about a pint of water; let them stew gently until reduced to half the quantity. Cut the remainder of the fowls into joints, strain the gravy and put in the fowl. When thoroughly hot, stir in a very little flour; well beat the yolks of a couple of new eggs, mix them with a quarter of a pint of fresh cream, and stir it gradually into the gravy. Make it very hot without letting it boil, and serve poured over the chickens.

Minced Fowl.
Time, one hour.

562. Cold roast fowl; peel and juice of half a lemon; one ounce and a half of butter; a dessertspoonful of flour; a bunch of savoury herbs; two eggs; a cupful of cream; a little mace, salt, and pepper.

Mince very fine all the white meat from some cold roast fowl, removing the bones and skin. Put the latter into a stewpan with all the trimmings, a bunch of savoury herbs, half a blade of mace, and a pint of broth or water; let this stew for nearly an hour, and then strain it off. Chop two hard-boiled eggs very fine, season the fowl with a little pepper, salt, and pounded mace, mix it with the eggs, pour in the gravy, having previously thickened it with the butter, flour, and cream; let it get very hot, but do not let it boil, and serve with sippets of toasted bread.

Grilled Fowl.
Time, a quarter of an hour to broil.

563. The remains of cold fowls; juice of half a lemon; pepper and salt; breadcrumbs; clarified butter; grated lemon peel.

Cut the remains of cold fowl into pieces, season them with pepper and salt, squeeze over them the juice of half a lemon, and let them stand for three-quarters of an hour; wipe them dry, dip them into clarified butter, and then into bread-crumbs with a little lemon peel grated. Put them on a gridiron and broil them over a clear fire. When fried instead of broiled, use the yolk of egg well-beaten instead of the clarified butter.

To Truss Pigeons.

564. A pigeon requires a great deal of care in cleaning. Wash it thoroughly and wipe it very dry before putting it to the fire. Pigeons should not be kept, or they will lose their flavour. Draw them directly they are killed; cut off the head and neck; truss the wings over the back, and cut off the toes at the first joint.

To Roast Pigeons.

Time, twenty minutes to half an hour.

565. Some pigeons; half a pound of butter; pepper and salt.

Well wash and thoroughly clean the pigeons; wipe them dry, season them inside with pepper and salt, and put a good-sized piece of butter into the body of each bird. Roast them before a clear bright fire, basting them well the whole of the time. Serve them with gravy and bread sauce.

Or send up a tureen of parsley and butter, in which case the birds must be garnished with fried parsley; but for very plain cooking, they can have a little water added to the butter in the dripping pan, and poured round them, adding a spoonful or two of gravy.

Stuffed Pigeons.

Time, half an hour.

566. Four pigeons; the livers minced, and their weight in beef suet, bread-crumbs and hard eggs; a little mace; nutmeg; pepper; salt; eggs; a glass of port wine; a bunch of sweet herbs.

Take four pigeons, make a forcemeat of the livers minced small, an equal quantity of beef suet or marrow, bread-crumbs, and hard eggs, seasoned with a little beaten mace, nutmeg, pepper, and salt; and a bunch of sweet herbs chopped fine. Mix all together with the yolk of a beaten egg; cut the skin of the pigeons between the legs and the bodies, and with your finger carefully raise the skin from the flesh, but take care you do not break it; then put in the forcemeat; truss the legs close to keep it in, roast and baste the birds well with butter; save the gravy which runs from them, and mix it with a glass of port wine, and some of the forcemeat, a little nutmeg, pepper and salt; thicken with the yolk of an egg well beaten (if not enough gravy for sauce, put in a little made gravy). Just boil it up, lay the pigeons in a hot dish, pour the sauce over them, and serve.

A Simple Receipt for Jugged Pigeons.

Time, to steam, one hour and a half.

567. Three pigeons; a little mace; pepper and salt; a quarter of a pound of butter; a glass of wine; a tablespoonful of ketchup; a sprig of sweet herbs; a piece of butter rolled in flour.

Pick the pigeons, wash and dry them in a cloth, and cut them into pieces. Season them well with a *little* pounded mace, pepper, and salt. Put them into a jar, and cover them well over to prevent the steam escaping. Place the jar in a saucepan of boiling water, and let it boil constantly. Then take out the pigeons, put the gravy from the jar into a stewpan with the wine, ketchup, and sprig of sweet herbs. Boil it a few minutes, and thicken it with butter rolled in flour. Serve the pigeons on a very hot dish, with the gravy poured over them.

To Truss a Roast Capon.

568. Pick it clean, cut a slit in the back of the neck, take out the crop, loosen the liver, and gut the breast with the forefinger. Then cut off the vent and draw it. Cut off the pinions at the first joint, and wipe out the inside. Beat the breastbone flat with a rolling-pin, put a skewer in the pinion, and bring the middle of the legs close. Then run the skewer through the legs, body, and the other pinion, twist the head, and put it on the end of the skewer with the bill fronting the breast. Put another skewer into the sidesman, and put the legs close on each side of the apron, and then run the skewer through all.

To Roast Capons.

Time, three-quarters of an hour to one hour.

569. A capon must be drawn and trussed as above, then placed on a spit, and roasted before a fine brisk fire for about three quarters of an hour, but if *very* large, a longer time. When done, put it on a hot dish, pour some good gravy round it, and serve with bread sauce.

To Truss a Capon for Boiling.

570. Pick the bird very clean, and cut the neck off close to the back. Take out the crop, and with the middle finger loosen the liver and other parts at the breast end. Cut off the vent, draw it clean, and beat the breastbone flat with a rolling-pin. Cut off the nails of the feet and tuck them down close to the legs. Put the forefinger into the inside, and raise the skin of the legs; then cut a hole in the top of the skin and

put the legs under. Put a skewer into the first joint of the pinion, and bring the middle of the leg close to it. Put the skewer through the middle of the leg, and through the body, and then do the same on the other side. Put the gizzard and the liver in the pinions, turn the points on the back, and tie a string over the tops of the legs to keep them in their proper places.

To Boil a Capon.

Time, one hour and three-quarters or two hours.

571. A capon; an onion; a bunch of sweet herbs; two carrots; a little salt.

Draw and truss a fine capon for boiling, and tie entirely over it a sheet of buttered paper, put it into a stewpan, cover it with water, and add two carrots cut across, one small onion, a little salt, and a bunch of sweet herbs; simmer very gently until tender. When done, dish it up, and garnish with bunches of cauliflowers. Pour over the capon white or Bechamel sauce, and serve.

Capon a la Francaise.

Time, one hour.

572. One capon; one lemon; three or four slices of bacon; one onion; half a pint of stock.

After having prepared and trussed the capon, scorch off with a lighted paper or over a flame every bit of feather and stubble remaining.

Wipe out the inside, rub it over outside with the juice of a lemon, put two or three slices of very fat bacon over the breast, and tie it up in thin strips of bacon very neatly. Put it in a stewpan, add an onion and half a pint of gravy or stock, and let it stew or boil gently till done.

Garnish:—Four eggs; one teacupful of rice; one ounce of butter.

The capon dressed this way may be served on rice, nicely boiled, and mixed with cream, or beat up with four yolks of eggs, and a little fresh butter.

Abd-el-Kader's Stewed Capon.

Time, one hour and a quarter.

573. Two onions; three spoonfuls of fine oil; one pinch of saffron; one pint of water; a little garlic; a capon; three spoonfuls of flour; a pint of good gravy or broth; a quarter of a pound of rice; two eggs; two capsicums.

Shred some onions *very* fine; fry them well in three tablespoonfuls of fine oil. Boil a tiny pinch of saffron in water. Take from time to time a little of this saffron water and put it into the stewpan where the onions are frying; add a little garlic. When the onions are partly done, cut up a capon or fowl in pieces, lay it on the onions and fry it. Thicken a pint of broth with the flour; have broth enough *to cover* the fowl; if a pint will not suffice, add more. When it is done, strain the broth from the fowl through a sieve. Boil some rice nicely as for curry, dry it, put it on a dish, and lay the fowl on it in the middle. Garnish it with slices of hard-boiled eggs cut in quarters, and capsicums, round the edge of the dish. Pour the gravy over it, and serve it very hot.

To Truss a Partridge.

574. Partridges should hang a few days.

Pluck, draw, and wipe the partridge inside and out, cut off the head, leaving sufficient skin on the neck to skewer back, bring the legs close to the breast—between it and the side bones, and pass a skewer through the pinions and the thick part of the thighs. If the head is left on, it should be brought round and fixed on to the point of the skewer, but it is generally removed from the bird at present.

To Roast a Partridge.

Time, twenty-five to thirty-five minutes.

575. Partridges; butter; gravy.

When the partridges are plumply trussed, roast them before a clear fire, basting them very frequently, and frothing them up with a little flour and butter just before serving them. Pour a little gravy over the birds, and serve them with bread sauce and gravy in tureens.

Salmi of Partridge.

Time, one hour and a quarter.

576. Some cold partridge; one small onion; one bay-leaf; a bunch of thyme and parsley; a glass of white wine; six pepper corns; a large cupful of broth; one pint and a half of water; a tablespoonful of browning.

Cut into joints a cold partridge or two, left from a previous dinner, remove the skin and put them into a stewpan. Put the bones and any trimmings you have minced small, a small onion cut into four, a bunch of thyme and parsley, a glass of white wine, and a bay-leaf, put these into a separate stewpan, pour in a pint and a half of water, and a large cupful of broth, add a spoonful of browning, and boil it altogether until reduced to half the quantity, skim it clean, and strain it over the partridges in the other pan. Warm the whole over the fire, and when hot, place the pieces of bird in a dish, and pour the gravy over them.

To Truss a Pheasant.

577. After the pheasant is picked and drawn, wipe it inside with a damp cloth, and truss it in the same way as a partridge. If the head is left on, as it ought to be, bring it round under the wing, and fix it on the point of the skewer.

Pheasant Roasted.

Time, from half an hour to one hour according to size.

578. A pheasant; butter; flour; brown gravy, and salt.

After the pheasant is trussed, spit it, and roast before a clear quick fire; baste it frequently with butter, sprinkle over it a little salt, and dredge it lightly with flour to froth it nicely. When done (which will be in about half an hour, or longer if a large bird), serve it up with a little good brown gravy poured round the pheasant, and the remainder in a tureen, with another of bread sauce.

Pheasant Broiled.

Time, half an hour.

579. A pheasant; a little lard; one egg; a few bread-crumbs; salt and Cayenne to taste.

Cut the legs off at the first joint, cut up the bird. Put the pieces into a frying-pan with a little lard, when browned on both sides and half done through take them up, drain them, brush them over with egg, dip them in bread-crumbs, well seasoned with salt and Cayenne; broil them for ten minutes, and serve with mushroom sauce.

Hashed Pheasant.

Time one hour for the gravy and a quarter of an hour for the pheasant.

580. Pheasant; butter; flour; a glass of port wine; a spoonful of colouring.

Cut some cold pheasant into pieces, and brown them lightly over the fire, in a piece of butter and a little flour. Pour into a stewpan a glass of port wine and a cupful of water, with a spoonful of browning, pepper, and salt; boil, skim, and stir it until very thick, then put in the pieces of pheasant, make them very hot, but do not let them boil. Place the meat on a dish, and strain the gravy over it. Garnish with sippets of fried bread.

A Boiled Pheasant.

Time, from half an hour to one hour, according to size.

581. A *hen* pheasant; half a pint of horseradish sauce.

Boil a hen pheasant nicely, as a fowl is done. Serve it covered with horseradish sauce.

This dish was recommended to an invalid friend by a celebrated physician. It is excellent.

To Truss a Hare.

582. When wanted for dressing, cut off the fore legs at the first joint, raise the skin of the back and draw it over the hind legs. Leave the tail whole, then draw the skin over the back and slip out the fore legs. Cut the skin from the neck and head, skin the ears and leave them on. Clean the vent, cut the sinews under the legs, bring them forward, run a skewer through one hind leg, through the body and the other hind leg. Do the same with the fore legs, lay the head rather back, put a skewer in the mouth, through the back of the head, and between the shoulders. Rinse the inside, wipe it dry, rub it with a little pepper and salt, and fill it with the proper stuffing. Sew up the body and pass a string over it to secure the legs on the skewers.

To Roast Hare.

Time, one hour and a quarter to one hour and a half or two hours.

583. A fine hare; some well-seasoned veal stuffing; milk; butter, and brown gravy.

After the hare is skinned and prepared, wipe it dry with a clean cloth, fill the belly with well-seasoned veal stuffing, and sew it up. Draw the fore and hind legs close to the body, and pass a long skewer through each. Tie a string round the body, from one skewer to the other, and secure it above the back. Fix the head between the shoulders with another skewer, and be careful to leave the ears on. Place it at some distance from the fire when first it is put down, and baste it well with milk and water for a short time, and afterwards with butter. Just before it is done, dredge over it a little flour, and baste it well with butter to make a fine froth. When done, take it up on a hot dish, remove the skewers, and pour a little good gravy into the dish. Serve gravy in a tureen.

Jugged Hare.

Time, four hours.

584. A hare; a small onion; a lemon;

two glasses of port wine; a tablespoonful of mushroom ketchup; one pound and a half of gravy beef; five cloves; pepper; salt, and a little Cayenne; butter and flour.

Skin the hare, and cut it in pieces, but do not wash it; dredge it with flour, and fry it a nice brown in butter, seasoning it with a little pepper, salt, and Cayenne. Make about a pint and a half of gravy from the beef. Put the pieces of hare into a jar, add the onion stuck with four or five cloves, the lemon peeled and cut, and pour in the gravy. Cover the jar *closely* to keep in the steam, put it into a deep stewpan of cold water, and let it boil four hours, but if a young hare three hours will be sufficient. When done, take it out of the jar, and shake it over the fire for a few minutes, adding a tablespoonful of mushroom ketchup, two glasses of port wine, and a piece of butter rolled in flour with some fried forcemeat balls. Serve with red currant jelly.

Hashed Hare.

Time, rather more than an hour.

585. Cold roast hare; three dessertspoonfuls of mushroom ketchup; four dessertspoonfuls of port wine; a bunch of savoury herbs; a little pepper, salt, and mace; butter and flour.

Take the remains of a cold roast hare, and cut the best parts into slices. Put the trimmings, head, and bones into a stewpan to make the gravy, pour in a pint of water, add the herbs and spice, with pepper and salt to your taste. Stew it gently for an hour, and then strain it through a sieve. Add a piece of butter rolled in flour, the ketchup, and wine, with a few forcemeat balls, or any stuffing left from the previous day. Put in the slices of hare and set it over the fire until very hot. Serve it up with toasted sippets and currant jelly.

To Roast a Leveret.

Time, three-quarters of an hour.

586. Leveret; half a pound of butter.

Clean and truss a leveret in the same manner as a hare, but roast it plain without any stuffing. Place it before a clear bright fire for about three quarters of an hour, and baste it often with the butter. About ten minutes before serving, dredge it lightly with flour to froth it nicely. Serve with gravy poured round it, and red currant jelly with it.

To Truss Roast Rabbits.

587. Empty, skin, wash, and soak the rabbit; stuff it with veal forcemeat; skewer back the head between the shoulders; cut off the fore joints of the legs and shoulders, draw them close to the body, and pass a skewer through them.

Roast Rabbit.

Time, three-quarters of an hour.

588. One large rabbit; pepper; salt; nutmeg; half a pound of butter; four dessertspoonfuls of cream; one tablespoonful of flour; yolks of two eggs; brown gravy; the peel of half a lemon grated.

Procure a fine large rabbit, and truss it in the same manner as a hare; fill the paunch with veal stuffing, and roast it before a bright clear fire for three-quarters of an hour, if a large one, basting it well with butter. Before serving, mix a spoonful of flour with four of cream to thicken it; stir in the yolks of two well-beaten eggs, and season with a little grated nutmeg, pepper, and salt; baste the rabbit thickly with this, to form a light coating over it. When dry, baste it with butter to froth it up, and when done place it carefully in a dish, and pour round it some brown gravy, boiled up with the liver minced, and a little grated nutmeg. Serve with gravy in a tureen, and red jelly. A rabbit can be baked instead of roasted, and will require the same time in a good oven.

Or—

Time, three-quarters of an hour for a large one.

589. One rabbit; sausage meat; veal stuffing; butter and flour.

Before trussing the rabbit, line the inside with sausage meat and veal stuffing, with the liver minced and added to it. Wrap the rabbit in buttered paper to prevent its burning, and roast it at a nice bright fire, baste it very frequently, and ten minutes before it is done, remove the paper and dredge over it a little flour to froth it up. When done, take out the skewers, put it on a hot dish, and serve with a brown gravy, and red currant jelly in a glass dish.

A small rabbit will only require about half an hour or thirty-six minutes at a brisk good fire.

Ragout of Rabbit.

Time, thirty-five minutes.

590. One rabbit; a quarter of a pound of bacon; one Spanish onion, or two common ones; half a lemon; a piece of butter the size of an egg; one tablespoonful of flour; and seasoning to taste.

Cut the onions into slices, dredge them

well with flour, and put them into a stewpan with a piece of butter the size of an egg; stir it over the fire until the onions are nicely browned, and then stir in a few spoonfuls of water, making it the consistency of melted butter. Cut the rabbit into joints, and the bacon into very thin slices, season it with pepper and salt to taste, put them into the stewpan and add half a lemon sliced thin. Set it over the fire, and let it simmer slowly for about thirty-five minutes, or until the meat is sufficiently tender; then pour in the glass of wine, shake it up, and serve hot.

To Truss Boiled Rabbits.

591. After well cleaning and skinning a rabbit, wash it in cold water, and then put it into warm water for about twenty minutes to soak out the blood. Draw the head round to the side, and secure it with a thin skewer run through that and the body.

To Blanch Rabbits, Fowls, &c.

592. To blanch or whiten a rabbit or fowl it must be placed on the fire in a small quantity of water, and let boil. As soon as it boils it must be taken out and plunged into *cold water* for a few minutes.

Boiled Rabbit.

Time, a very small rabbit, half an hour; medium size, three-quarters of an hour; a large rabbit, one hour.

593. A rabbit; six onions; liver sauce, or parsley and butter.

When the rabbit is trussed for boiling, put it into a stewpan, and cover it with hot water, and let it boil very gently until tender. When done, place it on a dish, and smother it with onions, or with parsley and butter, or liver sauce, should the flavour of onion not be liked. If liver sauce is to be served, the liver must be boiled for ten minutes, minced very fine, and added to the butter sauce. An old rabbit will require quite an hour to boil it thoroughly.

To Fricassee Rabbits White.

Time, three-quarters of an hour.

594. Two young rabbits; one pint of veal broth, or water; a bunch of sweet herbs; one onion; three shallots; half a blade of mace; half a pint of fresh mushrooms; peel of half a lemon; a piece of butter rolled in flour; yolks of two eggs; half a pint of cream; juice of half a lemon, and a little grated nutmeg.

Take two young rabbits, and cut them in small pieces, but do not use the head or neck, and put them into warm water to soak for an hour. Take them out, drain them dry, and then put them into a stewpan with a pint of veal broth *or water*, a bunch of sweet herbs, an onion, half a blade of mace beaten fine, three shallots chopped up, half a pint of mushrooms, the peel of half a lemon, and a little salt. Cover the pan close, and simmer them for half an hour; then take out the herbs, onion, and lemon peel, and stir in a piece of butter rolled in flour; boil it up, and skim it well. Add a liaison of the yolks of two beaten eggs mixed with the cream, grate in a little nutmeg, and shake the stewpan over the fire one way till the sauce is thick and smooth. Squeeze in the juice of half a lemon, shake it round, and serve it up. Garnish with sliced lemon.

To Fricassee Rabbits Brown.

Time, three quarters of an hour.

595. Two young rabbits; pepper; salt; flour, and butter; a pint of gravy; a bunch of sweet herbs; half a pint of fresh mushrooms; a few truffles if you have them; three shallots; a spoonful of ketchup; a lemon.

Take two young rabbits, cut them in small pieces, slit the head in two, season them with pepper and salt, dredge them with flour, and fry them a nice brown in fresh butter. Pour out the fat from the stewpan, and put in a pint of gravy, a bunch of sweet herbs, half a pint of fresh mushrooms, a few truffles if you have them, and three shallots chopped fine, seasoned with pepper and salt, cover them close, and let them stew for half an hour. Then skim the gravy clean, add a spoonful of ketchup, and the juice of half a lemon. Take out the herbs, and stir in a piece of butter rolled in flour, boil it up till thick and smooth, skim off the fat, and serve them garnished with lemon.

To Truss Woodcocks, Snipes, and Wheatears.

596. Pluck and wipe them very clean outside; truss them with the legs close to the body, and the feet pressing upon the thighs; skin the head and neck, and bring the beak round under the wing.

Woodcocks and Snipes.

Time, twenty to twenty-five minutes.

597. Some woodcocks or snipes; butter; bread toasted; two slices of bacon.

After the birds are picked and trussed, put a thin layer of bacon over them, and tie it on, run a bird spit through them, and tie it on to a common one. Toast and butter a slice of bread, and put it under them for the trail to drop on. Baste them continually with butter, and roast them, if large, for twenty-five minutes, if small, five minutes less. Froth them up, take up the toast, cut it in quarters, put it in the dish, and pour some gravy and butter over it. Take up the woodcocks and put them on it, with the bills outwards. Serve with plain butter sauce in a tureen.

Snipes are dressed the same as woodcocks, only roast the large ones twenty minutes, small ones a quarter of an hour.

Wheatears.

Time, about a quarter of an hour.

598. A slice of toasted bread; one lemon; half a pint of good brown gravy.

Do not draw them. Spit them on a small bird spit, flour them, and baste them well with butter. Have ready a slice of toasted bread (cut the crusts off), lay it in a dish, and set it on the dripping pan, under the birds, while cooking. When done, take them up, lay them on the toast, pour some good brown gravy round them, and garnish with slices of lemon.

To Truss Wild Duck.

599. Pick the bird very clean, and twist each leg at the knuckle; rest the claws on each side of the breast, and secure them by passing a skewer through the thighs and pinions of the wings.

To Roast Wild Ducks.

Time, twenty-five to thirty-five minutes.

600. Wild ducks; butter; flour, Cayenne pepper; one lemon; one glass of port wine.

When the ducks are trussed, spit them, and put them down to roast before a brisk fire, keeping the spit in rapid motion. Baste them plentifully with butter, dredge them lightly with flour, and send them up nicely frothed and browned, with a good gravy in the dish. Before carving it the breast should have a few incisions made across it with a knife, and a piece of fresh butter put on it; then cut a lemon across, on one half put a little salt, on the other a very small quantity of Cayenne pepper; put the lemon together and squeeze the juice over the ducks, then add a glass of warmed port wine, and your ducks will be ready to carve.

Hashed Wild Ducks.

Time, a quarter of an hour.

601. The remains of cold wild ducks; two glasses of port wine; one tablespoonful of mushroom ketchup; one of Harvey sauce; a little flour; pepper, salt, and Cayenne to taste; a little weak stock, or water.

Divide any remains of cold roast wild duck into pieces, and dredge them well with flour, put them into a stewpan with a tablespoonful of mushroom ketchup, and the same of Harvey sauce; add two glasses of port wine, and a very little water or weak stock. Season to your taste with pepper, salt, and Cayenne; and let it simmer for about a quarter of an hour, taking care it does not boil. Arrange the pieces of duck on toast, boil and skim the sauce, and when as thick as cream, pour it over the whole, and serve very hot.

Salmi of Wild Duck.

Time, nearly three-quarters of an hour.

602. Two wild ducks; a wineglass of port wine; one of gravy; six shallots; juice of a Seville orange, or a lemon; a little salt and Cayenne pepper.

Half roast the wild ducks, and cut them up; put a glass of port wine, and the same quantity of gravy, six shallots chopped fine, the juice of a Seville orange or a lemon, a little salt and Cayenne pepper, into a silver chafing dish, and set it over a spirit lamp till it boils up; then put in the wild duck, put on the cover, make it thoroughly hot, and send it to table in the dish. If you have not a chafing dish, stew it in a stewpan, and serve it on a hot dish, and pour over it a sauce made thus:—One glass of port wine or claret, sauce à la Russe one tablespoonful, one of ketchup, one of lemon juice, one slice of lemon peel, one large slice of shallot, four grains of Cayenne pepper.

Scald, strain, and add the above to the gravy which comes from the bird in roasting. The bird should be cut up in the silver dish which has a lamp under it, while the sauce is simmered with it.

To Truss a Peahen.

603. A peahen or peacock is trussed in the same manner as any other fowl, with the exception of the head, which is left on with the feathers on it, folded in buttered paper, and tucked under the wing. If the PEACOCK is roasted, a few of the tail feathers are saved to ornament the bird, as a pheasant sometimes is decked; but this is not done in the case of the peahen.

Peahen Larded and Glazed.

Time, one hour and a half.

604. A quarter of a pound of lardoons;

a quarter of a pound of forcemeat; glaze; watercresses.

Choose a *young* peahen; truss it as directed above. Then lard it on the breast and legs, as it is a dry bird, and is not nice unless larded. (For Larding, *see* page 33). Make a nice veal or turkey forcemeat and put into the inside of the bird, and roast it at a good fire. When it is done, remove the buttered paper from the head, put it on a hot dish, glaze it carefully, and pour round it a good gravy. Garnish with watercresses. Bread sauce served with it.

To Roast Grouse.
Time, half an hour.

605. Grouse; slices of fat bacon; vine leaves; melted butter.

Hang the grouse for some time; pick and truss them like a fowl for roasting, laying over them thin slices of bacon and vine leaves, which tie on with a thin thread. Roast them for half or three-quarters of an hour, and when done, serve them on a slice of toasted bread, and pour some good melted butter over them.

Or—
Time, half an hour.

606. Grouse; butter; bread-crumbs; toasted bread.

Grouse require to hang as long as possible, and, when ready to truss, should be wiped very dry, but not washed. Put a piece of butter and some bread-crumbs inside the birds, and truss them with the head under their wing. Put them down to a brisk fire, and baste them constantly to prevent them becoming dry. Froth them up, and serve them on a slice of buttered toast with bread sauce and gravy separately.

To Roast the Ptarmigan or White Grouse.
Time, half an hour.

607. Three or four birds; butter; fried bread-crumbs; some good, brown gravy.

Pluck, draw, and truss three or four young ptarmigans in the same manner as grouse, and roast them for about half an hour before a quick clear fire. Just before they are done, flour and froth them up, and serve them on a layer of fried bread-crumbs with a tureen of good brown gravy, and the same of bread sauce.

A Scotch Receipt for Dressing Grouse.
Time, thirty to thirty-five minutes.

608. Grouse; some butter; a thick slice of toasted bread.

Let the grouse hang for some time. Do not wash them, but wipe the inside and outside with a clean cloth, and truss them without the head, the same as a roast fowl: *Fill* the inside with *butter*, and put them down to a clear quick fire for half an hour or longer (if liked thoroughly done); and keep them constantly basted with butter the whole time they are roasting. Toast a slice of bread and well butter it, mince and pound the liver of the grouse (after boiling it in water for a few minutes) with a piece of butter and a little pepper and salt, until it is like a paste, and spread it over the buttered toast; then take the grouse from the fire, put them on the toasted bread, and serve with bread sauce and gravy in separate tureens.

Golden Plovers.
Time, ten minutes to a quarter of an hour.

609. Plovers; butter; salt; slice of bread toasted.

Truss them like woodcocks, put them on a bird spit, tie them on another, and put them before a clear fire to roast; place a round of toast under them, sprinkle a little salt over them, and baste them well with butter. When done, cut the toast into four pieces, put it into a hot dish with a little gravy and butter over it, place the birds on the toast, and serve them up hot.

Grey plovers must be drawn, and either roasted, or stewed with gravy, herbs, &c.

To Truss a Quail.

610. A quail must be plucked, singed, and drawn; then cut off the wings at the first pinion, leaving the feet, and pass a skewer through the pinions and the wings.

To Roast a Quail.
Time, about twenty minutes.

611. Quails; a little gravy; vine leaves; and bacon.

Pick, draw, and truss the birds. Cover the breasts with vine leaves, and a slice of fat bacon, secured with a skewer, which can be tied to the spit. Roast them for twelve or fifteen minutes before a very brisk fire; serve them up hot with a little good gravy poured round them.

Or—
Time, twenty minutes.

612. Draw and truss them like pheasants, run a long skewer through them, and fasten it on a common spit, roast them before a quick fire for a quarter of an hour or twenty minutes, and baste them frequently with butter. When done, serve them on a hot dish garnished with watercresses, and some gravy poured under the birds.

To Truss Blackcock.

613. Pluck and draw them, wipe them inside and out, cut off the heads and truss them the same as a roast fowl, scalding and picking the feet, and cutting off the toes.

Blackcock may also be trussed with the head on, if preferred, in which case it must be passed under the wing.

To Roast Blackcock.

Time, fifty minutes.

614. One blackcock; butter; three slices of bacon; three vine leaves.

Hang the birds for three or four days, and when thoroughly plucked and wiped, truss them neatly, and cover the breast with two or three very thin slices of bacon, over which place three vine leaves. Roast them at a quick clear fire, basting them frequently with butter. When done, serve them on a slice of buttered toast and bread sauce and gravy, in separate tureens.

These birds may be plainly roasted without the addition of the bacon and leaves; well basting and frothing them up.

To Truss Landrail.

615. Draw the birds, wipe them clean with a wet cloth, and truss them with their heads under their wings, and the thighs close to their sides, and run a small skewer through the body that the legs may be perfectly straight.

To Roast Landrail.

Time, fifteen to twenty minutes.

616. Five landrails; a quarter of a pound of butter; fried bread-crumbs; and a little good gravy.

After the birds are plucked and trussed, place them before a brisk fire, and baste them constantly with butter. They will take about a quarter of an hour or twenty minutes to roast, and when done, place them on a layer of fried bread-crumbs on a very hot dish. Serve with a tureen of bread sauce, and one of good gravy.

To Roast Larks.

Time, a quarter of an hour.

617. Two dozen larks; pepper; salt; nutmeg, and a sprig of parsley; egg; bread-crumbs; and melted butter.

Pick and clean the birds, and cut off the heads and legs, pick out the gizzards, and put a seasoning inside them of pepper, salt, nutmeg, and a *very* little chopped parsley; brush them over with the yolks of some well-beaten eggs, dip them into bread-crumbs, covering them very thickly, run a small bird spit through them, and fasten it on a larger one, and put them to roast before a bright fire, basting them constantly with butter, or they will burn. When done, arrange them in a circle round a dish, and fill the centre with a pile of crumbs of bread, fried crisp, and brown in a little butter. Serve them with melted butter, with the juice of half a lemon squeezed into it.

To Roast Larks the Dunstable Way

Time, twenty-five minutes.

618. Two dozen larks; some bread-crumbs; some butter.

Put two dozen larks on a bird spit, tie them on a common spit, and put them down to a moderate fire; rub the crumb of a stale loaf through a colander, baste the larks with butter, and sprinkle them with bread-crumbs. Baste them often, strew bread-crumbs on them repeatedly, and let them be a nice brown; in the meantime, take a good quantity of bread-crumbs, put some butter in a pan, and fry the crumbs crisp and brown. Place the larks in a dish, arranged in a circle, with the fried crumbs in the centre, nearly as high as the larks, or even higher. Serve them with plain butter in a tureen, or add the juice of a lemon and a pinch of Cayenne.

The Guinea Fowl.

When the guinea fowl is roasted plain, it is trussed like a turkey; when it is larded, it is trussed like a pheasant.

Roast Guinea Fowl—Larded.

Time, one hour and a quarter.

619. A guinea fowl; some lardoons; six ounces of butter.

When the guinea fowl is properly prepared, lard the breast with shreds of bacon, and truss it the same as a pheasant. Put it down to a clear brisk fire to roast, keeping it *well* basted; and about ten minutes before it is done dredge it with flour to make it froth nicely. Serve it with a little gravy poured round it, send up some also in a tureen, and the same of bread sauce. If the guinea fowl is not larded, but plainly roasted, truss it like a turkey. It will then require one hour to roast.

A guinea fowl may be roasted plain, as a pheasant. It will then take one hour to roast at a good fire. Baste it well with butter.

To Roast Ruffs and Reeves.

Time, twenty-six minutes to half an hour.

620. Some slices of toasted bread; some

good gravy; juice of half a lemon; some butter.

When the birds are plucked, run a thin wooden skewer through the thighs and the pinions of the wings, and tie a string round them to secure the shape. They must not be drawn. Put them on a lark spit and tie them on another spit, with a layer of bacon and vine leaves between them and over the breasts, and roast them for about twenty minutes, or rather more, before a clear fire, basting them frequently with butter; toast a round of bread and put it under the birds to receive their droppings. When done, serve them on the toast cut into squares; a good gravy poured round them, and a garnish of crumbs of bread crisped before the fire, or with watercresses if you have them; with some plain gravy or melted butter, with the juice of half a lemon squeezed into it, in separate tureens.

TEAL.

To Truss Teal.

621. Pick the bird carefully; twist each leg at the knuckle; rest the claws on each side of the breast, and secure them by passing a skewer through the thighs and pinions of the wings.

To Roast Teal.

Time, ten to fifteen minutes.

622. Teal should not be eaten till after the first frost, and should be plump and fat. Roast them before a bright hot fire, and baste them very frequently with butter. Serve with orange sauce. Garnish with watercresses. Send up a cut lemon on a plate with them, and a tureen of sauce or brown gravy.

WIDGEONS.

To be trussed the same as wild duck and teal.

To Roast Widgeons.

Time, eighteen or twenty minutes.

623. Roast these birds before a good fire; flour them and baste them continuously with butter. Send them to table very hot with brown gravy round them, or the gravy in a separate tureen. Send up a cut lemon with them.

Many persons prefer all game birds very under-dressed, "just shown the fire," they say. Our time allows for thorough dressing.

To Keep Game from Tainting.

624. Game may often be made fit for eating when apparently spoiled, by nicely cleaning it and washing it with vinegar and water.

If you have birds which you fear will not keep, pick and empty them; rinse them, and rub them over with salt outside and in; have in readiness a kettle of boiling water and plunge them in one by one, holding them by the legs and drawing them up and down, so that the water may pass through them, let them remain in it for five or six minutes, then hang them in a cool place; when perfectly drained, rub them outside and inside with black pepper, or better still, lightly powder them with charcoal. The most delicate birds may be preserved in this way. Thoroughly wash them before roasting or otherwise cooking them.

Pieces of charcoal put about meat or birds will preserve them from taint, and restore them when spoilt. Poultry or game drawn and wiped dry, and a knob of charcoal put into the body and powdered over the outside of each, will keep them nicely, or they may be kept in an ice safe. Pepper secures them from flies.

MADE DISHES, ENTREES, &c., &c.

"In the hands of an expert cook," says Majendie, "alimentary substances are made almost to change their nature, form, consistence, odour, savour, colour, chemical composition, &c.; everything is so modified that it is often impossible for the most exquisite sense of taste to recognise the substance which makes up the basis of certain dishes."

This is especially true of made dishes. There is a good old story of a French gentleman laying a bet with an epicure friend of his that he would not detect the basis of a made dish which his cook should prepare. The bet was accepted—and lost! The basis of the dish being a pair of old white kid gloves. So runs the legend in honour of good cookery which can make the most intractable substances tender by skill and care. Made dishes require *both* to be eatable and nice-looking; a greasy, badly-flavoured dish is an insult to those to whom it is offered. It is far better to send up meat or fish in its *plainest* form *well done*, than to serve some of the messes occasionally prepared by bad cooks—in which the gravy or sauce has the appearance of a paste, tastes of grease or flour, and has one predominating flavour strong enough to be unpleasant.

However, it is possible to prepare made dishes nicely. If a lady has only an inferior cook, she should see to their preparation herself, as a delicate palate is required, or an experienced one, for judging of flavours and seasoning.

In the receipts we are about to offer, the *time* must be considered as capable of being slightly modified by the degree of heat of either the fire or hot stove to which the preparation is subjected. Pepper and salt should be used with caution. Soyer advised *sprinkling* them in from the fingers, not throwing them in from the spoon.

The genius of a cook is shown in made dishes; his taste, in preparing them for the eye as well as for the palate. All made dishes should be served as hot as possible.

Rissoles of Lobster.

Time, ten minutes.

625. One lobster; bread-crumbs; two ounces of butter; yolks of two eggs; pepper; salt, and mace; half a pint of good gravy.

Mince up the meat from a boiled lobster very fine, season it with a little pounded mace, pepper, and salt, add two ounces of melted butter and a sufficient quantity of bread-crumbs to make it into balls, brush them over with the yolk of a well-beaten egg, strew bread-crumbs thickly over them, and fry in boiling fat a nice brown. Serve them in a dish with some good gravy.

Oyster Fritters—American Receipt.

Time, five or six minutes.

626. One quart of oysters; half a pint of milk; two eggs; a little flour; a little dripping, or butter.

Open a quart of oysters, strain the liquor into a basin, and add to it half a pint of milk, and two well-beaten eggs; stir in by degrees flour enough to make a smooth but rather thin batter; when perfectly free from lumps put the oysters into it. Have some beef dripping or butter made hot in a very clean frying-pan, and season with a little salt, and when it is boiling drop in the batter with a large spoon, putting one or more oysters in each spoonful. Hold the pan over a gentle fire until one side of the batter is a delicate brown, turn each fritter separately, and when both sides are done place them on a hot dish, and serve.

Kromeskies aux Huitres—An Entrée.

Time, to fry, six to eight minutes.

627. Turee or four dozen oysters; an equal quantity of chicken or other white meat; three chopped mushrooms; two spoonfuls of cream; three eggs; a teacupful of light frying batter; a few slices of fat bacon; a bunch of parsley to fry for garnishing.

Take three or four dozen oysters and blanch them, and after you have taken off the beards and hard parts, cut the remaining parts into small pieces. Chop the same quantity of chicken or white meat with two or three mushrooms. Make some sauce with the liquor the oysters were blanched in, and reduce it till it is very thick, adding a little cream—in fact, make a sauce as you would for croquettes—add to it the oysters, white meat, and mushrooms; add three yolks of eggs, stir it over the fire, and when it is done, spread the mixture on a dish to be put away till it is cold. When it is cold, roll it into pieces rather smaller than corks, each piece must then be rolled neatly in slices of fat bacon cut as thin as writing-paper. A few minutes before serving, you must dip the Kromeskies in a nice light frying batter, and fry them in fresh lard. Serve them immediately, garnished with fried parsley.

Beef au Miroton.

Time, five minutes.

628. Some slices of cold roast beef; a quarter of a pound of butter; one or two onions; half a pint of beef broth; pepper and salt.

Cut some thin slices of cold beef and one large onion or two small ones into slices, and fry them a nice brown in a quarter of a pound of butter, turn the pan round frequently to prevent the meat from burning. Then boil up half a pint of beef broth, seasoned with a little pepper and salt, put it over the meat, and serve it as hot as possible. This is a good and economical dish.

Croquettes of Beef—An Entrée.

Time, five minutes.

629. One pound and a half of lean cooked beef; one onion; one ounce of butter; a little flour; one teaspoonful of browning; half a pint of water; four eggs; pepper; salt; and bread-crumbs.

Mince rather fine a pound and a half of lean beef, chop up an onion, and fry it in a stewpan with about an ounce of butter until it is quite brown; then pour in half a pint of water or broth, a very little flour, and a teaspoonful of browning; let it boil for a few minutes; season the minced beef with pepper and salt, and add it to the gravy; then stir to it quickly the yolks of two well-beaten eggs, and pour it upon a dish to cool. When cold, make the mince into balls, roll them in bread-crumbs, then in the yolk of an egg, and then in bread-crumbs again, taking care that they look smooth and a nice shape. Fry them a pale colour in boiling fat, take them carefully out, and lay them to drain. Serve them in a pyramid piled on a napkin. Garnish with fried parsley.

Fricassee of Cold Roast Beef.

Time, twenty minutes to simmer.

630. Some slices of cold beef; one onion; a bunch of parsley; three-quarters of a pint of broth; yolks of four eggs; one spoonful of vinegar; three dessertspoonfuls of port wine; a little pepper and salt.

Cut the beef into very thin slices, season it with a little pepper and salt, shred a bunch of parsley very small, cut an onion into pieces, and put all together into a stewpan with a piece of butter and three-quarters of a pint of good broth. Let it all simmer slowly; then stir in the yolks of two well-beaten eggs, a teaspoonful of vinegar, or the juice of half a lemon, and a wineglass of port wine; stir it briskly over the fire, and turn the fricassee into a hot dish. If the flavour of shallot is liked, the dish can be previously rubbed with it.

Ox-tails Stewed.

Time, two hours and three-quarters.

631. Two ox-tails; a bunch of savoury herbs; pepper; salt: four cloves; half a blade of mace; juice of half a lemon; two dessertspoonfuls of ketchup; one onion.

Divide two ox-tails at the joints, put them into a stewpan, and cover them with cold water. When it boils take off the scum, and add a bunch of savoury herbs, a small onion cut into slices, four cloves, half a blade of mace, and a little pepper and salt. Let the tails simmer very slowly for about two hours and a half, or until they are quite tender, keeping the stewpan closely covered. When done, take them out, thicken the gravy with a lump of butter and a little flour, and let it just boil once more; then strain the gravy, add the ketchup and the juice of half a lemon strained, put in the tails, boil them up, and serve garnished with sippets of toasted bread.

Haricot of Ox-tails.

Time, two hours and a half.

632. Two ox-tails; one quart of water; three ounces of butter; eighteen button onions; one large onion; one large carrot; two turnips; one dessertspoonful of flour; salt to taste.

Divide two ox-tails into pieces about three or four inches long, and fry them (with one onion cut into slices) in a little butter. Boil a dozen and a half of button onions in about a quart of water until tender; put the ox-tails into a stewpan, and pour over them the onion liquor with sufficient water to cover them; put in a carrot cut in slices, and let it all simmer for twenty minutes; then add two turnips cut into slices, and stew it until the tails are very tender, skimming off the fat occasionally. Cover the meat closely over to keep it hot; melt some butter with a little flour, pour the gravy gradually to it, and stir it over the fire until it boils; then strain it through a hair sieve, and make it very hot. Lay the tails round a dish, and place the carrot and turnip in the centre; pour the gravy over the whole, and garnish with the button onions warmed in hot water.

Cuen de Bœuf.

Time, three hours at least.

633. The upper half of two ox-tails.

Cut the tails in pieces about three inches long, stew them for a long time till they are *very* tender. Stand them up, when done, on a dish and pour the brown gravy over them. Skim the gravy well.

Haricot Mutton.

Time, two hours and three-quarters to three hours.

634. Three pounds of the neck of mutton; three turnips; three carrots; two onions; a dessertspoonful of walnut ketchup; a little pepper and salt.

Take about three pounds of the best end of a neck of mutton, cut off some of the fat, and divide the chops. Fry them lightly in a little butter, but do not quite cook them; cut the onions into slices, and the carrots and turnips into any shapes you please; fry them a few minutes in the same butter in which the chops were done, but not sufficiently to change their colour. Put the mutton into a stewpan, lay the vegetables on it, and just cover the whole with hot water; allow it just to boil, and then draw it to the side of the fire to simmer until the chops are tender; season it with pepper and salt and two dessertspoonfuls of walnut ketchup; set it to cool, and then take off all the fat very carefully; put it again on the fire to get hot, and serve it.

Rechauffé of Salt Beef.

635. A bottle of piccalilli; slices of cold

beef; a little flour; a gill of water; potatoes; a little cream or butter.

Cut large and thin slices of cold silver side of beef. Pour out on a dish some of the sauce or vinegar of the piccalilli; drop a little vinegar into it to make it thinner. Dip each slice of beef into it; flour them; lay them on a dish. Pour the water over them; warm them in an oven, or before the fire. Mash some potatoes with a little cream, or butter. Lay the purée on a dish; place the slices when hot on it, and serve.

Sheep's Tongues Stewed.

636. Sheep's tongues; some good gravy; a little parsley; shallot; mushrooms; pepper; salt, and a piece of butter.

Put the tongues into cold water and let them boil until sufficiently tender to remove the skin easily, then split them and lay them in a stewpan with enough *good* gravy to cover them; chop a little parsley, mushrooms, and shallot finely, work a lump of butter with it, season with pepper and salt to your taste, add it to the gravy with the tongues, and stew them until tender, then lay them in a dish, strain the gravy, pour it very hot over the tongues, and serve.

House-Lamb Steaks—Brown.

Time, altogether half an hour.

637. Some steaks from a loin of lamb; pepper, salt, and nutmeg; peel of half a lemon; a sprig of parsley; one egg; a large cupful of rich gravy; three ounces of butter; one teaspoonful of flour; two dessertspoonfuls of port wine; twelve oysters.

Cut some nice steaks from a loin of house-lamb; dip them into the yolk of a well-beaten egg, and then season them with a sprig of parsley chopped very fine, the peel of half a lemon grated, and a little pepper, salt, and nutmeg. Fry the stakes a nice light brown in some butter, then thicken a *large* cupful of rich gravy with about an ounce of butter rolled in flour, add two dessertspoonfuls of port wine, and a dozen oysters bearded and washed clean; let the gravy boil and then put in the steaks. When they are thoroughly hot, serve them with forcemeat balls or plain.

Lambs' Sweetbreads—An Entree.

Time, thirty-five minutes.

638. Some lambs' sweetbreads; rather more than half a pint of good gravy; bread-crumbs; egg; one glass of sherry.

Thoroughly clean the sweetbreads and soak them in water for nearly an hour, then throw them into a basin of boiling water, which will blanch them and make them firm. Put them into a stewpan with some water and let them stew slowly for fifteen minutes, then dry them well on a clean cloth. Cover them with the yolk of an egg or two, pass them through bread-crumbs, and brown them in the oven. When done, put them on a hot dish and pour over them rather more than half a pint of good gravy boiled up with a glass of sherry.

Sheep's Kidneys a la Tartare.

Time, six to eight minutes.

639. Five or six kidneys; pepper and salt; bread-crumbs and butter.

Cut each kidney through without dividing it, take off the skins, and season highly with pepper and salt; dip each kidney into melted butter, and strew bread-crumbs over them; pass a small skewer through the white part to keep them flat, and broil them over a clear fire. Serve them with the hollow part uppermost, filling each hollow with sauce tartare.

Kidneys a la Brochette.

Time, six to eight minutes.

640. Four kidneys; one ounce of butter; one tablespoonful of chopped parsley and onion; a teaspoonful of lemon juice; pepper and salt.

Cut the kidneys nearly in halves, put them on a gridiron (well-greased) to grill. When they are quite done, have ready a piece of butter mixed with the chopped parsley and onion, and a *little* lemon juice; pepper and salt. Put this *in* the kidneys at the moment you send them to table.

Toad in a Hole.

Time, one hour and a quarter.

641. A chicken; some veal stuffing; three eggs; one pint of milk; some flour.

Draw, bone, and truss a chicken, fill it with a veal stuffing. Make a batter with a pint of milk, three eggs, and sufficient flour to make it thick; pour it into a deep buttered dish. Place the fowl in the centre of the batter, and bake it in the oven. Serve in the same dish.

Or—

Time, one hour and a half.

642. Two pounds of rumpsteak; pepper and salt; three eggs; one pint of milk; a little salt, and five or six dessertspoonfuls of flour.

Cut the steak into moderately-sized pieces, season them well with pepper and salt, and put them in a pie dish. Mix the flour to a smooth paste with a little milk, and the remainder very slowly with the eggs well beaten, and a very little salt. Stir the batter well together until thoroughly mixed, and pour it over the steak; bake it in a quick oven, and serve it.

Or—Of Cold Meat.
Time, one hour and a quarter.

643. Some slices of cold roast mutton; three or four sheep's kidneys; one pint of milk; a large cupful of flour; two eggs. Cut some nice slices of cold roast mutton, season them well with pepper and salt, and divide the kidneys into four. Mix with the milk sufficient flour to make a smooth batter, adding to it two well-beaten eggs. Butter a pie dish, pour in a little of the batter, then lay in the slices of meat and kidney; pour over them the remainder of the batter, and place the dish in the oven to bake, for an hour and a quarter. When done, serve it quickly, in the dish in which it was baked.

Beef Rissoles.
Time, ten minutes.

644. Some slices of cold roast beef; rather more than half their weight in grated bread; a bunch of savoury herbs; two or three eggs; rind of a lemon grated; half a pint of good brown gravy.

Take some slices of rather lean cold roast beef, and mince it very fine; season it highly with pepper and salt; and add a few savoury herbs chopped fine, and the peel of half a lemon, with rather more than half the weight of the beef in bread-crumbs. Mix all well together, and bind it with two eggs well beaten into a very thick paste. Form it into balls, egg and bread-crumb them, fry them a nice brown, and serve them with good brown gravy poured round them.

More frequently they are sent up *dry*, on a cloth garnished with fried parsley.

Rissoles of Sweetbread—An Entrée.
Time, to fry for use, six minutes.

645. Two sweetbreads; half a pound of veal; half a pound of ham; one shallot; a quarter of a head of celery; one spoonful of mushroom ketchup; one ounce of butter; one pint and a half of broth; one pint of cream; flour and butter; pepper and salt; bread-crumbs; three eggs.

Boil two sweetbreads for about an hour, and then set them in a cool place; when cold, mince them very fine with a large knife. Put into a stewpan half a pound of veal, and the same of ham, a large piece of celery, a minced shallot, a spoonful of ketchup, a piece of butter, and half a blade of mace; dredge in a little flour, and shake the pan over the fire for six or seven minutes. Then pour in the broth and cream, thicken it with a piece of butter rolled in flour, and stir in over a clear fire until it boils, then strain it through a hair sieve, and take just sufficient gravy to moisten the sweetbreads. Season the mince with pepper and salt; and let it boil up for five minutes, then turn it on a dish, and, when thoroughly cold, make it into small balls. Cover them with bread-crumbs, roll them in the yolks and whites of the eggs well beaten, then roll them again in bread-crumbs, and put them into a cool larder. When required, fry them in boiling fat, and serve them with fried parsley on a folded napkin.

Veal and Potato Rissoles.
Time to brown, six to eight minutes.

646. A few mashed potatoes; some cold roast veal; hard-boiled eggs.

Chop very fine about a pound, or as much as you require, of cold roast veal, and mix it with three-quarters of a pound of mashed-potatoes, and one or two hard-boiled eggs minced fine. Mix altogether with the yolk and white of an egg beaten separately—the white to a stiff froth; make it into balls, roll them in the yolk of an egg, and brown them in a Dutch oven before the fire.

Rissoles of Veal—An Entrée.
Time, to fry, about six minutes.

647. One pound of veal; ten pounds of crumb of bread; a quarter of a pound of suet; half a pint of milk; half a pint of good gravy; two eggs; pepper; salt, and pounded mace.

Scrape as fine as possible the veal and suet, and mix it with two pounds of crumb of bread—previously soaked in half a pint of milk for nearly a quarter of an hour; press the milk from the bread before mixing the latter with the other ingredients; season with pepper, salt, and a little pounded mace. Beat up the yolk of one or two eggs, to *moisten* the rissoles, roll them into balls; cover them thickly over with bread-crumbs, and fry them a nice brown. When done, serve them with a good gravy poured over them.

Minced Veal.
Time, one hour and a quarter altogether.

648. The remains of cold fillet, or loin of veal; a pint and a quarter of water; half a teaspoonful of minced lemon peel; a teaspoonful of lemon juice; a little mace if the flavour is liked; white pepper and salt to taste; three tablespoonfuls of milk; a

bunch of herbs; a small onion; one ounce of butter rolled in flour.

Put the bones of the cold veal, or any other bones you may have, into a stewpan with the skin and trimmings of the meat. Dredge in a little flour, pour in more than a pint of water, the onion sliced, the lemon peel, the herbs and seasoning. Simmer these ingredients for more than an hour; then strain the gravy, thicken it with the butter rolled in flour, boil it again, and skim it well.

While the gravy is making, mince the veal finely, but do not chop it up *too* fine. When the gravy is ready, put it in and warm it gradually; add the lemon juice, then put in the milk, or a little cream if you can afford it.

Do not let it *quite* boil, but as it is on the point of doing so, take it off the fire.

Cut some thin slices of bread, toast them, and cut them into sippets; garnish the dish the whole way round the edge with them. Pile the mince in the centre of the dish, garnish with tiny rolls of fried bacon, and quarter-slices of lemon.

Place three nicely poached eggs on the top, and you will have a very pretty as well as a nice dish for the table.

Calf's Heart Roasted.

Time, from half an hour to an hour, depending on the size.

649. Put the heart to disgorge in lukewarm water for an hour nearly; then wipe it dry, stuff it with a nice and highly seasoned veal stuffing or forcemeat. Cover it with buttered paper, and set it down to roast at a good fire. Serve it with good gravy, or any sharp sauce.

Send it up as hot as possible to table.

Scotch Collops—White.

Time, eighteen minutes.

650. One pound and a half of veal; half a pint of veal broth; a dessertspoonful of cream; two eggs; a few oysters; salt; nutmeg, and mace; the juice of half a lemon; two ounces of butter; a few forcemeat balls.

Cut about a pound and a half from the leg of veal into collops about the size of a crown piece, or rather thicker; season them with a little salt, nutmeg, and mace. Put a piece of butter into a stewpan, dredge in a little flour, lay in the collops, set the pan over a slow fire and stew them for five or six minutes, tossing it about until the collops look white. Then pour in the broth, or gravy (made from any bones or trimmings of veal), and four tablespoonfuls of cream. Let it simmer for ten or twelve minutes and then boil up. Place your collops in a dish, add a few oysters, and the juice of half a lemon to the gravy; thicken it with the yolks of two beaten eggs, pour it over, and serve with forcemeat balls.

Scotch Collops—Brown.

Time, a quarter of an hour.

651. Slices from a leg of veal; gravy made of any trimmings of veal and bones; juice of half a lemon; six ounces of butter; a little flour; salt; mace, and nutmeg.

Cut some collops from a leg of veal, rather thin, and larger than a crown piece; season them with a little salt, pounded mace, and a little nutmeg; fry them for about three minutes in two or three ounces of butter, then take them out and put them into the gravy. Brown the remaining butter in the pan, strain the gravy from your collops, and again fry them lightly; place them on a dish, pour off the butter from the pan into the gravy, add the juice of the lemon. Boil it up and pour it over the collops. Serve forcemeat balls as a garnish.

Veal Collops.

Time, a quarter of an hour.

652. Two pounds, or two pounds and a half of a leg of veal; three quarters of a pound of bacon; two eggs; two ounces of bread-crumbs; juice of one lemon; pepper; salt; pounded mace; a very little Cayenne; and two ounces of butter.

Cut some collops, not too thick, from the best part of a leg of veal, and lay over each a very thin slice of bacon the size of the veal; put a layer of forcemeat over the bacon, and season it with the smallest quantity of Cayenne pepper. Roll them up tightly, fasten them with a very small skewer, brush them over with egg, cover them with bread-crumbs, and fry them in butter, taking care that they do not burn. When they are done, put about two ounces of butter rolled in flour into the pan, pour in the juice of a strained lemon, or a spoonful of lemon pickle, some pepper, salt, and a very little pounded mace; add a cupful of hot water, and boil it up for a few minutes. Place the collops on a dish, pour the sauce over them and serve. Garnish with slices of lemon.

Ragout of Cold Veal.

Time, thirty-five minutes.

653. Some slices of cold roast veal; a large cupful of gravy; pepper; salt; and a little pounded mace; juice of a small lemon; two dessertspoonfuls of ketchup; and some forcemeat balls.

Cut some slices of cold roast veal, and fry them lightly in butter. Make a good gravy of the bones and any trimmings you may have, put a large cupful into the stewpan with the meat, and the butter in which it was fried; season it with pepper, salt, and a little pounded mace, and let it simmer slowly over a clear fire for rather more than half an hour. Then stir in a piece of butter rolled in flour, the ketchup, and strained lemon juice; let it boil for about five minutes, and serve with the forcemeat balls fried, and arranged round the edge of the dish, and a few over the ragoût.

A Fricandelle.

Time, half an hour.

654. Remains of cold veal or any other meat; bread-crumbs; half an ounce of butter; one egg; half a pint of gravy; seasoning; pepper and salt to your taste.

Chop some veal or any other cold meat, fat and lean together, season it with pepper and salt to your taste. Put grated bread-crumbs to it in proportion to the quantity of meat, about a teacupful generally suffices; add an ounce of butter, an egg, and a little good gravy. Mix these ingredients well together, and press them firmly into a basin or mould, which must be previously buttered. Boil it for half an hour, turn it out of the mould, and send it to table with a little brown gravy over it.

Stewed Sweetbreads—American.
(An Entree.)

Time, thirty-five minutes.

655. One or two sweetbreads; one pint of veal broth; some marjoram; mace; pepper; salt; flour; yolks of two eggs.

Soak the sweetbreads in warm water, and then put them into a stewpan with the veal broth, pepper, salt, and mace, with a little marjoram, and let them stew for rather more than half an hour. When done, place them on a hot dish; thicken the gravy with a little flour, and the beaten yolks of two eggs, pour the sauce over the sweetbreads, and serve.

Roast Sweetbreads—an Entree.

Time, half an hour.

656. Two sweetbreads; one egg; bread-crumbs; clarified butter; butter; juice of a lemon; a little Cayenne.

Trim off the tough part of the sweetbreads, and blanch them for nearly two hours in a stewpan of boiling water with a little salt. Then take them out, and put them into cold water until they are cool. Run a skewer through the sweetbreads, and fasten them on a spit, brush them over with the yolk of a well-beaten egg, shake bread-crumbs over them, sprinkle them with clarified butter, and again with bread-crumbs, roast them for a quarter of an hour. When done, take them from the skewers, and make a gravy of a little butter, a little lemon juice, and a pinch of Cayenne, make it hot, and serve it in the dish under the sweetbreads. Garnish with slices of lemon.

Boulettes an Fole de Veau.

Time, twenty minutes.

657. Two pounds of calf's liver; a bunch of sweet herbs; a few slices of ham or bacon; a cupful of cream; one or two eggs; one ounce of bread-crumbs; pepper and salt.

Mince the liver as fine as possible, and the slices of bacon or ham; stir into it the sweet herbs finely chopped, a little pepper and salt, the yolk of one or two well-beaten eggs, and a cupful of cream; put the whole when well mixed together into a stewpan. Set it over a slow fire until it becomes firm, and then roll it into balls with your hands, which should be well covered with flour. Brush them over with the white of the eggs well beaten, then roll them in bread-crumbs until they are quite covered, and fry them in boiling butter; drain them on a sieve before the fire, and serve them on a folded napkin, or if preferred with piquante sauce poured round them when sent to table, on a hot dish.

Ox-heart Roasted.

Time, about two hours to roast if large.

658. This is a very cheap dish. Put the heart into lukewarm water to disgorge the blood for one hour. Make during this time a good highly-seasoned veal forcemeat or stuffing (*see* Forcemeats).

Wipe the heart *well* with a cloth, stuff the interior with the forcemeat, tie it up in buttered paper, and pass a small spit through the sides. Set it before a good fire to roast, and baste it *well*. When done, remove the paper, and serve *very hot* with a little plain gravy or piquante sauce.

You may also stuff it with sage and onions, but this is not generally liked.

Haricot of Veal.
Time, twenty minutes.

659. Two pounds and a half of the best end of the neck; some good brown gravy; one pint of green peas; three cucumbers; two cabbage lettuces; four carrots; four turnips; one pint of broth.

Cut off the bones from the best end of a neck of veal quite short, but leave the neck whole; put all into a stewpan, and cover it with some good gravy. Just before serving, add a pint of green peas, then cucumbers cut into slices, the carrots and turnips cut into wheels, and the lettuces into four pieces, previously stewed in a little broth, and let them simmer with the veal for ten or twelve minutes. Dish up the meat, pour the vegetables and sauce over it, and garnish with the quarters of lettuce and forcemeat balls.

Calf's Head in a Shape.
Time, one hour.

660. Some cold boiled calf's head; eight eggs; half a pound of bacon or ham; a sprig of parsley; a large cupful of gravy; pepper; salt, and mace.

Boil eight eggs very hard, and arrange slices of them round a well-buttered mould, seasoned with a little pepper, salt, pounded mace, and minced parsley; then fill the mould with alternate layers of the calf's head cut into *very* thin slices; the bacon also cut thin; the sliced eggs, spice, &c.; pour in a large cupful of good veal gravy, make a paste to cover over the mould, and bake it. When done, set it in a cool place, and when it is cold turn it out and serve.

Calf's Brains à la Maître d'Hôtel.
Time, a quarter of an hour.

661. The brains; a spoonful of salt; one tablespoonful of vinegar; three ounces of butter; a lemon.

Take off all the fibres and skins which hang about the brains, and soak them in several waters; then boil them in salt and water and a tablespoonful of vinegar. Cut some thin slices of bread in the shape of scallop shells, and fry them in butter; lay these on a dish, divide the brains in two, and place them on the fried bread, pour gravy with lemon juice squeezed into it over them, and serve.

Croquettes of Brains.
Time, ten minutes.

662. Brains; one spoonful of sage leaves; one egg; some bread-crumbs; pepper and salt; a little milk.

Blanch the calf's brains, and beat them well together with a spoonful of sage leaves chopped very fine, seasoned with pepper and salt; mix them with bread-crumbs soaked in a little milk and a well-beaten egg. Make them into balls, and fry them in butter. Serve them piled up on a dish.

Boiled Calf's Feet.
Time, nearly three hours to stew.

663. Two calf's feet; parsley and butter.

Bone two or three calf's feet as far as the first joint, and soak them in warm water for two hours, then put them into a stewpan with sufficient water to cover them, and let them stew gently; take them out on a hot dish, and pour over them some good parsley and butter sauce.

Calf's Feet Roasted.
Time, altogether, two hours.

664. Two calf's feet; pepper and salt; three ounces of butter and a cupful of water; two wine-glasses of port wine; a teaspoonful of browned flour.

Thoroughly clean two calf's feet, and boil them just tender; then let them cool. When cold, dredge them with a mixture of pepper and salt, and tie them on a spit; baste them with two ounces of butter melted in a small cupful of water; when nearly done, dredge them with flour; baste them freely with butter, and let them finish roasting. When nicely browned take them up; add two wine-glasses of port wine to the gravy in the dripping-pan, put to it a spoonful of browned flour, and a piece of butter the size of an egg; stir it smooth, then strain it through a hair sieve, and serve in a tureen.

Veal Olives—An Entrée.
Time, twenty minutes.

665. Some slices of veal; a slice or two of fat bacon; some forcemeat; a shallot; Cayenne pepper; egg; some brown gravy.

Cut some thin slices of veal rather wide, but not more than three or four inches long, lay a *very* thin slice of fat bacon on each, then a layer of forcemeat, a little shallot sliced as thin and fine as possible, with pepper, salt, and Cayenne; roll them round, and fasten each securely with a small skewer, brush them over with egg, and fry them a nice brown. Boil a few mushrooms, pickled or fresh, with half a pint, or as much as your olives will require, of brown gravy, pour it round them, and garnish with egg-balls.

Veal Olives with Oysters.
Time, half an hour.

666. Some collops from a fillet of veal;

a little forcemeat; a sweetbread; a few mushrooms; twelve oysters; and half a pint of brown gravy.

Cut three large collops off a fillet of veal, trim them neatly, and spread a forcemeat over them, adding a few oysters chopped fine to each collop, roll them up, and fasten them with small skewers. Roast them in a Dutch oven before the fire, basting them with a little butter; or bake them in an oven. Make a regoût of a few oysters, the sweetbread cut into dice, and a few mushrooms, lay it in the dish with the olives, and pour a good brown gravy round.

Veal Cutlets—An Entree.

Time, twenty minutes.

667. Some cutlets from the best end of a neck of veal; some slices of bacon or ham; one tablespoonful of sweet herbs; peel of half a lemon; nutmeg; salt, and Cayenne; eggs; and bread-crumbs.

Take about two pounds from the best end of a neck of veal, and divide it into cutlets all of the same size—that of a crown-piece, and rather more than a quarter of an inch thick. Dip them into the yolks of some beaten eggs, and then cover them with bread-crumbs mixed with a little Cayenne, salt, and nutmeg, a tablespoonful of minced herbs, and the peel of half a lemon chopped as fine as possible. Fry them a nice brown in butter. Toast an equal number of very thin slices of bacon, or ham, as near the size of the cutlets as you can, and roll them round. Arrange the cutlets in a pile in the dish; surround them with the rolls of bacon. Pour a little good gravy into the centre, and serve with mushroom sauce or without.

Pork Cutlets Broiled.

Time, fifteen to twenty minutes.

668. Take some cutlets from a loin of pork, trim them neatly, and cut off nearly all the fat. Season them with pepper, and place them on a hot gridiron over a clear fire. Broil them for a quarter of an hour or twenty minutes, as pork requires to be very well done. Turn them as often as necessary while over the fire. When they are done, put them on a hot dish, and serve them with sauce piquante, or plain brown gravy.

Pork Cutlets Fried.

Time, twenty minutes.

669. Pork chops; bread-crumbs; egg; sage-leaves; pepper, and salt.

Take a sufficient number of cutlets from a loin of pork, trim them neatly, and scrape the top part of the bone clean. Dip them into a well beaten egg; cover them with bread-crumbs and a *very little* minced sage mixed together. Season the bread-crumbs with pepper and salt. Shake a little warmed butter over the cutlets, and fry them in boiling lard or beef dripping. When fried of a nice golden brown, take them up, and place them before the fire on a sieve turned upside down to drain all the grease from them.

Put a purée of mashed potatoes in a hot dish; lean the cutlets against it in a circle, and serve.

Pig's Liver.

Time, to bake, a little more than two hours.

670. Liver of a pig; five slices of bacon; two pounds and a half of potatoes; a bouquet of parsley; two sage leaves; one teaspoonful of pepper; two teaspoonfuls of salt; a gill of water; one onion.

Slice the liver and let it soak, and boil and mash the potatoes. Mince the parsley and sage (have about a tablespoonful of the two mixed), and chop up a Lisbon onion.

Lay part of the potatoes at the bottom of a well-buttered tin mould or dish. Then put in a layer of sliced liver and bacon; sprinkle it well with pepper and salt; lay over it a good sprinkling of sage, parsley, and onion. Then add a layer of potatoes, then one of liver and bacon; again season it with pepper and salt, and add the sage and onion once more. Cover with mashed potatoes. Add a little water.

Bake this dish for two hours, and then turn it out of the mould on a hot dish. Salamander it, and serve.

Pig's Fry.

Time, two hours and a quarter.

671. A pound and a half of fry; one onion; one teaspoonful of chopped sage leaves; two pounds and a half of potatoes; one saltspoonful of pepper; two saltspoonfuls of salt.

Boil a large Lisbon onion, then chop it up fine with a few sage leaves. Lay half the fry at the bottom of a pie dish, cover it with a thin layer of sage and onion, sprinkle it well with pepper and salt, cover it with a layer of sliced potatoes; then put in the other half of the fry, and again sprinkle it with pepper and salt, add another very thin layer of sage and onion, cover it with sliced potatoes, fill the dish with water, and put it in the oven. When it is done, brown it with a salamander, and serve.

Souffle of Chicken.

Time, half an hour, or less.

672. Chicken legs, &c.; three-quarters of a pint of white sauce; pepper and salt; one dessertspoonful of chopped parsley and sweet herbs; three eggs; a few bread-crumbs.

Take the meat from the legs of chicken, pheasant, or rabbit. Take out the sinews, mince the meat *very small* by putting it through the mincing machine twice. Boil it in a stewpan with white sauce, pepper, salt, and a little chopped parsley, or any other sweet herb. Stir it on the fire till it boils; put into it the yolk of three eggs, whipped to a firm froth that will bear an egg; stir them lightly into the mixture. Bake it in a plain mould, with paper round the top to allow it to rise. Bake it in a *very* quick oven. Serve white sauce or gravy round it. Butter the mould and shake bread-crumbs into it previous to putting the mixture into it.

Croquettes of Cold Fowl—An Entree.

Time, to fry the balls, ten minutes.

673. The white meat of some cold roast fowls; pepper; salt, and pounded mace; two or three ounces of ham; some bread-crumbs; a spoonful of milk; yolks of two or three eggs.

Pick off the white meat from some cold roast fowls, mince it fine, and season it with pepper, salt, and a very little pounded mace. Add about two or three ounces of grated ham, stir all together, and bind it with the yolk of egg, and a spoonful of milk; roll the mixture into oval balls, brush each over with the yolks of beaten eggs, and roll them in bread-crumbs once or twice; fry them a nice brown in butter, and serve them up on a border of mashed potatoes, and a little good gravy in the centre of the dish.

Minced Fowl—An Entree.

Time, ten minutes.

674. Cold roast fowl; half a cupful of white stock; the same of Béchamel sauce; one egg; bread-crumbs; thin melted butter; a little salt and pepper; half a teaspoonful of grated lemon peel.

Pick all the white meat from some cold roast fowls, and chop it up very fine, season it with a little salt, pepper, and half a teaspoonful of grated lemon peel, put it into a stewpan with half a cupful of Béchamel sauce, and the same of white sauce or stock; set it over the fire until it boils, stirring it all the time. When done, put it in the dish it is to be served in, piled up neatly, spread over it the white of an egg beaten very stiff, cover it with grated bread. Pour over it a *very* little *thin* melted butter, brown it in a Dutch oven before the fire, or with a salamander, and serve. Garnish with fried croûtons.

Chicken Cutlets—An Entree.

Time half an hour for the gravy; eight or ten minutes to fry.

675. Cold roast fowl; bread crumbs; egg; peel of half a lemon; a blade of pounded mace; a little pepper and salt; thin melted butter; fried bread; half a carrot; a few savoury herbs; a sprig of parsley; one ounce and a half of butter; eight or ten pepper corns; gravy made from the bones.

Fry half a carrot cut into slices, a few savoury herbs, a sprig of parsley, and the spice, in about an ounce and a half of butter, for a quarter of an hour; then add rather more than half a pint of the gravy from the bones, let it simmer for another fifteen minutes, strain it through a sieve, and when they are ready serve it with the cutlets. In the meantime, divide a cold roast fowl, or the remains of one, into a number of small cutlets. Cut an equal number of pieces of stale bread into sippets the size of the cutlets, and fry them lightly in butter. Dip the cutlets into *thin* melted butter mixed with the yolks of one or two well-beaten eggs, then spread over each some bread-crumbs seasoned with a little pounded mace, minced lemon-peel, salt, and pepper; fry them for eight or ten minutes, place a cutlet on a sippet, and pile them neatly on the centre of a dish.

To Fricassee Chickens—An Entree.

Time, one hour and a quarter altogether.

676. A chicken; pepper; salt, and nutmeg; a bunch of sweet herbs; two shallots; three anchovies; butter; eggs; and some gravy made of the bones.

Draw and wash the chickens, boil them till tender, and when cold cut them into pieces, fry them lightly in butter, and then take them out and drain them from the fat. Put some gravy made from the bones into a stewpan, add a glass of white wine, some pepper and salt, and grated nutmeg, two shallots, and three anchovies; stew it very gently, and thicken it with the yolk of egg well beaten, and a piece of butter; stir it until done, put in the chicken, toss it over the fire for a few minutes, and serve it up with sliced lemon and fried parsley.

Pigeon Compote.

Time, about forty-eight minutes.

677. Six pigeons; forcemeat; lardoons; gravy; butter; and flour.

Truss six young pigeons as for boiling, and fill their craws with a forcemeat, lard them down the breasts, and fry them brown in butter, then put them into a stewpan with a sufficient quantity of good gravy, and when they have stewed three-quarters of an hour thicken it with a piece of butter rolled in flour. Serve with the gravy strained over them, and garnish with forcemeat balls.

To Fricassee Pigeons—An Entree.

Time, half an hour to three-quarters of an hour to stew the pigeons; five minutes for the sauce.

678. Two pigeons; one pint of water; one pint of claret; one blade of mace; pepper and salt; one onion; a bunch of sweet herbs; one ounce and a half of butter rolled in flour; yolks of three eggs; half a nutmeg; a few fried oysters; and slices of bacon.

Cut the pigeons into pieces, wash and clean them well, and put them into a stewpan with a pint of water and the same of claret, season it with pepper and salt, a blade of mace, one onion, a bunch of sweet herbs tied together, and an ounce and a half of butter rolled in flour. Cover the stewpan closely, and let them stew till there is just enough for the sauce. Then take out the onion and the herbs, and place the pieces of pigeon on a dish and keep them hot. Beat the yolks of three eggs, and stir them into the gravy until it is thick and smooth, then put in the pigeon and shake all together over the fire. Put the pieces of pigeon into a dish, and pour the sauce over them. Scatter some fried oysters over the top, and lay slices of toasted bacon round.

Ragout of Snipes.

Time, ten to fifteen minutes.

679. Snipes; two spoonfuls of mushroom ketchup; juice of half a lemon; pepper and salt; a little butter or melted bacon fat.

Divide the snipes down the back, but do not remove the insides; sauté them with a little butter or melted bacon fat, two spoonfuls of mushroom ketchup, pepper and salt. When done, squeeze in the juice of half a lemon, and serve them on a hot dish, garnished with slices of lemon.

To Stew Pigeons.

Time, thirty-five minutes.

680. Six pigeons; one pint of good gravy; one onion; three or four shallots; a bunch of sweet herbs; pepper and salt; one pint of mushrooms; half a blade of mace; half a pint of white wine; and some grated bread.

Pick and wash six pigeons, put them into a stewpan with a pint of good gravy, an onion cut small, the shallots, a bunch of sweet herbs, a pint of mushrooms cut into small pieces, and a little pepper, salt, and half a blade of mace. Let the whole stew gently until tender, and add the wine just before you take the stewpan from the fire. Put the pigeons on a dish, brown the sauce, and pour it with the mushrooms over the pigeons. Strew over the whole some grated bread, and brown it with a salamander.

A good remove for a second course.

Spatchcock—English Fashion

Time, twelve minutes.

681. One fowl; three ounces of butter; a piece of puff paste.

Make about a pound or half a pound as required, of good puff paste. Roll it out about the thickness of two fingers. Cut the edge in vandykes. Rub together the pieces of paste left; cut them into the shape of crescent moons; wet one of the corners of each and the side of the vandyked paste, and stick crescents between each vandyke. Bake this crust a delicate golden colour. Cut up a freshly-killed fowl in joints, pepper and salt them and rub with butter; broil them, then pile them on the crust.

Spatchcock.—Indian Mode and Sea Fashion.

Time, half an hour.

682. One fowl; pepper and salt; two or three ounces of butter.

A fowl *freshly* killed, picked, and prepared. Split the fowl in halves through the middle of the breast and back; pepper and salt it; rub it over with butter; grease a gridiron, and broil it over a bright clear fire. Put a lump of fresh butter in a hot dish before the fire; let it dissolve; lay the fowl on it (or on a round of toasted bread), and serve very hot.

CURRIES AND INDIAN DISHES.

The author has the pleasure of offering in the next few pages original receipts direct from the East, presented to her by Anglo-Indian friends. Some of the dishes are quite unknown in England, as Ballachony, Bobotie, &c.

Malay Currie.

Time, half an hour.

683. Two ounces of almonds; one lemon; one dessertspoonful of currie powder; one chicken, half a pint of water; one teacupful of cream or milk; two ounces of butter. Blanch two ounces of almonds; fry them in a little butter until they are brown, but do not let them burn; pound them to a cream with an onion and the rind of half a lemon. Mix a dessertspoonful of currie powder with half a pint of water, and put this with the almonds into a stewpan, with a chicken cut up into joints. Let it simmer gently for nearly an hour; then add a teacupful of cream; let it nearly boil; squeeze into it the juice of a lemon, and serve up.

Kebobbed Currie.

Time, twenty-five minutes.

684. Equal number of slices of veal, onions, and apples; a little currie powder, and quarter of a pound of butter. Cut up some apples and onions into slices, and some uncooked veal into round slices the same size; have ready some small skewers (silver ones, if you have them), and put upon each skewer twelve slices of meat, apples and onions, alternately. Sprinkle well over them some currie-powder, and fry them in a stewpan, with sufficient butter to cover them. Send to table without removing the skewers.

Dry Currie.

Time, about two hours.

685. Two ounces of butter; one tablespoonful of currie-powder; a teacupful of stock; one fowl; one onion; three cloves; a small piece of cinnamon; three cardamom seeds; two bay-leaves. Melt two ounces of butter in a frying-pan until it is a little burnt; mix with it a tablespoonful of currie powder, and let it fry till brown; then put it with *very* little stock into a saucepan; cut up your fowl, or any *un*cooked meat, into pieces; add a little onion, cut very small, three cloves, a small piece of *stick* cinnamon, three cardamom seeds, and two bay leaves. Let all simmer together for two hours or longer. Be particular only to put very little stock, as there should be no gravy when served up.

Madras Currie.

Time, three hours.

686. One fowl; two tablespoonfuls of currie powder; a lemon; one cocoanut; one teaspoonful of salt; one onion; one clove of garlic; a small piece of butter rolled in flour. Skin a fowl, cut it up into small joints, and fry it in butter a light brown; put it into a saucepan with the currie powder, the juice of a lemon; the cocoanut *finely* grated; a little fried onion, and a clove of garlic. Season with salt, let it simmer slowly for three hours, adding a thickening of butter and flour, just before it is sufficiently cooked.

Curried Sweetbreads.

Time, about thirty-five minutes.

687. Two sweetbreads; three pints of veal gravy; one onion; a tablespoonful of vinegar; one lemon; a tablespoonful of currie powder; two ounces of butter. Have ready some good veal gravy, add to it a very small quantity of fried onion, a tablespoonful of vinegar or the juice of a lemon, the same quantity of currie powder, and salt to taste; rub two ounces of butter into enough flour to make this gravy (which ought to be about three-quarters of a pint) a proper thickness. Cut up two or three sweetbreads into pieces about two inches square, stew them gently in the gravy until sufficiently cooked, and serve.

Lobster Currie.

Time, half an hour.

688. One lobster; half an ounce of butter; two onions; one tablespoonful and a half of currie powder; half a pint of good gravy; a tablespoonful of vinegar. Fry two onions in half an ounce of butter, until they are nicely browned. Mix one tablespoonful and a half of currie powder, with half a pint of good gravy, and put this with the fried onions into a stewpan; then take the meat from a large lobster, cut it into rather small pieces, and add it to the gravy and onions with a tablespoonful of vinegar or lemon juice. Simmer slowly for about half an hour, and serve.

Prawn Currie.

Time, half an hour.

689. Two dozen large prawns; a table-

spoonful of currie powder; a little water; one teaspoonful of flour; half a pint of stock; one large onion; two ounces of butter; a tablespoonful of vinegar.

Mix one tablespoonful of currie powder, and one teaspoonful of flour, with a little water, into a smooth paste; then stir it into half a pint of good stock or gravy soup. Add a large onion, sliced and fried, and simmer it in a stewpan until it thickens. Have ready two dozen large prawns, taken whole from their shells, and put them into the stewpan, simmer for a quarter of an hour, stirring occasionally, care being taken not to break the prawns; then add two ounces of butter, and a tablespoonful of vinegar, and simmer for a quarter of an hour longer.

Curried Sole.
Time, half an hour.

690. One sole; half a pint of gravy; a tablespoonful of currie powder; one onion; two ounces of butter.

Take a filleted sole, a large thick one, cut it into pieces, not too small, lay them in vinegar for an hour. Have ready some gravy, prepared with fried onions and currie powder, as for prawn currie; add to it the pieces of sole, and a large lump of butter, about two ounces. Simmer gently for half an hour, or rather longer if the sole is thick.

Curried Cod.
Time, quarter of an hour.

691. Cod; one onion; stock; a teaspoonful of currie powder; one lemon; two ounces of butter.

Take a piece of cod, pull it into large flakes, and fry it till brown; put this into a stewpan, with half a fried onion. Pour over it sufficient good stock to cover it; add a teaspoonful of currie powder, and two ounces of butter, with salt to taste; also the juice of half a lemon. Simmer for a quarter of an hour, or until the fish is cooked, thicken the gravy, and serve.

Hard Egg Currie.

692. Two onions; a small piece of butter; one tablespoonful of currie powder; one pint of good stock; a cupful of cream; a little arrowroot or rice flour; six or eight hard boiled eggs.

Slice two onions, and fry them in butter, boil them with a tablespoonful of currie powder in a pint of good stock until quite cooked; then add a cup of cream, and thicken with arrowroot or rice flour. Simmer it slowly for a few minutes, adding six or eight hard boiled eggs cut into halves.

Heat the eggs thoroughly, but do not let them boil.

Vegetable Currie.

693. Four large potatoes; one ounce of butter; one pint of brown gravy; two onions; one small vegetable marrow, one handful of green peas; the same of French beans, of cucumber; one tablespoonful and a half of currie powder; one tablespoonful of vinegar; salt to taste; quarter of a pound of butter; one teaspoonful of flour.

Peel and cut up in square pieces four large potatoes, and fry them in butter until they are a light brown colour, put them into a stewpan with a pint of brown gravy, one raw onion, and one previously fried, half a small vegetable marrow cut into pieces, a handful of green peas, the same of French beans, and a few slices of cucumber; add one tablespoonful and a half of currie powder, a tablespoonful of vinegar, and salt to taste. Simmer very slowly, stirring carefully from time to time until the vegetables are nearly cooked, then add a quarter of a pound of butter mixed with a teaspoonful of flour to thicken the gravy, and simmer again until the vegetables are sufficiently cooked but not *broken*. A small piece of mint is by some considered an improvement.

Currie Powder.

694. One ounce and a half of cardamoms, six ounces of coriander seed, three ounces of black pepper, one ounce of Cayenne, one ounce and a half of cummin seed, three ounces of pale turmeric, one ounce of cloves, one ounce of cinnamon, and one ounce and a half of fenugreek.

Currie Powder No. 2.

695. Half an ounce of Cayenne, one ounce of mustard, half an ounce of black ground pepper, half an ounce of salt, a quarter of a pound of turmeric, a quarter of a pound of coriander seed, one ounce of pounded cinnamon, one ounce of ground ginger, two ounces of fenugreek, and a quarter of an ounce of allspice.

To boil Rice for Currie.
Time, seven minutes.

696. Wash the rice in several waters, then leave it in a basin of cold water to soak for two or three hours. Have ready a saucepan full of water, with a little salt in it. When the water boils, drain the rice and put it into the saucepan; let it boil very quickly for about seven minutes, then pour it into a colander, and place the colander on the top of the saucepan, that the water may

quite drain off. The rice ought to be stirred with a fork that the grains may be separated. It ought to be boiled in a large quantity of water, and it will be sufficiently cooked when the grains become a little soft, and *overdone* if they at all stick together. Rice should alway be served in a separate dish from the currie.

Pillau.

Time, about one hour.

697. Two pounds of rice; half a pound of butter; a little salt; peppercorns, cloves, and mace; two fowls; one pound and a half of bacon; hard boiled eggs and onions.

Wash two pounds of rice, boil it in a little water, with half a pound of butter, some salt, peppercorns, cloves, and mace. Keep the saucepan closely covered until the rice is sufficiently cooked; have ready a pound and a half of bacon and two fowls nicely boiled. Place the bacon in the middle of a dish and the fowls on each side; cover over with the boiled rice and garnish with hard boiled eggs and fried whole onions.

Pish Pash.

Time, an hour or more.

698. Fowl; half a teacupful of rice; one blade of mace; pepper and salt.

Put half a fowl into a saucepan with about a quart of water, let it boil to rags, then strain off the meat, and to the liquor add the other half fowl cut up into joints, half a teacupful of rice, a blade or two of mace, and pepper and salt to taste. Let this stew until the fowl is very tender and nearly all the gravy is absorbed, then send to table.

A Bengal Mutton Currie.

Time, two hours.

699. Two pounds of mutton; one onion; one clove of garlic; one or two tablespoonfuls of currie powder; two ounces of butter; some good gravy; a little tamarind juice or lemon juice.

Cut the mutton into pieces about an inch square; the best part for the purpose are cutlets from the leg, as there must not be any bone or fat. Put the pieces of meat into a stewpan, add an onion previously fried in butter, and a clove of garlic chopped fine. Sprinkle over the meat a spoonful (or two if the currie is required to be very hot) of currie powder, brown the butter in a frying pan, and pour it over the meat; add sufficient good gravy to cover it, and let it stew gently for two hours, then add the tamarind, or lemon juice, to make it the acid required, thicken the gravy and serve. Rabbits make a good currie.

Lord Clive's Currie.

Time, two hours and a half.

700. Six sliced onions; one green apple; one clove of garlic; a little good stock; one teaspoonful of currie powder; a few tablespoonfuls of stock; a saltspoonful of salt; and the same of Cayenne pepper and pepper; a piece of butter the size of a walnut; any uncooked meat.

Stew the sliced onions, green apple and garlic to a pulp in a little good stock; then add the currie powder, a few spoonfuls of stock; the Cayenne and pepper; add to this gravy any kind of uncooked meat, cut into small square pieces, adding the butter rolled in flour, stew slowly for two hours and a half.

Ballachony.

701. One hundred prawns; a little vinegar; two ounces of green ginger; half an ounce of Chili; peel of four lemons; two ounces of salt; juice of two lemons; four onions; two or three ounces of butter.

Boil a hundred prawns, take off the shells and clean them, then grind them in a currie stone with sufficient vinegar to keep the stone wet. Take one ounce of green ginger, half an ounce of Chili, and the peel of four lemons, pound them separately; then take two ounces of salt and the juice of two lemons, and mix all the ingredients with the prawns. Cut four onions in rings, and fry them with about two or three ounces of butter to keep them from burning. When the onions become soft and the ballachony dry, take it out and let it cool. To keep it any length of time, it must be put in jars with *orange* leaves on the top, and closed up with bladder.

Bobotee.

Time, half an hour.

702. One onion; one ounce of butter; one cupful of milk; one slice of bread; six or eight sweet almonds; two eggs; half a pound of minced cold meat or undressed meat; one tablespoonful of currie powder.

Slice an onion and fry it in butter, soak in milk a small slice of bread, and grate six or eight sweet almonds, beat two eggs into half a cupful of milk, and mix the whole *well* together, with half a pound of minced meat, a small lump of butter, and one tablespoonful of currie powder. Rub a pie dish with butter and the juice of a lemon, and bake the currie thus made in not too hot an oven. Serve it with boiled rice in a separate dish.

This currie is very little, if at all, known in England, and it is remarkably delicate and nice.

MEAT PIES AND PUDDINGS.

We believe that it is utterly impossible to teach verbally how to make good paste or pie-crust; a lesson from a good cook would be worth whole volumes on this subject. Some general directions, however, may be given on this important art. First, the cook should have smooth *cold* hands—very clean—for making paste or crust. She should wash them well, and plunge them in cold water for a minute or two in hot weather before beginning her paste, drying them well afterwards.

The pastry slab, if possible, should be made of marble; if it is a wooden pasteboard, it should be kept scrupulously clean. The crust used for homely pies need not be as delicate as that used for company; it may be made of clarified beef dripping or lard instead of butter.

Be very careful about the proper heat of the oven for baking pies, as if it be too cold the paste will be heavy, and have a dull look; if too hot, the crust will burn before the pie is done.

Try if the oven is hot enough by holding your hand inside it for a few seconds; if you can do so without snatching it out again quickly, it is too cold. It is best, however, to try it by baking a little piece of the crust in it first.

Always make a small hole with a knife at the top of the pie to allow the gases generated in it by the cooking to escape. This aperture is also useful for pouring gravy into the pie when it is done, if more is required. The hand of a pastrycook should be light, and the paste should not be worked more than is absolutely required for mixing it.

We give first three plain receipts for pie-crust, such as people of small means can use, and will find good—a puff paste (by Soyer), and one which will be found good enough for all ordinary purposes, of butter, flour, and egg, the last made stiff—will also suit raised pies.

We begin by giving instructions for clarifying dripping, so as to render it fit for making pie-crusts.

To Clarify Beef Dripping.

703. Put the dripping into a basin, pour over it some boiling water, and stir it round with a silver spoon; set it to cool, and then remove the dripping from the sediment, and put it into basins or jars for use in a cool place. Clarified dripping may be used for frying and basting everything except game or poultry, as well as for pies, &c.

To Make a Short Crust with Dripping—No. 1.

704. One pound of flour; three-quarters of a pound of clarified beef dripping; one wineglassful of *very* cold water; a pinch of salt.

Take care that the water you use is cold, especially in summer. Put the flour, well dried, into a large basin (which should be kept for the purpose) with a pinch of salt; break up the clarified beef dripping into pieces, and mix them *well* with the flour, rubbing them together till they are a fine powder. Then make a hole in the middle of the flour, and pour in water enough to make a smooth and flexible paste. Sprinkle the pasteboard with flour, and your hands also, take out the lump of paste, roll it out, fold it together again, and roll it out; fold it again, and roll it out—*i.e.*, roll it three times; the last time it should be of the thickness required for your crust, that is, about a quarter of an inch, or even thinner. It is then ready for use.

Or, a still Plainer Crust for Children—No. 2.

705. One pound of flour; five or six ounces of clarified beef dripping; and a cupful of water.

Put the flour into a bowl, and work it into a smooth paste with about a cupful of water. Divide the clarified dripping into three parts, roll out the paste, and put over it, in rows, one portion of the dripping broken into pieces the size of a bean; flour it, fold over the edges, and again roll it; repeat this folding, spreading, and rolling three times, dredging a very little flour over the paste and rolling-pin each time. It will be fit for any common purpose, or for children.

Or, Dripping Crust—No. 3.

706. One pound of flour; five or six ounces of good beef dripping; a large pinch of salt; one egg; water to moisten.

Put the flour into a bowl, and work into it five or six ounces of good beef dripping until as fine as the flour, add a pinch of salt, and mix the whole into a paste with one beaten egg and enough cold water; roll it out thin, and use it for meat pies, &c. If for fruit or jam tarts add an ounce and a half of sifted loaf sugar.

To Make Plain Crust with Lard—No. 4.

707. One pound of flour; three-quarters of a pound of lard; a pinch of salt.

II—2

Rub a little of the lard into the flour in the basin, a pinch of salt, and moisten it with water till it is a stiff paste; take it out, lay it on the floured pasteboard, flour the roller, and roll it out. Lay small knobs of lard dented into the paste in alternate rows all over the flat surface, then flour it, and fold over the edges all round till they meet in the centre; turn the roll of paste over, and roll it out again; repeat the spreading alternate rows of lard, flour it, and fold up the edges again. Roll it out a third time, spread the knobs of lard, flour it, fold it, and roll it out to the thickness required.

A Light Puff Paste—No. 5.

708. One pound of flour; half a pound of butter; half a pound of lard; water to moisten it; a pinch of salt.

Rub a little of the flour into the basin with a pinch of salt, then rub in a few knobs of butter; put in the salt; add water enough to make it into a stiff paste, then flour the pasteboard and your hands. Take out the paste, flour the roller, and roll it out to a thin flat surface. Spread over it in alternate rows knobs of butter and lard, fold it over from the edges, and let it stand in a *very cool* place for half an hour. Then roll it out again, sprinkle a little flour over it, and add another layer of alternate knobs of butter and lard. Let it stand for ten minutes. Roll and butter it twice, without letting it stand between the two last times. Roll it thinner for mince pies, which this crust suits very well.

Common Puff Paste—American.

709. One pound of sifted flour; a quarter of a pound of lard; half a teaspoonful of salt; half a pound of butter.

Put one pound of sifted flour on the slab, or in an earthen basin, make a hollow in the centre, work into it a quarter of a pound of lard and half a teaspoonful of salt. When it is mixed through the flour, add as much cold water as will bind it together, then strew a little flour over the pasteboard or table; flour the rolling-pin, and roll out the paste to half an inch in thickness; divide half a pound of butter in three parts; spread one evenly over the paste, fold it up, dredge a little flour over it and the paste-slab or table; roll it out again, spread another portion of the butter over, and fold and roll again; so continue until all the butter is used; roll it out to a quarter of an inch in thickness for use.

Benton Puff Paste.

710. Five ounces of beef dripping to one pound of flour, mixed with hot water, but not boiling. Put together lightly on the paste-board with a knife, and with the hands only to finish off. If the quantity makes more than is required it will keep well for two or three days. The great secret in making pastry well is to mix it lightly and make as quickly as possible.

Puff Paste—Very Good.

711. A quarter of a pound of butter; half a pound of lard; half a pound of flour; a little salt; all to be chopped up together and mixed with cold water till a proper stiffness, roll it out, and in making, use a knife, and not the hand. Make it in a cold place.

Suet Crust for Puddings.

712. One pound of flour; six ounces of beef suet; a cupful of cold water.

Strip the skin from the suet, chop it as fine as possible, rub it well into the flour, mix it with a knife, work it to a very smooth paste with a cupful of water, and roll it out for use.

Common Crust for Raised Pies.

713. Two pounds and a half of flour; three-quarters of a pint of water; four ounces of butter; four ounces of lard; half a saltspoonful of salt.

Put two pounds and a half of fine flour on the pasteboard, and put into a stewpan three-quarters of a pint of water with the above proportions of butter and lard. When the water boils, make a hole in the middle of the flour, pour in the water, butter, and lard by degrees, gently mixing the whole with a wooden spoon. When it is well mixed, knead it with your hands till it becomes stiff, dredging with a little flour to prevent it sticking to the board. When thoroughly kneaded, put it into a pan, cover it over with a cloth, and set it before the fire for five or six minutes, when it will be fit for any home purposes.

Salmon Pie.

The following is an old but good way of making salmon pie:—

714. Put pieces of butter at the bottom of the pie-dish, place in it a piece of salmon cut from the middle of the fish, pick out the flesh of a boiled lobster, chop up the solid parts, and mix all well with liquefied butter, season to taste, put on a crust, and bake it for about one hour.

French Pie.

Time, half an hour.

715. Half a pound of dressed beef; half a pound of potatoes; one egg; a piece of butter the size of a large walnut.

Chop the beef very small, mash and pound the potatoes, and mix them together with a well-beaten egg, and a piece of butter; season with pepper and salt. Put this mixture into a buttered mould, and bake it for half an hour, then turn it out, and brown it before the fire in a Dutch oven.

Pie a la Don Pedro.

There is a tin expressly made for this sort of pie.

Time, to bake, two hours.

716. Three or four pounds of *mashed* potatoes; four ounces of butter; loin of mutton; three or four slices of raw ham; a bunch of parsley; pepper and salt to taste.

Mash the potatoes with butter and salt *only*. Cut a loin of mutton into *very* small delicate cutlets, put them into a sauté-pan on the fire, with some chopped parsley, butter, pepper, and salt, sauté them like other cutlets, and then dish them into the pan in a turban, and cover them with very good brown gravy. Put in the middle of them some slices of raw ham. Put on the cover, which must rest on the supports, and *cover over the cover itself* with very nicely mashed potatoes, up to the brim of the pan, and garnish it with mashed potatoes made quite smooth. Put it into the oven and bake it gently as directed above.

Fillets of sole instead of mutton are also greatly approved.

Macaroni is a good substitute for ham.

Potato Pasty.

Time, nearly two hours.

717. One pound and a half of rumpsteak; a large cupful of stock or gravy; a piece of butter the size of an egg; pepper and salt to taste; a few spoonfuls of milk; some mashed potatoes.

Cut about a pound and a half of rumpsteak into thin slices, season it with pepper and salt to taste, lay it at the bottom of the Pedro-pan, and put small pieces of butter on the top, pour in a large cupful of stock or gravy, and put on the perforated plate. Mash some fine mealy potatoes with a few spoonfuls of milk, and fill up the whole space to the top of the tube of the pan, press the potato down, and mark it with a knife in any form you please. Bake it in a moderate oven a delicate colour. Send it to table with a folded napkin round it, and when served lift up the plate of potatoes.

Potato Pie.

Time, one hour.

718. One pound and a half of mutton-steaks or cutlets; five or six mealy potatoes; two eggs; and a little milk.

Boil five or six mealy pototoes, mash and rub them through a colander; then mix them with two well-beaten eggs, and sufficient milk to make a *thick* batter. Lay the steaks or cutlets, well-seasoned with pepper and salt, in a dish with alternate layers of the potato batter, the batter being placed at the top. Put it into a moderate oven, and bake it a nice brown.

Plain Beefsteak Pie.

Time, one hour and a half.

719. Two pounds and a half of beefsteak; a little pepper, salt, and Cayenne; a little water, or gravy if you have it; one tablespoonful of Worcestershire sauce; the yolk of one egg; half a pound of paste (Nos. 1 or 2).

Cut the steak into small pieces with a very little fat, dip each piece into flour, place them in a pie-dish, seasoning each layer with pepper, salt, and a very little Cayenne pepper, fill the dish sufficiently with slices of steak to raise the crust in the middle, half fill the dish with water or any gravy left from roast beef, and a spoonful of Worcestershire sauce; put a border of paste round the wet edge of the pie-dish, moisten it and lay the crust over it. Cut the paste even with the edge of the pie-dish all round, ornament it with leaves of paste, and brush it over with the beaten yolk of an egg. Make a hole with a knife in the top, and bake it in a hot oven.

Rumpsteak and Oyster Pie.

Time, to bake, two hours.

720. One pound of rumpsteak; a quarter of a hundred of oysters; half a blade of mace; one tablespoonful of walnut ketchup; one glass of port wine; a piece of lemon peel; a cupful of gravy; pepper and salt to taste; half a pound of paste (No. 7).

Cut a pound of steak into small collops, flour them, put a puff paste inside and round the edges of a pie-dish, and put in alternate layers of rumpsteak and oysters until the dish is full, seasoning each layer with pepper and salt. Pour in a spoonful of gravy, cover the top with the paste, make a hole in the top, egg it over and bake it.

Put the strained liquor and the beards of the oysters into a stewpan with a piece of lemon peel, half a blade of mace, a spoonful of walnut ketchup, and a glass of port wine and gravy. Make it very hot over a clear fire, and when the pie is done strain the gravy, and pour it into the dish through the hole in the top.

Mutton Pie.
Time, to bake, one hour and a half or two hours.

721. Two pounds of a loin of mutton; pepper and salt; a little forcemeat; three mutton kidneys; and gravy made from the bones; paste (No. 1).

Strip off the meat from the bones of a loin of mutton without dividing it, and cut it into nice thin slices, and season them with pepper and salt; put a pie-crust (No. 1) round the edge of a pie-dish, place in it a layer of mutton, then one of forcemeat, and again the slices of mutton with three or four halves of kidneys at equal distances; then pour in a gravy made from the bones seasoned and well cleared from fat. Moisten the edge with water. Cover with a paste half an inch thick, press it round with your thumbs, make a hole in the centre, and cut the edges close to the dish, ornament the top and border according to your taste, and bake it.

Veal and Ham Pie.
Time, one hour and a quarter.

722. Two pounds of veal cutlets; half a pound of ham; one ounce and a half of butter; a sprig of parsley; pepper and salt; a tablespoonful of ketchup; four or five mushrooms; six hard-boiled eggs; a large cupful of water or gravy and a little flour; three-quarters of a pound of puff paste.

Cut about two pounds of veal and half a pound of ham or bacon into rather small cutlets; fry three or four minced mushrooms and a sprig of parsley in a small piece of butter seasoned with pepper and salt. Then pour in a tablespoonful of ketchup, about half a pint of water (or gravy if you have it), dredge in some flour, and stir it all over the fire until it boils; place the veal and ham alternately in a pie-dish lined with puff paste, pour in the gravy, add five or six hard-boiled eggs cut across, and cover the pie with puff paste. make a hole at the top, ornament it with paste in any forms you please, and bake it. Pour in a little more gravy, when done, through the hole at the top.

Small Raised Yorkshire Pork Pies.
Time, one hour and a half.

723. Two pounds of neck of pork; a quarter of a pound of butter; a quarter of a pound of suet; one pound of flour; a teaspoonful of sage; pepper and salt.

Chop a quarter of a pound of suet very fine, mix it with a quarter of a pound of butter, and a pound of fine dry flour, and put it into a stewpan over a slow fire to become hot, and the suet and butter melted. Then knead it into a very stiff paste, and set it before the fire covered over with a cloth until required. Cut the pork into the smallest pieces and season them highly with pepper, salt, and a teaspoonful of powdered sage. Divide the paste into as many pieces as you think fit, reserving some for the tops; raise them into round forms, fill them with the small pieces of seasoned pork, cover the tops over, pinch them round with your thumb and finger, and bake them in a very hot brick oven.

Devonshire Squab Pie.
Time, to bake, one hour and a quarter.

724. A pound and a half of mutton steaks; some pippins; pepper and salt; two onions; and one pint of water; enough pie-crust.

Cover a pie-dish with a good pie-crust, and put at the bottom of it a layer of pippins pared, cored, and cut into slices, then a layer of mutton-steaks, cut from the loin, and well seasoned with pepper and salt; then put another layer of pippins, and two onions sliced thin (but previously boiled in two waters, to extract the strong flavour), and put over the pippins; then again with mutton, pippins, and onions until the dish is full; pour in a pint of water; put a cover over the pie with a hole in the top, glaze and ornament it, and bake.

Chicken and Ham Pie.
Time, to bake, one hour and a half.

725. One chicken; one pound of veal; a few slices of ham; some forcemeat; yolks of five or six eggs; three mushrooms; a sprig of parsley; pepper and salt; and a little gravy or stock; puff paste.

Line the edges of a pie-dish with puff paste, and place at the bottom a little forcemeat; cut up the chicken, ham, and veal in thin slices, place them alternately in your dish with the forcemeat, a seasoning of pepper and salt, the mushrooms, and parsley chopped very fine, and five or six hard-boiled eggs cut into slices; pour in a sufficient quantity of gravy, and cover it over with a puff paste, pass the point of a knife through the top, ornament it round the edges in any fanciful device, egg it over, and bake it in a well-heated oven.

Giblet Pie.

Time, nearly two hours to stew; one hour and a quarter to bake.

726. Two sets of giblets; three-quarters of a pound of rumpsteak; twelve pepper corns; one blade of mace; half a head of celery; a bunch of sweet herbs; half a carrot; one small onion; four cloves; a tablespoonful of ketchup; five or six eggs; sufficient puff paste.

Put the head, neck, pinions, and feet into boiling water to blanch, and take off the skin from the feet and break them; then put them into a stewpan with a bunch of sweet herbs, one small onion stuck with cloves, half a head of celery cut into pieces, half a carrot, a blade of mace, twelve pepper corns, and a little salt, pour in sufficient water to cover them, and let them stew for nearly two hours; then put them to drain and get cold, and cut them into pieces. Line a pie-dish with puff-paste, place a piece of steak at the bottom, then the giblets and the liver over them, more steak, and then the yolks of the hard-boiled eggs; add a spoonful of ketchup to the strained gravy, and pour it into the pie; cover it with puff paste, join it securely to the side, cut it close to the dish, and ornament the top and border, pass the point of a knife through the top, and bake it in a well-heated oven.

Hare Pie.

Time, to bake, one hour and a half.

727. Sufficient paste to line and cover the dish; an old hare; a little pepper, salt, nutmeg, and pounded mace; a quarter of a pound of bacon; one onion; a little winter savory; a glass of port wine; yolks of three eggs; one roll.

Cut the hare into small pieces, and season it with pepper, salt, nutmeg, and mace; put it into a jar, cover it close, and set it over the fire in a deep stewpan of boiling water, and let it stew until half done. Make a forcemeat with a quarter of a pound of scraped bacon, one onion minced fine, the crumb of a French roll grated, the liver chopped fine, a little winter savory, grated nutmeg, and a glass of port wine. Season it with pepper and salt, and mix it well together with the yolks of three well-beaten eggs. Line the side and edge of a dish with puff paste, put the forcemeat at the bottom, and then the pieces of hare, with the gravy that ran from it in the jar, cover it over with a puff paste, make a hole in the top, egg it over, and bake.

A Plain Rabbit Pie.

Time, to bake, one hour and a quarter.

728. A large rabbit; three-quarters of a pound of rather fat bacon; a sprig of parsley; pepper, salt, and one shallot; puff paste.

Skin and wash a fine large rabbit, cut it into joints, and divide the head. Then place it in warm water to soak until thoroughly clean; drain it on a sieve, or wipe it with a clean cloth. Season it with pepper and salt, a sprig of parsley chopped fine, and one shallot if the flavour is liked (but it is equally good without it). Cut the bacon into small pieces, dredge the rabbit with flour, and place it with the bacon in a pie-dish, commencing with the inferior parts of the rabbit. Pour in a small cupful of water, or stock if you have it; put a paste border round the edges of the dish, and cover it with puff paste about half an inch thick. Ornament and glaze the top, make a hole in the centre and bake it.

Venison Pasty.

Time, to stew, three hours and a half; three hours to bake.

729. A neck, or shoulder of venison; a quarter of a pint of port wine; three shallots; three blades of mace; pepper and salt; nine allspice; a little veal stock, or broth; raised pie crust.

For the gravy.—A glass of port wine; juice of a small lemon; a piece of butter, and flour; some stock from the stewed venison.

Take either of the above parts of venison, remove the bones and skin, and cut it into small square pieces. Put them into a stewpan with three shallots, pepper, salt, mace, and allspice. Add a quarter of a pint of port wine, and sufficient veal broth, or stock to cover it; put it on a gentle fire, and let it stew until three-parts done. Then take out the neatest pieces of venison for the pasty, and put them into a deep dish, in a cold place, with a little of the gravy poured over them. Pour the remainder of the gravy over the bones, &c., and boil it for a quarter of an hour. Cover the pasty with some raised pie crust (No. 11), ornament the top in any way you please, and bake it in a slow oven. When done, have ready the gravy left from the bones, strain and skim it clean, add a glass of port wine, the juice of a small lemon, and a piece of butter rolled in flour. Pour it into the pasty, and serve.

Lark Pie.—An Entree.

Time, to bake, about one hour.

730. Half a pound of beef; a quarter of

a pound of bacon; ten or twelve larks; peel of half a lemon; a sprig of parsley; a cupful of grated bread; pepper and salt to taste; one egg; a large breakfastcupful of stock; puff paste.

Cover the edges of a pie-dish with puff paste, pick and stuff ten or twelve larks with a cupful of grated bread, the peel of half a lemon minced, a sprig of chopped parsley, a seasoning of pepper and salt, and the egg well-beaten. Lay at the bottom of the dish half a pound of beef, and a quarter of a pound of bacon cut into small thin slices. Season with pepper and salt. Arrange the larks on the top. Season with pepper and salt, and a sprig of chopped parsley sprinkled on them; pour in a large cupful of stock, cover the top with puff paste, make a hole in it, and bake it in a gentle oven.

Pie of Larks or Sparrows.

Time, to bake, one hour and a half.

731. A dozen small birds; a rumpsteak; a small bunch of savoury herbs; the peel of half a lemon; a slice of stale bread; half a cupful of milk; six eggs; pepper and salt; two ounces of butter; puff paste.

Make a forcemeat with the slice of bread soaked in milk, and beaten up, a small bunch of savoury herbs chopped fine, and the peel of half a lemon minced, a seasoning of pepper and salt, a piece of butter, and the yolks of six eggs; mix all together, put it into a stewpan and stir it over the fire for a few minutes until it becomes very stiff, then fill the inside of each bird. Line a pie-dish with the rumpsteak, seasoned with pepper and salt and fried lightly; place the birds on it, cover them with the yolks of the hard-boiled eggs cut into slices, and pour in a sufficient quantity of gravy. Put a paste round the edge of the dish and cover it over, glaze it with the yolk of an egg brushed over it, make a hole in the top and bake it.

A Plain Pigeon Pie.

Time, to bake, one hour and a quarter.

732. Two or three pigeons; a rumpsteak; pepper and salt; a little gravy; two ounces of butter; puff paste.

Lay a rim of paste round the sides and edge of a pie-dish, sprinkle a little pepper and salt over the bottom, and put in a thin beefsteak; pick and draw the pigeons, wash them clean, cut off their feet, and press the legs into the sides; put a bit of butter and a seasoning of pepper and salt in the inside of each, and lay them in the dish with their breasts upwards, and the necks and gizzards between them; sprinkle some pepper and salt over them, and put in a wineglass of water; lay a thin sheet of paste over the top, and with a brush wet it all over; then put a puff paste half an inch thick over that, cut it close to the dish, brush it over with egg, ornament the top, and stick four of the feet out of it, and bake it. When done, pour in a little good gravy. You may put in the yolks of six hard-boiled eggs, or leave out the beefsteak, if you think proper.

Grouse Pie.

Time, three-quarters of an hour to one hour.

733. One grouse; three-quarters of a pound of rumpsteak; seasoning of pepper, salt, mace, and Cayenne; a bunch of sweet herbs; a glass of white wine; a quarter of a pint of gravy made from the bones; puff paste.

Cut three-quarters of a pound of rumpsteak in small pieces, lay them at the bottom of a pie-dish, and season them with pepper, salt, and Cayenne to taste. Cut the grouse into joints, place them on the steak, and pour in a few spoonfuls of broth. Cover it with a good puff paste, brush it over with the yolk of egg, and bake it from three-quarters of an hour to one hour. Make a gravy with the backbones, any trimmings, a glass of white wine, a small piece of mace, a bunch of sweet herbs, and as much water as will reduce to half a pint. When the pie is taken from the oven, pour in the gravy through a hole in the top. The grouse, if small, may be laid whole in the pie, and a large cupful of stock or gravy poured in before it is placed in the oven.

Rook Pie.

Rooks must be skinned and stewed in milk and water before being put into the pie-dish; they may then be treated as pigeons. Epicures assert that only the breast must be used, but if when the rook is drawn and skinned it is laid on its breast and an incision made on each side of the spine of about a finger width, *and that piece removed*, the whole of the bird is wholesome food, that being the really bitter part.

734. Four rooks; half a pound of puff paste; pepper; salt; three hard-boiled eggs; about two ounces of butter; a small piece of rumpsteak.

Lay the rumpsteak in the pie-dish, cut up the rooks as directed, and lay them in the dish well seasoned, add the butter in knobs, and some hard-boiled eggs. Bake as you would a pigeon pie.

Vols-au-Vent Crust.

Vols-au-vent are very difficult to make

1. *Vol-au-veut, small.*
2. *Curried Eggs.*
3. *Kippered Salmon.*
4. *Mayonaise de Saumon.*
5. *Pigeon Pie.*
6. *Veal Cake.*
7. *Lobster Salad.*
8. *Minced Veal.*
9. *Toad in the Hole.*
10. *Rissoles.*

Various Kinds of Patties.

even by an experienced cook, and cannot be made without a lesson from one. They are rather a test of the artist's skill. They should be made of puff paste rolled seven times and a half.

A Vol-au-Vent—Entree.

Time, half an hour.

735. Some good puff paste; yolk of egg; any mince; fricassee, &c.

Take a sufficient quantity of good puff paste, roll it out an inch in thickness, stamp it out with a fluted cutter the size of the dish in which it is to be served; mark it out with another of a smaller size, leaving about an inch and a half at the edge, brush it over with a beaten egg, and put it quickly into a brisk oven to rise and become brightly coloured. When done, carefully remove the piece marked out for the top with the point of a sharp knife, and scoop out all the soft part from the inside, taking care that the case is of a square thickness, and turn it on writing paper to drain and dry. When ready to serve, fill it with any mince or fricassee of fish you please, with a *small* portion of sauce.

Oyster Patties.

Time, twenty minutes in all.

736. Light puff paste; two dozen large oysters; one ounce of butter rolled in flour; half a gill of good cream; a little grated lemon peel; a little Cayenne pepper; salt; one teaspoonful of lemon juice.

Roll out puff paste less than a quarter of an inch thick, cut it into squares with a knife, cover eight or ten patty-pans, and put upon each a bit of bread the size of a walnut; roll out another layer of paste of the same thickness, cut it as above, wet the edge of the bottom paste and put on the top, pare them round and notch them about a dozen times with the back of the knife, rub them lightly with yolk of egg, and bake them in a hot oven about a quarter of an hour. When done, take a thin slice off the top, and with a small knife or spoon take out the bread and the inside paste, leaving the outside quite entire. Parboil two dozen large oysters, strain them from their liquor, wash, beard, and cut them into four, put them into a stewpan with an ounce of butter rolled in flour, half a gill of good cream, a little grated lemon peel, the oyster liquor strained and reduced by boiling to one half, a little Cayenne pepper and salt, and a teaspoonful of lemon juice; stir it over the fire five minutes, fill the patties, put the cover on the top, and serve.

Lobster Patties.

Time, twenty minutes.

737. Some puff paste; a hen lobster; one ounce of butter; half a tablespoonful of cream; half a tablespoonful of veal gravy; one teaspoonful of essence of anchovy; the same of lemon juice; one tablespoonful of flour and water; a little Cayenne pepper and salt.

Roll out the puff paste about a quarter of an inch thick, and prepare the patty-pans as for oyster patties; take a hen lobster already boiled, pick the meat from the tail and claws, and chop it fine, put it into a stewpan with a little of the inside spawn pounded in a mortar until quite smooth, with an ounce of butter, the halfspoonful of cream, the same of veal gravy, essence of anchovy, lemon juice, Cayenne pepper, and salt, and a tablespoonful of flour and water. Let it stew five minutes, fill the patties, and serve.

Veal and Ham Patties.

Time, a quarter of an hour.

738. Six ounces of ready dressed lean veal; three ounces of ham; one ounce of butter rolled in flour; one tablespoonful of cream; one of veal stock; a little grated nutmeg and lemon peel; some Cayenne pepper, and salt; a spoonful of essence of ham; one of lemon juice; puff paste.

Chop about six ounces of ready dressed lean veal, and three ounces of ham, very small, put it into a stewpan with an ounce of butter rolled in flour, a tablespoonful of cream, the same of veal stock, a little grated nutmeg and lemon peel, some Cayenne pepper and salt, a spoonful of essence of ham and lemon juice. Mix all well together and stir it over the fire until quite hot, taking care it does not burn. Prepare the patty-pans as for oyster patties, and bake them in a hot oven for a quarter of an hour; fill with the mixture and serve.

Moulded Veal, or Veal Cake.

Time, half an hour to bake.

739. Slices of cold roast veal; slices of ham; three eggs; some gravy; two sprigs of parsley; pepper and salt.

Cut a few slices of ham and veal *very* thin, taking off the skin from the veal, chop two sprigs of parsley fine, and cut the hard-boiled eggs into slices. Take any nice shaped mould, butter it, and put the veal, ham, eggs, and parsley in layers until the mould is full, seasoning each layer with a little pepper and salt, placing a few slices of egg at the bottom of the mould at equal

Meat Puddings.

distances, fill up with good stock and bake it When cold, turn it out and serve on a folded napkin, garnished with flowers cut out of carrots, turnips, and a little parsley.

Beefsteak Pudding.
Time, to boil, two hours, or a little longer.

740. One pound and a quarter of flour; half a pound of chopped suet; one teaspoonful of salt; two pounds of steak; salt and black pepper to taste; one gill of water.
Put a pound, or a little more, of flour in a basin, and mix it thoroughly with some very finely chopped suet; put in a good heaped saltspoonful of salt. Mix it to a paste with water; flour the pasteboard, the roller, and your hands. Take out the lump of paste, and roll it out about half an inch thick.
Butter a round-bottomed pudding-basin, line it with paste, turning a little over the edge. Cut up the steak into small pieces, with a little fat, flour them slightly, season highly with pepper and salt, then lay them in the basin, pour over them a gill of water. Roll out the rest of the paste, cover it over the top of the basin, pressing it down with the thumb.
Tie the basin in a floured pudding-cloth, and put it into a saucepan in a gallon of boiling water, keep it continually boiling for nearly two hours, occasionally adding a little more water.
Take it up, untie the cloth, turn the pudding over on the dish, and take the basin carefully from it. Serve.
Some persons, of delicate digestion, like this pudding boiled without a basin, on account of the superior lightness the crust thus acquires, but it does not look nearly as well when served.

Beefsteak and Kidney Pudding.
Time, to boil, two hours.

741. One pound of rumpsteak; one beef kidney; pepper and salt; and a little flour; suet paste.
Take a pound of nice tender beef, or rumpsteak and beef kidney, cut them into pieces about a quarter of an inch thick, season them well with pepper and salt, and dredge a little flour over them. Lightly butter a round-bottomed pudding-basin, roll out the paste to about half an inch in thickness, and line the basin, then put in the beef and kidney, pour in three or four tablespoonfuls of water, cover a piece of paste over the top, press it firmly together with your thumb, then tie the pudding-basin in a floured cloth, and put it into a saucepan with about four quarts of water; keep it constantly boiling, adding more boiling water if required.

Mutton Pudding.
Time, nearly two hours.

742. One pound and a half of mutton cutlet; pepper and salt; suet crust.
Line a well-buttered basin with paste, and lay in the mutton cut into small neat pieces, and well seasoned with pepper and salt, cover it over with a crust, cut it evenly round the edge of the basin, moisten the paste, and pinch it together, tie it in a cloth, and put it in boiling water. Take off the cloth, and turn it out carefully on a hot dish.

Rabbit Pudding.
Time, two hours to boil.

743. A small rabbit; a few slices of bacon or ham; pepper and salt; suet paste.
Cut a small rabbit into small neat pieces, and have ready a few slices of bacon, or ham. Line a basin with a good suet crust. Lay in the pieces of rabbit with the bacon, or ham intermixed, season to your taste with pepper and salt, and pour in a cupful of water. Cover the crust over the top, press it securely with the thumb and finger, and boil it.

Suet Pudding.
Time, to boil, one hour and a quarter.

744. One pound of flour; half a pound of beef-suet; one egg; a pinch of salt; a gill of water.
Mix the flour very dry with finely chopped suet; add the eggs and a pinch of salt; make it into a paste with the water, beating it all rapidly together with a wooden spoon. Flour a pudding cloth, put the paste into it, tie the cloth tightly, and plunge it into boiling water. The shape may be either a roll or a round ball. When it is done, untie the cloth, turn the pudding out, and serve very hot.

VEGETABLES, VEGETABLE PUREES, SALADS, AND SALAD MIXTURE.

To Steam Potatoes.
Time, twenty to forty minutes.

745. Pare the potatoes thin, and throw them into cold water for about five minutes; then put the strainer over the saucepan filled with boiling water, and let them steam from twenty to forty minutes, or until a fork goes through them easily. Then take them up, and serve them quickly, or they will lose their colour.

To Boil Potatoes.
Time, eighteen to twenty minutes after the water boils; large ones, half an hour.

746. Pare some potatoes as near the same size as possible, and throw them into cold water. Then put them into a saucepan, cover them with cold water and a pinch of salt. When the water boils, check it several times by throwing cold water in, as the slower they are boiled the better. When done, throw away the water, and sprinkle a little salt over them. Put them at the side of the fire to dry, with the lid of the saucepan off, and then serve them quickly on a napkin.

To Boil Potatoes with their Skins on.
Time, twenty to twenty-five minutes after the water boils; three-quarters of an hour, or longer, if very large.

747. Choose the potatoes as nearly the same size as possible. Wash and scrub them thoroughly clean, put them into a saucepan, just cover them with water and a little salt. Let them boil, and then draw the saucepan to the side, and let them simmer slowly until tender and sufficiently done, which may be ascertained by trying them with a fork. Then drain the water from them, raise the lid, and let them dry by the side of the fire. Peel them carefully and quickly, and serve them, in a very hot vegetable dish, with or without a napkin.

To Mash Potatoes.
Time, half an hour, or three-quarters of an hour if large.

748. Potatoes; a piece of butter; a little milk and salt.

Old potatoes, when unfit for boiling, may be served mashed. Cut out all imperfections, take off all the skin, and lay them in cold water for an hour; then put them into an iron saucepan with a teaspoonful of salt, cover them with water, and let them boil for half an hour, unless they are large, when three-quarters of an hour will be required. When done, drain the water thoroughly from them, put them into a wooden bowl or mortar, and mash them fine with a potato pestle. Melt a piece of butter the size of a *large* egg with a little milk; mix it with the mashed potatoes until it is thoroughly incorporated, and they are become a smooth mash, taking care the potatoes are not too wet. Then put the mash into a dish, smooth it neatly with a knife, and serve. Or it may be greatly improved by browning them in the oven, or in a Dutch oven before the fire. Or you may rub them through a *coarse sieve*, and brown them with a salamander, without smoothing them over.

To Boil New Potatoes.
Time, a quarter to half an hour.

749. Scrape the skins from new potatoes and lay them in cold water for an hour or two, then put them into an iron saucepan and cover them with water; cover them over and let them boil for half an hour. Try one; if not quite done, cover them for a few minutes longer. Then drain the water off, let them stand for a couple of minutes over the fire to dry, and send them to table plain; or you may pour a little melted butter over them.

Baked Potatoes.
Time, one hour.

750. Take as many large and equally-sized potatoes as you wish, wash them perfectly clean in two or three changes of water, then wipe them dry, and put them in a quick oven for one hour. Serve them on a napkin with cold butter, and pepper and salt separately.

Fried Potatoes.
Time, to fry, ten minutes.

751. Boil some potatoes in their skins; when cold, peel them and cut them in slices a quarter of an inch thick, and fry them in butter, or beef dripping, a nice delicate brown. When done, take them out with a slice to drain any grease from them, and serve piled high on a dish; or they may be chopped up small, seasoned with a little pepper and salt, and fried lightly in butter, turning them several times that they may be nicely browned. Serve in a covered dish.

Potato Ribbons.
Time, ten minutes.

752. Wash and remove any specks from

some nice large potatoes, and when peeled, lay them in cold water for a short time; then pare them round and round like an apple; but do not cut the curls too thin, or they are likely to break. Fry them very slowly in butter a light colour, and drain them from the grease. Pile the ribbons up on a hot dish and serve.

Potato Croquettes.
Time, to fry, ten minutes.

753. Eight large potatoes; one ounce and a half of butter; pepper and salt; a little nutmeg; a sprig of parsley; two or three eggs; and some bread-crumbs.

Wash eight large potatoes, and roast them in the oven, take out the inside, and when cold pound them in a mortar with about an ounce, or an ounce and a half of butter; then stir in a seasoning of pepper, salt, and nutmeg, with a sprig of parsley chopped up fine; mix and pound all well together, and then bind with the yolks of two or three eggs and the white of one. Make them up into balls, roll them two or three times in bread-crumbs, and fry them in boiling fat. When done, drain them and serve.

To Broil Potatoes.

754. Eight or nine potatoes; a little flour; butter; pepper and salt.

Cut some cold boiled potatoes lengthwise, a quarter of an inch thick, dip each piece in flour, and lay them on a gridiron over a *clear* fire. When both sides are nicely browned, put them on a hot dish with a piece of butter over them, and a little pepper and salt. Serve them up hot.

Potatoes à la Maître d'Hôtel.

755. Some boiled potatoes; a little melted butter; pepper; salt; a sprig of parsley; a few chives; and the juice of half a lemon.

Take some potatoes boiled and peeled; when nearly cold, cut them into rather thick slices and put them into a stewpan with a little melted butter, seasoned with pepper, salt, a sprig of parsley, a few chives chopped fine, and the juice of half a lemon. When very hot, put them into a dish and serve with the sauce over them.

Kolcannon—as Dressed in Ireland.

756. Six large potatoes; three cabbages; half an ounce of butter; one spoonful of cream; pepper and salt.

Boil the potatoes with the skins on, bruise them to meal, and mix them with the cabbage boiled, pressed from the water, and chopped fine; then add to them the butter, cream, pepper and salt; stir the whole over the fire until *hot*, and press it into a mould, or into the shape of a cake, before seasoning.

Potato Puffs.

757. Three ounces of flour; three ounces of sugar; three well-boiled potatoes; a piece of butter the size of a nutmeg; two eggs; a little grated nutmeg.

Boil and mash three mealy potatoes; mix them with three ounces of sugar, three ounces of flour, a little grated nutmeg, a small piece of butter, and two well-beaten eggs. Make them into cakes, fry a nice brown, and serve them with white sauce.

To Brown Potatoes under Meat.

758. Boil some fine large mealy potatoes, take off the skins carefully, and about an hour before the meat is cooked put them into the dripping-pan, having well dredged them with flour. Before serving, drain them from any grease, and serve them up hot.

Potato Cones, or Loaves.

759. Some mashed potatoes; a little raw shallot; pepper and salt; two ounces of butter.

Boil and mash some potatoes, mix with them a seasoning of pepper, salt, and minced shallot, beat into it a sufficient quantity of fresh butter to bind it, divide it into equal parts, and form them into loaves, or cones, and place them under roast beef or mutton, to slightly brown, allowing a little gravy to fall on them.

Rolled Potatoes with Sweet Sauce

Time, fifteen to twenty minutes to brown the roll; five or six minutes to boil the sauce.

760. Four pounds of boiled potatoes; a glass of white wine; a little nutmeg; beaten mace; yolks of six eggs; bread-crumbs; half a pint of white wine; two ounces of sugar; and a little melted butter.

Beat four pounds of boiled potatoes in a mortar with a glass of white wine, a little grated nutmeg, and beaten mace; mix it together with the yolks of two or three eggs, and a very little melted butter; make it into a roll, brush it over with the yolks of some well-beaten eggs, and roll it in bread-crumbs; butter a dish, put it in, and bake it in a gentle oven a nice brown. When done, put it on a hot dish, have ready a sauce made with half a pint of white wine, two ounces of pounded sugar, the yolks of two beaten eggs, and a little grated nutmeg. Mix all together and stir it over the fire till it is rather thick, then pour it over the rolled potatoes, and serve.

Potatoes with Parmesan Cheese.
Time, twenty minutes.

761. Eight or nine boiled potatoes; two tablespoonfuls of gravy; four ounces of butter; juice of half a lemon; four ounces of Parmesan cheese; yolks of four eggs; some bread-crumbs; pepper, salt, and nutmeg.

Put two small tablespoonfuls of white gravy into a stewpan with a quarter of a pound of butter, two ounces of grated cheese, the juice of half a lemon, a seasoning of pepper, salt, and nutmeg, and the yolks of four well-beaten eggs, and set it over the fire to become hot. Place a border of croûtons of fried bread round a dish. Put a row of potatoes cut into slices within the border, pour over it some of the above sauce, then arrange some more slices of potato in a smaller circle, then a layer of the sauce, and so on until you form a raised centre; put a little sauce over the top, and cover it well over with the remaining two ounces of cheese and the bread crumbs. Bake it for about twenty minutes, and serve it up hot.

To Boil Green Peas.

Time, twelve to fifteen minutes if young; twenty to twenty-five minutes if large.

762. Half a peck of peas; a knob of butter; a sprig or two of mint; and a teaspoonful of white sugar, if you like.

Shell half a peck of green peas, and put them into a saucepan of boiling water with a teaspoonful of salt, and a sprig or two of mint, let them boil about half an hour with the pan closely covered. When tender, drain them through a colander, and put them in a dish with a bit of butter stirred into them, a very little pepper, and the sprigs of mint on the top. Serve them up very hot.

To Stew Peas.
Time, one hour.

763. A piece of butter the size of an egg; a few onions; a bunch of mint and parsley; half a spoonful of flour; one ounce of sugar; a pinch of salt.

Put the butter into a stewpan with the onions, herbs, and salt; stew the peas in a little water slowly for one hour, stirring them frequently; when they are done, add the flour mixed in a little butter very smooth, and the sugar pounded; simmer them with the herbs, having removed the onions.

Peas Stewed with Mint and Lettuces.
Time, forty minutes.

764. One quart of green peas; two cabbage lettuces; a slice of ham or bacon; one onion; some green mint; a quarter of a pound of butter; a little flour; a cupful of cream; a quarter of a pint of gravy; pepper and salt.

Take a quart of green peas, and two cabbage lettuces cut small, and washed clean, put them into a stewpan with some green mint chopped, a little pepper and salt, and a large piece of butter, a piece of lean ham or bacon, an onion, and a quarter of a pint of gravy; mix all well together carefully without bruising the peas, cover them close and stew them for twenty minutes or half an hour, shaking the pan all the time to prevent its burning. When done, take out the onion and slice of ham, and stir in a piece of butter rolled in flour, and a little cream, just boil them up, put them in a dish, and serve them quickly.

To Boil Carrots.

Time, twenty minutes; if large, one hour and a half to one hour and three-quarters.

765. When young and small, carrots need only be washed without scraping, and the skin wiped off if necessary after they are boiled. Put them into a stewpan with hot water to cover them and half a spoonful of salt. Let them boil fast for twenty minutes, then take them out, with a clean cloth rub off the skins, and put them whole into the dish. If old carrots, scrape the skins very clean, and wash them; if large, cut them in halves, and boil them in plenty of soft water till they are tender. Put them in a dish, and serve.

Carrots Flemish Way.
Time, forty-five minutes, to boil.

766. Six or eight good-sized carrots; five small onions; a sprig of parsley; salt and pepper; three-quarters of a pint, or a pint of gravy, or a quarter of a pound of butter.

Boil six or eight good-sized carrots for about three-quarters of an hour, or until they are tender. Cut them into stars or dice, then stew them with five small onions, a sprig of chopped parsley, a little pepper and salt, three-quarters of a pint of good gravy, or a little melted butter.

Serve very hot.

To Stew Carrots.

Time, to parboil them, fifty minutes: nearly twenty minutes to simmer.

767. Some carrots; five tablespoonfuls of cream; a quarter of a pint of water, or weak stock; a piece of butter rolled in flour.

Cut into large slices some fine carrots

scraped and washed, parboil them, and then simmer until tender in about a quarter of a pint of weak broth and five large spoonfuls of cream. Add a seasoning of pepper and salt, and a piece of butter rolled in flour. When done, serve on a hot dish.

Mashed Carrots (American).

Time, to boil the carrots, one hour and a half to one hour and three-quarters.

768. Some carrots; butter; pepper, and salt.

Scrape off all the skin, wash them well, and boil them tender in a stewpan of boiling water. Then take them up with a skimmer, mash them smooth, add a piece of butter, and season with pepper and salt. Place them in the centre of a dish, piled up, and marked over with a knife. Serve with boiled or roast meat.

To Boil Artichokes.

Time, half an hour to three-quarters of an hour.

769. Two tablespoonfuls of salt and a piece of soda the size of a sixpence to every gallon of water.

Gather the artichokes two or three days before they are required for use. Cut off the stems, pull out the strings, and wash them in two or three waters that no insects may be in them. Have a large saucepan of boiling water with the above quantities of salt and soda. Put the artichokes with the tops downwards, and let them boil quickly until tender. About half an hour or three-quarters will boil them, but that can be ascertained by pulling out one of the leaves; (if it comes out easily they are done) or by trying them with a fork. Take them out and lay them upside down to drain. Serve them on a napkin, with a tureen of melted butter, allowing a teacupful to each artichoke.

They may be served without a napkin on a hot dish, with white sauce poured over them.

To Stew Artichokes in Gravy.

Time, twenty to twenty-five minutes to boil the artichokes.

770. Artichokes; one ounce and a half of butter; a quarter of a pint of gravy; two spoonfuls of ketchup; juice of half a small lemon.

Strip off the leaves from the artichokes, remove the choke, and soak them in warm water for several hours, changing it two or three times. Put them into a stewpan, pour in a quarter of a pint of good gravy, two spoonfuls of any ketchup, with the juice of half a small lemon, and thicken the sauce with an ounce and a half of butter rolled in flour. Set the stewpan over a moderate fire, and let it stew until the artichokes are quite tender, and serve on a hot dish, with the sauce poured over them.

Jerusalem Artichokes—An Entree.

Time, twenty minutes.

771. Half a pint of white sauce; sufficient artichokes for a dish.

Wash and peel a sufficient number of Jerusalem artichokes to fill a dish. Cut them in the shape of a pear, with a piece from the bottom, that they may stand upright in the dish. Boil them in salt and water until tender. Then place them neatly on a dish, and pour over them about half a pint of white sauce. Garnish with a few Brussels sprouts between each.

To Boil Jerusalem Artichokes.

Time, twenty minutes.

772. To each gallon of water, two tablespoonfuls of salt.

Wash the artichokes very clean, peel and cut them into a round, or oval form, and put them into a large saucepan of cold water, with the salt and water in the above proportions. They will take about twenty minutes from the time the water boils to become tender. When done, drain them and serve them with a little white sauce, or melted butter poured over them. Or on a napkin, with melted butter in a separate tureen.

To Boil Asparagus.

Time, fifteen to eighteen minutes after the water boils.

773. One tablespoonful of salt to half a gallon of water.

Scrape very clean all the white part of the stalks of the asparagus, and throw them into cold spring water, tie them up in bundles, cut the root ends even, and put them in a piece of muslin to preserve the tops. Have a wide stewpan of spring water, with the above proportion of salt; and when it boils, lay in the asparagus and boil it quickly for fifteen minutes, or until it is tender. Have a thin slice from a loaf nicely toasted, cut it in square pieces, dip them in the asparagus water, and put them in the dish. Take up the asparagus, lay it on the toast with the white end outwards, and the points meeting in the centre. Serve with melted butter in a tureen.

Asparagus in French Rolls.

Time, about half an hour to boil.

774. Three French rolls; one hundred asparagus; half a pint of cream; yolks of four eggs; salt and nutmeg.

Cut the green part off a hundred young asparagus, wash them well, boil and strain them. Take three French rolls, cut a piece neatly out of the top crusts, taking care that they will fit again; pick all the crumb out of the inside, and crisp them before the fire or fry them brown in butter; then take half a pint of cream, with the yolks of four or five eggs, beat up in it a little salt and nutmeg, and stir it well together over a slow fire till it begins to thicken; put in three parts of the asparagus cut small; then fill the rolls with them, put on the tops, and with a sharp skewer make holes in the tops, and stick some asparagus in, as if it were growing; put them on a dish and serve them very hot.

To Boil Cauliflowers.

Time, twelve to fifteen minutes, longer if very large.

775. A tablespoonful of salt to each gallon of water.

Make choice of some cauliflowers that are close and white, pick off all the decayed leaves, and cut the stalk off flat at the bottom; then put them with the heads downwards in strong salt and water for an hour, to draw out all the insects. Drain them in a colander, and put them into a saucepan with plenty of fast boiling water, keep the pan uncovered, and boil them quickly until tender, which will be from twelve to fifteen minutes, or longer if they are very large. Skim the water clean, and when done, take them up with a slice, and serve with sauce in a separate tureen.

Cauliflowers in Sauce.

Time, ten minutes to parboil; twenty minutes to simmer.

776. Three heads of cauliflowers; three-quarters of a pint of weak broth; two ounces of butter; a little flour; three tablespoonfuls of cream; pepper and salt.

Parboil three heads of cauliflowers; then cut them into bunches, and put them into a stewpan with three-quarters of a pint of weak broth, and a seasoning of pepper and salt. Let them simmer for twenty minutes, and then stir in three large spoonfuls of cream, and about three ounces of butter rolled in flour. Set the pan over the fire for six or seven minutes, shaking it constantly to prevent its burning; and serve the bunches of cauliflowers with the sauce poured over them.

Or have one whole head in the centre of the dish, and the small sprigs arranged round it.

Moulded Cauliflowers with Sauce.

Time, to boil cauliflowers, ten to fifteen minutes if small.

777. Three heads of very white cauliflowers; a little flour; some maître d'hôtel sauce, piquante or tomato sauce.

Put a small quantity of flour into a saucepan of water, and when it boils put in three very white heads of cauliflowers. When sufficiently done, cut off the stalks, place the pieces head downwards into a *hot* basin, and press them gently together. Put either of the above sauces into a dish, and turn the moulded cauliflowers out of the basin on it, which, if quickly and carefully done, will have a very good appearance, forming one large cauliflower.

Cauliflower au Gratin.

Time, to boil cauliflowers, ten to fifteen minutes if small; twenty minutes or longer if large.

778. Cauliflowers: clarified butter; four ounces of grated Parmesan cheese; a seasoning of pepper, salt and nutmeg.

Arrange some neatly-cut pieces of cauliflower, previously boiled, on a dish, pour over them a cupful of clarified or melted butter, strew over a quarter of a pound of grated Parmesan cheese, and season with pepper, salt, and nutmeg to taste. Brown with a salamander, or set them in the oven until lightly coloured.

Or—

Time, to boil the cauliflowers, ten to fifteen minutes if small; twenty or twenty-five minutes if large; ten or twelve minutes to bake.

779. Two or three cauliflowers; a little garlic; pepper; salt; bread-crumbs; a few capers; two anchovies; a little clarified butter.

Boil two or three cauliflowers until tender, cut off the stalk, and arrange them neatly, piled up on a hot dish previously rubbed with a *very* little garlic. Wash and mince one or two anchovies very fine with a few capers, mix them with a seasoning of pepper and salt, and a small cupful of bread-crumbs, strew it over the cauliflowers; and pour over the whole sufficient clarified butter to *well* moisten it. Bake it in a moderate oven for about ten or twelve minutes, or until it is lightly coloured.

To Boil Brocoli.

Time, ten to fifteen minutes if small; twenty to twenty-five minutes if large.

780. Two or three heads of brocoli; two quarts of water; and a little salt.

Strip off all the dead outside leaves, and cut the inside ones even with the flower; cut off the stalk close, and put them into cold salt and water for an hour before they are dressed to cleanse them from all insects; put them into a large saucepan of boiling salt and water, and boil them quickly for about twelve or fifteen minutes with the pan uncovered. When tender, take them carefully out, drain them dry, and serve them with a little melted butter poured over them, and some in a separate tureen.

Brocoli and Buttered Eggs.

Time, to boil, as above.

781. Three heads of brocoli; some toasted bread; four ounces of fresh butter; six eggs.

Boil one large and two small heads of brocoli tender. Put four ounces of fresh butter into a stewpan, and when warm, stir in six well-beaten eggs until of the consistency of good cream. Pour it over a piece of toasted bread, previously placed in a hot dish. Lay the large head of brocoli in the centre, and the two small ones cut into sprigs and arranged round it.

To Boil large Cabbages.

Time, half an hour to three quarters.

782. A tablespoonful of salt to half a gallon of water.

Pick off all the dead leaves, and cut the stalk as close as possible from the cabbages; cut them across at the stalk end, or if very large divide them into quarters Soak them in cold water to get out any insects, and drain them dry; then put them into plenty of fast boiling water, with the salt and a *very small* piece of soda; press them down in the water once or twice, keep them uncovered, and let them boil quickly until tender. When done, take them up into a colander to drain, covering them over, and, when dry, serve them neatly arranged on a hot dish.

A very small piece of soda may be added to all greens when boiling.

To Boil Brussels Sprouts.

Time, ten to twelve minutes after the water boils.

783. Some sprouts; a tablespoonful of salt; half a gallon of water.

Pick carefully off all the dead leaves from a pint of Brussels sprouts, and wash them clean; then put them into a saucepan of boiling salt and water, with a *very small* piece of soda. Boil them very quickly, with the pan uncovered, until tender; then drain them through a colander, and serve them arranged in a light pile in the centre of the dish, with a tureen of melted butter.

To Boil Sprouts or young Greens.

Time, young greens twelve minutes; brocoli sprouts, ten to twelve minutes after the water boils.

784. Pick any dead leaves from the sprouts or greens, and put them into cold water to soak, with a little salt to take away any insects; then drain them through a colander and put them into a saucepan of fast boiling water with a little salt. Boil them quickly, with the lid off, until tender; and when done, take them up, drain them well, and serve quickly.

To Boil Cabbage or Savoys.

Time, a large cabbage or savoys, half an hour to three-quarters; young summer greens, twelve minutes.

785. Remove any dead or decayed leaves. Cut off as much of the stalk as convenient, and cut the cabbages across twice at the stalk end, unless very large, then they must be quartered; wash them and soak them in cold water to prevent any insects being in them, drain them in a colander, and put them into a saucepan of *boiling water*, with a spoonful of salt. Stir them down frequently, and let them boil very quickly until tender, taking care to keep the saucepan uncovered. When done, take them up quickly, drain them through a colander, covered over to keep them warm; dish and serve them very hot, arranged in quarters round the vegetable dish.

Cabbage with Forcemeat—a la Francaise.

786. A large cabbage; a slice of bacon; a sprig of thyme; two carrots; one bay-leaf; some stock; pepper and salt; mincemeat or forcemeat.

Take off the outer leaves, and cut off the stalk from a fine cabbage; scald it in hot water for ten minutes, make a hole in the middle by the side of the stalk, and fill it *between each leaf* with minced beef, or mutton highly seasoned, or with some sausage forcemeat, bind it round neatly, and stand it in a stewpan with some stock, a slice of bacon, a sprig of thyme, the bay-leaf, and two carrots; let all stew gently, and when done place the cabbage on a dish, untie the string, and pour the strained gravy round it. Garnish with carrots and turnips, and serve it up very hot.

Fregarhed Greens.

787. Three onions; one Chili; two ounces and a half of butter; some greens; a little salt.

Take the onions and the Chili, and put a sufficient quantity of butter with them to stew the greens in; fry the onions and Chili till soft; then wash the greens, and put them with the butter, onions, and Chili into a stewpan, without any water. Season the whole with salt, cover the stewpan, and let them simmer gently over the fire, till all the water from the greens is dried up.

You may add prawns if you like.

To Boil Spinach.

Time, ten to fifteen minutes to boil the spinach; four or five minutes to warm.

788. Two large basketfuls of spinach; a piece of butter the size of an egg; pepper and salt.

Pick the spinach very clean, and put it into several waters, until not a particle of grit is remaining; then put it into a *very* large saucepan, with just sufficient water to prevent its burning, sprinkling in a large spoonful of salt. Press it down with a wooden spoon several times, and when it is quite tender, drain it in a colander, and chop it up very fine; then put it into a stewpan with a piece of butter the size of an egg, and a little pepper. Stir it over the fire until very hot, put it into a dish, and garnish with sippets of bread, or press it into a hot mould and turn it carefully out. Lay seven poached eggs at the top.

Spinach à la Creme.

Time, twenty minutes.

789. Two large bowlfuls of spinach; quarter of a pound of butter; two teaspoonfuls of pounded sugar; a little salt, and nutmeg; three tablespoonfuls of cream.

When the spinach has boiled until quite tender, chop it very fine, and rub it through a *coarse* wire sieve; season it with pepper, salt, and a little grated nutmeg. Put it into a stewpan: stir it over the fire until warm, then pour in three tablespoonfuls of cream, add a quarter of a pound of butter, and a teaspoonful of pounded sugar, stir it over the fire for five or six minutes, and serve it piled high in the centre of the dish,' and garnished with croûtons; or press it into a form.

Boiled Turnips.

Time, one hour to one hour and a quarter; young ones, twenty minutes.

790. Turnips; a spoonful of salt to every half gallon of water.

Pare the turnips, and cut them into quarters, put them into a stewpan of boiling water, and salt in the above proportion, and boil them until quite tender; then drain them dry, and rub them through a colander with a wooden spoon (add a tablespoonful or two of cream, or milk) and put them into another stewpan with a large piece of butter and a little white pepper; stir them over the fire until thoroughly mixed and very hot. Dish them up, and serve them with boiled mutton, &c.

Turnips may be served whole, plainly boiled, if very young.

Turnips in White Sauce.

Time, three-quarters of an hour.

791. Some turnips; a large cupful of white sauce; and a little butter.

Wash and peel as many nice white turnips as you require for a dish; peel and cut them into forms as for Jerusalem artichokes, and boil them tender in a saucepan of water with a piece of butter the size of a large walnut. When done, drain them on a colander, and place them on your dish neatly. Pour over them some white sauce, and serve them up hot.

To Boil French Beans.

Time, moderate size, fifteen to twenty minutes.

792. French beans; a little salt; and water.

Take as many French beans as you may require, cut off the tops and bottoms, and remove the strings from each side; then divide each bean into three or four pieces, cutting them lengthways, and as they are cut put them into cold water with a little salt. Have ready a saucepan of boiling water, drain the beans from the cold water, and put them in. Boil them quickly with the saucepan uncovered, and as soon as they are done, drain them in a colander. Dish and serve them with a small piece of butter stirred into them.

French Beans à la Creme.

Time, to boil the beans, fifteen minutes if young; longer if a moderate size.

793. A pint and a half of French beans; a little salt and a great deal of water; the yolks of three eggs; two tablespoonfuls of cream; two ounces of good butter; and one spoonful of vinegar.

String a pint and a half of French beans, or as many as you may require, and boil them in a large quantity of water with a little salt until tender, and then drain them. Beat the yolks of three new-laid eggs in two large spoonfuls of cream, and about two ounces of good butter, put it when thoroughly beaten together into a stewpan, and set it over a clear fire. When very hot, stir in a large spoonful of vinegar, add the beans, and let it simmer for five or six minutes, stir it constantly with a wooden spoon, and serve it up very hot.

To Boil Broad Beans.

Time, a quarter of an hour if young; twenty to twenty-five minutes if of a moderate size.

794. One peck of beans; one tablespoonful of salt; and half a gallon of water.

After shelling the beans put them into a saucepan of boiling salt and water, and boil them quickly for a quarter of an hour if young, or longer if of a moderate size. When done, drain them on a colander, and serve them with parsley and butter in a separate tureen. Boiled bacon should always be served with broad beans.

White Kidney Beans Fricasseed.

Time, a quarter of an hour to stew.

795. One quart of beans; half a pint of veal broth, or water; a bunch of sweet herbs; a little salt; nutmeg; and beaten mace; a glass of white wine; a piece of butter; yolks of two eggs; half a pint of cream; juice of half a lemon.

Take a quart of white kidney beans; if they are dried soak them in salt water all night; if fresh gathered, blanch them and take off the skins. The dried ones must be boiled till they are tender and the skins slip off; put them into a stewpan with half a pint of veal broth or water, a bunch of sweet herbs, a little beaten mace, pepper, salt, and nutmeg, and a glass of white wine; cover them close, and let them stew very gently for a quarter of an hour; then take out the herbs, add a piece of butter mixed with flour, and shake it about till it is thick. Beat the yolks of two eggs in cream, put it in, and keep shaking the pan one way till it is thick and smooth; squeeze in the juice of half a lemon, and pour the fricassee into a hot dish. Garnish with pickled French beans.

To Boil Haricot Beans.

Time, two hours to two hours and a half.

796. One quart of beans; a piece of butter the size of a walnut; half a gallon of water; a spoonful of salt. Shell a quart of haricot beans, and soak them in cold water for three or four hours, then put them into a large pan of cold water and salt in the above proportions, and when boiling draw them to the side to simmer for two hours, or longer if necessary. When done, drain the water from them, and let them stand uncovered until dry, then add a seasoning of pepper and salt, and a piece of butter the size of a walnut. Shake them over the fire for a few minutes until hot, then turn them carefully out without breaking the haricots, and serve them quickly.

Haricot Blancs à la Maitre d'Hotel.

Time, to boil and stew the beans, two hours to two hours and a half.

797. One quart of haricot beans; a sprig of parsley; a teaspoonful of chopped chives; pepper and salt; four ounces of butter, and half a lemon, or a spoonful of vinegar.

Soak a quart of haricot beans in cold water for two or three hours, then boil them in salt and water until tender; drain them well, and put them hot into a stewpan with four ounces of butter mixed with a teaspoonful of chopped chives, a sprig of parsley minced fine, and a seasoning of pepper and salt. Place it over the fire, and shake the pan, as stirring with a spoon may break the beans. When hot and all thoroughly mixed together, serve with the juice of half a lemon, or a spoonful of vinegar or not, according to your taste.

Haricot Beans with White Sauce.

Time, to boil two hours.

798. Beans; a little white sauce; and cream.

Soak the beans for twenty-four hours in cold water with a little salt in it, then let them boil slowly till quite tender. Pour the water off, and having some white sauce ready-made, toss the beans up in it over the fire for a few minutes, and add a little cream when they are turned into the dish.

To Boil Beetroot.

Time, one hour, one hour and a half, or two hours.

799. Beetroot; vinegar; salt; and pepper.

Winter beets should be soaked over night, and before boiling washed very clean, then put them into a stewpan of boiling water, and boil them quickly. If not very large, one hour will be sufficient for them, but if large a longer time must be allowed. When done, put them into cold water, and rub off the skins with your hands, then cut them into thin slices, put them into a dish, and pour over them some cold vinegar; add a little salt and pepper.

If served with cold or boiled meat, mix a large tablespoonful of butter with a cupful of vinegar; season with pepper and salt, make it very hot, and pour it over the beetroots.

If beetroot is in the least broken before dressed, the colour will be gone entirely.

Boiled Vegetable Marrow.

Time, ten to twenty minutes.

800. Some marrows; one tablespoonful of salt to half a gallon of water.

Peel the marrows and put them into a saucepan of boiling water and salt. When tender, take them out, cut them into quarters if large, if not, halve them. Serve them in a vegetable dish on toast, with a tureen of melted butter sent to table with them.

Stewed Vegetable Marrow.

Time, twenty minutes.

801. Six or eight vegtable marrows; juice of half a lemon; one ounce of butter or fat bacon; a little salt.

Take off all the skin of six or eight vegetable marrows, put them into a stewpan with water, a little salt, the juice of half a lemon, and an ounce of butter or fat bacon. Let them stew gently till quite tender, and serve them up with a rich Dutch sauce or any other sauce you please that is piquante.

Fried Vegetable Marrows.

Time altogether, fifteen minutes.

802. Six vegetable marrows; egg; breadcrumbs; pepper and salt.

Cut six vegetable marrows in quarters, take off the skin, remove the seeds, stew them in the same manner as for table. When done, drain them *dry*, dip them into beaten egg, and cover them well with breadcrumbs, make some lard or butter hot, and fry them a nice light colour, strew a little pepper and salt over them, and serve them up quite dry.

Or—

803. Six or eight vegetable marrows; pepper and salt.

Take six or eight vegetable marrows as near of a size as possible, slice them with a cucumber slice, dry them on a cloth, and fry them in very hot lard or butter, dredge them with pepper and salt, and serve up on a napkin. Care must be taken that the fat is *very* hot, as they are done in a minute, and will soon spoil. If not hot enough, they will be tough and greasy.

Vegetable Marrow Rissoles.

Time, about half an hour.

804. One or two large vegetable marrows; some well-seasoned minced beef, and a little good gravy.

Pare the marrows very thin, cut them across, take out the seeds, and fill the centre with well-seasoned minced cold beef or veal. If the latter, add a little minced lemon peel, tie them securely together, and stew them in a little good gravy made from the beef bones. Serve on a hot dish with the gravy poured round them.

Parsnips Boiled.

Time, one hour to one hour and a half; if small, half an hour to one hour.

805. A tablespoonful of salt to half a gallon of water.

If the parsnips are young they require only to be scraped before boiling, old ones must be pared thin and cut into quarters. Put them into a stewpan of boiling salt and water, boil them quickly until tender, take them up, drain them, and serve in a vegetable dish. They are generally sent to table with boiled beef, pork, or salt cod, and also added as a garnish with boiled carrots.

Fried Parsnips.

Time, one hour to one hour and a half.

806. Parsnips; butter; and pepper.

Boil the parsnips until they are tender, then skin them, and cut them in slices lengthwise of a quarter of an inch in thickness; fry them in boiling butter or beef dripping. When one side is brown, turn them over to brown the other; then put them on a dish and dredge them with a little pepper. Serve them with fried or roast meat.

Parsnip Fritters.

Time, one hour and a half to boil, if large; if small, half an hour to one hour.

807. Four or five parsnips; a teaspoonful of flour; one egg; some butter or beef dripping.

Boil four or five parsnips until tender, take off the skins and mash them very fine, add to them a teaspoonful of flour, one egg well beaten, and a seasoning of salt. Make the mixture into small cakes with a spoon, and fry them on both sides a delicate brown in boiling butter or beef dripping. When both sides are done, serve them up very hot on a napkin or hot dish, according to your taste.

These resemble very much the salsify or oyster plant, and will generally be preferred.

Parsnips Boiled and Browned under Roast Beef.

Time, half an hour to one hour; one hour to one hour and a half, according to size.

808. Parsnips; one large spoonful of salt to five pints of water; pepper and salt.

Wash and scrape the parsnips, and if very large cut them across. Put them into boiling salt and water, and boil them very quickly until tender. Take them up, drain them dry, and place them in the dripping-pan under roast beef, dust over them a little pepper and salt, and let them brown nicely. Serve them in a separate dish, with a few as a garnish round the meat.

Parsnips Mashed.

Time, one hour to one hour and a half.

809. Parsnips; a little cream; pepper; salt; two ounces of butter.

Boil and scrape the parsnips, then mash them smooth with a few spoonfuls of cream, two ounces of butter, and a little pepper and salt; warm over the fire, and serve.

Stewed Parsnips.

Time, one hour to one hour and a half.

810. Four large parsnips; half a pint of cream; a piece of butter mixed with flour; a little grated nutmeg; some salt.

Pare and boil four parsnips very tender, cut them in rather thin slices, and put them into a stewpan with half a pint of cream, a piece of butter rolled in flour, grated nutmeg, and salt. Keep shaking the pan round till it is well mixed, and is thick and smooth. When done, put it in a hot dish and serve.

Baked Spanish Onions.

Time, two hours.

811. Some Spanish onions; half a pint of good brown gravy.

Wash the onions very clean, but do not remove their skins. Put them into boiling water with a little salt, and let them boil rapidly for an hour. Then take them out, wipe them dry, roll them separately in a piece of thin paper, and bake them for an hour in a slow oven. When done, peel them, put them into a vegetable dish, and pour over them some good brown gravy; or they may be browned in a Dutch oven before the fire without removing their skins, and when done, a piece of cold butter placed on the top of each, and a little pepper and salt sprinkled over them.

To Stew Onions Brown.

Time, two hours.

812. Some Portugal onions; good beef gravy.

Strip off the skin and trim the ends neatly, taking care not to cut the onions; place them in a stewpan that will just hold them in one layer, cover them with some very good beef gravy, and let them stew very slowly for two hours, or until they are perfectly tender without breaking. The onions may be dredged lightly with flour, and fried a light colour before they are stewed, if preferred.

Onions à la Creme.

Time, two hours.

813. Four or five Spanish onions; three ounces of butter; a little flour; pepper; salt; and half a cupful of cream.

Boil the onions in two or three waters to take off the strong taste, then drain them on a sieve, and put them into a stewpan with about three ounces of butter, a little flour rubbed smooth, pepper and salt, and half a cupful of cream. Put it over a slow fire, and stir them frequently until sufficiently done. Serve them with the sauce poured over them.

To Stuff Onions.

Time, ten minutes to fry; two hours to stew.

814. Some large Portugal onions; a little fat bacon; a little lean beef; bread-crumbs; a sprig of parsley; lemon peel; pepper; salt; and mace; one or two eggs; a piece of butter; some brown gravy.

Peel some large Portugal onions, par-boil and drain them, then take out the inside, but be careful to keep the onions whole. Chop up the inside of the onion, a little beef, and a little fat bacon, add some bread-crumbs, a sprig of parsley, and lemon-peel minced up, and a seasoning of pepper, salt, and mace, beat it all up with a well-beaten egg or two into a paste, and stuff the onions with it, dredge them over with flour, and fry them a nice brown, then put them into a stewpan with sufficient brown gravy to cover them, and stew them gently over a slow fire for two hours. If stewed in water a little flour and butter must be added.

To Serve Celery.

815. Wash the roots free from dirt, and cut off all the decayed leaves; preserve as much of the stalk as you can, removing any specks or discoloured parts. Divide it lengthwise into quarters, curl the top leaves, and place

it with the roots downwards in a celery glass nearly filled with cold water.

Celery à la Creme.

Time, to boil the celery, three-quarters of an hour.

816. Six heads of celery; half a pint of cream; a piece of butter rolled in flour; nutmeg, and salt.

Take six heads of celery, cut them about three or four inches long, wash them very clean, and boil them in water until they are tender. Have ready half a pint of cream, mix it with a piece of butter rolled in flour, and a little salt, and a grated nutmeg, boil it up till it is thick and smooth, put in the celery, warm it up, and serve with the sauce poured over it.

Celery with Cream.

Time, three-quarters of an hour, to boil the celery; six or eight minutes to thicken the sauce.

817. Three or four heads of celery; yolks of four eggs; half a pint of cream; a little salt, and grated nutmeg.

Cut the white part of three or four heads of celery into lengths of three or four inches long, boil it until quite tender, and strain it from the water. Beat the yolks of four eggs, and strain them into the cream; season with a little salt and grated nutmeg. Put it into a stewpan with the celery, set it over a stove until it boils and is of a proper thickness, and then send it to table on toasted bread.

Stewed Celery.

Time, one hour and twenty minutes.

818. Four heads of celery; half a pint of veal gravy; half a pint of water; three or four tablespoonfuls of milk.

Wash four heads of celery very clean, take off the dead leaves, and cut away any spots, or discoloured parts. Cut them into pieces about three or four inches long, and stew them for nearly half an hour. Then take them out with a slice, strain the water they were stewed in, and add it to half a pint of *veal gravy*, mixed with three or four tablespoonfuls of cream. Put in the pieces of celery, and let it stew for nearly an hour longer. Serve it with the sauce poured over it.

Celery Fried.

Time, twenty minutes.

819. Three heads of celery; two eggs; salt; nutmeg; two ounces of butter; four spoonfuls of white wine; two ounces of flour; two ounces of lard.

Cut the green tops off three heads of celery, remove the outside stalks, and clean the roots well. Make a batter with the yolks of two eggs well-beaten, the white wine, salt, and nutmeg, and stir the flour in thoroughly. Dip each head of celery into the batter, and fry in lard. Serve quite hot, with melted butter poured over them.

To Stew Cucumbers.

Time, five or six minutes to fry; six or seven to stew.

820. An equal quantity of cucumbers and onions; two ounces of butter; three tablespoonfuls of gravy; two tablespoonfuls of white wine, and half a blade of mace; a little salt, and Cayenne; a piece of butter rolled in flour.

Cut into slices an equal quantity of cucumbers and onions, and fry them in two ounces of butter. Strain them from the butter, and put them into a stewpan with the gravy, wine, and mace. Set it over a slow fire, and let it stew for about six or seven minutes. Then stir in a piece of butter rolled in flour, a seasoning of salt, and a *very* little Cayenne. Shake it over the fire until the sauce thickens, and then serve it up hot.

To Stuff and Stew Cucumbers.

Time, one hour and five minutes.

821. Two large cucumbers; a little forcemeat; three-quarters of a pint of stock; two ounces of butter; a bunch of sweet herbs.

Peel two large cucumbers, cut a piece off the large end, and scoop out the seeds; fill it with forcemeat, replace the piece from the end, and secure it with a very small skewer. Put about a pint of gravy into a stewpan with two ounces of good butter, and a bunch of sweet herbs. Put in the cucumbers, set the pan over a moderate fire, and let them stew very slowly for one hour. Then take them out, and boil down the sauce for a few minutes, pour it over the cucumbers, and serve hot.

To Roast Cucumbers.

Time, twenty minutes or half an hour.

822. Two large cucumbers; some forcemeat; a little butter; half a pint of gravy.

Boil two large cucumbers for about ten or twelve minutes, then peel them, cut them down, and take out all the inside. Fill them with forcemeat, and tie them neatly together; dredge over them a little flour, and place them before a bright fire in a Dutch oven to become brown, basting them frequently with fresh butter. When done, put them on a hot dish, remove the string carefully, that they should not come apart, and serve them up with a little rich gravy poured round them.

To Dress Cucumbers.

823. Five tablespoonfuls of vinegar; three of salad oil; pepper and salt.

Pare the cucumbers, and commence cutting them at the thick end with a sharp knife, or a cucumber cutter. Shred them as thin as possible on a dish, sprinkle them with pepper and salt, and pour over them the above proportion of oil and vinegar.

Cucumbers à la Poulette.

Time, twenty-five minutes.

824. Three large cucumbers; a little salt; two tablespoonfuls of vinegar; yolks of two eggs; a piece of butter; a little flour; two spoonfuls of cream; and half a pint of broth.

Take three large cucumbers, pare off the rind, and cut them into slices of an equal thickness. Pick out the seeds, and boil the cucumbers tender in boiling water, with a teaspoonful of salt, and a tablespoonful of vinegar. When done, take them carefully out with a slice, and when drained, put them into a stewpan with half a pint of broth, a piece of butter rolled in flour, and two teaspoonfuls of cream. Skim off any fat which may rise, and boil it gently for a quarter of an hour, taking care that the slices of cucumbers are not broken. When ready to serve, stir in the yolks of two eggs, beaten with a spoonful of vinegar.

Endive Stowed with Cream.

Time, ten minutes to boil; six or seven minutes to stew.

825. Four or five heads of endive; a large piece of butter; three parts of a wineglass of cream; two dessertspoonfuls of white sauce; two lumps of sugar, and a little salt.

Wash and free the endive thoroughly from insects. Pick off the outer green leaves, leaving only the white part, which must be carefully examined. Put them into a stewpan of boiling water with a spoonful of salt, and let them boil quickly until tender. When done, drain them in a colander, squeeze them dry, cut off the roots, and chop them very fine. Rub them through a coarse wire sieve into a stewpan, add a large piece of butter, and a pinch of salt. Stir it over a slow fire for a few minutes, then mix in the white sauce, cream, and a couple of lumps of pounded sugar. Stir them over the fire, until sufficiently thick to pile in a dish, and garnish with sippets.

To Choose Mushrooms.

826. The greatest care is requisite in the choice of mushrooms, as the death of many persons has been occasioned by carelessly using the poisonous kinds.

The eatable ones first appear very small and of a round form, on a little stalk. They grow very fast, and the upper part and stalk are white. As the size increases, the under part gradually opens, and shows a fringy fur of a very fine salmon-colour, which continues more or less till the mushroom has gained some size, and then turns to a dark brown. These *marks* should be attended to, and likewise whether the skin can be easily parted from the edges and middle. Those that have *white* or *yellow* fur should be carefully avoided, though many of them have the same smell (but not so strong) as the right sort.

Stewed Mushrooms.

Time, twenty-one minutes.

827. Button mushrooms; salt to taste; a little butter rolled in flour; two tablespoonfuls of cream, or the yolk of one egg.

Choose buttons of uniform size. Wipe them clean and white with a wet flannel, put them in a stewpan with a little water, and let them stew very gently for a quarter of an hour. Add salt to taste, work in a little flour and butter, to make the liquor about as thick as cream, and let it boil for five minutes. When you are ready to dish it up, stir in two tablespoonfuls of cream, or the yolk of an egg, stir it over the fire for a minute, but do not let it boil, and serve it. Stewed button mushrooms are very nice, either in fish stews or ragoûts, or served apart to eat with fish.

Another way of doing them is to stew them in milk and water (after they are rubbed white), add to them a little veal gravy, mace, and salt, and thicken the gravy with cream or the yolks of eggs.

Mushrooms Grilled.

Time, about twelve minutes, to broil.

828. Six large mushrooms; quarter of a pound of butter; pepper and salt; juice of a lemon.

Peel and score the under part of six fine sound fresh mushrooms, put them into an earthen dish, and baste well with melted butter; strew with pepper and salt, and leave them for an hour and a half. Broil on both sides over a clear fire. Serve quite hot, with a lump of butter on each and a little pepper, or with a little melted butter, and the lemon juice poured over them.

Baked Mushrooms.

Time, from twenty to thirty minutes.

829. Twenty mushroom flaps; quarter of a pound of butter; pepper and salt.

Peel the tops of twenty mushrooms; cut off a portion of the stalks, and wipe them carefully with a piece of flannel dipped in salt. Lay the mushrooms in a tin dish, put a small piece of butter on the top of each, and season them with pepper and salt. Set the dish in the oven, and bake them from twenty minutes to half an hour. When done, arrange them high in the centre of a *very* hot dish, pour the sauce round them, and serve quickly, and as *hot* as you possibly can.

Seakale.

Time, twenty minutes.

830. Some toasted bread; and melted butter.

Tie the seakale up in bundles, and put it into a stewpan of boiling water with a teaspoonful of salt; let it boil for about twenty minutes, or until tender. Drain and serve it up on a slice of toast, with a tureen of melted butter.

Seakale Stewed.

Time, twenty-five minutes.

831. Trim and wash it well, tie in bundles, put it in boiling water, into which a handful of salt has been thrown; and after having been boiled twelve minutes, lay it to drain, and when free from the water, put it in a stewpan, cover it with a rich gravy, and stew until quite tender. It should be sent to table in the gravy.

Salsify, or Vegetable Oyster.

Time, to boil, thirty to forty minutes.

832. Six ounces of butter; two dessertspoonfuls of white sauce; a little pepper and salt; some vinegar or lemon juice.

After you have washed and scraped the salsify very white, throw it into very weak vinegar and water, or lemon juice and water, for a few minutes; then put it into a pan of boiling water with two ounces of butter, a little salt, and a tablespoonful of vinegar or lemon. When it is quite tender, put it to drain on a sieve; then cut it into short pieces, and again put it into a stewpan with the white sauce, the remainder of the butter, and a little lemon juice. Shake it over the fire for a few minutes until it is well mixed and very hot, and serve it piled high in the centre of a dish, garnished with croûtons arranged round it.

Stewed Tomatoes—American.

Time, one hour.

833. Six or eight large tomatoes; one teaspoonful of salt; a piece of butter half the size of an egg; one tablespoonful of grated bread.

Pour boiling water over six or eight large tomatoes, or a greater number of small ones; let them remain for a few minutes, then peel off the skins, squeeze out the seeds and some of the juice, put them in a well-tinned stewpan with a teaspoonful of salt, a saltspoonful of pepper, a piece of butter, and a tablespoonful of grated bread. Cover the stewpan close, and set it over the fire for nearly an hour, shake the pan occasionally that they may not burn, and serve them hot.

Baked Tomatoes—American.

Time, nearly one hour.

834. Five or six tomatoes; a saltspoonful of salt; half as much of pepper; a piece of butter the size of a nutmeg.

Wash five or six smooth tomatoes; cut a small piece from the stem end, and put a little salt, pepper, and a piece of butter the size of a nutmeg in each, place them in a dish, and bake them in a moderate oven for nearly an hour. Serve them up hot.

Scalloped Tomatoes—American.

Time, half an hour.

885. Six tomatoes; two tablespoonfuls of bread-crumbs; a teaspoonful of salt; a saltspoonful of pepper; a piece of butter the size of an egg; a teaspoonful of sugar.

Peel six fine tomatoes (pour scalding water over them if the skins do not come off readily) and press the seeds and juice from them; butter a scallop dish; add to the tomatoes two tablespoonfuls of bread-crumbs, the pepper and salt, and a piece of butter the size of a small egg, cut small. Put the prepared tomatoes into the buttered tin, and bake them half an hour in a quick oven. When done, turn them out. A teaspoonful of sugar added to the preparation is considered an improvement.

To Boil Green Truffles.

Time, one hour.

836. Twelve large truffles; equal quantities of white wine and water; a little salt; three cloves; and a little mace.

Take twelve large truffles, pair the outside skins off very thin, wash them, and put them into a stewpan that will just hold them, and cover them with half white wine, half water, two or three cloves, a little salt, and a quarter of a blade of mace. Cover them close, and boil them gently for an hour, then fold a napkin, lay it in a dish, and serve the truffles on it.

Green Truffles Stewed.
Time, one hour.

837. Six or eight truffles; half a pint of gravy; a glass of white wine; a bunch of sweet herbs; a little beaten mace; pepper and salt; a piece of butter; juice of half a lemon.

Pare off the outside from six or eight large green truffles, cut them in thin slices, and put them into a stewpan with half a pint of gravy, a glass of white wine, sweet herbs tied together, pepper, salt, and mace. Cover them close, and let them simmer very slowly for one hour, then add a piece of butter mixed with flour. Stew it until thick, and squeeze in the juice of half a lemon, crisp the top of a French roll, put it in the centre of a dish, take out the bunch of sweet herbs, and put the truffles over the roll.

Green Morels Stewed.
Time, one hour and a quarter.

838. A glass of white wine; some gravy; pepper; salt, and beaten mace; juice of half a lemon; a piece of butter and flour; and some morels.

Take the quantity you want, wash them very clean, cut the large ones in quarters, and let the small ones remain whole. Put them into a stewpan with gravy enough to cover them, a glass of white wine, pepper, salt, and beaten mace. Cover them closely, and let them stew gently for an hour, then stir in a piece of butter mixed with flour and the juice of half a lemon. Boil it up until of a proper thickness and serve.

To Stew Cardoons.
Time, boil until tender.

839. Four cardoons; one pint of gravy; a glass of white wine; a small bunch of sweet herbs; pepper; salt, and a very little pounded mace; the juice of half a lemon; a piece of butter in flour.

Take four cardoons, pull off the outside leaves, string the white part, cut them about two inches long, wash them very clean, and put them into a stewpan with a pint of white gravy, a glass of white wine, a small bunch of sweet herbs, a little pounded mace, pepper and salt. Cover them over and stew them gently till they are tender, then put to them a piece of butter mixed with flour, and boil it gently till of a proper thickness, take out the herbs, squeeze in the juice of half a lemon, and dish them up.

To Boil Cardoons.
840. Butter and cardoons.

Cut the cardoons into pieces of six inches long, and put them on a string, boil them till quite tender, then have some butter in a stewpan, flour them, and fry them a nice brown. Put them on a sieve to drain, and serve with melted butter poured over them. You may tie them in bundles and boil them like asparagus. Put a toast under them; serve melted butter in a tureen.

Cardoons Fried.
Time, till tender.

841. A dish of cardoons; two ounces of butter; pepper; salt.

Cut the cardoons into pieces about eight or nine inches long, string and tie them into bundles or cut them into dice. Boil thoroughly, and serve hot with melted butter, pepper, and salt.

Cardoons à la Fromage.
Time, stew till tender.

842. A dish of cardoons; one pint of red or port wine; pepper and salt; one ounce of butter floured to thicken; juice of an orange; a quarter of a pound of Cheshire cheese.

String the cardoons and cut them into pieces about an inch long, stew them in the port wine until quite tender, add the flour, butter, pepper, and salt. Put them into a dish in which they are to be served, add the juice of an orange, and grate over all the cheese. Brown with a salamander, and serve quite hot.

Horseradish.
843. Wash the horseradish very clean, and lay it in cold water for nearly an hour; then scrape it into very fine shreds with a sharp knife. Place some of it in a glass dish, and arrange the remainder as a garnish for roast beef, or many kinds of boiled fish.

Radishes.
844. Radishes are of three sorts, the long red, the small turnip, and the winter or white radish.

Radishes should be fresh pulled and tender to be in perfection. Cut off all the leaves, leaving about an inch of the stalk, trim them neatly, and lay them in cold water for an hour. Serve the long ones in a celery glass half filled with water, and the small ones arranged on a plate with the stalk ends outwards and a saltcellar in the centre. They may also be added to a salad.

Purée of Turnips.
Time, ten or twelve minutes.

845. Seven or eight large white turnips;

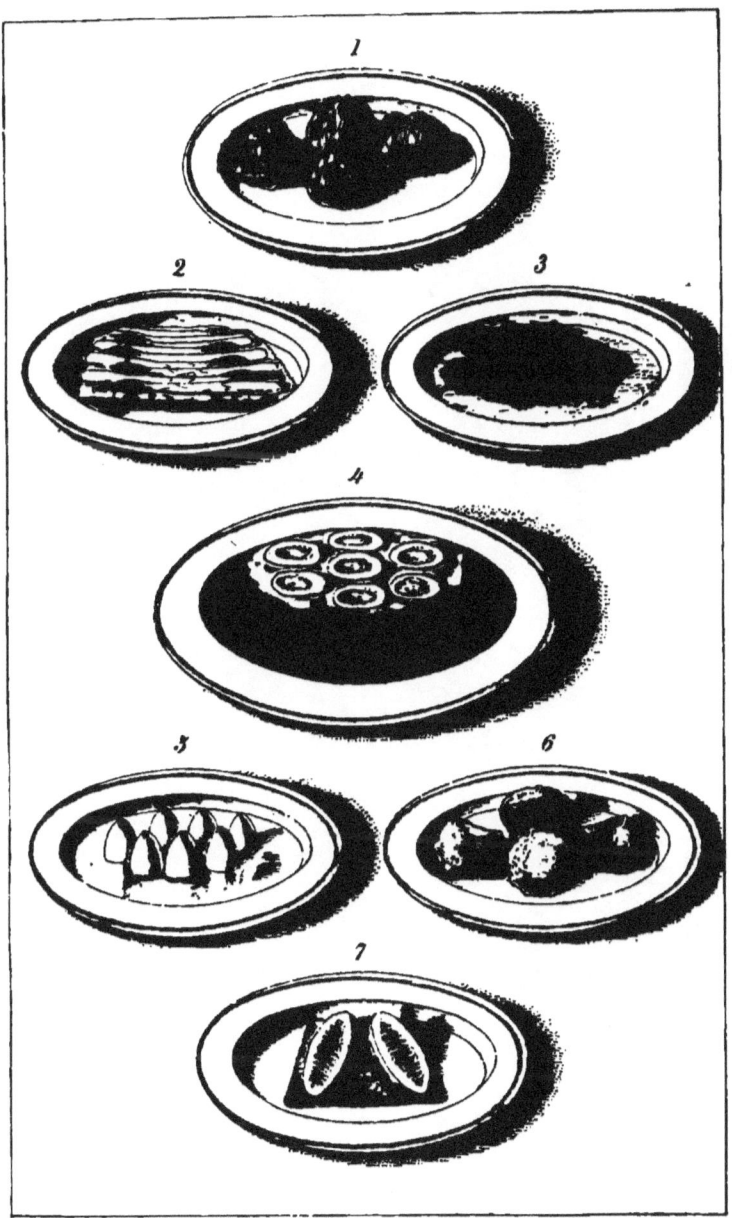

1. *Artichokes.*
2. *Asparagus.*
3. *Beetroot.*
4. *Spinach and Eggs.*
5. *Jerusalem Artichokes.*
6. *Cauliflowers.*
7. *Vegetable Marrow.*

a quarter of a pound of good butter; pepper; salt, and a little nutmeg, if the flavour is liked; two tablespoonfuls of cream.

Peel, slice, and well wash seven or eight very white turnips. When tender enough to pulp press them through a wire sieve, mix in a quarter of a pound of good butter, two tablespoonfuls of cream, and a seasoning of pepper, salt, and grated nutmeg, if the flavour is not disliked. Stir the whole over a clear fire for about ten or twelve minutes, and serve with boiled mutton.

Purée of Potatoes.

Time, half an hour to thirty-five minutes to boil the potatoes, if large.

846. Six or seven large mealy potatoes; two dessertspoonfuls of cream; three or four ounces of butter; pepper and salt.

Boil and mash six or seven large mealy potatoes, press them very smooth through a wire sieve, or beat them smooth with a wooden spoon. Mix them with the butter, pepper, salt, and two spoonfuls of cream. Stir over a clear fire until hot, and serve with cutlets, piling the purée in the centre of the dish.

Purée of Green Peas for Lamb Cutlets, &c.

Time, ten to fifteen minutes to boil the peas, if young.

847. One pint and a half of green peas; a sprig of green mint; three or four ounces of butter; pepper; salt, and a lump of sugar.

Boil a pint and a half of green peas and a sprig of mint until the peas are sufficiently soft to pulp, then drain them dry and either press them through a sieve or pound them in a mortar; mix with them three or four ounces of butter, a lump of sugar, and a little pepper and salt. Put the purée into a small stewpan over a clear fire until hot, stirring it all the time, and when done, pile it in the centre of the lamb cutlets.

Purée of Celery.

Time, nearly an hour.

848. Six heads of very white celery; three ounces of fresh butter; two or three ounces of flour; three-quarters of a pint of milk, or half a pint of milk and a quarter of a pint of cream; pepper and salt.

Wash six heads of white celery very clean, cut them into small and thin slices, and put them into a stewpan with three ounces of fresh butter, pepper and salt. Cover it closely, and let it stew until the celery is sufficiently tender to pulp, taking care it does not become coloured, then pour in the milk, or milk and cream. Boil it up for twenty minutes or more, stirring it constantly. When done, rub it through a wire sieve, make it hot, and serve it piled up in the centre of cutlets, game, poultry, or any entrée.

Purée of Red Carrots.

Time, two hours.

849. Eight or nine carrots; half a pint of stock; one lump of sugar; half a pound of butter; pepper; salt; a small onion.

Shave off the red part of eight or nine carrots, and scald them in a stewpan of hot water for a few minutes. Then put them into a stewpan with a quarter of a pound of butter, a quarter of a pint of stock, pepper, salt, and a small onion. Set it over the fire to simmer slowly for about two hours, or until the carrots will pulp. Then rub them through a coarse sieve into another stewpan; stir in the remainder of the butter, the stock, and a lump of sugar, and stir it constantly over a moderate fire until thick enough to pile in the centre of cutlets, or anything for which it may be required.

A purée may be made of any vegetables, the same directions serving for all.

Purée of Chestnuts.

Time, one hour and a half to boil the chestnuts.

850. Half a hundred of chestnuts; two ounces of butter; two tablespoonfuls of cream; pepper; salt, and nearly a pint of milk.

Pick and scald the skins from half a hundred of chestnuts, put them into a stewpan, pour over them nearly a pint of new milk, and stew them until they are sufficiently soft to pulp. Drain the milk from them, if any remains, and press them through a sieve. Stir into the pulp two ounces of fresh butter, two spoonfuls of cream, and a seasoning of pepper and salt. Make it hot, stirring it all the time, and serve with cutlets round it.

Salad Mixture.

851. Three tablespoonfuls of oil; half a spoonful of tarragon vinegar, and the same of common vinegar; a little black pepper; a teaspoonful of salt.

Mix the above ingredients very smooth, cut the lettuce into it, and do not stir it until used.

Salad Mixture.

852. One boiled potato; one saltspoonful of salt; two of white powdered sugar; one mustardspoonful of mustard; one table-

spoonful of oil; one teaspoonful of Harvey sauce, and some vinegar.

Boil a nice mealy potato, and mash it very smooth. Add all the other ingredients, and when the whole is well mixed, add some vinegar by degrees till it is the consistency of thick cream.

Another Salad Dressing.

853. One teaspoonful of made mustard; one ditto of pounded sugar; two tablespoonfuls of salad oil; four of milk; two of vinegar; Cayenne and salt to your taste.

Put the mixed mustard into a salad bowl with the sugar, and add the oil, drop by drop, carefully stirring and mixing all the ingredients well together. Proceed in this manner with the milk and vinegar, which must be added very gradually, or the sauce will curdle, then put in the seasoning of Cayenne and salt. It ought to have a creamy appearance, and when mixing, the ingredients cannot be added too gradually, or stirred too much.

Italian Sauce for Salads.

854. Three tablespoonfuls of sauce tournée; one of mustard; a little tarragon and chervil; three tablespoonfuls of Florence oil; a little salt, and a glass of tarragon vinegar.

Mix well together three tablespoonfuls of sauce tournée, with one of mustard, some tarragon and chervil shred fine, and three tablespoonfuls of Florence oil, dropped in by degrees. When quite smooth, add a glass of tarragon vinegar, a little at a time, and a little salt. This sauce cannot be too much mixed.

Salad Sauce.

855. Three hard-boiled eggs; one tablespoonful of made mustard; three of salad oil; white pepper; salt; Cayenne; a dust of sugar; five spoonfuls of thick Béchamel sauce; one tablespoonful of tarragon vinegar; one of Chili vinegar; two of common vinegar; half a wineglass of cream.

Rub the *yolks* of the hard-boiled eggs in a basin, add to them the mustard and the salad oil, and mix it very smooth. Then add the pepper, salt, Cayenne. dust of sugar, the Béchamel, tarragon, Chili, and common vinegar, and mix all well together with hal; a glass of cream. If this sauce is required for fish salads, add a few drops of essence of anchovies, and sprinkle over the sauce a little finely-chopped parsley the last thing.

Salad (Bohemia).

856. Yolk of one or two raw eggs; one or two young onions, or leeks; three tablespoonfuls of salad oil; one of vinegar; some lettuce; and slices of beetroot; salt, and mustard.

Take the yolk of one or two *raw* eggs, according to the size of the salad you require, beat them up well, add a little salt and mustard, and chop up one or two young onions, or leeks, about the size of grass, then add the salad oil and the vinegar, and beat the whole up into a thick sauce. Cut in the salad, and put thin slices of beetroot at the top. Sprinkle a little salt over it, and do not stir it up till the moment you use it. For a small salad three *dessertspoonfuls* of oil, and one of vinegar will do.

Chicken Salad.

857. Cold fowl; two or three white-heart lettuces; two hard-boiled eggs; two dessertspoonfuls of butter melted, or salad oil; two teaspoonfuls of made mustard; one of loaf sugar; one large cupful of vinegar.

Wash and dry two or three white-heart lettuces, reserving the centre leaves, cut them fine, and lay them at the bottom of a dish, mince all the white meat from a boiled chicken, or fowl, without the skin, and place it on the lettuce. Rub the yolks of two hard-boiled eggs to a smooth paste with the butter melted, or salad oil. Add to it two tablespoonfuls of made mustard and one of pounded loaf sugar, and stir very gradually in a large cupful of vinegar. Arrange as a border the centre leaves of the lettuces, with some small delicate cress between the chicken and edge of the dish, and when *ready* to serve, pour over the chicken the salad dressing.

Salad of Chicken and Celery.

858. The white meat of a chicken; the weight in celery; the yolk of one raw egg, and one hard-boiled; a teaspoonful of salt; the same of pepper; half a tablespoonful of mustard; a tablespoonful of salad oil; one of white wine vinegar.

Take the white meat of a chicken, either roasted, boiled, or fricasseed, cut it small, or mince it fine; take the same quantity, or *more*, of white tender celery cut small, and mix the celery and chicken together an hour or two before it is wanted, then add the dressing made thus:—Break the yolk of a hard-boiled egg very fine with a silver fork, add to it the yolk of a raw egg, and the pepper and salt, with half a tablespoonful of made mustard, work all smoothly together, adding gradually a tablespoonful of salad oil, and the same of white wine vinegar. Mix the chicken with the dressing, pile it up in the dish, and spread some of the dressing over the outside. Garnish with the delicate leaves of the celery, the white of the egg cut into rings, green pickles cut in slices, pickled beetroot in slices and stars, and placed alternately with the rings of egg, and the leaves.

Endive as a Winter Salad.

Time, twenty minutes to boil the eggs.

859. Endive; celery; beetroot; six hard-boiled eggs.

Make a salad mixture in the usual way, and place it at the bottom of the bowl, then wash and dry some endive, place it in the centre of the dish, piled rather high, and arrange round it slices of boiled beetroot, and hard-boiled eggs cut across, and placed alternately, garnishing the edge thickly with the delicate part of celery curled with the small green of the leaves.

Do not stir the mixture with the vegetables.

To Make a Salad (ascribed to the Rev. Sydney Smith.)

860.

Two boiled potatoes strained through a kitchen sieve,
Softness and smoothness to the salad give;
Of mordant mustard take a single spoon,
Distrust the condiment that bites too soon;
Yet deem it not, thou man of taste, a fault,
To add a double quantity of salt.
Four times the spoon with oil of Lucca crown,
And twice with vinegar procured from town.
True taste requires it, and your poet begs,
The pounded yellow of two well-boiled eggs.
Let onions' atoms lurk within the bowl,
And scarce suspected animate the whole;
And lastly, in the flavoured compound toss,
A magic spoonful of anchovy sauce;
Oh, great and glorious! oh, herbaceous meat!
'Twould tempt the dying anchoret to eat,
Back to the world he'd turn his weary soul,
And dip his finger in the salad bowl.

Lobster Salad.

861. One hen lobster; lettuces; endive; mustard and cress; radishes; beetroot; cucumber; some hard-boiled eggs.

Pour the salad mixture into the bowl, wash and dry the lettuces and endive, and cut them fine with a silver knife, add them to the dressing, with the pickings from the body of the lobster, and *part* of the meat from the shell cut into small pieces. Rub the yolks of two or three hard-boiled eggs through a sieve, and afterwards the coral of the lobster, then place the salad very lightly in the bowl, and garnish it with the coral, yolks of the hard-boiled eggs, sliced beetroot, cucumber, radishes, and the pieces of lobster. Place as a border hard-boiled eggs cut across, with the delicate leaves of the celery and endive between them.

Lobster Salad.

862. A lobster; yolks of two eggs; a spoonful of made mustard; three tablespoonfuls of salad oil; a taste of Chili vinegar; a little salt; some fresh lettuces.

Pick all the meat out of the lobster, thoroughly beat the yolks of two new-laid eggs, beat in made mustard to taste, and continuing to beat them drop in three tablespoonfuls of salad oil, add whatever flavouring may be preferred, a taste of Chili vinegar, and some salt. Mix in six tablespoonfuls of vinegar, and the soft part of the lobster. Moisten the remainder of the lobster with this, and lay it at the bottom of the bowl, cut up the lettuce, take care that it is well rolled over in the dressing, and put it over the lobster. Mustard can be left out if it is not liked. The above quantity is given for the proportions, and can be increased according to the lobster employed.

Or—

863. Two lobsters; three new-laid eggs; half a pint of salad oil; half a pint of vinegar; two tablespoonfuls of made mustard; Cayenne pepper; and salt; three lettuces; a sprig or two of mint; half a root of beet.

To make the dressing, beat three new-laid eggs thoroughly, and mix in gradually half a pint of salad oil, beat in half a pint of vinegar or less, two tablespoonfuls of made mustard, Cayenne pepper and salt. Wash three fine white lettuces, and drain them dry, cut them up with the meat of two large lobsters, or of four smaller (which is better) adding a sprig or two of mint if the flavour be not disliked. Cut up also three hard-boiled eggs, and slice about half a root of beet. A deep dish is prettier to use than a salad bowl. Mix all the ingredients well together on the dish, and let them lie on it heaped up in the middle, pouring in dressing enough to moisten all thoroughly, and to collect in the dish below. Sprinkle the spawn and coral over the top. When the lobster salad is well mixed it must also be well helped, with due care that each person has sufficient lobster with the green.

The lettuces should not be cut up until the salad is going to be eaten. If it be not convenient to do the final mixing then, it is better to mix the dressing with the lobster, and to let some one, when the time arrives, arrange the lettuce round it, cut in quarters.

Canadian Salad.

864. Two large apples; one cucumber; one large onion; twelve Chilies; one teaspoonful of Cayenne pepper; a spoonful or two of salt; sufficient vinegar to cover it.

Mince very fine the apples, cucumber, onion, and Chilies. Put the whole into a large basin, and sprinkle them with salt and the Cayenne pepper, then pour over the whole sufficient vinegar to cover the mixture and stir it well together.

To Boil Green Corn or Maize.

865. Get the short full ears of sugar corn, trim off all the husks, leaving only the last inside leaves. Have a stewpan of boiling water, with a small teaspoonful of salt to each quart of water, put in the corn and let it boil quickly for half an hour, if young and tender, or longer if less tender. When done, drain off all the water and take off the remaining husks, lay a napkin on a dish, place the corn on it and serve, or when drained place them on toast and send melted butter to table with them.

It may also be served in the following manner :—Take off all the husks, and with a sharp knife cut it from the cob and put it into a stewpan with a cupful of water to a quart of corn cut from the cob, cover it close, and let it simmer for an hour, then add a large tablespoonful of butter, pepper and salt to taste, and send it up very hot.

CURING BACON, HAMS, &c.—POTTING, COLLARING, &c.

The important art of pickling or salting meat calls for the housekeeper's best attention. There are many modes of doing it, both in England and America. In England North and South make bacon in a different manner. In Hampshire, Wiltshire, and Berkshire, they singe the hog. In Yorkshire, Lincolnshire, &c., they scald the hog. The American mode of pickling pork we consider especially good. Great care must be taken in preparing the meat for salting. It must be carefully examined to see that it is fresh and good, then wiped, sprinkled with salt, and afterwards left to drain a few hours before it is rubbed with the salt. The meat will thus be thoroughly cleansed from the blood, which will prevent it from turning and tasting strong. It should then be placed in the pickling pan and turned every morning, also should be rubbed with the pickle. The cover of the pickling-pan should fit very closely, and have a weight on it to keep it down. If a large quantity of salt meat is frequently required, the pickle may be boiled up, skimmed well, and when cold poured over any meat that has been sprinkled and well drained as above directed.

To Pickle Pork.

866. For a pig of twenty stones weight, half a bushel of salt; half a pound of saltpetre; four pounds of coarse moist sugar.

Cover the bottom of the tub with salt. Then cut off the hams, shoulders, spareribs, and griskins of the pig. Rub the remaining part of the pork with the above ingredients, lay it in the tub with salt between each layer, and in three or four days, if the brine from the pork does not cover it, there must be some made, according to the quantities you may require. Put two pounds of salt and a quarter of an ounce of saltpetre to a quart of water. Boil it half an hour, and when cold pour it over the pork.

The pork must on no account *swim* in the brine. To prevent it, have a piece of wood cut the size of the rib, and on that lay very heavy stones. If done in this way, it will keep good for two years.

To Pickle Pork—an American Receipt.

867. Four pounds and a half of common and fine salt; three gallons of water; one pound of brown sugar; one ounce of saltpetre; half an ounce of saleratus.

Dissolve the saltpetre and saleratus in the water, then add the two pounds and a quarter of common and the same of fine salt, and the brown sugar; put it into a large saucepan and boil and skim it clear. Then put it into the pickle-pan, and when cold, it will be fit for use.

Pork for boiling should be laid in this pickle for a few days, taking care to always keep the meat under the brine, by a suitable piece of board and a weight.

A Pickle for Hams, Beef, or Pork.

Time, half an hour.

868. Six pounds of common salt; one

pound of coarse sugar; four ounces of saltpetre; two gallons of water.

Boil the above ingredients for half an hour, and skim the liquor well. Let it stand till cold before you put the pickle into the tub. Place a weight on the meat so as to keep it quite immersed. It will keep good for five or six months.

To Cure Bacon.

Time, three weeks.

869. One pound of saltpetre; one pound of bay salt; one gallon of coarse salt; one pound of salprunella; one pound of moist sugar.

Pound the salprunella and bay salt very fine, mix the coarse salt and the sugar well together, and rub it into your bacon, hams, and cheeks, putting all in the same brine. Turn and rub the bacon for a week every day; afterwards every other day. Let it remain in the brine three weeks, and then send it to be smoked or dried. Large sides of bacon take a month to dry, small ones three weeks.

West Country Way to Cure Bacon, Hams, &c.

Time to boil the pickle, twenty minutes.

870. To every fifteen pounds of meat allow the following quantities—five pounds and a quarter of common salt; two ounces of salprunella; two ounces of saltpetre; three pounds of bay salt; six pounds and a half of coarse sugar; three pounds and a quarter of treacle; four gallons of water.

Mix the salprunella, saltpetre pounded, and a quarter of a pound of common salt well together; and rub it into every part of the meat, lay it in a salting-pan, and repeat the rubbing for three days. Boil up the coarse sugar, salt, and treacle, with four gallons of water, for twenty minutes, skimming it quite clean. Pour it over the bacon, cheeks, &c., and turn and rub them for a fortnight, or longer should the pig be large. At the end of the time it will be ready for smoking.

To Salt a Ham of Twelve Pounds.

Time, ten weeks.

871. One pound of common salt; one pound of bay salt; two ounces of saltpetre; ten ounces of black pepper; one pound and a half of treacle.

With these ingredients well mixed and pounded, rub the ham every day for half an hour until it becomes soft and pliable. Let is also remain covered over with this pickle for four days, then add one pound and a half of treacle. Rub and turn it every day for a month, at the expiration of that time soak it for twenty-four hours in water, dry it with a cloth, and hang it up for a month in the kitchen. Then remove it to the storeroom, and hang it where the sun does not fall, and where there is a free current of air.

If the ham weighs more than twelve pounds, you must let it lie in the pickle for *more* than four days before you put the treacle to it, and rather more than a month in the pickle. But, a day or two before the treacle is added, the ham should not be touched or rubbed, only suffered to lie in the pickle, taking care that the salt does not fall off.

The best time for curing hams by this receipt is from Michaelmas to Christmas.

The aitchbone should be taken out to the cup, and the blood well drained off, as it is in that part insects are generally found to come.

To Cure Hams.

Time, five weeks to cure.

872. For four hams: four pounds of common salt; half a pound of bay salt; three ounces of saltpetre; two pounds of coarse brown sugar; two ounces of allspice; one ounce of whole black pepper; two quarts of ale.

Rub the hams well with this mixture for a quarter of an hour each—the first time. Then turn and rub them seven days following, after which add to them a pickle made thus:—The allspice, coarse brown sugar, and whole pepper boiled with two quarts of ale. When cold, pour it to the hams, and turn them every day for five weeks, when they will be fit for drying.

Or—

873. Two pounds of salt; half a pound of bay salt; one ounce of black pepper; one ounce of treacle.

The ham should be well rubbed with the salt, bay salt, and pepper, for two days. Then rub well in a pound of treacle, and turn it every day for a fortnight. If the ham is large, a pound and a half of treacle will be better.

Pickle for Westphalia Hams.

Time, two or three weeks; small pork, for present use, four or six days.

874. Seven pounds of bay salt; three ounces of saltpetre; three gallons of water.

Boil the above ingredients together over a slow fire, skim it while boiling, and when cold pour it over the meat so as to cover it. Hams for drying must be left in it for two or three weeks; small pork for present use four or six days. Before putting the meat into the pickle, wash it in water, press out the blood, and wipe it dry. When the pickle becomes weak by constant use, boil it over again, and add half the quantity of the ingredients, and with more water make it up to three gallons, and skim it clean whilst it is boiling.

Hams, Tongues, and Beef, Yorkshire Fashion.

875. One pound and a half of ham sugar; two ounces of saltpetre; one pound of common salt; half a pound of bay salt; two ounces of pepper.

The meat should be well rubbed over night with common salt, and well rubbed in the morning with the above ingredients. If *hams*, they should be rubbed before the fire every day and turned.

To Cure Hams with Hot Pickle.

876. One ounce of saltpetre; half a pound of bay salt; half a pound of common salt; half a pound of coarse brown sugar; one quart of old strong beer.

Beat an ounce of saltpetre very fine, rub it over the ham, which must remain one night; then boil the salt, common salt, and coarse brown sugar in a quart of old strong beer, and pour it over the ham boiling hot. Let it remain three weeks, turning the ham every day. Dry it in wood smoke.

Berkshire Way of Curing Hams.

Time, two months six days.

877. Two hams from fifteen to eighteen pounds each; one pound of salt; one pound of coarse sugar; two ounces of saltpetre; one bottle of vinegar.

Lay the hams to drain three days; then cover them with the salt, saltpetre, and sugar for three days. Add the vinegar and leave them for one month.

To be smoked one month; hung high up from the fire, not to melt the fat. When cooked, they should be softly simmered, not over-done. The hams should be large and of finely-fed pork.

Bacon.

878. For every forty or fifty pounds of meat, allow one pound of bay salt; one pound of saltpetre; two ounces of salprunella; four pounds of common salt.

In Yorkshire and the northern counties, pigs are scalded; the hams, spareribs, and chine cut off, and then afterwards salted thus :—Rub them well with common salt, and lay them on a board for the first brine to run away, for twenty-four hours; then take for every side of forty or fifty pounds, the above quantity of bay salt, saltpetre, salprunella bruised fine, and mixed with four pounds of common salt. Rub the pork well with salt, and put it in the pans at full length; turn and rub it in the brine every day for a fortnight, then take it out, strew it all over with bran or sawdust, and hang it in a wood smoke till it is dry; place it in a cool dry place, taking care that it does not touch the wall, as that would spoil it.

To Cure Hams by the American Mode.

879. One ounce of saltpetre; some molasses; salt and water.

Take one ounce of saltpetre for a fourteen pound ham; make it very fine, and dissolve it in a little molasses; rub it well over the cut side of the meat, around the bone, and over the whole ham. Then pack as many hams as you have, with the small end downwards, in a barrel, with fine salt sprinkled between and over them; let them remain for two or three days; then make a cold brine of salt and water, which will bear an egg, and cover the hams with it. After three weeks they are fit to smoke, or they may remain in the brine three months without injury. Any part of pork may be salted in this manner. The cheeks or head split in two, or any other pieces for boiling or smoking, are much finer cured in this way. Beef tongues may also be done in this manner.

To Pickle Pork.

880. One-third of saltpetre; two-thirds of white salt.

Some people prefer pork pickled with salt alone (legs especially), others in the following manner :—Put a layer of salt at the bottom of a tub; then mix the salt and saltpetre beaten; cut the pork in pieces, rub it well with the salt, and lay it close in the tub, with a layer of salt between every layer of pork, till the tub is full. Have a cover, just large enough to fit the inside of the tub, put it on, and lay a great weight at the top, and as the salt melts it will keep it close. When you want to use it take a piece out, cover the tub over again, and it will keep good a long time.

To Cure Neats' Tongues.

Time, ten to fourteen days.

881. Three tongues; one ounce and a half of salprunella; one ounce and a half of saltpetre; one pound and a half of common salt.

Take three neats' tongues, cut off the roots without removing the fat that is under the tongue, wash them very clean, and dry them in a cloth; then rub them well over with the saltpetre and salprunella, and repeat this for three or four days. Cover them with a pound and a half of common salt, and let them remain for three weeks, turning them every morning. Wipe them dry, rub some dry bran over them, and hang them to smoke for a fortnight, or dress them out of the pickle.

A very Cheap Way of Potting Birds.
Time, one hour and a half.

882. Birds; mace; allspice; white pepper; some butter.

Clean the pigeons or any other birds nicely, and season them with mace, allspice, white pepper, and salt, in fine powder. Rub every part well; then lay the breasts downwards in a pan, and pack the birds as closely as you can. Put a large piece of butter on them; then cover the pan with a coarse flour paste, and a paper over, tie it close, and bake them in the oven. When baked and grown cold, cut them into proper pieces for helping, pack them closely in a large potting-pot, and (if possible) leave no space for the butter about to be added to run between them. Cover them with butter; one-third part less will be wanted then when the birds are done whole.

The butter that has covered potted things will serve for basting, or for paste for meat pies.

To Pot Rabbits.
Time, two hours to two hours and a half.

883. Two or three young rabbits; pepper; mace; a little Cayenne; salt and allspice; and a large piece of butter.

Cut up and wash two or three young, but full-grown rabbits, and take the legs off at the thigh. Pack them as closely as possible in a small pan after seasoning them with pepper and salt, mace, allspice, and a very little Cayenne, all in fine powder. Make the top as smooth as you can, keep out the heads and carcases, but take off the meat from about the neck. Put in a good deal of butter, and bake the whole gently, keep it two days in a pan, then shift it into small pots, adding butter. The livers also may be added, as they eat well.

Potted Neat's Tongue.
Time, two hours, to boil.

884. One neat's tongue; one ounce of saltpetre; four ounces of coarse sugar; pepper; salt, and mace; one pound of clarified butter.

Take a fine neat's tongue, and rub it all over with an ounce of saltpetre, and four ounces of coarse sugar, and let it remain for two days. Then boil it until quite tender and take off the skin and side bits, cut the tongue in very thin slices, and beat them in a mortar with nearly a pound of clarified butter, seasoning it to your taste with pepper, salt, and pounded mace. Beat all as fine as possible, then press it closely down in small potting-pots, and pour over them some clarified butter.

Potted Ox-tongue.

885. One pound and a half of boiled tongue; six ounces of butter; a little Cayenne; a small spoonful of pounded mace; nutmeg and cloves.

Cut about a pound and a half from an unsmoked boiled tongue, remove the rind. Pound it in a mortar as fine as possible with the butter, and the spices beaten fine. When perfectly pounded, and the spice well blended with the meat, press it into small potting-pans, and pour clarified butter over the top. A little roast veal added to the potted tongue is an improvement.

To Pot Beef.
Time, three hours and a half.

886. Two pounds and a half of lean beef; five ounces of butter; pepper; salt; mace.

Take a piece of lean beef and free it from the skin and gristle, put it into a covered stone jar with three dessertspoonfuls of hot water, and stand it in a deep stewpan of boiling water to boil slowly for nearly four hours, taking care that the water does not reach to the top of the jar. When done, take it out, mince it fine, and pound it in a mortar with a seasoning of pepper, salt, and pounded mace. When smooth and like a thick paste, mix in some clarified butter and a very little of the gravy from the jar, press it into pots, pour butter over the tops, and tie down for use.

Strasburg Potted Meat.
Time, three hours and a quarter, to stew in the water.

887. Two pounds of rump of beef; six ounces of butter; four cloves; allspice; nutmeg; salt, and Cayenne to your taste; six ounces of oiled butter; six anchovies.

Cut about two pounds of lean beef into very small pieces, and put it into an earthen jar with six ounces of butter; set the jar in a deep stewpan or saucepan of boiling water, and let it boil until half done, then stir in the seasoning of pepper, salt, cloves, allspice, nutmeg, and Cayenne. Set the beef again in the stewpan of water and boil it until quite tender, take it out, and when cold, add six anchovies washed and boned; pound it well in a mortar, and add six ounces of the butter oiled, with the gravy from the jar, colour it with a little cochineal, make it warm, and then press it into small pots, and pour melted suet over the tops.

Potted Beef like Venison.

Time, to bake, two hours to two hours and a half.

888. Four pounds of the buttock of beef; two ounces of saltpetre; two ounces of bay salt; a quarter of a pound of common salt; half an ounce of salprunella; half an ounce of cloves and mace; a quarter of an ounce of pepper; half a nutmeg.

Take four pounds of buttock of beef and cut the lean into four pieces, beat the saltpetre, bay salt, common salt and salprunella very fine, mix them well together, and rub them into the beef. Let it remain in the pan four days, turning it night and morning, after that put it into a pan, cover it with water and a little of the brine. Send it to the oven and bake it until very tender, then drain it from the gravy, and take out all the skin and sinews, pound the beef in a mortar, put it on a broad dish, and strew over it the mace, cloves, and pepper, all beaten very fine, and grate in half a nutmeg, mix the whole well with the pounded meat, and add a little fresh butter clarified to moisten it. Then *press* it down into pots, set them at the mouth of the oven just to settle, and then cover them two inches deep with clarified butter. When quite cold, cover them with white paper tied over, and set them in a dry place. The beef will keep good a considerable time.

To Pot Venison.

Time, all night in the oven.

889. A pound of butter; three-quarters of a pint of port wine; pepper, salt, and beaten mace; any part of venison.

Rub the venison all over with a little port wine, season it with pepper, salt, and beaten mace, put it into an earthen dish, and pour over it half a pint of port wine, add a pound of butter, and place it in the oven. If a shoulder of venison, let it remain in the oven all night. When done pick the meat from the bones, and pound it in a mortar with the fat from the gravy. Should you find it not sufficiently seasoned, add more, with some clarified butter, and beat it until it becomes a fine paste, then press it hard into pots, pour clarified butter over it, and place them in a dry place.

Potted Fowl and Ham.

890. Some cold roast fowl; a quarter of a pound of lean ham; six ounces of butter; pepper; salt; nutmeg, and a pinch of Cayenne.

Cut all the meat from a cold fowl, and remove the bones, skin, &c., then cut it into shreds, with a quarter of a pound of lean ham and six ounces of butter, the pepper, salt, nutmeg, and Cayenne, and pound it all in a mortar until reduced to a smooth paste. Then mix it thoroughly together, fill the potting-pots, pour over them a thick layer of clarified butter, and tie them down with a bladder. Set them in a dry place, and it will keep good for some time. A little grated lemon peel is an improvement to the fowl.

Potted Head.

Time, five or six hours.

891. Half an ox head; two cow-heels; pepper, salt, and mace.

Take half a head, and soak it in salt and water. When well cleansed from the blood, put it with two cow-heels into a large stew-pan, and *cover* them with cold water. Set it over the fire, and let it boil till tender. Strain the meat from the liquor, and when cold, cut the meat and gristle into very small pieces. Take all the fat from the cold liquor in which the meat, &c., was first boiled, put the mince with it, and boil the whole slowly till perfectly tender and thick enough to jelly; give it a quick boil, and put it in shapes. Before boiling the second time, add pepper and salt to your taste, and a little pounded mace if approved.

To Pot Partridges.

Time, one hour and a half.

892. Two partridges; pepper; salt; mace, and allspice; half a pound of butter.

Pick and clean the birds, and season them with a little pepper, salt, mace, and allspice pounded fine, and rubbed well over them. Then put them into a deep dish as close together as possible, with half a pound of butter on them. Make a common paste of flour and water, cover it over the dish, with a piece of paper over it, and bake them in an oven. When done, and quite cold, cut them into joints, and lay them as closely as possible in a potting-pan, cover them with clarified butter, tie them over close, and keep them in a dry place.

To Pot Moor Game or Pheasants.

Time, one hour.

893. A little beaten mace; cloves, pepper,

salt, and nutmeg; a large piece of butter, and the pheasants.

Pick and draw the game, wipe them clean with a cloth, singe them, season them inside with a little beaten mace, cloves, pepper, salt, and grated nutmeg. Break the breastbones, and press them down as flat as you can; put them in an earthern pan, cover them with butter, and bake them one hour. When they are taken from the oven, lay them on a coarse cloth to drain till they are cold, then put them into pots breast downwards, and cover them half an inch thick above the breasts with clarified butter. When cold, tie white paper over them, and keep them in a dry place.

Potted Hare—A Luncheon Dish.
Time, three or four hours.

894. One hare; a little mace; cloves; pepper, and salt; a pound of butter.

Hang a hare up for four or five days, then case it and cut it in quarters. Put it into a stone jar, season it with beaten mace, cloves, pepper, and salt, put a pound of butter over it, and bake it for four hours in a slow oven. When done, pick the meat from the bones, and pound it in a mortar with the butter that it was baked in skimmed clean from the gravy. Season it with beaten cloves, mace, pepper, and salt to your taste, pound it until it is a smooth paste, then fill the potting-pots, press it down, cover it with clarified butter, and tie white paper over the tops.

Marble Veal.
Time, two hours and a half or three hours to boil the tongue; two hours to stew the veal.

895. A pickled tongue; a pound of fresh butter; four pounds of lean veal; a little beaten mace, and some clarified butter.

Boil, skin, and cut a pickled or dried tongue as thin as possible, and beat it in a mortar with a pound of fresh butter, and a little pounded mace, till it is like a paste. Stew four pounds of lean veal, and pound it in the same way. Then put some of the veal into a large potting-pot, and lay some *tongue* in *lumps* over the veal in different parts; then nearly fill the pots with veal, press it hard down, and pour clarified butter over it. When served, cut it across in thin slices, put them on a dish, and garnish with curled parsley. Keep it in a cold place, tied over with paper.

Potted Herrings.
Time, two hours.

896. Herrings; white wine vinegar; a few bay-leaves.

Cut off the heads and tails of the fish, clean, wash, and dry them well, sprinkle them with pepper and salt within and without, lay them in an earthen pan, and cover them with white wine vinegar. Set them in an oven not too hot (the roes at the top, but they are not to be eaten), till the bones are quite soft, which will be in about two hours. Some cut the fish down by the bone so as to open them, and then roll them up from the tail to the head. The bay-leaves are an improvement, and a little water may be added to the vinegar if preferred. Cover them with paper.

To Pot Herrings.
Time, three hours, to bake.

897. One or two dozen herrings; two ounces of salt; two of allspice; one of saltpetre; one ounce of nutmegs; the same of mace; white pepper and salt; one clove and some butter; two or three bay-leaves and clarified butter.

Pound the saltpetre, salt, and allspice to the finest powder, rub it well over the herrings, and let them remain with the spice upon them eight hours to drain; then wipe off the spice very clean, and lay them in a pan on which butter has been rubbed; season them with grated nutmeg, pounded clove, pepper, mace, and salt, lay over them two or three bay-leaves, cover them with pieces of butter, and bake them slowly. When cool, drain off the liquor, place the fish in the pan intended for their use, cover them with clarified butter sufficiently melted just to run, but not hot, and they will be fit for use in two days.

Worcester Receipt for Potting Lampreys.
Time, three hours, to bake.

898. Six good-sized fish; one ounce of white pepper; one blade of mace; six cloves; a little salt; half a pound of clarified butter; half a pound of beef suet.

Leave on the skin, but remove the cartilage and the string on each side of it down the back. Clean the fish thoroughly, wipe them dry, and leave them to drain all night. For half a dozen fish of pretty good size, take the above quantity of white pepper, mace, cloves, and salt, beat all to a fine powder, season the fish with it, and arrange the lampreys in a stone jar curled round, with the seasoning sprinkled in and about them. Pour clarified butter mixed with beef suet over the fish, tie thick paper over to keep in the steam, and bake them for three hours in a moderate oven. Look at them frequently after they are potted, and take off the oil as it rises. They will keep some time, but the butter must be taken off occasionally, the dish warmed in the oven, and then covered with fresh clarified butter.

Potted Pike.

Time, one hour to bake.

899. Pike; a little bay salt; and pepper. Scale and clean the fish, cut off the head, split it down the back, and take out the bone. Sprinkle over the inside some bay salt and pepper, roll it up tight, and lay it in the pot. Cover it closely, and let it bake an hour. Take it out, and lay it on a coarse cloth to drain; when cold put it into a pot that will just hold it, and cover it with clarified butter.

Potted Char.

Time, three hours.

900. Char; a few cloves; mace; nutmeg; pepper and salt; a little clarified butter.

Cut off the fins and gill covers of the char, clear them from the internals, and the blood from the backbone, dry them well with a soft cloth, and lay them out on a board, strew a large quantity of salt over them, and let them lie all night. Next day clear them from the salt, and wipe them dry; pound some cloves, mace, and nutmeg together very fine, sprinkle a little *inside* each fish, and a good deal of salt and pepper outside. Put them close down in deep pots with their backs downwards, pour clarified butter over them, set them in the oven, and let them remain there three hours. When they are taken out of the oven pour off from them as much butter as will run off, lay a board over the pots, and turn them upside down to let the gravy run from the fish. Scrape off the salt and pepper, lay them close in pots of the right shape and size with the backs upwards, and pour clarified butter over them. In a cold, dry place they will keep good some time.

To Pot Lobsters.

Time, three-quarters of an hour to one hour.

901. One large or two small lobsters; two ounces of fresh butter; beaten cloves; mace; pepper; salt, and nutmeg; clarified butter.

Take a fine lobster (or two small ones) and boil it for three-quarters of an hour. When done, pick all the meat out of the body, claws, and tail, add the spawn, and beat it to a paste in a mortar; melt a quarter of a pound of fresh butter, add it to the meat with a seasoning of beaten mace, cloves, pepper, salt, and nutmeg. When all

is beaten and wel press it down as clo over them some cla an inch thick. Wl over with white pa meat from the lobst Take it out of the t it as close as you c above, and pour cl;

Time, three-quarte to boil

902. One lobster Cayenne pepper; 1 clarified butter.

Take from a hen flesh, and pickings pound well and sea pepper, and mace, it to a firm paste v Pound and season and put it into a pi other paste. Cove clarified butter, an

Pott

Time, three-c

903. Smelts; pe butter.

Draw the smelts to leave the roes) them thoroughly, s salt, and a little r pot with pieces of them, tie them dov stove oven for thi When they are tak them aside until t them carefully out tight down in ov; and cover them wi

Potte

904. Shrimps; Shell the shrin pepper, salt, and cloves, and put th the closer the bette butter to run in b¢ put a little butter c few minutes into when cold just cove butter.

Potte

905. One hund three ounces of fr and mace.

Pick out the mea fish, and pound the

butter to a paste, seasoning them at the same time with the pounded mace, pepper, and salt. Put the paste into pots, pour over it clarified butter, and tie it closely over to exclude the air, and to prevent it from spoiling.

To Collar Beef.
Time, six hours and a half.

906. Eight pounds of beef; a bunch of savoury herbs; a large sprig of parsley; pepper; salt; allspice, and nutmeg.

For the Pickle.—One ounce of saltpetre; two ounces of brown sugar; seven ounces of salt.

Take about eight pounds from a thin flank of beef, and rub it well with the above proportions of salt, saltpetre, and coarse sugar; turn and rub it every morning for ten or twelve days. Then take out the bones and gristle, chop very fine a large sprig of parsley, and a bunch of savoury herbs, pound a dozen allspice, and add it to the herbs with pepper, salt, and grated nutmeg. Mix it all well together, and lay it over the beef. Roll the meat up as tightly as you can in a round form. Cover it with a cloth, bind it with a wide tape, and boil it in a large quantity of water for six hours and a quarter. When done, put it between two boards, under a weight, and let it remain until cold. Then remove the tape and cloth, put a silver skewer through it, and it will be fit to serve for luncheon, or breakfast.

To Collar a Breast of Mutton, or Lamb.
Time, a quarter of an hour to the pound.

907. A breast of mutton, or lamb; some bread-crumbs; pepper; salt; mace, and cloves well pounded; yolks of three hard-boiled eggs; peel of half a lemon; five anchovies.

Cut off the red skin, and take out all the bones and gristle from a breast of mutton, or lamb. Then place it flat and even on a table, and season it with pepper, salt, mace, and cloves pounded. Take bread-crumbs, five anchovies washed and boned, the peel of half a lemon grated, and the yolks of three hard-boiled eggs bruised small. Mix all these together, lay the mixture over the meat, and then roll it up in a collar, tie it with wide tape, and either bake it in the oven, or roast or boil it.

To Collar a Breast of Veal.
Time, two hours and a half.

908. A breast of veal; yolk of an egg; a quarter of an ounce of beaten cloves; a mace; half a nutmeg; pepper and salt; a bunch of sweet herbs; a sprig of parsley; peel of a small lemon.

For the Pickle.—A pint of salt and water; half a pint of vinegar.

Take a fine breast of veal, bone it, and take off the outside skin; beat it well with a rolling-pin, rub it over with the yolk of an egg, and strew over it the beaten mace and cloves, half a nutmeg grated, a little pepper and salt, some sweet herbs and parsley shred fine, and the peel of a small lemon minced. Then roll it up tight, wrap it in a clean cloth, bind it round with wide tape, and boil it two hours and a half in a large quantity of *boiling* water. When it is done, take it out, tie it at each end afresh with packthread, and put it between two boards, with a heavy weight upon it, till cold. Then take it out of the cloth, and put it into a pickle made of a pint of salt and water and half a pint of vinegar. Boil together, and set it to cool.

To Collar a Calf's Head.
Time, three hours.

909. A calf's head; a quart of milk; pepper; salt; pounded mace; cloves, and half a nutmeg; a sprig of scalded parsley, and a small bunch of savoury herbs; six or seven hard-boiled eggs.

For the Pickle.—A pint of vinegar; pepper; salt, and spice.

Take a calf's head with the skin on, scald off the hair, take out all the bones very carefully, and lay it in some warm milk for a short time to make it white. Boil the tongue, peel it, and cut that and the palate into thin slices. Then make a seasoning of pepper, salt, the pounded cloves, and mace, half a nutmeg grated, the peel of a small lemon minced, and the scalded parsley, and herbs chopped very small. Spread the yolk of an egg over the veal, put a layer of the seasoning, the slices of tongue, and the palate, with the yolks of six hard-boiled eggs, here and there. Roll it up very tightly, put a cloth round it, then bind it with wide tape, and boil it gently for three hours in sufficient water to cover it. When taken out, season the liquor with salt, pepper, and spice, and add a pint of vinegar. When cold, put in the collar. Serve it cut in handsome slices, and garnished with curled parsley.

To Collar a Calf's Head with Oysters.
Time, two hours.

910. A calf's head; a little milk; white of one egg; a teaspoonful of pepper; one of salt; two blades of pounded mace; a nutmeg; half a pound of beef marrow; a sprig or two of parsley; forty oysters.

Scald the hair from a calf's head, but leave on the skin. Divide it down the face, and take out all the bones carefully from the meat. Steep it in warm milk until it looks white, then lay it flat, rub it with the white of a beaten egg, strew over it the spice, pepper, salt, and nutmeg, forty oysters bearded and chopped fine, a sprig or two of chopped parsley, and the beef marrow minced. Lay these ingredients all over the inside of the head, roll it up tight, wrap it in a clean cloth, bind it with tape, and boil it two hours. When almost cold, bind it up with a fresh fillet, and put it in a pickle of salt and water, with a pint of vinegar.

Collared Mackerel.

Time, twenty minutes.

911. Mackerel; pepper; salt; mace; nutmeg; a bunch of parsley; a little vinegar.

Clean the mackerel, take off their heads, and cut them open, taking care not to cut through the tender flesh. Lay them flat, and season the insides with pepper, salt, pounded mace, and nutmeg, and a bunch of parsley minced fine, evenly spread over them. Roll them up, each one separately in a cloth, tie them, and boil them gently in vinegar and water, with a little salt, for twenty minutes. Take them out, put them in something deep, and pour the liquor over them to prevent the cloth sticking. The next day, take off the cloth, and replace the fish in the pickle with a little more vinegar added to it. When they are sent to table, put some of the pickle in the dish with them, and garnish them with sprigs of fennel.

Collared Eels.

Time, to boil, three-quarters of an hour.

912. Some large eels; twelve sage leaves; a sprig of parsley; a little mixed spice; a pint of vinegar; a little knotted marjoram and thyme; twelve whole peppers; two bay-leaves.

Take some of the finest eels that can be procured, and carefully extract the bones, without removing the skin. Spread the fish out, and rub it well over with the sage leaves and parsley finely chopped, and some mixed spices. Then bind the eels tightly up with some broad tape, and put them into a stewpan of water with a handful of salt and two bay-leaves. Boil them for three-quarters of an hour, and then hang them to dry for twelve hours. Add to the liquor in which the fish were boiled a pint of vinegar, the pepper, marjoram, and thyme. Boil it up for twelve minutes, and set it to cool for the time the eels are hung up. The fish must be unrolled carefully, and put into the pickle. Serve whole, or in slices, garnished with parsley.

Sprats Preserved like Anchovies.

913. To half a peck of sprats allow one pound of common salt; two ounces of bay-salt; two ounces of saltpetre; one ounce of salprunella; a pinch of cochineal.

For half a peck of sprats, prepare the above seasoning pounded together in a mortar. If *possible*, the sprats should be fresh from the sea, not even wiped, unless brought from market. Arrange them in a pan, with seasoning between each layer of fish, press them tightly down, and cover them close, and in about four or six months they will be fit for use. For anchovy toast, or to make anchovy paste, fry them in butter, turning them *carefully*, not to break them. Take off the heads, tails, and remove the bones, beat them to a paste, put them into pots, and pour clarified butter over them.

TO MAKE PASTES AND PASTRY.

In the article on meat-pies and puddings we have already given several modes of making puff paste. For tarts, tartlets, &c., however, we shall here insert some of a finer character.

German Paste.

914. Three-quarters of a pound of flour; half a pound of butter; half a pound of sugar; peel of a lemon; two eggs; half an eggshell of water.

Take three-quarters of a pound of fine flour, put into it half a pound of butter, the same of powdered sugar, and the peel of a lemon grated: make a hole in the middle of the flour, break in the yolks of two eggs, reserving the whites, which are to be well beaten, then mix all well together. If the eggs do not sufficiently moisten the paste, add half an eggshell of water. Mix all thoroughly, but do not handle it too much. Roll it out thin, and you may use it for all sorts of pastry. Before putting it into the oven, wash over the pastry with the white of the beaten eggs, and shake over a little powdered sugar.

Feuilletage, or French Puff Paste.

915. One pound of fresh butter; one pound of flour; yolks of two eggs; a large pinch of salt; a little water.

Put a pound of flour dried and sifted into a bowl or on the pasteboard, break into it about two ounces of butter, then beat the yolks of two eggs, stir into them a few spoonfuls of water, and add them gradually to the flour, forming the whole into a smooth paste. Press the moisture from the remainder of the butter, put it into the centre of the paste, and fold it over. Then dredge the board and rolling-pin with flour, roll the paste out very thin, fold it in three, roll it out and fold it again, and put it in a cold place for three or four minutes. Again roll it out twice, taking care the butter does not break through the paste; set it in a cold place, and repeat again. It will then be fit for use.

A Light Puff Paste—American.

916. One pound of sifted flour; one pound of fresh butter; two teaspoonfuls of cream of tartar; one teaspoonful of soda; a little water.

Work one-fourth of the butter into the flour until it is like sand; measure the cream of tartar and the soda, rub it through a sieve, put it to the flour, add enough cold water to bind it, and work it smooth; dredge flour over the paste-slab or board, rub a little flour over the rolling-pin, and roll the paste to about half an inch thickness; spread over the whole surface one-third of the remaining butter, then fold it up; dredge flour over the paste-slab and rolling-pin, and roll it out again; then put another portion of the butter, and fold and roll again, and spread on the remaining butter, and fold and roll for last time.

Very Rich Short Crust.

917. Ten ounces of butter; one pound of flour; a pinch of salt; two ounces of loaf sugar, and a little milk.

Break ten ounces of butter into a pound of flour dried and sifted, add a pinch of salt, and two ounces of loaf sugar rolled fine. Make it into a very smooth paste as lightly as possible, with two well-beaten eggs, and sufficient milk to moisten the paste.

Paste for Custards.

918. Six ounces of butter; half a pound of flour; yolks of two eggs; three tablespoonfuls of cream.

Rub six ounces of butter into half a pound of flour. Mix it well together with two beaten eggs and three tablespoonfuls of cream. Let it stand a quarter of an hour, then work it up, and roll it out very thin for use.

Light Paste, for Tartlets, &c.

919. One pound of flour; twelve ounces of butter; one egg.

Wash the butter in water, to take out the salt, and melt it without its being oiled. When it is cool mix with it a well-beaten egg, and then stir it into a pound of flour, dried and sifted; work it into a thin paste, roll it out thin, and line the patty-pans as quickly as possible with it. When putting the tarts into the oven brush the crust over with water, and sift some pounded sugar over them. Bake them in a lightly heated oven, and serve on a napkin, filling them with any preserve you please.

Croquante Paste.

920. One pound of flour; half a pound of sifted loaf sugar; and the yolks of eggs.

Pound and sift half a pound of loaf sugar; mix it with a pound of flour, and stir in a sufficient number of the yolks of eggs to form it into a smooth paste. Beat and knead it well, roll it out to the size of the croquante form, and about a quarter of an inch thick. Rub the form with butter or beef-suet, and press the paste closely over it to cut the pattern well through. Then lay it on a baking-tin, brush it lightly over with the white of a beaten egg, sift sugar over it, and bake it in a slow oven. When done, take it carefully from the tin, and cover it with any preserves. If kept in a dry place it can be used several times.

Frangipane Paste.

921. Half a pound of flour; six eggs; a little milk.

Just moisten half a pound of flour with a little milk, put it into a delicately clean saucepan, and beat it well together, then turn it out, and stir in six well-beaten eggs until sufficiently cold to make into a paste with your hand. Use it for all sorts of tartlets or entremets.

Brioche Paste.

922. Put in a bowl four ounces of the finest flour, add to it half an ounce of German yeast, beat up in a little warm water, so as to make a very soft paste. Cover it with a floured cloth, and then with a cover. Put it by the fire, and let it rise till it is more than double its original size. Meantime, spread on the slab or pasteboard eight

ounces of flour, make a hole in the middle into which put about six ounces of fresh butter, a little salt, five whole eggs, and two spoonfuls of rich cream. Mix it all well up with the flour till it is a paste. Work it *well* with the hands, and then rub it to and fro on the slab with the palm of the hand three or four times. Roll it out, spread the sponge or piece of leaven if ready over it, then thoroughly but lightly mix the two, the sponge and paste together. The paste must be delicate and soft, but firm enough not to run on the pasteboard. If it should be too slack add a little flour, if *too* firm, add another egg. When it is made, flour a cloth, lay it in a basin, and put the paste on it, cover it with the cloth, and let it stay for twelve hours untouched.

Then take it out of the basin on the slab, shake flour over it, and knead it well. Replace it under its cover, and let it remain for two or three hours.

It will require kneading again when used or formed into the shape or shapes intended, which may be just what you please.

There is no end to the modes of using brioche paste. Alone, as a large brioche, in balls for soup, with preserves in it, or as the crust of sweet vols-au-vent, it is equally excellent.

But it will not keep long, and should be made up and used the day after you have begun making it, according to the preceding directions.

Pate aux Choux.

923. Half a pint of water; four ounces of butter; a little lemon peel or lemon flavouring; two ounces of sugar; a little salt; about four ounces of flour; seven or eight eggs; a pinch of salt.

Put into a stewpan the water, the butter, the salt, and the sugar. Add the flavouring of lemon, or the peel minced as fine as possible. As soon as the water begins to boil, dredge in flour with your left hand, and stir with your right, till it forms a *very thick paste,* which will be in a few minutes. Take it off the fire, and let it grow cold. Break an egg into it, beat it together, and continue doing so till the paste is soft and will detach itself easily from the spoon.

The paste is then ready for use.

Nougat.

924. Nougat, which is a useful paste for forming pretty sweet dishes, may be made as follows :—

Take a pound of sweet (Jordan) almonds, blanch them, *i.e.,* put them in scalding water, and then rub off their skins with a cloth. Throw them into cold water, take them out and dry them on a table napkin. Cut each almond into two or three pieces, or cut them in shavings. Put them in a slow oven, and let them get nicely coloured while you melt three-quarters of a pound of powdered white sugar over the fire, stirring it lightly with a wooden spoon to prevent it from burning. When it begins to bubble, and is a nice gold colour, put in the almonds *hot.* Lift the stewpan off the fire, and mix the sugar and almonds together. Keep the nougat very hot; warm and slightly oil a tin sheet, and spread the nougat on it, pressing it very thin with half a lemon. Have ready your mould or moulds nicely oiled, and drained after oiling, and put in the nougat as quickly as you possibly can, pressing it flat with the lemon.

If the nougat gets cold, it will be brittle, and you will not be able to form it. You must not mind burning your fingers with it.

When the nougat is *quite cold,* turn it out of the mould, or moulds, fill it with whipped cream flavoured with vanilla, and serve on a napkin.

To Ice or Glaze Pastry, or Sweet Dishes.

925. Whites of two eggs to three ounces of loaf sugar.

To ice pastry or any sweet dishes, break the whites of some new-laid eggs into a large soup plate, and beat them with the blade of a knife to a *firm* froth. When the pastry is nearly done, take it from the oven, brush it well over with the beaten egg, and sift the pounded sugar over it in the above proportion. Put it again into the oven to dry or set, taking care it is not discoloured.

Or beat the yolks of eggs and a little warm butter well together, brush the pastry over with it; when nearly baked, sift pounded sugar thickly over it, and put it into the oven to dry.

For raised, or meat pies, the *yolks* of eggs must be used.

To Glaze Pastry.—Icing another Way.

926. White of an egg; four ounces of double-refined sugar, with as much gum as will lie on a sixpence.

Beat the white of an egg to a stiff froth, add by degrees four ounces of powdered sugar, with as much gum as will lie on a sixpence beaten and sifted fine; beat or whisk it well for half an hour, then lay it over your tarts, and put them in a slow oven to set.

Red Currant and Raspberry Tart.

Time, to bake, three-quarters of an hour.

927. A pint and a half of picked red cur-

rants; three-quarters of a pint of raspberries; a quarter of a pound of moist sugar; half a pound of puff paste.

Pick the currants and raspberries from their stalks, mix them together in a pie-dish with the moist sugar. Wet the edge of the dish, place a band of puff paste round it; wet that also. Cover the top with puff paste, pressing it round the edge with your thumbs. Cut the overhanging edge off evenly. Then scallop the edge by first chopping it in lines all round, and then giving them a little twist at regular intervals with the knife. Take the edges you have cut off, flour them, roll them out, and cut them into leaves to ornament the top. Egg it over and bake it. When done, dredge it with white sugar, and salamander it.

Cherry Tart.

Time, to bake, thirty-five to forty minutes.

928. About one pound and a half of cherries; half a pound of short crust; moist sugar to taste.

Pick the stalks from the cherries, put a tiny cup upside down in the middle of a deep pie-dish, fill round it with the fruit, and add moist sugar to taste. Lay some short crust round the edge of the dish, put on the cover as directed before, ornament the edges, and bake it in a quick oven. When ready to serve, sift some loaf sugar over the top.

Black and Red Currant Tarts.

Time, to bake, half an hour to three-quarters of an hour.

929. One quart of black currants; five tablespoonfuls of moist sugar; half a pound of short crust.

Strip a quart of currants from the stalks, and put them into a deep pie-dish with a small cup placed in the midst, bottom upwards, place a border of paste round the edge of the dish, put on the cover as before directed, ornament the edges and top, and bake it in a brisk oven. When served, sift pounded sugar over it.

Gooseberry Tart.

Time, to bake, about three-quarters of an hour.

930. One quart of gooseberries; rather more than half a pound of short crust; five or six ounces of moist sugar.

Cut off the tops and tails from a quart of gooseberries, put them into a deep pie-dish, with five or six ounces of good moist sugar, line the edge of the dish with short crust, put on the cover, ornament the edges and top in the usual manner, and bake it in a brisk oven. Serve with boiled custard or a jug of good cream.

Cranberry Tart.

Time, to bake, three-quarters of an hour or one hour.

931. One quart of cranberries; one pint of water; one pound of moist sugar; puff paste.

Pick a quart of cranberries free from all imperfections, put a pint of water to them, and put them into a stewpan, add a pound of fine brown sugar to them, and set them over the fire to stew gently until they are soft, then mash them with a silver spoon, and turn them into a pie-dish to become cold. Put a puff paste round the edge of the dish, and cover it over with a crust; or make an open tart in a flat dish with paste all over the bottom of it and round the edge; put in the cranberries; lay crossbars of paste over the top, and bake.

Rhubarb Tart.

Time, to bake, three-quarters of an hour to one hour.

932. Some stalks of rhubarb; one large teacupful of sugar; some puff paste.

Cut the large stalks from the leaves, strip off the outside skin, and cut the sticks into pieces half an inch long. Line a pie-dish with paste rolled rather thicker than a crown-piece, put in a layer of rhubarb, strew the sugar over it, then fill it up with the other pieces of stalks, cover it with a rich puff paste, cut a slit in the centre, trim off the edge with a knife, and bake it in a quick oven. Glaze the top or strew sugar over it.

Plain Apple Tart.

Time, to bake, one hour, or, if small, half an hour.

933. Apples; a teacupful of sugar; peel of half a lemon or three or four cloves; half a pound of puff paste.

Rub a pie-dish over with butter, line it with short pie-crust rolled thin, pare some cooking apples, cut them in small pieces, fill the pie-dish with them, strew over them a cupful of fine moist sugar, three or four cloves, or a little grated lemon peel, and add a few spoonfuls of water; then cover with puff paste crust, trim off the edges with a sharp knife, and cut a small slit at each end, pass a gigling iron round the pie half an inch inside the edge, and bake in a quick oven.

Open Apple Tart.

Time, to bake in a quick oven, until the paste loosens from the dish.

934. One quart of sliced apples; one tea-

cupful of water; one of fine moist sugar; half a nutmeg; yolk of one egg; a little loaf sugar and milk; puff paste.

Peel and slice some cooking apples and stew them, putting a small cupful of water and the same of moist sugar to a quart of sliced apples, add half a nutmeg, and the peel of a lemon grated, when they are tender set them to cool. Line a shallow tin pie-dish with rich pie paste, or light puff paste, put in the stewed apples half an inch deep, roll out some of the paste, wet it slightly over with the yolk of an egg beaten with a little milk, and a tablespoonful of powdered sugar, cut it in very narrow strips, and lay them in crossbars or diamonds across the tart, lay another strip round the edge, trim off the outside neatly with a sharp knife, and bake in a quick oven until the paste loosens from the dish.

Apple Tart and Custard.

Time, to bake, three-quarters of an hour.

935. Two pounds of apples; a quarter of a pound of sugar; peel of half a lemon; one tablespoonful of lemon juice; one pint of custard; puff paste.

Make about a pound of good puff paste, put a border of it round the edge of a pie-dish, and fill it with the apples pared, cored, and cut into slices; add the sugar, the grated lemon peel, and the juice with a small quantity of water. Cover it with a crust, cut the crust close round the edge of the dish, and bake it. When done, cut out the middle of the crust, leaving only a border at the edge of the dish, pour in a good boiled custard, grate a little nutmeg on the top, and serve it up cold.

Apple Tart with Quince.

Time, to bake, three-quarters of an hour to one hour.

936. Six or eight apples; the rind of a lemon; three ounces of sugar; one quince; one ounce of butter; puff paste.

Pare, core, and cut into slices as many apples as required for the dish, and arrange them neatly in it, then slice the quince and stew it in a little water with some sugar and a piece of butter until quite tender; add it, and sufficient sugar to sweeten the apples, and the rind of a lemon grated; place a band of paste round the edge of the dish, wet it, and place the cover of puff paste over it, press it down all round, cut the edge evenly, scallop it with a spoon or knife, decorate the top with paste cut into leaves or forms, brush an egg over it, and bake in a moderate oven.

Damson Tart.

Time, to bake, three-quarters of an hour.

937. One pint and a half of damsons; five or six ounces of moist sugar; half a pound of puff paste.

Pick any stalks from the damsons and pile them high in a dish, strew the sugar well amongst the fruit, and pour in two or three spoonfuls of water. Line the edge of the pie-dish with a good puff paste, cover it with paste, and bake it in a well-heated oven. A short time before the tart is done, brush it over with the white of egg beaten to a stiff froth, sift pounded sugar over it, and return it to the oven for about ten minutes.

Apricot Tart.

Time, to bake, half an hour to three-quarters of an hour.

938. Some ripe apricots; puff paste; good moist sugar to taste.

Divide a sufficient number of ripe apricots to fill the dish; take out the stones, crack them, and blanch the kernels. Fill the dish with the fruit and some moist sugar to taste; lay the kernels at the top of the fruit; line the edge of the dish with puff paste, and put on the cover as before. Glaze it a few minutes before it is done, and put it into the oven again to set the sugar.

Portuguese Tart.

Time, to bake, half an hour.

939. Puff paste; twelve golden pippins; some apricot jam; one pint of milk; four bitter almonds; a quarter of a pound of sugar; a little cinnamon; twelve eggs; a quarter of a pound of puff paste.

Cover the inside of a pie-dish with puff paste, lay in twelve golden pippins peeled, cored, and quartered, put over them a layer of *apricot jam;* then boil, in a pint of new milk, four bitter almonds, a quarter of a pound of loaf sugar, and a piece of cinnamon. When cool, stir in the yolks of twelve eggs well beaten, pour it over the apples and jam, and bake.

Vols-au-Vent of Fruit.

Time, three-quarters of an hour.

940. Only a really skilful cook can make a vol-au-vent well.

It should be made of feuilletage paste (*see* page 197).

Before folding the paste for the last time, brush it over with lemon juice.

Lay it rolled the thickness you require on a baking-sheet; put on it a plate or tumbler, and cut the paste neatly all round it, removing the trimmings; then brush it over with egg on the top, but take care not to egg the edges, or it will not rise.

Mark a circular incision on the top, an inch from the edge, with the knife, held slanting towards the centre, so as not to cut *quite* through, but to push the edges away from each other. Put it in a moderate oven to rise. It will be ready to take up in three-quarters of an hour. Then lift out the marked-out cover, and hollow out the doughy centre, without hurting the outside; fill the centre with bread.

Make it hot in the oven, brush it over with egg, and sift sugar thickly over it. Dry the glaze, and with care remove the bread.

Pound a pint and a half of strawberries or raspberries with finely rolled sugar, and fill the inside of the vol-au-vent with it.

Crown it with whipped cream, and serve.

Brunswick Tart.

941. Crust; eight or ten golden pippins; one glass of sweet wine; four ounces of sifted sugar; peel of half a lemon; one small stick of cinnamon; half a blade of mace; some good custard; vol-au-vent puff paste.

Raise a crust as for vol-au-vent, pare and core eight or ten golden pippins, put them into a stewpan with a glass of sweet wine, four ounces of sifted loaf sugar, the peel of half a lemon grated, half a blade of mace, and a small stick of cinnamon. Set them over a clear fire, and stew them slowly until the apples are tender; set them in a cool place, and when cold place them in the tart or vol-au-vent, and pour over them a little good custard.

Meringue Tart.

942. An open tart of any preserves, jams, or stewed fruit; whites of two eggs; a quarter of a pound of loaf sugar; flavouring of vanilla or lemons.

Make any nice rich tart of preserves, jams, or stewed fruit; whisk the whites of two eggs with a quarter of a pound of pounded loaf sugar and a flavouring of vanilla or lemon until it can be moulded with a knife, lay it over the tart nearly an inch thick, and put it into the oven for a few minutes until it is slightly coloured. Serve it hot or cold.

Sweet Casserole of Rice.

Time, three-quarters of an hour.

943. Three-quarters of a pound of Patna rice; three pints of milk; two ounces and a half of butter; peels of two lemons; three ounces of loaf sugar.

Well wash and drain three-quarters of a pound of Patna rice, pour over it three pints of milk, and stir it over or near a slow fire until the rice begins to swell; then draw it to the side, and let it simmer gently until tender. Then stir in two ounces and a half of butter, and three ounces of powdered sugar, with a few lumps previously rubbed on the peel of two lemons to extract the flavour; let it simmer again slowly for half an hour, as the rice must be perfectly dry and tender. Press it as smooth as possible into a mould which opens at the end, and let it stand until cold. Mark round the top rim with the point of a knife.

Puffs.

Time, half an hour.

944. Fine puff paste; jam, or marmalade.

Roll the paste to rather more than half an inch in thickness, and cut it in cakes with a tin cutter the size of the top of a tumbler, then with a cutter the size of a wineglass mark a circle in the centre of the larger round. Lay the puffs on tins, wet the tops over with a brush dipped in an egg beaten with a little sugar. Bake them in a quick oven. When done, take out the centre, and fill with jam or marmalade.

Mince Pies.

Time, twenty-five to thirty minutes.

945. Puff paste; any of the mincemeats given at page 205.

Roll out the puff paste to the thickness of a quarter of an inch, line some good-sized patty-pans with it, fill them with mincemeat, cover with the paste, and cut it close round the edge of the patty-pan. Put them in a brisk oven. Beat the white of an egg to a stiff froth, brush it over them when they are baked, sift a little powdered sugar over them, replace them in the oven for a minute or two to dry the egg. Serve them on a tablenapkin very hot. Cold mince pies will re-warm and be as good as fresh.

Fanchonettes—Entremets.

Time, to bake, twenty minutes.

946. One pound and a half of rich puff paste; some apricot or strawberry jam; some sifted loaf sugar.

Roll a pound and a half of *rich* puff paste out very thin, and lay half of it on a tin; cover it smoothly with apricot or strawberry jam, leaving a margin round the edge about half an inch wide, moisten it with a little water or egg, and lay the other half of the paste carefully over it, pressing the edges securely together, brush the top lightly over with water, and sift powdered loaf sugar thickly over it; mark the paste with the back of a knife in equal divisions, and put the tin in a well heated oven to bake. When done, take it out and cut it with a very sharp knife quickly through the divisions marked; pile them, crossed, in a pyramid on the centre of a dish.

Canellons.

Time, ten or fifteen minutes.

947. A quarter of a pound of flour; two ounces of white sugar; a teacupful of melted butter; a teaspoonful of essence of lemon; some marmalade, or preserve.

Make the flour, pounded sugar, and melted butter into a stiff paste flavoured with a spoonful of essence of lemon; beat the paste well with a rolling-pin, and roll it as thin as a crown piece. Make small canes of card paper of about three inches in length, and one in diameter. Butter the outside well, and wrap each in some of the paste, close it neatly on one side, and bake them in a quick oven. When they are done and cooled a little, take out the paper, and fill them with marmalade, or preserve.

Canellons Glacés.

Time, ten to fifteen minutes.

948. Some puff paste; a piece of butter; the yolks of one or two eggs; some powdered loaf sugar.

Roll out some puff paste quite thin to about eighteen inches square, and cut it into about twenty-four strips. Have as many pieces of beechwood turned, or as many made of cardboard, let them be about six inches long, three-quarters of an inch in diameter at one end, and not more than half an inch at the other. Rub them over with butter, moisten one side of the strips of paste, and wind one round each of the moulds. Begin at the smallest end, so as to form a screw four inches in length, lay them on baking tins, rather distant from each other, and half bake them in a quick oven. Then take them out, wet them over with beaten egg, roll them lightly in powdered loaf sugar, and return them to the oven for a few minutes, to give them a colour. As soon as you take them from the oven, remove the moulds, and lay them to cool. When served, fill them with preserved apricot jelly, or any marmalade that you may prefer.

Crusades.

Time, a quarter of an hour.

949. Slices of stale bread; apricot, or any other jam, or preserve.

Cut some rather thick slices of stale bread, and stamp them out with two fluted tin cutters, one, *half* the size of the other, press the small piece of bread on the top of the larger piece, and then carefully scoop out a hollow in the centre, leaving a border round the edge. Fry them a bright colour in good fresh butter, drain them dry, and then pile apricot, or any other preserve in the centre, and serve them.

Darioles—Entremets.

Time, twenty to thirty minutes.

950. Yolks of six eggs; half a tablespoonful of flour; one teaspoonful of grated lemon peel; sugar to your taste; about a pint and a half of cream; a little puff paste; enough to line the moulds.

Line some small dariole moulds with puff paste, then make a batter as follows:—Beat together the yolks of six eggs, half a tablespoonful of flour, a little lemon peel, and sugar to your taste. Add as much good cream to the above ingredients as will fill your moulds. Bake the darioles in a quick oven.

Almond Darioles—Entremets.

Time, twenty-five to thirty-five minutes.

951. Half a pint of cream; half a pint of milk; about three or four ounces of pounded sugar; two ounces of flour; two ounces of fresh butter; seven eggs; a little essence of almonds, and enough puff paste to line the moulds.

Line some dariole moulds with puff paste. Then make a smooth batter with seven well-beaten eggs, the milk and cream sweetened with the pounded sugar, the butter beaten to a cream and the two ounces of fine flour. Flavour it with essence of almonds, and three parts fill the dariole moulds. Bake them in a well-heated oven for the time specified. When done, turn them *very carefully* out, strew sifted sugar over them, and serve.

Vanilla, or any other flavouring that may be preferred, may be substituted for the almonds, from which they take their name.

Spanish Puffs.

Time, to fry, twenty minutes.

952. One pint of milk; one pint of

Tartlets of Various Kinds.

flour; a little cinnamon; a very little almond powder, and sugar to your taste; four eggs.

Put a pint of milk into a stewpan and let it boil. Add the same quantity of flour by degrees, a teaspoonful at a time, stirring it together fill it becomes a very stiff smooth paste. Put it into a basin, or mortar, add a little cinnamon, a little almond powder, and sugar to your taste. After you have put in all the ingredients, beat them well together for half an hour, adding, *as you beat it, and by degrees*, four eggs. Make some lard or dripping hot in an omelet-pan, drop into it pieces of this paste of about the size of a walnut and fry them.

Pyramid of Paste.

953. Some puff paste; apricot, strawberry, and raspberry jam; dried fruit; spun sugar; yolks of eggs.

Roll out some rich puff paste about half an inch thick, and cut it out with an oval fluted cutter in different sizes, the first being the size of the dish intended for use, and the last the size of a two-shilling piece. Arrange them on a paper placed on a baking plate, brush them over with the yolk of egg, and bake them lightly. When done, and quite cold, place the largest on the dish, spread a layer of strawberry jam over it; then the next size piece of paste, cover that with jam, and repeat until you have piled them all up. Place tastefully on the top a few dried cherries, and spin over it a caramel of sugar.

German Pastry.
Time, fifteen minutes.

954. The weight of two eggs in butter, flour, and sugar; any preserve you like.

Take two eggs well beaten, and mix them with their weight in flour and sugar. Beat well together with a fork, lay half the paste on a tin, and put it into a brisk oven. When a little set, spread over it preserve of apricot or strawberry jam. Then add the remainder of the paste, and bake it again till quite set. When cold, sift a little sugar over it, and cut it into narrow strips.

Tartlets.
Time, fifteen to twenty minutes.

955. Some rich puff paste; any preserve you please, or marmalade.

Cut as many rounds of rich puff paste with a tin cutter as you require. Then cut an equal number, and press a smaller cutter inside them to remove the centre and leave a ring. Moisten the rounds with water, and place the rings on them. Put them into a moderate oven for ten or twelve minutes, and when done, fill the centre with any preserve of apricot, strawberry, or orange marmalade. Stamp out a little of the paste rolled very thin in stars, &c. Bake them lightly, and place one on the top of each tartlet. Serve them hot or cold.

Orange Tartlets.

Time, to bake, fifteen to twenty minutes.

956. Two Seville oranges; a piece of butter the size of a walnut; twice the weight of the oranges in pounded sugar; puff paste.

Take out the pulp from two Seville oranges, boil the peels until quite tender, and then beat them to a paste with twice their weight in pounded loaf sugar, then add the pulp and the juice of the oranges with a piece of butter the size of a walnut, beat all these ingredients together, line some patty-pans with rich puff paste, lay the orange mixture in them, and bake them.

Green Apricot Tartlets.
Time, fifteen minutes.

957. Some green apricots; six ounces of sugar; puff paste.

Take some green apricots before the stone is hardened, and stew them gently in a very little water and four ounces of loaf sugar. When tender, add two ounces more sugar, reduce the syrup until rather thick, add it to the apricots, and put the mixture into patty-pans lined with puff paste, and bake them.

Paganini Tartlets.
Time, fifteen minutes.

958. Whites of three eggs; five ounces of loaf sugar; some apricot jam or orange marmalade; puff paste.

Beat the whites of the eggs to a froth, then stir in the loaf sugar pounded fine, and whisk it well to a *very* stiff froth; have ready some patty-pans lined with puff paste; put a spoonful of apricot jam or orange marmalade at the bottom of each and bake them, and when taken from the oven pile the froth on each.

Lemon Turnovers.
Time, to bake, twenty minutes.

959. Three dessertspoonfuls of flour; one of powdered sugar; rind of one lemon; two ounces of butter; two eggs; and a little milk.

Mix the flour, sugar, and the grated rind of the lemon with a little milk to the consistency of batter, then add the eggs well beaten and the butter melted. Butter some tin saucers, pour in the mixture, and bake them in rather a quick oven. When done, take them out of the tins, cut them across, fold them together, and place them on a napkin with sifted sugar sprinkled over them.

Lemon Puffs.

Time, six or eight minutes to bake.

960. One pound and a quarter of loaf sugar; peel of two lemons; whites of three eggs.

Beat and sift a pound and a quarter of loaf sugar, and mix with it the peel of two lemons grated, whisk the whites of three eggs to a firm froth, add it gradually to the sugar and lemon, and beat it all together for one hour. Make it up into any shape you please, place the puffs on oiled paper on a tin, put them in a moderate oven and bake

Lemon Tartlets.

Time, half an hour

961. Four lemons; a quarter of a pound of sweet almonds; a quarter of a pound of loaf sugar; rich puff paste.

Cut the peels from four lemons, boil them tender, and beat them to a paste, add a quarter of a pound of sweet almonds blanched and minced fine, a quarter of a pound of loaf sugar pounded, and the juice of four lemons strained with the peel of one grated. Put the whole when well mixed into a stewpan, let it simmer to a very thick syrup, and pour it into a shallow dish lined with rich puff paste, put small bars of paste across it, and bake it in a moderate oven a light colour.

Lemon Patties.

Time, about fifteen to twenty minutes.

962. Two penny loaves; half a pint of boiling milk; peel of two lemons; a quarter of a pound of butter; three eggs; sugar to your taste.

Grate the crumb of two penny loaves, and pour on it half a pint of boiling milk. When cold, grate in the peels of two lemons, add the quarter of a pound of butter beaten to a cream and the three eggs, adding pounded sugar to your taste; well butter some small cups, pour in the mixture, and bake them. When done, turn them out, and pour wine sauce over them.

Chocolate Tarts.

963. A quarter of a pound of chocolate; one small stick of cinnamon; peel of one lemon; two spoonfuls of flour; six eggs; two spoonfuls of milk; sugar to taste; a pinch of salt; puff paste.

Rasp a quarter of a pound of chocolate, a small stick of cinnamon, and add the peel of half a lemon grated, a pinch of salt, and sugar to taste; well beat the yolks of eggs with two spoonfuls of milk, add it to the other ingredients, and set them over the fire in a stewpan for about ten minutes, add the peel of half a lemon cut small, and then set it to cool; beat up the whites of the eggs, put the mixture into a tart-dish lined with puff paste, cover it with the whisked egg, and bake it. When baked, sift sugar over it, and glaze it with a salamander.

Jersey Wonders.

964. A quarter of a pound of sugar; four ounces of butter; one pound of flour; three large or four small eggs; a little nutmeg.

Work the sugar and butter together till quite soft, throw in the eggs that have been previously well beaten, and then add the flour and a little nutmeg, knead twenty minutes and let it rise; then roll between your hands into round balls the size of a small potato, but do not add any more flour; flour your pasteboard lightly and each ball roll out into a thin oval the size of the hand, cut with a knife *three* slits like bars in the centre of the oval, cross the two centre ones with your fingers, and draw up the two sides between, put your finger through and drop it into boiling lard, which must be ready in a small stewpan. Turn as they rise, and when a nice brown, take them up with a fork, and lay them on a tray with paper underneath them. The lard must be boiling before putting them in; a stewpan wide enough to put three in at once answers best, and when the lard would froth too much add a little fresh before putting in any more. When all are done save the lard in a basin, as it will answer, by adding a little more fresh, to use again.

Choux à la Comtesse.

Time, to bake, till crisp.

965. A quarter of a pint of water; two pieces of butter the size of a walnut; two large spoonfuls of flour; two eggs; two tablespoonfuls of very strong coffee; some very stiff icing; half a pint of cream whipped.

Put a quarter of a pint of water in a stewpan with a piece of butter the size of a walnut. When it boils, add two large spoonfuls of flour; work this in with a wooden spoon, keeping it on the fire all the time. When sufficiently done, add a piece more butter the size of the first, and two whole eggs. Work it all thoroughly with a spoon, have the baking sheet ready, and drop the paste on it about the size of a very small egg. Bake them in rather a quick oven, and be sure they are crisp enough or they will fall when cold. When done, take a small round piece out of the bottom of each (keep the piece to put back again), and whatever can be spared must be scraped out of the pastry. Make about two tablespoonfuls of very strong coffee, some *very* stiff icing, and add the coffee to it, immerse the pastry in it, and let them stand on a dish in the screen to dry. When quite dry change them to a clean dish. The icing that has run off must be put back in the basin. Whip half a pint of cream, mix the rest of the icing with it, and just before sending to table fill each of the choux with it, using a paper cornet or funnel to do so. Put the pieces back again to keep the cream in.

MINCE MEAT FOR MINCE PIES.

Mince Meat.

966. Two pounds of beef suet; two pounds of apples; two pounds of currants; two pounds of raisins; half a pound of moist sugar; half a pound of citron; quarter of a pound of candied lemon; quarter of a pound of candied orange peel; two nutmegs; half an ounce of salt; half an ounce of ginger; half an ounce of allspice; half an ounce of cloves; juice and peel of one lemon; quarter of a pint of brandy; quarter of a pint of white wine.

Take two pounds of beef suet chopped fine, add the apples pared and minced fine, the currants washed and picked, the raisins stoned and chopped fine, the moist sugar, citron, orange and lemon peel cut fine, the nutmegs grated, the salt, the ginger, allspice, and cloves all ground fine, and the juice of the lemon, with the rind grated. Mix all these ingredients well together, with the brandy and sherry, or any white wine. Put all into a jar, and keep it in a cool place.

Apple Mince Meat.

967. One pound of currants; one pound of peeled and chopped apples; one pound of suet chopped fine; one pound of moist sugar; quarter of a pound of raisins stoned and cut in two; the juice of four oranges and two lemons, with the chopped peel of one; add of ground mace and allspice each a spoonful, and a wineglass of brandy. Mix all well together and keep it closely covered in a cool place.

Lemon Mince Meat.

968. Eight lemons; one pound of loaf sugar; one pound and a half of raisins; one pound of suet; juice of three or four lemons; a teacupful of brandy.

Peel the lemons as thickly as possible without cutting into the pulp; boil the peel in plenty of water till soft, then beat it well with the sugar until it becomes a sweetmeat. Then mix the raisins and the suet well minced and chopped *very* fine, with the sweetmeat; add the juice of three or four lemons, or more according to your taste, and a teacupful of brandy. Mix all well together, and tie it down quite close in pots, or in a jar. It will keep a year.

Banbury Mince Meat.

969. Three quarters of a pound of currants; two ounces of beef suet; quarter of a pound of candied orange peel; three ounces of ratafias; and a little nutmeg.

Wash and dry three-quarters of a pound of currants, and mix them with two ounces of beef suet chopped as fine as possible, a little nutmeg, the candied orange peel shred very fine, the ratafias crushed up, and a slip of lemon peel. Mix all well together, and when required, use it to spread over your paste.

Egg Mince Meat.

970. Six hard-boiled eggs shred very fine; double the quantity of beef suet chopped very small; one pound of currants washed and dried; the peel of one large or two small lemons minced up; six tablespoonfuls of sweet wine; a little mace, nutmeg, and salt, with sugar to your taste; a quarter of a pound of candied orange and citron cut into thin slices. Mix all well together, and press it into a jar for use.

Lemon Mince Meat.

971. One large lemon; three large apples; four ounces of beef suet; half a pound of currants; four ounces of white sugar; one ounce of candied orange and citron.

Chop up the apples and beef suet; mix them with the currants and sugar; then squeeze the juice from a large lemon into a cup. Boil the lemon thus squeezed till tender enough to beat to a mash; add it to the mince meat. Pour over it the juice of the lemon, and add the citron chopped fine.

BAKED AND BOILED PUDDINGS.

For boiled puddings you will require either a mould, a basin, or a pudding-cloth: the former should have a close fitting cover, and be rubbed over the inside with butter before putting the pudding in it, that it may not stick to the side; the cloth should be dipped in boiling water, and then well floured on the inside. A pudding-cloth must be kept very clean, and in a dry place. Bread-puddings should be tied very loosely, as they swell very much in boiling.

The water must be boiling when the pudding is put in, and continue to boil until it is done. If a pudding is boiled in a cloth it must be moved frequently whilst boiling, otherwise it will stick to the saucepan.

There must always be enough water to cover the pudding if it is boiled in a cloth; but if boiled in a tin mould, do not let the water quite reach the top.

To boil a pudding in a basin, dip a cloth in hot water, dredge it with flour, and tie it closely over the basin. When the pudding is done, take it from the water, plunge whatever it is boiling in, whether cloth or basin, suddenly into cold water, then turn it out immediately; this will prevent its sticking. If there is any delay in serving the pudding, cover it with a napkin, or the cloth in which it was boiled; but it is better to serve it as soon as removed from the cloth, basin, or mould.

Baked Puddings.

Bread or rice puddings require a moderate heat for baking; batter or custard require a quick oven. The time needed for baking each particular pudding is given with the receipt. Eggs for puddings are beaten enough when a spoonful can be taken up clear from strings. Soufflés require a quick oven. These should be made so as to be done the moment for serving, otherwise they will fall in and flatten.

Acid Pudding.

972. Five lemons; one pint and a half of water; one large Seville orange; three-quarters of a pound of sugar; three ounces of almonds; three plain sponge cakes; strawberry or raspberry jelly.

Steep the thin peel of five lemons and one Seville orange in a pint and a half of boiling water, to extract the flavour and the colour; then add the lemon juice strained, and the sugar pounded. When cold, pour it over three plain sponge cakes, previously placed in the dish in which they are to be served. Let them thoroughly soak, taking care not to break them. Blanch three ounces of sweet almonds, cut them into long shreds, and stick them over the soaked cakes. Pour over the whole a little strawberry or raspberry jelly dissolved, and serve.

The Adelaide Pudding.

Time, to bake, twenty minutes.

973. A quarter of a pound of butter; a quarter of a pound of sugar; four eggs; rind of one lemon.

Beat the butter to a cream, add the sugar pounded and sifted, the rind of the lemon grated, and four well-beaten eggs; beat all these ingredients well together, and bake it in a slow oven. Serve it with wine sauce poured over it.

Apple, Gooseberry, Currant, or other Fruit Puddings.

Time, one hour and a half.

974. One pound of flour; six ounces of suet; water; fruit.

Make a paste as for beefsteak pudding, roll it out thin, and line a well-buttered basin with part of it, fill it with the apples pared and cored, a slice or two of lemon peel cut very thin, or a few cloves. Moisten the edges of the paste, cut out a piece and put it over the top, press it well together, and cut it neatly round that it may be of an equal thickness. Put the mould or basin into a floured cloth and tie it closely over. Then put it into a saucepan of boiling water and boil it. When done, turn it carefully from the basin on a hot dish.

If boiled in a cloth, without a basin, the cloth must be dipped in hot water, dredged with flour, and laid into an empty basin, that the crust may be formed in it.

All fruit puddings are made in the same

manner, whether of gooseberries, currants, damsons, greengages, &c.

Boiled Apple Pudding.

Time, two hours.

975. Three eggs; one pint and a half of milk; one pint of flour; five or six large apples; a little salt.

Make a batter with three eggs well beaten, and a pint and a half of milk, with nearly or quite a pint of flour; beat it until light and smooth. Pare, quarter, and core five or six large tart or sour apples, and stir them into the batter with a little salt; tie it up in a pudding cloth or buttered mould, and boil it. When done, turn it out on a dish, and serve with sugar, butter, and nutmeg sauce.

Baked Apple Pudding.

976. Half a pound of *grated* apples; half a pound of butter; half a pound of sugar; yolks of six eggs; whites of three; juice of half a lemon; peel of one; a little puff paste.

Grate half a pound of apples and add them to the butter beaten to a cream, the sugar pounded, the yolks of six whole eggs, and the whites of three beaten separately, the peel of one lemon grated, and the juice of half a one. Mix all thoroughly together, and put it into a dish with puff paste round the edge.

Rich Apple Pudding.

Time, to bake, three-quarters of an hour.

977. One pound of apples; half a pound of sugar; six eggs; one lemon; a quarter of a pound of butter; puff paste.

Pare and core a pound of apples, put them into a stewpan with sufficient water to prevent their burning, and stew them until they will pulp, then add to them the sugar pounded, the rind of the lemon grated, and six well-beaten eggs. Stir all well together, and just before putting it into the oven, melt the butter, and stir it into the other ingredients. Put a puff paste round a pie-dish, pour in the pudding, and bake it.

Boiled Apple Dumplings.

Time, to boil, one hour.

978. Eight apples and some suet crust.

Pare and core eight fine apples, and cut them into quarters. Roll a nice suet crust half an inch thick, cut it into round pieces, and lay in the centre of each piece as many pieces of apple as it will contain. Gather the edges up, and pinch them together over the apple. When all the dumplings are made drop them into a saucepan of boiling water, and let them boil gently for nearly or quite an hour, then take each one carefully out with a skimmer, place them all on a dish, and serve them quickly with butter, sugar, and nutmeg. To be eaten cut open, and the butter and sugar put into them.

Baked Apple Dumplings.¹

Time, three-quarters of an hour.

979. Some baking apples; white of eggs; some pounded sugar; puff paste.

Make some puff paste, roll it thin, and cut it into square pieces, roll one apple into each piece, put them into a baking dish, brush them with the white of an egg beaten stiff, and sift pounded sugar over them. Put them in a gentle oven to bake.

Amber Pudding.

Time, three hours.

980. Half a pound of suet chopped fine; half a pound of bread-crumbs; six ounces of powdered sugar; a little candied mixed peel cut up small, the grated rind and juice of a fresh lemon;. four eggs and a small pot of orange or apricot marmalade.

To be well beaten up together and boiled in a mould or basin, tied up in a cloth like a plum pudding for three hours.

Sauce for Same.

981. Put into a stewpan two eggs, a little powdered sugar, a wineglassful of sherry, mull this quickly on the hot hearth, till it is quite warm. Then remove it to the table, and quickly whisk it for fifteen minutes, or until the last minute of sending it to table.

Apple and Crumb Pudding.

Time, to bake, half an hour.

982. Bread-crumbs; apples; butter; sugar; and cinnamon powder.

Put a layer of bread-crumbs over the bottom of a well-buttered and rather deep dish, on the crumbs small pieces of butter, then a layer of apples pared, cored, and cut into slices, then sugar and the powdered cinnamon; repeat this, beginning with the bread-crumbs, until your dish is full, and bake it in a moderate oven. When done, turn it out of the dish, and serve it with fresh cream poured over it, or the cream in a jug separately.

Agnew Pudding.

Time, half an hour.

983. Eight russets; rind of half a lemon; yolks of three eggs; three ounces of butter; sugar; puff paste.

Pare and core the apples, and boil them to a pulp with the lemon peel ; well beat the eggs, and add them to the butter warmed, sweeten to your taste, and beat all well together. Lay a puff paste round a dish, pour in the mixture, and bake it a light brown.

Almond Pudding.
Time, three-quarters of an hour.

984. Yolks of five eggs ; whites of three ; twelve bitter almonds; one pint and a quarter of milk ; a quarter of a pound of sugar.

Blanch and pound the bitter almonds in a mortar, put them into a basin, and pour over them a pint and a quarter of hot milk to take the flavour, let them stand ten or twelve minutes, strain, and when nearly cold add the eggs well beaten, and the sugar sifted, beat it all well together and boil it very slowly in a well-buttered basin. When done, let it stand until cold, then turn it out on a dish, and serve it with any preserve round the pudding.

Small Almond Puddings.
Time, half an hour.

985. One pint of milk ; three eggs ; three tablespoonfuls of flour ; two ounces of almonds ; one teaspoonful of essence of lemon ; one ounce of butter ; four ounces of sugar.

Boil the milk and let it cool, beat the eggs lightly with the flour, blanch and pound the almonds in a mortar to a paste with the lemon essence, or peach water. Melt the butter in the milk, add the sugar pounded, and beat all well together. Bake it in buttered cups, or small moulds.

Almond and Raisin Pudding.
Time, three hours.

986. Two ounces of beef-suet ; one teacupful of milk ; a quarter of a pound of bread-crumbs ; a quarter of a pound of currants ; half a pound of raisins ; three ounces of almonds ; four eggs ; two tablespoonfuls of rum ; two ounces of sugar ; a little nutmeg.

Chop two ounces of suet very fine, and mix it with the bread-crumbs, a little grated nutmeg, the sugar pounded, and the currants washed and dried. Butter a mould, and put the raisins in rows all over it, with the almonds blanched and laid between the raisins. Well beat four eggs, and add them with two spoonfuls of rum to the other ingredients. Put it all carefully into the mould and boil it. When done, turn it out, and serve a wine sauce with it.

A Rich Boiled Almond Pudding.
Time, half an hour.

987. One pound of almonds ; one tablespoonful of orange flower-water ; one glass of wine ; half a pound of fresh butter ; yolks of five eggs ; whites of two ; one quart of cream ; a quarter of a pound of loaf sugar ; half a nutmeg ; one tablespoonful of flour ; three of bread-crumbs.

Blanch and pound the almonds to a paste in a mortar with the orange water, well beat the yolks of the eggs, and the whites separately, and mix them with the butter melted, then stir in the cream, the pounded sugar, the almond paste, flour, and bread-crumbs ; add a little grated nutmeg and a glass of wine. Mix all these ingredients thoroughly together, butter a mould, pour it in, and let it boil for half an hour, then turn it out on a dish and send it to table. Half milk and half cream would be less expensive, and very good.

Baked Almond Pudding.
Time, to bake, half an hour.

988. A quarter of a pound of sweet almonds ; five bitter ones ; four eggs ; three ounces of butter ; one pint of milk and cream mixed ; two ounces of sugar ; one glass of white wine ; one lemon ; puff paste.

Blanch and pound the almonds in a mortar with a little water, melt the butter and mix it with the almonds, well beat the eggs, and add them with the juice of half a lemon, the rind grated, the glass of wine, the sugar, the milk and cream to the other ingredients, and mix them all well together. Line a pie-dish with puff paste, put in the mixture, and bake it.

The Alexandra Pudding.
Time, half an hour.

989. Three eggs ; three ounces of sugar ; three ounces of bread-crumbs ; half a lemon ; a teacupful of milk ; a little jam ; puff paste.

Line a pie-dish with puff paste, and cover the bottom with apricot or strawberry jam, mix the bread-crumbs, pounded sugar, juice of the lemon, and the rind grated with the milk and the eggs well beaten ; beat all thoroughly together, pour it into the dish over the jam, and bake it.

The Albert Pudding, or Cake.
Time, three hours.

990. Half a pound of flour ; half a pound of butter ; five eggs ; a quarter of a pound of sugar ; half a pound of dessert raisins ; one lemon ; candied peel.

Beat the butter to a cream, and mix it by degrees to the sugar pounded and sifted. After they have been well beaten together, add the yolks of the eggs, and then the whites which have been separately whisked. Strew in the flour dried and sifted, the raisins stoned, and the rind of the lemon grated. Butter a mould, and lay thickly over it slices of candied orange and lemon peel. Then put all the other ingredients, perfectly mixed, into it, tie it closely over, and boil or steam it. Serve it with punch sauce.

For a change, this pudding may be baked, when it is called Prince Albert's Cake.

Anna's Pudding.

Time, one hour and a half to steam.

991. A quarter of a pound of suet; a quarter of a pound of bread-crumbs; one tablespoonful of ground rice; three ounces of loaf sugar; two eggs; rind of a lemon.

Chop the suet very fine, and add to it the stale bread-crumbs, the ground rice, and the rind of the lemon grated. Mix it well together with the yolks of two eggs well beaten. Butter a basin, and place the ingredients in it. Steam it. When served, pour over it a little melted butter and sugar, with half a glass of white wine, or serve the sauce in a tureen.

Steamed Arrowroot Pudding.

Time, one hour.

992. Two tablespoonfuls and a half of arrowroot; one pint of milk; four eggs; sugar and flavouring to your taste.

First mix the arrowroot smooth in a few spoonfuls of cold milk, stir into it the remainder. Add four well-beaten eggs, and sugar and flavouring to your taste, put it into a buttered basin, tie it securely over, and steam it for one hour, with the lid of the saucepan close on.

Baked Arrowroot Pudding.

Time, one hour to one hour and a quarter.

993. Three dessertspoonfuls of arrowroot; a pint and a half of new milk; peel of half a lemon; a piece of butter the size of a walnut; moist or loaf sugar to taste; three eggs, and a little nutmeg; puff paste.

Mix into a rather thick smooth batter three spoonfuls of arrowroot with a little cold milk. Put the remainder of the milk into a clean saucepan with the peel of half a lemon, and sugar to taste. When it boils, strain it gradually into the batter, stirring it all the time, adding a piece of butter the size of a walnut. When nearly cold, stir in three well-beaten eggs, and pour the whole into a pie-dish, round which has been placed a border of puff paste. Grate a little nutmeg over the top, and bake it in a moderate oven.

If boiled, it will take the same time.

Asparagus Pudding.

Time, two hours.

994. Two dessertspoonfuls of minced ham; a little milk; half a pint of asparagus; three dessertspoonfuls of flour; four eggs.

Mince a little lean ham *very* fine, and mix it with four well-beaten eggs, a seasoning of pepper and salt, a little flour, and a piece of butter the size of a walnut. Cut the green parts of the asparagus into very small pieces, not larger than a pea, and mix all well together. Then add a sufficient quantity of fresh milk to make the mixture the consistency of thick butter, and put it into a well-buttered mould that will just hold it; dredge a cloth with flour, tie it over the pudding, and put it into a saucepan of boiling water. When done, turn it carefully out on a dish, and pour some good melted butter *round* it.

Brown Bread Pudding.

Time, three hours.

995. A large slice of brown bread; nearly the weight in suet; peel of half a lemon; nutmeg, and mace; two or three ounces of sugar; two ounces of orange peel; a spoonful of brandy; four eggs.

Grate a slice of brown bread, and mix with it nearly an equal quantity of suet shred very fine, a little nutmeg and pounded mace, the peel of half a lemon, and two ounces of candied orange peel chopped *very* small, two or three ounces of powdered sugar, and a spoonful of brandy. Mix all well together. Then add four well-beaten eggs, butter a pudding mould, put in the mixture, and boil it.

Plain Bread Pudding.

Time, one hour and a half.

996. A quart of milk; a few slices of bread; three eggs; a little grated nutmeg; sugar to taste.

Pour a quart of boiling milk over some slices of bread, cover it over, and when cold, beat it quite smooth. Stir in three beaten eggs sweetened to your taste. Add a little grated nutmeg, or lemon peel if preferred, put it into a buttered basin, or a wet floured cloth, and boil it. Serve with sweet, or wine sauce.

Bread Pudding.

Time, one hour, or more.

997. A pint of bread-crumbs; some new milk; peel of a lemon; a little nutmeg; a piece of cinnamon; sugar to your taste; four eggs.

Take a pint of bread-crumbs; put them into a stewpan with as much milk as will cover them; add the peel of a lemon grated, and a little nutmeg and cinnamon. Boil it for ten minutes, and then sweeten it to your taste. Take out the cinnamon, and stir in the four well-beaten eggs. Beat all well together, and bake it for one hour. If boiled, it will require rather more than the hour.

Bread and Butter Pudding.

Time, to bake, one hour.

998. Slices of bread and butter; eight teaspoonfuls of white sugar; three laurel leaves; a pint and a half of milk; four or five eggs.

Put into a deep dish that will hold a quart very thin slices of bread and butter, only half filling it. Stir into a pint and a half of cold milk eight teaspoonfuls of white pounded sugar, three Spanish laurel leaves, and four or five eggs well beaten. When all are well mixed, pour it into the dish over the bread and butter, and bake it in a quick oven.

An Economical Bread Pudding.

Time, to bake, one hour and a half.

999. Any pieces of bread, crumb and crust; half a pound of raisins or currants; peel of a small lemon grated; a little nutmeg; two eggs; sufficient hot water or milk to soak the bread.

Take any pieces of bread that may be left from making stuffing or from other dishes, cut it into very small pieces, and pour over it sufficient boiling water or milk to soak it; then beat it smooth with a fork, and stir into it three ounces of fine moist sugar, a little nutmeg, the peel of a lemon grated, and half a pound of raisins or currants. Mix all well together with two or three beaten eggs, and bake it in a buttered pie-dish.

Bombay Pudding.

Time, three-quarters of an hour.

1000. Half a pound of cocoa-nut; one pint of milk; five eggs; a quarter of a pound of loaf sugar; a quarter of a pound of fresh butter; half a glass of brandy; one penny spongecake; puff paste.

Scrape off the brown part from a cocoa-nut, grate the nut fine, and boil it for about eight or ten minutes in a pint of new milk. Beat five eggs well up with a quarter of a pound of fresh butter and loaf sugar to taste, and when very light and well mixed, strew in the spongecake grated or crumbled. Then stir it gradually into the cocoa-nut and milk, which must have been previously set to cool; add the brandy, and pour the mixture into a dish lined with a rich puff paste, and bake it from one half to three-quarters of an hour.

Bakewell Pudding.

1001. Some puff paste; raspberry or any other preserve; yolks of eight and whites of two eggs; a quarter of a pound of sifted sugar; a little almond flavour, or the peel and juice of two lemons; four ounces of butter.

Line a dish with puff paste, and put in it raspberry or any other preserve, about half an inch thick. Mix with a quarter of a pound of sifted sugar the grated peel and juice of two lemons; then stir in the yolks of eight and the whites of two eggs well beaten, and lastly the butter, which only requires melting and pouring off clear. Stir all together until it is thoroughly mixed, then pour it over the preserve, and bake in a quick oven. Half the quantity will make five or six puddings, baked in buttered saucers lined with puff paste.

Bakewell Pudding with Almonds.

Time, twenty minutes.

1002. Three ounces of raspberry or strawberry jam; three ounces of almonds; three ounces of bread-crumbs; three ounces of sugar; three ounces of butter; three eggs; half a lemon; puff paste.

Line a pie-dish with puff paste, and lay the jam over the bottom, mix the bread-crumbs with the pounded sugar, the butter melted, the grated rind and juice of a lemon, a little nutmeg, and the yolks of the eggs well beaten. Stir all well together, and lay it over the jam; twenty minutes will bake it.

Bishop's Pudding.

Time, three-quarters of an hour.

1003. One teacupful of ground rice; one quart of milk; four eggs; a flavouring of lemon; sugar to taste; a piece of puff paste, two or three tablespoonfuls of jam; a round of bread and butter.

Lay a covering of nice puff paste over a pie-dish, spread on it a layer of jam; cut a thin round of bread, taking off the crust; butter it well, and spread on it the jam, then mix a teacupful of ground rice very smoothly with a quart of milk, add to it four eggs *well* beaten, sugar and lemon to taste; pour it over the bread and butter, and bake in a quick oven.

Boiled Batter, Boston, and Biscuit Puddings.

Boiled Batter Pudding.
Time, to boil, one hour and a quarter.

1004. One pint of milk; one ounce of butter; three eggs; two tablespoonfuls of flour.

Mix two spoonfuls of flour to a smooth batter with a little cold milk, then add the remainder of the milk, and stir in the butter, which should be previously dissolved; add three well-beaten eggs, and when the batter is perfectly smooth, stir in a pinch of salt; pour it into a buttered basin, tie it over very lightly with a cloth dredged with flour, and plunge the basin into a saucepan of boiling water. Move the basin about for two or three minutes to prevent the flour settling in any part, and boil it. When done, turn it out of the basin, and serve it with wine or sweet sauce.

Rich Batter Pudding.
Time, one hour to bake; two hours to boil.

1005. Six eggs; six tablespoonfuls of flour; one quart of milk.

Beat six eggs with the flour until very light, then stir it into a quart of milk, beat them well together; butter a dish, and put in the mixture; bake it an hour in a hot or quick oven. Serve with brandy or sweet sauce, or, instead of brandy or wine, lemon juice may be used.

This pudding may be tied in a cloth or put into a basin, and boiled two hours.

Cheap Batter Pudding.
Time, to bake, one hour; to boil, two hours.

1006. Three eggs; six dessertspoonfuls of flour; one quart of milk; two tablespoonfuls of sugar; one of butter; half a nutmeg; a little salt and essence of lemon or peach water.

Beat the eggs with the flour until very light, then stir into it very gradually a quart of new milk, add the butter dissolved and the sugar, flavour it with a teaspoonful of essence of lemon or peach water, and half a nutmeg grated. Beat it all well together, and bake it in a buttered basin or mould for one hour. When done, turn it out and serve, or it may be boiled for two hours and served with white sauce.

Boston Pudding.
Time, to bake, half an hour.

1007. Eighteen apples; two cloves; a little cinnamon; juice and peel of two lemons; sugar to taste; yolks of four eggs; white of one egg; a quarter of a pound of butter; half a nutmeg; puff paste.

Peel a dozen and a half of apples, take out the cores, cut them small, put them into a stewpan that will just hold them with a little water, a little cinnamon, two cloves, and the peel of a lemon. Stew over a slow fire till quite soft, then sweeten with moist sugar, and pass it through a hair sieve, add to it the yolks of four eggs, and white of one; a quarter of a pound of butter, half a nutmeg, the peel of a lemon grated and the juice; beat all well together, line the inside of a pie-dish, with good puff paste, put in the pudding and bake it.

Biscuit Pudding.
Time, twenty minutes.

1008. Four or five plain biscuits; half a pint of milk; peel of half a lemon; three ounces of butter; two ounces of loaf sugar; four eggs; and a spoonful of brandy.

Break four or five plain biscuits into small pieces, and boil them in half a pint of milk, with the peel of half a small lemon grated very fine; beat it smooth, and then stir in the butter warmed, the sugar powdered, and the four eggs well beaten; mix all together, pour it into a buttered basin, and boil it. When done, turn it out, and serve with wine sauce.

Black Cap Pudding.
Time, one hour.

1009. One pint of milk; three tablespoonfuls of flour; two ounces of butter; four eggs; half a pound of currants.

Beat the flour into the milk until quite smooth; then strain it into a stewpan, and simmer it over the fire until it thickens; stir in the butter, and when cold add the yolks of the eggs well beaten and strained, and the currants washed and dried; put the batter into a buttered cloth, tie it tightly together, and plunge it into boiling water, moving it about for a few minutes that it may be well mixed, or it may be boiled in a buttered basin, which is far better.

Black or Red Currant Pudding.
Time, two hours and a half to three hours.

1010. One quart of currants; four ounces of fine moist sugar; suet crust.

Make with about a quart of flour a nice suet crust, and line a well-buttered basin with half of it; pick the stalks from the currants, and put them into the basin with the sugar; cover over the top with a piece of the crust, press it tightly together round the edge, moistening it with a little water to make it stick, and cut it evenly round; tie

14—2

it up in a floured cloth, and put it into a saucepan of boiling water. If the pudding is made of red currants, add a pottle of fresh raspberries. It will take from two to three hours boiling in a basin, but if in a cloth half an hour less will be sufficient.

Brandy Pudding.
Time, to boil, one hour.

1011. Eight ounces of jar raisins, or some dried cherries; slices of a French roll; four ounces of ratafias or macaroons; two glasses of brandy; four eggs; peel of half a lemon; half a nutmeg; one ounce and a half of sugar; one pint of milk or cream.

Line a pudding-mould with jar raisins or dried cherries, then with slices of French roll, next to which put ratafias or macaroons, then the fruit, roll, and cakes in succession until the mould be full; sprinkle in at times two glasses of brandy; beat four whole eggs, add to them a pint of milk or cream, the peel of half a lemon finely grated, and half a grated nutmeg. Let the liquid sink into the solid part; then flour a cloth, tie it tight over the mould, and boil it, keeping it the right side up. Serve it out of the mould, and with sweet sauce.

Brazenose College Pudding.
Time, three hours and a half to boil.

1012. Half a pound of bread-crumbs; six ounces of beef-suet; six ounces of stoned raisins; two tablespoonfuls of the best moist sugar; two tablespoonfuls of flour; half a teaspoonful of mixed spice; a little salt; four drops of essence of almonds; one egg; a glass of sherry; nearly half a pint of milk.

Mix the above quantities well and *gradually* together, and when thoroughly beaten up, put the pudding into a well-buttered mould, and boil it. Serve with brandy or wine sauce.

Bath Pudding.

1013. Three-quarters of a pint of milk; three spoonfuls of flour; six ounces of butter; six eggs; nutmeg and sugar to taste; peel of one lemon; half the juice; a little brandy or ratafia; some puff paste.

Mix the milk and flour into a smooth hasty pudding. Pour it into a basin on the butter, and stir it till the butter is melted. When cold, add the eggs well beaten, sugar, nutmeg and the rind of a lemon, the juice of half a lemon, and a little ratafia or brandy. Bake it in a dish with a puff paste on the edge. Put it in a brisk oven. Serve with wine sauce.

Wyvern Puddings.
Time, to bake, twenty minutes.

1014. Three-quarters of a pint of milk; three eggs; enough flour to make a thick batter; raspberry jam.

Make a nice batter of the milk, flour, and eggs. Butter some patty-pans. Pour the batter into them till they are three-parts full. Bake them. When done, place them on a folded napkin, and put jam on the top of them.

Green Bean Pudding.
Time, to boil, one hour.

1015. Some old green beans; pepper and salt; yolk of one egg; and a little cream; parsley; and butter sauce.

Boil and blanch some old beans, beat them in a mortar with very little pepper and salt, some cream, and the yolk of an egg; boil the pudding in a basin that will just hold it, and pour parsley and butter over it. Serve bacon to eat with it.

Brown Charlotte Pudding.
Time, to bake, three hours.

1016. Some thin slices of bread and butter; a little brown sugar; some good baking apples; two ounces of candied citron; one ounce of orange peel; peel of half a lemon grated.

Butter a pudding-mould thickly, sprinkle brown sugar over the butter, and then line the mould with slices of bread thickly buttered; cut some good baking apples into slices, place them in the mould in layers, with grated lemon peel, candied citron, and orange peel, and a little sugar between each layer of apples. When the mould is full, cover the top with a slice of bread, previously soaked in a little warm water. Bake it in a moderately-heated oven, turn it out of the mould, and serve it.

Cheese Pudding.
Time, to bake, twenty-one minutes.

1017. Two eggs; half a teacupful of cream; a little salt and pepper; two large tablespoonfuls of rich grated cheese.

Well beat two eggs, add to them a teacupful of cream, a little salt and pepper, and two *large* spoonfuls of rich grated cheese. Mix all well together, and bake it in a quick oven.

Or—
Time, forty minutes, to boil.

1018. One egg; two tablespoonfuls of milk; a quarter of a pound of grated cheese; one tablespoonful of bread-crumbs.

Cabinet, College, Cherry, Citron Puddings, &c.

Well beat one egg, mix it with two tablespoonfuls of milk, one of bread-crumbs, and a quarter of a pound of grated cheese. If the cheese be dry, add half an ounce of butter warmed in the milk. This pudding may be put into a mould and boiled forty minutes, or baked with bread-crumbs and salamandered.

A Plain Cabinet Pudding.

Time, one hour.

1019. Three ounces of stoned raisins; four eggs; peel of a lemon grated; one pint of milk; slices of bread and butter; sugar to taste.

Stone three ounces of jar raisins, and arrange them over the inside of a buttered pudding basin, then nearly fill the basin with slices of bread and butter with the crust cut off, and sprinkle the grated lemon peel over each slice. Add the eggs well beaten to the milk, sweeten to taste, and pour it over the bread and butter, let it stand for a quarter of an hour, then tie a floured cloth over it, boil for an hour, and serve with cabinet pudding or sweet sauce.

Cabinet Pudding.

Time, to steam, one hour.

1020. Seven or eight small spongecakes; a large cupful of white wine; three ounces of loaf sugar; seven eggs; one quart of new milk.

Pour a large cupful of white wine over seven or eight small spongecakes to soak them through. Sweeten a quart of new milk with about three ounces of loaf sugar, stir into it seven well-beaten eggs, and mix it well together, pour it over the soaked spongecakes, and then carefully turn the whole into a buttered mould, tie it securely over and steam it. Serve it with the cabinet pudding sauce given below.

Cabinet Pudding Sauce.

1021. Yolks of two eggs; two tablespoonfuls of pounded sugar; four or five spoonfuls of white wine.

Well beat the yolks of two eggs, and mix them with the pounded sugar and the white wine. Simmer it over a slow fire for a few minutes, stirring it constantly, and pour it round the pudding.

College Puddings.

Time, fifteen to twenty minutes.

1022. A quarter of a pound of breadcrumbs; a quarter of a pound of Naples biscuits; a quarter of a pound of beef-suet; two ounces of candied orange or lemon peel; a quarter of a pound of currants; two ounces of loaf sugar; yolks of four eggs.

Mix the bread-crumbs. Naples biscuits pounded, beef-suet chopped *very* fine, the candied orange peel cut into shreds, the sugar pounded, and the currants washed and dried. Mix the above with the yolks of four beaten eggs till all becomes a paste, then cut them in pieces of a flat shape, fry them in lard over a gentle fire till brown, and put them on a napkin. Sauce in a tureen.

Cherry Pudding.

Time, to boil, two hours.

1023. One pint of milk; three tablespoonfuls of flour; one ounce of butter; three eggs; one pound of cherries.

Mix the flour to a smooth paste with a little milk, then add the remainder, warm the butter and stir it in, stirring the mixture well, then add the eggs well beaten, and a pinch of salt. Take the stones from a pound of cherries, stir them into the batter, tie it in a pudding cloth, and boil it. Serve with butter sauce.

Citron Puddings.

Time, half an hour.

1024. One tablespoonful of flour; two ounces of loaf sugar; half a pint of cream; a little nutmeg; yolks of six eggs; two ounces of citron.

Mix a spoonful of flour with two ounces of sugar, a little nutmeg, and half a pint of cream, add the six eggs well beaten, and two ounces of citron cut into very thin pieces. Stir all thoroughly together, and put it in buttered teacups or small tins. Bake the puddings in a quick oven and turn them out, and serve them with wine sauce.

Citron and Almond Puddings.

Time, three-quarters of an hour.

1025. Half a pint of cream; one tablespoonful of flour; six ounces of sugar; yolks of three eggs; white of one; two ounces of citron; ten almonds.

Mix a spoonful of flour to a smooth paste with a little cream or milk, then add half a pint of cream, six ounces of pounded sugar, the almonds blanched and minced fine, and the citron cut into thin shreds. Beat all well together with the yolks of three eggs, and the whites whisked to a froth. Butter four small moulds, fill them with the mixture, and bake them in a quick oven, turn them out, and serve with sweet or wine sauce.

Baked Chocolate Pudding.

Time, to bake, from three-quarters of an hour to one hour.

1026. Ten squares of chocolate; peel of one *small* lemon; a large cupful of milk; a quarter of an ounce of gelatine; three ounces of loaf sugar; whites of six eggs; yolk of one; puff paste.

Dissolve a quarter of an ounce of gelatine in a large breakfastcup of milk, and add it to the peel of a small lemon and nine or ten squares of chocolate grated; whisk the whites of six eggs and the yolk of one to a stiff froth, and stir it gradually into the other ingredients, pour it into a dish, put a rich puff paste round the edge, and bake it in a slow oven.

Cream may be used instead of the milk, but with the latter it is very good.

Curd Puddings or Puffs.

Time, a quarter of an hour.

1027. Two quarts of milk; a piece of rennet; a quarter of a pound of butter; crumb of a French roll or penny loaf; two tablespoonfuls of cream; half a nutmeg; one ounce and a half of sugar; a glass of white wine; one spoonful of orange flower water.

Turn two quarts of milk with rennet, press the whey from it, rub the curd through a sieve, and mix with it a quarter of a pound of butter, the crumb of a French roll or a penny loaf, two spoonfuls of cream, a little pounded sugar, and a glass of white wine mixed with a spoonful of orange flower water. Butter small cups or patty-pans, fill them three-parts full with the mixture, and bake them in a moderately-heated oven. When done, turn them out, and stick over them a few slips of blanched almonds and orange peel cut into thin shreds. Sift sugar over them, and serve with a sweet sauce in a tureen.

Duke of Clarence's Pudding.

Time, one hour.

1028. Half a pound of sultana raisins; one French roll; one glass of brandy; one of white wine; four eggs; one pint of milk; two ounces of citron; and a little sugar.

Take a basin that will hold rather more than a pint, butter it well, and flour it, after that turn the basin up to shake off any loose flour; stick some raisins in various devices over it, up to the top. Take a French roll without the crust, grate it, and strew it thin and lightly over the raisins, then slices of citron and fruit alternately, with a glass of brandy and white wine poured over it. Well beat four eggs, and stir them into a pint of milk, with sugar to your taste, pour it by degrees into the basin on the other ingredients, and *let it stand* one hour. Then dip the pudding cloth into boiling water, put the basin carefully into it, tie closely down, and boil it one hour.

Chester Pudding.

Time, to bake, half an hour.

1029. A quarter of a pound of loaf sugar; two ounces of butter; four eggs; twelve bitter almonds; twelve sweet almonds; the rind and juice of one lemon; puff paste.

Put the butter into a stewpan with the grated rind and juice of the lemon, the sugar, yolks of the eggs, and the almonds blanched and pounded; set them on the stove, and stir them till they are hot. Line a dish with paste, pour the mixture in, and bake it. Beat up the whites of the eggs to a strong froth, and mix a little powdered sugar with it. After it is baked put the white froth on the top, dust some sugar well over it, and put it in a cool oven to take a little colour, take it out of the dish, and put it very carefully on a folded napkin, and serve.

Cream Pudding.

Time, half an hour.

1030. One large cupful of rice; a little milk; two ounces of pounded sugar; three-quarters or half a pint of cream.

Boil the rice in a little water, strain it off, and then boil it in milk until *quite* tender, add the pounded sugar, and put it into a dish. Warm some preserved fruit in a little cream, put it into the centre of the rice, and pour more cream over the whole.

Rich Cream Pudding.

Time, thirty-five minutes.

1031. One pint of cream; the crumb of a penny roll; eight ounces of almonds; one spoonful of rose-water; yolks of six eggs; six ounces of citron and candied orange peel; one glass of white wine; a little salt.

Boil a pint of cream, and then slice the crumb of a roll into it. When cold, beat it very smooth. Mix in the almonds blanched and pounded in a mortar with a spoonful of rose-water, a pinch of salt, the yolks of six beaten eggs, and the citron and orange peel sliced thin. Mix all well together, adding sugar to your taste, and bake it in a buttered pie-dish.

Small Cocoa-Nut Puddings.

Time, half an hour.

1032. Two ounces of butter; two ounces of sifted sugar; two ounces of cocoa-nut;

two ounces of citron; juice of half a lemon; peel of a whole one grated; four eggs.

Melt the butter cut small, stirring in the pounded and sifted sugar, and boil for one minute. When cool, grate in the cocoa-nut, add the shred citron, the grated peel of a lemon, and the eggs beaten well with the juice. Mix and put it into coffee cups, and bake them for half an hour. The same quantity may be made into one pudding and baked longer.

Grated Cocoa-Nut.—American.

1033. One cocoa-nut; a clear strawberry or currant jelly.

Take a large cocoa-nut, break it in pieces, pare off the dark outside, and throw them into cold water; grate the white meat of the cocoa-nut on a very coarse grater, and with a broad fork heap it on a flat dish, and serve it with any preserve. Or arrange it round a jelly flavoured with raspberry, strawberry or any other fruit.

Apple Custard Pudding.

Time, to bake, thirty to thirty-five minutes.

1034. Ten or twelve good-sized boiling apples; a quarter of a pint of water, sugar to taste; the grated peel of one lemon; four eggs; two ounces of loaf sugar; half a pint of cream; half a pint of milk.

Peel and core ten or twelve apples, and boil them as for apple sauce, in a very clean saucepan, with a quarter of a pint of water, the peel of a large lemon grated, and moist sugar to taste, beat them to a pulp and set them to cool.

Make a custard with half a pint of cream, half a pint of milk, two ounces of sugar, and four eggs well-beaten. Put the apple at the bottom of a pie-dish, pour over it the custard, and bake it in a moderate oven.

Cocoa-Nut Pudding.

Time, three-quarters of an hour.

1035. Half a pound of cocoa-nut; one pound of white sugar; six ounces of butter; six eggs; one wineglass of brandy; one teaspoonful of essence of lemon; half a nutmeg; puff paste.

Grate half a pound of the white meat of a cocoa-nut; work a pound of powdered sugar into the butter, beat six eggs light, and add them to the sugar and butter, sprinkle the cocoa-nut gradually in, stir it well, add the brandy and the lemon flavouring with half a nutmeg grated. Line a pie-dish with a rich puff paste, put the pudding into it, set it in the oven for half an hour. Have ready some of the paste rolled thin and cut out into leaves; make them into a wreath round the edge of your dish, and return it to the oven for a quarter of an hour.

Cream Custard Pudding.

Time, three-quarters of an hour.

1036. Six eggs; one quart of cream; half a nutmeg; sugar to your taste; a teaspoonful of vanilla.

Beat the eggs very light, stir them into the cream, sweeten it to your taste, and add the nutmeg and vanilla. Bake it one hour in a quick oven in a dish, with or without a bottom crust.

Boiled Custard Pudding.

Time, three-quarters of an hour.

1037. Half a pint of milk; half a pint of cream; four eggs; three ounces of sugar; a little cinnamon.

Boil a little cinnamon with the sugar pounded and the milk and cream. When cold, add the eggs well beaten, and stir it over the fire until it thickens, then set it to get quite cold. Butter and flour a cloth, and tie the custard in it, put it into a saucepan and boil it three-quarters of an hour. When done, put it in a basin to cool, then untie the cloth, put a dish over it, and turn the pudding carefully out. Serve it with sifted sugar over it, and with wine sauce in a tureen.

Baked Custard Pudding.

Time, to bake, half an hour.

1038. One pint of milk; one of cream; rind of half a lemon; eight eggs; one tablespoonful of flour; a glass of brandy; a little nutmeg and sugar; puff paste.

Boil the milk and cream with the lemon peel and the nutmeg, for half an hour; then strain it into a basin to cool, add the eggs well beaten with the brandy, pounded sugar, and the flour. Mix all thoroughly together, and put it into a pie-dish lined at the bottom and round the edge with puff paste. Bake it for half an hour.

This pudding may be boiled in a mould, and served with wine, brandy, or arrowroot sauce poured over it.

Custard for Puddings.

1039. One pint of milk; two or three eggs; three ounces of loaf sugar; one bay-leaf; a little nutmeg; a saltspoonful of powdered cinnamon.

To a pint of milk stir in the yolks of two or three beaten eggs, a little nutmeg and cinnamon (should the flavour be liked), one bay-leaf, and the sugar pounded. Stir all well together, and boil it to the thickness you require. When done, take out the bay-leaf.

Curate's Puddings.

Time, twenty to thirty minutes.

1040. Four ounces of flour; a quarter of an ounce of sugar; one-third of an ounce of butter; yolks of four eggs; whites of three; one pint of milk; peel of half a lemon.

Make the butter very hot in the milk, and then pour it into a basin to cool. Stir in the flour very gradually, add the sugar pounded, and the peel of the lemon grated. Whisk the yolks of four and the whites of three eggs separately, and then beat them well into the other ingredients. Butter some cups, half fill them with the mixture, and bake them for twenty or thirty minutes, according to the size of your puddings. When served, turn them out on a dish, and pour a little custard or wine sauce over them.

Chancellor's Pudding.

Time, one hour.

1041. Two spongecakes; one French roll; one pint of milk; peel of half a lemon; one ounce and a half of sugar; four eggs; four ounces of currants; three ounces of sultanas; some candied peel; nutmeg.

Cut the citron or peel into long slices, and put them in a star or any other form at the bottom of a pudding mould, which has been greased in every part with warm butter; fill in the spaces between the citron with currants and sultanas. Then put over them a layer of spongecake or of roll, with a few drops of melted butter over it, and then add some currants; commence again with the cake, placing some citron in occasionally, and repeat it until the mould is nearly full. Then add the sugar, grated lemon peel, and a little nutmeg to the milk, and stir it into the eggs well beaten. Mix all well together, and pour it into the mould over all the other ingredients, taking care it is quite full; tie a buttered paper over it, and let it stand to soak for nearly two hours. Then tie a thick cloth over it, *plunge* it into a saucepan of boiling water, and let it boil slowly for an hour. When done, take it out of the water, and let it stand for four or five minutes before removing the cloth, then turn it out on a hot dish, and serve it with a sweet or wine sauce in a tureen.

Carrot Pudding.

Time, to bake, one hour.

1042. Three-quarters of a pound of carrots; half a pound of bread-crumbs; a quarter of a pound of raisins; four ounces of suet; three ounces of loaf sugar; three eggs; some nutmeg; and a little milk.

Boil and pulp the carrots, add to them the bread-crumbs, the raisins stoned, the suet chopped *very* fine, a little nutmeg, and three ounces of sugar pounded. Well beat the three eggs, and add them to a sufficient quantity of milk to make the ingredients into a thick batter, then put it into a buttered pie-dish and bake it. When done, turn it out and sift sugar over it.

Rich Carrot Pudding.

Time, to bake, one hour.

1043. Half a pound of carrots; half a pound of bread-crumbs; yolks of eight eggs, whites of four; half a pint of cream; half a pound of fresh butter; a glass of brandy; three spoonfuls of orange-flower water; nutmeg and sugar to your taste; puff paste.

Scrape and grate the carrots, and add the bread-crumbs, beat up the eggs, and mix them with the cream, then stir in the carrots and the bread-crumbs, the butter melted, the brandy, orange-flower water; sugar, and nutmeg. Mix all well together, and if not sufficiently thin add a little more cream or milk, as it must be a moderate thickness. Put puff paste round your dish, pour in the pudding, and bake it for one hour.

Cassel Pudding.

Time, twenty or thirty minutes.

1044. The weight of two eggs in butter, sugar, and flour; peel of half a lemon grated.

Take the weight of two eggs, in the shell, in butter, sugar, and flour; half melt the butter, beat the yolks and the whites of the eggs separately, mix the butter and sugar together, then the eggs with the grated lemon peel, then stir in the flour. Butter your tins and fill them rather more than half full. Bake them in a moderate oven for about twenty minutes or half an hour.

Cold Pudding.—No. 1.

Time, forty minutes.

1045. One pint of cream; peel of one lemon; one blade of mace; sugar to the taste; yolks of six eggs; some melted currant or raspberry jelly.

Take a pint of cream, the peel of a lemon, a blade of mace, and sugar to the taste; boil these gently together until the peel is tender; take out the peel, beat it in a mortar, pass it through a sieve, and put it to the cream; pass the whole again through the sieve, and let it stand till nearly cold, then stir it gently to the yolks of the eggs well beaten, mix all together and pour it into a mould. Stand the mould in a pan of boiling water, cover it over, and put hot cinders on the lid. Set the pan over a slow fire, or stove, and let the pudding boil gently for half an hour, putting more hot cinders on the lid as the others get cold. Turn it out of the mould whilst it is warm, and let it stand until quite cold. Serve it plain, or pour melted currant or raspberry jelly over it.

No. 2.
Time, forty minutes.

1046. Two ounces of arrowroot; two ounces of sugar; one ounce of butter; two ounces of crystallized fruit; one cupful of cream; one of milk; and some ratafias.
Mix the arrowroot very smooth in the milk, add the sugar, butter, and cream; boil it all together in a stewpan like a *soufflé*, until it leaves the pan; flavour it with whatever you may fancy. Then stir in the crystallized fruit cut into small pieces, put it into a wet mould, and when quite cold turn it out, and stick it all over with ratafia cakes. Make a thick custard, and when served, pour it over the pudding.

No. 3.
Time, to boil, one hour.

1047. Four eggs; one pint of milk; rind of half a lemon; two ounces of sugar; two ounces of raisins; four tablespoonfuls of marmalade; and six spongecakes.
Line a well-buttered mould with the two ounces of raisins stoned and cut in halves; spread the cakes cut into slices with marmalade, and place them over the raisins in the mould. Well beat the four eggs, add then to the pint of milk and sugar, with the grated peel of half a lemon, stir all thoroughly together, and pour it on the cakes and marmalade, tie it down with buttered paper and a cloth, and boil it slowly.

Duke of Cambridge Pudding.
Time, to bake, three-quarters of an hour.

1048. One ounce of lemon peel; one ounce of orange peel; one ounce of citron; six ounces of butter; six ounces of pounded sugar; yolks of four eggs; puff paste.
Line a pie-dish with a rich puff paste, and lay over the bottom the candied orange, lemon, and citron cut into thin slices; warm the butter and the sugar, add the yolks of the eggs well beaten, and stir it over the fire until it boils, then pour it into the dish over the sweetmeats, and bake it in a slow oven.

Cup Puddings.
Time, to bake, twenty minutes

1049. Three ounces of flour; three ounces of butter; two ounces of sugar; half a pint of milk.
Beat the butter to a cream, add to it the sugar pounded, stir in the flour, and mix it with a pint of milk. Put the mixture into buttered cups, and bake them.

The Coburg Pudding.
Time, three-quarters of an hour.

1050. Some apples; half a pint of cream; half a pint of milk; two tablespoonfuls of arrowroot; two of sugar; some butter and jam, or marmalade.
Fill a deep dish three parts full with apples sliced very thin, sprinkle over them some pounded sugar, and a layer of butter, and then a layer of apricot jam, or of marmalade; mix the sugar and the arrowroot in a little milk quite smooth, then add it gradually to the cream and the remaining milk, and stir it over the fire until it boils, pour it over the apples and jam, and bake it a nice brown in a moderate oven.

Currant Dumplings.
Time, half an hour.

1051. One pound of currants; three-quarters of a pound of suet; nine dessertspoonfuls of flour; three teaspoonfuls of powdered ginger; four eggs; one pint of milk.
Wash, pick, and dry a pound of currants, and lay them on a plate before the fire; mix nine dessertspoonfuls of flour with the powdered ginger, a pinch of salt, and the beef-suet chopped very fine, add the currants, and mix all thoroughly together; make the whole into a light paste with four well-beaten eggs and a pint of milk, roll it into large balls and put them into a saucepan of boiling water; move them frequently that they may not stick; and when done, serve them hot.
Or make the pudding in the shape of a bolster, rolled in a cloth (previously dipped into hot water and floured) tied tightly at each end, and put into a saucepan of boiling water. It will take an hour and a half to boil in this form.

Damson Pudding.
Time, three hours.

1052. A pint and a half of damsons; six ounces of moist sugar; suet crust.
Make about three-quarters of a pound of suet crust, line a buttered basin with it, reserving a piece for the top; fill the basin with the fruit, add the sugar, and two table-

spoonfuls of water; put on the lid, pinch the edges of the crust firmly together; tie over it a floured cloth, put the pudding into a saucepan of boiling water, and boil it from two hours and a half to three hours. When done, turn it carefully out.

Date Pudding.
Time, four hours.

1053. Half a pound of dates; half a pound of bread-crumbs; five ounces of suet; six ounces of white sugar; two eggs; a pinch of salt; and a little nutmeg.
Chop the dates and the suet very fine; add five ounces of sugar, half a pound of bread-crumbs, a pinch of salt, and a little nutmeg; mix all together with the eggs well beaten, and boil it in a basin or a pudding shape for four hours.

Devonshire Pudding.
Time, one hour.

1054. Five eggs; one pint of milk; two wineglassfuls of brandy; slices of good plum-pudding; the peel of half a lemon; and a little nutmeg.
Make a custard with a pint of milk and five eggs well beaten, and flavoured with the rind of half a lemon and a little nutmeg. Cut some cold plum-pudding into long narrow slices, and let them soak in a little brandy for a few minutes, then put them into a buttered mould, crossing them over each other, and pour the custard over it. When the mould is quite full, tie a cloth over it, and boil it for one hour. Send it to table with custard flavoured with brandy poured over it.

Dutch Pudding or Souster.
Time, to bake, one hour.

1055. One pound of butter; half a pint of milk; two pounds of flour; eight eggs; four spoonfuls of yeast; one pound of currants; a quarter of a pound of sugar.
Melt a pound of butter in half a pint of milk; mix it into two pounds of flour, eight beaten eggs, and four spoonfuls of yeast; add a pound of currants washed and dried, and a quarter of a pound of sugar beaten and sifted. Bake it in a quick oven.
This is a very good pudding hot; and equally so as a cake when cold. If for the latter, caraways may be used instead of currants.

Eve's Pudding.
Time, to boil, three hours.

1056. Six ounces of suet; six ounces of bread-crumbs; six ounces of currants; six ounces of apples; six ounces of sugar; six eggs; rind of one lemon; a little nutmeg and allspice; a glass of brandy.
Chop the suet very fine, and add it to the grated bread, with the currants washed and dried, the apples minced up, the sugar pounded, the grated lemon peel, and the spice; stir all thoroughly together, and mix it with the eggs well beaten. Boil it in a buttered basin.

Fig Pudding.
Time, to boil, four hours.

1057. Half a pound of bread-crumbs; half a pound of figs; six ounces of brown sugar; two eggs; a little nutmeg; a quarter of a pound of suet; and a little milk; two ounces of flour.
The figs and suet to be minced very fine, and well mixed with the bread-crumbs, flour, sugar, and nutmeg; then stir all the ingredients well together, and add two eggs well beaten, and a little milk; press the whole into a buttered mould, tie it over with a thick cloth, and boil it. Serve it with wine sauce or without, as you please.

Fun Pudding.
Time, twenty minutes.

1058. Some apples; a little sugar and butter; apricot jam; two spoonfuls of arrow-root; half a pint of cream; half a pint of milk.
Fill a large dish three-parts full with apples sliced very thin. Sprinkle some finely powdered sugar over them, and a very thin layer of butter, and over the butter put a layer of apricot jam. Then take a stewpan with two spoonfuls of arrowroot, a little loaf sugar, half a pint of cream, and half a pint of milk. Stir it over the fire till it boils, pour it over the apples, and bake it in a moderate oven until brown.

General Satisfaction.
Time, about half an hour

1059. Some preserve; finger sponge-cakes; a gill of milk; an ounce of butter; a spoonful of flour; the peel of a lemon; yolk of an egg; a little nutmeg, and sugar to taste; whites of three eggs; puff paste.
Line a pie-dish with rich puff paste. Put a layer of raspberry or strawberry preserve at the bottom, then a layer of the finger spongecakes, then a layer of the following mixture:—Take a gill of milk, one ounce of butter, a spoonful of flour, and the peel of a lemon grated, and boil it until it thickens. When cold, add the yolk of a beaten egg, a

little nutmeg, and sugar to your taste. Cover the edge of the paste to prevent its burning, and bake it in a moderate oven. Whisk the whites of three eggs to a stiff froth, lay it on the pudding when baked, and put it again into the oven for a few minutes before serving.

Preserved Ginger Pudding.

Time, one hour and a half to steam; half an hour to bake.

1060. Six ounces of butter; six ounces of flour; a pint and a half of boiling milk; six eggs; a little sugar; half a pound of preserved ginger.

Stir the butter and flour over a slow fire. Have ready a pint and a half of boiling milk, and mix it gradually with the above over the fire. Add the beaten yolks and half a pound of preserved ginger cut up fine, with the syrup belonging to it, and a little powdered sugar. Well whisk the whites of the eggs, add them the last thing, place the pudding in a mould, and let it steam. It is *extremely* good baked in a dish with puff paste round it for half an hour in a moderate oven. It may then be served hot or cold.

Half the quantity is enough for a *moderate* sized pudding.

A George Pudding.

Time, three-quarters of an hour.

1061. Half a cupful of whole rice; a little milk; peel of half a lemon; twelve large apples; a glass of white wine; yolks of five eggs; two ounces of orange peel and citron; whites of five eggs; puff paste.

For the sauce.—Two glasses of wine; a large spoonful of sugar; yolks of two eggs; a piece of butter the size of a walnut.

Boil the rice very tender in a small quantity of milk, with the peel of half a lemon cut thin. Let it drain, then mix with it a dozen large apples boiled to a dry pulp. Add a glass of wine, the yolks of five eggs well beaten, two ounces of orange peel and citron cut thin, and two ounces of sugar. Line a mould, or basin with a rich puff paste; whisk the whites of the eggs to a very strong froth, and mix them with the other ingredients. Fill the mould, and bake it a fine brown. Serve it turned out on a dish with the following sauce:—Two glasses of wine, a spoonful of sugar, yolks of two beaten eggs, and a piece of butter the size of a walnut. Simmer without boiling, and pour it to and from the saucepan till of a proper thickness, then pour it into the dish.

Gingerbread Pudding.

Time, to boil, two hours.

1062. Six ounces of bread-crumbs; six ounces of suet; two ounces of flour; half a pound of treacle; a teaspoonful of ground ginger.

Grate six ounces of stale bread, and mix it with the suet chopped *very* fine, and two ounces of flour. Add the ground ginger, and mix all well together with half a pound of treacle. Put it into a mould, and boil it.

German Pudding.

Time, three hours to boil.

1063. Half a pound of treacle; quarter of a pound of flour; a quarter of a pound of suet; a teaspoonful of carbonate of soda; a quarter of a pint of milk; one ounce or more of candied peel.

Mix the milk and treacle first; put the soda with the suet, flour, and peel; rub all these together dry. Pour the treacle in, and boil it in a basin.

Baked German Pudding.

Time, to bake, ten or twelve minutes.

1064. Yolks of four eggs; whites of three; two spoonfuls of flour; half a pint of cream; two spoonfuls of butter melted; two of wine; a little nutmeg, and sugar to your taste.

Mix the above ingredients well together; rubbing the flour smooth in a little cream, and then adding the eggs, butter, some sugar, and nutmeg. Bake it in cups in a brisk oven.

German Pudding.

Time, to boil, one hour and a quarter.

1065. Two dessertspoonfuls of flour; one of arrowroot; a pint and a half of milk; a good sized piece of butter; rind of a small lemon; five eggs; a wineglass and a half of brandy; sugar to your taste.

Extract the flavour of a small lemon in a pint and a half of boiling milk, rub very smooth the arrowroot and the flour in a spoonful or two of cold milk, and pour the pint and a half of hot very gradually to it. Add the butter and the sugar, and stir it over the fire until it boils. Then take it off, and stir in the yolks of five eggs, and then the whites well whisked. Well butter a mould, dust over a thick coating of sugar, pour in the brandy, and then put in the pudding. Tie it closely over with a cloth, and boil it.

Rich German Pudding.

Time, one hour to boil.

1066. A sufficient quantity of bread for

the size of the pudding; a little milk; five ounces of butter; five eggs; three ounces of loaf sugar; peel of a lemon; orange marmalade.

Pour some milk over some slices of stale bread, and when thoroughly soaked, press it dry, and beat it into crumbs. Beat five ounces of fresh butter to a cream, with the yolks of the eggs, and the peel of the lemon grated. Beat these ingredients well into the bread, and the whites of the eggs whisked to a firm froth. Put a thick layer of this mixture in a buttered mould, then a layer of orange marmalade, then of the mixture, repeating this until the mould is full. When boiled, turn it out on a dish, cover the top with marmalade mixed with the juice of the lemon strained, and sweet sauce poured round it.

Ginger Puffs.

Time, half an hour.

1067. Half a pound of flour; four eggs; one teaspoonful of grated ginger; a little nutmeg; a tablespoonful of loaf sugar; half a glass of white wine.

Add the grated ginger, pounded loaf sugar, and nutmeg to the flour, and mix all together with four eggs well beaten and the half glass of wine. Bake them in cups in a quick oven, and pour a little wine sauce over them before they are sent to table.

German Puffs with Almonds.

Time, a quarter of an hour.

1068. Half a pint of cream; yolks of six eggs; whites of four; one tablespoonful of flour; two ounces of sweet almonds; and a little orange-flower water.

Beat the yolks of six eggs and the whites of four separately, add them to half a pint of cream, the flour mixed very smoothly in a very little cream previously, the orange-flower water, and the almonds blanched and pounded. Beat all well together, and bake them in buttered cups or in tins in a Dutch oven before the fire for about ten or fifteen minutes. Serve them with wine sauce.

Gloucester Puddings.

Time, half an hour.

1069. Three eggs; their weight in flour and butter; twelve bitter almonds; and five ounces of sugar.

Weigh the eggs in their shells, and take their weight in flour and in butter; blanch and pound twelve bitter almonds, roll the five ounces of sugar, whisk it well together for half an hour, then put the mixture into pudding cups well buttered, only half full, and bake them.

Gateau de Riz.

Time, one hour to bake; three-quarters of an hour to swell the rice.

1070. One quart of milk; four ounces of good rice; four ounces of fresh butter; peel of one large lemon; three ounces of sugar; six eggs; some grated bread.

Well wash, pick, and drain four ounces of rice; put it into a stewpan with a quart of new milk, and the peel of a large lemon cut very thin. Let the rice swell slowly for three-quarters of an hour, then take out the lemon peel and stir in the butter and three ounces of pounded sugar, the yolks of the eggs well beaten, and the whites whisked separately. Butter a pudding mould, and strew over it some grated bread; then pour in the rice, and bake the pudding in a slow oven. Turn it out, and garnish with any preserve or dried fruit.

Greengage Pudding.

Time, one hour, or an hour and a half.

1071. Plain suet paste; some greengages.

Roll out some plain suet paste, and put it over the inside of a buttered basin, then fill it with greengages picked from the stalks, and some good moist sugar; put a cover of paste over the top, cut it even all round, tie it in a floured cloth, and boil it for an hour or an hour and a half. When done, turn it out of the basin, cut a hole in the top of the pudding, put in more sugar, and serve.

Gooseberry, currant, or any ripe fruit, are all made in the same manner.

Ginger Pudding.

Time, three hours.

1072. A quarter of a pound of suet; half a pound of flour; a quarter of a pound of moist sugar; one good teaspoonful of ground ginger.

Chop a quarter of a pound of beef-suet very fine; mix it with the flour, sugar, and ginger. Mix all *dry*, and put it into a well-buttered basin. Boil it three hours, and, when done, turn it out, and serve with white wine sauce.

Dry Ginger Pudding.

Time, two hours.

1073. Two ounces of brown sugar; two ounces of fresh sweet suet; four ounces of flour; two teaspoonfuls of grated ginger.

Mix all well together, and put it *dry* into a half pint basin, boil it two hours, and take great care that the water does not get into the pudding when boiling.

Golden Pudding.
Time, two hours and a half.

1074. Quarter of a pound of flour; quarter of a pound of bread-crumbs; quarter of a pound of suet; quarter of a pound of sugar; quarter of a pound of marmalade; one egg.

Mix these ingredients well together, put them in a buttered basin, and boil for the specified time.

Louis-Philippe's Pudding.
Time, half an hour.

1075. Two pounds of apples; a spoonful of brandy; two ounces of sugar; a piece of cinnamon; four macaroons; orange, or candied lemon peel; apricot jam; a little vanilla cream.

Peel and core the apples without dividing them, and put them into a stewpan with a little water, and the bottom of the pan well buttered; add a little cinnamon, the brandy, and the sugar. Put the pan over a *slow* fire to keep the apples whole. When tender, take them carefully out and put them into a dish or mould—the latter is the best—so that they may rise rather above the level of it. Put into each apple a spoonful of apricot jam and a piece of orange or candied lemon peel; powder the macaroons, and sprinkle them over the apples. Pour a thick cream flavoured with vanilla over it, sufficient to cover the whole, and bake it in a moderate oven.

This dish is excellent iced.

Halliday's Warwickshire Pudding.
Time, twenty minutes.

1076. A quarter of a pound of fresh butter; a quarter of a pound of pounded sugar; a quarter of a pound of fine flour; four eggs; two tablespoonfuls of good cream; two of brandy; two ounces of candied orange or lemon peel; the juice and peel of one lemon.

Take a quarter of a pound of fresh butter, and the same of pounded loaf sugar, put both into a basin, and stir them briskly with a *wooden* spoon until quite light, then add a quarter of a pound of fine flour, four well-beaten eggs, two large spoonfuls of thick cream, and the same of brandy, a little candied orange or lemon peel cut fine, the juice of a lemon strained, and the peel grated. Stir all well together, and bake it in small tins for twenty minutes in a moderate oven. It will make five small puddings. Serve them with sauce in a separate tureen, made with the juice of half a lemon, a spoonful of brandy, and a little pounded sugar mixed and warmed in some good melted butter.

Hannah More's Pudding.
Time, to boil, three hours.

1077. Six ounces of apples; of beef-suet; of bread; of raisins; of sugar; and six eggs; three ounces of candied peel; half a nutmeg; and a glass of brandy.

Mix the six ounces of suet chopped very fine with the bread grated, the apples minced up, the raisins stoned and chopped, the sugar pounded, the citron cut into slices, and the nutmeg grated. Well beat the six eggs, add them to the glass of brandy, and stir all together; boil it in a well-buttered quart mould for three hours, mixing the pudding the day before.

To Make Hasty Puddings.
Time, twenty minutes.

1078. Half a pint of milk; one egg; one heaped tablespoonful of flour, and a little salt; half a teacupful of cold milk.

Put half a pint of fresh milk into a saucepan to boil; beat an egg, yolk and white together *well*, add to it a good tablespoonful of flour and a little salt, beat the egg and flour together with a little cold milk to make a batter. Pour it to the boiling milk, and keep stirring it until it is well boiled together.

Oatmeal Hasty Pudding.
Time, twenty minutes.

1079. Half a pint of boiling milk; half a teacupful of cold milk; one dessertspoonful of flour; one of oatmeal; a little salt.

Boil half a pint of milk, beat the flour and oatmeal into a paste with cold milk, add to it the boiling milk, and keep stirring it always in the same direction till it is done.

Ice Pudding.

1080. Make a thin custard with the yolks of four eggs and one pint of milk, keeping out a little to mix with some currants, raisins, crumbs of spongecake, candied lemon peel, citron and ginger, apricots, or any thing that is nice. Scald the currants and raisins, and mix them with the cold milk, then mix all together and put it into a deep jar. Plunge the jar into a bucket of ice pounded with salt, turning the jar every two hours, and the inside occasionally. Flavour with vanilla.

Cheap Indian Puddings.
Time, to bake, two hours.

1081. Half a pint of Indian (yellow) corn meal; one quart of milk; half a teacupful of suet; one teaspoonful of ground ginger;

two ounces of sugar; half a teacupful of butter; one egg; a little salt.

Stir the corn meal very gradually to a quart of boiling milk. When it has cooled, add a little salt and half a cupful of suet chopped very fine, or the same quantity of butter, put to it half a nutmeg grated, a teaspoonful of ground ginger, one well-beaten egg, and two ounces of pounded sugar, or sugar made into a syrup; put it into a buttered dish and bake it.

Jam Roly-poly Pudding.

Time, two hours.

1082. Half a pound of suet crust; half a pound of jam.

Make a light suet crust and roll it out rather thin, spread any jam over it, leaving a small margin of paste where the pudding joins. Roll it round, and tie it in a floured cloth, put it into boiling water, and in two hours it will be ready to serve.

Jenny Lind Pudding.

Time, half an hour.

1083. One lemon; four eggs; one breakfastcup of white wine; four sponge biscuits; a quarter of a pint of cream; half a small pot of any preserve; and some whipped cream.

Put the juice and the grated peel of the lemon into a stewpan, with the yolks of four eggs well beaten, and stir the whole over the fire until nearly boiling. Have ready the whites of the eggs whipped to a stiff froth, and stir them into the yolks, adding half the breakfastcup of wine. Put the sponge biscuits into a dish, pour over them the remainder of the wine, and when soaked, lay over them some preserve, and pour the custard made from the lemon and the yolks of the eggs over them, then pile some whipped cream on the top, and ornament it with harlequin comfits.

Josephine Puddings.

Time, half an hour.

1084. The weight of three eggs with their shells on in flour, sugar, and butter; two small lemons.

Beat the butter to a cream, then add gradually the sugar pounded, and the grated lemon peel; stir in the eggs well beaten, and then the flour dried before the fire. Beat all well together, half fill some cups or moulds, well buttered, with the mixture, and put them into the oven the moment the flour is added. Bake them in a quick oven for half an hour, or longer should it be a slow one. Serve them quickly with wine sauce poured over them.

Leche Crema

Time, from eight to ten minutes.

1085. Three eggs; a pint and a half of milk; four tablespoonfuls of best wheat flour; two ounces of finely-powdered loaf sugar; grated rind of one lemon; half a pound of macaroons.

Beat up three eggs, leaving out two of the whites, and add to them gradually a pint and a half of milk; then mix carefully four tablespoonfuls of fine wheat flour, and two ounces of finely-powdered loaf sugar, with grated lemon peel to give a flavour. Boil these ingredients over a slow fire, stirring constantly to prevent their burning, until the flour is quite dissolved. Prepare a shallow dish, with half a pound of ratafia cakes at the bottom, and when the créma is sufficiently boiled, pour it through a sieve upon the cakes. This delicious dish is always served cold; just before sending it up some finely-powdered cinnamon should be dusted thickly over it.

Leicester Pudding.

Time, two hours and a half.

1086. One teaspoonful of carbonate of soda; two teacupfuls of flour; a quarter of a pound of suet; half a pound of stoned raisins; one tablespoonful of sugar; half a pint of milk; peel of half a lemon; and some nutmeg.

Mix the carbonate of soda with the flour, the suet chopped very fine, the raisins stoned, the sugar, grated lemon peel, and nutmeg; mix all together with a pint of milk, put it into a basin or mould, boil it two hours and a half, and serve it with sweet sauce.

Lemon Dumplings.

Time, three-quarters of an hour.

1087. Half a pound of grated bread; half a pound of suet; one lemon; four ounces of loaf sugar; two eggs.

Chop the suet very fine and mix it with the grated bread, the sugar pounded, and the peel of the lemon grated; mix these all well together with two well-beaten eggs; make it into small balls, or boil it in a basin.

Lemon Pudding.

Time, to bake, one hour.

1088. One pint of bread-crumbs; nine teaspoonfuls of crushed sugar; a lump of butter the size of a small egg; a pint and a half of milk; six or seven eggs; peel of one *large* lemon.

Sift a pint of stale bread-crumbs through

a colander, add nine teaspoonfuls of sugar crushed small, and a lump of butter the size of a small egg. Boil a pint and a half of milk, pour it over the bread, stir it together, and leave it until cold, then stir into it six or seven well-beaten eggs, and the peel of a large lemon grated. Put it into a mould or basin, and bake it in a quick oven for one hour. To be eaten hot or cold.

Plain Boiled Lemon Suet Pudding.

Time, to boil, three hours and a half.

1089. Three-quarters of a pound of bread-crumbs; six ounces of beef suet; four ounces of flour; a quarter of a pound of fine moist sugar; one large or two small lemons; three eggs; and milk.

Add to three-quarters of a pound of bread-crumbs, six ounces of suet finely chopped, the sugar, and the peel of the lemon minced or grated, with the juice strained; mix all thoroughly together, and then stir into it three well-beaten eggs, and sufficient milk to make the whole into a *thick* batter, pour it into a buttered mould, and boil it for three hours and a half. Serve with sifted sugar over it, wine sauce in a tureen.

Leamington Pudding.

Time, one hour.

1090. Two ounces of flour; two ounces of sugar; two ounces of butter; yolks of three eggs, white of one; a little apricot jam; half a pint of cream.

Stir into two ounces of flour the same weight of pounded sugar, and mix with it the butter melted, the cream, and the yolks of three eggs, with the white of one. When all are well stirred together, put the mixture into three oval-shaped moulds, or *tins*, about an inch deep, but each one smaller than the other. Bake them for one hour, and when done, put them on a hot dish, the largest at the bottom, then a thin layer of jam, then the next size, then jam, and the smaller one at the top. Serve it with wine sauce. This pudding may be placed on a dish in the same way, without the jam, and sugar sifted over it.

Aunt Louisa's Pudding.

Time, three-quarters of an hour.

1091. One pint of grated bread; a pint and a half of milk; half a pint of cream; six ounces of loaf sugar; two ounces of fresh butter; peel and juice of one lemon; five eggs.

Pour over a pint of grated bread a pint and a half of warm milk, stir it well together, and then add the cream, the peel of a lemon grated, three ounces of pounded sugar, a piece of butter the size of an egg, and the yolks of five or six eggs well beaten. Mix all thoroughly together, pour it into a dish, and bake it carefully. Put the juice of the lemon into a basin, add three ounces of sifted sugar, beat it well, and stir it into the whites of the eggs whisked to a very stiff froth. Put a layer of apricot preserve over the top of the pudding, pile the whisked whites of eggs over it, and place it in the oven to bake lightly.

The Kensington Pudding.

Time, to boil, two hours and a quarter.

1092. Two ounces of flour; two ounces of bread-crumbs; quarter of a pound of pounded loaf sugar; quarter of a pound of finely-chopped suet; the juice of a lemon, and the peel grated; one spoonful of marmalade; yolks of two eggs, the white of one well beaten.

Mix all these ingredients well together, and garnish the top with raisins.

The sauce: Two ounces of white sugar; one spoonful of marmalade; juice of a lemon; half a wineglass of sherry. To be put in the last thing; all to be well mixed together, and poured over the pudding cold.

Queen Mab's Pudding.

Time, half an hour.

1093. One pint and a half of cream, or a pint of milk and half a pint of cream; peel of one lemon; six bitter almonds; one ounce of isinglass; five ounces of sugar, yolks of six eggs; two ounces and a half of dried cherries; three ounces of preserved ginger; two ounces of candied orange peel; one ounce of pistachio-nuts.

Blanch and bruise about six bitter almonds, cut the peel of a lemon very thin, and put both into a clean stewpan with a pint of milk; stir it at the side of the fire until at the point of boiling, and the flavour of the lemon and almonds is well drawn out. Then add an ounce of isinglass, and a very little salt. When the isinglass is dissolved, strain the milk through a muslin into another stewpan, and add the sugar broken, and the cream; just allow it to boil, then stir quickly in the yolks of the eggs well beaten, and stir it *constantly* and carefully to prevent its curdling, until it becomes the thickness of a good custard; then pour it out, and again stir it until nearly cold; then mix with it the dried cherries, and the citron cut into shreds. Rub a drop of oil over a mould, pour in the mixture, and set it in a cold place or on ice, for some time before it is turned out.

Preserved ginger may be substituted for the dried cherries, and the pistachio-nuts blanched and cut for the candied citron, with the syrup of the ginger poured round it; currants may also take the place of the cherries, but must be steamed for a quarter of an hour before used; and a sauce of sweetened raspberry, strawberry, or any other juice of fresh fruit may be served as sauce instead of the ginger syrup.

Muffin Pudding with Dried Cherries.
Time, one hour.

1094. Four muffins; one pint and a half of milk; a piece of lemon peel, and sugar to your taste; half a pound of dried cherries; a wineglass of brandy; six eggs; two ounces and a half of sweet almonds; a little nutmeg; puff paste.

Boil a pint and a half of milk for ten or twelve minutes with a piece of lemon peel, and loaf sugar to your taste, pour it over four muffins. When cold, add half a pound of dried cherries, a glass of brandy, the almonds blanched and pounded, and the egg well beaten. Mix all these well together, and either boil it in a basin or bake it in a dish lined with puff paste.

Baked Marmalade Pudding.
Half an hour to bake, quarter of an hour to boil.

1095. Three table-spoonfuls of marmalade; three spoonfuls of melted butter; yolks of three eggs; puff paste.

Mix the melted butter with the marmalade, and the eggs well beaten, and beat the whole together for a quarter of an hour. Line a shallow dish with puff paste, pour in the mixture and bake in a slow oven.

Baked Maizena Pudding.
Time, to bake, half an hour.

1096. Five tablespoonfuls of maizena; two eggs; two ounces of loaf sugar; one quart of milk; some orange marmalade, or any preserve.

Mix the maizena with the eggs well beaten, and a pinch of salt; put the milk over the fire, and when on the point of boiling, pour in the mixed maizena and stir quickly for a few minutes until very thick and smooth.

Put a layer of marmalade, or any other preserve, at the bottom of a pie-dish, and pour in the maizena. Bake in a moderate oven.

Monmouth Pudding.
Time, to bake, twenty minutes.

1097. One pint of boiling milk; three ounces of bread; peel and juice of one lemon; three eggs; a quarter of a pound of butter; two ounces of sugar; a little jam.

Pour the boiling milk on the bread, let it stand till tolerably cool; then add the juice and grated peel of the lemon, two ounces of sugar pounded, the eggs well beaten, and the butter dissolved; put in a layer of raspberry or strawberry jam at the bottom of a dish, pour the pudding over it, and bake it.

Malvern Pudding.
Time, ten or twelve minutes.

1098. Some slices of stale bread; one pint and a half of currants; half a pint of raspberries; four ounces of sugar; some whipped cream.

Dip a pudding basin into cold water, and line it with rounds of rather stale bread; stew the currants and raspberries with the sugar for ten or twelve minutes after they are hot, fill the basin with the fruit, and cover it over with rounds of bread, put a plate on it with a weight, and set it in a cold place until the next day. Then turn it very carefully out, cover it with whipped cream, and pour round it a little of the currant and raspberry juice.

Malvern Apple Puddings.
Time, four hours.

1099. One pound of apples; two pounds of currants; three or four large spoonfuls of moist sugar; a wineglass of brandy; four eggs; peel of half a lemon; one pound of grated bread.

Chop a pound of apples very small, mix them with two pounds of currants washed and picked, three or four large spoonfuls of moist sugar, a glass of brandy, the peel of half a lemon grated, and four well beaten eggs; add to the whole a pound of bread grated very fine; butter and flour the cloth, tie the puddings up *quite close*, or they will break when turned on the dish, and boil them. This quantity makes *two* large puddings.

Bread and Marmalade Pudding.
Time, twenty or twenty-five minutes.

1100. Thin slices of bread; orange marmalade; one pint of new milk; five eggs.

Cut some thin slices of bread, well butter a plain pudding-mould, and lay in some marmalade, then slices of bread, then of marmalade, and repeat until the mould is almost full. Mix in a pint of warm milk, five well-beaten eggs, pour it over the bread and marmalade, and tie the mould tightly over; put it into a saucepan of boiling water, and let it boil twenty or twenty-five minutes. When done, turn it out, after allowing it to settle for a minute or two, and serve with a plain pudding sauce or not.

Macaroni Pudding.

Time, one hour and a quarter, to bake and simmer.

1101. Two ounces and a half of macaroni; one quart of milk; four eggs; a wineglass of brandy or raisin wine; peel of one small lemon.

Simmer the macaroni in a pint of new milk, and the peel of a small lemon, for about three-quarters of an hour, or until it is tender; take out the lemon peel, and put the macaroni into a pie-dish with a good puff paste laid round the edges. Well beat the eggs, add the sugar pounded, the glass of brandy or raisin wine, and stir all into the other pint of milk; pour it over the macaroni, and bake the pudding in a moderate oven.

Baked Macaroni Pudding with Almonds.

Time, one hour; three-quarters of an hour to simmer the macaroni.

1102. A quarter of a pound of pipe macaroni; one pint of good cream; one quart of new milk; a piece of butter the size of an egg; a quarter of a pound of loaf sugar; six or seven eggs; a little nutmeg; one ounce of bitter and sweet almonds.

Break a quarter of a pound of pipe macaroni into small pieces, and soak it for a few hours in a pint of cream and a quart of new milk; then set it over a slow fire to simmer until tender, adding an ounce of sweet and bitter almonds blanched and chopped fine. Then mix with six or seven well-beaten eggs, a piece of butter the size of an egg, and a quarter of a pound of loaf sugar pounded fine. Add it to the macaroni and milk, beat all well together, and pour it into a buttered dish, grate a little nutmeg and lemon peel over the top, and bake it for an hour in a moderately-heated oven.

Michael Angelo.

1103. Two pounds and a half of curd, prepared as for cheese; eight or ten eggs; one pound and a quarter of raisins; six ounces of white sugar; half an ounce of cinnamon powder; a quarter of a pint of mixed brandy and rum; three ounces of citron; some grated crust of bread; some butter.

For sauce.—Yolks of four eggs; milk or cream; brandy or rum; citron or orange cream.

Mix the curd prepared as for cheese, with the yolks of eight or ten well-beaten eggs, and the whites whisked to a stiff froth, the raisins stoned and soaked in brandy, the pounded sugar, cinnamon powder, citron cut into slices, and the brandy and rum. Well and carefully mix all these ingredients together in a large basin. Then take a *small* well-cleaned stewpan, and butter the inside *thickly;* add two handfuls of crust of bread grated fine; shake it round so as to line the stewpan; then put in the pudding, and let it bake gently for two hours and a half, till the outside is brown.

Should it be difficult to obtain the curd, a compound of milk or cream and fine crumbs of bread will answer the purpose.

When done, the pudding must be placed in a hot dish, and a sauce poured over it made of the yolks of four well-beaten eggs, mixed with milk or cream, and a glass of brandy or rum mixed with it, and some citron. Or, instead of the sauce, orange cream if preferred.

Montreal Pudding.

Time, three hours.

1104. Three eggs; a wineglass of milk; two ounces of brown sugar; a quarter of a pound of flour; seven ounces of breadcrumbs, and a little nutmeg.

Beat and strain the eggs through a sieve, and mix them with the milk, sugar, and nutmeg. Add the flour gradually, and mix it well together. Then stir in the breadcrumbs, and beat all together for at least *half an hour* before putting it into the saucepan. Well butter an earthen mould, or basin, put in the mixture, tie it tightly over, and let it boil three hours without stopping.

Half a pound of stoned raisins may be added for a change.

Boiled Meal Pudding—American.

Time, two hours.

1105. Half a pint of Indian, or corn meal; a quart of milk; three or four eggs; a teaspoonful of salt.

On half a pint of Indian meal pour a quart of boiling milk, stirring it all the time. Add a teaspoonful of salt, beat three or four eggs very light, and when the batter is nearly cold, stir them into it. Put the pudding into a tin mould, or a cloth, and boil it for two hours. When done, serve it with butter and syrup, or with any sauce you please.

Madeira Pudding.
Time, fifteen minutes.

1106. The weight of two eggs in flour, and sugar; two ounces of butter.

Well beat the eggs, and stir them into the flour, and sugar pounded fine, and mix the whole with two ounces of butter warmed. Bake the puddings in cups, or moulds, and serve with sweet sauce.

Marlborough Pudding.
Time, three-quarters of an hour.

1107. Puff paste; one ounce of candied citron; one ounce of lemon peel; one ounce of orange peel; six ounces of butter; six ounces of sugar; yolks of four eggs.

Cover a dish with a thin puff paste; then take an ounce of candied citron, one of orange, and the same of lemon peel sliced very thin, and lay them over the bottom of the dish. Dissolve six ounces of butter without water, and add to it six ounces of pounded sugar, and the yolks of four well-beaten eggs. Stir them over the fire till the mixture boils, then pour it over the sweetmeats, and bake the pudding in a moderate oven for three-quarters of an hour.

Marrow Pudding.
Time, two hours.

1108. One pint of grated bread; one pint of milk, or cream; one pound of beef marrow; four eggs; a wineglass of brandy; sugar and nutmeg to taste; two ounces of citron.

Grate sufficient stale bread to fill a pint basin, pour over it a pint of boiling milk, or cream. When cold, slice into it a pound of beef marrow very thin; add four well-beaten eggs, sugar and nutmeg to taste, and a wineglass of brandy. Mix all well together, and boil it in a buttered mould two hours. Cut the citron into very thin shreds, and when the pudding is served, stick the citron over it.

Madonna Pudding.
Time, one hour.

1109. Ten ounces of bread; half a pound of fine Lisbon sugar; half a pound of suet; a large lemon; an egg; a tablespoonful of brandy.

Chop the suet very fine, mix it with the bread-crumbs and sugar, and the grated rind of one large, or two small lemons. Then add the rind of the lemon grated, and the brandy and egg well beaten. Stir and beat all these ingredients together for a quarter of an hour. Put it into a pudding mould, and boil it nearly one hour.

Northumberland Pudding.
Time, half an hour.

1110. One pint of milk; one pint of flour; sugar; a quarter of a pound of butter; six ounces of currants; two tablespoonfuls of brandy; two ounces of candied lemon peel.

Mix the flour and milk into a hasty pudding the day before the Northumberland pudding is required. Mash it with a spoon, add the butter clarified, the currants well picked and mashed, the sugar, brandy, and lemon peel cut in small pieces. Bake in small cups, buttered, in a moderate oven, and serve with wine sauce.

Nottingham Pudding.
Time, to bake, one hour.

1111. Six large apples; two ounces of sugar; one pint of batter for pudding.

Peel the apples, and take out all the core; fill them up with sugar, and place them in a pie-dish. Cover them with a light batter, and bake.

Newmarket Pudding.
Time, half an hour.

1112. One pint of milk; peel of half a lemon; one bay-leaf; a little cinnamon; sugar to your taste; yolks of five eggs; whites of three; a quarter of a pound of currants; slices of bread and butter.

Boil a pint of new milk with the peel of half a lemon, a little cinnamon, and a bay-leaf. Boil it gently for ten minutes, sweeten it with loaf sugar. Break the yolks of five eggs, and the whites of three into a basin. Beat them well, add the milk, beat all well together, and strain it through a fine hair sieve. Have some bread and butter cut very thin, put a layer of it in a pie-dish, and then a layer of currants, and so on till the dish is nearly full, then pour the custard over it, and bake.

Newcastle Pudding.
Time, to boil, one hour and a half.

1113. A quarter of a pound of sultanas, or dried cherries; six or eight slices of bread; one pint of custard.

Put dried cherries, or sultanas thickly round a buttered mould, and next to them a thin slice of bread-crumb soaked in milk. Fill up the mould with layers of thin bread and butter without any crust, until three parts full. Pour in the custard, and boil.

Norfolk Dumplings.

Time, to boil, a quarter of an hour.

1114. Take about a pound of dough from a baking of light bread, and divide it into small pieces, mould them into dumplings, drop them into a saucepan of fast boiling water, and boil them quickly. Send them to table the instant they are dished up with wine sauce, or melted butter sweetened.

Boiled Neapolitan Pudding.

Time, one hour to boil.

1115. Half a pound of puff paste; some apricot or any red preserve; three quarters of a pint of boiled custard.

Butter a cake tin, from which the bottom can be removed, and lay on it a piece of puff paste; over the paste a layer of apricot jam, then of paste, and on that any red preserve, Repeat the layers of paste and preserve until the mould is full, tie it over, and take great care that the water does not get into it.

When done, *carefully* remove it from the tin mould, and serve it with boiled custard poured over it. Eggs chopped fine may be used instead of preserve.

Orange Pudding.

Time, twenty minutes.

1116. A piece of butter the size of a walnut; five yolks of eggs; rind and juice of two oranges; two teaspoonfuls of powdered white sugar, or to your taste; puff paste.

Put a small piece of butter into a stewpan; break into it the yolks of five eggs, then grate the rind of the two oranges into it, and squeeze the juice in through a sieve to catch the seeds and pulp. Add as much lump sugar as will make it pleasant, the quantity depending on the acidity of the oranges, and stir it over the fire till it becomes as thick as custard. Line a tart dish with puff paste, put in the orange custard, and bake it.

Small Orange Pudding.

Time, a quarter of an hour.

1117. Two eggs, with their weight in butter and sugar; five tablespoonfuls of grated bread; six tablespoonfuls of orange marmalade.

Well beat the eggs with their weight in sugar and butter, then stir in the breadcrumbs and the marmalade. Mix all well together, and put the mixture in small tins well buttered. Bake them in a moderate oven.

Orange and Batter Pudding.

Time, one hour.

1118. One pint of milk; two ounces of sugar; four dessertspoonfuls of flour; four eggs; and a small jar of orange marmalade.

Mix the flour very smooth in a little milk, then add the remainder with the pounded sugar and the eggs well beaten. Stir it well together, and put it into a buttered basin; tie it closely over, and boil it for one hour. When done, turn it out, and put the marmalade on the top.

Boiled Rhubarb Pudding.

Time, two hours to two hours and a half.

1119. Four sticks of rhubarb; four ounces of moist sugar; rather more than half a pound of suet crust.

Line a buttered basin with a good suet crust, wash and wipe a few sticks of rhubarb, and pare off the outside skin, cut it into small pieces, fill the basin with it, strewing in the moist sugar, and cover it with the crust. Pinch the edges together, tie over it a floured cloth, put it into a saucepan of boiling water, and boil from two hours to two hours and a half. When done, turn it out of the basin and serve with sugar handed.

Oxford Puddings.

Time, until brown.

1120. Two ounces of bread-crumbs; four ounces of currants; four ounces of suet; three tablespoonfuls of flour; peel of two lemons; two ounces of sugar; two eggs; half a pint of milk; one ounce and a half of orange peel.

Grate the bread, and mix it with the suet chopped *very* fine, the flour, peel of the lemons grated, the sugar, the currants washed and dried, and the candied peel cut up very small. Mix all well together with the eggs well beaten, divide it into equal portions, and fry them a nice brown. Serve them with sweet sauce. Flour may be used instead of the bread.

Omnibus Pudding.

Time, to boil, four hours.

1121. Four ounces of raisins; four ounces of currants; four ounces of suet; a quarter of an ounce of fine moist sugar; four ounces of carrot; four ounces of potato; a little salt and nutmeg.

Grate the carrots and the potatoes, and add them to the raisins stoned, the currants washed and dried, the suet chopped very fine, and the moist sugar; flavour with a little grated nutmeg, and add a pinch of

15—2

salt. Put it into a basin, and boil it. When done, turn it out and serve with brandy sauce.

A Plain Pudding.
Time, rather more than half an hour.

1122. One pint and a half of milk; three eggs; a large dessertspoonful of flour; sugar to your taste; peel of a lemon grated.

Mix a large dessertspoonful of flour with sufficient cold milk to make it a cream; then pour gradually to it a pint and a half of boiling milk, stirring it all the time. Set it to *cool*, and then stir into it three well-beaten eggs and the peel of half a lemon grated, pour it into a buttered dish, and bake it in a moderate oven rather more than half an hour. When done, let it stand for a quarter of an hour or twenty minutes before serving, as it is extremely good cold with any fruit tart.

Polka Pudding.
1123.—A large spongecake; some vanilla cream; apricot jam.

Bake a large spongecake in the tin made on purpose for this pudding, and when cold cut off the bottom of the cake, and then with a small knife remove the inside as near as possible without breaking the top or sides, so as to leave it about a quarter of an inch thick; then put a layer of cream ice (flavoured with vanilla, orange-flower water, or any other flavouring you like), then a layer of apricot jam, then of cream ice, and repeat this until the cake is full, then put on the bottom of the cake and the *lid* of the *tin* mould, which prevents the ice from melting. When the pudding is to be served up turn it out on the dish, warm a little brandy, pour it round the dish, and sprinkle some over the pudding. Set the brandy on fire just outside the door of the dining-room, and bring it in in flames. The cake should be in the mould when the inside is cut out, and it is filled with the ice and cream.

Polka Pudding.
1124. Four tablespoonfuls of arrow-root; one quart of new milk; four eggs; three ounces of butter or three large spoonfuls of rich cream; three ounces of bitter almonds; two tablespoonfuls of orange or rose water.

Mix four spoonfuls of arrowroot in a pint of cold milk. When quite smooth add four eggs well beaten, and either three ounces of butter cut into small pieces or three large spoonfuls of rich cream. Pound three ounces of bitter almonds in two tablespoonfuls of orange or rose water to prevent their oiling. Boil the remaining pint of milk, and when quite boiling add it to the mixture, stir it till quite smooth and thick, and put it into a mould. *Ice* it if convenient, otherwise keep it in a very cold place till wanted. Turn it out, and serve it with the polka pudding sauce.

Portugal Pudding.
Time, one hour.

1125. Three tablespoonfuls of ground rice; one pint of cream; a quarter of a pound of butter; yolks of six eggs; whites of four; a quarter of a pound of white sugar; some sweetmeat or jam.

Put three tablespoonfuls of ground rice into a stewpan with a pint of cream and a quarter of a pound of butter; stir it until it just boils, then let it stand to cool, and add the yolks of six and the whites of four eggs with the sugar pounded and sifted, put the whole into a dish well buttered, and bake it nearly an hour. When done, turn it out bottom upwards, and cover the top with mixed sweetmeats or with apricot and strawberry jam.

One tablespoonful of arrowroot rubbed down in half a pint of cold cream, to which add half a pint of boiling milk and the butter, boiling the whole a short time, will be better than the rice and cream.

Pumpkin Pudding.
1126. Half a large pumpkin; one pint of milk; three eggs; a glass of white wine; peel of a small lemon; two ounces of currants; two ounces of sugar; puff paste.

Pare half a large pumpkin and cut it in slices; boil it until quite soft, drain it from the water, and beat it very fine; add to it a pint of milk, two or three ounces of powdered sugar, the peel of a small lemon grated, two ounces of currants washed and picked, and three eggs well-beaten. Beat the whole together for a few minutes, put a puff paste over a dish, pour in the mixture, and bake it in a moderate oven.

Christmas Plum Pudding.
Time, six hours.

1127. One pound and a half of raisins; half a pound of currants; three-quarters of a pound of bread-crumbs; half a pound of flour; three-quarters of a pound of beef-suet; nine eggs; one wineglass of brandy; half a pound of citron and orange peel; half a nutmeg; and a little ground ginger.

Chop the suet as fine as possible, and mix it with the bread-crumbs and flour; add the currants washed and dried, the citron and

1. Pears and Rice.
2. Queen Mab Pudding.
3. Plum Pudding.
4. Trifle.
5. Jelly of two colours.
6. Blanc Mange.
7. Chantilly Basket.
8. Oranges and Jelly.

Rich and Plain Plum Puddings, Cottage Puddings, &c.

orange peel cut into thin slices, and the raisins stoned and divided. Mix it all well together with the grated nutmeg and ginger, then stir in nine eggs well-beaten, and the brandy, and again mix it thoroughly together that every ingredient may be moistened ; put it into a buttered mould, tie it over tightly, and boil it for six hours. Serve it ornamented with holly, and brandy poured round it.

This pudding may be made a month before using, boiled in a cloth, and hung up in a dry place, and when required put into a saucepan of boiling water, and boiled for two hours or two hours and a half, then turned out, and served with sauce as above.

Christmas Pudding.

Time, to boil, six hours.

1128. One pound of raisins ; one pound of currants ; a quarter of a pound of sultanas ; one pound of suet ; half a pound of bread-crumbs ; a pint of milk ; ten eggs ; three-quarters of a pound of flour and same of citron and orange peel mixed ; one small nutmeg ; one glass of brandy.

Stone the raisins and divide them, wash and dry the currants and sultanas, and cut the peel into slices. Mix all these with the bread-crumbs, flour, and suet chopped very fine, add the grated nutmeg, and then stir in the eggs well-beaten, the brandy, and the milk. When the ingredients are well blended, put it into a mould, tie a floured cloth over it, and boil it. When done, turn it out, and serve it with brandy or arrowroot sauce.

Rich Plum Pudding without Flour.

Time, five hours.

1129. One pound and a half of grated bread ; one pound and a half of raisins ; one pound and a half of currants; one pound of beef-suet; peel of one large lemon; three ounces of almonds ; a little nutmeg or mixed spice ; sugar to taste ; three-quarters of a pound of candied orange ; lemon and citron ; eight or nine eggs ; half a pint of milk ; two wineglasses of brandy.

Stone the raisins, wash and pick the currants, chop the suet very fine, and mix with them a pound and a half of grated bread; add the candied peel cut into shreds, the almonds blanched and minced, and the mixed spice and sugar to taste. When all are thoroughly blended, stir it well together with eight or nine well-beaten eggs, two glasses of brandy, and half a pint of milk, tie it in a cloth, and boil it for five hours or five hours and a half, or divide it into equal parts, and boil it in moulds or basins for half the time.

Cottage Plum Pudding.

Time, five hours.

1130. A pound and a half of flour; four or five eggs ; a pinch of salt ; a little nutmeg ; one pound of raisins ; half a pound of currants ; sugar to taste, and a little milk.

Make a thick batter with five well-beaten eggs, a pound and a half of flour, and a sufficient quantity of milk. Then add the currants washed and picked, the raisins stoned, a little nutmeg, and sugar to taste. Mix all well together, and boil it in a basin or floured cloth for quite five hours.

The peel of a lemon grated, and a few pieces of citron cut thin may be added.

Plain Plum Pudding.

Time, two hours and a half or three hours.

1131. Eight ounces of flour; eight ounces of beef-suet ; half a pound of raisins ; half a pint of milk; two eggs.

Chop the suet very fine, mix it with the flour, add half a pound of raisins stoned, and mix the whole with half a pint of milk and two well-beaten eggs. Tie it up in a floured cloth, or put it into a basin. Plunge it into a saucepan of boiling water, and *keep* it boiling for two hours and a half or three hours.

Plum Pudding.

Time, three hours.

1132. Six ounces of raisins ; six ounces of currants ; six ounces of bread-crumbs ; six ounces of suet ; half a nutmeg ; a little lemon peel ; five eggs ; half a wineglass of brandy.

Mix these ingredients together, and put the pudding into a mould, and boil it.

A Good Plum Pudding without Eggs.

Time to boil, four hours.

1133. One pound of raisins ; half a pound of suet ; one pound of flour; four ounces of bread-crumbs ; two tablespoonfuls of treacle ; one pint of milk ; nutmeg, and grated ginger.

Chop the suet very fine, and mix it with the flour. Add the bread-crumbs, ginger, and nutmeg, and the raisins stoned, and mix it all well together with the milk and treacle. Put it into a basin, or floured cloth, and boil it.

Duke of Portland's Pudding.

Time, to boil, six hours.

1134. Half a pound of flour ; a quarter of a pound of sugar ; five eggs ; six ounces of butter, one pound of raisins ; two ounces of candied orange; a pinch of salt and a little nutmeg.

Put the flour into a basin with the pounded sugar, and rub in the eggs, well-beaten, one at a time. When mixed, stir gently in the fresh butter just melted, and beat it up like a cake. Then add the raisins stoned, a little spice, and the candied peel cut into shreds. Put it into a mould, or basin, leaving room for it to rise. Put it into *boiling* water, let it boil the time specified, and when done, turn it out and serve with sauce.

Prune Pudding.

Time, to boil, two hours.

1135. Two eggs; a quart of milk, and sufficient flour to make a rather thick batter; a handful of prunes.

Well beat two eggs, stir them to a quart of milk, and enough fine flour to make a rather thick batter; rinse, or wash a handful of prunes, sprinkle a little flour over them, then stir them into the batter, tie it in a pudding cloth, and boil it. Serve with butter and sugar, or wine sauce.

Palm Tree Pudding.

Time, altogether, twenty minutes.

1136. Two ounces of flour; two ounces of loaf sugar; half a pint of milk; a piece of butter the size of an egg.

For the Syrup.—A quarter of a pound of sugar; one egg; half a pint of water; juice of two small lemons.

Mix two ounces of flour and two ounces of pounded sugar with half a pint of water, put it into a stewpan, and stir it over a moderate fire for two or three minutes. Take it off the fire and place the mixture on a dish to become perfectly cold. Then cut it into *diamonds* about an inch and a half each way, and fry the pieces in butter. Make a syrup with a quarter of a pound of loaf sugar, one egg well beaten and half a pint of water; put it into a small stewpan over a slow fire, and as the scum rises, skim it clean. Continue stirring it until the side of the pan becomes slightly encrusted; then take it off the fire and set it to cool. When cold, pour it round the fried pudding (with the juice of two lemons), and serve.

Peas Pudding.

Time, three hours and a half.

1137. A pint and a half of split peas; a piece of butter the size of an egg; pepper, and salt.

Soak a pint and a half of split peas for several hours. Then tie them loosely in a cloth, and put them into a saucepan of cold rain water to boil, allowing about two hours and a half after the water has simmered. When the peas are tender, drain them from the water, and rub them through a colander with a wooden spoon. Stir in the butter, a little pepper and salt, and the eggs well beaten. Then tie it tightly in a cloth, boil it another hour, turn it out on a dish, and serve it very hot with boiled leg of pork.

Porcupine Pudding.

Time, one hour and a half.

1138. Half a pint of Patna rice; half a pint of milk; six eggs; peel of one lemon; a spoonful of ratafia flavouring; sugar to your taste, and some sweet almonds.

Boil the rice in the milk until very tender; then add the eggs well beaten, the pounded sugar, the peel of a lemon grated, and a flavouring of ratafia, or essence of lemon. Mix all the ingredients well together, and boil them in a mould for an hour and a half. When done, turn it out, cut the almonds (after they have been blanched) into long shreds, and stick them all over the pudding. Serve it with a very rich custard poured over it.

Quaking Pudding.

Time, two hours to boil; one to bake.

1139. A large cupful of grated bread; six eggs; one dessertspoonful of rice flour; one quart of milk; peel of half a lemon.

Add to the grated bread six well-beaten eggs, and the spoonful of rice flour; stir them into a quart of milk. Add a teaspoonful of salt, and the peel of half a lemon grated. Tie it in a well-floured pudding cloth, and boil it for two hours. Or it may be baked in a buttered basin, then turned out, and served with wine sauce over it.

Queen's Pudding.

Time, to boil, twenty minutes.

1140. A quarter of a pound of raisins; bread and butter; three ounces of candied orange peel; one pint of milk; four eggs; two ounces of sugar; peel of a small lemom; three ounces of bitter and sweet almonds.

Butter a mould, or basin, well, and stick it all over with raisins. Put layers of bread and butter with three ounces of bitter and sweet almonds mixed, blanched, and cut into shreds, three ounces of candied orange peel cut thin, the peel of a lemon grated, sugar to your taste, four well-beaten eggs, and a pint of milk. Fill the basin with layers of bread and butter with the almonds on the raisins. Then mix the milk, eggs, and sugar, pour it in, cover the mould closely over, and boil it.

Quince Pudding.
Time, three-quarters of an hour.

1141. Seven quinces; one pint of cream; yolks of four eggs; a little powdered ginger and cinnamon; sugar to taste; puff paste.

Boil seven large quinces until very tender, then pare and core them, beat them to a pulp, and add sugar to your taste; well beat the yolks of four eggs, and stir them gradually into a pint of cream, mix it with the pulp of the quince, flavour it with a little powdered ginger and cinnamon, and put it into a buttered dish with a puff paste round the edge. Bake it in a moderate oven, and serve with sifted sugar over it.

Plain Rice Pudding.
Time, one hour.

1142. Three eggs; one quart of milk; a little salt; a wineglass of rice; two tablespoonfuls of sugar; one of butter; half a nutmeg.

Beat three eggs light, and stir them into a quart of milk, with a little salt, and a wineglass of rice well washed; put to it two tablespoonfuls of sugar, half a nutmeg grated, and a tablespoonful of butter. Bake one hour in a quick oven.

Rice and Apple Pudding.
Time, ten minutes for rice; pudding one hour.

1143. One cupful of rice; six apples; two cloves; a little lemon peel; two teaspoonfuls of sugar.

Boil the rice for ten minutes, drain it through a hair sieve until it is perfectly dry. Put a cloth into a pudding-basin, lay the rice all round it like a crust. Quarter some apples as you would do for a tart, and lay them in the middle of the rice, add a little chopped lemon peel and two cloves, and two teaspoonfuls (or to your taste) of sugar, cover the apples with rice. Boil the pudding for an hour. Serve it with melted butter poured over it.

Plain Boiled Rice for Children.
Time, two hours.

1144. Three-quarters of a pound of rice ; jam, or melted butter and sugar.

Wash the rice in water, tie it in a cloth rather loosely, to give it room to swell, and put it into a saucepan of cold water. When done, turn it out on a dish, and serve with sweet sauce or jam.

Ground Rice Pudding.
Time, three-quarters of an hour.

1145. Half a pound of ground rice; two quarts of milk; three ounces of sugar; seven eggs; a little nutmeg; a glass of brandy; and a small piece of butter.

Mix the rice in a little milk quite smooth, add it to the remainder, and set it over the fire to boil till it becomes thick, stirring it all the time, or it will be in lumps; then add the butter, sugar, and yolks of seven well-beaten eggs, with the whites of four; grate in a little nutmeg, and pour in the glass of brandy. Mix all well together, and bake it in a quick oven for three-quarters of an hour.

Rice Pudding without Eggs.
Time, two hours.

1146. A small cupful of rice; one quart of milk; a cupful of sugar; a teaspoonful of salt; half a nutmeg.

Wash the rice in two waters, and add it to the sweetened milk, the salt, and grated nutmeg. Put it into a pie-dish, and bake it in a moderate oven for two hours.

Rice Pudding with Preserve.
Time, one hour.

1147. Half a pound of rice; one quart of new milk; peel of one lemon; two ounces of fresh butter; two ounces and a half of pounded sugar; four eggs; apricot preserve.

Wash half a pound of rice, drain it on a hair sieve. Put it into a very clean stewpan, and pour over it a quart of new milk and the peel of half a lemon cut thin; let it simmer very gently for half an hour. Then mix with it two ounces of fresh butter, and two ounces and a half of pounded sugar, and let it continue to simmer till the rice is quite tender. Take it off the fire, and when cooled a little add four well-whisked eggs, put it into a round mould. and bake it about half an hour in a slow oven. Serve it hot or cold, with apricot or any other preserve spread round the bottom.

Small Rice Puddings.
Time, thirty-five to forty minutes.

1148. Six ounces of whole rice; one quart of milk; three ounces of fresh butter; six eggs; peel of half a lemon; three ounces of candied orange peel; loaf sugar to taste; flavouring of almonds.

Put the rice into a small stewpan with three-quarters of a pint of milk, and when soft stir in the butter and the remainder of the milk. When nearly cold, stir in six eggs well whisked, with the loaf sugar rolled, and a few drops of almond flavouring. Cover the inside of some small buttered moulds with the candied orange peel cut into very thin shreds, fill them rather more than half full with the rice, and bake them from thirty-five to forty minutes. When done, turn them out. Serve them on a folded napkin, with sweet or wine sauce in a tureen.

Rice Meringue.
Time, ten minutes to bake.

1149. A quarter of a pound of rice; one pint of milk; a piece of fresh butter the size of a small egg; two ounces and a half of loaf sugar; peel of one lemon; yolks of six eggs; whites of five.

Boil a quarter of a pound of rice in about a pint of new milk until it is sufficiently tender to swell the grains; draw it to the side to cool, and then stir in two ounces and a half of pounded loaf sugar, the peel of a lemon grated, and the yolks of six beaten eggs. Mix all thoroughly together, and then pour it into a buttered dish. Whisk the whites of five eggs to a very stiff froth, and lay it over the top. Bake it in a slow oven, and serve quickly.

Iced Rice Pudding.
Time, two hours boiling; two hours freezing.

1150. Three-quarters of a pound of whole rice; three-quarters of a pint of good thick cream; half a pound of finely-crushed loaf sugar; a few drops of ratafia (or vanilla, if preferred).

Take three-quarters of a pound of whole rice well washed and picked; boil it in water for one hour until it is quite soft; then drain it well from the water, and boil the rice in nearly a pint of good thick cream until it is very much done, adding by degrees half a pound of crushed loaf sugar and the flavouring. Put this mixture into a plain mould, and freeze the pudding for two hours, or less if it is not liked very well frozen. Turn it out on a dish for table (with or without a napkin under it) just before it is wanted. This is an excellent pudding.

Lemon Rice.
Time, half an hour to boil the rice; two hours to stew the peel.

1151. Half a pound of rice; one quart of new milk; one lemon; sugar to taste.

Boil the rice in a quart of new milk, and some white sugar till it is very soft; put it into a mould, and set it in a cold place. Peel a *large* lemon, very thickly, cut the peel into shreds about three-quarters of an inch long, put them into a little water, boil them and drain them from the water. Then pour a teacupful of fresh water over the lemon shreds, squeeze and strain the *juice* of the lemon, add it with some white sugar to the water and shreds, and let it stew gently for two hours. When cold, it will be a syrup. Having turned out the jellied rice from the mould on a dish, pour the syrup gradually over it, taking care that the shreds of lemon peel are equally distributed over the whole.

Croquettes of Rice.
Time, three-quarters of an hour.

1152. Half a pound of rice; one pint and a half of milk; a quarter of a pound of butter; half a pound of sugar; one lemon; five eggs; and some bread-crumbs.

Put the rice and the milk into a stewpan, and stir it over the fire until it boils; then cover the stewpan, and let it simmer until quite tender. Rub the rind from the lemon with the sugar, then pound the sugar in a mortar, add it to the rice and the yolks of the eggs well beaten; again stir it over the fire until the eggs thicken, but do not let it boil. When cold, form it into small balls; whisk four eggs well in a basin, dip each ball into the egg, and then into the bread-crumbs, smooth them with a knife, repeat the egg and crumbs, and put them into a wire basket made for the purpose, place it in a stewpan of boiling lard, and fry them lightly. When done, drain them from the fat on a very clean cloth, and pile them very high in the centre of a dish on a folded napkin, sift powdered sugar over them, and serve.

Roseberry Puddings.
Time, to bake, a quarter of an hour.

1153. Three eggs; their weight in flour; sugar and butter.

Mix the sugar with the flour, and then stir into it three well-beaten eggs and their weight in butter. Mix all together into a paste, fill small cups, and bake them in a moderate oven. This pudding is very good cold.

Ratafia Puddings.
Time, to boil, one hour and a half.

1154. Half a pound of ratafias; six penny queencakes; one pint of thick cream; yolk of six eggs; a glass of brandy; a little pounded sugar; three ounces of dried cherries.

Take half a pound of ratafia cakes and six queencakes, and beat them up in the cream. Add the yolks of six beaten eggs, a small glass of brandy, and sufficient white sugar to sweeten the whole. Butter the mould thickly, stick into the butter three ounces of dried cherries, then pour in the pudding, and boil it.

Boiled Ratafia Pudding.
Time, one hour.

1155. Six spongecakes; a quarter of a pound of ratafias; six eggs; one pint of milk, and a little sugar.

Butter a mould and put some ratafias all over it, then fill it with layers of the spongecakes cut into slices, and ratafias. Mix the well-beaten eggs with the milk, and sugar to your taste. Pour it over the other ingredients, taking care to fill the mould, tie it closely over, and boil it for an hour. When done, turn it out, and serve it with wine sauce.

Plain Ratafia Pudding.
Time, to bake, twenty minutes.

1156. A little sherry or raisin wine; one spongecake; yolks of five, whites of two eggs; one pint of milk; two ounces of sugar; a little nutmeg; four ounces of ratafias; any preserve you like.

Put into the bottom of a buttered dish a sixpenny spongecake cut across, and sprinkle over it four ounces of ratafias. Then pour over them the wine, and when soaked add a layer of preserve. Whisk the yolks and whites of the eggs, mix them with the sweetened milk and a little flavouring if you like, pour it over the soaked cake, put the ratafias on the top, and bake it.

Very Rich Ratafia Pudding.
Time, to boil, half an hour.

1157. One quart of cream; half a pound of dry spongecakes or Naples biscuits; one teacupful of butter; one glass of wine; a quarter of a pound of sugar; two ounces of almonds; a little lemon juice or brandy; yolks of four eggs, and some nutmeg.

Break into small pieces the dry spongecakes, and boil them in the cream, add the butter, the wine, grated nutmeg, and the white sugar. Blanch and pound the almonds in a mortar to a smooth paste with a little lemon juice to keep them from oiling. When the cream, &c., is cold, add to it the yolks of the eggs well beaten, and the almond paste. Mix and beat them well together, put it into a pie-dish, grate some sugar over the top, and bake it in a quick oven.

Boiled Raisin Pudding.
Time, to boil, four hours and a half.

1158. Half a pound of flour; half a pound of bread-crumbs; half a pound of beef suet; half a pound of raisins; three ounces of sugar; two ounces of citron; four eggs; half a teacupful of milk; a little nutmeg; and ground ginger; one tablespoonful of brandy.

Chop half a pound of kidney suet very fine, add it to the bread-crumbs with a little grated ginger and nutmeg, the raisins stoned, the sugar pounded, and the citron cut into slices. Mix it all together, and then stir with it the well-beaten eggs, the milk, and a tablespoonful of brandy. Beat the mixture well together, and boil in a floured cloth.

Economical Raisin Pudding.
Time to boil, four hours.

1159. One pound of flour; half a pound of suet; ten ounces of raisins, and some milk; two ounces of sugar.

Chop half a pound of suet very fine, and mix it with the flour dried. Stone the raisins, and stir them into the flour and suet with two ounces of fine brown sugar. Mix all well together, and pour in sufficient milk to make it into a rather stiff paste, tie it in a floured cloth, and put it into a saucepan of boiling water, and boil it. When done, serve it with sifted white sugar over it.

Baked Raisin Pudding.
Time, to bake, one hour and three quarters.

1160. One pound and a quarter of flour; one pound of raisins; half a pound of suet; two ounces of sugar; one ounce and a half of citron; some milk; a little nutmeg and grated ginger.

Mix the suet chopped very fine with the flour, two ounces of pounded white sugar or very fine brown, a little grated nutmeg and ginger, and the raisins stoned and cut into pieces. When all the ingredients are mixed together with the citron cut into slices, moisten the whole with sufficient milk to make it a very thick batter, put it into a buttered pie-dish, and bake it. Eggs may be added or not, as you please.

Snow Ball—for Children.
Time, one hour.

1161. Half a pound of rice; one quart of water or milk.

Pick all imperfections from half a pound of rice, put it in water, and rub it between the hands. Then pour that water off, put more in, stir it about, let the rice settle, and then drain it from the water. Put the rice in a two-quart stewpan with a quart of water or milk, cover the pan, and let it boil gently for one hour, or until the water or milk is all absorbed. Dip some teacups into cold water, fill them with the boiled rice, and press it to their shape. Then turn them out on a dish, and serve with butter and sugar, or wine sauce.

Potato Pudding.
Time, three-quarters of an hour, to bake.

1162. Fourteen ounces of mashed potatoes; four ounces of butter; four ounces of sifted sugar; the grated peel of a lemon; five eggs; a pinch of salt; three ounces of candied peel; a few spoonfuls of clarified butter.

Well beat the potatoes, and rub them through a wire sieve before they are cold. Add to them the butter beaten to a cream, with the sifted sugar, grated peel, and pinch of salt. Mix all well together with the beaten eggs, put a layer of candied peel at the bottom of a dish, put in the pudding, pour a few spoonfuls of clarified butter on the top, and sifted sugar over the butter. Bake it carefully a delicate brown, and serve it with currant jelly or marmalade round it.

Boiled Sago Pudding.
Time, three quarters of an hour.¹

1163. Two ounces of sago; one pint of milk; five eggs; two Naples biscuits; one glass of brandy; sugar to your taste.

Boil the sago in the milk until it is quite tender. When cold, add five well-beaten eggs, the biscuits, brandy and sugar, beat all together, and put it into a buttered basin. Boil it three-quarters of an hour, and serve it with wine sauce poured over it.

Baked Sago Pudding.
Time, one hour.

1164. One quart of milk; four tablespoonfuls of sago; rind of one lemon; five eggs; two ounces of butter; two ounces and a half of sugar; puff paste.

Boil in a quart of new milk the peel of a large lemon cut as thin as possible, then strain it through muslin, and stir in the sugar and sago. Set it over a slow fire, and let it simmer for twenty minutes. Then put it into a basin to cool. Add the butter and the eggs well beaten. Put it into a pie-dish with some rich puff paste round the edge, and bake it for an hour in a moderate oven.

Semolina Pudding.
Time, ten minutes.

1165. A pint and a half of new milk; half a teacupful of semolina; orange marmalade.

Put a pint and a half of milk over the fire, and when boiling stir in half a cupful of semolina, and continue to stir it over the fire for ten minutes; then put it into a mould to cool; turn it out, and serve with jam or marmalade round it. It is delicious iced.

Swansea Pudding.
Time, three-quarters of an hour.

1166. Seven ounces of melted butter; seven ounces of loaf sugar; three ounces of candied peel; yolks of seven eggs; puff paste.

Butter a pie-dish, and cover the bottom with the citron shred up. Then pound the sugar, add it to the yolks of the eggs well beaten, and the butter melted; stir it over the fire until very hot, but *do not* let it *boil*. Put a puff paste round the edge of the dish, pour the mixture over the shred peel, and bake it in a hot oven for about three-quarters of an hour, or until it is very firm.

Strawberry and Crumb Pudding
Time, to bake, half an hour.

1167. A quart of new milk; four eggs; a little nutmeg; two ounces of sugar; one small pot of strawberry jam; half a pound of bread-crumbs.

Butter a pie-dish, and put a small pot of strawberry jam at the bottom, then a good layer of bread-crumbs. Well beat four eggs, stir into them two ounces of powdered sugar, and a little grated nutmeg; add a quart of new milk, and stir it over the fire until it is sufficiently thick, pour it over the preserve very gradually, and bake the pudding in a very moderate oven.

Spanish Puddings.
Time, ten or twelve minutes to fry.

1168. Half a pint of milk; one ounce of butter; some flour; yolks of three eggs.

Put the milk and butter into a stewpan, over a clear fire, and just before it boils dredge in sufficient flour to make it a thick dough, stirring it all the time with one hand, as you add the flour; then take it off the fire, and stir in, *one* at a time, the yolks of three well-beaten eggs, mixing each well in before adding the other. Then put it on a dish. Fry it in small round pieces in boiling butter, until a light brown. When done, drain them from the fat, and serve on a folded napkin, with sifted sugar over them.

Snowdon Pudding.
1169. Two pounds of bread-crumbs; two

pounds of suet; three pounds of moist sugar; three nutmegs; one pound of candied peel; juice of three lemons; yolks of six eggs; whites of three, and one ounce of ground cinnamon.

Mix all together and press tightly into a basin, and boil for four hours.

Sauce for the Above.

1170. Two quarts of water; two pounds of loaf sugar; the rinds of twelve lemons, cut in strips and boiled in it until quite soft.

A Plain Swiss Pudding.
Time, to boil, four hours.

1171. Eight ounces of bread-crumbs; six ounces of beef suet; half a pound of apples; six ounces of sugar; juice and peel of one lemon; and a pinch of salt.

Chop very fine six ounces of beef-suet, and mix it well with eight ounces of bread-crumbs, half a pound of apples, pared, cored, and minced fine, add eight ounces of powdered white sugar, the juice of one lemon, and the peel grated, with a pinch of salt. Well mix all the above ingredients, and put it into a buttered mould, boil it, and when done turn it out and serve.

Cheap Spongecake Pudding.
Time, to bake, half an hour.

1172. Three penny spongecakes; peel and juice of half a lemon; one egg; a small piece of butter; a very little sugar and milk.

Soak the cakes in a little milk, and mix them with the juice, and grated peel of half a lemon, a piece of butter, a very little loaf sugar, and one egg. Beat all together, and bake it in a quick oven.

Spongecake Pudding.
Time, one hour.

1173. Cherries; almonds, or raisins; some small spongecakes soaked in wine; and some rich custard.

Butter a mould thickly, stick it all over with dried cherries, almonds, or raisins. Fill the mould three parts with small sponge-cakes soaked in wine, and fill up the mould with a rich custard. Then butter a piece of paper, put it on the mould, tie it securely over, and boil it.

Baked Spongecake Pudding.
Time, to bake, one hour.

1174. One stale spongecake; some hot milk; a quarter of a pound of currants; a piece of butter; a quarter of a pound of sugar; white of an egg; one glass of white wine; some puff paste.

Grate a stale spongecake, and add enough hot milk to make it a batter; put to it a piece of butter and the currants washed and dried. Line deep dishes with puff paste, put the mixture in, and bake them in a quick oven. Beat the white of the egg with the pounded sugar, and a glass of wine, until it is light and white, and will stand in a form; heap it on the top of each pudding or pie as soon as taken from the oven, and serve them.

Boiled Sponge Pudding.
Time, three-quarters of an hour.

1175. Three eggs; the weight of them in sugar, flour, and butter; eighteen bitter almonds; peel of half a lemon.

Beat the butter to a cream, then add the pounded sugar, the lemon peel grated, and the egg well beaten. Then stir in the flour, and the almonds blanched and pounded. Boil it in a buttered basin (filling it only half full), with a piece of buttered paper under the cloth to prevent the water from getting in.

Souffle Pudding.
Time, two hours.

1176. Five ounces of butter; six ounces of flour; one pint of milk; peel of half a lemon; three ounces of sugar; yolks of six eggs; whites of four.

Well work five ounces of fresh butter into six ounces of dried flour; boil the peel of half a lemon in a pint of new milk, stir it gradually into the butter and flour, set it over a clear fire, and when it boils stir in the yolks of six eggs well beaten with three ounces of powdered sugar; pour it out, and when cold add the whites of four eggs whisked to the stiffest froth. Put any dried fruit, or candied peel, at the top of a *very* large plain mould. Butter the inside, pour in the mixture, tie a piece of buttered white paper round the top, and steam or boil it for two hours. When done, let it stand for ten or twelve minutes to settle before turning it out, and serve with sweet or brandy sauce.

Vanilla Souffle Pudding.
Time, one hour and a half.

1177. One pint of milk; five spoonfuls of flour; five eggs; two ounces of sugar; some dried cherries; and a flavouring of vanilla.

Put half a pint of milk into a very clean stewpan, and make it scalding hot; mix the other half pint with the flour as smoothly as possible, and stir it gradually into the stew-pan. Scald it for four or five minutes, keeping it *constantly* stirred. Then mix in the yolks of the eggs well beaten, the sugar pounded, and the flavouring of vanilla, or essence of lemon; whisk the whites to a stiff froth, and when the other ingredients are cold, stir in the whites and strain it. Butter a mould, stick some dried cherries over it, put in the mixture, and tie it over with a cloth, putting a buttered paper over the pudding under it. Boil it for an hour and a half, and when done let it stand a few minutes before turning it out.

Baked Souffle Pudding.

Time, rather more than half an hour.

1178. Nine ounces of flour; nine ounces of fresh butter; five ounces of powdered sugar; seven eggs; two dessertspoonfuls of orange juice.

Beat the nine ounces of butter to a cream, add it to nine ounces of flour, and five of powdered sugar, beaten with the yolks of seven eggs, and a flavouring of orange juice. Stir all together until perfectly smooth, and then add the whites of the eggs whisked to a very stiff froth. Pour it into a buttered dish (only half filling it), and bake in a moderate oven.

Plain Souffle Pudding.

Time, half an hour.

1179. Three-quarters of a pint of new milk; two ounces of butter; two spoonfuls of flour; three eggs.

Put three-quarters of a pint of new milk into a stewpan, and when it boils add two spoonfuls of flour mixed smooth with a little milk; boil it up again, and set it to cool. Then take the yolks of three eggs well beaten, stir them in, and the whites whipped to a very stiff froth. When all are thoroughly well mixed together, butter a baking dish, put it in, and bake it in a quick oven.

Ginger Souffle Pudding.

Time, one hour.

1180. Two ounces of butter; one ounce of flour; four eggs; one pint of milk; six ounces of sugar; one ounce of preserved ginger; some dried cherries and citron.

Put the butter into a stewpan, and when melted stir in the flour to make a stiff paste; add the eggs well beaten very gradually, forming the whole into a batter, then add the milk with the sugar dissolved in it, and the preserved ginger cut into very little pieces. Butter a mould, and ornament the inside by placing over it dried cherries, and pieces of citron cut into thin slices. Fill the mould with the batter, and cover over the top a piece of buttered paper; let it steam for one hour, or boil it in a stewpan with the water about half way up the mould, taking great care that it does not touch the top of the pudding. When done, turn it out on a dish, and serve it with sweet sauce.

Cream Souffle Pudding.

Time, one hour and a half.

1181. Half a pint of cream; peel of one lemon; two ounces of sugar; a quarter of a pound of butter; five eggs; a teacupful of flour.

Put half a pint of cream, with two ounces of sugar, and the peel of a lemon cut very thin, into a stewpan, boil it, take out the peel, and set it to cool. Put the quarter of a pound of butter with the cupful of flour mixed very smoothly in a stewpan, and when the butter is melted, stir into it the sweetened cream, and the yolks of the five eggs *one* at a *time;* stir it over the fire until well mixed, then pour it out, and add the whites whisked to a very stiff froth. Put it into a buttered mould with a piece of buttered paper over the top, then tie a cloth closely over it and boil it for nearly an hour and a half. When done, let it stand for a few minutes before serving.

Plain Suet Pudding.

Time, two hours and a half to three hours.

1182. One pound of flour; four ounces of beef-suet; a pinch or two of salt; half a pint of water.

Chop the suet very fine, and mix it with the flour, and a pinch or two of salt, and work the whole into a smooth paste with about half a pint of water. Tie the pudding in a cloth, the shape of a bolster, and when done, cut it in slices and put butter between each slice. Or boil it in a buttered basin, turn it out when done, and serve it whole and without butter.

One or two beaten eggs added to the above, with a less quantity of water, may be used.

Tapioca Pudding.

Time, one hour to bake.

1183. One quart of new milk; three ounces of tapioca; an ounce and a half of butter; four eggs; grated lemon peel, or any other flavouring; three ounces of sugar; puff paste.

Put the tapioca into a stewpan with a quart of milk, and let it simmer by the side of the fire for nearly twenty minutes, stirring it frequently to prevent its burning, turn it out to cool, and then stir into it the sugar, the flavouring, and the eggs well-beaten. Bake it in a well-buttered pie-dish with a puff paste round the edge, or without, as you may prefer. One hour will bake it in a moderate oven.

Plain Tapioca Pudding.
Time, one hour.

1184. One ounce and a half of tapioca; a pint of milk; three eggs; sugar to taste; grated lemon peel.

Soak an ounce and a half of tapioca in cold water until soft, stirring it now and then; well beat three eggs with sugar to taste, and mix them with a pint of cold milk; stir the tapioca into it, and pour the whole into a buttered pie-dish. Grate the peel of a lemon on the top, and bake it in a moderate oven.

Thatched Pudding.
Time, twenty minutes.

1085. Three ounces of butter; two dessertspoonfuls of flour; peel of one lemon; half a pint of milk; four eggs; some preserves; a few sweet almonds; sugar to your taste.

Melt the butter; mix the flour with a little cold milk very smooth, and pour over it the remainder boiling hot, add the sugar and grated lemon peel, and mix all well together. When cool, stir in the yolks of the eggs well-beaten, and add the whites whisked to a stiff froth, and stirred into the pudding the last thing before putting it into the oven. Bake it for twenty minutes. When done, turn it out of the dish, spread some preserves over it, and stick the almonds in cut into thin shreds.

Transparent Pudding.
Time, half an hour.

1186. Eight eggs; half a pound of butter; half a pound of sugar; and some nutmeg; puff paste.

Warm the butter and mix with it the eight eggs well beaten, the sugar pounded, and the nutmeg grated; put it over the fire and stir it till the thickness of batter, then put it into a basin to cool. Put a puff paste round the edge of a dish, pour in the ingredients, and bake it in a moderate oven.

Teacake Pudding.
Time, one hour.

1187. One teacake; three ounces of citron or orange peel; three eggs; half a pint of milk; a little butter; sugar to taste.

Cut the cake into slices, buttering each slice slightly, then place the top slice at the bottom of a buttered basin, and add the remainder, with a layer of orange peel or of citron put thin between each slice of cake. Beat the sugar, eggs, and milk together, and pour it over the cakes; tie the basin over and when done, serve with wine sauce, or the juice of any preserved fruit poured round it.

Maizena Blanc Mange.

1188. Five tablespoonfuls of maizena; two eggs; one quart of new milk; two ounces of sifted loaf sugar; two or three ounces of candied peel, or citron; the peel and juice of one lemon.

Well mix to a smooth cream the maizena with two beaten eggs, and a few spoonfuls of milk if not sufficiently smooth, and stir in the juice of a lemon. Put the milk over a clear fire, adding the sugar and the peel of the lemon cut very thin; when on the point of boiling, stir in the maizena *very quickly*, to prevent it getting into lumps, and boil it until very thick, stirring it constantly. Cut the citron into any form you please, and place it over the bottom and sides of a mould, previously wet with cold water: pour in the boiling maizena, dropping a few pieces of citron in by degrees.

Iced Venice Pudding.

1189. Yolks of four eggs; two ounces of isinglass; three or four spongecakes; some preserve; two ounces of sweetmeats; and sufficient brandy to soak the cakes.

Make a custard with the yolks of four eggs and two ounces of isinglass, ornament the bottom of a mould with sweetmeats according to taste. Pour a little of the custard into the mould, then add spongecake soaked in brandy, then preserve, &c., and at last the custard. Set it in a cold place, or ice it. Serve with clear brandy sauce.

Victoria Pudding in a Mould.

1190. One pint of new milk; or half a pint of cream and half a pint of milk; five eggs; two dessertspoonfuls of brandy; three-quarters of an ounce of isinglass; a little vanilla; six small spongecakes; two glasses of white wine.

Make a good custard with five well-beaten eggs, half a pint of cream and the same quantity of milk, or milk alone; add three-quarters of an ounce of isinglass, and flavour it with a small piece of shred vanilla tied in muslin. When cold, stir in two dessertspoonfuls of brandy. Have ready any ornamental mould, dip it in water, and fill the pattern at the bottom with custard, then place in slices of spongecake in layers with raspberry jam between each, and fill up the mould with the remainder of the custard; put it in a cold place until the next day, or ice it. Turn it out, and ornament it with crystallized fruit or jelly.

The Volunteer's Puddings.

Time, three-quarters of an hour.

1191. Three-quarters of a pound of bread-crumbs; ten ounces of suet; three-quarters of a pound of fine moist sugar; two lemons; two ounces of candied orange peel.

Mix the bread-crumbs with the suet chopped as fine as you can, the grated lemon peel, the candied orange or lemon cut very small; add the sugar and juice of the lemons, grate in a little nutmeg, and bake them in small buttered moulds for about three-quarters of an hour. When done, turn them out on a dish, and pour some lemon, or any sweet sauce you may prefer, over them.

Vermicelli Pudding.

Time, to boil the vermicelli, a quarter of an hour; to bake, one hour.

1192. Three ounces of vermicelli; three teacupfuls of milk; two ounces of butter; three eggs; three tablespoonfuls of powdered sugar.

Wash three ounces of vermicelli and put it into a saucepan with three cupfuls of milk, boil it for a quarter of an hour, then add two ounces of butter. Well beat three eggs with three spoonfuls of powdered sugar, and when the vermicelli is *quite* cold stir in the eggs and sugar. Bake it one hour, and serve with brandy sauce.

Windsor Pudding.

Time, three hours.

1193. Half a pound of apples; half a pound of currants; half a pound of raisins; five eggs; half a pound of suet; half a pound of French roll; peel of one lemon; one glass of raisin wine; half a teaspoonful of nutmeg and a pinch of salt.

Grate the French roll and add to it the suet finely chopped, the nutmeg and lemon peel. Stone and chop the raisins, and mince the apples, then mix with the roll, adding the currants, raisin wine, eggs well beaten, and salt. Mix thoroughly and boil in a well-buttered basin. Sift some white sugar over the pudding when turned out, and serve with wine sauce quite hot.

Wrexham Pudding.

Time, one hour.

1194. Half a pound of bread-crumbs; half a pound of suet; two ounces of sago; six eggs; two dessertspoonfuls of brandy; five ounces of moist sugar; seven ounces of orange marmalade; and a few raisins.

Chop the suet very fine, and mix it with the bread-crumbs and sago, the moist sugar, orange marmalade, and the well-beaten eggs and brandy. When all the ingredients are thoroughly mixed together, butter a mould, and lay over it, in any device you like, some jar raisins scalded in a little hot water for a few minutes. Put in the mixture, tie it securely over, and boil it for one hour. When done, turn it out, and serve it with marmalade sauce.

Wafer Puddings.

Time, twenty to thirty minutes.

1195. One pint of cream; a quarter of a pound of flour; half a pound of butter; yolks of seven eggs; whites of four; two ounces of sugar.

Stir a pint of cream and half a pound of butter over the fire, and when the butter is melted beat into it a quarter of a pound of flour well dried before the fire; then turn it out into a bowl. Well beat the yolks of seven, and the whites of four eggs, stir into them two ounces of powdered sugar, and mix them with the other ingredients in the bowl. Set it before the fire for nearly an hour, then put the mixture into small patty-pans buttered, and bake them in a quick oven until of a nice brown colour. When done, place them on a dish, and pour over them a good wine sauce.

Sir Watkin's Pudding.

Time, eight hours; two hours for a small one.

1196. One pound of marrow; one pound of sugar; one pound of bread-crumbs; four lemons; and eight eggs.

Mix the marrow with the sugar, bread-crumbs, peel of the lemons grated, and the juice strained. Beat the yolks and the whites of the eggs separately, and add them to the other ingredients, and boil it in a basin or mould for eight hours. A small one can be made with a quarter of the quantity and boiled for two hours.

Yeast Dumplings.

Time, twenty minutes.

1197. Some dough; butter; and sugar.

Take some dough from the baker's, and set it to rise before the fire, covered closely over, for ten or twelve minutes. Divide it into as many pieces as you may require, roll them into balls, and drop them into a large saucepan of boiling water. Twenty minutes will be long enough to boil them. They must be sent to table the moment they are done, or they will become heavy, and when eaten they should be divided with forks, and not with a knife. If made at home, the dough may be mixed with milk instead of water. They may be served with sweet sauce or eaten with gravy.

Or,—With Home-made Dough.
Time, half an hour.

1198. One pound and a half of flour; one tablespoonful of baker's yeast; one teaspoonful of salt; one of warm milk.

Make a dough of a pound and a half of flour, the spoonful of yeast, the salt, and the spoonful of warm milk. Set it in a warm place to rise for *two hours*. When light, flour your hands, knead it down, and make it into balls the size of a small teacup. Have a large saucepan of *boiling* water, take off any scum that may have risen in boiling, drop the dumplings in, and boil them fast for half an hour, take them up with a skimmer, and serve with boiled meat or with a sweet sauce of butter and sugar. They must be served as quickly as possible after they are taken out of the water.

Hard Dumplings.
Time, half an hour.

1199. Half a pound of flour; a little milk or water; a pinch of salt.

Mix half a pound of flour into a stiff paste with a little milk or water and a pinch of salt. Roll it into balls, and throw them into boiling water; or make it into a roll, boil it in a cloth, and when done, cut it in slices with butter between.

Yorkshire Pudding.
Time, one hour and a half.

1200. One pint and a half of milk; seven tablespoonfuls of flour; three eggs; and a little salt.

Put the flour into a basin with a little salt and sufficient milk to make it into a stiff, *smooth* batter, add the remainder of the milk and the eggs well beaten. Beat all well together, and pour it into a shallow tin which has been previously rubbed with butter.

Bake it for an hour, then place it under the meat for half an hour to catch a little of the gravy that flows from it; cut the pudding into small square pieces, and serve them on a hot folded napkin with hot roast beef.

Cold Pudding.

1201. Boil in half a pint of milk the peel of a lemon and a little cinnamon; when it has gained the flavour pretty strongly, strain it, and add to it a pint of cream, one ounce of bitter and sweet almonds mixed, blanched, and pounded fine, the yolks of eight eggs, with sugar to taste. Put all the mixture into a mould, then put the mould into water and put it into a slow oven. Bake it until it sets quite equally in the mould, take it out of the oven, and when cold turn it out and pour round it some syrup or any kind of sweetmeats.

White American Pudding.
Time, to bake, three-quarters of an hour.

1202. Two eggs; one pint of cream; a small teaspoonful of salt; three slices of bread; a quarter of a pound of raisins.

Beat the eggs very light, and add them to the cream with the salt. Butter a tin pudding-pan, cut the bread an inch thick from a baker's loaf, pick and stone the raisins, lay them in the pudding-pan, cut the bread into small pieces, and put them on the raisins, pour the cream over the whole, and bake it in a quick oven. Serve it with wine sauce.

Soupon, or Corn Meal Pudding.

1203. Two quarts of water; one tablespoonful of salt; some corn meal.

Mix the ingredients in a batter as thick as you can stir easily, or until the stick will stand in it, stir it a little longer, let the fire be gentle, and when it is sufficiently done it will bubble or puff up. Then turn it into a deep dish, and eat it hot or cold, with milk or with butter and syrup or sugar, or with meat and gravy, the same as potatoes or rice.

PANCAKES AND FRITTERS.

Pancakes should be eaten hot. They should be light enough to toss over in the pan. *Snow* will serve instead of eggs for pancakes. It should be taken when *just* fallen, and quite clean. Two tablespoonfuls of snow will supply the place of one egg. Time to fry a pancake, five minutes. Whenever the time differs on account of the ingredients it will be specified.

Cream Pancakes.

1204. Half a pint of cream; yolks of six eggs; whites of three eggs; a quarter of a pound of butter; some pounded loaf sugar; and some flour.

Well beat the yolks of six and the whites of three eggs, mix the cream with them, and add sufficient flour to make the batter a proper thickness; break into it a quarter of a pound of butter in pieces not too small. Cover the bottom of the pan with butter, and turn it out again, as they will fry themselves. When done, strew pounded sugar between the pancakes as you lay them on the dish.

They are better laid on a saucer, placed in the middle of the dish, as it raises them up, gives a better effect at table, and they are helped better.

French Pancakes.
Time, five minutes.

1205. Six eggs; one pint of cream; one ounce of butter.

Beat the whites and yolks of the eggs separately. Beat a pint of cream till it is stiff. Then beat the eggs and cream together. Put a little piece of butter into an omelet-pan over a quick stove, put into it a large spoonful of the mixture, fry it very quickly, put it into a dish in the oven, rolling it as you take it from the pan, and putting a little grated sugar between it. The pancake will rise in the oven. Do not fry them till they are required, as they must be sent in *very* hot.

French Pancakes with Preserves.
Time, twenty minutes.

1206. Three-quarters of a pint of good cream; five eggs; two dessertspoonfuls of flour; two of pounded sugar; apricot or raspberry jam.

Whip three-quarters of a pint of cream to a froth, and strain it. Whisk the yolks and whites of five eggs separately, and stir them into the flour and sifted white sugar. Mix gradually with the frothed cream, and pour it into shallow tins; put them into a moderate oven for about twenty minutes; and when done, place one on the other with a layer of raspberry or apricot jam between them.

The peel of half a lemon grated is an improvement.

Ground Rice Pancakes.

1207. Three-quarters of a pint of new milk; two spoonfuls of ground rice; a quarter of a pound of butter; two ounces of sugar; a little nutmeg; four eggs; a pinch of salt.

Set a pint of new milk over the fire in a very clean stewpan, and when it is scalding hot, stir in two spoonfuls of ground rice, previously mixed smooth in a quarter of a pint of cold milk. Keep it on the fire till it thickens, but do not let it boil, put it into a basin to cool, stirring in gently a quarter of a pound of fresh butter. When cold, add some white pounded sugar, a little nutmeg, and four eggs well beaten, with a pinch of salt. Drop enough of this mixture to make a pancake, into as little lard as possible, and fry it a nice light brown colour; sift sugar over them, roll them round and serve, with lemon cut and laid round the dish.

Ginger Pancakes.

1208. Yolks of six eggs; whites of three; one quart of milk; two spoonfuls of grated ginger; a pinch of salt; a wineglassful of brandy; six ounces of flour.

Beat six eggs (leaving out the whites of three), and stir them into a quart of milk. Mix the flour smooth with a few spoonfuls of the milk, and add the remainder by degrees; then put in the grated ginger, pinch of salt, and a glass of brandy, stir all thoroughly together. Put a large piece of butter into a fryingpan, and when very hot, pour in a ladleful of the batter, shake the pan, and when one side is sufficiently done turn it on the other, to lightly brown both sides. Raise the pan at the handle that the pancakes may drain. Sift loaf sugar over them, and serve quickly.

Prussian Pancakes.

1209. One pound of flour; one ounce of yeast; a little milk; two ounces of loaf sugar; four eggs; three ounces of butter; the peel of half a lemon; orange marmalade or apricot jam.

Put a pound of flour into a bowl, and put into the centre an ounce of liquid yeast; add sufficient milk to form a stiff dough, and set it by the fire to rise. Melt three ounces of butter, add it to four eggs, a little grated lemon peel, and about two ounces of sifted sugar. Beat it all well together, add it to the dough, and again beat it until it will separate from the bowl. Roll this mixture into a number of balls any size you prefer, fill each with marmalade or apricot jam, and set them to rise inside a screen on a sheet of tin with a floured paper under them. Then put them into a large pan of boiling lard and fry them nicely.

Irish Pancakes.

1210. Yolks of eight eggs; whites of four; one pint of cream; a little grated nutmeg; two ounces of sugar; peel of a lemon grated; three ounces of fresh butter; six ounces of flour.

Warm a pint of cream over a slow fire, and strain into it the yolks of eight well-

New England, American, Snow, Common Pancakes, &c. 241

beaten eggs, and the whites of four, with two ounces of pounded sugar, a little nutmeg and the peel of a lemon grated; warm the butter and stir it into the cream. Then mix in six ounces of flour to form a smooth batter. Put a piece of butter at the bottom of the pan, pour in the batter, and fry the pancakes very thin. When done, place them on a hot dish on one another, and serve them quickly, and as hot as possible.

New England Pancakes.

1211. One pint of cream; six spoonfuls of flour; eight yolks, four whites of eggs; two ounces and a half of powdered sugar; some grated lemon peel or cinnamon.

Mix in a pint of good cream six spoonfuls of flour very smooth; then add the yolks of eight eggs, and the whites of four. Put the pancakes into a pan of hot butter, fry them very thin, and between each strew some pounded sugar, and grated lemon peel or cinnamon, and send up several rolled separately in the same dish.

Pancakes with Marmalade.

1212. Four eggs; four ounces of dried flour; a quarter of a pint of milk; a quarter of a pint of cream; a quarter of a pound of loaf sugar, and some orange marmalade.

Make a smooth batter with the flour, eggs, milk, and cream, and when well mixed pour half a small teacupful into a pan of very hot butter, brown it nicely on one side, toss it over, and turn it on a dish. When all are done, spread some orange marmalade over each. Roll them up, cut off the ragged edges, place them on a sheet of tin, sift some pounded sugar over them, and lightly glaze the whole with a hot salamander: fold a napkin on a dish, and serve the pancakes up on it.

Plain American Pancakes.

1213. Six eggs; one pint of flour: a pinch of salt: a little sugar and powdered cinnamon: a piece of butter and some milk.

Beat six eggs very lightly with a pint of flour, add a pinch of salt, and stir gradually into it enough milk to make a smooth thin batter. Put an omelet-pan over the fire to become hot, rub it over with butter, and put in sufficient batter to run over it, as thin as a crown piece: shake the pan when you think one side is done enough, and toss it up so as to turn it. When both sides are a delicate brown, place it on a dish, put a little butter over it, and some grated white sugar and cinnamon; fry another, lay it on the first one, sprinkle it likewise, and so continue until you have enough, cut them in quarters, and serve very hot.

Pancakes without Lard or Butter.

1214. A pint of cream: six eggs: half a nutmeg: a quarter of a pound of sugar: and some flour.

Well beat six eggs, and stir them into a pint of cream: add half a grated nutmeg, and a quarter of a pound of sifted sugar: mix all well together with sufficient flour to make it a rather thick batter. Heat your frying-pan, wipe it over with a clean cloth, drop in the batter, and fry lightly. Serve with sifted sugar and the juice of a lemon.

Common Pancakes.

Time, five minutes.

1215. Three eggs: one pint of milk: sufficient flour to make a batter: a pinch of salt: and a little nutmeg.

Beat three eggs, and stir them into a pint of milk: add a pinch of salt, and sufficient flour to make it into a thick, smooth batter: fry them in boiling fat, roll them over on each side, drain and serve them very hot, with lemon and sugar.

Snow Pancakes.

1216. Four ounces of flour: a quarter of a pint of milk: a little grated nutmeg: a pinch of salt: sufficient flour to make a thick batter: and three large spoonfuls of snow to each pancake.

Make a stiff batter with four ounces of flour, a quarter of a pint of milk, or more if required, a little grated nutmeg, and a pinch of salt. Divide the batter into any number of pancakes, and add three large spoonfuls of *snow* to each. Fry them lightly, in very good butter, and serve quickly.

Batter for Fritters.

1217. Eight ounces of flour; half a pint of water; two ounces of butter; whites of two eggs.

Mix eight ounces of fine flour with about half a pint of water into a smooth batter, dissolve the butter over a slow fire, and then stir it by degrees into the flour. Then add the whites of two eggs whisked to a stiff froth and stir them lightly in.

Arrowroot Fritters.

Time, about half an hour.

1218. One pint of new milk; one pint of cream; ten ounces of arrowroot; a little vanilla; yolks of eight eggs; sugar to taste; bread-crumbs; greengage or apricot jam.

Put the milk and cream in a good-sized stewpan over the fire until it boils; have the arrowroot ready mixed, and stir it into the milk as quickly as possible, add the vanilla and yolks of eggs, the sugar the last. Stir it for about twenty minutes over a quick fire; then put it into a deep cutlet-pan, and bake it about ten minutes in a quick oven. When it is quite cold, cut out the fritters with a round cutter, and egg and bread-crumb them, glaze and send them up quite hot, with greengage or apricot sauce in the dish.

Apple Fritters.
Time, six minutes.

1219. Yolks of seven eggs; whites of three; one pint of new milk; a little grated nutmeg; a glass of brandy; and sufficient flour for the batter; six apples.

Beat and strain the yolks of seven eggs, and the whites of three; mix into them a pint of new milk, a little grated nutmeg, a pinch of salt, and a glass of brandy. Well beat the mixture, and then add gradually sufficient flour to make a thick batter. Pare and core six large apples, cut them in slices about a quarter of an inch thick, sprinkle pounded sugar over them, and set them by for an hour or more; dip each piece of apple in the batter, and fry them in hot lard about six minutes; the lard should not be made too hot at first, but must become hotter as they are frying. Serve on a napkin, with sifted sugar over them.

Apricots are extremely good done in the same way.

Potato Fritters.
Time, ten minutes.

1220. Two large or three small potatoes; four yolks, three whites of eggs; one tablespoonful of cream; a little nutmeg; a little lemon juice; and half a wineglass of raisin wine.

Boil and scrape very fine two large or three small mealy potatoes; well beat the yolks of four eggs and the whites of three, and add them to the potato with a spoonful of cream, the raisin wine, nutmeg, and a little lemon juice. Beat this well together for rather more than half an hour. Drop a spoonful at a time of the batter into a pan of boiling fat, and fry the fritters a light colour, drain them, and serve on a napkin. A separate sauce may be served with these fritters, made of a spoonful of loaf sugar, the juice of half a lemon, and a glass of sherry.

German Fritters.

1221. Six large apples; a quarter of a pint of brandy; one tablespoonful of pounded sugar, and a little cinnamon.

Pare, core, and cut the apples into round pieces. Put into a stewpan a quarter of a pint of brandy, a tablespoonful of pounded sugar, and a little cinnamon; put the slices of apple into this liquor, and set them over a gentle fire, stirring them often, but taking care not to break them. Have a pan of boiling lard or butter, drain the apples, dip them into a little flour, and put them into the pan. Strew some sugar over a dish, set it near the fire, lay in the apples piled up, strew sugar over them, and glaze them with a red-hot salamander.

Royal Fritters.

1222. One quart of new milk; one pint of white wine; six eggs; a little nutmeg; and two ounces of pounded sugar.

Put a quart of new milk into a stewpan, and when it begins to boil pour in the wine. Then take it off, let it stand five or six minutes, skim off the curd, and put it into a basin. Beat it up well with six eggs and a little nutmeg with a whisk, and add sufficient flour to form it into a smooth batter, adding the sugar pounded. Have ready a pan of hot lard or butter and fry the fritters quickly. Put them on a sieve to drain, and serve them garnished with sweetmeats.

Danish Fritters.

1223. Five eggs; half a pint of flour; a pinch of salt; one teaspoonful of cinnamon powder; one of grated lemon peel; an ounce and a half of candied citron; and some powdered sugar.

Well beat five eggs, add them to the flour, and stir in sufficient milk to work it smooth; then add a pinch of salt and work it again; then the powdered cinnamon, the grated lemon peel, and the citron cut into very small pieces. Rub the bottom of a delicately-clean stewpan with fresh butter and put it over a gentle fire, and let it be done slowly, without sticking to the pan. When it is in a manner baked, take it out and lay it on a dish. Set on a pan with a large quantity of lard or butter, when it boils cut the paste the size of a finger, and then cut it across at each end to make it rise and be hollow, put them into the pan and fry them carefully, as they rise very quickly. When done, sift sugar on a dish, lay the fritters on it, and sift sugar over them; or serve on a napkin.

Cake Fritters.

1224. A stale pound cake; strawberry, or any other preserve; a few spoonfuls of cream.

Cut a stale cake into slices an inch and a half in thickness, pour over them a little good cream, and fry them lightly in fresh butter; and when done, place over each slice of cake a layer of strawberry or any other preserve.

Rice, or Portuguese Fritters.

Time, twenty minutes in all.

1225. One pint of new milk; six ounces of rice; three ounces of loaf sugar; peel of a lemon; three eggs; two ounces of fresh butter; and a very little cinnamon.

Put into a small stewpan one pint of new milk, with the rice, butter, lemon peel grated, the sugar, and a very little cinnamon; boil all slowly until the rice has absorbed all the moisture. Mix in the yolks of three well-beaten eggs, and then make the rice into balls, placing in the centre of each some orange marmalade, brush them over with egg, and the crumb of some grated bread, place them in a wire basket and fry them in boiling fat, of a light brown colour, drain and serve them on a napkin with sifted sugar over them.

Bread Fritters.

1225. A quart basinful of bread; one quart of milk; two eggs; half a nutmeg; one tablespoonful of brandy; one of butter; a little salt.

To a quart basinful of stale bread broken small, put a quart of boiling milk, cover it for ten or fifteen minutes. When quite soft, beat it with a spoon until it is smooth, add two well-beaten eggs, half a nutmeg grated, a tablespoonful of brandy, one of butter, and a little salt. Beat it light; make an omelet-pan hot, put in a small piece of butter, and when dissolved pour in sufficient batter to run over the pan; let it fry gently. When one side is a fine brown turn the other, put butter and sugar with a little grated nutmeg over, lay one on the other, cut them through in quarters, and serve them hot.

Custard Fritters.

1227. Yolks of three eggs; one tablespoonful of flour; half a nutmeg; a little salt; half a pint of cream, or rich boiled milk; one glass of brandy; sugar to taste; one pint of milk; two eggs; a little flour.

Whip the yolks of three eggs with a tablespoonful of flour, half a nutmeg grated, and a little salt, add half a pint of cream or rich boiled milk, flavour with a glass of brandy, sweeten it to your taste, and bake it in a buttered dish. When cold, cut it in slices, and again into small squares or diamonds; make a batter of two eggs beaten very light to a pint of milk, and sufficient flour to make a thin batter; dredge the pieces of custard with flour, put some lard or butter into a pan, and a little salt. When boiling, take up one of the pieces with a spoonful of batter, put it into the pan, and repeat this until the pan is full, let them fry gently; when one side is done turn the other. Serve with white sugar grated over them.

Spanish Fritters.

1228. Crumb of a French roll; a little grated nutmeg, and pounded cinnamon; an ounce and a half of sugar; half a cupful of cream.

Cut the crumb of a French roll about an inch thick in any shape you please; soak the pieces in half a cupful of cream, with a little grated nutmeg, and cinnamon, and an ounce and a half of pounded sugar. When well soaked, take them carefully out and fry them a nice brown. Serve butter, wine, and sugar sauce.

Orange Fritters.

1229. Three oranges; batter; pounded sugar.

Take the peel and white skin from three large oranges; then cut them across into slices, pick out the seeds, and dip each slice of orange into a thick batter. Fry them nicely, and serve them with sugar sifted over each.

Pineapple Fritters.

Time, to fry, seven or eight minutes.

1230. One pineapple; three-quarters of a pint of cream; three eggs; a pinch of salt; sufficient flour to make a batter; two glasses of curaçoa; two ounces and a half of loaf sugar.

Make a *thick* and smooth batter with three-quarters of a pint of cream, the yolks and whites of three eggs beaten separately, a pinch of salt, and sufficient flour to make it a proper consistency. Take the peel from the pine, cut it into slices, and let them soak in two glasses of curaçoa, mixed with two ounces and a half of powdered sugar, for several hours. When well flavoured with the liqueur, dip the pieces into the thick batter, and fry them on each side in boiling fat. When done, drain them on white blotting-paper before the fire to absorb the grease. Serve them on a white doyley, and sift loaf sugar over them quickly.

Strawberry Fritters.

1231. One dessertspoonful of salad oil; peel of half a lemon; a little flour; whites of three or four eggs; some white wine; some fine ripe strawberries.

Mix a spoonful of salad oil with a little

flour, and the peel of half a lemon grated, or minced *very* fine. Whisk the whites of three or four eggs, stir them in, and add sufficient white wine to make a *very thick* batter; then mix in some fine ripe strawberries, and drop the mixture from a spoon about the size of a walnut into a pan of boiling butter, with a strawberry in each fritter. When done, take them carefully out, drain them on a sieve reversed, and serve them with sifted sugar over them.

Beetroot, or Pink-Coloured Fritters.

1232. A large red beetroot; yolks of four eggs; two spoonfuls of flour; three spoonfuls of cream; sugar to your taste; a little grated nutmeg; grated peel of half a lemon; a glass of brandy.

Boil a large beetroot till it is tender, and then beat it fine in a mortar. Add the yolks of four beaten eggs, two spoonfuls of flour, and three spoonfuls of cream. Sweeten it to your taste, grate in some nutmeg and the peel of half a lemon, and add a glass of brandy. Mix all well together, and fry the fritters in butter. Garnish them with green sweetmeats, apricots preserved, or green sprigs of myrtle.

Almond Frase.

1233. Half a pound of almonds; half a pint of cream; yolks of five eggs; whites of two; two ounces of sugar, and some grated bread.

Steep the almonds (blanched) in half a pint of cream, the yolks of five well-beaten eggs, and the whites of two. Then take out the almonds, and pound them fine in a mortar; mix them again with the cream and eggs, adding the pounded sugar, and a little grated bread. Stir all well together, put some butter into a pan, and when very hot, pour in the batter, stirring it in the pan till it is very thick. When done enough, turn it out on a dish, and sift sugar over it.

Backings.

1234. Three ounces of buckwheat flour; one spoonful of yeast; four eggs, and milk.

Mix three ounces of buckwheat flour with a teacupful of warm milk and a spoonful of yeast. Let it rise before the fire for about an hour, then mix four well-beaten eggs, and as much milk as will make the batter the usual thickness for pancakes, and fry them in the same manner.

Raspberry Fritters.

1235. Two Naples biscuits; half a gill of boiling cream; yolks of four eggs; two ounces of loaf sugar; some raspberry juice; a little citron, and a few blanched almonds.

Grate two Naples biscuits, pour over them half a gill of boiling cream, and set it to cool. Beat the yolks of four eggs to a strong froth; and then beat them into the soaked biscuits. Add the sugar pounded fine, and as much raspberry juice as will flavour and give it a pink colour. Drop it from a spoon the size of a large walnut into a pan of boiling fat, and when done, drain them from the fat, stick shreds of citron into some, and blanched almonds cut lengthwise in others; lay round them green and yellow sweetmeats, and serve.

FLUMMERY, BLANCMANGE, SYLLABUBS, &c.

Flummery.

1236. One ounce of sweet; one ounce of bitter almonds; one pint of calf's-feet stock; sugar to taste; one pint of cream; a little orange-flower water.

Blanch one ounce of bitter, and the same of sweet almonds, and beat them in a mortar with a little orange-flower water to keep them from oiling. Put them into a pint of calf's-feet stock, set it over the fire, and sweeten it to your taste. As soon as it boils, strain it through a piece of muslin, and when it is quite cool, put it into a pint of thick cream, and keep stirring it often till it becomes thick and cold. Then pour it into a mould which has been oiled or laid in cold water. Let it stand six or seven hours before you turn it out, as if very stiff it will greatly improve the appearance of the flummery, and it will turn out without putting the mould in hot water, which gives a dulness to the flummery.

Dutch Flummery.

Time, half an hour for the isinglass; two or three minutes to scald.

1237. Two ounces of isinglass; a pint and a half of water; one pint of sherry, or raisin wine; juice of three, and peel of one lemon; yolks of seven eggs; sugar to taste.

Boil two ounces of isinglass in three half-pints of water very gently half an hour. Add a pint of sherry, or raisin wine, the juice of three lemons, and the peel of one, and rub a few lumps of sugar on another lemon to extract the essence, and with them add more sugar to your taste. Well beat the yolks of seven eggs, mix them with the

Flummeries—Iced and Orange Custards.

other ingredients, and give the whole one scald, stirring it all the time. Pour it into a basin, and stir it till half cold. Then let it settle, and pour it into a mould that has been oiled, or laid in water for a short time. Put it in a cold place to set; but it is better made the day before.

French Flummery.

1238. Two ounces of isinglass, or gelatine; one quart of cream; sugar to your taste; two spoonfuls of orange-flower water.

Boil two ounces of isinglass, or gelatine, in a quart of cream for a quarter of an hour. Add sugar to your taste broken into small pieces, and two spoonfuls of orange-flower water. Stir it constantly, and then strain it into a mould. Turn it out on a dish when firm, and place round it some baked pears.

Rice Flummery.

1239. Four ounces and a half of ground rice; six tablespoonfuls of milk; three ounces of loaf sugar; twelve drops of almond flavouring.

Boil four ounces and a half of ground rice in six tablespoonfuls of milk, stirring it all the time. When tolerably thick, add three ounces of powdered loaf sugar, and twelve drops of almond flavouring. Then pour it into an oiled mould, set it in a cold place, and the next day turn it out, and serve with baked pears round it, or with cream and preserve.

Almond Flummery.

1240. One quart of new milk; two ounces of almonds; one ounce of isinglass; one spoonful of orange-flower water; loaf sugar to taste.

Add to a quart of new milk two ounces of almonds blanched, and pounded to a paste, and one ounce of isinglass; boil the whole over a gentle fire until the isinglass is dissolved; then strain it through a fine sieve, add a spoonful of orange-flower water, sweeten it with pounded loaf sugar to your taste, and stir it until cold, and put it into a mould to set.

Green Melon in Flummery.

1241. One pint of clear calf's-feet jelly; half an ounce of isinglass; half a pint of cream; a few sweet almonds; sugar to taste; sufficient juice of spinach to colour the flummery.

Boil slowly half an ounce of isinglass in half a pint of cream, with a few sweet almonds pounded in a mortar, and as much juice of spinach as will make it a pale green.

When it becomes as thick as good cream, wet a melon-shaped mould, and put it in. Then put a pint of clear calf's-feet jelly into a large mould, and let it stand all night. The next day turn out the melon, and lay it in the middle of the mould of jelly; then fill it up with jelly that is beginning to set, and again let it stand all night. The next morning set the mould in hot water, and when you see it is getting loose from the mould lay the dish over it, and turn the jelly carefully out. Ornament it with flowers.

Iced Custard with Preserved or Dried Fruit.

Time, five hours to ice.

1242. One pint of boiling cream; one glass and a half of curaçoa, or any other liqueur; yolks of twelve eggs; a quarter of an ounce of isinglass; different kinds of dried or preserved fruits.

Flavour a pint of cream with a glass and a half of curaçoa, or any other liqueur, add it boiling to the yolks of twelve eggs well beaten and strained; add a quarter of an ounce of isinglass dissolved and clarified to the cream; whip it until nearly cold. Have ready a mould, cover the inside with different kinds of dried or preserved fruits, set the mould in ice, and pour some of the custard in it, about three inches high, then throw in the trimmings, and a little of the fruit chopped very fine. When set, add more custard; continue to do so until the mould is full, and let it stand in ice at least five hours before it is served.

Orange Custards.

1243. One large Seville orange; one spoonful of brandy; a quarter of a pound of pounded sugar; yolks of six eggs; one pint of boiling cream; juice of the orange; some candied orange peel.

Pare a large Seville orange very thin, and boil the peel in plenty of water until it is tender, then beat it in a mortar till very fine; put in a spoonful of brandy, the sugar pounded, and the yolks of four well-beaten eggs. Beat all well together for ten minutes, then, by degrees, pour in a pint of boiling cream, stirring it all the time *until* it is *cold*. Squeeze in the juice of the Seville orange, taking care that none of the seeds get in. Pour the custard into cups; put them into a stewpan of boiling water and let them stand until set—but only let the water be half way up the cups—then take them out, and stick over the tops small slips of candied orange peel. When cold, serve them on a dish, with a spoon between each cup.

Lemon Custards.

1244. Half a pound of loaf sugar; juice of two lemons; peel of one; yolks of four eggs; the whites of two; pint of white wine.

Take half a pound of loaf sugar, the juice of two lemons, the peel of one pared *very* thin, boiled tender and rubbed through a sieve, and a pint of white wine. Let all boil for a quarter of an hour, then take out the peel and a little of the liquor, and set them to cool. Pour the rest into the dish you intend for it. Beat the yolks of the eggs and the whites, and mix them with the cool liquor. Strain them into your dish, stir them well up together, and set them on a *slow* fire in boiling water. When done, grate the peel of a lemon on the top, and brown it over with a salamander. This custard may be eaten hot or cold.

Almond Custards.

1245. Quarter of a pound of almonds; one pint of cream; two spoonfuls of rosewater; yolks of four eggs; sifted sugar to taste.

Blanch and pound in a mortar a quarter of a pound of almonds, and add them to a pint of cream, two spoonfuls of rosewater, and the yolks of four well-beaten eggs. Stir it well together always the same way over a clear fire until sufficiently thick, and then pour it into a glass dish, or into custard cups.

Cheese Custards.

Time, to bake, ten minutes.

1246. Three ounces of cheese; two ounces of butter; two eggs; one tablespoonful of milk.

Grate the cheese very fine; beat the butter to a cream, taking care not to oil it. Well beat two eggs. Mix the cheese and butter together first, then add the eggs and milk, beating all well together. Put the mixture into a flat dish, and bake in a quick oven. Serve immediately.

Custard Mould.

1247. A pint and a half of milk; two laurel leaves; yolks of four eggs; three-quarters of an ounce of isinglass, or one packet of Nelson's gelatine; sugar to taste; peel of one lemon.

Pour a pint and a half of boiling milk, in which two laurel leaves have been boiled, over a packet of gelatine, or three-quarters of an ounce of isinglass. When dissolved, and a little cool, stir in the yolks of the beaten eggs, sugar to taste, and the peel of a lemon grated. Stir it over a clear, slow fire until it thickens; but do not let it boil. Then pour it into a basin, stir it until nearly cold, and pour it into a mould.

Plain Boiled Custard.

Time, about twenty minutes to infuse the peel; ten or fifteen minutes to stir the custard.

1248. One quart of milk; ten eggs; peel of one lemon; three laurel leaves; a quarter of a pound of sugar.

Pour a quart of milk into a delicately-clean saucepan with three laurel leaves and the peel of a lemon, set it by the side of the fire for about twenty minutes, and when on the point of boiling strain it into a basin to cool. Then stir in a quarter of a pound of loaf sugar and the ten eggs well beaten, again strain it into a jug, which place in a deep saucepan of boiling water, and stir it one way until it thickens; then pour it into a glass dish, or into custard cups. You may put a knob of coloured jelly on the top of each custard cup if you please.

Custard with Cream.

1249. Half a pint of new milk; half a pint of thick cream; white of one egg; yolks of six; and two laurel leaves.

Add the yolks of six eggs and the white of one well beaten to half a pint of new milk, half a pint of cream, and two laurel leaves. Mix the whole well together and stir it over the fire until it begins to thicken, taking care it does not boil, or it will run to curd, then strain it into your glasses.

Jaunemange.

Time, a quarter of an hour to dissolve the isinglass.

1250. One ounce of isinglass; half a pint of boiling water; yolks of eight eggs; half a pint of white wine; juice and peel of one small lemon; sugar to taste.

Steep the peel of the lemon in half a pint of boiling water, and then pour it over an ounce of isinglass; add to it the yolks of eight well-beaten eggs, half a pint of white wine, the juice of the lemon, and sugar to taste. Set it over a brisk fire until the isinglass is dissolved, stirring it all the time, then strain it through a fine hair sieve, and pour it into a mould to become cold.

Lemon Blancmange.

1251. Three gills of milk; half an ounce of isinglass; four eggs; peel of two lemons; sugar to taste.

Dissolve half an ounce of isinglass in three

gills of milk; add four well-beaten eggs and the peel of two lemons rubbed in a few lumps of sugar; sweeten it to taste, and stir it over a slow fire until on the point of boiling, add a little brandy, if liked, and pour the whole into a mould.

Blancmange.
Time, fifteen minutes.

1252. One ounce of isinglass or gelatine; two ounces of blanched and pounded almonds; one ounce of bitter ones; one pint and a half of milk; one pint of cream; one lemon; a spoonful of rosewater; and two ounces of loaf sugar.

Put into a delicately-clean stewpan the isinglass or gelatine, the sweet and bitter almonds blanched and pounded, the new milk and cream, the lemon juice and the peel grated, with loaf sugar to taste. Set the stewpan over a clear fire, and stir it till the isinglass is dissolved, then take it off and continue stirring it till nearly cold before putting it into the mould. This quantity will fill a quart mould, but if you wish to make it in a smaller shape, you must not put more than a pint of milk and half a pint of cream. Colour the top ornament with cochineal, and let it get cold before you add the rest of the blancmange.

Isinglass Blancmange.

1253. One ounce of isinglass; one quart of spring water; whites of four eggs: one spoonful of rice water: sugar to taste: one ounce of blanched bitter almonds.

Boil an ounce of isinglass in a quart of spring water until reduced to a pint: then stir in the whites of four eggs with a spoonful of rice water to prevent the eggs from poaching: add sugar to taste, and just scald an ounce of bitter almonds in the jelly. Strain the whole through a hair sieve, pour it into an oiled mould, and the next day turn it out, and stick it all over with blanched almonds cut into spikes. Ornament it with green leaves and flowers.

Arrowroot Blancmange.
Time, about half an hour.

1254. Two ounces of arrowroot: one pint and a half of milk: three laurel leaves: sugar to taste: one tablespoonful of brandy or noyeau.

Mix the two ounces of arrowroot with a large cupful of the milk into a smooth thick batter: boil the remainder of the milk with three laurel leaves until sufficiently flavoured: then strain the milk into a jug and pour it over the arrowroot, stirring it constantly: add sugar to taste, and stir it over a clear fire until very thick, add a tablespoonful of brandy or of noyeau, and pour it into an oiled mould. Set it in a cold place or in ice if you have it. When firm, turn it carefully out on a dish, and garnish it with fruit or flowers.

Strawberry Blancmange.

1255. One quart of ripe strawberries; two ounces of isinglass; half a pound of loaf sugar; juice of one lemon; one pint and a quarter of cream; one pint of milk.

Crush a quart of strawberries with a silver or a wooden spoon, and strew over them a quarter of a pound of powdered sugar, let them stand for several hours, and then press them through a hair sieve reversed. Dissolve two ounces of isinglass in a pint of boiling milk and the remaining quarter of a pound of sugar, then strain it through muslin, and stir it into the cream, and continue to stir it until nearly cold; then pour it gradually to the strawberries, whisking it quickly together. Add the lemon juice, a few drops at a time, to prevent its curdling, and then put it into an oiled mould in a cold place to set, for twelve or fourteen hours.

Quince Blancmange.
Time, half an hour.

1256. Two pounds of quinces; four pints of water; one ounce of isinglass; nine ounces of loaf sugar to every pint of quinces; half a pint of cream.

Simmer two pounds of quinces in four pints of water until they are quite tender; then set them by in a bowl with the liquor until the next day. Put them into a jelly bag, or strain them through a closely-woven cloth, without pressing the fruit, suspending the bag or cloth over a pan until all the juice has dripped through. To every pint of juice put nine ounces of pounded sugar, and stir the whole over a clear fire until the juice falls in a jelly from the spoon; skim it carefully, and pour the boiling jelly very gradually to half a pint of cream, stirring it quickly together as they are mixing, and continue to stir until nearly cold. Then pour the mixture into an oiled mould, or a mould soaked in cold water, and place it in a cool spot to set.

Ribbon Blancmange.
Time, half an hour.

1257. One quart of blancmange.

Make a sufficient quantity of blancmange for one or two moulds, and divide it into equal portions. Add to one, sufficient prepared spinach juice to colour it green, to another a small quantity of cochineal, to a third a little saffron, or if objected to, stir into the boiling blancmange the yolks of two or three eggs well beaten, and stirred over the fire (with a few spoonfuls of milk) to the consistency of the other parts. A little boiled chocolate will also give an additional colour. The different colours should be poured into an oiled mould about an inch deep, and each colour must be let get perfectly cold before the other is added, or it will spoil the beauty of the ribbon.

When full, put the mould in a cold place to set, and turn it carefully out.

Raspberry Blancmange.
Time, a quarter of an hour.

1258. Two pottles of raspberries; one ounce and a half of isinglass; half a pound of sugar; three-quarters of a pint of cream.

Put the raspberries into a bowl, press them with a wooden spoon, and strain the juice. Add to it half a pound of powdered sugar and the ounce and a half of isinglass. Boil it over a clear fire until the isinglass is dissolved, strain it, and stir it gradually into three-quarters of a pint of cream. When nearly cold, pour it into a mould, and put it in a cold place to set.

Cheap Blancmange.
Time, fifteen minutes altogether.

1259. One quart of new milk; one ounce of isinglass; two tablespoonfuls of boiling water; a quarter of a pound of sugar; one large lemon; a stick of cinnamon; half a teaspoonful of vanilla flavouring.

Pour two spoonfuls of boiling water over an ounce of isinglass, rub part of the sugar on the lemon, and when the flavour and colour are well extracted, put it with the remainder of the sugar into a stewpan with a quart of milk and a stick of cinnamon. Let it all simmer until the sugar and isinglass are dissolved. Then strain it through muslin into a jug, add the vanilla flavouring, strain it again, and then pour it into a china mould, and let it stand all night in a very cold place.

Ground Rice Blancmange.
Time, a quarter of an hour to boil the rice.

1260. Four ounces of ground rice; one quart of milk; two ounces and a half of loaf sugar; flavouring of essence of lemon, or almonds.

Simmer a pint of milk with two ounces and a half of loaf sugar, add the flavouring until on the point of boiling. Then stir in the rice, previously mixed to a smooth thin batter, with the remaining pint of milk. Boil the whole for about ten minutes, stirring it all the time until very thick. Moisten a mould with salad oil, pour in the rice, and when perfectly cold and firm, turn it out, and serve it with any preserve, jam, or compote round it.

Whole Rice in a Mould.
Time, twenty minutes altogether.

1261. One cupful of whole rice; two cupfuls of thin cream; one laurel leaf; peel of half a lemon; a small piece of cinnamon; two ounces of sugar.

Wash a cupful of whole rice, and put it into a stewpan with sufficient water to cover it. Let it simmer at the side, and when boiling, add two cupfuls of thin cream, the peel of half a lemon cut thin, a piece of cinnamon, two ounces of sifted sugar, and one laurel leaf. Boil it carefully together until the rice is soft, put it into a mould, press it down tight, and when cold turn it out, and send it to table with any preserve round it.

If put into a cylindrical mould, the centre may be filled with fruit, or sweetmeats.

London Syllabub.
1262. A pint and a half of sherry; two ounces of sugar; grated nutmeg; two quarts of milk.

Sweeten a pint and a half of sherry with the loaf sugar in a bowl, and add nutmeg. Milk into it from the cow about two quarts of milk.

Somerset Syllabub.
Time, twenty minutes.

1263. One pint of port; one pint of sherry; three pints of milk; one pint of clouted cream; a quarter of a pound of sugar; one ounce of nonpareil comfits; nutmeg; cinnamon.

Put the port, sherry, and sugar into a china bowl, and milk into it about three pints of milk. Let it stand twenty minutes, and pour over the top one pint of clouted cream. Grate nutmeg over all. Add powdered cinnamon to taste, and strew thickly with comfits.

Whipped Syllabubs.
1264. Six or seven ounces of loaf sugar; peel of three lemons, and juice of two; four tablespoonfuls of brandy; four of sherry; one pint of cream.

Cut the peel of three lemons very thin, and let them infuse in the juice of two for three or four hours; then strain it over six or seven ounces of pounded sugar. Add four tablespoonfuls of brandy, and the same of sherry; pour in a pint of cream, and whisk the whole to a stiff froth. Take off the froth as it rises, and put it into glasses. These syllabubs should be made, if possible, the day before they are required.

Devonshire Junket.

1265. One quart of milk; half a pint of cream; three ounces of sugar; one glass and a half of white wine; one glass of brandy, and a little nutmeg; two spoonfuls and a half of rennet.

Put two ounces of loaf sugar to the quart of new milk, and turn it to a curd, with two spoonfuls and a half of rennet; then add one ounce of loaf sugar, one glass of brandy, one glass and a half of white wine, and half a pint of cream, mixed together, and poured over the curd, grating some nutmeg on the top. Great care must be taken not to break the curd, and that it is quite hard before pouring these ingredients over it. To be served in the dish it is made in.

Devonshire cream should be put on the top if you have it.

SOUFFLES AND OMELETS.

A soufflé must be ready *only* at the instant it is required; not a minute *too soon*, or it will fall. Both soufflés and omelets require good cooking. Take our advice and see them made by a good cook. The mode of doing them *well* must be taught by example, not by words.

Milan Souffle.

1266. Four lemons; six eggs; half a pint of whipped cream; two ounces of sugar; one ounce of isinglass.

Take four lemons, rub the peel on the sugar, put to it the yolks of six eggs made into a custard, add the juice of the lemons. Let it stand till cold, then add nearly half a pint of whipped cream and an ounce of isinglass. The whites of the eggs to be well whipped to a strong froth, and put round it with the whipped cream when cold.

York Souffle.

1267. Five eggs; half a pound of loaf sugar; peel and juice of two lemons; two ounces of butter; puff paste.

Well beat five eggs; stir with them half a pound of powdered sugar, and the juice and grated peel of two lemons. Melt the butter, pour it into the eggs, and bake the whole in a dish with puff paste round it.

Omelet Souffle.

1268. Twelve eggs; two ounces of powdered sugar; one dessertspoonful of orange-flower water; one ounce of fresh butter.

Separate the whites from the yolks of twelve eggs. Put the whites into a basin and beat them extremely fast till they form a very thick snow. Then beat six yolks separately, with two ounces of sugar, and a dessertspoonful of orange-flour water, or just enough to flavour it to your taste.

Before beating the eggs have ready a round tin, well greased all over the inside with fresh butter.

When you have finished beating the six yolks, mix them *very quickly* with the whites, lest the snow should turn—that is, melt into water. Put it then into the buttered tin, and place it in the oven. It will be so thick, if it is well and skilfully mixed, that there will be no fear of its running over. Watch it well; glancing at it from time to time through a little opening of the oven door, to see how it is going on; as soon as it has risen very high, and is of a golden colour, take it out of the oven.

Do not suffer the omelet soufflé to remain long in the oven. If it is not watched it will fall in and become a mere *galette*. Let the oven be of a very gentle heat, or the bottom of the omelet will be burnt before the top is done.

Before putting the tin in the oven, you may powder the snow with fine sugar; it crystallizes and produces a very pretty effect. As soon as the omelet is done it must be sent to table. If it waits for longer than ten minutes it falls in. The eggs should be beaten with a fork or a little whisk.

If this soufflé is liked a little more solid, add to the yolks of the eggs when beaten two dessertspoonfuls of rice boiled in milk, and flavoured with vanilla. In this case do not put in the orange-flower flavouring. The rice must be very well cooked, and well sweetened before it is added to the eggs.

Apple Souffle.

Time, ten minutes.

1269. Six or eight apples; some white sugar; yolks and whites of three eggs; a quarter of a pint of cream, or new milk; one tablespoonful of brandy; and sugar to taste.

Peel and cut six or eight apples; boil

them with a little white sugar, and mash them smooth. Make a custard with the yolks of three well-beaten eggs, a quarter of a pint of cream or new milk, and a tablespoonful of brandy, and white sugar to taste. Have the apples and custard ready; make a ring round the dish with the apples, and put the custard in the middle. Whisk the whites of the eggs to a *stiff* froth, and put them over the custard and apples; sift sugar over it, and bake it in a moderate oven.

Apple Souffle in Paste

1270. Ten or twelve large apples; peel of half a lemon; whites of four eggs; three ounces of loaf sugar; half a pound of puff paste.

Well butter the *outside* of a tin or pie-dish, cover it with good puff paste, and bake it a nice light colour. When done, take out the dish carefully, and fill the inside of the paste with ten or twelve large apples, three ounces of pounded sugar, and the peel of half a lemon stewed until perfectly soft. Whisk the whites of four eggs very stiff, pile it on the apples, strew sifted sugar over it, and brown it lightly in a gentle oven. Serve hot, with a napkin round it.

Orange Souffle.

1271. One ounce of isinglass; one pint of water; juice of one lemon; one Seville orange; fifteen China oranges; sweeten to taste.

Put an ounce of isinglass into a pint of cold water, and boil it until reduced to half a pint; strain it, and add the juice of one lemon, one Seville orange, and of fifteen China oranges. Sweeten it to your taste, and whisk it all together until almost cold; dip a mould into cold water, put in the soufflé, and set it by for use. Before turning it out, put the mould into warm water, then turn it out on a dish, and serve ornamented with flowers, or in any way you please.

Lemon Souffle.

Time, half an hour.

1272. Three ounces and a half of fresh butter; a little flour; yolks of six eggs; whites of nine; one pint of milk; three ounces of loaf sugar; juice of one lemon; peel of three.

Boil the peel of three lemons cut very thin in a pint of sweetened milk. When cool, add the yolks of six well-beaten eggs and the juice of a lemon strained. Dissolve nearly four ounces of fresh butter, and stir in sufficient flour to form a stiff paste; then take out the lemon peel, mix it with the flour and butter, and stir the whole over a clear fire for five or six minutes. Set it to cool, and about an hour before placing it in the oven whisk the whites of nine eggs to a very stiff froth; stir them gradually and lightly in, and pour it into a souffle-dish well buttered with a wide band of white buttered paper tied round the top. Bake it for half an hour. When done, remove the paper and serve.

Strawberry Souffle.

1273. Three pints of ripe strawberries; peel of half a lemon; a quarter of a pound of loaf sugar; one pint of milk; four eggs.

Simmer three pints of ripe strawberries with a little loaf sugar and the peel of half a lemon grated; then place it round a dish as high as the quantity will allow, forming a wall, leaving the centre hollow. Make a custard with the yolks of four eggs well beaten, a pint of milk, and sugar to taste; fill the centre of the strawberry wall, and cover the whole with the whites of the eggs whisked sufficiently firm to bear an egg; sift over it powdered sugar, and brown it with a salamander, or serve white if preferred.

Apricot, or Strawberry Souffle.

Time, fifteen to twenty minutes, to bake.

1274. One dozen ripe apricots, or one quart of ripe strawberries; four ounces of sugar; a large cupful of water; a large cupful of good cream; yolks of six eggs; whites of ten; four tablespoonfuls of fine flour; a piece of butter the size of an egg.

Take the stones from a dozen or fourteen ripe apricots (or take a quart of strawberries), put them into a stewpan with the sugar pounded and a cupful of water; stir it constantly over a clear fire until the fruit will pulp; then press it through a sieve. Mix it with four spoonfuls of flour rubbed smooth, half a pint of good cream, and a piece of fresh butter; stir it briskly over the fire until it boils; then stir in the yolks of six well-beaten eggs, and the whites of ten whisked to a stiff froth; fill the souffle-mould, and bake it.

French Souffle.

Time, about one hour.

1275. Two tablespoonfuls of flour; a piece of butter the size of a walnut; two tablespoonfuls of cream; half a pint of milk; yolks of five eggs; whites of eight; two ounces of sugar; a large spoonful of noyeau or maraschino.

Stir over the fire two spoonfuls of flour and a piece of butter until thick, taking care it does not become coloured; then stir gradually in two spoonfuls of boiling cream and half a pint of boiling milk. Beat it together until smooth and thick, and then pour it into a basin; stir in the yolks of the eggs well beaten, and the sugar pounded with a spoonful of noyeau or maraschino. Whisk the whites to a stiff froth, and stir them very lightly into the other ingredients. Pour it into a souffle-dish, and bake it carefully.

Punch Souffle.

Time, half an hour.

1276. Yolks of ten, whites of eleven eggs; some bread-crumbs; three ounces of loaf sugar; a dessertspoonful of orange-flower water; three dessertspoonfuls of potato flour; three ounces of ratafias; half a pint of custard flavoured with rum and lemon peel.

Beat the yolks of ten eggs with three ounces of pounded sugar, three ounces of ratafias bruised fine, three spoonfuls of flour, and a flavouring of orange-flower water. Well butter a plain oval mould and a strip of paper; tie the paper round the top, and strew bread-crumbs over the interior.

Whisk the whites of eleven eggs to the stiffest froth, and stir them lightly into the other ingredients; pour the whole into the mould, and bake it in a slow oven for half an hour; turn it out of the mould, and pour round it about half a pint of custard flavoured with rum and lemon peel.

Rice Souffle.

Time, to bake, three-quarters of an hour.

1277. A quarter of a pound of rice; three ounces of loaf sugar; three-quarters of a pint of milk; a quarter of a pint of cream; yolks of six eggs; whites of eight; one glass of white wine; a piece of butter the size of an egg.

Soak a quarter of a pound of the best rice in boiling water for about a quarter of an hour, then boil it in a small stewpan with the milk, cream, wine, sugar, and piece of butter, and let it simmer slowly until it is quite soft; then beat the yolks of six eggs, add them to the rice, and stir lightly in the whites of eight beaten to a firm froth. Put a paper round a souffle-dish, pour in the mixture, and bake it in a moderate oven.

Souffle in Cases.

Time, quarter of an hour to bake.

1278. Peel of two small lemons; six eggs; two tablespoonfuls of cream; five ounces of flour; one pound of loaf sugar.

Rub the peel of two lemons with the sugar, then pound it, mix it with the yolks of six eggs, and beat it well together; then add two tablespoonfuls of whipped cream, and four or five ounces of fine flour. Stir all together for about five minutes, and then add gradually the whites of the eggs whisked to a *very* stiff froth. Three parts fill some small and neatly shaped white paper cases with the mixture, and bake them in a moderate oven. Sift powdered sugar over them, and serve piled high on a folded napkin.

A Plain Souffle.

Time, half an hour to bake.

1279. One ounce and a half of fresh butter; one ounce and a half of pounded sugar; four dessertspoonfuls of arrowroot, or rice flour; six eggs; rather more than a pint of new milk; a little vanilla.

Mix into a very smooth paste four dessertspoonfuls of arrowroot, or rice flour, in a basin, then pour in the remainder of the milk, sweeten it with a little pounded sugar, and put it into a very clean stewpan with an ounce and a half of fresh butter. Stir it over a clear fire until it is the consistency of thick cream, then add the yolks of six well-beaten eggs, and then stir in the whites, *whisked* stiff enough to bear the weight of an egg; pour it into the souffle-dish, and bake it in a moderately-heated oven. When done, hold a salamander over it for a few minutes, and serve it with a napkin pinned round the mould, or place it inside another ornamental one, dust a little sifted sugar over the top, and serve as quickly as possible. Vanilla, or any flavouring may be added.

Omelet aux Confitures.

1280. Four eggs; two tablespoonfuls of good cream; three dessertspoonfuls of flour; any preserve you may fancy.

Well beat four eggs; add them to two tablespoonfuls of good cream, and three dessertspoonfuls of flour. Mix all well together. Put it into an omelet-pan, and fry it only one side, like a pancake, then fill it with any preserve you may have, or fancy, turn it over on the dish, and sift sugar over it.

Friar's Omelet.

1281. Eight or nine large apples; two ounces of fresh butter; sugar to taste; bread-crumbs.

Boil eight or nine large apples to a pulp, stir in two ounces of butter, and add pounded sugar to taste. When cold, add an egg well-beaten up. Then butter the bottom of a deep baking-dish, and the sides also. *Thickly* strew crumbs of bread, so as to stick all over the bottom and sides. Put in the mixture, and strew bread-crumbs plentifully over the top. Put it into a moderate oven, and when baked turn it out, and put powdered sugar over it.

Cream Omelet.

1282. Ten eggs; three tablespoonfuls of rice flour; a piece of butter the size of an egg; four ounces of loaf sugar; peel of half a lemon; one pint of cream; one ounce of bitter and sweet almonds mixed.

Boil a pint of cream with three large spoonfuls of rice flour, mixed smooth in a little of the cream, four ounces of powdered sugar, and a piece of butter the size of an egg. When thick, set it to cool, and then stir in the yolks of six eggs, the grated lemon peel, and the almonds blanched and pounded in a mortar. Stir all well together, and lightly add the whites of the six eggs beaten to a stiff froth. Line a mould with buttered paper on both sides, pour in the mixture, and bake it in a moderate oven. When done, let it settle for a minute, turn it very carefully out, and strew sugar over the top.

Omelet Souffle.

1283. Six eggs; four dessertspoonfuls of sugar; peel of one large lemon; quarter of a pound of fresh butter.

Beat six eggs, the whites and yolks separately; put to the yolks four dessertspoonfuls of white sugar powdered, and the peel of a large lemon chopped very fine; mix them thoroughly. Whisk the whites to a high froth, and add them to the yolks. Put a quarter of a pound of butter into a pan over a brisk fire, and as soon as it is completely melted, pour in the mixture; stir it that the butter may be well incorporated with the eggs. When it is so, put it in a buttered dish, and set it over hot embers or ashes; strew powdered sugar over the top, and colour it with a salamander. This may be done in the oven. Serve quickly, or the omelet will fall and its appearance be spoiled.

Omelet Souffle with Vanilla.

Time, quarter of an hour.

1284. Yolks of seven eggs; whites of eight; quarter of a pound of sugar; two dessertspoonfuls of flour; a flavouring of vanilla.

Beat the yolks of seven eggs with two spoonfuls of flour, rubbed smooth in a spoonful of milk, add a quarter of a pound of powdered sugar, and a flavouring of vanilla. Well beat all these together, and stir lightly in the whites of eight eggs whisked to a stiff froth. Put the souffle in the centre of a dish, and bake it in a moderate oven for a quarter of an hour. When done, sift sugar over it, and serve as quickly as possible.

Omelet Souffle in a Mould.

Time, half an hour.

1285. Six eggs; three spoonfuls of powdered sugar; one dessertspoonful of rice flour; and a teaspoonful of orange-flower water.

Break six fresh eggs, separate the whites from the yolks, add to the latter three spoonfuls of powdered sugar, a spoonful of rice flour, and a little orange-flower water; stir these well together. Whip the whites of the eggs to a stiff froth, and *stir* them to the yolks. Pour the mixture into a buttered mould, rather more than half full; bake it in a moderate oven for half an hour. When done, turn it on a dish, and serve quickly. This omelet must be clear, and shake like a jelly.

Omelet Glace.

1286. Six eggs; a little salt; five or six macaroons; the peel of half a lemon.

Break and separate the yolks from the whites of six fresh eggs, add a pinch of salt, the peel of half a lemon minced fine, and five or six pounded macaroons; mix all well together. Then whip the whites to a stiff froth, beat them well into the yolks, and then pour the mixture into a pan of hot butter, stir them round, and raise the edges to separate it from the pan; turn them over, and then turn the omelet on a dish, sprinkle sugar over it, and lightly brown with a salamander. Serve quickly.

Omelet with Sweetmeats.

1287. Nine eggs; five tablespoonfuls of white sugar; a teaspoonful of lemon extract or peach water; a teacup of butter; and preserved apricot, strawberry, or any other jam.

Beat nine eggs, the yolks and whites separately; put five spoonfuls of white sugar to the yolks; add the flavouring of lemon or peach-water. Whisk the whites to a stiff froth, and stir them lightly to the yolks. Put a cupful of butter into an omelet-pan, let it become hot, put in the omelet, draw it from the edges of the pan to the middle, and stir it so that it may be evenly done, and shake it occasionally. When done, spread either of the above-named preserves over it. Roll it in the form of a muff, strew powdered sugar over it, and serve.

Sweet Omelet.

1288. Six eggs; three tablespoonfuls of pounded sugar; one tablespoonful of flour; peel of one lemon; a quarter of a pint of cream; some sweetmeat.
Part the yolks of six eggs from the whites, stir in the pounded sugar to the yolks, a spoonful of flour, and a quarter of a pint of cream. Mix all well together, then whisk the whites to a stiff froth, and mix them gently with the other ingredients just as you are about to fry it. Put in half at a time, cover minced sweetmeats on it, fry the other, and turn over it, and glaze with a salamander.

Omelet Souffle.

1289. Six eggs; four dessertspoonfuls of powdered sugar; peel of one lemon; a quarter of a pound of butter.
Beat the whites and yolks of six eggs separately, put to the yolks six dessertspoonfuls of powdered sugar and the peel of a lemon cut very thin and chopped as fine as possible. Mix them thoroughly, whip the whites to a stiff froth, and add them to the yolks. Then put a quarter of a pound of butter into an omelet-pan over a quick fire, and as soon as it is melted pour in the mixture, stir it that the butter may be well mixed with the eggs; then put it into a buttered dish, and set it over hot ashes, strew powdered sugar over the top, and colour it with a salamander, or put it into the oven. This must be served as soon as possible, as it soon falls, and the appearance would be spoiled.

CREAMS.

Apple Cream.

Time, half an hour to three-quarters of an hour.

1290. One pound of apple pulp; half a pint of cream; peel of half a lemon; two spoonfuls of brandy; half an ounce of powdered sugar, or to taste.
Pulp boiled apples till you have a pound weight of them. Add to them half a pint of cream, the lemon peel grated, and two spoonfuls of brandy. Whisk the whole till it is a fine white cream, and leave a white froth at the top. Sweeten it to taste before whisking it. The quantity of sugar required must depend on the acidity or sweetness of the apple pulp.

Apricot Cream.

Time, twenty-five to thirty minutes.

1291. A dozen ripe apricots; one pint of milk; half a pint of cream; yolks of nine eggs; eight ounces of isinglass; eight ounces of loaf sugar.
Make a thin syrup with part of the sugar boiled in a *small* cupful of water, and in the syrup boil the apricots to a pulp, having first removed the stones. Press them through a sieve, and set them in a cool place. Boil a pint of milk and half a pint of cream, and when cool, stir in the yolks of nine eggs well beaten with the remainder of the sugar. Put it into a jug with a lip; set the jug in a deep saucepan of boiling water, and stir it one way until the cream thickens, without allowing it to boil, or it will curdle. Then strain it into a basin, add the ounce of isinglass (previously dissolved in hot water), and stir in the pulped apricots. Mix it thoroughly together, and put it into an oiled mould. Set it in a cold place.

Superior Apricot Cream Iced.

1292. Twelve apricots; six ounces of sugar; one pint of cream.
Pare, stone, and scald twelve ripe apricots, beat them to a pulp in a mortar. Put to them six ounces of double-refined sugar and a pint of scalding cream, work it through a hair sieve, put it into a tin that has a close cover, set it in a tub of ice broken small, with a large quantity of salt put amongst it. When the cream grows thick round the edge of the tin stir it, and again place it in the ice till it becomes quite thick. When all the cream is thoroughly frozen take it out of the tin, and put it into the mould you intend it to be turned out of. *Cover it over* with the lid, place the mould in the centre of another tub of ice and salt, laying the ice over the top of the mould, and let it stand four or five hours. When ready to serve, dip the mould into warm water, or hold a cloth round it for a minute which has been dipped into boiling water, and it will come out easily.

Creme Brulee.

1293. Ten ounces of loaf sugar; peel of two lemons; one pint of cream; yolks of eight eggs; a little salt; half a pint of whipped cream; one ounce and a half of clarified isinglass.
Put two ounces of pounded sugar into a stewpan with the grated peel of two lemons;

stir these with a wooden spoon over a slow fire until the sugar begins to assume a rather light brown colour, then pour in a pint of cream, and add to this eight ounces of sugar, the yolks of eight eggs, and a little salt. Stir the whole over a *stove fire* until the eggs are set, then strain the cream through a hair sieve into a large basin, and mix with it half a pint of whipped cream and one ounce and a half of clarified isinglass. Pour the cream into a mould embedded in rough ice.

Ground Rice Cream.
Time, three minutes.

1294. Four tablespoonfuls of ground rice; yolks of four eggs; whites of two; one pint of new milk; two ounces of loaf sugar.
Mix four tablespoonfuls of ground rice very smooth with a spoonful or two of milk, add the yolks of four well beaten eggs, and the whites of two; sweeten it to taste, or add about two ounces of pounded sugar, boil a pint of milk, pour it over the rice and eggs, boil it three minutes, and put it into a mould. When turned out, serve it with either custard, preserves, or whipped cream over it.

Stone Cream.
Time, to boil, one minute; to stand, one night.

1295. One pot of preserved apricots or plums; half an ounce of isinglass; one pint of cream; one lemon; two teaspoonfuls of crushed white sugar (more or less, to taste).
Take a glass dish and line it at the bottom about an inch thick with preserved apricots or plums, dissolve half an ounce of isinglass in a little water, strain it, add to it a pint of thick cream, the peel of the lemon grated, enough sugar to make it pleasant to your taste. Let it boil one minute; then put it into a jug that has a spout. When it is *nearly* cold, but not quite set, squeeze into it the juice of the lemon (or rather, squeeze the lemon in a cup and add it to the cream, lest a pip should fall into the jug). Pour it into the dish (from a jug with a spout) over the sweetmeat, and let it stand all night. Place on the top a few ratafias.
Any very nice jam may be substituted for the apricot, but the latter is best of all. Wine sours are perhaps the best substitutes for apricots.

Velvet Cream.
Time, until the isinglass is dissolved.

1296. One ounce of isinglass; a breakfast-cup of white wine; juice of one large lemon; the peel rubbed with sugar; one pint of cream.
Put the ounce of isinglass into a stewpan with a *large* cupful of white wine, the juice of a large lemon, and sufficient sugar to sweeten it rubbed on the peel to extract the colour and flavour. Stir it over the fire until the isinglass is dissolved, and then strain it to get cold. Then mix with it the cream, and pour it into a mould.

Chocolate Cream.
Time, twenty minutes.

1297. One bar of chocolate; one pint and a half of cream; yolks of five eggs; one tablespoonful and a half of good moist sugar.
Break a bar of chocolate into small pieces, and pour over them a pint and a half of cream, let it remain until it is dissolved, and then boil it slowly for ten minutes. Well beat the yolks of five eggs with a spoonful and a half of good moist sugar, mix it with the cream, and pour it into cups. Stand them in a stewpan of boiling water, which must only cover half way to the edge of the cup, and let them remain simmering twenty minutes with the cover of the stewpan kept on. When done, place them in a very cold place. Milk may be used instead of cream if a less expensive cream is required.

Iced Chocolate Cream.

1298. Half a pint of strong made chocolate; one pint of milk; yolks of eight eggs; half a pint of thick cream; half a pound of loaf sugar.
Make a pint of milk very hot, sweetened with half a pound of loaf sugar; then stir carefully into it the yolks of eight well-beaten eggs and half a pint of strong made chocolate. Put it into a jug, stand it in boiling water over a clear fire, and stir it one way until the eggs are set in the milk, but do not let it boil, then strain it through a fine silk or hair sieve, and stir into it about half a pint of thick cream. Freeze and mould it as other iced creams.

Coffee Cream.

1299. One *large* cupful of made coffee; four ounces of sugar; three-quarters of a pint of milk; yolks of eight eggs; two ounces of gelatine.
Put three-quarters of a pint of boiled milk into a stewpan with a *large* cupful of made coffee, and add the yolks of eight well-beaten eggs and four ounces of pounded loaf sugar. Stir the whole briskly over a clear fire until it begins to thicken, take it off the fire, stir it for a minute or two longer, and strain it through a sieve on the two ounces of gelatine. Mix it thoroughly together, and when the gelatine is dissolved,

pour the cream into a mould, previously dipped into cold water, and set the mould on rough ice to set.

Tea Cream.

1300. A quarter of an ounce of Hyson tea; half a pint of milk; half a pint of cream; two spoonfuls of rennet; sugar to taste.

Boil a quarter of an ounce of fine Hyson tea with half a pint of milk; strain off the leaves, and put to the milk half a pint of cream and two spoonfuls of rennet. Set it over a stove in the dish it is to be served in, and cover it with a tin plate. When it is thick it will be sufficiently done. Garnish with sweetmeats.

Maraschino Cream,

Time, about ten minutes.

1301. One pint of fine red strawberries; a quarter of an ounce of isinglass; four tablespoonfuls of maraschino; and some good strawberry cream.

Dissolve a quarter of an ounce of isinglass in a very little boiling water; pick the stems from a pint of fresh red strawberries, dip each into the dissolved isinglass and then into the maraschino. Line the inside of a mould with the strawberries as thickly as they can be placed; fill the interior with strawberry cream or any other you may prefer. Place the mould in ice, or in a *very* cold place until the next day.

Lemon Cream.

1302. One pint of water; peel of three large lemons; juice of four lemons; six ounces of fine loaf sugar; whites of six eggs.

Pare into a pint of water the peel of three large lemons; let it stand four or five hours; then take them out, and put to the water the juice of four lemons and six ounces of fine loaf sugar. Beat the whites of six eggs and mix it altogether, strain it through a lawn sieve, set it over a slow fire, stir it one way until as thick as good cream, then take it off the fire and stir it until cold, and put it into a glass dish.

Orange cream may be made in the same way, adding the yolks of three eggs.

Lemon Cream without Cream.

Time, five or six minutes.

1303. Two ounces of gelatine or isinglass; three-quarters of an ounce of bitter almonds; three lemons; one quart of new milk; yolks of seven eggs; ten ounces of loaf sugar.

Put a quart of new milk into a stewpan with the peel of three small lemons cut thin, ten ounces of loaf sugar pounded, three-quarters of an ounce of bitter almonds, blanched and pounded to a paste, and about two ounces of gelatine or isinglass. Boil the whole over a moderate fire for eight or nine minutes, until the gelatine or isinglass is thoroughly dissolved. Then strain it through a fine sieve into a jug with a lip to it; stir in the yolks of seven well-beaten eggs, and pour the mixture from one jug to another until barely cold; then add the strained juice of three small lemons, stir it quickly together, and pour it into an oiled mould.

Ratafia Cream.

Time, fifteen minutes.

1304. Six bay-leaves; one quart of new milk; a little essence of ratafia; yolks of four eggs; four spoonfuls of cream; sugar to taste.

Put a quart of new milk into a stewpan with six bay-leaves and a little ratafia. When it has boiled up, take out the leaves, beat up the yolks of four eggs with four spoonfuls of cream, and add sugar to your taste. Stir it into the ratafia cream to thicken it, and set it over the fire to get hot, without allowing it to *boil*. Keep stirring it all the time *one way*, or it may curdle, and then pour it into a glass dish. To serve when cold.

Iced Ratafia Cream.

Time, about a quarter of an hour, or until it thickens.

1305. Half a pound of ratafias; seven eggs; one pound of curaçoa; the rind of one Seville orange; five ounces of sugar; one pint of milk; two ounces of gelatine; two ounces of preserved ginger; the same of candied orange and cherries; one ounce of candied lemon; half a pint of cream.

Put into a stewpan the yolks of seven eggs, the glass of wine, the rind of the Seville orange, the ratafias, the sugar pounded, and a pint of boiled milk; stir it over the fire until it thickens, press it through a hair sieve into a bowl, and add the gelatine previously dissolved, the cream well whisked, and the preserves cut up into very small pieces, and well mixed in with the other ingredients. Dip the mould into water, put in the mixture, and set it in ice.

Raspberry Cream in a Mould.

Time, about ten minutes.

1306. One ounce of isinglass; a pint and a half of cream; a sufficient quantity of raspberry jelly to sweeten and colour it.

> Boil an ounce of isinglass in a small quantity of water until quite dissolved. Take a pint and a half of cream, boil half of it, then strain the isinglass to it. Put a sufficient quantity of raspberry jelly to sweeten and colour the cold cream, whisk it well until the jelly is dissolved, then add the warm cream to it, and strain it into a well-oiled mould.

Raspberry Cream without Cream.

Time, one hour.

1307.—A quarter of a pound of raspberry jam or jelly; a quarter of a pound of sugar beaten fine; whites of four eggs.

Pound and sift the sugar, mix it with the jam or jelly, and the whites of four eggs. All to be beaten together for one hour, and then put in lumps in a glass dish.

Orange Cream.

Time, ten or twelve minutes.

1308. One ounce of isinglass; quarter of a pound of loaf sugar; one lemon; seven oranges; half a pint of cream.

Squeeze and strain the juice from the oranges and the lemon, put it into a saucepan with the isinglass and sufficient water to make a pint and a half with the orange and lemon juice included. Rub some sugar over the orange and lemon peel, add it to the other ingredients, and boil all together for about ten or twelve minutes. Then strain it through a muslin bag, let it stand until cold, and beat it up with the cream. Dip the mould in cold water, or oil it, pour in the cream, and put it in a very cold place to set, or in ice if you have it.

Seville Orange Creams.

Time, ten or twelve minutes.

1309. One pint of cream; one spoonful of brandy; a quarter of a pound of loaf sugar; one Seville orange; yolks of four eggs.

Boil the peel of a Seville orange in several waters to take off the bitter taste, and then pound it in a mortar. Add a quarter of a pound of sifted loaf sugar to the yolks of four eggs, beat it smooth, and then add a spoonful of brandy, the juice of the orange strained, and the pounded peel. Beat all together for ten or twelve minutes, then pour gradually in a pint of boiling cream, and stir it briskly together until cold, pour it into a basin with a spout and stand it in boiling water till cold, then pour it into glass custard cups.

Preserved Ginger Cream.

Time, about ten or twelve minutes.

1310. One pint and a half of good cream; five ounces of preserved ginger; three tablespoonfuls of the syrup; yolks of six eggs; one ounce of isinglass or gelatine; two ounces of loaf sugar.

Add the yolks of six well-beaten eggs to a pint and a half of cream, three tablespoonfuls of ginger syrup, and the five ounces of preserved ginger minced very fine. Add about two ounces of pounded sugar, and stir the whole when thoroughly mixed over a slow fire for ten or twelve minutes. When sufficiently thick stir in the isinglass previously dissolved and strained, whisk it for about twenty minutes, or until lukewarm, and pour it into a glass dish. When set, lay over the top slices of preserved ginger or crystallized fruit.

Bohemian Cream.

1311. One ounce and a half of isinglass; one pint of cream; half a pint of water; six ounces of sugar; one lemon; one pint of strawberries.

Rub through a sieve a pint of fresh strawberries; add the six ounces of sugar pounded, and the juice of the lemon. Dissolve the isinglass in half a pint of water. Mix these ingredients well together, and set the bowl upon ice, stirring it until it begins to set. Whisk a pint of cream to a light froth, and stir it into the strawberries. Fill the mould, and place it upon ice until served.

Brandy Cream.

Time, about a quarter of an hour in all.

1312. Twenty sweet and twenty bitter almonds; yolks of five eggs; two wineglasses of brandy; one quart of cream; three ounces of loaf sugar; a few spoonfuls of milk.

Boil twenty sweet and twenty bitter almonds blanched and pounded in a few spoonfuls of milk. When cold, stir in the yolks of five eggs well beaten with a spoonful of cream. Add three ounces of loaf sugar pounded and sifted, and two glasses of the best brandy. When thoroughly mixed, pour in a quart of cream, set it over the fire, but do not let it boil; stir one way till it thickens, and pour it into custard cups with a ratafia on the top of each.

Italian Cream.

Time, half an hour.

1313. One pint of thick cream; juice of two lemons; half a glass of white wine; a quarter of an ounce of isinglass; a quarter of a pound of loaf sugar; a teacupful of new milk.

Mix the wine, lemon juice, and sugar well together. Add the cream by degrees, stirring it all the time, and then whisk it for a quarter of an hour. Dissolve the isinglass in a cupful of hot new milk; stir it lukewarm into the other ingredients, and whisk it all together for another quarter of an hour, and then put it into the mould.

Spanish Cream.

Time, until very thick.

1314. Three tablespoonfuls of sifted ground rice; yolks of three eggs; three spoonfuls of water; two of orange-flower water; one pint of cream; two spoonfuls of pounded sugar.

Sift three tablespoonfuls of ground rice; add it to two of pounded sugar, and mix it smooth with the water and orange-flower water. Then stir gradually in a pint of cream, and stir the whole over a clear fire till it is of a proper thickness, then pour it into a glass dish.

Spanish Cream—To Ornament Preserves.

1315. One ounce of isinglass; half a pint of rosewater; yolks of four eggs; three-quarters of a pint of cream; sugar to taste.

Dissolve an ounce of isinglass in half a pint of rosewater. Beat the yolks of four eggs with three-quarters of a pint of cream. Add sugar to taste. Boil it up, pour it into a shallow dish, and when cold turn it out, and cut it into any shape you please, and lay it in rings round different coloured sweetmeats.

Burnt Cream.

Time, to boil, ten minutes.

1316. One pint of cream; peel of half a lemon; a stick of cinnamon; one ounce and a half of sugar; yolks of four eggs.

Boil a pint of cream with the peel of the lemon and the stick of cinnamon. Take it off the fire, and pour it very slowly on the well-beaten yolks of the four eggs, stirring till half cold. Add the sugar pounded and sifted. Take out the spice and lemon peel, pour it into a dish, and when cold strew over it some pounded sugar, and brown it with a salamander.

Imperial Cream.

Time, five minutes to boil the cream.

1317. One quart of cream; peel of one lemon; juice of three, and about eight ounces of loaf sugar.

Boil a quart of cream with the thin peel of one lemon to extract the flavour, and then stir the cream until nearly cold, adding eight ounces of powdered loaf sugar. Strain the juice of three lemons into a glass dish, and pour the cream over it from a jug with a spout, holding it as high as possible, and moving it about to mix it with the juice of the lemons.

Rhenish Cream.

Time, about a quarter of an hour.

1318. One ounce of isinglass; one pint of water; three lemons; four ounces of loaf sugar; yolks of four eggs; half a pint of white wine.

Dissolve an ounce of isinglass in a pint of boiling water, and let it stand till cold; then add the yolks of four well-beaten eggs, the peel of three lemons grated, the juice strained, and four ounces of powdered sugar, with half a pint of white wine. Stir these ingredients together, and boil them slowly until the mixture thickens; then pour it into a mould.

Pistachio Cream.

1319. Half a pound of pistachio-nuts; one spoonful of brandy; yolks of two eggs; one pint and a half of cream; sugar to taste.

Blanch half a pint of pistachio-nuts and pound them to a paste with a spoonful of brandy. Add the paste to a pint and a half of good cream; sweeten it to your taste, and stir it over the fire, until it becomes thick. Pour it into a glass dish, and when cold stick long shreds of pistachio-nuts over the top.

Noyeau Cream.

Time, nearly half an hour.

1320. Two ounces of isinglass; one quart of cream; peel of one, juice of three lemons; a quarter of a pound of loaf sugar; one or two glasses of noyeau.

Dissolve two ounces of isinglass in a small cupful of boiling water with the peel of a lemon cut very thin. When the isinglass is dissolved, and the essence extracted from the peel, strain it into a quart of good cream, stirring it constantly to prevent its curdling; sweeten it with a quarter of a pound of sifted loaf sugar, and add a glass or two of noyeau. Whisk the whole thoroughly together for a few minutes; then pour it into an oiled mould, and set it in ice or a very cold place until well set. Garnish with flowers or fruit.

Chester Cream.

1321. One pint of rich cream; peel of one lemon; a teaspoonful of the juice; one glass of raisin wine; sugar to taste; three ounces of macaroons.

17

Mix the peel of a lemon shred very fine with a pint of very rich cream; squeeze in a teaspoonful of lemon juice, loaf sugar to taste pounded and sifted, and a glass of raisin wine. Whisk the whole to a very strong froth, and lay it on a sieve all night; then put it on a glass dish piled very high, and a border of macaroons round the edge.

Cream à la Vanilla.
Time, ten or twelve minutes, to stir the cream.

1322. One ounce of isinglass; one pint of new milk; a quarter of a pint of cream; one pod of vanilla; five or six ounces of loaf sugar; yolks of eight eggs.

Add a pod of vanilla and five or six ounces of pounded loaf sugar to half a pint of new milk, and a quarter of a pint of cream, and set it over a moderate fire until it is very hot, and sufficiently flavoured with the vanilla. Well beat the yolks of eight eggs, and stir them gradually into the milk and cream; pour the whole into a jug, and stand it in a deep stewpan of boiling water, stirring it with a silver or wooden spoon until it is thick. Then add it to an ounce of isinglass previously dissolved and boiled in the half pint of milk. Mix all well together, and pour it into an oiled mould. Set it on ice, or a very cold place, to set, and then turn it out very carefully on a dish; garnish with flowers, or crystallized fruit. Or make some little vases of Nougat Paste, (moulds may be bought of the shape) and fill them with this cream. Serve them prettily decorated.

Vanilla, or Lemon, Ice Cream.
Time, until boiling hot.

1323. Two drachms of Vanilla or lemon peel; one quart of milk; half a pound of loaf sugar; one pint of cream; yolks of three eggs.

Beat the yolks of three eggs, and add them to a quart of milk: then stir in two drachms of vanilla or lemon peel, half a pound of sifted loaf sugar, and a pint of good cream; set it over a gentle fire, and stir it constantly with a silver spoon until it is *boiling hot*, then take out the lemon peel, *or vanilla*, and when cold freeze it.

Pineapple Ice Cream.
Time, about ten minutes.

1324. One quart of milk; six ounces of sugar; five eggs; pineapple juice.

Set a quart of milk over the fire to boil, stir it occasionally; well beat five eggs, and stir them gradually into the boiling milk, adding six ounces of pounded sugar, stir it for five or six minutes, and then set it to cool. Bruise a pineapple, strain the juice, add it to the cream when cool, and freeze it.

Spring Cream.
Time, about twenty minutes.

1325. Two dozen sticks of rhubarb; peel of one lemon; two cloves; a piece of cinnamon; and as much moist sugar as will sweeten it; two ounces of isinglass.

Clean the rhubarb, cut it into pieces, and put it into a stewpan with the peel of a lemon grated, two cloves, a piece of cinnamon, and as much good moist sugar as will sweeten it. Set it over the fire, and reduce it to a marmalade, pass it through a hair sieve, and add to it a pint of good thick cream. Serve it in a deep dish. If wanted in a shape, dissolve the isinglass in a little hot water, and strain it when nearly cold to the cream, pour it into a mould, and when perfectly set turn it out on a dish.

Barley Cream.
Time, about fifteen minutes to boil the barley.

1326. A quarter of a pint of pearl barley; a pint and a half of milk and water; one quart of cream; six eggs; one tablespoonful of flour; two teaspoonfuls of orange flower water; sugar to taste.

Boil a quarter of a pint of pearl barley in milk and water till tender; strain off the liquor, and put the barley into a quart of cream. Let it boil slightly; then beat up the whites of five eggs, and the yolk of one with a tablespoonful of flour, and two teaspoonfuls of orange-flower water.

Remove the cream from the fire, mix the eggs in by degrees, and set the whole over the fire to thicken. Sweeten to taste, and pour it into cups for use.

German Cream.
1327. One pint of cream; six ounces of loaf sugar; peel of half a lemon, and the juice of two; one wineglass of brandy.

Boil a pint of cream with six ounces of loaf sugar, and the peel of half a lemon cut thin. As soon as it boils, take it off the fire, and let it stand till nearly cold; then add the juice of two lemons, and a wineglass of brandy. Pour the whole from one jug to another quickly for a quarter of an hour, and it will be ready to serve. This cream should be made at *least* twelve hours before it is served.

Almond Cream.
1328. Five ounces of sweet almonds; six bitter almonds; one quart of cream; three ounces of loaf sugar; juice of two large lemons.

Blanch and pound five ounces of sweet, and six bitter almonds, and stir the paste into a quart of cream, sweetened with three ounces of loaf sugar, mixed with the strained juice of two large lemons. Whisk the whole to a stiff froth, and lay it on a sieve to drain as the froth rises; fill glasses with the drained liquor, and pile the froth on the top.

Spongecake Cream.

1329. Nine small spongecakes; a glass of brandy; a quarter of a pint of sherry; raspberry jam; a little boiled custard.

Cut some small spongecakes in two, and place them at the bottom and sides of a glass dish; pour half the quantity of the wine and brandy over them, and over the wine and brandy put some raspberry jelly, or raspberry jam made warm and strained through a sieve. Cover the jelly with another layer of sliced cakes, and pour the remainder of the wine and brandy on them. Have ready rather more than half a pint of cold boiled custard, and when ready to serve, pour it over the top, and arrange a few rings of candied fruit, or a few ratafias on the top.

Crème à la Comtesse.

Time, six or seven minutes.

1330. Twenty chestnuts; half a pint of cream; half a pint of milk; one ounce of isinglass; nine bitter almonds; a quarter of a pound of loaf sugar; peel of half a large lemon; a glass of curaçoa or maraschino.

Blanch about twenty chestnuts, throw them into cold water as the peel is removed, pound them in a mortar, and press them through a hair sieve into half a pint of good cream. Dissolve an ounce of isinglass in half a pint of milk, stir into it eight or nine bitter almonds blanched and bruised, the peel of a lemon, and a quarter of a pound of sifted loaf sugar. Set it over a gentle fire, to simmer for six or seven minutes, and when the milk is sufficiently flavoured, strain and press it through a piece of muslin, and add the glass of maraschino or curaçoa. Then stir it gradually to the chestnuts and cream, beat the whole well together, and pour it into a mould rubbed over with oil.

Sicilian Cream.

1331. One pint of cream; one glass of noyeau, or maraschino; two ounces of isinglass; five ounces of sugar.

Whip a pint of rich cream until it becomes a froth, add to it a glass of noyeau or maraschino, five ounces of sugar rolled and sifted, with two ounces of clarified isinglass. Mix all lightly and thoroughly together, and fill a mould, put it in a cool place until quite firm, or on ice, and, when served, ornament it with dried cherries, &c.

Snow Cream.

1332. One quart of cream; whites of three eggs; two glasses of raisin wine; two ounces of sugar; the peel of half a lemon.

Well beat the whites of three eggs, and put to them a quart of cream; stir them well together, and add the glass of raisin wine, sugar, and lemon peel. Whip all together to a froth, remove the peel, and serve it in a glass dish.

Housewife's Cream.

1333. Half a pint of cream; quarter of a pint of sherry; three ounces of sugar; peel and juice of one lemon.

Cut the peel of lemon into small pieces; mix the cream, wine, powdered white sugar, peel and juice of lemon together, whisking it until quite thick. Put into glasses and keep cool. This cream is better made the day before it is required.

Fruit Ice Creams.

Time, thirty-five minutes to freeze.

1334. To every pint of juice allow one pint of cream; a quarter of a pound of lump sugar; and two ounces and a half of isinglass.

Strip the fruit from some ripe currants, raspberries, or any other fruit; put them into a bowl, strew over them half the sugar sifted, bruise them with a spoon, and let them stand for two hours to draw out the juice, then press it through a sieve with a wooden spoon, and add the remainder of the sugar. Dissolve half an ounce of isinglass for every pint of juice, and whisk it with the cream for eight or ten minutes, then stir it into the juice, and whisk all well together.

Put it into the freezing-pot, and stir it together often that the whole may be thoroughly frozen, then fill a mould, put on the lid, plunge it into the ice pot, cover it over with a wet cloth and ice, and let it remain until served; then turn it out on a dish. The isinglass will not be required if served in glasses or ice plates.

Holwell Cream.

1335. One pint of thick cream; one lemon; sugar to taste; one teaspoonful of ground rice; one spongecake.

Sweeten to taste a pint of thick cream, add to it the peel of a lemon pared thin, and let it boil slowly. Mix a teaspoonful of ground rice with a little cream, until it is

Creams—Jellies and Sweet Dishes.

quite smooth, add the juice of the lemon to it, mix it with the boiled cream, and let it boil again for a few minutes. Cut a spongecake in slices, lay them in a glass dish, and pour the cream over them.

Apple Cheese and Cream.

1336. An equal weight of apples and sugar; one pint of cream, or new milk; oiks of two eggs; peel and juice of one lemon; a little cinnamon; and a spoonful of orange-flower water.

Boil the sugar in water, and as the scum rises, carefully take it off. When clear, put in the weight of the sugar in apples pared, cored, and cut into quarters, with the juice of a lemon and the peel cut very fine. Set the stewpan over a clear fire, and stew it until it is boiled to a thick jam. Put it into a mould, and when cold turn it out.

Add the yolks of two beaten eggs to a pint of cream or new milk, a stick of cinnamon, a spoonful of orange-flower water, and the thin peel of a lemon; boil it for a few minutes, stirring it constantly, and when cold, pour it round the apple cheese.

Peach Cream Ice.

1337. Twelve peaches; six ounces of sugar; one pint of scalding cream.

Pare and stone twelve ripe peaches, scald them over a clear fire, and beat them to a pulp in a mortar; then mix with them six ounces of loaf sugar pounded and sifted, and a pint of scalding cream. Stir all thoroughly together, and rub it through a sieve; put it into a tin ice-mould that has a cover, and set it in the ice-pail; when the cream grows thick round the edges of the mould, stir it well, and set it in again till it becomes thick, then take it out of the tin mould, and place it in the shape it is intended to be turned out of, put on the lid, and set it in the ice

again for four or five hours before it is to be turned out.

Garnish it with preserved peaches.

Spinach Cream.

1338. Yolks of nine eggs; one pint of thick cream; one pint of milk; seven ounces of loaf sugar pounded; a small teacupful of spinach juice; two ounces of preserved orange; or two ounces of citron; one stick of cinnamon.

Whisk the yolks of nine eggs, with seven ounces of loaf sugar pounded; then add a pint of thick cream, and a pint of new milk, with a stick of cinnamon. When all the ingredients are well mixed together, stir in a small teacupful of spinach juice, put the mixture into a stewpan, and stir it one way over a clear fire until it is *very* thick. Lay at the bottom of a glass dish some slices of preserved orange, or about two ounces of citron, cut very thin. Pour the warm cream over the preserve, and put it in a cold place until the next day. Ornament it with shreds of preserved orange or citron.

Chantilly Basket, with Whipped Strawberry Cream and Fruit.

1339. Sixty-two macaroons; some melted barley-sugar; strawberry cream; and twenty-four strawberries.

Take any tin mould that will serve to form a basket, and rub it over with fresh butter to prevent the candy sticking to it. Dip the cakes in the barley-sugar, which must be kept hot, and fasten them together with it, each row of cakes being cold and firm before the next is put on; then take it from the mould and keep it in a dry place until wanted. Fill it with a whipped strawberry cream which has been drained on a sieve the preceding day, and put into the whip ripe strawberries.

JELLIES AND SWEET DISHES.

To Prepare Cochineal to Colour Red or Pink.

1340. One ounce of powdered cochineal; one ounce of cream of tartar; two drachms of alum; half a pint of water.

Take an ounce of powdered cochineal, an ounce of cream of tartar, and two drachms of alum. Put these ingredients into a saucepan with half a pint of water. When it boils take it from the fire and let it cool, pour it off into a bottle as free from sediment as possible.

To keep cochineal any length of time, boil an ounce of it (finely powdered) in three-quarters of a pint of water until reduced to half; then add to it rock-alum and cream of tartar, of each half an ounce (pounded fine). Boil them together for a short time, then strain it. When cold, bottle it. If to be kept any *great* length of time, boil an ounce of loaf sugar with it.

To Clarify Isinglass.

1341. One ounce of isinglass; half a pint of water.

Break an ounce of isinglass small, pour over it half a pint of boiling water, and set it over a gentle heat to dissolve. When

Strawberry Acid for Jelly.

Time, to stand, twenty-four hours.

1342. Twelve pounds of strawberries; three quarts of spring water; five ounces of tartaric acid; one pound and a half of loaf sugar to each pint of strawberry juice.

Put twelve pounds of ripe strawberries into a pan, and pour over them three quarts of spring water previously acidulated with five ounces of tartaric acid. Let them remain twenty-four hours, and then strain them without *bruising* the fruit. To each pint of strained liquor add a pound and a half of powdered loaf sugar; stir it frequently until it is dissolved, and then bottle it for use. This quantity fills twelve bottles, and the process must be cold.

To make one quart of jelly, take one bottle of the syrup, half an ounce of isinglass, or half an ounce of gelatine dissolved in half a pint of water; strain it off, and add it to the syrup. Mix all well together, and pour it into a jelly mould.

The Foundation of all Jelly.

1343. One shilling packet of Nelson's gelatine; half a pint of cold water; one pint of hot water; the rind of five lemons; one small stick of cinnamon; six cloves; juice of six lemons; half a pint of sherry; a quarter of a pound of loaf sugar; whites of five eggs.

Take a packet of gelatine, dissolve it in half a pint of cold water, and then add a pint of hot water, the rind of five lemons without the pith, a small stick of cinnamon, the cloves, the juice of the lemons, the sherry, and the loaf sugar. When done, clarify it with the shells and whites of five eggs.

If you wish to make any other kind of jelly *omit the sherry*, and add for instance orange juice for orange jelly, or the juice of strawberries, cherries, pineapple, or any other fruit. The jelly takes its name from its flavouring. No jelly of several colours should be set warm, as the different colours run and weaken it extremely.

Calf's Feet Stock for Jellies.

1344. Three calf's feet; four quarts of water; half an ounce of isinglass; whites and shells of six eggs.

Take three calf's feet thoroughly cleaned, split them down the middle, and take all the fat from the claws. Put them into a stewpan with four quarts of cold spring water, set it over a clear fire, and when it boils skim it well, and let it simmer slowly until reduced to rather more than two quarts, then strain it through a hair sieve and set it to cool. When cold, put it into another stewpan with the whites and shells of six eggs, stir it well together, and set it over the fire to become gradually hot, but do not stir it after it begins to heat. Let it boil for nine or ten minutes. Pour in a cupful of cold water; let it boil again, and then set it near the fire covered over for half an hour. Dip the jelly-bag into boiling water, squeeze it dry, and strain the stock through it until perfectly clear. It will then be fit for use.

Calf's Feet Jelly.

Time, to boil the feet, until reduced to one quart; to reboil the jelly, a quarter of an hour.

1345. Two calf's feet; two quarts of water; half a pound of loaf sugar; one pint of white wine; a wineglass of brandy; four lemons; whites of four eggs.

Cut two feet in small pieces after they have been well cleaned and the hair taken off. Stew them very gently in two quarts of water until it is reduced to one quart. When cold, take off the fat and remove the jelly from the sediment. Put it into a saucepan with half a pound of loaf sugar, a pint of white wine, with a wineglass of brandy in it, four lemons with the peel rubbed on the sugar, the whites of four eggs well beaten and their shells broken. Put the saucepan on the fire, but do not stir the jelly after it begins to warm. Let it boil a quarter of an hour after it rises to a head; then cover it close, and let it stand about half an hour; after which, pour it through a jelly-bag, first dipping the bag in hot water to prevent waste, and squeezing it quite dry. Pour the jelly through and through until clear, then put it into the mould.

Jelly from Cowheels.

Time, to boil the cowheels, seven hours, or until reduced to three pints; boil five minutes after the wine is added.

1346. Two cowheels; one gallon of water; one pint of white wine; half a pound of loaf sugar; juice of five, peel of four lemons; whites of six eggs.

Put two thoroughly clean cowheels into a stewpan with a gallon of spring water, and let it boil until reduced to three pints. When cold, skim off the cake of fat, and take the jelly carefully from the sediment at the bottom; put the jelly into a stewpan with the white wine, loaf sugar, and the

Juice of the lemons. Beat up the whites of six eggs, throw them into the jelly; stir it all together, and let it boil five minutes. Then pour it into a jelly-bag, and let it run on the peels of four lemons placed in the basin the jelly runs into, as the peel will give a fine flavour and colour. If not perfectly clear, run it through again.

Pour it into a mould, and turn it out the next day.

Isinglass Jelly.

Time, about three-quarters of an hour.

1347. One ounce of isinglass; one pint of water; half a pint of white wine; juice of one large lemon, peel of half; loaf sugar to taste; whites of four eggs.

Simmer one ounce of isinglass for half an hour in a pint of water; then add half a pint of white wine, the peel of half a lemon, and the juice of one, and sweeten to taste with loaf sugar.

Beat the whites of four eggs to a very strong froth, and add them to the other ingredients with their shells broken, stirring them well in. Boil the whole from ten to fifteen minutes, keeping the mixture stirred all the time; then strain it through a jelly-bag into the mould, previously soaked in cold water or brushed over with oil.

Strawberry Jelly.

Time, twenty to twenty-five minutes.

1348. One quart of scarlet strawberries; three-quarters of a pound of loaf sugar; one ounce and a half of isinglass; juice of one lemon; half a pint of red currant jelly.

Boil three-quarters of a pound of loaf sugar in one pint of water for about twenty or twenty-five minutes; pour it over a quart of scarlet strawberries, and let them stand all night. Clarify an ounce and a half of isinglass in a pint of water. Drain the syrup from the fruit, adding the melted currant jelly and the juice of a lemon. When the isinglass is nearly cold mix all together, adding more sugar if required. Put it into a mould, and place the mould in ice.

Lemon Jelly.

Time, altogether, one hour.

1349. Peel of four lemons, juice of six; three glasses of sherry; three-quarters of a pound of loaf sugar; one ounce and a half of isinglass; one pint of spring water.

Steep the thin peel of four lemons in half a pint of boiling water until strongly flavoured with the peel. Put the sugar pounded, with the isinglass into a stewpan, and boil it slowly for about a quarter of an hour or twenty minutes; then add the strained lemon juice and the water from the peel. Let it just boil up; skim it well; add the wine, and strain it until quite clear.

Orange Jelly.

Time, until it almost candies.

1350. Peel of two Seville, two China oranges, and two lemons; juice of three of each; a quarter of a pound of loaf sugar; a quarter of a pint of water; two ounces of isinglass.

Grate the rinds of the Seville, China oranges, and lemons; squeeze the juice of three of each; strain it, and add the juice to the sugar and the water, and boil it until it almost candies. Have ready a quart of isinglass jelly made with two ounces of isinglass; put to it the syrup, and boil it once up. Strain off the jelly, and let it stand to settle before it is put into the mould.

Open Jelly, with Whipped Cream.

Time, three-quarters of an hour.

1351. One pint and a half of clear jelly; three-quarters of a pint of cream; one glass of white wine; sugar to taste.

Prepare a pint and a half of nicely flavoured and clear isinglass or calf's foot jelly. Have ready an open mould, previously soaked for an hour in cold water; fill it with the jelly, and put it in a cold place to set. When firm, turn it carefully out on a dish, and pile about three-quarters of a pint of whipped cream in the centre, flavoured with a glass of white wine, and sugar to taste.

Apple Jelly in a Mould.

Time, rather more than one hour.

1352. Apples; ten ounces of sugar to every pound of pulp; peel of half a lemon.

Pare and core some fine boiling apples; cut them into slices, and boil them with a little water to a pulp. Boil the sugar with a little water to a thick syrup; add it to the apple pulp, with the peel of half a large lemon grated. Put the whole over a clear fire, and boil it for about twenty minutes or until the apples are a thick marmalade, stirring it all the time.

Then put it into a mould which has been previously soaked in cold water. When cold and set, turn the jelly out on a glass dish; stick blanched almonds over it in any form you please, and pour a little good custard round it.

If for dessert, serve it up without the custard and almonds.

Clear Apple Jelly.

Time, one hour and a half to boil the apples; a quarter of an hour the jelly.

1353. Two dozen and a half of pippins;

one quart of spring water to every pint of juice; three-quarters of a pound of loaf sugar; ten ounces of isinglass; the peel of one small lemon.

Pare, core, and boil two dozen and a half of pippins in a pint and a half of water with the peel of a small lemon. When they are tender, pour the juice from the pippins and strain it through a jelly-bag; then put to the strained juice the sugar pounded, and the isinglass, boiled till dissolved in half a pint of water. Boil the whole in a very clean stewpan for about fifteen minutes, and then pour it into moulds.

Riband Jelly—or Jelly of Two Colours.

Time, three-quarters of an hour to make the jelly.

1354. One quart of calf's foot jelly; a few drops of prepared cochineal.

Have ready a quart of calf's foot jelly, flavoured in any way that may be preferred, leaving one pint of a pale colour, and adding a few drops of prepared cochineal to colour the remainder a bright red. Pour a small quantity of the red into a mould previously soaked in cold water. Let this set; then pour in a small quantity of the pale jelly, and repeat this until the mould is full, taking care that each layer is perfectly firm before pouring it on the other. Put it in a cold place, and the next day turn it out; or the mould may be partly filled with the yellow jelly, and when thoroughly set, filled up with the pink.

Riband jelly and jelly of two colours can be made in any pretty fancy mould (there are many to be had for the purpose), as in the coloured plates of jelly of two colours and riband jelly. Of course one colour must be always firm before the other is put in. In order to hasten the operation it is best to *ice* the jelly each time, by placing the mould in an ice-pail.

Noyeau Jelly with Almonds.

Time, ten minutes.

1355. Two ounces of gelatine; eight lemons; peel of one; a quarter of a pint of noyeau; a quarter of a pint of brandy; a quarter of a pint of sherry; whites of four eggs; a pint and a half of water; three ounces of almonds; sugar to taste.

Soak the gelatine for ten minutes in half a pint of filtered water, then dissolve it in another half pint of water over a gentle fire, stirring it the whole time. When thoroughly dissolved, add the strained juice of the lemons, the peel of one large one cut very thin, the noyeau, brandy, and sherry, with pounded white sugar to taste, half a pint more water and the whites and shells of the eggs. Let it just boil up, and then draw it to the side of the fire, cover it over and let it stand five minutes. Blanch the almonds, and as they are blanched throw them into cold water to preserve their colour, and then cut them into long thin shreds. Soak a mould in cold water for two or three hours, or brush it over with salad oil, and let it drain. Strain the jelly until perfectly clear, and as it cools throw in the shreds of almonds, fill the mould, and set it in a cold place, or in ice, and when turned out surround it with whipped cream.

French Jelly.

1356. One quart of calf's foot or clear isinglass jelly; some ripe fruit; or any preserved, or brandy cherries.

Have ready one quart of *very clear* jelly; select ripe and nice-looking fruit, and pick off the stalks; commence by putting some jelly at the bottom of a mould, and let it remain about two hours to harden, then arrange some fruit according to taste round the edge of the mould. If currants, lay them in as they come from the tree, on their stalks, and pour in more jelly to make the fruit adhere, and let that layer also harden, then add more fruit and jelly until the mould is full. If peaches, apples, apricots, &c., are used, they are better boiled first in a small quantity of syrup, but strawberries, grapes, cherries, or currants may be put in uncooked. An extremely pretty jelly may be made from *preserved* fruits, or brandy cherries. It may be garnished with any fruit, or an open jelly may have some strawberries piled in the centre, or a whipped cream piled up, with strawberries stuck in it, which has a very good effect.

Rice Jelly.

Time, five minutes when it boils.

1357. Half a pound of rice flour; milk or cream enough to fill a mould; peel of one lemon; two ounces of loaf sugar; a piece of butter the size of a walnut; two ounces of clarified isinglass.

To half a pound of rice flour add sufficient milk or cream to fill a mould. Rub the peel of a lemon on the sugar, and add a piece of butter the size of a walnut, put it on the stove, continue stirring it, and let it boil five minutes. Add half an ounce of clarified isinglass, put it into a mould on ice, or on the cellar floor. Melted currant jelly or any syrup may be poured round it when sent to table.

Punch Jelly.

Time, five minutes.

1358. Two ounces and a half of isinglass; a pint and a half of water; two pounds and a quarter of loaf sugar; the peel of a large lemon, and juice of two; two large wine-glasses of brandy; the same of rum.

Dissolve in a pint and a half of water two ounces of isinglass, with the peel of one large lemon cut thin; put the juice of the lemons and two pounds of loaf sugar to the two wineglasses of brandy and the same of rum, strain the water in which the isinglass has been dissolved upon the lemon juice and spirits, place it over the fire to become hot, but do not allow it to boil; let it stand a few minutes to settle, strain it through a fine hair sieve into the mould, and turn it out the next day.

Italian Jelly.

1359. One pint and a half of clear isinglass jelly; some very stiff blancmange.

Half fill a mould with clear isinglass jelly, and when it is set, lay round it a wreath of very stiff blancmange cut out with a cutter in small rounds. Then fill up the mould with jelly nearly cold, and put it into ice.

Oranges Filled with Jelly.

1360. Some large China oranges, and some jelly of two colours.

With the point of a small knife cut out from the top of each orange a round about the size of a shilling; then, with the small end of a teaspoon, empty the pulp from them, taking care not to break the rinds. Throw them into cold water. Make jelly of the juice pressed from the pulp, and strained quite clear. Colour one half a bright rose colour with prepared cochineal, leaving the other very pale. When the jelly is nearly cold, drain and wipe the oranges, and fill them with alternate stripes of the different-coloured jelly. Each colour being allowed to get quite cold before the other is poured in. When they are perfectly cold, cut them into quarters *with a very sharp* knife, and arrange them tastefully on a dish, with sprigs of myrtle between them.

Gaufres.

1361. Two eggs; one pint of warm milk; two ounces of butter; a little nutmeg; sugar to taste; one spoonful of yeast; sufficient flour to make a thick batter.

Mix two well-beaten eggs with a pint of warm milk, two ounces of butter, a little grated nutmeg and pounded loaf sugar to taste, add sufficient flour to make a smooth paste or thick batter, and put in a spoonful of yeast. Set it to rise about two hours. Then work it lightly, and let it stand half an hour. Put about two spoonfuls of the mixture into the gaufring-irons, having previously made them hot, and rubbed them over with butter; close the irons, and bake the gaufres for a few minutes. When done of a light colour, turn them out, and sift over them pounded sugar and cinnamon mixed together.

Almond Gaufres.

1362. Six ounces of almonds; three ounces of pounded sugar; one ounce of flour; two eggs; a tiny pinch of salt; a little lemon flavouring.

Blanch the almonds and shred them very fine; then mix them in a bowl with the sugar, flour, and flavouring, the salt, and well-beat up eggs. Heat a baking sheet in the oven, rub it over with white wax. Spread the gaufre mixture thinly over it with a fork. Put it in the oven, which must not be very hot. When half done, take the sheet out, and with a round tin cutter stamp out as many gaufres as the sheet will admit, and put them back again in the oven to *just* colour them. Then take them out, and form them into small cornucopiæ. This must be done as quickly as possible, as if they get cold they will break in doing, being very brittle.

These tiny horns can be filled with any preserve you please; or being first covered with white of egg and sugar, may be dipped in finely-chopped pistachio-nut or angelica, and then dried before the fire; or they may be filled with whipped cream.

Dominoes.

Time, half an hour.

1363. Four eggs; half a pound of loaf sugar; seven ounces of flour; essence of lemon or almonds; coloured icing.

Beat the yolks of four eggs for ten minutes with half a pound of powdered loaf sugar, and seven ounces of flour; whisk the whites of the eggs to a *high* froth, flavour them with essence of lemon; add them to the yolks, stir all gently together, and put the mixture into a shallow square tin lined with buttered paper, and bake it in a quick oven for half an hour. When done, take it from the tin, cut it with a sharp knife into oblong pieces the shape of a domino. Cover them with icing, smooth it over, and drop small spots on each to resemble dominoes, of icing coloured with chocolate or prepared cochineal. Dry the icing in a cool oven, and serve.

Custard with Jelly.

1364. One pint of milk; three peach leaves; five eggs; sugar to taste; peel of half a lemon.

Put into a delicately-clean saucepan a pint of milk, three peach leaves, sugar to taste, and the peel of a small lemon cut thin. When it boils pour it out; whisk the whites and yolks of five eggs, and stir them gradually to the milk, pour it into the stewpan and stir it over the fire one way until it thickens, or put it into a jug with a lip, and stand the jug in a saucepan of boiling water until the custard is sufficiently thick. When cool, pour it into custard glasses, and put a spoonful of clear jelly on some, and of dark coloured jelly on the others. Place the cups on a dish and serve.

Gateau de Pommes.

Time, three-quarters of an hour.

1365. One pound of sugar; one pint of water; two pounds of apples; juice and peel of one large lemon; some rich custard.

Boil one pound of sugar in a pint of water until the water has evaporated, then add two pounds of apples pared and cored, the juice of a large lemon, and the peel grated. Boil all together till quite stiff, then put it into a mould, and when cold turn it out, and serve it with rich custard round it.

Apple Hedgehog.

1366. Fifteen or sixteen large apples; four or five pounds of boiling apples for marmalade; three ounces of loaf sugar; whites of three eggs; some apricot or strawberry jam; half a pound of sweet almonds; half a pint of water; half a pound of sugar for the syrup.

Pare and core fifteen or sixteen large apples, make a syrup with half a pint of water and half a pound of sugar, and simmer the apples until tolerably tender; drain them, and fill the part from which the core was taken with apricot or strawberry jam, then arrange them on a dish in the form of a hedgehog. Stew the boiling apples down to a smooth dry marmalade and fill the spaces between the apples with it, covering it also entirely over them. Whisk the whites of three eggs and three ounces of sifted loaf sugar to a solid froth, spread it evenly over the hedgehog, and sift sugar over it. Blanch and cut into long spikes half a pound of sweet almonds, and stick them thickly over the surface; place the dish in a moderate oven to slightly colour the almonds, and make the apples hot through.

Apples and Rice.

Time, twenty minutes, to boil the rice.

1367. Twelve apples; three ounces of butter; peel of one large lemon; four ounces of pounded loaf sugar; one quart of milk; six or seven ounces of rice; a very little powdered cinnamon; and some apricot jam.

Divide the apples in halves, take out the cores, and pare them; spread them on a stewpan *well* buttered, strew over them the lemon peel grated, and part of the sugar pounded; put the lid on the stewpan and bake the apples without allowing them to take any colour. Boil the rice in a quart of milk, and the remainder of the sugar, butter, and cinnamon. When thoroughly done, mix it well up with a spoon, and place it in the centre of a dish in the form of a dome. Arrange the apples neatly upon this, cover them with apricot jam, and serve quite hot.

Apple de Par.

1368. One pound of loaf sugar; half a pint of water; peel and juice of one lemon; a pound and a half of apples.

To a pound of loaf sugar add half a pint of cold water, and the peel of a lemon cut thin; let it boil about ten or fifteen minutes. Take out the peel and put in a pound and a half of apples cut in slices and the juice of the lemon. When they have boiled until soft enough to pulp, press them through a hair sieve, put them back into the stewpan, and let them boil until quite stiff, stirring all the time; then put it into small moulds, or into a soup plate, and cut it in slices of any form you please for dessert.

If not boiled so stiff, it may be turned out of teacups, and custard poured over it as a second course dish.

Lemon Floating Island.

1369. Yolks of twelve eggs; juice of four lemons; loaf sugar to taste.

Beat the yolks of twelve eggs; add to them the juice of four lemons strained, and loaf sugar to taste. Set the mixture over a chafing dish of coals, or a stove, stir it until it becomes thick, then pour it into a dish. Whisk the whites of the eggs to a high froth, and pile it on the cream, previously placed in a glass dish.

Vanilla Floating Island.

1370. One quart of rich milk, or a pint and a half of milk and a quarter of a pint of cream; two tablespoonfuls of loaf sugar; yolks and whites of six eggs; flavouring of vanilla.

Put a quart of rich milk, or a pint and a

half, with a quarter of a pint of cream, into a clean stewpan; put it over a clear fire, and when it boils, stir in two tablespoonfuls of pounded sugar, the beaten yolks of six eggs, and a flavouring of vanilla; stir it constantly until it is a thick custard; then pour it into a deep glass dish, and pile the whites of the eggs, whisked to a stiff froth, on the top of the custard, with small pieces of any bright jelly here and there; or ornament it as you please.

Gooseberry Fool.

1371. Two quarts of gooseberries; one quart of water; sugar to taste; two quarts of new milk; yolks of four eggs; a little grated nutmeg.

Put two quarts of gooseberries into a stewpan with a quart of water; when they begin to turn yellow and swell, drain the water from them and press them with the back of a spoon through a colander, sweeten them to your taste, and set them to cool. Put two quarts of milk over the fire beaten up with the yolks of four eggs, and a little grated nutmeg; stir it over the fire until it begins to simmer, then take it off, and stir it gradually into the cold gooseberries, let it stand until cold, and serve it. The eggs may be left out and milk only may be used. Half this quantity makes a good dishful.

Rice Snow Balls.

Time, twenty minutes, to boil the rice.

1372. A quarter of a pound of Carolina rice; one pint and a half of new milk; two ounces of loaf sugar; two ounces of sweet almonds; and some preserve or marmalade.

Put a quarter of a pound of rice into a stewpan with a pint and a half of new milk, two ounces of pounded sugar and two ounces of sweet almonds blanched and minced fine, and boil it until the rice is tender. Dip some small cups into cold water, fill them with the rice, and set them to become cold; turn them out on a dish, arrange a border of preserve or marmalade all round them, and pour a little rich cream into the centre, if you have it.

Apple Snow.

Time, one hour.

1373. Eight apples; half a pound of sugar; juice of one lemon; whites of three eggs.

Add to the pulp of eight baked apples half a pound of powdered sugar, the juice of one lemon, and the whites of three eggs; whisk the whole together for one hour. Put some cream or custard in a dish, and drop the whisked froth on it in large flakes. A pinch of alum makes the whisk firmer.

Snow.

1374. Half an ounce of isinglass; half a pint of soft spring water; two ounces of sugar; one large, or two small lemons; whites of two eggs.

Dissolve half an ounce of isinglass in half a pint of soft water, rub two ounces of sugar on one large or two small lemons, strain the isinglass and water on the sugar, whisk it together, and add the juice of the lemon by degrees; then add the whites of two eggs well beaten. Whisk it all together until it becomes thick and white; then put it into the mould.

Œufs a la Neige, or Snow Eggs.

1375. Six or eight eggs; one quart of milk; some custard made from the yolks and the milk; some sugar.

Divide the yolks from the whites of six or eight eggs, and whisk the whites with a little pounded sugar until they are a stiff froth. Put a quart of milk slightly sweetened over the fire in a stewpan, and when it boils put in the egg froth in a tablespoon, and when set on one side, turn it on the other. When all are done, drain the milk they were boiled in from the eggs, and make it into a custard by adding the yolks well beaten, a little sugar if required, and any flavouring you like. When cold, pour it into a glass dish, place the eggs on the top, and either serve them white, or sprinkle over them a few coloured sugar plums, and serve.

Green Caps.

1376. Twelve large green codlings; whites of six eggs; pounded loaf sugar; and some custard.

Take twelve large green apples, green them as for preserving, and put them on a tin plate or dish; whisk the white of eggs to a *very* stiff froth, rub them over with it, sift loaf sugar over them, and put them in the oven until they look bright and sparkle like frost; then take them out and arrange them carefully in the dish you intend to serve them on, pour some good custard round them, and stick a flower on every apple.

Frosted Pippins.

Time, half an hour.

1377. Twelve large pippins; whites of three eggs; lemon peel; pounded sugar.

Divide twelve pippins, take out the cores, and place them close together on a tin, with the flat side downwards. Whisk the white of egg quite firm, spread it over them, then strew some lemon peel cut very thin and in shreds, and sift double-refined sugar over the whole. Bake them half an hour, and then place them on a hot dish, and serve them quickly.

Rice and Pears.
Time, one hour and a half.

1378. One breakfast cup and a half of rice ; one pint of milk ; a large tablespoonful of sugar ; three eggs ; a little cinnamon and nutmeg ; baked pears.

Boil the rice till tender in the milk, then put in the cinnamon, sugar, and nutmeg. Take it up, let it get nearly cold, beat the eggs well, and mix them with the rice. Butter a mould, put the rice in, tie it down tightly in a floured cloth, and let it boil for an hour. Turn it out ; lay round it baked pears. Garnish it with slices of lemon stuck into the rice.

Flanc of Apricots or Peaches—Entremets.

Time, about twenty minutes to bake the flanc ; ten minutes to simmer the fruit.

1379 About three-quarters of a pound of short crust ; ten ounces of loaf sugar ; three-quarters of a pint of water ; peel of a lemon; ten or twelve apricots, or peaches.

Make about three-quarters of a pound of good short crust. Well butter the inside of a mould, and press the paste round it to take the form. Pinch the paste that rises above with the paste pinchers, and fill the case with flour. Put it in a moderate oven for a quarter of an hour, then take out the flour, carefully remove the paste from the mould, and put it back in the oven to dry and colour. Boil ten ounces of loaf sugar pounded, with three-quarters of a pint of water, and the thin peel of a lemon until it makes a nice syrup. Take out the stones from the fruit, and simmer the apricots in the syrup until tender. Serve them in the case.

A Charlotte de Pomme.

Time, three-quarters of an hour to one hour.

1380. The crumb of a stale loaf; apple marmalade ; apricot jam.

Butter a plain mould, and line it with thin slices of the crumb of a stale loaf dipped into clarified butter, joining each slice neatly to prevent the syrup from escaping, which would spoil the appearance of the Charlotte when done. Then fill the mould with apple marmalade and apricot jam ; cover the top with slices of bread dipped into butter, and on the top of the bread put a plate with a weight on it. Set the mould in a quick oven from three-quarters of an hour to one hour, according to the size. Turn it out with care, having drained any butter from it before it is taken from the mould. Sift loaf sugar over it, or cover it with clear jelly, and serve it hot.

Swiss Apple Charlotte.
Time, fifty minutes.

1381. Ten or twelve apples ; bread and butter ; a quarter of a pound of moist sugar; two lemons.

Take the crust from a stale loaf, and cut slices of bread and butter from the crumb. Butter the inside of a pie-dish, and line it with the bread ; then put in a layer of apples pared, cored, and cut into slices. Strew over them some lemon peel minced very fine, and some sugar ; then slices of bread and butter, then apples, lemon peel and sugar, until the dish is full. Squeeze over the whole the juice of two lemons, and cover it with the bread crusts and the peel of the apples, to prevent its burning, or browning. Bake it for about fifty minutes in a quick oven, and when done, take off the crusts and apple peels, and turn it out on the dish carefully.

A Charlotte à la Parisienne.
Time, till the icing is dry.

1382. One Savoy cake; pot of preserve; five ounces of loaf sugar ; whites of four eggs.

Cut a Savoy cake horizontally into rather thin slices ; cover each slice with any preserve preferred, and replace the slices in their original form. Whisk the whites of four eggs with five ounces of sifted loaf sugar to a fine froth, and spread it smoothly over the cake. Sift finely powdered sugar over the icing in every part, and put it into a slack oven to dry the icing.

A Charlotte Russe.—Entremets.
Time, to set, six minutes.

1383. Some Savoy biscuits; three-quarters of a pint of good cream ; rather more than half an ounce of isinglass; two dessertspoonfuls of curaçoa, or vanilla ; one ounce of loaf sugar ; a large slice of spongecake ; one egg.

Take as many Savoy biscuits as will cover the inside of a mould ; lightly moisten the edges with the beaten white of an egg, and place them upright all round the sides of the mould, slightly over each other, or sufficiently close to prevent the cream from escaping. Arrange them at the bottom of the mould in a star, or rosette, taking care that it is well covered, and then set it in the oven for five or six minutes to dry. Whisk the cream with the curaçoa, or wine, the isinglass dissolved, and loaf sugar to taste. When sufficiently firm, fill the inside of the Charlotte Russe, and place over it a slice of spongecake, or of bread cut the same shape and size. Cover it with the cream, and ornament it with sweetmeats or coloured sugar. Place it in ice till set.

To Make a Pyramid of Macaroons, or Meringues.

1384. Half a pound of loaf sugar; one ounce of gum arabic; two tablespoonfuls of water; macaroons.

Put half a pound of loaf sugar, one ounce of gum arabic, and two tablespoonfuls of water into a basin; stir it until it is dissolved; then set it over a slow fire, stirring it all the time until it is like melted glue.

Have a tin mould, rub butter over the outside to prevent the candy from sticking, set it firmly on a dish, or table, begin at the bottom by putting a row of macaroons, or meringues around it; stick them together with the prepared sugar (which must be kept hot). When this row is firm and cold, add another above it, let that also become firm, then add another, and so continue until the pyramid is finished. When the whole is cold and firm, take it from the form.

These pyramids may be filled with whipped cream, fruit, &c.

A Cake Trifle.

1385. A Savoy cake, or a Naples cake; a pint of milk; yolks of four eggs; whites of two; two ounces of sugar; one teaspoonful of peach water.; any jam you please.

Take a Savoy, or Naples cake; cut out the inside about an inch from the edge and bottom, leaving a shell; fill the inside with a custard made of the yolks of four eggs beaten with a pint of boiling milk, sweetened with two ounces of powdered sugar, and flavoured with a teaspoonful of peach water. Lay on it some strawberry, or any other jam you may prefer; beat the whites of two eggs with a little sifted sugar, until they will stand in a heap. Pile it up on the cake over the preserve, and serve.

Trifle, or Swiss Cream.

Time, to simmer, five minutes.

1386. One pint of cream; peel of a lemon; one drachm of cinnamon; four teaspoonfuls of flour; juice of two lemons; four ounces of macaroons; two ounces of ratafias; two ounces of candied citron, or orange peel.

Flavour a pint of cream with the peel of a lemon, and a drachm of cinnamon. Put it over the fire, and when it boils, stir gradually in four teaspoonfuls of flour, previously mixed to a thin smooth batter, with a few spoonfuls of cream. Let it simmer for about five minutes, *stirring it all the time;* then pour it out of the stewpan, and when cold, mix with it the juice of two lemons strained. Cover the bottom of a glass dish with half the macaroons and half the ratafias, then pour over them part of the cream, then add another layer of cakes, and then the cream. Cut an ounce of candied citron, or orange peel into shreds, and strew them lightly over the top of the cream.

Gooseberry Trifle.

Time, fifteen to twenty-five minutes to boil the gooseberries.

1387. Three pints of gooseberries; three-quarters of a pound of good moist sugar; one pint of custard; some whipped cream.

Boil three pints of gooseberries with about three-quarters of a pound of good moist sugar, or sugar to taste. When sufficiently soft to pulp, put them at the bottom of a glass trifle-dish, and pour over them about a pint of good custard, and set it in a cool place. When ready to serve, pile a whipped cream over it, and ornament the top with rings of preserved or crystallized fruit.

Apple Trifle.

1388. Ten or twelve apples; peel of one lemon; sugar to taste; three-quarters of a pint of milk; a quarter of a pint of cream; yolks of two eggs; whipped cream.

Pare, core, and scald ten or twelve apples with the peel of a lemon grated, and sugar to taste. When tender, beat them to a pulp, and put them at the bottom of a trifle-dish; add three-quarters of a pint of milk and a quarter of a pint of cream to the yolks of two eggs, with a few lumps of sugar; stir it over the fire or in a jug placed in hot water until it thickens, and when cold lay it over the apple, and pile a whipped cream over the whole.

To Make a Rich Trifle.

1389. Eight spongecakes; four ounces of macaroons; four ounces of ratafias; three ounces of sweet almonds; the grated peel of one large lemon; a pot of raspberry jam; half a pint of sherry, or raisin wine; three wineglasses of brandy; one pint of rich custard.

For the Whip.—One pint of cream; whites of two eggs; one glass of white wine; three ounces of loaf sugar.

Put the cream, pounded sugar, glass of white wine, and the whites of two new-laid eggs into a bowl, and whisk them to a stiff froth. As the froth rises take it off with a skimmer, and put it on the reversed side of a sieve to drain, and when the whole is finished, set it in a cool place until the next day. Then put the spongecakes at the bottom of the glass trifle-dish; then the macaroons and the ratafias, and pour over them the wine and brandy. When well soaked, grate over them the peel of a large lemon, then add the almonds blanched and cut into thin shreds, and the raspberry jam. Pour over the whole a pint of rich custard, and pile the whip lightly over the top. Ornament it with flowers or with crystallized fruits of any bright colour.

Tipsy Cake.

Time, one hour and three-quarters or two hours, to soak the cake.

1390. One large round stale spongecake; one glass and a half of brandy; sufficient sherry or raisin wine to soak it; juice of half a lemon; three ounces of sweet almonds; one pint of rich custard.

Place a large spongecake in the glass dish in which it is to be served; make a small hole in the centre, and pour in over the cake a sufficient quantity of sherry or raisin wine (mixed with a glass and a half of brandy and the juice of half a lemon), to soak it thoroughly. Then blanch two or three ounces of sweet almonds; cut them into long spikes, stick them all over the cake, and pour round it a pint of very rich custard.

Orange Sponge.

Time, twenty minutes.

1391. One ounce of isinglass; one pint of water; juice of six or seven oranges; juice of one lemon; sugar to taste; whites of three eggs.

Dissolve an ounce of isinglass in a pint of boiling water, strain it and let it stand till nearly cold; then mix with it the juice of six or seven oranges, and the juice of one lemon; add the whites of eggs and sugar to taste, and whisk the whole together until it looks white and like a sponge. Put it into a mould, and turn it out the next day.

Lemon Sponge.

Time, half an hour.

1392. Two ounces of gelatine; one pint and a half of water; juice of four lemons; peel of two; whites of three eggs; three-quarters of a pound of loaf sugar.

Pour over two ounces of gelatine a pint of cold water; let it simmer for a quarter of an hour, then add half a pint of boiling water. If not sufficiently dissolved, set the stewpan over the fire until it be so. Add to this three-quarters of a pound of pounded loaf sugar and the juice of four lemons. When the gelatine is cold (but before it begins to get firm), add the whites of three eggs which have been well beaten. Whisk the whole for a quarter of an hour, or until the mixture is quite white and begins to thicken; then put it into a mould which has been previously soaked in cold water. Set it in a cold place until firm, then turn it carefully out, and garnish it with dried fruit or flavouring.

Meringues.

1393. Whites of four small eggs; half a pound of finely-powdered sugar; lemon or vanilla flavouring.

Whisk the whites of four small eggs to a high froth, then stir into it half a pound of finely-powdered sugar; flavour it with vanilla or lemon essence, and repeat the whisking until it will lie in a heap; then lay the mixture on letter paper, in the shape of half an egg, moulding it with a spoon, laying each about half an inch apart. Then place the paper containing the meringues on a piece of hard wood, and put them into a quick oven; do not close it. Watch them; and when they begin to have a yellow appearance take them out; remove the paper carefully from the wood, and let them cool for two or three minutes; then slip a thin-bladed knife very carefully under one, turn it into your left hand, take another from the paper in the same way, and join the two sides which were next the paper together.

The soft inside may be taken out with the handle of a small spoon, the shells filled with jam, jelly, or cream, and then joined together as above, cementing them together with some of the mixture.

Apple Meringue.

Time, four or five hours to stew; one hour to bake.

1394. Twelve large apples; some preserved wine sours; sugar to your taste; some sugar icing.

Pare and core twelve large apples; stew them gently for four or five hours; sweeten them to your taste. Spread a layer on a soufflé-dish, then add a layer of preserved wine sours *stoned;* then the remainder of the apples. Bake for an hour, and a short time before it is wanted, put on an icing of fine white sugar. Put it again in the oven to brown, and send it up quite hot as a remove at second course.

Almond Meringues.

1395. A quarter of a pound of almonds; a quarter of a pound of double-refined sugar; whites of two large eggs.

Whisk the whites of two large eggs to a high froth; then add to it a quarter of a pound of finely-powdered double-refined sugar, and again whisk it until it is light and *firm*, so as to take any form you may place it in; add to it a quarter of a pound of almonds blanched and cut into *very* thin small slices, drop the meringues on letter paper, placed on baking tins, and put them for a few minutes into a quick oven without closing it. When done, take them from the papers with a thin-bladed knife.
Cocoa-nut may take the place of the almonds, if finely chopped.

Apple and Apricot Meringue.

1396. Eight or ten apples; two ounces of white sugar; apricot jam; whites of five eggs.
Cut eight or ten apples into quarters, and after removing the peel and cores put them into a stewpan, sprinkle over them two ounces of sugar, and stew them until tender. Strain the juice. Put them in a dish with a layer of apricot jam over them; whisk the whites of five eggs to a stiff froth like snow, spread it over the top, sprinkle sifted sugar over the whole, and dry it thoroughly in a very slow oven.
This dish can be made of rhubarb, gooseberry, or any other fruit, and makes a very pretty dish.

Rice Meringue.
Time, twenty minutes.

1397. One teacupful of rice; half a pint of milk; three eggs; one teaspoonful of moist sugar; apricot or any other jam; two teaspoonfuls of loaf sugar.
Put a teacupful of rice into half a pint of milk, and stand it at the side of the fire to simmer until quite soft. Then add the yolks of three beaten eggs to the rice in the stewpan, and beat the whole up with a teaspoonful of fine moist sugar. Then turn it out into the tin that it is to be baked in, piling it up *high* in the centre, and spread a thick layer of apricot or any other jam over it. Whisk the whites of the three eggs to a firm froth with a teaspoonful of powdered loaf sugar, spread it all over the jam, and sprinkle loaf sugar on the top of it, then drop a little of the froth about it in different shapes. Put it into the oven for about twenty minutes, taking care to leave the oven door open.
Raspberry, strawberry, or currant jam may be used.

Neapolitan Pastry.
Time, twelve to fifteen minutes.

1398. Some rich puff paste; raspberry or strawberry jam; coloured icing.

Roll out some rich puff paste to about half an inch in thickness, and cut it into strips about an inch and a half wide, and two inches in length; place them on a baking sheet some distance from each other, to allow them room to spread. Bake them in a quick oven. Spread a layer of raspberry or strawberry jam over half of them, take the others and stick them together in pairs. Ice them with coloured icing, and ornament them as preferred. Serve them piled high on a napkin.

Croquettes of Rice.

Time, three-quarters of an hour, or longer, to swell the rice; ten minutes to fry the croquettes.

1399. Eight ounces of rice; one quart of milk; six or seven ounces of pounded sugar; flavouring of almonds or vanilla; yolk of egg and bread-crumbs.
Put eight ounces of rice into a stewpan with a quart of milk, flavour it with almonds or vanilla, and let the rice gradually swell until the milk is dried up, and the rice tender. Turn it out, and when cold, form it into round balls, dip them into the yolk of egg beaten up with a little pounded sugar, sprinkle them with bread-crumbs, and fry them in boiling lard, turning them frequently, that they may get browned all over. Place them on a clean napkin before the fire to drain, and serve them piled high on a folded napkin.

Curd for Cheesecakes—Yorkshire Receipt.
Time, till it curds.

1400. One quart of water; two eggs; one quart of new milk; two spoonfuls of lemon juice or good vinegar.
Boil the water in a stewpan. Beat two eggs and mix them with a quart of new milk; add them to the water with two spoonfuls of lemon juice or good vinegar. When the curd rises lay it on a sieve to drain.

Another Way.
Time, till it curds

1401. Four quarts of mixed old and new milk; three pints of buttermilk; four eggs.
Set the old and new milk to boil, then add three pints of buttermilk with four eggs beat up in it. Stir all together till it turns to curd.
More eggs must be added when it is to be made into cheesecakes, with a little butter and cream.

Cheesecakes.

Time, fifteen to twenty minutes.

1402. Half a pint of good curd; four eggs; three spoonfuls of rich cream; a quarter of a nutmeg; one spoonful of ratafia; a quarter of a pound of currants; puff paste.

Beat half a pint of good curd with four eggs, three spoonfuls of rich cream, a quarter of a nutmeg grated, a spoonful of ratafia, and a quarter of a pound of currants washed and dried. Mix all well together, and bake in patty-pans lined with a good puff paste.

Apple Cheesecakes.

Time, fifteen to twenty minutes.

1403. Twelve large apples; juice of two large lemons, and the peel grated; half a pound of fresh butter; yolks of five eggs; sugar to taste; puff paste.

Pare and core twelve large apples, and boil them as for apple sauce, with a small quantity of water. Mash them very smooth, and stir in the juice of two lemons and the peel grated, the yolks of five or six eggs, and four ounces of butter beaten to a cream, sweeten to your taste with pounded loaf sugar, and bake them in patty-pans lined with a rich puff paste.

Lemon Cheesecakes.

Time, fifteen to twenty minutes.

1404. A quarter of a pound of warmed butter; peel of two lemons, juice of one; a quarter of a pound of loaf sugar; a few almonds; puff paste.

Just warm the butter; stir into it the sugar pounded fine, and when dissolved, mix with it the peel of two lemons grated, and the juice of one strained. Mix all well together, and pour it into patty-pans lined with puff paste. Put a few blanched almonds on the top of each.

Potato Cheesecakes.

Time, half an hour.

1405. Six ounces of potatoes; a quarter of a pound of lemon peel; a quarter of a pound of sugar; a quarter of a pound of butter; a little cream; puff paste.

Boil and mash some mealy potatoes, and beat them fine; boil a quarter of a pound of lemon peel, and beat it in a mortar with a quarter of a pound of sugar pounded; then add it to the beaten potato, with a quarter of a pound of butter melted in a little cream. When well mixed, let it stand to grow cold. Line some patty-pans with a rich puff paste; rather more than half fill them with the potato mixture, and bake them in a quick oven, sifting some double refined sugar over them when going into the oven.

Almond Cheesecakes.

Time, fifteen to twenty minutes.

1406. A quarter of a pound of sweet almonds; six bitter almonds; one spoonful of water; a quarter of a pound of loaf sugar; one spoonful of cream; whites of two eggs; puff paste.

Blanch and pound the sweet and bitter almonds with a spoonful of water; then add a quarter of a pound of sugar pounded, a spoonful of cream, and the whites of two eggs well beaten. Mix all as quick as possible, put it into very small patty-pans lined with puff paste, and bake in a warm oven nearly twenty minutes.

Citron Cheesecakes.

Time, a quarter of an hour.

1407. One pint of curds; a quarter of a pound of almonds; one spoonful of orange-flower water; yolks of four eggs; two Naples biscuits; two ounces and a half of sugar; two or three ounces of green citron; puff paste.

Beat a pint of curds in a mortar until they are perfectly smooth; blanch and pound four ounces of sweet almonds with a spoonful of orange-flower water, to prevent their oiling; well beat the yolks of four eggs, and mix them with the curds and almonds, then add the biscuits grated, the loaf sugar pounded small, and some green citron shred very fine. Mix all these ingredients well together, line some patty-pans with a rich paste, fill them with the mixture, put slips of citron on the top of each, and bake them.

Cheap Ratafia Cheesecakes.

Time, fifteen to twenty minutes.

1408. One quart of milk; a little rennet; two ounces of butter; three eggs; a little nutmeg; one ounce of pounded sugar; one ounce and a half of ratafias; half a glass of brandy; puff paste.

Turn a quart of milk to a curd with a little rennet, beat it smooth in a mortar, and when well drained from the whey, add two ounces of butter dissolved, three eggs well beaten, one ounce of pounded sugar, half a glass of brandy, and an ounce and a half of crushed ratafia cakes. Mix all well together. Line some patty-pans with rich puff paste, pour in the mixture, and bake them carefully.

Bread Cheesecakes.

Time, fifteen to twenty minutes.

1409. One French roll; one pint of boiling cream; eight eggs; half a pound of butter; a little grated nutmeg; half a pound of currants; half a glass of wine or brandy. Slice a French roll as thin as possible, pour over it a pint of boiling cream, and let it stand two hours; then beat eight eggs with half a pound of fresh butter, mix them with the bread and cream, grate in a little nutmeg, add half a pound of currants washed and dried, and half a glass of white wine or brandy. Mix and beat all together, and bake them in patty-pans, or in small raised crusts.

Rice Cheesecakes.

Time, fifteen to twenty minutes.

1410. A quarter of a pound of Patna rice; half a pint of cream; half a pound of fresh butter; half a pound of loaf sugar; a little lemon peel; six eggs; a glass of brandy; a spoonful of orange-flower water; puff paste.

Wash and pick the rice and boil it tender in two quarts of water, strain it through a sieve, and let it drain; put it into a stewpan with the cream, butter, pounded sugar, orange-flower water, and the lemon peel minced fine. Mix all together with six well-beaten eggs and a glass of brandy, put it over the fire and stir it till it is thick; then take it off the fire and let it cool. Put some rich puff paste over some patty-pans, crimp them round the edge with a knife, and when the mixture is cold, fill the pans nearly full and bake them in a slow oven.

Maids of Honour.

Time, fifteen to twenty minutes, to fry.

1411. Four quarts of milk; a piece of rennet; nine ounces of fresh butter; yolks of six eggs; ten ounces of sifted sugar; two ounces of sweet, one ounce of bitter almonds; juice of two small lemons; peel of four; two large potatoes; four tablespoonfuls of brandy; puff paste.

Mix ten ounces of powdered sugar with the yolks of six well-beaten eggs, the almonds blanched and pounded fine, the juice of two small lemons, the grated peel of four, and two mealy potatoes drained dry and well-beaten. Turn two quarts of milk to a curd with a piece of rennet, and when quite dry, crumble and sift it through a coarse sieve, and beat it up with nine ounces of fresh butter until it is perfectly smooth, add it to the sugar, eggs, &c., and mix all thoroughly together with four tablespoonfuls of brandy. Line some tartlet-pans with some *very* light puff paste, fill them with the mixture, and bake them quickly a light colour.

Lemon Cheesecakes.

1412. One pound of loaf sugar; six eggs; juice of three large lemons, peel of two; a quarter of a pound of butter.

Take a pound of loaf sugar, broken as for tea, add to it six eggs well beaten, leaving out the whites of two, the juice of three large lemons strained, the peel of two grated, and a quarter of a pound of butter. Put these ingredients into a stewpan and stir them gently over a slow fire till as thick as honey, then pour it into small jars, tie papers dipped in brandy over them, and keep them in a dry cool place.

Lemon Cheesecakes to Keep Several Years.

1413. A quarter of a pound of butter; one pound of loaf sugar; six eggs; the peel of two lemons, the juice of three.

To a quarter of a pound of butter put a pound of loaf sugar, broken into lumps, six eggs well beaten, leaving out two whites, the peel of two lemons grated, and the juice of three. Put all into a nice brass pan, and let it simmer over the fire till it is dissolved and begins to look like honey, then pour it into jars, and tie it down tightly with bladders. Keep it in a dry place. When you use it, have ready some very small tins, make a good puff paste, and fill them *half* full with cheesecakes, as they will rise very much. When cold, add a little grated sugar.

N.B.—It must be stirred gently all the time it is on the fire.

Fairy Butter.

1414. Yolks of four eggs; a quarter of a pound of butter; two ounces of sugar; one large teaspoonful of orange-flower water.

Take the yolks of four hard-boiled eggs, a quarter of a pound of butter, and two ounces of sugar in a large teaspoonful of orange-flower water; beat it together until a fine paste; let it stand two or three hours, then rub it through a colander on a small dish.

Orange Butter.

Time, eight minutes to boil the eggs.

1415. Six hard-boiled eggs; two ounces and a half of sugar; three ounces of fresh butter; two ounces of sweet almonds; a few spoonfuls of orange-flower water.

Beat six hard-boiled eggs in a mortar with two ounces and a half of pounded loaf sugar, three ounces of fresh butter, and two ounces of sweet almonds blanched and beaten to a smooth paste. Moisten the whole with a few spoonfuls of orange-flower water, and press it through a colander on a dish.

Arrange round it sweet or any ornamental biscuits.

Spanish Butter.
Time, ten minutes.

1416. One wineglass of rosewater; half an ounce of isinglass; six bittter almonds; half a pint of cream; yolks of three eggs; sugar to your taste.

To a wineglass of rosewater add half an ounce of isinglass, and six bitter almonds blanched and sliced; let it stand by the fire for rather more than an hour, then add half a pint of cream, the yolks of three beaten eggs; sweeten to your taste. Set it over a slow fire until thick, then stir it until cold, wet the mould with rosewater, and pour in the butter.

Snow Cheese.
Time, twenty-four hours.

1417. One pint of thick cream; a quarter of a pound of double-refined loaf sugar; juice of two lemons, peel of three grated. Mix with a pint of thick cream a quarter of a pound of double-refined sugar, the juice of two lemons, and the peel of three grated. Whisk the whole up until quite thick, put it into a lawn sieve just large enough to hold the quantity, and let it stand twenty-four hours before you turn it into a dish for the table.

Banbury Cakes.
Time, half an hour.

1418. Some good puff paste; Banbury mincemeat; white of eggs, and some sugar.

Make a good puff paste, and roll it out thin, divide it into equal parts, and cover one half over with Banbury mincemeat, then moisten the edge with the white of an egg, cover the other paste over it, press it together, and mark it out in oval forms. Glaze it over with the white of egg and pounded sugar, and bake it on a tin in a well-heated oven for half an hour. When done, divide the cakes with a sharp knife the moment they are taken from the oven, and serve them when required.

Or the paste may be cut into rounds with a cutter, some of the mince laid on each, covered with puff paste, and closed in the form of an oval, placing the join underneath, with sifted sugar over them.

SECOND COURSE DISHES, RELISHES, &c.

Macaroni as usually served.
Time, to boil the macaroni, half an hour; to brown it, six or seven minutes.

1419. Half a pound of pipe macaroni; seven ounces of Parmesan or Cheshire cheese; four ounces of butter; one pint of new milk; one quart of water and some bread-crumbs; a pinch of salt.

Flavour the milk and water with a pinch of salt, set it over the fire, and when boiling, drop in the macaroni. When tender, drain it from the milk and water, put it into a deep dish, sprinkle some of the grated cheese amongst it, with part of the butter broken into small pieces, place a layer of grated cheese over the top, and cover the whole with fine bread-crumbs, pouring the remainder of the butter lightly warmed over the crumbs. Brown the top of the macaroni with a salamander, or before the fire, turning it several times that it may be nicely browned.

Serve it quickly, and as hot as possible.

Macaroni.
Time, half an hour to boil; five minutes with cream.

1420. Four ounces of macaroni; two tablespoonfuls of good cream; one ounce and a half of butter rolled in flour; some toasted cheese.

Boil the macaroni until quite tender, and lay it on a sieve to drain; then put it into a tossing-pan with the cream, and the butter rolled in flour, boil it five minutes, pour it on a dish, spread toasted cheese all over it, and serve it up very hot.

Fish Macaroni.
Time, to boil macaroni, half an hour; to brown it, five minutes.

1421. Some cold cod; twice its weight in macaroni; six ounces of cheese; a large piece of butter.

Chop any quantity of cold cod very fine, mix with it twice its weight in macaroni boiled tender, and three ounces of grated cheese; mix the whole well together, put it on a dish with a few pieces of butter on the top. Grate cheese thickly over it, and brown it before the fire in a Dutch oven.

Timbale de Macaroni.
Time, half an hour to boil the macaroni; one hour to steam.

1422. Half a pound of macaroni; water

18

and salt ; yolks of five eggs ; whites of two ; half a pint of cream ; four dessertspoonfuls of Parmesan cheese ; a few slices of ham; and the white meat of a fowl.

Put half a pound of macaroni into a stewpan with a little salt, and well cover it with water, simmer it until *quite* tender, taking care to preserve the form, and when done strain it through a sieve. Mince the white meat of a cold fowl and a few slices of ham very fine, season it with pepper and salt, and mix it with the Parmesan cheese finely grated. Well beat the yolks of five and the whites of two or three eggs, add them to the minced fowl, &c., with half a pint of good cream. Well mix the whole with the macaroni, put it into a buttered mould, steam it for an hour, and serve with a good gravy.

Admiral Ross's Indian Devil Mixture.

1423. Four tablespoonfuls of cold gravy ; one of Chutney paste ; one of ketchup ; one of vinegar ; two teaspoonfuls of made mustard ; two of salt ; two tablespoonfuls of butter.

Mix all the above ingredients as smooth as possible in a soup plate, put with it the cold meat, or whatever you wish to devil. Stew it gently until thoroughly warmed, and then you will have a good devil.

Devilled Biscuits.

Time, ten minutes.

1424. Some thin slices of kippered salmon ; three captain's biscuits ; clarified butter or oil ; some devil mixture.

Soak some thin captain's biscuits in clarified butter or salad oil ; then rub each side well over with devil mixture, and toast them on the gridiron over a clear fire ; put them on a dish ; place on each a very thin slice of kippered salmon, and brown with a salamander or before the fire. Serve it quickly and *very* hot.

Devilled Oysters.

Time, three or four minutes.

1425. Some fine large oysters ; one ounce and a half of butter ; a little lemon juice ; pepper, salt, and Cayenne.

Open a sufficient number of oysters for the dish, leaving them in their deep shells and their liquor, add a little lemon juice, pepper, salt, and Cayenne ; put a small piece of butter on each, and place the shell carefully on a gridiron over a clear bright fire to broil for a few minutes. Serve them on a napkin with bread and butter.

Salmagundy.

1426. Some cold veal or fowl; the whites and yolks of hard-boiled eggs ; four anchovies ; some grated tongue and ham ; red cabbage and beetroot.

Chop the white part of some veal or fowl very fine, and all the other ingredients *separately*. Then place at the bottom of a small flat dish a saucer or small china basin ; make rows of the veal, eggs, &c., round it wide at the bottom, and smaller as you reach the top, arranging the ingredients according to their colour—as the white of egg on the beetroot, and so on. Salmagundy may be served in a variety of ways, placed on a dish without the basin ; or the white of hard-boiled eggs filled with each ingredient, a small piece of the egg cut from the bottom to make them stand evenly on the dish, and garnished with double curled parsley.

Indian Kabob.

Time, to fry, quarter of an hour.

1427. Apples ; one pound of small collops of beef or mutton ; five ounces of butter ; half a drachm of red pepper ; a quarter of a drachm of turmeric ; two onions.

Procure a sufficient number of silver skewers for the kabob ; cut about a pound of apples into slices, and the same weight of beef or mutton into collops of the same size. Skewer them alternately on the skewers : first apple, then meat, then onion, and commence again until about four of each are on. Sprinkle over them the onions, pepper, and turmeric, all pounded in a mortar, and fry them in butter over a clear fire. Serve them hot, with a separate dish of boiled rice.

This dish does nicely for luncheon or supper.

Chicken and Ham Sandwiches.

Time, about five minutes.

1428. Some cold chicken and a little ham; a cupful of gravy ; one large tablespoonful of curry paste ; a little Cheddar cheese; and some butter.

Mince up some cold chicken, and add a little minced ham to it, then stir it into a cupful of boiling gravy and a spoonful of curry paste ; set it over the fire for a few minutes, and turn it out. Stamp some slices of thin stale bread in a round with a tin cutter, and fry them carefully. Spread a layer of the fowl and ham between two of them, and place on the top a small piece of cheese and butter, pressed together with a spoon to form a paste. Put the sandwiches on a sheet of tin in a quick oven for a few

Plain Sandwiches.—Dutch and Bread Ramakins, &c. 275

minutes. When done, serve them very hot on a folded napkin for supper.

Plain Sandwiches.

1429. Cut some very thin slices of bread and butter from a square loaf baked in a tin, and place very thin slices of ham, beef, or game between the slices. Season them with salt and mustard, press them on a clean board with the blade of a large knife, cut off the crust evenly, and divide them into oblong squares. Pile them on a table-napkin, and serve.

Cheese Fingers.

Time, quarter of an hour.

1430. A quarter of a pound of puff paste; a pinch of salt; two ounces of Parmesan cheese; half a teaspoonful of Cayenne.
Take a quarter of a pound of puff paste and roll it out thin, then take two ounces of grated Parmesan cheese, half a teaspoonful of Cayenne, and a pinch of salt. Mix these, and strew the cheese over half the paste, turn the other over it, and cut it with a sharp knife half an inch wide, and any length you like. Bake in a quick oven, and serve them *quite hot*, shaking a little grated cheese over them. No cheese will answer except *Parmesan*. The fingers must be piled in a dish crossing each other at right angles.

Cheese Canapees.

Time, altogether, about twenty minutes.

1431. Cut some thin slices from a stale loaf of bread, stamp them out in any form you please with a tin cutter, and fry them lightly in fresh butter; cover the top of each with some Cheshire or Parmesan cheese, seasoned with pepper and a little mustard. Set them before a brisk fire to dissolve the cheese, and serve as hot and as quickly as possible on a folded napkin.

Grilled Kippered Salmon.

1432. Cut some dried salmon in long narrow pieces, and broil them over a clear fire; then rub them over with fresh butter. Season with lemon juice and Cayenne, and serve very hot.

Pulled Bread.

Time, five minutes.

1433. Pull out the crumb of a hot loaf, and divide it into small rough-looking pieces, place them on a baking sheet, and lightly brown and crisp them in the oven.

Ramakins.

Time, to bake, a quarter of an hour.
1434. Two eggs; one teaspoonful of flour; two ounces of melted butter; two ounces of grated cheese; two tablespoonfuls of cream.
Mix a teaspoonful of flour with two ounces of grated cheese, two ounces of melted butter, two tablespoonfuls of cream, and two well-beaten eggs. Stir all together, and bake it in small tins. You may add a little Cayenne pepper if you please.

Dutch Ramakins.

Time, to brown, about ten minutes.

1435. A quarter of a pound of good Cheshire cheese; yolks of two eggs boiled hard; one ounce and a half of butter; slices of toasted bread buttered.
Scrape a quarter of a pound of good Cheshire or Gloucester cheese; mix with it about an ounce and a half of butter and the yolks of two hard-boiled eggs. Put it in a mortar and pound it into a smooth paste. Toast some slices of bread, butter them and cut them into square pieces, spread the mixture thickly over them, brown them with a salamander, or in a Dutch oven, and serve as hot as possible.

Ramakins with Ale.

Time, to bake, a quarter of an hour.

1436. Four ounces of Cheshire cheese; four ounces of Gloucester cheese; four ounces of fresh butter; four eggs; one French roll; a cupful of cream or milk; a wineglass of good ale.
Scrape four ounces of Cheshire, and the same of Gloucester cheese, add four ounces of fresh butter, and beat all well together in a mortar with the crumb of a roll boiled in a cupful of cream, the yolks of four well-beaten eggs, and a wineglass of good ale. Mix the paste when smooth with the whites of the four eggs beaten to a stiff froth, and put the mixture into small paper cases. Bake them in a Dutch oven before the fire, and serve them very hot.

Bread Ramakins.

Time, ten minutes.

1437. Two ounces of cheese; yolk of one egg; one ounce of melted butter; one anchovy; a very little pepper; and some toasted bread.
Scrape two ounces of cheese, add to it the yolk of a beaten egg, an ounce of butter melted, one anchovy, and a very little pepper. Beat all thoroughly in a mortar, and spread the mixture very thick on small pieces of toasted bread. Brown it before the fire, or with a salamander.

18—2

Eggs and Artichokes—An Entree.

Time, to boil the artichokes, half an hour; ten or twelve minutes to boil the eggs.

1438. Six artichokes; three hard-boiled eggs; a little good gravy, or melted butter.

Strip the leaves from six artichokes, and boil the bottoms in hard water until sufficiently done. Boil three eggs for ten or twelve minutes. Cut them across, and place on each artichoke half an egg, leaving the round end uppermost. Put them on a hot dish, and pour over them a little good melted butter, or some rich gravy.

Frothed Eggs.

Time, to brown, five minutes.

1439. Eight eggs; one tablespoonful of water; a pinch of salt; juice of one lemon; sugar to taste; vanilla or lemon flavouring; one pound of sugar.

Beat the yolks of eight and the whites of four eggs with a spoonful of water, a pinch of salt, the juice of one lemon, and sugar to taste. Fry them as an omelet, and put it on a dish. Have ready the four remaining whites whipped to a high froth with a pound of white pounded sugar and a flavouring of vanilla or lemon; heap it on the omelet very high, and set it before the fire, or in the oven, for a few minutes to lightly brown.

Toasted Cheese.

Time, about ten minutes.

1440. Cut some Parmesan or Cheddar cheese into *very* thin slices or shreds. Put it into a tin toasting dish, and set in the oven, or before a strong fire to toast, and when thoroughly dissolved, stir into it a good-sized piece of butter, a spoonful of made mustard, and a little very fine pepper, and serve it in a dish as hot as possible with pulled bread, or placed on toast.

Welsh Rabbit.

Time, ten minutes to brown.

1441. A quarter of a pound of Cheshire or Parmesan cheese; yolks of two eggs; five ounces of grated bread; a quarter of a pound of butter; one tablespoonful of mustard; a little salt.

Mix with a quarter of a pound of grated cheese five ounces of bread-crumbs and a quarter of a pound of good butter; add a tablespoonful of mustard and a little salt. Mix all well together, and then beat it smooth in a mortar. Lay the mixture neatly on slices of toasted bread, and place them in a Dutch oven before the fire to become thoroughly hot and slightly brown. Placing a thick white paper over the dish until hot, and then removing it prevents the cheese from becoming too brown or dry.

Mayonnaise de Saumon.

Time, to boil the eggs, twenty minutes.

1442. One pound and a half of cold salmon; small salad of endive and mustard and cress; one teaspoonful of chopped tarragon; four or six white-heart lettuces; Mayonnaise or tartare sauce.

Wash and carefully clean the salad and lettuces, shred the latter up fine. Cut part of the salmon into small pieces, boil the eggs quite hard. Make some Mayonnaise or tartare sauce. Put the salad into the bowl, mix a little of the salmon with it, and add the sauce. Cut some rather longer pieces of salmon, season them with oil, vinegar, pepper, and salt. Pile the salad up in the middle, lay the pieces of salmon upon it.

Mock Crab.

1443. Three-quarters of a pound of pickled shrimps; a quarter of a pound of good mellow cheese; a spoonful of made mustard; a little salad oil; two spoonfuls of vinegar; a little salt and Cayenne pepper.

Take about a quarter of a pound or more of good made mellow cheese, mix with it a spoonful of made mustard, a little salad oil, two spoonfuls of vinegar, a little salt, and Cayenne pepper. Pound it well in a mortar until it is of the consistency of cream. Stir into it the pickled shrimps, and serve it in a crabshell garnished with lemon and parsley. Keep a crabshell for this purpose.

Mock Crab—Sailor Fashion.

1444. A large slice of Gloucester cheese; a teaspoonful of mustard; the same of vinegar; pepper and salt to taste.

Cut a slice of Gloucester cheese rather thin, but of good size round. Mash it up with a fork to a paste, mix it with vinegar, mustard, and pepper. It has a great flavour of crab.

ICES.

Ice is no longer a luxury confined to the splendid homes of the rich. Sold at the cheap rate of one penny or twopence the pound, it is within the reach of the middle classes, and is found of the greatest service to the cook and housekeeper. During the

Receipts for Making Ices.

heat of summer, when our butter threatens to become oil, a few lumps of ice placed round and on the pot (if no refrigerator is possessed by the housewife), will render it good and eatable at a very slight expense.

And, if the outlay of a few pounds can be afforded, we recommend every housekeeper to purchase one of the new "Piston" Freezing Machines, invented by Mr. Ash. The lowest price will be only £2 10s. for one to be used with *ice and salt* only. These pretty little machines can be used by a lady herself with the greatest ease. The writer has assisted in the manufacture of an ice with one, and found it a pleasant and amusing task, and at a *very* small expense iced creams, puddings, &c., &c., can be produced whenever required.

The Piston Freezing Machines may be had either to be used with ice and salt only, or it may be used with the chemical freezing mixture. The latter, however, is expensive.

There is a new icing machine recently patented which is said to be likely to surpass those named here.

Receipts for Making Ices.

Nesselrode, or Frozen Pudding.

1445. Take one pint of cream, half a pint of milk, the yolks of four eggs, one ounce of sweet almonds pounded, and half a pound of sugar. Put them in a stewpan on a gentle fire; set it as thin as custard. When cold, freeze, *and when sufficiently congealed* add one pound of preserved fruits, and two wineglasses of brandy, with a few currants. Cut the fruit small, and mix well with the ice. Let it remain to set in the moulding pots, as directed.

Custard Ice Cream.

1446. Take a pint of fresh cream, add the yolks of six new-laid eggs, stir them up well with a whisk, add a thin slice of lemon peel as for custard. Put the pan on a gentle fire, or in hot water, stirring it until the cream appears to be setting, remove it from the fire, and add pulverized sugar to palate. Place it in a vessel of cold water, and continue stirring a few minutes to prevent its curdling. Give it any flavour you please, strain it through a sieve, then put it into the freezer, and proceed as before directed. One quart.

Strawberry Ice Cream.

1447. Pick some strawberries (the scarlets are considered the best) into a basin or pan, add sugar in powder, with a quantity of strawberry jam equal to the fruit, the juice of a lemon or two, according to palate, a small quantity of new milk, and a pint of fresh cream. Mix and add a little colour, from cochineal, saffron or spinach juice; freeze. One quart. Or, when fresh strawberries cannot be procured, take one pound of strawberry jam, the juice of one or two lemons, one pint of cream, and a little milk. Colour; freeze. One quart.*

* Should the cream be found not to freeze so quickly as you wish, add a little more new milk. This applies to all ice creams.

Raspberry Ice Cream.

1448. To one pound of raspberry jam, add the juice of one or two lemons, one pint of cream, and a little milk; colour; freeze. One quart. If raspberries are in season, it may be made with equal portions of raspberries and jam, and a small quantity of sugar.

Lemon Ice Cream.

1449. Take one pint of cream, rasp two lemons on sugar, scrape off into the vessel you are about to mix in; squeeze them, and add the juice, half a pound of sugar; mix; freeze. One quart.

* Vanilla Ice Cream.

1450. Pound two sticks of vanilla, or sufficient to flavour it to palate in a mortar, with half a pound of sugar; pass through a sieve, put it into a stewpan, with half a pint of milk; boil over a slow fire, with the yolks of two eggs, stirring all the time, the same as custard; add one pint of cream, and juice of one lemon; freeze. One quart.

Plain Ice Cream.

1451. To one pint of cream, add the juice of one lemon, half a pound of sugar, a little nutmeg; mix; freeze. If too rich, add a little new milk.

Noyau Ice Cream.

1452. One pint of cream; the juice of one lemon; half a pound of sugar; two glasses of noyau: mix; freeze. One quart.

Coffee Ice Cream.

1453. Take six ounces of the best Turkey coffee berries, well roasted; put them on a tin, and place them in an oven for five minutes; boil one pint of cream and half a pint of milk together, and put them into a can; take the berries from the oven, and put them with the scalding cream. Cover till cold; strain, and add one ounce of arrowroot; boil like custard, and add half a pound of sugar; freeze. One quart.

Tea Ice Cream.

1454. One pint of cream; half a pound of sugar, one ounce of tea, or a sufficient quantity to make one cup; mix with the cream; freeze. One quart.

Chocolate Ice Cream.

1455. Infuse four or six ounces of chocolate: mix it well with a pint of cream, a little new milk, and half a pound of sugar; strain; freeze. One quart.

To Clarify Sugar for Ices.

1456. Take twelve pounds of sugar, twelve pints of water, half the white of one egg, well beaten up; add to it the water; boil ten minutes. This is used in all water ices.

Claret Cup.

1457. To each bottle of claret add one of soda-water, a glass of sherry or curaçoa, the peel of a-lemon cut thin, and powdered sugar to taste. Add some lumps of ice, and let it remain half an hour before serving. A few slices of raw cucumber or some sprigs of burridge may be added.

Instead of the lemon peel as above, a pint of ripe raspberries or four or five peaches or nectarines, cut in slices, will make a most delicious beverage.

Moselle Cup.

1458. To each bottle of still or sparkling Moselle add one of soda-water, a glass of sherry or brandy, four or five thin slices of pineapple, the peel of half a lemon cut thin, powdered sugar to taste, and some lumps of block ice. A pint of strawberries or some peaches or nectarines may be used instead of pineapple.

To Mould Dessert Ice when not Frozen in the Patent Moulding Pots.

1459. Dessert ices, iced puddings, &c., when required to be moulded, must not be frozen too hard, or they will not fill the crevices of the mould.

After the mould is filled with the dessert ice, secure it air-tight by placing a piece of writing paper round the edges, and then shutting the top and bottom cover of the mould upon it.

The mould should be immediately inserted into a tub of rough ice and salt, seeing that every part of the mould is well covered, and in contact with the ice and salt. In about an hour, or longer, if convenient, the mould may be withdrawn, and the ice turned out and sent to table.

All dessert ices and puddings should contain only a certain amount of sweetness; the proper richness is shown by using a saccharometer. For ascertaining the correct amount of saccharine (or sweetness) that should be contained in dessert ices, iced puddings, &c., when using either ice and common salt, or the chemical freezing powders, as a refrigerating medium, use the saccharometer.

Directions for its Use.

1460. Nearly fill a tumbler with the sweet confection; place the saccharometer gently into it, and if mixed correctly, for freezing with ice and salt, it will sink to the lowest red mark. For freezing with freezing powders it will sink to the highest red mark. To make the saccharometer sink, add milk to a cream ice, and water to a water ice. To make it rise, add more sugar or sweet syrup.

Ices, &c., will not freeze well unless mixed by this scale.

BAKING BISCUITS AND CAKES.

An oven to bake well should have a regular heat throughout, but particularly at the bottom, without which bread or cakes will not rise, or bake well.

An earthen basin is best for beating eggs, or cake mixture.

Cake should be beaten with a wooden spoon, or spatula; butter may be beaten with the same.

Eggs should be beaten with rods, or a broad fork; a silver fork, or one made of iron wire, is best, as it is broadest; eggs should be clear and fresh for a cake.

It is well, as a general rule in cake making, to beat the butter and sugar (which must be made fine) to a light cream; indeed, in the making of pound cake, the lightness of the cake depends as much upon this as upon the eggs being well beaten; then beat the eggs and put them to the butter, and gradually add the flour and other ingredients, beating it all the time.

In common cakes, where only a few eggs are used, beat them until you can take a spoonful up clear from strings.

In receipts in which milk is used as one ingredient, either sweet or sour may be used, but not a mixture of both.

Sour milk makes a spongy light cake; sweet milk makes a cake which cuts like pound cake.

To blanch almonds, pour boiling water on them, and let them remain in it until the skins may be taken off; then throw the almonds into cold water to whiten them, drain them from the water, but do not wipe them; the moisture will prevent their oiling.

In making cakes, if you wish them to be pleasing to the palate, use double refined sugar, although light brown sugar makes a very good cake.

For icing cakes, the sugar must be rolled and sifted, or pounded in a mortar.

For making lady-fingers, have a tin tube as long as your finger, like the spout of a funnel; to the upper part of this a little bag must be attached, and the cake mixture put in, and pressed out on to the paper the length and size desired; the point of the tube may be larger or smaller as may be required. Savoy biscuit mixture may be baked as lady-fingers for making Charlotte Russe.

To ascertain whether a cake is baked enough, if a small one, take a very fine splint of wood and run it through the thickest part; if not done enough, some of the dough, or unbaked cake will be found sticking to it; if done, it will come out clean. If the cake is large, pass a small knife-blade through it instead of the splint. Cakes to be kept fresh should be placed in a tin-box tightly covered, in a cool dark place.

Preparation of Sugars.

1461. To prepare sugars properly is a material point in the business of confectionery; and as some rules are undoubtedly necessary to be given in a work of this kind, we shall begin with the first process, that of clarifying sugar, which must be done in this manner:—

Break the white of an egg into the preserving-pan, put in four quarts of water, and beat it up to a froth with a whisk. Then put in twelve pounds of sugar, mix all together, set it over the fire, and when it boils, put in a little cold water. Proceed in this manner as many times as may be necessary till the scum appears thick on the top; then remove it from the fire, and let it settle; take off the scum, and pass it through a straining bag. If the sugar should not appear very fine, you must boil it again before you strain it, otherwise, in boiling to a height, it will rise over the pan. Having thus finished the first operation, proceed to clarify the sugar to either of the five following degrees.

First Degree, called Smooth or Candy Sugar.

1462. Having clarified the sugar as above directed, put any quantity over the fire, and let it boil till it is smooth. This may be known by dipping the skimmer into the sugar, and then touching it between the forefinger and thumb (previously dipped into cold water) and immediately opening them; a small thread will be drawn between, which will instantly break, and remain as a drop on the thumb. This will be a sign of its being in some degree smooth. Then boil it again, and it will draw into a larger string, and will have acquired the first degree above mentioned.

Second Degree, called Souffle.

1463. To obtain this degree, boil the sugar longer than in the former process, and then dip in the skimmer, shaking off the sugar into the pan. Then with the mouth blow strongly through the holes, and if certain bladders or bubbles blow through, it will be a proof of its having acquired the second degree.

Third Degree, called Feathered Sugar.

1464. This degree is to be proved by dipping the skimmer in when the sugar has boiled longer than in the former degree. First shake it over the pan, then give it a sudden flirt behind, and if it is boiled enough, the sugar will fly off like feathers.

Fourth Degree, called Crackled Sugar.

1465. Having let the sugar boil longer than in the preceding degree, dip a stick into the sugar, and immediately put it into a basin of iced water. Draw off the sugar that hangs to the stick into the water, and if it becomes hard, and snaps in the water, it has acquired the proper degree; but if otherwise, boil it till it answers that trial. Take particular care that the water used for this purpose is very cold, otherwise it will lead to errors.

Fifth Degree, called Caramel Sugar.

1466. To obtain this degree, the sugar must boil longer than in either of the former operations; prove it by dipping in a stick, first into the sugar, and then into cold water; but observe, when it comes to the caramel height, it will, the moment it touches the cold water, snap like glass, which is the highest and last degree of boiled sugar. Take care that the fire is not very fierce when this is boiling, lest, flaming up the sides of the pan, it should cause the sugar to burn, which will discolour and spoil it.

Little Devices in Sugar.

1467. Steep gum-tragacanth in rose-water, and with some double-refined sugar make it up into a paste; colour the paste with powders and jellies according to fancy, and then make them up into the requisite shape. Moulds may be made in any shape, and they will be pretty ornaments placed on the tops of iced cakes.

To Boil Sugar to Caramel.

1468. To every pound of refined sugar allow one gill of spring water; juice of half a lemon.

Break a pound of refined sugar into a delicately-clean stewpan, pour in one gill of spring water. Set it on a clear fire and let it boil very quickly, skimming it very carefully as soon as it boils.

Keep it boiling until the sugar snaps, which may be known by dipping a teaspoon into the sugar, and letting it drop to the bottom of a pan of cold water. If it remains hard, the sugar has attained the right degree; then squeeze in the juice of half a lemon, and let it remain one minute longer on the fire. Then set the pan in another of cold water, and the caramel will be fit for use.

Have ready moulds of any form, rub the insides with oil, dip a fork or spoon into the sugar, and throw it over the moulds in fine threads or net-work.

Syrup for Compotes.

Time, a quarter of an hour to twenty minutes.

1469. One pound of refined sugar; one pint and a half of water.

Boil a pound of refined sugar in a pint and a half of spring water, carefully remove the scum as it rises, and the syrup will then be fit for use when required.

To Colour Sugar Red.

1470. Crush the sugar roughly with a rolling-pin, but do not pound it fine. Put it in a plate and drop a little prepared cochineal over it. Set it before the fire to dry. It will then be ready for use.

Clarified Sugar or Syrup.

Time, four or five minutes to boil.

1471. Two pounds of double-refined loaf sugar; one pint of spring water; half of the white of one egg.

Break into small pieces two pounds of double-refined loaf sugar, put it into a clean stewpan with a pint of cold spring water. When the sugar is dissolved, add half the white of an egg, which should be well beaten. Watch it, and when it boils take off the scum, keep it boiling till no scum rises, and it is perfectly clear, then run it through a clean napkin, and the sugar will be fit for use.

Or it may be put into a close stoppered bottle, when it will keep for some time.

Spun Sugar.

1472. Having boiled the sugar to the fifth degree, oil the handle of a wooden spoon, tie two forks together, the prongs outward, dip them into the sugar lightly, take them out and shake them to and fro. Let the sugar run from them over the spoon, forming fine silken' threads. These you can form with your hands into whatever you may require for garnishing. Or, which is really better, you may do so from the lip of the sugar-pan. However, it requires practice. A good cook will have sugar spinners.

Icing for Cakes.

1473. Whites of three eggs; one pound of sugar; flavouring of vanilla or lemon.

Beat the whites of the eggs to a high froth, then add to them a quarter of a pound of white sugar pounded and sifted, flavour it with vanilla or lemon, and beat it until it is light and very white, but not quite so stiff as meringue mixture. The longer it is beaten the more firm it will become. Beat it until it may be spread smoothly on the cake.

To Ice or Frost a Cake.

1474. When the icing is made as directed, place the cake on the bottom of the tin in which it was baked. Then spread the icing on the sides with a piece of cardboard about four inches long and nearly three wide. Then heap what you may think sufficient for the top in the centre of the cake, and with the cardboard spread it evenly over. Set it in a warm place to dry and harden, after which ornament it as you please. If sugar ornaments are put on, it must be done whilst it is moist or soft; or if the icing is required coloured, pink may be made with cochineal syrup, blue with indigo, yellow with saffron, green with spinach syrup, and brown with chocolate.

Almond Icing for Bridecake.

1475. The whites of three eggs; one pound of sweet almonds; one pound of loaf sugar; a little rosewater.

Beat the whites of the eggs to a *strong* froth, beat a pound of almonds very fine with a little rosewater, mix the almonds with the eggs lightly together, and one pound of common white sugar beaten very fine and put in by degrees. When the cake is sufficiently done take it out, lay the icing on, and then put it back to brown.

Sugar Icing for the Top.

1476. Two pounds of double-refined sugar; whites of five eggs; a little lemon juice.

Whisk the whites of the five eggs stiff enough to bear the weight of an egg, then with a spatula or wooden spoon mix gradually with them two pounds of sugar which has been dried and sifted, work them together for a few minutes, and add a teaspoonful of strained lemon juice. Spread it *all* over the cake, covering the almond icing thickly and evenly. Dry it *very slowly* in a cool oven, or if it is put on as soon as the cake is taken from the oven, the icing will be hard by the time the cake is cold.

Ornamental Frosting.

1477. Whites of eggs; sugar and colouring.

For this purpose have syringes of different sizes, draw any one you may choose full of the icing, and work it in any designs you may fancy. *Wheels, Grecian borders* or *flowers* look well, or borders of *beading*. The cake must first be covered with a plain frosting, which may be white, or coloured pink with cochineal powdered, blue with a little indigo, or brown with a little chocolate finely grated, green with a little spinach juice.

Spongecake.

Time, three-quarters of an hour to one hour.

1478. Five eggs; half a pound of sifted loaf sugar; the weight of two eggs and a half (in their shells) of flour; one lemon.

Take half a pound of sifted loaf sugar, break five eggs over it, and beat all together for *full half an hour* with a steel fork. Previously take the weight of two eggs and a half (in their shells) in flour. After you have beaten the eggs and sugar together for the time specified, grate into them the peel of a lemon, and add the juice if approved. Stir the flour into this mixture and pour it into a tin. Put it instantly into a cool oven.

Cocoa-nut Spongecakes.

Time, half an hour.

1479. Six eggs; half a pound of sugar; a quarter of a pound of flour; one teaspoonful of lemon essence; one of salt; half a nutmeg; one cocoa-nut.

Beat the yolks of six eggs with half a pound of sugar, then add the flour, salt, essence of lemon, and half a nutmeg grated. Beat the whites of the eggs to a stiff froth, and stir them to the yolks, &c., and the white meat of the cocoa-nut grated. Line square tin pans with buttered paper, and, having stirred the ingredients well together, put the mixture in, an inch deep in the pans. Bake them in a quick oven half an hour, cut it into squares, and serve it with or without icing.

A Rich Pound Cake.

Time, one hour.

1480. One pound and a half of flour; one pound of butter; one pound of white sugar; ten eggs; a wineglassful of brandy; half a nutmeg, a teaspoonful of vanilla, or essence of lemon.

Beat the butter and pounded sugar to a cream, whisk the eggs to a high froth, then put all the ingredients together, and beat until light and creamy. Put it into a tin lined with buttered paper, and bake it in a moderate oven for one hour. When done, turn it gently out, reverse the tin, and set the cake on the bottom until cold. Let the paper remain on until the cake is to be cut.

Cocoa-nut Pound Cakes.

Time, half an hour.

1481. One pound of pounded sugar; half a pound of butter; one teacupful of new milk; one pound of flour; the peel of half a lemon grated, or a teaspoonful of essence of lemon; four eggs; one cocoa-nut; one teaspoonful of carbonate of soda.

Mix a pound of sifted white sugar with half a pound of butter beaten to a cream, the peel of a lemon grated, or a teaspoonful of essence of lemon, a teacupful of new milk, and four eggs, beaten separately. Stir all well together, then add the soda, or the same quantity of powdered saleratus, and beat it all thoroughly together with a pound of sifted flour, or as much as will make it as thick as a pound cake, then lightly stir in the white meat of a cocoa-nut grated. Line square tins with buttered paper, put the mixture in an inch deep, and bake it in a quick oven. When done, take out the cakes and set them to cool. It may be baked in one tin, but will require a longer time, and either way it must be iced or frosted over.

Plain Almond Cake.

Time, three-quarters of an hour to one hour.

1482. Three ounces of sweet almonds; a quarter of a pound of white sugar; four eggs; a quarter of a pound of fine flour; one ounce of citron.

Stir into the yolks of four well-beaten eggs, two ounces of white sifted sugar, and then add it by degrees to three ounces of sweet almonds blanched and pounded in a mortar with another two ounces of sugar. Whisk the whites of the eggs to a very stiff froth, stir them into the mixture, and add the flour sifted and dried before the fire. Mix all thoroughly together, and put it into a buttered tin, and bake it in a moderate oven.

Rice Cake.
Time, one hour.

1483. A quarter of a pound of ground rice; a quarter of a pound of flour; half a pound of sifted sugar; six ounces of butter; four eggs; and a few seeds.

Mix the sugar, rice, butter, and flour together, then add the *whites* of the eggs, having been previously beaten to a stiff froth. When it begins to look white add the yolks. Stir all well together. Line a tin with buttered paper, and bake it.

Lady Freakes' Cake.

1484. Three-quarters of a pound of flour; quarter of a pound of butter; three eggs; quarter of a pound of currants; quarter of a pound of sugar.

Beat the butter to a cream, add the sugar, beat the eggs and all well together but by degrees, mix in the flour and currants, then add a very little milk.

Small Rice Cakes.
Time, half an hour.

1485. A quarter of a pound of rice; a quarter of a pound of butter; a quarter of a pound of sugar; four eggs.

Beat the butter to a cream, add it to the ground rice and the sugar pounded and sifted. Well beat the yolks and whites of four eggs separately, stir in the yolks first, and mix all well together; then add the whites whisked to a stiff froth, mix it until it becomes a paste, and bake it in small tins.

Rice Cake.
Time, half an hour.

1486. Half a pound of ground rice; yolks of six eggs; whites of four; eight drops of essence of almonds; six ounces of loaf sugar.

Beat the yolks and whites of the eggs separately, mix the yolks with the rice; add the sugar, the lemon essence, and the whites well beaten. Put all into a tin and bake.

Manx Cake.

1487. Half a pound of rice flour; half a pound of white sugar; eight eggs; peel of half a lemon.

Well beat eight eggs for half an hour, and stir them into half a pound of rice flour, half a pound of white sugar pounded, and the peel of the lemon grated. Mix all well together, and bake it in a buttered tin.

Josephine Cake.
Time, one hour.

1488. Half a pound of butter; half a pound of brown sugar; five eggs; one pound of flour; half a pound of currants; one glass of white wine.

Beat half a pound of butter to a cream, then beat in the sugar, and the five eggs well beaten. Mix it gradually into a pound of flour, add half a pound of currants washed and dried, and a glass of white wine, and bake it, when well beaten together, in a buttered tin.

Rich Seed Cake.
Time, one hour.

1489. Half a pound of butter; half a pound of sugar; one pound of patent flour; six eggs; and some caraway seeds.

Beat half a pound of butter before the fire to a cream, then stir in the pounded sugar, and beat it together for some minutes; add the yolks of six, and the whites of three eggs, one at a time; then stir in gradually a pound of patent flour, and a few caraway seeds to taste. Bake it in a tin lined with a buttered paper in a moderate oven.

Common Seed Cake.
Time, two hours.

1490. Two pounds and a half of flour; half a pound of loaf sugar; one tablespoonful of thick yeast; half a pint of warm milk; half a pound of butter; one ounce of caraway seeds.

Mix half a pound of pounded loaf sugar, or good moist, with two pounds and a half of dried flour; mix a spoonful of yeast, and half a pint of warm milk with a sufficient quantity of flour to make it the thickness of cream, and pour it into the middle of the flour and sugar, and set it by in a warm place for one hour. Melt the butter to an oil, and stir it into the sponge, with the caraway seeds and sufficient milk to make the dough of a middling stiffness; line a tin, or hoop, with buttered paper, put in the mixture, and again set it before the fire to rise, bake it for one hour in rather a hot oven. When done, brush the top over with milk.

A Light Cake.
Time, one hour.

1491. One pound of flour; half a pound

of butter; half a pound of sugar; three teaspoonfuls of German yeast; a little milk, and nutmeg.

Put the flour, sugar and nutmeg into a bowl, and mix it thoroughly with three teaspoonfuls of German yeast. Set it to rise, and *just* before setting it in the oven mix it up with the butter, warmed in a little milk, as stiff as you can, and bake it one hour. Add a few caraway seeds or citron, if you please.

Spongecake.

Time, one hour and twenty minutes.

1492. Three-quarters of a pound of loaf sugar; half a pound of flour; peel of one lemon; seven eggs.

Put the sugar over the fire to melt, with rather more than half a cupful of boiling water, and the lemon peel; whisk seven eggs, leaving out the whites of three, to a froth, pour the sugar to them, whisking it all the time, and whisk it together for twenty minutes, then add the flour by degrees, stirring it gently. Line a tin with buttered paper, and only half fill it with the mixture, put a piece of white paper over the top, as great care is required to prevent its burning, and bake it for one hour. Do not open the oven until the cake has been in a quarter of an hour.

Lafayette Cake.

1493. A Savoy cake; some jelly or jam.

Make a Savoy cake, and bake it in a round tin five inches in diameter, with straight sides. When cold, cut it in slices a quarter of an inch thick, spread each with jam or jelly; put it together again, placing one slice on the other, three or four for each cake, ice the top and sides, and while it is soft, mark it to cut in wedge-shaped pieces when served. This cake may be served without icing, and may be made of poundcake, or Dover cake.

Lemon Cake.

Time, one hour.

1494. Six eggs; half a pound of pounded sugar; seven ounces of flour; peel of one large, or two small lemons.

Beat the pounded sugar with the yolks of the eggs until it is smooth; whisk the whites to a froth stiff enough to bear the weight of an egg, and add it to the beaten yolks; then stir in gradually seven ounces of flour, and the grated peel of one large, or two small lemons. Line a tin with buttered paper, pour in the cake mixture and bake it.

A Very Rich Lemon Cake.

Time, one hour and a half.

1495. Eighteen eggs; three-quarters of a pound of flour; a pound and a half of sifted sugar; four lemons; a pound and a half of butter; one glass of brandy.

Break the eggs, and leave out six whites, beat them separately for quite half an hour; add to them by degrees three-quarters of a pound of well dried flour, one pound and a half of sifted loaf sugar. Grate into the peel of four lemons. Beat a pound and a half of butter to a cream, and add all together, beating the ingredients well up with a glass of spirits.

Savoy Cake.

Time, to bake, one hour.

1496. Nine eggs; their weight in pounded loaf sugar; the weight of six in flour; the peel of one lemon grated.

Break the eggs into a round-bottomed preserving-pan with the loaf sugar pounded and sifted, and the peel of the lemon grated. Set the pan over a *very* slow fire, and whisk it till quite warm (but not hot enough to set the eggs), remove the pan from the fire, and whisk it till cold, which may be a quarter of an hour; then stir in the flour slightly with a spattle. Take a round mould, be very careful it is quite dry, rub it all over the inside with butter, put pounded sugar round the mould upon the butter, and shake it well to get it out of the crevices; tie a slip of paper round the mould, fill it three parts full with the mixture, and bake it in a cool oven. When done, let it stand for a few minutes, and take it from the mould, which may be done by shaking it a little.

Soda Cake.

Time, one hour and a half to two hours.

1497. One pound of flour; a quarter of a pound of sugar; six ounces of butter; half a pound of currants; fifty grains or a small teaspoonful of carbonate of soda; half a pint of milk; and two eggs.

Rub the quarter of a pound of butter into the flour and sugar. Mix the soda *thoroughly* with the milk, which must be cold. Mix all the ingredients well together, put the mixture into a tin, and bake directly.

Plain Cake.

Time, one hour, or one hour and a half.

1498. One pound of flour; a quarter of a pound of beef dripping; a quarter of a pound of moist sugar; two eggs; two spoonfuls of yeast; two ounces of caraway seeds.

Rub the flour, beef dripping, and moist sugar well together, beat up the eggs, add the yeast and caraway seeds, and beat up all well together. Bake in a tin.

Real Scotch Short Bread.

Time, twenty-five to thirty minutes.

1499. One pound of butter; two pounds of flour; half a pound of sifted sugar; some sweet almonds; a few caraway comfits, and some citron.

Put a pound of butter into a basin, and squeeze it near the fire with the hand till quite soft. Then squeeze into it two pounds of flour and half a pound of sifted loaf sugar with a few sweet almonds chopped very fine. Mix all well together. Take portions of it and shape into cakes of half an inch thick with the hand. Bake in a slow oven. To this may be added caraway comfits and citron.

Plain Short Bread.

Time, twenty-five to thirty minutes for three cakes.

1500. One pound of flour; half a pound of butter; three ounces of brown sugar.

Mix these ingredients and roll them out thick, and bake.

Beaulieu Cake.

Time, two hours.

1501. One pound of butter; eight whole eggs; one pound of flour; three-quarters of a pound of sifted sugar; a teaspoonful of cloves; nutmeg and cinnamon in a fine powder; one glass of wine; three-quarters of a pound of currants.

Beat the butter to a cream and mix with it the whites and yolks of eight eggs beaten separately. Have ready warm by the fire a pound of flour and the same of sifted sugar. Mix them with a few cloves, nutmeg, and cinnamon in a fine powder; then by degrees work the dry ingredients into the butter and eggs. When well beaten, add a glass of wine, and the currants picked and washed. Beat it well for one hour. Put it into a buttered tin, and bake it in a quick oven for one hour.

Leaving out four ounces of butter and the same of sugar makes a less luscious cake.

Adelaide Cake.

Time, one hour and a half.

1502. Yolks of fifteen, whites of seven eggs; ten ounces of loaf sugar; half a pound of ground rice; a little orange-flower water or brandy; peel of two lemons grated.

Whisk the yolks of fifteen eggs for nearly half an hour, add to them the loaf sugar sifted fine, and mix them well together. Then stir in the rice, a little orange-flower water or brandy, and the peel of two lemons grated. Then add the whites of seven eggs well beaten, and stir the whole together for half an hour. Put the mixture in a hoop lined with buttered paper, and bake it in a quick oven for half an hour.

To Clean Currants for Cakes.

1503. Pick out all the sticks and stones; put the currants in a pan, and more than cover them with water; rub them between your hands, take them up by the handful, pick out any imperfections, and put them into another pan. When all are done, cover them with water, shake them about, take them up in the hand, press the water from them and spread them on a thickly folded cloth, lay them in the sun or near the fire to dry, turn them, and spread them that they may be thoroughly dried. Keep them in glass jars or boxes lined with paper. Some dried currants require only to be picked over, rinsed in one water, and dried.

Plain Plum Cake.

Time, two hours and a half.

1504. Two pounds of flour; three spoonfuls of yeast; four eggs; three-quarters of a pound of sugar; one glass of sweet wine; one teaspoonful of ginger; peel of one lemon; one pound of currants, or a few caraways.

Rub eight ounces of butter into two pounds of dried flour; mix it with three spoonfuls of yeast—not bitter—to a paste, and let it rise an hour and a half; then mix in the yolks and whites of four eggs beaten separately, one pound of sugar, some milk to make it a proper thickness, a glass of sweet wine, peel of a lemon grated, and a teaspoonful of ginger. Add at the last a pound of currants washed and dried, or a few caraway seeds.

Small Plum Cakes.

Time, half an hour.

1505. One pound of flour; a quarter of a pound of sugar; yolks of two eggs, white of one; a quarter of a pound of butter; three spoonfuls of cream; three-quarters of a pound of currants.

Well rub a quarter of a pound of butter into a pound of dried flour; then beat up the yolks of two eggs and the white of one. Warm three tablespoonfuls of cream, and mix the flour and butter with them. Wash and dry the currants; stir them well in, and

A Rich Plum Cake.
Time, two hours, or more.

1506. One pound of fresh butter; twelve eggs; one quart of flour; one pound of moist sugar; half a pound of mixed spice; three pounds of currants; one pound of raisins; half a pound of almonds; half a pound of candied peel.

Beat the butter to a cream with your hand, and stir into it the yolks of the twelve eggs well beaten with the sugar; then add the spice and the almonds chopped very fine. Stir in the flour; add the currants washed and dried, the raisins chopped up, and the candied peel cut into pieces. As each ingredient is added, the mixture must be beaten by the hand; then butter a paper, place it round a tin, put in the cake, and bake it for two hours, or more, if required.

Then make it into small cakes. Bake them on a tin in a hot oven, and when they are a nice colour on both sides, open the oven door that they may well soak through for a short time.

Raisin Cake.
Time, one hour and a quarter.

1507. One pound of flour; one pound of sugar; one pound of butter; six eggs; one wineglass of brandy in which rose-leaves have been steeped; one small nutmeg; one small teaspoonful of soda or saleratus; one pound of raisins.

Beat a pound of butter to a cream, and add it to the same weight of flour, and of sugar pounded fine and stirred into the yolks of six eggs; then beat in the whites whipped to a stiff froth, a glass of brandy, a small nutmeg grated, and a *small* teaspoonful of soda or saleratus dissolved in a tablespoonful of hot water. Beat the whole together until it is light and creamy; then add a pound of raisins stoned and chopped. Strew a cupful of flour over them before putting them into the cake; line a tin with buttered paper; put in the cake mixture, and bake it in a quick oven.

Neapolitan Cake.

1508. One pound of flour; ten ounces of sweet almonds; four ounces of bitter almonds; peel of two small lemons; three-quarters of a pound of sifted loaf sugar; one spoonful of orange-flower water; three-quarters of a pound of good butter; yolks of four eggs.

Blanch and pound the sweet and bitter almonds with a spoonful of orange-flower water to a smooth paste. Mix them with the flour and butter broken into pieces; rub the sugar on the peel of the lemons; pound it very fine, and add it to the flour and the almonds, mixing the whole together with the yolks of four well beaten eggs. Roll the paste about a quarter of an inch thick; cut it out with a fluted cutter, and place each piece on a tin lightly dredged with flour. When firm and of a nice bright colour, take them out, and when cool, spread on one side of each slice a layer of different coloured preserves, and pile them evenly on each other to form one entire cake. Ornament the top with pistachio-nuts or coloured sugar in any form you please, or serve plain.

Small Venetian Cakes.

1509. Half a pound of flour; five ounces of sweet almonds; two ounces of bitter almonds; yolks of two eggs; peel of one lemon; six ounces of butter; a quarter of a pound of sugar; a little orange-flower water; two ounces of white sugarcandy.

Blanch and pound the almonds with a little orange-flower water to a smooth paste. Mix it with the flour and the butter broken into small pieces. Rub the sugar on the peel of the lemon to extract the flavour; then pound it fine, and mix it with the flour and almonds. Bind the whole into a paste with the beaten yolks of the eggs, roll it into small balls, and press each with your hand to form a round cake about an inch thick. Brush them over with egg, and strew *thickly* over them coarsely pounded white sugarcandy. Bake them in a slow oven.

Vienna Cake.

1510. One large spongecake; five ounces of loaf sugar; whites of three or four eggs; strawberry, raspberry, and apricot jam.

Take a large round spongecake and cut it very carefully into thin slices; spread each with a layer of strawberry, raspberry, and apricot jam, and replace them in their original form; pound and sift five ounces of sugar, and whisk it with the whites of three or four eggs until it will bear the weight of a whole one; spread this over the cake; sift sugar over the whole, and put it in a cool oven to harden the icing.

A Delicate Cake.
Time, about one hour.

1511. One pound of sugar; one pound of flour; seven ounces of butter; whites of eight eggs; half a nutmeg grated; a little lemon extract.

Beat the butter to a cream, and stir into it a pound of powdered sugar and a pound of sifted flour; then add the whites of eight eggs beaten to a froth, half a small nutmeg grated, and a little lemon extract. Beat all well together, and put it into a tin lined with buttered paper. Five or six ounces of pounded almonds may be added to this cake, according to your taste.

Portugal Cakes.
Time, twenty minutes to half an hour.

1512. One pound of flour; one pound of sugar; one pound of butter; two spoonfuls of rose or orange-flower water; ten eggs; two glasses of white wine; eight ounces of currants.

Mix into a pound of flour the same weight of sifted white sugar, and rub into it a pound of fresh butter till it is thick like grated white bread; then put to it two spoonfuls of orange-flower or rose-water, two glasses of white wine, and the ten eggs well beaten. Work all together with a whisk, and put in the currants washed and dried. Butter some small tin pans, fill them half full, and bake them in a quick oven.

Tablets de Patience, or Lady-fingers.

1513. Four eggs; three ounces of sugar; three ounces of sifted flour; a quarter of a pint of rose or orange-flower water.

Take four eggs, whisk the whites to a firm snow. In the meantime have the yolks beaten up with three ounces of powdered sugar; each of these should be beaten separately. Then mix all together, with three ounces of sifted flour, and when incorporated stir in a quarter of a pint of rose or orange-flower water, and stir them together for some time. Rub some tins with butter, take a funnel with three or four tubes, fill it with the paste, and press out the cakes on the tins, to the size and length of a finger; grate white sugar over each, let them lay till the sugar melts and they shine, then put them in a moderate oven until they have a fine colour; when cool, take them from the tin, and lay them together in couples by the backs. These cakes may be formed with a spoon on writing-paper.

Galettes.
Time, thirty-five minutes.

1514. A pound and a half of butter; two pounds of flour; yolks of four eggs; two ounces of white sugar; and a little milk.

Rub a pound and a half of butter into two pounds of flour; add two ounces of pounded sugar, and mix all together with the yolks of four eggs; and sufficient milk to make it into a paste. Form it into three round cakes about an inch thick, sift a little pounded sugar over them, and bake them in a quick oven for half an hour, or more if required. If very superior cakes are desired, cream may be substituted for the milk, but they are extremely good without it.

Rutland Cake.
Time, one hour and a half to bake.

1515. A quarter of a stone of flour; half a pound of butter; half a pound of loaf sugar; six eggs; three large spoonfuls of yeast; three pints of milk; one pound of currants; peel of two lemons.

Melt half a pound of butter in three pints of milk, and mix it, when quite cool, with a quarter of a stone of flour, six eggs well beaten, half a pound of loaf sugar pounded fine, the peel of two lemons chopped small, a pound of currants washed and picked, and three large spoonfuls of yeast. Beat all well together, and set it at some distance from the fire for three hours, covered over. Divide it into two cakes, and bake them.

Canadian Cakes.
Time, fifteen minutes, to bake.

1516. A pound and a half of sifted flour; one pound of loaf sugar; one pound of fresh butter; ten eggs; two tablespoonfuls of orange-flower water; two tablespoonfuls of wine or brandy; half a pound of currants; peel of half a grated lemon.

Mix a pound and a half of sifted flour with a pound of powdered sugar; rub into it a pound of fresh butter, then add ten well beaten eggs, two spoonfuls of orange-flower water, and two tablespoonfuls of wine or brandy, with half a pound of well cleansed and dried currants. Beat the mixture until it is light and creamy, have some square tins lined with buttered paper, put the mixture into them half an inch deep, and bake in a quick oven. When served, cut it in squares or diamonds. This cake may be iced, but it must be marked as it is to be cut, before the icing is done.

Yeast Cake.
Time, two hours and a half.

1517. Two pounds and a half of flour; half a pound of loaf sugar; half a pint of warm milk; one tablespoonful of yeast; thirteen ounces of oiled butter; one pound and a quarter of currants; half a pound of candied lemon and orange peel; three-quarters of an ounce of mixed spice.

Mix the flour with half a pound of good Lisbon, or pounded loaf sugar. Mix a spoonful of thick yeast with half a pint of lukewarm milk, and enough flour to make it the thickness of cream, pour it into the centre of the flour, and put the pan before the fire for one hour to set the sponge. Then mix with it the fresh butter oiled, the currants washed and dried, the mixed spice, and the candied peel cut into thin pieces. Put it into a hoop or tin lined with a buttered paper, and bake it in a well-heated oven for one hour and a half. When done, it may be iced, and ornamented, or plain.

Sledmere Gingerbread.
Time, three-quarters to one hour.

1518. Half a pound of butter; half a pound of sugar; half a pound of treacle; one pound of flour; half an ounce of ginger; one teaspoonful of carbonate of soda; four eggs.

Put the butter, sugar, and treacle into a saucepan together, and place it over the fire to melt. Then beat four eggs, and stir the melted butter, sugar, and treacle into the eggs, add the powdered ginger and carbonate of soda. Stir all together into the flour, and bake.

Ginger Cakes.
Time, half an hour.

1519. One pound of moist sugar; half a pound of butter; four tablespoonfuls of milk; one pound and three-quarters of flour; half an ounce of grated ginger.

Put a pound of moist sugar, half a pound of butter, and four tablespoonfuls of milk into a saucepan; let it boil until the butter is melted. Whilst it is *quite* hot, mix it with a pound and three-quarters of flour and half an ounce of grated ginger. Roll it out thin, prick it, and cut it into any shape you please. If the paste gets stiff before you have rolled all out, set it before the fire a little. Bake these cakes in a slack oven.

Cheap Gingerbread Cakes.
Time, three-quarters of an hour.

1520. One pound of flour; one pound of treacle; a quarter of a pound of butter; two eggs; one ounce of ground ginger; a teaspoonful of soda; two ounces of citron; a little milk.

Mix the ground ginger with the pound of flour, warm the butter and the treacle, and mix it well with the flour and ginger. Make a few spoonfuls of milk warm, dissolve a teaspoonful of soda in it, and mix the whole up lightly with two eggs well beaten; cut two ounces of citron into slices, stir it into the mixture, and bake in a long buttered tin for three-quarters of an hour. Just before it is removed from the oven, brush it over with the yolk of one egg well beaten with a little milk; put it back in the oven and finish baking it. The time, of course, must be according to its size.

Gingerbread Loaf.
Time, three-quarters of an hour to one hour.

1521. One pound of flour; one pound of treacle; six ounces of butter; four ounces of moist sugar; half an ounce of coriander seeds; half an ounce of caraway seeds; half a tablespoonful of pearlash mint; a quarter of a teacupful of cream; four eggs.

Melt the treacle and the butter together, add the moist sugar, the coriander and caraway seeds ground together, and ginger to your taste; mix with the flour. Bruise fine half a tablespoonful of pearlash mint with a very little cream. Mix all together. Beat four eggs and add them to the gingerbread the very last thing. Line a tin with paper, butter it, and put the mixture in it. Bake in a slow oven.

Honeycomb Gingerbread.
Time, ten minutes.

1522. Half a pound of flour; half a pound of coarse sugar; a quarter of a pound of butter; half an ounce of ginger; half an ounce of lemon peel; juice of one lemon; six ounces of treacle; a quarter of an ounce of butter for the tin.

Add to half a pound of flour half a pound of coarse sugar; rub into it a quarter of a pound of butter; add half an ounce of ginger; mix it up. Put half an ounce of lemon peel, well grated, over it. Pour in the juice of a whole lemon. Use enough treacle to make it into a very thin paste that will spread over a sheet of tin, first having rubbed the tin with butter. Bake it in a moderate oven, and watch it carefully. When it is baked enough, cut it into strips upon the tin, and roll it round your finger like a wafer.

These rolls must be kept in a tin case; if they should chance to get moist they must be renewed in the oven when wanted.

Cocoa-nut or Almond Gingerbread.
Time, three-quarters of an hour.

1523. One pound of treacle; nine ounces of wheaten flour; nine ounces of rice flour; one ounce of ground ginger; half a pound of fresh butter; half a pound of moist sugar; seven ounces of grated cocoa-nut or of pounded almonds; peel of two small lemons; one ounce and a half of candied orange peel.

Put a pound of treacle into a saucepan with half a pound of fresh butter, and when hot pour it into the flour and rice flour, previously mixed with the sugar, ginger, grated lemon peel, and sliced citron. Beat the mixture well together, and set it to become cold; then stir or beat into it seven ounces of grated cocoa-nut or of sweet almonds pounded small in a mortar; beat it for a few minutes, and then drop the mixture from a tablespoon on a buttered tin any size you prefer the cakes to be, and bake them in a slow oven.

Orange Gingerbread.

Time, a quarter of an hour.

1524. Two pounds and a quarter of flour; one pound and three-quarters of treacle; eight ounces of candied orange peel; three-quarters of a pound of moist sugar; one ounce of ground ginger; one ounce of allspice; three-quarters of a pound of butter; one teacupful of milk; yolk of one egg. Mix with the flour a pound and three-quarters of treacle, the candied orange peel cut very small, the moist sugar, ground ginger, and allspice; melt the butter till it is oiled, mix it well with the flour, &c., and put it in a cool place for ten or twelve hours. Roll it out about half an inch thick. Cut it into any form you please, or divide it into pieces rather longer than square, brush them over with milk mixed with the yolk of an egg, and bake them in a cool oven.

Hunting Nuts.

Time, fifteen to thirty-six minutes.

1525. One pound of flour; half a pound of treacle; half a pound of brown sugar; six ounces of butter; and grated ginger. Mix the above ingredients well together, make them into small nuts, and bake them on a baking sheet.

Gingerbread Nuts.

Time, twenty minutes to half an hour.

1526. One pound of Lisbon sugar; two pounds of treacle; three-quarters of a pound of butter; four pounds of flour; four ounces of ginger; one ounce of allspice; two spoonfuls of coriander seed; some candied orange peel; two spoonfuls of brandy; yolks of four eggs. Mix the sugar, treacle, and butter, and melt all together; then stir in the flour, ground ginger, allspice, coriander seed, and the orange peel cut very small. Mix all into a paste with the eggs well beaten, and the brandy, and make them into nuts or cakes.

Ginger Snaps.

Time, twenty minutes to bake.

1527. Half a pound of treacle; quarter of a pound of brown sugar; one pound of flour; one tablespoonful of ground ginger; one of caraway seeds. Work a quarter of a pound of butter into a pound of fine flour, then mix it with the treacle, brown sugar, ginger, and caraway seeds. Work it all well together, and form it into cakes not larger than a crown piece, place them on a baking tin in a moderate oven, when they will be dry and crisp.

Irish Luncheon Cake.

1528. Two pounds of flour, a quarter of a pound of powdered sugar; six ounces of washed and dried currants; one ounce of candied peel; a quarter of a pound of butter; one teaspoonful of carbonate of soda; one of salt; whites of four eggs, and some buttermilk. Rub the butter into the flour, and add to it the powdered sugar, the currants washed and dried, the citron cut into pieces, the salt and carbonate of soda. Mix all these ingredients together. Then whip up the whites of four eggs to a *stiff* froth, and mix up the cake with them and some buttermilk to a moderate thickness, but not too stiff. Grease the cake tins with lard, and dust them with flour; half fill them with the cake mixture, and bake them in rather a quick oven of a light brown. To know when they are done, pass a clean skewer through the middle of each cake, if the skewer is sticky put the cake back into the oven, but should the skewer come out clean the cake is done. Turn them out on a sieve to let the steam go off.

Sydenham Cake.

Time, one hour, to bake.

1529. Half a pound of flour; a quarter of a pound of butter; three ounces of pounded sugar; one teaspoonful of caraway seeds; a little ginger and nutmeg; half a teaspoonful of pounded salts of ammonia. Rub the butter into the flour, and then mix in the seeds, and the ginger and grated nutmeg; add the yolks of two well-beaten eggs, and the whites whisked separately to a stiff froth. Then mix all together with the salts, by putting them into a spoon, holding them over the cake, and pouring from a *kettle* sufficient *boiling* water to make all into a paste. Then put it into a tin lined with a buttered paper, and bake it. To ascertain when it is done, plunge a knife into the centre, and if it comes out clean the cake is ready.

1. Blanc Mange.
2. Open Jelly, with Whipped Cream.
3. Méringues.
4. Tartlets.
5. Wedding Cake.
6. Milan Souffle.
7. Twelfth Cake.
8. Custards with Jelly.

Twelfth Cake.

Time, four hours and a half.

1530. Two pounds of flour ; two pounds of butter ; two pounds of loaf sugar; twenty eggs; four pounds of currants; half a pound of almonds ; one pound of citron ; half a pound of orange; half a pound of candied lemon peel; one wineglassful of brandy; one nutmeg; a quarter of an ounce of ginger and a little mixed spice.

Work the butter to a smooth cream with the hand, mix it with the pounded sugar and the spice, and work it well together for ten minutes. Then break in the eggs by degrees, and beat it for twenty minutes. Add the brandy and then the flour, again stirring it well together; add the currants washed and dried, the citron, and the candied peel cut into thin shreds, and the almonds blanched and chopped very fine. Mix all thoroughly but lightly together, and put it into a hoop lined with buttered paper; smooth it on the top with your hand dipped into milk, and put the hoop on a baking sheet, and then on a raised stand in the oven to prevent the bottom of the cake from burning, and bake it four hours and a half in a slow oven. When nearly cold, ice it over, and ornament it with fancy articles of any description, with a high ornament in the centre.

Rich Bridecake.

1531. Four pounds of flour; four pounds of fresh butter beaten to a cream; two pounds of white powdered sugar; six eggs for each pound of flour; one ounce of mace and nutmeg mixed; one tablespoonful of lemon extract ; four pounds of currants picked clean; four pounds of raisins cut in two and stoned; and one pound of almonds blanched and chopped ; half a pint of brandy.

Beat the yolks of the eggs to a smooth paste, beat the butter and flour together, and add them to the yolks and sugar. Then mix in the whites beaten to a *stiff* froth, the spice, and half a pint of brandy. Stir all together for some time. Strew half a pound of flour over the fruit, mix it thoroughly, then by degrees stir it into the cake.

Butter a *large* tin mould, line it with white buttered paper ; put in the mixture, and bake in a moderate oven. Ice and ornament delicately.

Gateau de Chocolat.

Time, to bake the cake, about one hour.

1532. Fourteen eggs ; two pounds of fine sugar; a little lemon essence; four ounces of fine flour; five ounces of patent flour; four ounces of chocolate ; whites of three eggs ; half a lemon.

Beat up with a wooden spoon the yolks of the eggs with one pound of powdered sugar flavoured with lemon, until it looks nearly white ; whip the whites of the eggs *very stiff*, add them to the beaten yolks and sugar, and mix the flour well in but lightly. Fill a *well* buttered mould three-parts full with this mixture, and place it in a slow oven, keeping the door shut. When done, turn it out of the mould, and let it get cold.

Meantime, make some chocolate icing thus :—Pound and sift the other pound of sugar, put it into a basin with the whites of three eggs, and beat it well together, adding the juice of half a lemon. It is not done till it hangs in flakes from the spoon. Melt about a quarter of a pound of chocolate over the fire, when quite melted stir it in with the icing till it is dark enough. Glaze the gâteau with it. Decorate with spun sugar.

Gateau.

Time, one hour, to bake.

1533. Twenty eggs; their weight in fine sugar; the weight of eleven eggs in flour; one pound of Jordan almonds; green sweetmeats; one pot of apricot jam; a quarter of a pint of white wine ; one glass of brandy ; peel of half a lemon; half a pint of custard.

Beat the yolks of the eggs with the flour *well*, then beat the whites to a very stiff froth. Take care that not the least speck of the yolk falls into them, or they will not beat up so stiffly; by degrees mix them with the sugar, then all together, and beat the whole for half an hour. Take two nice moulds, one larger round than the other, butter them well, fill them with the cake batter, and bake them in a quick oven for an hour. When the spongecakes are baked, take them up. Keep them one day. Cut the top of the larger one smoothly off and scoop out the inside, cut it in slices, cover them with layers of jam and replace them. Cut off the top of the smaller cake, make a hollow in the centre, put the cake you have removed into a basin, and soak it in the wine and brandy for some hours. Then mix it with half a pint of good custard, and replace it in the hollow, put on the top, glaze it with pale chocolate glazing, ornament it with almonds, and decorate the top with green sweetmeats. Put a frill of pink and white cut paper round the bottom of the cake. This is a nice dish for a supper.

Gateau Nourmahal.

1534. A large stale spongecake ; strawberry, raspberry, and greengage jam; one glass of brandy; one glass of white wine; three eggs; fourteen ounces of loaf sugar; half a pint of cream; half a pint of milk; peel of one lemon.

Cut four or five slices from the bottom of a round spongecake, and spread over each slice a layer of the different preserves; replace them in their original form, covering the top layer with a thin slice of cake, press it lightly, and with a sharp knife cut out the centre of the cake, leaving a wide margin all round. Put the part removed into a basin, pour over it the brandy and wine, adding the peel of a lemon grated. When well soaked, mix it with a good custard made with the milk and cream, the yolks of the eggs, and *two* ounces of loaf sugar. Beat it all well together, pour it into the centre of the cake, and put the top over it.

Whisk the whites of the eggs with the remainder of the sugar pounded fine to a *stiff paste*, and spread it thickly and very smoothly round the bottom of the gâteau, form a scroll of icing coloured with a little cochineal syrup round it, and the same on the top, put it into a cool oven to set the icing, and ornament it with leaves, fruit, and almonds.

Chocolate Cakes.

1535. One pound of flour; one pound of sugar; one pound of butter; eight eggs; two tablespoonfuls of brandy; a pinch of salt; chocolate glazing.

Mix the above ingredients well together with a wooden spoon, putting the butter (melted before the fire) in last. Spread a baking sheet with butter, put over it the mixture half an inch thick, and bake it. Cut the cake into oblong pieces and glaze them thickly with chocolate.

Rich Spice Cakes.

Time, ten or twelve minutes.

1536. A pound and a half of flour; three-quarters of a pound of sugar; three-quarters of a pound of butter; half a teacupful of mixed spice.

Well work the butter, flour, and sugar together with the spices, until thoroughly incorporated; roll it thin. Cut it into small cakes, and bake them in a moderate oven.

Wine Cakes.

Time, ten or twelve minutes.

1537. Eight ounces of flour; half a pound of sugar; a quarter of a pound of butter; one wineglassful of wine; four eggs; a few caraway seeds.

Mix eight ounces of flour with half a pound of finely-powdered sugar; beat four ounces of fresh butter with a glass of wine, then make the flour and sugar into a paste with it, and four eggs beaten light, add a few caraway seeds, and roll the paste as thin as paper. Cut the cakes with the top of a tumbler, brush the tops over with the beaten white of an egg, grate sugar over, and bake them ten or twelve minutes in a quick oven. Take them from the tins when cold.

Snow Cake.

Time, one hour and a quarter to one hour and a half.

1538. One pound of arrowroot; eight ounces of loaf sugar; eight ounces of fresh butter; whites of seven eggs; flavouring of essence of lemon.

Beat eight ounces of fresh butter to a cream before the fire, and add the sugar pounded and the arrowroot, beating the mixture all the time. When well mixed, stir in the whites of the eggs whisked to a very stiff froth and the essence of lemon to your taste. Again whisk the mixture for nearly half an hour, pour it into a buttered tin, and bake it in a moderately-heated oven.

Honey Cakes.

Time, twenty-five minutes.

1539. Three pounds and a half of flour; one pound and a half of honey; half a pound of sugar; half a pound of butter; half a nutmeg grated; one tablespoonful of ground ginger; one teaspoonful of saleratus, or carbonate of soda.

Mix the sugar with the flour and grated ginger, and work the whole into a smooth dough with the butter beaten to a cream, the honey and saleratus, or soda, dissolved in a little hot water. Roll it a quarter of an inch thick, cut it into small cakes, and bake them twenty-five minutes in a moderate oven.

Madeline Cake.

Time, one hour.

1540. Four eggs; half a pound of flour; half a pound of butter; half a pound of sugar; peel of half a lemon.

Beat half a pound of butter to a cream with the same weight of pounded sugar, and when thoroughly mixed, add the yolks of four well-beaten eggs, one at a time, then stir in the flour, and then the whites of the eggs beaten as stiff as possible. Put it into a tin lined with buttered paper, and bake it in a quick oven.

Webster Cakes.

Time, a quarter of an hour, to bake.

1541. One pound and a half of flour; one pound of sugar; one pound of butter; ten eggs; two tablespoonfuls of orange-flower water; two of wine or brandy; half a pound of currants; two ounces of citron.

Mix a pound and a half of flour with a pound of white sugar sifted, rub into it a pound of butter, add ten well-beaten eggs, two spoonfuls of wine or brandy, and half a pound of currants washed and dried. Beat the mixture until it is light and creamy. Put it half an inch deep in square tin pans lined with buttered paper, and bake it in a quick oven; or it may be baked in one tin, and iced over.

Dover Cake.

Time, one hour, or more.

1542. Half a pound of butter; one pound of white sugar; half a pint of milk; four eggs; one glass of brandy; two tablespoonfuls of orange-flower water; one teaspoonful of ground cinnamon; one nutmeg; half a *small* teaspoonful of carbonate of soda; two ounces of citron and orange peel; and sufficient flour to make it as thick as pound cake mixture.

Beat half a pound of butter to a cream with a pound of white sugar, add half a pint of new milk, four well-beaten eggs, two spoonfuls of orange-flower or rosewater, a wineglass of brandy, one small nutmeg grated, a teaspoonful of ground cinnamon, and half a *small* teaspoonful of carbonate of soda, dissolved in a tablespoonful of hot water, Beat in as much flour as will make it as thick as a pound cake mixture, beat all well together, and bake it in a buttered tin in a quick oven.

Madeira Cake.

Time, one hour.

1543. Six eggs; nine ounces of flour; nine ounces of sugar; six ounces of butter; one ounce and a half of candied orange peel; peel of half a large lemon; half a teaspoonful of carbonate of soda.

Break six eggs into a basin, and whisk them for at least ten minutes; then whisk in nine ounces of sifted white sugar, nine of sifted flour, the peel of half a large lemon grated, and six ounces of butter just warmed sufficiently to whisk lightly in. Add the candied peel cut into thin slices, and when ready to place in the tin, beat in the soda quickly, and bake it in a moderately-heated oven for about an hour. The cake must be constantly whisked and beaten until put into the oven, and the tin lined with a buttered paper.

Cream Cakes.

1544. Eight eggs; to each egg the grated peel of one large lemon; and one tablespoonful of double-refined sugar.

Whisk the whites of eight eggs to a *stiff* froth, until they will bear the weight of an egg on them, then stir in the grated peel of one lemon to each egg, and a tablespoonful of double-refined sugar. Put a sheet of wet wafer paper on a tin, and with a large spoon drop the froth on it in small lumps, at a little distance from each other; sift a quantity of finely pounded sugar over them, and set the tin in a very slow oven, close it up, and when the froth rises they are sufficiently done; then take them out, put the bottoms of two cakes together, lay them on a sieve, and put them to dry in a cool oven. Before you close the bottom of your cakes to dry, you may lay raspberry or any other jam between them. Serve arranged in pyramid.

Cakes a la Polonaise.

1545. The white of an egg; some powdered sugar; puff paste.

Take some good puff paste, roll it a quarter of an inch thick, and cut it in pieces four or five inches square, gather up the four corners of each, have ready some round moulds, dip them in warm water, and put them inside the cakes; then put them in a quick oven. When they are three parts done, take them out, and brush them over with the white of a beaten egg, sprinkle powdered sugar over, and finish baking. When done, take out the moulds; whip the white of egg and powdered sugar to a froth, and fill the cakes with it.

Queen Cake.

Time, one hour.

1546. One pound of butter; one tablespoonful of orange-flower water; one pound of white sugar; ten eggs; one pound and a quarter of flour; half a pound of almonds.

Beat the butter to a cream, with a spoonful of orange-flower water; then add the sugar pounded, the eggs beaten very light, and a pound and a quarter of sifted flour. Beat the cake well together, then add half a pound of blanched almonds, beaten to a paste; butter some tin moulds, line them with white paper, put in the mixture an inch and a half deep. Bake in a quick oven.

Small Queen Cakes.

Time, a quarter to half an hour.

1547. One pound of flour; half a pound of butter; six ounces of sugar; half a pound of currants; a quarter of a pint of good cream; three eggs; one teaspoonful of carbonate of soda; a quarter of a pound of almonds.

Beat half a pound of fresh butter to a cream, sift in the flour gradually, add six ounces of pounded sugar, a quarter of a pound of sweet almonds, blanched and pounded to a paste, and the currants washed and dried; whisk the eggs separately, add them to the cupful of cream, and stir it into the flour; put the soda into the centre, and beat it all thoroughly together for nearly a quarter of an hour. Then put it into small buttered tin pans, and bake them from twenty minutes to rather more than half an hour.

Derby Short Cakes.

Time, ten minutes.

1548. Half a pound of butter; one pound of flour; one egg; a quarter of a pound of sugar; half a pint of milk.

Rub the butter and flour well together, and mix into a paste with one egg and half a pint of milk, add a quarter of a pound of sifted sugar. Roll out very thin, and cut into shapes. Strew with sugar or ice the top of each, and bake on tin plates.

Bread Cake.

1549. Three pounds of dough; one pound of butter; one pound of sugar; one pound of currants; six eggs; one glass of brandy; one nutmeg; half a teaspoonful of allspice.

Work the butter, sugar, and eggs well together, with a glass of brandy, then work it into the risen dough, adding the spice, and currants picked and washed. Make it into a loaf, and bake the same as bread.

Jumbles.

Time, ten minutes.

1550. A pound and a half of flour; three-quarters of a pound of butter; half a pound of sugar; three eggs; a quarter of a grated nutmeg; half a teaspoonful of lemon extract, or of ground cinnamon.

Work three-quarters of a pound of butter into a pound and a half of flour, half a pound of sugar, and three well beaten eggs; add a quarter of a nutmeg grated, a little lemon extract, or ground cinnamon. Mix it all well together, and then roll it out to the eighth of an inch in thickness, grate loaf sugar over it, cut it into round cakes, make an aperture in the centre of each, lay them on tin plates, and bake them ten minutes in a quick oven.

Almond Jumbles.

Time, ten or twelves minutes.

1551. Half a pound of butter; half a pound of loaf sugar; one pound of flour; a quarter of a pound of almonds; juice of a lemon.

Beat half a pound of butter to a cream, with half a pound of loaf sugar pounded fine; mix it with a pound of flour, and a quarter of a pound of almonds blanched and shred fine, or beaten to a paste with the juice of a lemon. Work it well together, then roll it thin, cut it into small round cakes, and bake them in a quick oven.

Strawberry Shortcake.

1552. One large tablespoonful of butter; two of loaf sugar; one well-beaten egg; two even teaspoonfuls of cream of tartar; three cupfuls of flour; one small teaspoonful of soda; one cupful of milk; strawberries and sugar.

Beat a large tablespoonful of butter with two of pounded sugar to a cream; add one well beaten egg, rub two even teaspoonfuls of cream of tartar in three cupfuls of flour, and add them. Dissolve a *small* teaspoonful of carbonate of soda in a cupful of milk; add it last. Bake in a flat pan in a quick oven. When done, let it get cold, cut it in three layers, or in half, cover one layer with strawberries, and sprinkle them with sugar; put on a layer of the cake, another layer of strawberries and sugar, lay on the top layer, and dust sugar over it.

The strawberries may be bruised in a syrup made with three large spoonfuls of sugar and three dessertspoonfuls of water, and boiled to a syrup for a few minutes, and when cold, spread over the cake.

Shrewsbury Cakes.

Time, twelve to fourteen minutes.

1553. Half a pound of butter; half a pound of sifted loaf sugar; one pound of flour; half a teaspoonful of powdered cinnamon; a quarter of a pound of currants; two or three eggs; or instead of currants half an ounce of grated ginger.

Take half a pound of butter, the same of sifted loaf sugar, and one pound of flour. Mix them well together. Add a little pounded cinnamon, and a quarter of a pound of currants; wet the ingredients with the yolks and whites of two eggs. If two are not enough, add a third yolk. Roll the paste out rather thin, cut the cakes out of it the size of a saucer, pinch them round the edges. Bake them in a cool oven to a nice brown.

N.B.—The currants may be left out, and grated ginger used instead, if preferred.

Citron Cakes.
Time, fifteen or twenty minutes.

1554. Half a pound of butter; six eggs; half a pound of sugar; ten ounces of flour; one wineglassful of brandy; a quarter of a pound of citron.

Beat half a pound of butter to a cream, take six new-laid eggs, beat the whites to a *stiff* froth, and the yolks with half a pound of white powdered sugar, and rather more than half a pound of sifted flour. Beat these well together, add a glass of brandy and a quarter of a pound of citron cut into thin slips. Bake it in small heart-shaped tins, or in any form you please, rubbing the tin over with melted butter, and bake in a quick oven.

Rock Cakes.
Time, half an hour.

1555. Half a pound of butter; one pound of flour; half a pound of moist sugar; forty drops of essence of lemon; two eggs; half a glass of brandy or white wine.

Rub half a pound of butter into a pound of dried flour and half a pound of fine moist sugar. Mix the whole with two beaten eggs and half a glass of brandy or white wine. Drop them on a baking sheet, and bake them half an hour.

Cocoa-nut Rock Cakes.
Time, half an hour.

1556. Half a pound of cocoa-nut; seven ounces of sifted loaf sugar; three eggs.

Grate the cocoa-nut, mix it with the sifted lump-sugar and the whites of three eggs. Put a piece of buttered paper on a flat tin, and with a fork drop the cake mixture in little cakes on it. Bake in a moderate oven.

Italian Macaroons.
Time, half an hour.

1557. One pound of Valencia or Jordan almonds; two pounds and a half of sifted loaf sugar; whites of fourteen eggs.

Pound the almonds quite fine with the whites of four eggs, add the sifted loaf sugar, and rub them well together with the pestle. Put in by degrees ten more whites, working them well as you put them in. Put the mixture into a biscuit funnel, and lay them out on wafer paper in pieces about the size of a walnut. Put three or four pieces of blanched almonds cut into slips on each, and bake them on a baking plate in a slow oven.

Riband Wafers.
Time, fifteen minutes.

1558. One pound of pounded sugar; three-quarters of a pound of flour; nine eggs; two lemons.

To one pound of loaf sugar pounded and sifted very fine, add a quarter of a pound of flour and the peel of two lemons. Beat the eggs for half an hour, then add the other ingredients to them. Oil some butter, grease the copper sheets with it, and roll out the paste very thin. When half done, roll them round your finger, and return them to the oven to crisp.

To Make Light Wigs.

1559. Three-quarters of a pound of fine flour; half a pint of warm milk; two or three spoonfuls of light yeast; a quarter of a pound of sugar; a quarter of a pound of butter; a few seeds.

To three-quarters of a pound of fine flour put half a pint of milk made warm. Mix in it two or three spoonfuls of light yeast. Cover it up, set it to rise for half an hour by the fire, and then work into the paste a quarter of a pound of sugar and a quarter of a pound of butter. Make it into light wigs with as little flour as possible, and a few carraway seeds. Set them in a quick oven to bake.

In addition to this receipt put a little more butter, sugar, and a few currants, instead of the seeds, and it makes a good common cake.

Rout Drop Cakes.

1560. One pound of butter; one pound of flour; one pound of sugar; one pound of currants; two eggs; one tablespoonful of orange-flower water; one of brandy.

Mix a pound of butter into the same weight of flour and powdered sugar. Add the currants washed and dried, and wet it into a stiff paste with two well-beaten eggs, the orange-flower water, and a tablespoonful of brandy. Mix it well together, and drop it on a floured tin. Bake them lightly.

Indian Griddle Cakes.

1561. Two eggs; one quart of milk; one teaspoonful of salt, and some flour.

Beat two eggs very light, and stir them into a quart of milk, with a little salt, and sufficient flour to make a good batter. Bake it as soon as it is mixed, on a hot griddle, rubbed over with a piece of suet, or butter. A tablespoonful of batter will be sufficient for each cake.

Tea Cakes.
Time, twenty minutes.

1562. One pound and a quarter of flour; one tablespoonful of yeast; two eggs; a little salt, and one ounce and a half of sugar; half a pint of milk; two ounces and a half of butter.

Beat two eggs in a large basin, or bowl, and mix with it a tablespoonful of yeast. Then pour on it the butter and milk warmed together; stir in the flour, salt, and pounded sugar; beat it to a *very* light dough, and set it to rise for twenty minutes or half an hour, covered over before the fire. Divide it into as many tea cakes as you please, and bake them in a moderate oven for twenty minutes, or less time, if small.

Iced Rolls.
Time, ten to twelve minutes.

1563. A quarter of a pound of fine flour; two ounces of butter; two or three ounces of sifted sugar; two eggs; a quarter of a cupful of cold water; a quarter of a pint or more of good custard; a little candied sweetmeat.

Take a quarter of a pound of fine flour, two ounces of butter, and one ounce of sifted crushed white sugar; rub these ingredients well together. Beat up the yolk of an egg with a little water. Add it to the flour and butter, and make them into a paste. Work it well with your hands for *one minute*, and roll it cut. Have ready some mince-pie tins, butter them, line them with the paste, put a little ball of paper in each (to keep the lid of paste raised), then put a lid of the paste over them. Bake them in a quick oven. When you take them out of the tins, turn them bottom upwards. When they are cold, take a penknife and cut a hole the size of a sixpence, and take the paper out.

Beat the whites of two eggs to a strong froth; cover the rolls with it, and dust them well with sifted sugar. Put them in a slack oven to brown.

When you send them to table, fill them with good custard, and put a little sweetmeat on the top. Six will make a dish.

Cheshire Rolls.
Time, half an hour to bake.

1564. Two pounds of dried flour; two ounces of sugar; a pinch of salt; a quarter of a pound of butter; two eggs; two tablespoonfuls of yeast; one pint of milk.

Mix with two pounds of dried flour a pinch of salt, a quarter of a pound of butter, the sugar, and two eggs well beaten with two spoonfuls of yeast. Pour in a pint of new milk, knead it well, and set it before the fire to rise. Divide it into equal portions, butter a tin, put them on it, and again place them to rise for a few minutes, and then bake them.

To Make Buns.
Time, to bake, twenty minutes.

1565. Half an ounce of caraway seeds; half a pound of currants; a little nutmeg; a little lemon peel; two eggs; one quart of new milk; one ounce of butter; two pounds of flour; a quarter of a pound of sifted sugar; one or two spoonfuls of yeast; one egg.

Make a hole in the middle of the flour, and pour the milk in, with one or two spoonfuls of yeast. Stir the dough, cover it over, and let it stand before the fire to rise for one hour. Then mix the caraway seeds, lemon peel, and nutmeg with one half, and the currants with the other, and cover all up together till the oven is ready. Make up the buns to a proper size, and put them on a tin baking sheet buttered. Beat up an egg, and brush them over with it. Cover them over again, and put them before the fire for another half an hour. Then bake them. Do not make them too large.

Light Buns.
Time, twenty to twenty-five minutes to bake,

1566. One pound of flour; half a pound of butter; half a pound of sugar; yolks of four eggs; whites of two; three ounces of candied orange or lemon peel; a quarter of a pint of milk; a little nutmeg; a teaspoonful of carbonate of soda.

Work into a pound of well dried flour, half a pound of good butter, until it is like crumbs of bread. Add the sugar pounded, a little grated nutmeg, a pinch of salt, and the candied peel minced fine (or half a pound of currants if preferred). Pour the boiling milk over the whole, mix it lightly for a minute or two, and then add quickly the yolks and whites of the eggs well beaten. When all are thoroughly mixed, shake the carbonate of soda over it, and beat it well into the mixture. Drop the cakes upon a buttered tin, and bake them in a moderate oven.

Bath Buns.
Time, twenty minutes.

1567. One pound of flour; half a pound of butter; half a pound of white sugar; peel of three lemons; a small cupful of cream;

one teaspoonful of yeast; a few caraway comfits.

Mix with a pound of dried flour, half a pound of sifted sugar, the peel of three lemons grated, half a pound of good butter melted in a small cupful of cream, three well-beaten eggs, and a spoonful of yeast. Work all well together, set it to rise, and then make it into buns of any size you like. Put a few caraway comfits on the top.

Cross Buns.
Time, twenty minutes.

1568. Four pounds of sifted flour: one pound of moist sugar; one gill of yeast; an ounce and a half of allspice; one pint of milk; one pound of butter.

Mix with four pounds of fine flour an ounce and a half of allspice, or the same quantity of mixed spice, and a pound of good fine moist sugar. Make a hole in the centre, and stir in a gill of yeast and a pint of lukewarm milk, made the thickness of cream with a few spoonfuls of the flour. Cover the pan over with a folded cloth and set it to rise for two hours. Then just dissolve until lukewarm a pound of butter, stir it into the other ingredients to make a soft paste, adding a little more warm milk if required. Set it again to rise for nearly an hour, then roll it the size you wish with your hands, and place the buns on a baking tin rubbed over with butter, laying them in rows about four inches apart. Set them in a warm place for half an hour, or until they have half risen to double their size. Then press the form of a cross on each with a tin mould, or mark them with the back of a knife, set them in a hot oven to bake, and when done, brush them over with milk as they are drawn from the oven.

Sally Lunn Cakes.
Time, twenty minutes.

1569. One pint of boiling milk; half a tumbler of yeast; sufficient flour to form a stiff batter; two eggs; two ounces of powdered sugar; a quarter of a pound of butter.

Put a pint of boiling milk into a pan, and when it has become lukewarm pour half a tumbler of yeast upon it, stir it well, and add as much flour as will form a *stiff* batter. Cover the pan with a cloth, and place it before the fire for two hours; beat up the eggs with the powdered sugar. After the dough has stood to rise the time specified, mix the butter with the sugar and eggs, add it to the dough, knead it, and let it remain in the pan for half an hour, then divide it into cakes, put them on a baking tin, and bake them in a well-heated oven.

Egg Rusk.
Time, twenty minutes to bake.

1570. Four ounces of butter; seven eggs; three ounces of sugar; a gill of yeast; and some wheat flour; one pint of warm milk.

Melt four ounces of butter in a pint of warm milk; beat seven eggs until you can take them up by the spoonful, and with these, three ounces of sugar, a gill of yeast, and as much flour as may be necessary to make a soft dough, shake a little flour over it, and set it in a warm place to rise. When light (which it will be in two hours), work it down, cover it, set it to rise again for one hour; again work it down. Rub a baking tin with butter, make the rusks in cakes the size and shape of an egg, lay them on the tin, so as to touch each other, dip a brush into milk and pass it lightly over the cakes, let them set for ten minutes, and then bake them in a quick oven for twenty minutes. A few minutes before they are done pass a brush dipped in milk over them.

Potato Muffins.

1571. Three large mealy potatoes; a little salt; two ounces of butter; two eggs; a small teaspoonful of soda; a teacupful of yeast; three pints of flour; one pint of warm water.

Boil and mash three large mealy potatoes, and beat them smooth with about two ounces of butter and a little salt, adding sufficient warm water to make it the consistency of *very* thick cream. Well beat two eggs, mix them in, and then stir to the whole three pints of fine dried and sifted flour; mix these well together and add a pint of lukewarm water, then stir in the soda and yeast, and set it to rise all night. The next morning bake the muffins in rings on a griddle.

Brown Bread Biscuits.
Time, six or seven minutes.

1572. One pound of coarse brown flour; two ounces of butter; and a little water.

Make the butter and water boiling hot, add it to the flour, keeping it very firm. Roll the biscuits out not too thin, and bake them in rather a quick oven.

Caraway Biscuits.
Time, ten minutes.

1573. A quarter of a pound of butter; a quarter of a pound of sugar; two eggs; a few caraway seeds; and some flour.

Beat a quarter of a pound of butter to a cream; beat two eggs with four ounces of powdered sugar to a good froth, put them together and mix them well; add flour enough to make it into a stiff paste, put in a few caraway seeds, roll it thin, and cut out the biscuits with a glass or small tin. Prick them, and bake in a slow oven.

French Biscuits.

1574. Three eggs; their weight in flour, and powdered sugar; half an ounce of candied lemon peel.

Whisk the whites of three new-laid eggs until they are *very* stiff, then whip in the candied lemon peel cut thin and fine, add by degrees the flour, and sugar pounded, and then whip all together with the yolks of the eggs until it is thoroughly blended; shape the biscuits on fine white paper with a spoon, and sift white sugar over them. Bake them in a moderate oven, giving them a light colour on the top; then with a fine knife cut them from the paper, and put them in tin boxes to dry.

Naples Biscuits.

Time, about ten minutes.

1575. One pound of flour; one pound of loaf sugar; nine eggs; a little rosewater.

Beat the eggs well, leaving out the whites of two; pound and sift the sugar, and then whisk it with the beaten eggs and a spoonful of rosewater; add the flour gradually. Mix all well together, and make them up long or round.

Nun's Biscuits.

1576. Yolks and whites of six eggs; half a pound of almonds; one pound of loaf sugar; quarter of a pound of flour; peel of two lemons grated; two ounces of citron.

Whisk the whites of six eggs to a froth, blanch half a pound of almonds, and beat them well; with the froth as it rises; then take the yolks of the eggs and beat them with a pound of sifted loaf sugar. Mix the almonds and froth with the sugar and eggs; add a quarter of a pound of flour, the peel of two lemons grated, and the two ounces of citron sliced. Butter some small cake pans, fill them *half* full, put them into a quick oven, and when the biscuits are lightly coloured, turn them out on tins to harden the bottom of the biscuits.

Lemon Biscuits.

Time, fifteen minutes.

1577. One pound and a half of flour; a quarter of a pound of butter; one pound and a half of loaf sugar; three lemons; two eggs.

Dry well before the fire a pound and a half of flour, rub into it a quarter of a pound of butter *as fine as possible*, mix with it a pound and a half of loaf sugar pounded, and the peel of three lemons chopped very fine. Well beat two eggs; add to them the juice of two lemons, and stir thoroughly. Put the mixture into the flour, and mix all well together till you have a stiff paste; roll it out to the thickness of a penny piece, and divide it into biscuits with a paste cutter. Bake them on a tin.

These biscuits should be kept in a tin box near the fire till wanted, as they are apt to give.

Orange Biscuits.

Time, five or six minutes.

1578. Eight eggs; two Seville oranges; quarter of a pound of flour; half a pound of butter; half a pound of sugar; and some candied orange peel.

Beat half a pound of fresh butter until it is a cream, and stir into it the same weight of pounded white sugar previously rubbed on the rinds of two or three Seville oranges. Add the candied orange peel cut into thin slices, then mix in the flour, and stir in gradually the yolks of eight eggs beaten well; whisk the whites until they will bear an egg on them, and mix them with the other ingredients. Fill some buttered moulds, pour in the mixture, sift some powdered sugar over, and bake them in a slow oven.

Damascus Biscuits.

Time, fifteen minutes.

1579. Four eggs; five ounces of beef-suet; half an ounce of almonds; six ounces of loaf sugar; two ounces and a half of flour; lemon to taste.

Beat the whites of four eggs to a froth, chop the suet and almonds separately very fine, and beat well together. Mix with the yolks of the eggs the loaf sugar finely sifted; beat well, and pour into the almond mixture; shake in the flour, and add the lemon. Bake in small tins in a quick oven.

German Biscuits.

Time, six or eight minutes.

1580. Half a pound of dried flour; five ounces of butter; seven ounces of sugar; two eggs; two dessertspoonfuls of cream; peel of a small lemon grated.

Beat five ounces of butter to a cream, and mix in the loaf sugar pounded, the grated lemon peel, half a pound of dried flour, and the cream and well-beaten eggs, to form a nice light dough. Mix all well before kneading it, roll it in thin, long narrow strips, and bake on a tin in a quick oven.

American Biscuits.

Time, about twenty minutes.

1581. One pound of flour; a quarter of a pound of butter; a quarter of a pound of sugar; half a pint of milk; half a teaspoonful of salt of tartar; half a teacupful of water.

Mix a pound of flour with a quarter of a pound of butter. Make half a pint of new milk warm, and sweeten with a quarter of a pound of white sugar; pour it gradually into the butter paste. Dissolve the salt of tartar in half a teacupful of cold water, and add to the mixture, working the paste to a good consistency; roll it out, and cut into small biscuits. Bake in a quick oven directly they are made.

Sponge Biscuits.

Time, half an hour to bake.

1582. Twelve eggs; one pound and a half of sugar; fourteen ounces of flour; peel of two lemons.

Beat the yolks of twelve eggs for half an hour, then add a pound and a half of sifted white sugar, and whisk it till you see it rise in bubbles; then whisk the whites of the eggs to a strong froth, and beat them well with the sugar and yolks; stir in fourteen ounces of flour, and the peel of two lemons grated. Bake in tin moulds well buttered, in a quick oven; but before you put the biscuits in, sift pounded sugar over them.

Spanish Biscuits.

Time, ten or twelve minutes.

1583. Eight eggs; eight spoonfuls of sugar; eight ounces of flour; the peel of one lemon grated.

Beat the yolks of eight eggs for half an hour, and then stir in eight spoonfuls of powdered sugar; beat the whites of the eggs to a very stiff froth, and work them into the sugar and yolks; then mix in the flour and the peel of a lemon grated, beat it all well together, and drop the mixture on paper placed on a tin.

Ginger Biscuits.

Time, seventeen or eighteen minutes.

1584. Eight ounces of flour; four ounces of butter; four ounces of loaf sugar; yolks of three eggs; and some ground ginger.

Beat the butter to a cream before the fire; add the flour by degrees, then the sugar pounded and sifted, and a flavouring to taste of ground ginger, and mix the whole with the yolks of three well-beaten eggs. When thoroughly mixed, drop the biscuit mixture on buttered paper, a sufficient distance from each other to allow the biscuits to spread, and bake them a light colour, in a rather slow oven.

Almond Spice Biscuits.

Time, one hour.

1585. Three pounds of flour; three pounds of almonds; one ounce of mace; one ounce of cinnamon; one pound of loaf sugar; three pounds of moist sugar.

Take three pounds of sifted flour, three pounds of almonds pounded fine, an ounce of mace, and the same of cinnamon beaten up, and one of powdered sugar. Dissolve three pounds of good brown sugar in a teacupful of water; set it over the fire, and when boiling take off the scum, add it to the other ingredients, and make it into a paste the size of a rolling-pin, lay it on a sheet of paper, flatten it with your hands, keeping it higher at the middle than at the ends; put it into a quick oven for nearly one hour. When done, take it out, and whilst hot cut it in slices the eighth of an inch thick, and dry them in a cool oven. Keep them in a tin box for use.

Half this quantity can be used.

Arrowroot Biscuits.

Time, fifteen minutes.

1586. Eight ounces of flour; eight ounces of butter; six ounces of arrowroot; eight ounces of loaf sugar; six eggs.

Beat the butter to a cream, add it to the eggs well whisked, stir in the flour gradually, and beat all thoroughly together. Roll the arrowroot, mix it with the sugar pounded fine, and mix it well into the other ingredients. Drop the dough from a spoon on a buttered tin in small pieces, and bake them in a slow oven.

Spoon Biscuits.

Time, twenty-two minutes.

1587. The yolks and whites of four eggs; a quarter of a pound of fine loaf sugar; peel of one lemon.

Put to the yolks of four eggs a quarter of a pound of fine loaf sugar, and the peel of a lemon grated; mix them together for ten minutes, then whip the whites to a firm froth, and put about half of them to the yolks; mix it well, then add the remainder, stir it very gently, and lay it with a spoon on sheets of paper; let each biscuit be the thickness and length of a finger, and some little distance apart. Strew them with fine white sugar; lay the papers on baking-tins, and as soon as the sugar dissolves, and the biscuits shine, put them in a moderate oven, let the door remain open for seven or eight minutes, then close it for a quarter of an hour. When cold, take the biscuits from the paper with a knife blade. Almonds blanched and cut in slips across, may be stirred into the mixture before putting it on the paper.

Pistachio Biscuits.

Time, twenty-five minutes.

1588. One pound of pistachio-nuts; two ounces of sweet almonds; whites of sixteen eggs; yolks of eight; one pound of loaf sugar; two ounces of flour; peel of one lemon grated.

Blanch and pound the pistachio-nuts and almonds, moistening occasionally with the white of egg; beat the whites of the eggs to a high froth, and the yolks with half of the sugar, and the peel of a lemon grated. When both are thoroughly beaten, put them together, beat constantly; whilst doing so, sift over the remainder of the sugar and the flour, and then add the almonds and pistachios. Make some paper cases, put in the biscuits half as thick as a finger, bake in a moderate oven. Whip the white of an egg with a tablespoonful of sugar to a smooth paste and brush the biscuits over with it.

Cocoa-nut Biscuits.

Time, fifteen minutes.

1589. Six ounces of cocoa-nut; three eggs; nine ounces of loaf sugar.

Well whisk the eggs, sift in the sugar by degrees, and add the grated cocoa-nut. Take a piece of the paste nearly the size of an egg, roll it between your hands in the form of a cone. When all are thus shaped, place them on tins covered with paper, and bake them a light colour in a gentle oven.

Plain Biscuits.

Time, ten minutes to bake.

1590. One pound of flour; half a pint of milk; two ounces and a half of fresh butter.

Dissolve the butter in the milk made warm but not hot, and stir it into the flour to make a firm paste, roll it out thin, and cut it with a plain tin shape or a tumbler; prick each biscuit and bake.

DESSERTS.

To Prepare Apples for Dessert.

1591. Apples; a thin syrup of sugar and water; strawberry or any other *pink* jelly.

Peel and core as many apples as will fill a dish, and put them in a stewpan over a hot plate, with a thin syrup of sugar and water (the same as for compotes) until tender, then set them to cool. Lay them on a dish, pour the syrup round them, and fill the centre of the apples with strawberry, or any pink jelly.

To Prepare Oranges for Dessert.

1592. Oranges; a quarter of a pound of loaf sugar; a little cochineal.

Strip off the peel from a sufficient number of oranges to fill a dish, and take off part of the white skin, being careful not to break through to the orange. Pound a quarter of a pound of loaf sugar, lay it in a dish, and pour over it as much cochineal as will make it a bright colour; dry it before the fire, and then roll the oranges about in the sugar until they are well *covered* with it. Serve in a glass dish.

Iced Fruit for Dessert or Garnish.

Time, three or four hours to dry.

1593. Some barberries, or any fresh fruit; a quarter of a pint of water; whites of two eggs and some finely powdered sugar.

Break the whites of two eggs into a bowl, well whisk them, and then beat them into a quarter of a pint of cold water. Take some of the largest bunches of barberries, dip them into the beaten egg, drain them, and then roll them thrice in some loaf sugar pounded very fine. When done, place them separately on sheets of paper, and put them in a dry place for three or four hours, or longer, to crystallize. Send them to table arranged as taste directs on a dessert dish, or garnish with them when required.

Apricots, peaches, or any fresh fruit may be crystallized in the same manner, and have a very good effect.

To Ice Oranges.

Time, three-quarters to one hour.

1594. The whites of two eggs; one pound of loaf sugar; oranges.

Take off the skin and pith from some fine China oranges, taking care not to cut them through, and pass a double thread through the centre of each. Pound and sift the sugar, add it to the whites of two eggs, and whisk it for about twenty minutes, or not quite so long. Hold the oranges by the thread, and dip them into the beaten eggs and sugar, covering every part with it, then pass a piece of thin stick through the thread, and fix it across a very slow oven for the sugar to dry.

Iced and Stewed Fruits for Desserts. 299

Iced Currants for Dessert.

Time, to dry, about three hours.

1595. Red or white currants ; a quarter of a pint of water ; pounded loaf sugar; whites of two eggs.

Procure some of the finest bunches of red or white currants ; well beat the whites of two eggs, and mix them with a quarter of a pint of spring water, dip each bunch of currants separately into the egg and water, drain them for two minutes, and roll them in some finely-powdered loaf sugar, repeat the rolling in sugar, and lay them carefully on sheets of white paper to dry, when the sugar will become crystallized. Arrange them on a dish, or with a mixture of any other fruit. Plums, grapes, or any fruit may be iced in the same manner for dessert.

Stewed French Plums.

Time, one hour to stew the plums separately ; one hour and a half in the syrup.

1596. One pound and a half of French plums ; three-quarters of a pint of syrup ; two tablespoonfuls of port wine; peel and juice of one lemon ; one pound of loaf sugar.

Stew a pound and a half of French plums in a little water. When tender, strain them, and put to the water a pound of loaf sugar, boil it for a quarter of an hour, skimming it carefully. When clear, add the port wine, peel of the lemon, and the juice ; put in the plums, and let the whole simmer very slowly for about an hour and a half. When done, take out the plums in a glass dish, and pour the syrup over them. Set them in a cold place.

Stewed Fruit—A Compote.

Time, twenty minutes.

1597. To two pounds and a half of fruit, and three-quarters of a pound of sugar, one pint of water.

The fruit should be freshly gathered. Make a syrup of three-quarters of a pound of loaf sugar in a pint of water, *for each two pints and a half* of fruit. Let this syrup boil gently for ten or twelve minutes, and skim it thoroughly, then throw in the fruit. Let it boil up quickly, and afterwards simmer until quite tender, which it will be usually in eight or ten minutes. Be careful that the fruit does not crack.

Compote of Oranges.

Time, twenty-five minutes.

1598. One pound of sugar; one pint and a half of water ; eight oranges.

Boil a pound of sugar in a pint and a half of water with the peel of eight oranges cut very thin, for nearly twenty minutes, removing the scum as it rises. After the oranges are peeled, remove all the white pith without breaking the inner skin, divide them into quarters, and put them into the syrup, and let them simmer for five or six minutes ; then take them carefully out with a skimmer or spoon, and arrange them in the centre of a glass dish piled one on the other with the skins downwards. Boil the syrup until thick, and when cool pour it carefully over the orange quarters, and set them in a cold place until ready to serve.

Compote of Apricots.

Time, three-quarters of an hour.

1599. Twelve ounces of sugar to one pint of water ; some ripe apricots.

Boil twelve or fourteen ounces of sugar in a pint of water for a quarter of an hour, removing all the scum as it rises. Put as many ripe apricots into it as required, and let them simmer gently for a quarter of an hour or twenty minutes, until they are tender, but do not let them break. Then take each apricot carefully out on a glass dish, arranging them as taste directs, and when the syrup is cool pour it over them and set it in a cold place.

Orange Wafers.

Time, four hours and a half.

1600. Four dozen Seville oranges, and their weight in loaf sugar.

Take four dozen of the finest Seville oranges, squeeze out the juice, take out the core, and boil the peel in three quarts of water until quite soft. Then take them out and dry them from the water, chop them very fine, and put them into a mortar with their weight in fine loaf sugar, and pound them for four hours. Spread them on tins or glasses very thin, and dry them in the sun. They must be taken off the tins or glasses before quite dry, and cut into the shapes you wish, taking care they are flat.

Apricot Cakes.

Time, a quarter of an hour to simmer.

1601. One pound of ripe apricots ; half a pound of double-refined sugar ; one spoonful of water.

Scald and peel a pound of fine ripe apricots, take out the stones, and beat them in a mortar to a pulp. Boil half a pound of double-refined sugar with a spoonful of water, skim it well, then put in the apricot pulp, and simmer it over a slow fire for a quarter of an hour, stirring gently all the time. Then put it into shallow flat glasses, and when cold turn the cakes out on glass plates, put them in a cool oven, and turn them once a day till they are dry.

Apricot Chips.

1602. Some apricots; three-quarters of their weight in sugar.

Take some fine ripe apricots, pare them, and cut them very thin into chips; take three-quarters of their weight in pounded sugar, and put it into a stewpan with the apricot chips. Set it over a slow clear fire to dissolve the sugar, and then take it off the fire. Take the chips out of the syrup and let them stand till the next day. Then *warm* them again in the syrup, but do not let them *boil*, and keep turning them until they have drunk up all the syrup. Place them on a plate, and set them in a cool oven to dry.

Orange Chips.

1603. Some fine Seville oranges; one pound of sugar to a quart of water for the syrup.

Pare some of the finest Seville oranges aslant, about a quarter of an inch broad, and keep the parings as whole as you can, as they will then have a better effect. Put them into spring water and salt for a day or two. Then boil them in a large quantity of water until quite tender, and when done drain them on a sieve. Make a thin syrup with a pound of sugar to a quart of water, put in the chips and boil them a few at a time, to keep them from breaking, till they look clear; then put them into another syrup of pounded sugar, as much water as will dissolve it, and boil to candy height. Then take them out very carefully and lay them on a sieve; grate or *sift* double-refined sugar over them, and dry them in the oven.

Orange Biscuits for Dessert.

1604. Seville oranges and their weight in sugar.

Boil the oranges in two or three waters, till most of the bitterness is gone, cut them across, and take out the pulp and juice; beat the peels very fine in a mortar, and add to them an equal weight of pounded sugar. When mixed to a paste, spread it thin on dishes; set it before the fire. When half dry, cut it into any forms you please; turn them to dry the other side, and keep them in a box with layers of paper between them.

Damson Cakes.

1605. To each pound of damsons one pound of loaf sugar; whites of six eggs.

Put the damsons into the oven to bake, then pour the syrup from them through a sieve. To each pound of damsons add a pound of sifted loaf sugar, a little of the damson juice, and the whites of six eggs; beat the whole together till it becomes quite thick; put the mixture into a Dutch oven, in little cakes about the size of small queen cakes, smooth them on the top with a knife, and bake them very slowly with the door of the oven shut.

To Bake Pears.

Time, four or five hours to bake; half an hour to stew.

1606. Twelve pears; a few cloves; a glass of port wine; one pound of white sugar; a little water; peel of one lemon.

Pare, halve, and core the pears; put them into an earthen pan, with a few cloves, a glass of port wine, a pound of white sugar pounded, and a little water. Bake them in an oven not too hot, then set them over a slow fire and let them stew gently. Cut the peel from a lemon very thin in small shreds, and add it to the pears when stewing. Should the syrup not be rich enough, add more sugar. Half the number of pears can be done, allowing half a pound of sugar, or more if necessary, but the same quantity of wine and lemon peel.

Stewed Pears.

Time, three or four hours.

1607. Nine or ten large pears; seven ounces of loaf sugar; seven cloves; six allspice; rather more than half a pint of water; a quarter of a pint of port wine; a few drops of cochineal.

Pare and core nine or ten large pears, dividing them with part of the stalk on each piece; put them into a very clean stewpan with seven ounces of loaf sugar, rather more than half a pint of water, a quarter of a pint of port wine, seven cloves, six allspice, and a few drops of prepared cochineal. Let them stew gently over a clear fire until tender, and when done take them carefully out, and place the slices of pear in a glass dish. Boil up the syrup for a few minutes, and when cool pour it over the pears, and put them by to get cold. The peel of a lemon cut thin is an improvement to the flavour of the fruit.

To Ice Evergreens.

1068. One pound of alum; one quart of boiling water.

Dissolve a pound of alum by boiling it in a quart of water; pour it into a deep vessel, and as it cools the alum will be precipitated.

Choose the lightest sprays, and hang them with the stems upwards on cords stretched across the top of the vessel so that they do not touch the bottom. They will attract the alum in the process of crystallization like the threads in sugarcandy. The warmer the solution when they are put in the smaller will be the crystals attached to them, but care must be taken that it be not hot enough to destroy the leaves or fronds, and if there be any berries like holly it must be hardly lukewarm.

The same solution warmed again will do two or three bouquets.

PRESERVES AND PICKLES.

Lime Preserves.

Time, to stand, forty-eight hours; to boil, ten or twelve minutes.

1609. The limes; double their weight in sugar; one pint of water to each two pounds and a half of sugar.

Weigh the limes and set aside double their weight in loaf sugar. Boil them until a pin's head or a straw will easily pierce the rind. Change the water once or twice whilst they are boiling. When cold, slice the limes, removing the pips, and put the lime slices into an earthen vessel.

Boil the sugar, adding a pint of water to each two pounds and a half of sugar. When it is a clear syrup, pour it boiling hot over the limes; let it stand two days and nights; then boil the whole together for ten minutes or a quarter of an hour, and it will be ready to pour into pots.

To Preserve Damsons.

Time, to boil and simmer, one hour.

1610. Ten ounces of loaf sugar to every quart of fruit.

Pick the stalks from the damsons, and put them into a stone jar with the loaf sugar pounded fine and sprinkled between each layer of damsons very thickly. Tie the jar over securely, and set it in a deep stewpan of cold water. Bring it slowly to a boil, and then let it simmer until the damsons are soft without being broken; pour off the juice, and boil it for about a quarter of an hour. Put the damsons carefully into pots. Strain the juice through very thick double muslin, or through a jelly-bag, and pour it over the damsons which have been previously set to cool. When the jam is cold, cover the pots over with brandy papers, and the tops with paper moistened with the white of an egg.

Damson Cheese.

Time, one hour and a half, to boil.

1611. To every quart of damsons allow a quarter of a pound of loaf sugar; and to every pound of pulp add half a pound of sugar.

Gather the damsons when full ripe, put them into a jar, and to every quart of damsons put a quarter of a pound of loaf sugar pounded. Bake them in a moderate oven until they are soft; then rub them through a hair sieve. To every pound of pulp add half a pound of loaf sugar beaten fine. Boil it over a slow fire, and stir it all the time. Pour it into *shapes;* tie brandy paper over them, and keep them in a dry place. They will not be fit to use for three or four months. All cheese may be made by this receipt except greengage, which does not require so much sugar.

Clear Damson Cheese.

1612. To every pint of damson juice allow one pound of loaf sugar.

Put the damsons into a stone jar. Set it in the oven, and when the juice is thoroughly drawn from them strain it through a sieve (but not the pulp), and to every pint of damson juice put a pound of loaf sugar. Boil it to the consistency of other jellies, and pour it into shallow saucers or moulds.

Red Gooseberry Jam.

Time, one hour and a quarter.

1613. Three pounds of loaf sugar; six pounds of rough red gooseberries.

Pick off the stalks and buds from the gooseberries, and boil them carefully but quickly for rather more than half an hour, stirring continually; then add the sugar pounded fine, and boil the jam quickly for half an hour, stirring it all the time to prevent its sticking to the preserving-pan. When done, put it into pots, cover it with brandy paper, and secure it closely down with paper moistened with the white of an egg.

Green Gooseberry Jam.

Time, forty-five minutes.

1614. Three pounds of gooseberries; two pounds and a half of loaf sugar.

Gooseberry Jam.—Jelly, and Preserves.

Pick off the stalks and buds from the gooseberries, bruise them lightly, put them into a preserving-pan, and boil them quickly for eight or ten minutes, stirring all the time; add the sugar pounded and sifted to the fruit, and boil it quickly for three-quarters of an hour, carefully removing the scum as it rises. Put it into pots, and when cold cover it as directed above.

To Preserve Green Gooseberries Whole.

1615. To one pound of gooseberries allow one pound and a half of double-refined sugar, and one pint and a half of water.

Pick off the black eye, but not the stalk, from the largest green gooseberries you can procure, and set them over the fire to scald, taking care they do not boil. When they are tender, take them out, and put them into cold water. Then clarify a pound and a half of sugar in a pint and a half of water, and when the syrup is cold, put the gooseberries singly into your preserving-pan, add the syrup, and set them over a gentle fire. Let them boil slowly, but not quick enough to break them. When you perceive the sugar has entered them, take them off, cover them with white paper, and let them stand all night. The next day take out the fruit and boil the syrup until it begins to be ropy. Skim it well, add it to the gooseberries, and set them over a slow fire to simmer till the syrup is thick. Then take them out. Set them to cool, and put them with the syrup into pots. Cover them over, and keep them in a dry place.

Green Gooseberry Jelly—An excellent substitute for Guava Jelly.

Time, one hour and twenty-five minutes, to boil the jelly.

1616. Six pounds of gooseberries; four pints of water; one pound of sugar to each pound of fruit.

Wash some green gooseberries very clean after having taken off the tops and stalks; then to each pound of fruit pour three-quarters of a pint of spring water, and simmer them until they are well broken, turn the whole into a jelly-bag or cloth, and let the juice drain through, weigh the juice, and boil it rapidly for fifteen minutes. Draw it from the fire, and stir into it until entirely dissolved an equal weight of good sugar sifted fine; then boil the jelly from fifteen to twenty minutes longer, or until it jellies strongly on the spoon. It must be perfectly cleared from scum. Then pour it into small jars, moulds, or glasses. It ought to be pale and transparent.

Gooseberries Preserved as Hops.

Time, twenty minutes.

1617. Two quarts of green walnut gooseberries, and their weight in loaf sugar.

Cut some large green gooseberries at the stalk end into quarters about half way down, and fasten five or six together with a coarse piece of cotton or a sprig of scraped thorn, and throw them into a basin of water. When all are done, and the seeds carefully taken out, put them into a preserving-pan, with their weight in pounded sugar, and boil them over a clear fire until they look clear. Then put them into wide-mouthed glass bottles or pots, put a piece of brandy paper over them, and tie them closely over, or secure them with a paper cover moistened with the white of an egg.

To Preserve Strawberries Whole.

Time, nearly one hour to simmer.

1618. The largest strawberries to be had; their weight in fine loaf sugar.

Take equal weights of strawberries and fine loaf sugar, lay the fruit in deep dishes, and sprinkle half the sugar over them in fine powder, give a gentle shake to the dish, that the sugar may always touch the under part of the fruit. The next day make a syrup with the remainder of the sugar and the juice drawn from the strawberries, and boil it until it jellies; then *carefully* put in the strawberries, and let them simmer nearly an hour. Then put them with care into jars or bottles, and fill up with the syrup, of which there will be more than required, but the next day; the jars will hold nearly or quite the whole. Cover the jars or bottles with bladder or brandy papers.

Strawberry Jam.

Time, one hour.

1619. To six pounds of strawberries allow three pounds of sugar.

Procure some fine scarlet strawberries, strip off the stalks, and put them into a preserving-pan over a moderate fire; boil them for half an hour, keeping them constantly stirred. Break the sugar into small pieces, and mix them with the strawberries after they have been removed from the fire. Then place it again over the fire, and boil it for another half hour very quickly. Put it into pots, and when cold, cover it over with brandy papers and a piece of paper moistened with the white of an egg over the tops.

Strawberry Jelly.

Time, half an hour.

1620. Equal weight of sugar and strawberry juice.

Press some ripe strawberries through a delicately clean cloth, then strain the juice very clean, and stir it into an equal weight of loaf sugar dried and pounded very fine. When the sugar is dissolved, put it into a preserving-pan over a clear fire, and let it boil for half an hour, skimming it carefully as the scum rises. Put it into glass jars or pots, and when cold cover it over as before directed.

Strawberries Stewed for Tarts.

1621. One pound of sugar; half a pint of water; whites of one or two eggs; one quart of strawberries.

Make a syrup with a pound of loaf sugar and a quarter of a pint of water; add the whites of one or two eggs; let it boil, and skim it until only a foam rises, then put in a quart of strawberries free from the stems. Let them boil till they look clear, and the syrup is quite thick, when they will be fit to use.

Raspberry Jam.
Time, forty minutes.

1622. One pound of fruit; one pound of sugar.

To every pound of raspberries use the same weight of sugar, but always boil the fruit well before you add the sugar to it, as that will make it a better colour. Put the fruit in a preserving-pan, mashing it well with a long wooden spoon. After boiling it a few minutes, add the same quantity of sugar as fruit, boiling it half an hour, keeping it well stirred. When done and sufficiently reduced, fill the jars, and when cold, cover them over with white paper moistened with white of eggs.

Raspberry Jelly.
Time, thirty-five minutes.

1623. To four pounds of raspberry juice allow three pounds and a half of loaf sugar.

Put the raspberries on a slow fire to simmer for a few minutes, pressing them lightly with a wooden spoon; strain clear, and weigh the juice. Then put it into a preserving pan lined with china, and set it over a quick fire to boil for nearly twenty minutes; then stir into it the sugar broken into small pieces, and when it is thoroughly dissolved, place it again over the fire, and boil it very quickly for a quarter of an hour. Skim it well, and keep it constantly stirred all the time it is boiling. Pour it into glass or stone pots, and when cold, cover it, and set it in a cool place.

To Preserve Greengages.
Time, three-quarters of an hour.

1624. To three pounds of greengages allow three pounds of sugar.

Prick the plums with a fine needle, to prevent their breaking, put them into a preserving-pan with only sufficient water to cover them, and set them over a gentle fire until the water simmers; then take them out and set them on a sieve to drain; add to the water in which the plums were boiled the above quantity of pounded sugar, boil it quickly, skimming it as the scum rises, until the syrup sticks to the spoon. Then put in the greengages, and let them boil until the sugar bubbles, then pour the whole into a basin, and let it stand until the next day. Drain the syrup from the fruit, boil it up quickly, and pour it over the plums—repeat this for four days, then boil the fruit in it for five or six minutes, put them into jars, pour the syrup over them, and cover them over with brandy papers. The kernels must be blanched and boiled with the fruit.

To Preserve and Dry Greengages.
Time, ten or twelve minutes.

1625. Two pounds of greengages; two pounds of loaf sugar; half a pint of water.

Take two pounds of greengages before they are quite ripe, with the stalks left on. Boil the sugar and water to a thick rich syrup in a stewpan lined with china. Put in the greengages, boil them for ten or twelve minutes, and then drain them on a sieve until the next day. Then boil up the syrup, put in the fruit, boil it for a few minutes, and again drain it; repeat this for a week, and then drain and place the fruit on the reversed side of a sieve in a cool oven to dry. Place them when done in boxes, with paper between each layer of plums, and set them in a cool, dry place.

Put a cut paper over the fruit, under the lid of the box.

To Brandy Greengages.
Time, twenty-five minutes.

1626. Half a pound of loaf sugar to every pound of fruit; an equal measure of syrup and pale brandy.

Make a syrup of half a pound of sugar for each pound of greengages, with half a teacupful of water for each pound of sugar. When boiling hot, pour it over the plums, let them remain for a day or two; boil them in the syrup until they are clear; very slowly, that they may not break; then take them out very carefully with a skimmer, boil the syrup fast for a few minutes, skim it, let it cool and settle, then mix with it an equal measure of pale brandy, and pour it over the greengages; put them into glass jars, and cover them well over, first with a piece of tissue-paper, moistened with a little sugar boiled in water, and then a piece of thick paper.

Rhubarb Marmalade.

Time, three-quarters of an hour, if young rhubarb; an hour and a half if old.

1627. To one pound of loaf sugar one pound and a half of rhubarb stalks; peel of half a large lemon; a quarter of an ounce of bitter almonds.

Cut the rhubarb stalks into pieces about two inches long, and put them into a preserving pan with the loaf sugar broken small, the peel of the lemon cut thin, and the almonds blanched and divided. Boil the whole well together, put it into pots, and cover it as directed for other preserves.

Rhubarb and Orange Preserve.

Time, one hour.

1628. Six oranges; one quart of rhubarb; one pound and a half of loaf sugar.

Peel the oranges carefully, take away the white rind and the pips, slice the pulps into a stewpan, with the peel cut very small, add one quart of rhubarb cut very fine, and from a pound to a pound and a half of loaf sugar. Boil the whole down in the way usual with all preserves.

To Preserve Apricots.

Time, three-quarters of an hour to boil the jam.

1629. One pound of apricots; half a pint of the juice of white currants; one pound and a quarter of loaf sugar.

Stone and pare a pound of the finest apricots, put them into a preserving pan, dusting some double-refined sugar over them. Have ready half a pint of the juice of white currants pressed out raw, and a pound and a half of loaf sugar. Boil them over a slow fire, with half the quantity of sugar, throwing in the other half twice during the time of boiling. Take care not to break them in the skimming, and when they are done enough, put two or three into a small glass. A little more boiling makes it jam.

To Dry Apricots.

Time, six or seven minutes.

1630. The weight of the fruit in white sugar.

Pare and stone the apricots, they must not be over ripe, and place them in a dish in even rows; pound and sift their weight in loaf sugar, and strew it thickly over them. Let them remain until the next day, then put them into a preserving pan with the sugar, and set them over a moderate fire to become gradually heated, let them simmer for six or seven minutes, or until the apricots are quite tender. Take them carefully out, and let them stand in the syrup for two days, after which drain them on a sieve, and then spread them on dishes to thoroughly dry before storing them away. Keep them in a dry place.

Brandy Apricots.

1631. Twenty-four apricots; half a pound of sugar; a little water, and brandy.

Put half a pound of loaf sugar into a stewpan, with sufficient water just to cover the bottom of the pan; take off the scum as it rises, and then put in the apricots. Let them just boil up in the syrup. Set them by till cold; put them into a jar, or bottles, and fill up the jar with the best brandy. Keep them *close* from the air.

Apricot Marmalade.

Time, three-quarters of an hour.

1632. The weight of the fruit in double-refined sugar.

Put the weight of the fruit in double-refined sugar into a delicately clean stewpan, just moistening it with cold water. Set it over a very slow fire, and when boiled to a candy, take it out, pound and sift it. Then take the skin from the apricots, taking care they are not too ripe, cut them into slices, and set them over the fire with the pounded sugar, and let them *simmer* until clear. Then put them into small preserving pots, and tie closely over.

A few bitter almonds blanched and cut into very thin slices, will be an improvement.

To Preserve Nectarines.

Time, three-quarters of an hour.

1633. Three-quarters of a pound of sugar to each pound of fruit.

Take the nectarines when nearly ripe, pare them, and cut them in halves, put them into a stewpan of boiling water, and let them simmer until they rise to the surface, then put them on a sieve to drain. Clarify three-quarters of a pound of sugar to one of fruit, put in the nectarines, and let them boil until nearly clear, then set them aside in the syrup. The next day, drain the syrup from them, and boil it until quite thick, then put in the fruit, and let it boil for a short time. Drain off the syrup, and repeat the boiling on the following day, then put it into a deep dish, and let it stand for two days, after which put the preserve into pots, and cover it over as hitherto directed.

To Candy Nectarines.

1634. Half the weight of the fruit in loaf sugar.

Split the nectarines, and take out the

stones, clarify half their weight of sugar; put in the fruit, and boil it slowly until clear, taking off the scum as it rises. Then take them out with a skimmer, place them on flat dishes, and cover them over until the next day. Boil the syrup until it is rather thick, put in the fruit, and let them boil gently until hot through. Put them again on flat dishes, as free from syrup as possible, and let them remain all night. Again boil the syrup, and put in the fruit for a short time. Then spread them out to dry, and set them in a warm oven; dust fine white sugar over them, and turn them until dry and candied.

Peach Preserve.

Time, about three-quarters of an hour.

1635. One pound of sugar to three pounds of peaches; a quarter of a pint of water to each pound of sugar; white of one egg to every four pounds.

Pare and cut in halves some ripe peaches, and dry them in a hot sun, or warm oven for two days; then weigh them, and make a syrup of a pound of sugar for three pounds of fruit. Put a teacupful of water to each pound of sugar, and the white of an egg to four pounds. Stir it until it is dissolved, then set it over the fire, boil and skim it until only a light scum rises, then put in the peaches, and let them boil gently until the syrup is thick and clear. Put in the kernels blanched, and when cold, put a piece of paper to fit the inside of the pots, or jar, dipped in thick sugar syrup, over the top of the preserve, and close it over securely with tissue paper moistened with the white of an egg.

To Preserve Peaches.

Time, about three-quarters of an hour.

1636. Peached brandy; quarter of a pint of water to each pound of sugar for the syrup.

Make a strong syrup, which boil and skim well. Have ready some fine peaches, gathered before they are *over* ripe; rub the lint off them carefully with a cloth, then take a needle and run it down the seam of each peach to the depth of the skin, and place them in a jar, covering them with good brandy, and let them remain two hours; then take them out and put them into a preserving pan, so that each may lie *singly*. Pour the syrup over them, and boil them until they look clear, but be careful not to break them. Remove the peaches with a spoon into glasses, and when the syrup is cold, mix it with the brandy, and pour it on the peaches. The glasses must be well tied down with a bladder, and the air carefully excluded, or the peaches will turn black.

Peach Marmalade.

Time, three-quarters of an hour.

1637. Three-quarters of a pound of sugar to each pound of fruit; a quarter of a pint of water to every pound of sugar.

Peel, stone, and cut small some ripe peaches, weigh three-quarters of a pound of sugar to each pound of cut fruit, and a quarter of a pint of water to each pound of sugar; set it over the fire; when it boils, skim it clear; then put in the peaches, let them boil fast; then mash them smooth, and let them boil until the whole is a jellied mass, and very thick; put it into jam-pots, and when cold cover it closely over.

To Preserve Plums.

Time, three-quarters of an hour.

1638. To every pound of fruit allow three-quarters of a pound of sugar.

Divide the plums, take out the stones, and put the fruit on a dish with pounded sugar strewed over; the next day put them into a preserving-pan, and let them simmer gently by the side of the fire for about thirty minutes, then boil them quickly, removing the scum as it rises, and keep them constantly stirred, or the jam will stick to the bottom of the pan. Crack the stones, and add the kernels to the preserve when it boils.

To Preserve Plums for Dessert.

Time, fifteen to twenty minutes.

1639. To every pound of sugar a teacupful of water; plums.

Gather the plums before they are quite ripe; slightly prick them, and put them into a stewpan with sufficient cold water to cover them, set them over a slow fire, and when on the point of boiling take them out carefully and put them into a stewpan with the syrup, previously made with the above proportions of sugar and water, boil them from a quarter of an hour to twenty minutes, skimming them frequently; then set them by until the next day. Add a small quantity of sugar, boiled almost to candy, to the syrup and plums, put all in a wide-mouthed jar, and set it in a cool oven for two nights; then drain the syrup from the plums, sprinkle pounded sugar over them, and dry them in a cool oven.

Almack Preserve.

1640. Two dozen apples; two dozen pears; four dozen plums; one pound of fine moist sugar to every pound of fruit.

Split the plums and take out the stones;

pare, core, and slice the pears and apples, and put the whole into a stone jar in layers; put them into a cool oven, and when sufficiently tender, press them through a rather coarse sieve into a preserving-pan. Stir in some fine moist sugar, or loaf sugar pounded fine if preferred, and stir them over a moderate fire until very firm; cut the preserve into slices after it has become sufficiently cool.

To Preserve Lettuce Stalks.

Time, thirty-five minutes the first time.

1641. The stalks of large lettuces; one pound and a half of sugar to six pints of water; three dessertspoonfuls of ground ginger; three ounces of whole ginger.

Cut into pieces of about three inches in length some stalks of large lettuces, and soak them in cold water for ten minutes, washing them very clean. Put a pound and a half of sugar into a preserving-pan with six pints of water and three large dessertspoonfuls of ground ginger. Set it over a clear fire and boil it for twenty-five minutes, then pour it into a deep dish to remain all night. The next day repeat the boiling for half an hour; do this for five or six days, and then drain them free from moisture on a sieve reversed. Make a rich syrup with sugar, water, and three ounces of whole ginger, just *bruised*, put the lettuces again into a preserving-pan, pour the syrup over them, and boil them several times until the stalks become clear, taking care the syrup is sufficiently strong of the ginger.

Vegetable Marrow Preserve.

Time, twenty minutes.

1642. To every pound of vegetable marrows allow one pound of loaf sugar, one lemon, one ounce of dried ginger, and half a glass of whisky.

Peel and slice the marrows, pour over them a syrup made of brown sugar and boiling water, and let them stand for two or three days; then make a syrup of one pound of loaf sugar, the juice and peel of one lemon, an ounce of dried ginger, and as little water as is necessary to make it into a syrup. When boiling, put in the marrows, having previously drained them. Let them simmer for twenty minutes, then pour in half a glass of whisky for every pound of vegetable and sugar, and boil it until quite clear—which ought to be soon after the spirit is thrown in—put them when done into pots covered closely over.

Preserved Pumpkin

Time, three-quarters of an hour.

1643. Allow one pound of loaf sugar to every pound of pumpkin; juice of two large lemons; peel of one.

Pare off the rind and pick out the seeds from a very fresh pumpkin, cut it into slices, and put it into a deep pie-dish with the sugar pounded and put between each layer; squeeze the lemon juice from two large, or three small lemons, strain it over the slices, and let them remain in it for two days; then put them into a preserving-pan with a quarter of a pint of water to every pound and a half of crushed sugar, and the peel of a large lemon cut very thin. Let it boil until the slices are tender; then put it into a deep bowl, and let it stand covered over for five or six days. Put the pumpkins into pots, boil and skim the syrup until it is very thick and rich, and pour it over the preserve. When cold, cover it with brandy papers and tie it closely down with thick brown paper, or white paper moistened with egg.

Blackberry Jam.

Time, three-quarters of an hour.

1644. To every quart of blackberries allow a pound of loaf sugar and a wine-glass of brandy.

Crush a quart of fully ripe blackberries with a pound of the best loaf sugar pounded very fine, put it into a preserving-pan, and set it over a gentle fire until thick, add a glass of brandy, and stir it again over the fire for about a quarter of an hour; then put it into pots, and when cold tie them over.

Barberry Jam.

Time, three-quarters of an hour the first day.

1645. Three pounds of sugar to three pounds of barberries.

Pick the fruit from the stalks, and put them into a jar with their weight of pounded loaf sugar, set the jar in a deep saucepan of boiling water until the sugar is dissolved and the barberries quite soft; then let them stand all night. The next day put them into a preserving-pan and boil them for a quarter of an hour or twenty minutes; then put them into pots, tie them over, and set them in a dry place.

To Preserve Barberries in Bunches.

Time, half to three-quarters of an hour.

1646. Barberries; to every pint of juice allow a pound and a half of loaf sugar, and to every pound of sugar half a pound of barberries in bunches.

Select the finest barberries, taking the

largest bunches to preserve whole. Pick the rest from the stalks, and put them into a preserving-pan, with sufficient water to make a syrup for the bunches; boil them till they are soft, then strain them through a hair sieve, and to every pint of juice put a pound and a half of pounded sugar. Boil and skim it well, and to every pint of syrup put half a pound of barberries tied in bunches. Boil them till they look very clear, then put them into pots or glasses, and when cold tie them down with paper dipped in brandy.

Black Currant Jam.

Time, three-quarters of an hour to an hour.

1647. To every pound of currants allow three-quarters of a pound of sugar.

Gather the currants when they are thoroughly ripe and dry, and pick them from the stalks. Bruise them lightly in a large bowl, and to every pound of fruit put three-quarters of a pound of finely-beaten loaf sugar; put sugar and fruit into a preserving pan, and boil them from three-quarters to one hour, skimming as the scum rises, and stirring constantly; then put the jam into pots, cover them with brandy paper, and tie them closely over.

Black Currant Jelly.

Time, two hours.

1648. To every five quarts of currants, allow rather more than half a pint of water; to every pint of juice one pound of loaf sugar.

Gather the currants when ripe on a dry day, strip them from the stalks, and put them into an earthen pan, or jar, and to every five quarts allow the above proportion of water; tie the pan over, and set it in the oven for an hour and a quarter; then squeeze out the juice through a coarse cloth, and to every pint of juice put a pound of loaf sugar, broken into pieces, boil it for three-quarters of an hour, skimming it well; then pour it into small pots, and when cold, put brandy papers over them, and tie them closely over.

Red Currant Jelly.

Time, forty minutes.

1649. To one quart of currant juice, one pound of powdered lump sugar.

Pick the currants from the stalks into a broad earthenware pan. To about one gallon of the picked currants put half a pound of sifted lump sugar. Put the sugar over the picked currants the day before you make the jelly. Set the currants over a slow fire to simmer gently for about twenty minutes; the slower they simmer the greater quantity of juice they will discharge. There should be an equal quantity of red and white currants. When all the juice is discharged, strain it through a hair sieve, and then through a jelly-bag while quite hot. Now to each quart of juice put one pound of powdered loaf sugar. Put it into a preserving-pan, and set it over a quick stove to boil for twenty minutes. If any scum rises, skim it off. When done, put it into small white pots or little glasses, and cover it with brandied paper. Tie down.

Red Currant Jam.

Time, three-quarters to one hour.

1650. Three-quarters of a pound of loaf sugar to every pound of currants.

Pick the stalks from the currants when they are quite ripe and dry, put them into a preserving-pan with three-quarters of a pound of loaf sugar broken into small pieces to every pound of fruit. Bring it gradually to a boil, and then let it simmer for three-quarters of an hour or one hour, removing the scum as it rises, and stirring it constantly. When done, put it into pots with brandy paper over them, and tie them closely over.

White Currant Jelly.

Time, one hour and a quarter.

1651. White currants; to every pint of juice three-quarters of a pound of loaf sugar.

Pick the currants when quite ripe and dry, put them into a stone jar, place the jar in a deep saucepan of boiling water, and let it simmer for nearly an hour. Then strain the fruit carefully through a fine cloth without pressing them too much, and put the juice with the sugar into a preserving-pan. Let it simmer slowly until clear and well set, and keep it constantly stirred all the time, carefully removing the scum as it rises, or the jelly will not be clear. Pour it into pots, cover it over, and keep it in a dry place.

Lemon Store.

Time, till thick as cream.

1652. A quarter of a pound of fresh butter; one pound of beaten sugar; six eggs; three large lemons.

Put into a clean saucepan the fresh butter, sugar beaten to a powder, the yolks of six eggs, and the whites of four, the grated peel of two large lemons, and the juice of three. Keep the whole stirred over a gentle fire until it is as thick as cream. When it is cold pour it into jars. This makes a nice substitute for preserve in small tarts.

To Preserve Lemons Whole.
Time, fifteen minutes the first day.

1653. Lemon; sugar; and vine leaves.
Pare the lemons very thin, then cut a hole at the top the size of a shilling, and take out all the pulp and skin. Rub them with salt, and put them into spring water as you do them, which will prevent them from turning black. Let them lie in it five or six days, and then boil them in fresh salt and water fifteen minutes. Have ready made a thin syrup of a quart of water and a pound of loaf sugar. Boil them in it for five minutes once a day for four or five days, and then put them into jars. Let them stand for six or eight weeks, as it will make them clear and plump. Then take them out of the syrup. Make a fresh syrup of double-refined sugar with only sufficient water to moisten it, boil and skim it, then put in the lemons, and boil them slowly until they are clear. Put them into small jars with brandy paper over them, and tie them closely over.

Lemon Marmalade.
Time, two hours and a half.

1654. To one pound of lemons, one pint of water; to one pound of fruit, two pounds of loaf sugar.
To every pound of fruit put one pint of water, and boil it for two hours; change the water and add the same quantity of boiling water.
Then cut the lemons in small thin slices, taking care to extract all the pips. To every pound of fruit then add two pounds of loaf sugar. Put the sugar on in the stewpan, and add to it half a pint of water to every pound of sugar. When the sugar is quite dissolved add the fruit, and boil it half an hour.

To Preserve Oranges Whole.
Time, half an hour to three quarters.

1655. Some large Seville oranges; to every pound of oranges allow two pounds of loaf sugar, and *one* pint of spring water.
Procure some of the largest and clearest Seville oranges, cut a small hole at the stalk end and scoop out the pulp very clean; tie them singly in muslin, and lay them *two days* in spring water, changing the water *twice* a day. Boil them in the muslin until they are tender, be careful to keep them covered with water. Before you scoop the oranges weigh them, and to every pound add two pounds of loaf sugar pounded, and a pint of spring water. Boil the sugar and water with the orange juice to a syrup, skim it well, and let it stand till cold. Take the oranges out of the muslin and put them into the syrup, then put them over a slow fire, boil them till they are *clear*, and put them by till they are cold. Drain the oranges out of their syrup, and if quite *tender* put them into a small stone jar the size of the orange, and pour the syrup over them. Then put brandy papers and tie the covers over them.

Orange Marmalade.
Time, two hours and ten minutes.

1656. Six pounds of Seville oranges; eight pounds of loaf sugar.
Take six pounds of Seville oranges; cut the peel so as to make it peel off in four pieces. Put all the peels on the fire in a preserving-pan, with a large quantity of water, and boil them for two hours, then cut them in very thin slices. While they are boiling press the inside of the oranges through a splinter sieve, narrow enough to prevent the seeds and skin from going through. When this is done, and the peels cut into the thinnest shreds, put the whole on the fire in a copper or brass pan, with eight pounds of loaf sugar broken small. Boil it all together for ten minutes, it may then be taken off the fire and put into preserving jars.

Transparent Marmalade.
Time, half an hour.

1657. To every pound of fruit allow one pound and a half of double-refined sugar.
Cut some very pale Seville oranges into quarters, take out the pulp, and pick out the seeds. Put the peels into a little salt and water, and let them stand all night. Then boil them in a large quantity of spring water till they are tender, cut them in *very* thin slices and put to the pulp. To every pound of marmalade add a pound and a half of double-refined sugar finely beaten, and boil together gently for twenty minutes; but if not clear and transparent enough in that time, boil eight or ten minutes longer, keep stirring gently all the time, and take care you do not break the slices. When it is cold, put it into sweetmeat glasses or into pots, and tie them down with brandy paper, and a cover of thick paper over them.

RECEIPTS FROM SCOTLAND.
Grated Marmalade.
Time, half an hour.

1658. Four pounds of oranges; one gill of water; four pounds of sugar; one lemon.

Grate the outside of the oranges off. Squeeze the pulps through a sieve, using about a gill of water to four pounds of fruit. Put it on to boil with the sugar (one pound of sugar to one pound of oranges) and the gratings. Boil till you find the gratings getting soft, *i.e.*, for about half an hour.

You may add the juice, pulp, and peel of one lemon if you please.

Marmalade with Chips.
Time, four hours.

1659. To one pound of oranges two pints of water and two pounds of sugar; two lemons to six pounds of oranges.

Peel the oranges and cut the peel into thin chips, bruise the pulps and juice together, but keep out the seeds. Put the whole into a stewpan, and boil it for three hours and a half. Then *add* the sugar, and boil it for half an hour longer on a regular slow fire.

To Preserve Green Figs.
1660. The weight of the fruit in loaf sugar; peel of one large lemon and a little ginger.

Lay the figs in cold water for twenty-four hours, then simmer them until tender; put them again into cold water, and let them remain two days, changing the water each day. Then, if you do not find them quite soft, give them another simmer and put them again into cold water until the next day. Then take their weight in loaf sugar, and with two-thirds of it make a syrup, and simmer the figs in it for ten minutes. In two days take the third of the sugar pounded fine, and pour the syrup from the figs on it. Make a rich syrup with the peel of a lemon and a little raw ginger, and boil the figs in it. Then mix all together and put it into large jam pots, and tie them closely over. The figs may be cut in two if you prefer it, after they have simmered until soft.

To Preserve Mulberries.
Time, one hour and a quarter.

1661. Three pounds of mulberries; three pounds and three-quarters of sugar to a pint and a half of juice.

Put about half a pound of mulberries into a preserving-pan, with a gill of water to prevent burning, and set it over a slow fire to simmer until all the juice is extracted. Then strain it through a fine sieve, and add three pounds and three-quarters of sugar to every pint and a half of juice. Put the sugar pounded into the preserving-pan and pour over it the strained juice, boil it up, and skim it well. Then add three pounds of ripe mulberries, and let them stand in the syrup until warm, then boil them slowly for about a quarter of an hour, and turn them carefully out into a china bowl until the next day. Repeat the boiling for the same time until the syrup is thick, and will jelly when cold. The fruit may then be put into pots, and covered closely over; care must be taken not to break the mulberries when boiling.

To Preserve Cherries.
1662. One pound of sugar to every pound of cherries; and three tablespoonfuls of red currant juice.

Lay some pounded sugar at the bottom of the preserving-pan, and place some cherries on it, then another layer of sugar, then of cherries, repeating this until all are in, leaving out a little of the sugar to strew in as they boil; add three spoonfuls of currant juice to each pound of fruit, and set it over a clear fire. Boil them quickly, *shaking* them round frequently to prevent their burning, but do not stir them. Take off the scum as it rises, and when the syrup is thick and they look clear, put them into pots, and when cold, cover them over.

To Bottle Cherries.
1663. Cherries; three ounces of sugar to each bottle.

Have ready some wide-mouthed bottles quite clean and dry; *cut* each cherry from the stalk into the bottle, be sure *not* to *pull* them off. To every bottle of cherries put three ounces of powdered sugar, then tie them tightly over with bladder. After drawing the bread leave the oven door open. About nine o'clock at night put in the bottles and close the oven door. Take them out the first thing in the morning, and put them in a dry place for use.

To Dry Cherries.
Time, five days.

1664. Seven pounds of cherries; two pounds of loaf sugar.

Stone seven pounds of cherries, put a layer of them at the bottom of a stewpan, cover it with a layer of the best white sugar pounded, then put in another layer of cherries; continue putting the fruit and sugar in layers till your ingredients are all in the stewpan. Let them stand all night. The next day set the stewpan over a *charcoal* fire, and scald the fruit, but take great care not to let it boil. Repeat this for four following days. Then lift the cherries out of the syrup one by one, lay them on earthenware dishes, and dry them in the sun. Should the weather be wet or gloomy, they can be dried in a very slow oven. But they are best sun-dried.

To Candy Cherries.

1665. Boil some sugar to a candy height, and put it over some fine ripe cherries stoned; move them gently about, and when almost cold take them out and dry them by the fire, or in a cool oven.

To Dry Cherries with their Leaves and Stalks.

1666. A little vinegar; syrup of sugar and water.

Take some large cherries with a little stalk and a leaf or two on, dip the *leaves* and *stalk* in a little boiling vinegar, stick the sprig upright in a sieve till they are dry; in the meantime make a strong syrup with double-refined sugar, and dip the cherries, stalks, and leaves into it, and let them just scald; take them out and lay them on a sieve, and boil the syrup to candy height; then dip the cherries, stalks, and leaves all in; then stand the branches in sieves and dry them in a slow oven, or before the fire.

To Preserve Cucumbers.

1667. Some cucumbers; salt and water; a syrup of a quarter of a pound of sugar to a pint of water; two ounces of whole ginger.

Gather large and small cucumbers *when dry*, with the stalks and flowers on, put them into a stone jar with some salt and water, cover them with vine leaves, set them on the hob by the fire for a fortnight till they turn quite yellow; strain the leaves and salt and water from them; put the cucumbers into a bell metal skillet with the same salt and water, set them over the fire covered with cabbage leaves till they turn green. When very green and clear take them off and drain them from the salt and water, changing them twice a day for two days, then dry them in a cloth, split them, and take out the seeds. Have ready a thin syrup of sugar, allowing a quarter of a pound to a pint of water, with two ounces of whole ginger. When cold, pour it on the cucumbers. Warm up the syrup every day twice for three or four days, and pour it on them quite cold, then tie them over for use.

To Preserve Pears.

Time, six or seven hours.

1668. Three-quarters of a pound of loaf sugar to each pound of pears; peel of a lemon.

Weigh the pears when pared, and put three-quarters of a pound of loaf sugar to a pound of fruit; add the peel of a small lemon cut very thin, and just water enough at the bottom of the stewpan to prevent the fruit burning; stew it *gently* for six or seven hours, and it will keep good for three months.

A few drops of cochineal may be added, which will improve the colour, and the pears may be served in a glass dish or to garnish rice.

To Preserve Jargonelle Pears.

Time, about half an hour, to simmer the pears in water; five minutes in the syrup.

1669. Jargonelle pears; to every pound of fruit rather more than half a pint of water, and one pound of sugar.

Pare some jargonelle pears very thin, and simmer them in just sufficient water to cover them until they are tender, but do not allow them to break. Boil and skim the sugar and water for five or six minutes, skimming it clear, then put in the pears, previously drained from the water, and simmer them in the syrup for about five minutes; repeat the simmering for three or four days (taking care that the pears do not break) until they are clear, then drain and dry them in the sun, or put them in a cool oven for a very short time. They may be then kept in the syrup and dried when wanted, which makes them more moist and rich.

Apple Jam.

Time, altogether, two hours and a half.

1670. To every pound of apples after being pared, three-quarters of a pound of loaf sugar; juice of one small lemon, and the peel of one large one grated.

Pare and core the apples, cut them into very thin slices, and put them into a stone jar; set the jar in a deep saucepan of boiling water, and let the apples stew for about two hours; then put them into a preserving-pan, with the sugar pounded, and the juice and grated peel of the lemon. Simmer the whole over a clear fire for about half an hour; after it begins to simmer all over carefully remove the scum as it rises, and when done, put the preserve into pots. When cold, cover them with paper dipped into white of egg, and stretched over the top, with a piece of oiled paper next the jam.

Apple Marmalade.

Time, half an hour and ten minutes.

1671. One peck of apples; one gallon of water to every quart of pulp; one pound of loaf sugar.

Take a peck of apples full grown but not the least ripe, of all or any sort; quarter them and take out the cores, but do not pare them, put them into a preserving-pan with one gallon of water, and let them boil moderately until you think the pulp will run, or suffer itself to be squeezed through a cheese cloth, only leaving the peels behind. Then to each quart of pulp add one pound, *good weight,* of loaf sugar, either broken in small pieces or pounded, and boil it all together for half an hour and ten minutes, keeping it stirred. Then put it into pots, the larger the better, as it keeps longer in a large body.

Apple Ginger.

Time, about three-quarters of an hour.

1672. Two pounds of apples; one pint and a half of water; two pounds of loaf sugar; and a little of Oxley's concentrated ginger.

Put into a preserving-pan two pounds of loaf sugar pounded fine, and about a pint and a half of water; boil and skim it well, and then add the concentrated ginger; pare, core, and divide some *golden pippins,* and put them into a preserving-pan with the syrup. Boil them quickly until they are very clear, then lay them carefully on a dish, put the syrup into a jar, and when cold put in the slices of apples. and tie it closely over to exclude the air. This preserve can only be made of golden pippins.

To Preserve Golden Pippins.

1673. Peel of one Seville orange; juice of one lemon; two pounds of sugar; one quart of golden pippins; twelve common pippins.

Having boiled the peel of a Seville orange very tender, let it lie in water two or three days. Take a quart of golden pippins, pare, core, quarter, and boil them to a strong jelly, and run it through a jelly-bag. Then take twelve pippins, pare them and scrape out the cores; put the sugar into a preserving-pan with nearly a pint of water. When it boils, skim it and put in the pippins with the orange peel cut into shreds. Let them boil quickly until the syrup is very thick, and will almost candy, then add a pint of the pippin jelly, and boil them quickly until the jelly is clear. Squeeze in the juice of a lemon, give it one boil, and put them into pots or glasses with the orange peel. When cold, cover it over with brandy paper, and tie the pots closely down.

Normandy Pippins.

Time, about two hours.

1674. One pound of pippins; one quart of water; half a pound of loaf sugar; one large lemon; one glass of wine.

Soak a pound of pippins in cold water for four hours, or until they are twice their size: then pour off the water they have not absorbed, and mix with a large cupful of the strained water half a pound of loaf sugar, and the peel of the lemon cut thin. Boil the sugar and water to a syrup, pour in a glass of white wine, put in the pippins, and set them over a clear fire to simmer until they are tender, but not broken. When nearly done, squeeze in the juice of a lemon, take the fruit out, and send to table with the peel of the lemon laid on each pippin.

Tomatoes Preserved.

1675. One pound of sugar to every pound of tomatoes; and a quarter of a pint of water to each pound; two lemons.

Take the small plum-shaped yellow or red tomatoes, pour boiling water over them, and peel off the skins. Make the syrup of an equal weight of sugar and a quarter of a pint of water to each pound; set it over the fire. When the sugar is dissolved and boiling hot, put in the tomatoes, let them boil very gently, and stir in two lemons boiled in water until the peels are tender, and cut into very thin slices; let it boil until the fruit is clear throughout, and the syrup rich. Then place the tomatoes on flat dishes, and set them to become cold. Boil the syrup until very rich and thick, and then set it to cool and settle. Put the tomatoes into jars or pots, pour the syrup over them free from any sediment, or strain it through muslin. Cover them over as directed, and keep them in a dry place.

To Candy Tomatoes.

Time, three and a half or four hours.

1676. For every four pounds of tomatoes clarify one pound of loaf sugar; two lemons.

Choose the fig or plum-shaped tomatoes, and for every four pounds clarify one pound of loaf sugar, pour boiling water over the tomatoes, cover them for a few minutes, and then peel them. When the syrup is boiling hot, put them in, let them simmer very slowly until they look clear, then take them out with a skimmer, and place them on a sieve reversed to become cold. Boil the syrup until it is quite thick, then put the tomatoes in again, simmer them slowly for nearly an hour, then take them out and lay them again on sieves. Boil the syrup an hour longer, then put in the tomatoes for the last time, simmer them for half an hour, take them out, *flatten* them, and dry them in a warm oven. When dry put them into glass jars. Two lemons boiled tender, then sliced, and preserved with the tomatoes, impart a fine flavour.

To Preserve Siberian Crabs.

Time, half an hour.

1677. One quart of water; two pounds and a quarter of loaf sugar; one small lemon; crab apples.

Put two pounds of loaf sugar into a preserving-pan with the peel of a small lemon and a quart of water, boil it until it become a thin syrup. Take some fine red crab apples with their stalks on, just prick them with a needle, and put them into the syrup. When you see the skins begin to crack, take them carefully out and drain them separately on a dish; add the remainder of the sugar to the syrup, and again boil it up. Put the crabs into wide-mouthed bottles or jars. When the syrup is cool pour it over them, and tie the jars tightly over.

To Preserve Carrots.

1678. Three pounds of carrots; three pounds of sugar; one pound of ginger; four lemons; three pints and a half of water.

Boil the ginger in a quart of water until very strong, then add the carrots (which must be very clear and bright coloured) cut into slices, and boil them until tender. Take them out, put them into a deep pan, pour over them the ginger and water, and let them stand four or five days, stirring them each day four or five times. Make a syrup with the sugar and a pint and a half of water, the juice of three lemons, the peel of four, and a few pieces of white ginger cut into slices. Boil and skim it until the syrup is rich and good, rub the skin off the carrots, wipe them dry, and boil them for about ten minutes in the syrup. Then take it from the fire, and let it remain for a week. Drain off the syrup, boil it up with another half pound of sugar, put in the carrots and boil them for another quarter of an hour, or longer. Then put them into pots, pour the syrup over them, cover the tops with brandy paper, and tie them closely over.

To Preserve Melons.

Time, half an hour the first day.

1679. One or two melons; two lemons; one pound of sugar to each pint of water for the syrup; a quarter of a pound of white sugar.

After scraping off the thin skin of the melons, scoop out the seeds at the end by making a small hole at the stem; put them into water, and let them remain all night; then put them into a preserving-pan with about four or five ounces of loaf sugar and sufficient water to cover them, cover the pan, and set it over a slow fire for half an hour. Repeat this for three days, never allowing it to *boil* Make a thin syrup with a pound of loaf sugar to each half pint of water, drain the melons, and put them into the syrup, set them over the fire for half an hour covered close, and repeat this as before for three days. Put the melons into jars, boil the syrup with the peel of a lemon cut very thin, and the strained juice of two, until it is very rich, then pour it over the preserves, and when cold, cover them.

Pineapple Preserve.

Time, half an hour to boil the pine.

1680. One pound of white sugar for each pound of fruit.

Twist off the top and bottom, and pare off the rough outside of one or more pineapples, then weigh and cut them in slices; to each pound of fruit put a teacupful of water. Put the slices into a preserving pan, cover it, and set it over the fire to boil gently until they are tender and clear, then take them from the water with a skimmer, or by placing a fork in the centre of each slice. Add to the water a pound of sugar to each pound of fruit, stir it until it is dissolved, then put in the slices of pine, cover the pan, and let them boil gently until transparent through, then take them out, let them cool, and put them into glass jars. Let the syrup simmer gently until it is thick and rich, and when nearly cold pour it over the fruit. The next day secure the jars by putting closely-fitting corks in the top, and dip them in melted sealing wax. Put them away in a cool dark place until the cold weather, or put a tissue paper wet with melted sugar over the top, and a closely-fitting tin over it.

To Preserve Pineapples without Cooking.

1681. One pound of white sugar to each pound of pineapple.

Pare off the rough outside of the pine, and cut it into thin slices. Have ready a pound of finely-pounded sugar for each pound of fruit; put the sugar half an inch deep at the bottom of a small glass jar, then put a layer of sliced pineapple nearly an inch deep, on that sugar as thick as at first. Press it down with a spoon as closely as possible; then add another layer of pineapple, then one of sugar, and so continue until the jar is full, the sugar being the last. Put closely-fitting corks in the top with a piece of tissue paper wet with melted sugar under them, and a closely-fitting tin cover over them

To Preserve Pineapples in Brandy.

1682. One pound of sugar to each pound of fruit; brandy.

Pare off the rough outside of the pine, and cut it into slices. Have ready a preserving-pot the size of the slices of pine, put a layer of pounded white sugar at the bottom of the jar or pot, then of pineapple, then of sugar, repeating this until full, but do not press it down. When the jar is lightly filled, pour in sufficient brandy to rather *more* than cover the slices, taking care that the pounded sugar is the last layer. Cover it closely over, and keep it in a dark cool place.

To Preserve whole Quinces.

1683. Six or seven pounds of apples; one pound of loaf sugar to every pint of juice; as many quinces as you may require.

Cut six or seven pounds of golden pippins into slices without paring them, and put them into a preserving pan with four pints of water; boil them quickly, covered closely over until the water is a thick jelly, to every pint of which add a pound of loaf sugar pounded fine. Set it over the fire to boil, and skim it thoroughly. Scald the quinces until they are tender, and then put them into the syrup. Let it boil quickly, skim it well, and when the quince is clear put a small portion of the syrup into a glass, and if the jelly is sufficiently firm put the quinces into jars, and pour the syrup over them. Set them to cool, and then cover them with brandy paper, and paper dipped into the white of an egg pressed closely over the top of the pots.

Quince Marmalade.

1684. To every pound of pulp three-quarters of a pound of loaf sugar.

Pare the quinces and well core them, place them in a jar, cover them with water, adding half a pound of sugar. Tie down the jar the same as for damsons, and put them in the oven all night. The next day pulp them through a wire sieve, and to every pound of pulp add three-quarters of a pound of loaf sugar. Boil all together till they look a nice purple colour. When stiff enough, fill your pots. Keep them in a dry place, and cover them closely over.

Quince Cheese.

1685. A quarter of a pint of water to each pound of fruit; half a pound of fine Lisbon sugar to each pound of quinces.

Pare and core some ripe quinces, cut them very small, put the parings into a preserving pan, and turn a plate over them large enough to cover them. Then put in the cut quinces with a quarter of a pint of water to each pound, cover the pan closely, and set it over a gentle fire until they are quite soft, and then take them out. Strain the water from the parings to the sugar, set it over the fire, and stir it until it is dissolved. Let it boil, taking off the scum, until only a light foam rises. Mash the quinces, put them into the syrup, cover it over, and let them boil slowly (taking care that it does not burn) until it is thick like a stiff jelly. Line earthen flat dishes with tissue paper, and put the marmalade or cheese in to fill them. When cold, lay tissue paper over, and cover with earthen lids. Apples or pears may be put with the quinces, or done in the same manner without the quinces, lemon cut small being added to pears or apples to flavour them.

To Preserve Grapes in Brandy for Winter Dessert.

1686. Grapes; white sugarcandy; brandy.

Take some fine close bunches of grapes, prick each twice with a fine needle, and lay them carefully in jars, cover the grapes thickly over with pounded sugarcandy, and then fill up the jars with good brandy. Tie the jars tightly over with a bladder, and set them in a cool dry place.

Greengage Jam.

Time, one hour.

1687. To six pounds of greengages, four pounds of loaf sugar.

Take off the skins, and stone some ripe greengages, and boil them quickly for three-quarters of an hour with sugar, keeping them constantly stirred; then add four pounds of pounded sugar to six pounds of fruit. Boil the preserve for eight or ten minutes longer, skimming it frequently as the scum rises. Put it into pots or jars, cover it closely over, and keep it in a dry place.

Rules to be observed in Pickling.

1688. Procure always the best *white wine vinegar*. Orleans vinegar, although the dearest, is the best. *The success of your pickles depends on the goodness of your vinegar.*

Use glass bottles for your pickles; if earthen jars, they must be unglazed, as the vinegar acting upon the glaze produces a mineral poison. Use saucepans lined with earthenware, or stone pipkins to boil your vinegar in. If you are compelled to use tin, do not let your vinegar remain in it one moment longer than actually necessary. Employ also wooden knives and forks in the preparation of your pickles. Fill the jars three-parts full with the articles to be pickled, and then fill the bottle or jar with vinegar.

When greening, keep the pickles covered down, as the evaporation of the steam will injure the colour. A little nut of alum may be added to crisp pickles, but it should be *very small* in proportion to the quantity, or it will give a disagreeable flavour.

A List of Vegetables, and their Season for Pickling.

1689. Cauliflowers, for pickling. — July and August.
Capsicums, yellow, red, and green.—The end of July and August.
Cucumbers.—The middle of July and August.
Chilies.—End of July and August.
Gherkins.—The middle of July and August.
Onions.—The middle of July and August.
Shallots.—Midsummer to Michaelmas.
Garlic.—The same time.
Melons as mangoes.—Middle of July and August.
Tomatoes.—End of July and August.
Nasturtiums.—Middle of July.
Walnuts.—About the 14th of July.
Radish pods.—July.
French Beans.—July.
Red Cabbage.—August.
White Cabbage. — September and October.
Mushrooms, for pickling and ketchups.—September.
Artichokes.—July and August, pickling.
Jerusalem Artichokes.—July to November, pickling.
Samphire.—August.
Horseradish.—November and December.

Indian Pickle.

1690. One pound of raw ginger; two ounces of long pepper; one pound of garlic; some brine; a quarter of a pound of mustard seed; half an ounce of turmeric; half a pound of made mustard, and plenty of Cayenne pepper, and a gallon of the best vinegar.

Take one pound of raw ginger, soak it in water one night, then cut it into thin slices, lay it on a clean sieve, or cloth to dry on the kitchen dresser. Take two ounces of long pepper, cut it in the same way as the ginger. Then take a pound of garlic, lay it in strong brine for three days, and then dry it in the same way as the ginger. Then mash it well, or cut it in slices. Put the mustard seed in a mortar with half an ounce of turmeric, half a pound of made mustard, and plenty of Cayenne pepper. When all these ingredients are prepared, put them into a large stone jar with a gallon of vinegar. Stir it well and often for a fortnight, and tie it over closely. Into this pickle you can put any kind of vegetables, taking care that they are well dried before putting into the pickle. The whole process is to be quite cold. The vinegar not to be boiled. This pickle will keep good for seven or ten years, but it requires replenishing with vinegar. Keep it filled up with vegetables as they come in season.

Piccalilly.

Time, ten weeks altogether.

1691. One pound of ginger; one pound of garlic; one pound of black pepper; one pound of mustard seed; three-quarters of an ounce of turmeric; a little Cayenne pepper; one quart of vinegar.

Take a pound of ginger, let it lie in salt and water one night, then cut it in thin slices; take one pound of garlic, peel, divide, and salt it three days, then wash and dry it in the sun on a sieve; take the pound of black pepper, the mustard seed, and the turmeric bruised very fine, and a little Cayenne pepper, put all these ingredients into a quart jar, with the vinegar boiled and poured over them, and when cold fill the jar three-parts full, and let it stand for a fortnight. Everything you wish to pickle must be salted and dried in the sun for three days. The jar must be full of liquor, and after it is finished for use, stop it down for six weeks or two months before fit for use. The vinegar must be thrown over when the spices and garlic are hot.

Melon Mangoes.

Time, five days.

1692. Late, small, smooth, green melons; sliced horseradish; very small cucumbers; green beans; small white onions; mustard seed; capsicums; whole pepper; cloves, allspice, and vinegar.

Get some late, small, smooth, green melons the size of a teacup, take a piece from the stem end, large enough to allow you to take the seeds from the inside, scrape out all the soft part, without cutting the other, then secure each piece to its own melon; lay them in rows in a stone or wooden vessel as you do them. Make a strong brine of salt and water, pour it over the melons, and let them remain twenty-four hours. Prepare the followiag stuffing:—Sliced horseradish, very small cucumbers, green beans, capsicums, small white onions, and the spice. Put the beans with the onions in a little water; having peeled them, and set them over the fire, give them one scald, and spread them out to cool; scald the pickles, and set them to cool; rinse the melons in clear water, wipe each dry, and put a cucumber, one or two small onions, two or three beans, one capsicum, sliced horseradish, and mustard seed into each melon, put on the piece belonging to it, and sew it with a coarse needle and thread; lay them in stone jars, or one jar, the cut side up. When all are in, strew over the cloves and pepper, make a sufficient quantity of vinegar boiling hot, pour it over them, cover the jar with a folded towel, and let them stand all night; then drain off the vinegar, make it hot, pour it over the melons, and cover them as before, repeat this scalding four or five times, if necessary, until the mangoes are a fine green; three times is generally enough. Be sure that the melons are green and fresh gathered; the proper sort are the last on the vines, and are very firm.

Should you wish to keep some until the next summer, choose the most firm, put them in a jar, and cover them with fresh vinegar, tie thick paper several thicknesses over them, and set them in a dry place.

Cucumber Mangoes.
Time, five hours over the fire.

1693. Cucumbers; to every gallon of vinegar—one ounce of mace; one ounce of cloves; two ounces of ginger; two ounces of long pepper; two ounces of Jamaica pepper; three ounces of mustard seed; four ounces of garlic; and a stick of horseradish.

Take the largest cucumbers you can get, before they are too ripe, or yellow at the ends, cut a piece out of the side of each, and take out the seeds with a teaspoon; put them into very strong salt and water for eight or nine days, or until they are very yellow, stirring them two or three times each day; then put them into a pan with a large quantity of vine leaves both under and over them, pour the salt and water they came out of over the cucumbers, and set the pan over a very slow fire for four or five hours, till they are a bright green; then take them out, and drain them on a hair sieve. When they are cold, put into them a little horseradish, then mustard seed, two heads of garlic, a few pepper corns, a capsicum, then horseradish and the same as before, until you have filled them, then take the piece you have cut out, and sew it on with a needle and thread, repeating this to each cucumber. Put into a stewpan a gallon of vinegar, or as much as your cucumbers may require, and to every gallon add one ounce of mace, the same of cloves, two of ginger sliced, two of long pepper, and the same of Jamaica pepper, three ounces of mustard seed tied up in a bag, four ounces of garlic, and a stick of horseradish cut in slices. Boil all these ingredients for about five minutes, then pour it upon your pickles, which have been previously placed in jars. Tie them down close, and set them by for use.

To Pickle Cucumbers.
Time, ten days.

1694. Brine; vinegar; whole pepper; mustard seed; allspice; and cucumbers; a small piece of alum.

Make a brine of salt and water which will bear an egg; let your cucumbers or gherkins remain in that for twenty-four hours; then take them from the brine, and lay them in a pan. Make a sufficient quantity of vinegar boiling hot, adding whole pepper, allspice, and mustard seed, pour it over the pickles, and let them remain until the next day, then drain it off, boil it again, pour it over, and cover the pickles with a thickly-folded cloth; drain off the vinegar the next day, add a few bits of alum the size of a pea to it, make it boiling hot, and again pour it over the pickles; let them remain for a day or two, then cut one across, and if it is not green through, scald the vinegar again, and pour it over them. In a few days divide the pickles, and put them of an equal size into jars, cover them with the cold vinegar, and cover them down for use.

Or they may be put into jars for immediate use, with a cloth folded over the top, and a plate over the cloth.

To Pickle Plums like Olives.
Time, twenty-four hours.

1695. Green plums; vinegar; mustard seed; and salt.

Make a pickle of vinegar, mustard seed, and salt, make it boiling hot, then pour it over green plums, gathered before they begin to turn, or before the stone is formed; let them stand all night, then drain off the vinegar, make it hot again, and pour it over the plums. When cold, cover them closely over.

To Pickle Peaches.
Time, eight or ten days.

1696. Peaches; one gallon of vinegar;

four pounds of brown sugar; five or six cloves into each peach.

Take some sound-cling-stone peaches, remove the down with a brush; make the vinegar hot, add to it the sugar, boil and skim it well, stick five or six cloves into each peach, then pour the vinegar boiling hot over them, cover them over, and set them in a cold place for eight or ten days; then drain off the vinegar, make it hot, skim it, and again pour it over the peaches, let them become cold, then put them into glass jars, and secure them as for preserves.

Walnuts Pickled Black.

1697. Walnuts; vinegar.

For the Pickle.—To every two quarts of vinegar—half an ounce of mace; half an ounce of cloves; the same of black pepper, Jamaica pepper, ginger, and long pepper; two ounces of salt.

Gather the walnuts when the sun is on them and before the shell is hard, which may be known by running a pin into them. Put them into strong salt and water for nine days, stir them twice a day, and change the water every three days; then place them on a hair sieve and let them remain in the air until they turn black; put them into stone jars and let them stand until cold, then boil the vinegar three times, pour it over the walnuts, and let it become cold between each boiling; tie them down with a bladder and let them stand three months. Then make a pickle with the above proportions of spice, vinegar, and common salt, boil it ten minutes, pour it hot on the walnuts, and tie them over with paper and a bladder.

To Pickle Mushrooms.

1698. Some button mushrooms; pepper, and salt; two or three cloves, and a very little mace; some vinegar.

Gather some mushroom buttons, wipe them very clean with a piece of flannel dipped in vinegar, then put them into an iron saucepan with pepper, salt, two or three cloves, and a very little mace pounded; let them stew over the fire, and after they have produced a great deal of liquor, let them stand by the fire till they have consumed all that liquor up again; but the saucepan must be shaken now and then to prevent their sticking to the bottom. Put them into large-nosed bottles, and pour *cold* vinegar that *has been boiled* over them, and then cork them up.

They will keep for seven years. If the vinegar should dry away, add a little more. Should they be wanted to put over a broiled fowl or veal cutlets, take a few out of the bottle and pour some boiling water over them to take off the sourness, then put them immediately over the cutlets.

Brown Mushrooms.

Time, one hour and a half over the fire.

1699. Mushrooms; vinegar; cloves; mace; allspice; and whole pepper.

Choose the mushrooms of nearly a pink colour underneath, clean them thoroughly, put them into a pan that will close, in layers sprinkled with salt, and let them stand two days; then add some whole pepper. Again cover them close, and stand them in the oven for an hour. Strain off the liquor and boil it for half an hour with the cloves, mace, and allspice; then put in the mushrooms for a short time, remove the stewpan from the fire, and when perfectly cold, put them into a glass or stone jar, and add a little vinegar.

To Pickle Radish Pods.

1700. Radish pods; one quart of white wine vinegar; two blades of mace; two ounces of ginger; one ounce of long pepper; and some horseradish.

Gather the radish pods when they are quite young, and put them into salt and water all night. The next day boil the salt and water they were laid in, pour it upon the pods, and cover the jar to keep in the steam. When it is nearly cold, make it boiling hot, and pour it on again, and continue doing so till the pods are quite green; then put them into a sieve to drain, and make a pickle for them of white wine vinegar, the mace, ginger, long pepper, and horseradish, pour it boiling hot upon the pods, and when it is almost cold make the vinegar twice as hot as before, and pour it upon them. Tie them down closely, and set them in a dry place.

To Pickle French Beans.

1701. French beans; vinegar; a blade of mace; whole pepper and vinegar; two ounces of each.

Gather the beans when they are young, and put them into strong salt and water until they become yellow; drain the salt and water from them, and wipe them quite dry. Then put them into a stone jar with a small piece of alum, boil the vinegar with the mace, ginger, and whole pepper, and pour it boiling on the beans every twenty-four hours, preventing the escape of steam. Continue this for a few days until they become green. Put them by in bottles for use.

To Pickle Cauliflowers, Beetroots, Onions, Capsicums, &c. 317

To Pickle Cauliflowers.

1702. Three ounces of coriander seed; one ounce of mustard seed; one ounce of ginger; half an ounce of mace; half an ounce of nutmeg; three quarts of vinegar.

Gather on a dry day some of the whitest and closest cauliflowers you can procure, break them into bunches and *scald* them in salt and water, taking care they do not boil, or it would spoil their colour. Set them to cool, covering them over; then put them on a colander, sprinkle them with salt, and let them drain for a day and night. Then place the bunches in jars, pour boiling salt and water over them, and let them remain all night; then drain them through a hair sieve, and put them into glass jars. Boil the vinegar with the ginger, mustard, nutmeg, and coriander seed, and when cold pour it over the cauliflowers, and tie them closely over.

To Pickle Beetroots.

Time, three-quarters of an hour to one hour and a half.

1703. Three quarts of vinegar; half an ounce of mace; half an ounce of ginger; some horseradish; the beetroots.

Boil the beetroots from three-quarters of an hour to an hour and a half, according to their size, cut them into any form you please, or gimp them in the shape of wheels, and put them into a jar. Boil three quarts of vinegar with the mace, ginger, and a few slices of horseradish, and pour it while very hot over the roots, tie them over, and set them in a dry place.

To Pickle Onions.

1704. Onions; vinegar; ginger; and whole pepper.

Take some nice onions; peel and throw them into a stewpan of boiling water, set them over the fire, and let them remain until quite clear, then take them out quickly, and lay them between two cloths to dry. Boil some vinegar with the ginger and whole pepper, and when cold, pour it over the onions in glass jars, and tie them closely over.

To Pickle Capsicums.

1705. Some capsicums; vinegar; three-quarters of an ounce of mace; three-quarters of an ounce of nutmeg; salt and water; one quart of vinegar to the above quantity of spice.

Pick some fine capsicums with the stalks on, just before they turn red, and remove the seeds by opening a small place at the side. Set them in strong salt and water for three days, changing it three times, then take them out and place them between a thick cloth to become dry. Put them into a jar, and cover them with vinegar previously boiled with the mace and grated nutmeg, and let get cold.

To Pickle Gherkins.

1706. Two quarts of water; one pound of salt; two quarts of white wine vinegar; a quarter of an ounce of cloves; a quarter of an ounce of mace; half an ounce of allspice; half an ounce of mustard seed; half a stick of horseradish; three bay leaves; two ounces of ginger; half a nutmeg; and a little salt.

Put the salt and water into an earthen jar, and throw in the gherkins; let them remain for two hours, and then drain them on a sieve, and when thoroughly dry put them into jars. Boil the vinegar with the cloves, mace, allspice, ginger, mustard seed, horseradish, bay leaves, nutmeg, and salt, and pour it over the gherkins, cover them closely over and let them stand twenty-four hours, then put them in a stewpan, and set them over the fire to *simmer* until they are green, taking care they do not boil, for that would spoil their colour; then put them into jars or wide-mouthed bottles, and cover them over until they are cold. Tie the corks over with leather, and set them in a dry place.

To Pickle Tomatoes.

1707. One peck of tomatoes; vinegar; one ounce of cloves; and white pepper; two ounces of mustard seed.

Mode : Prick each tomato with a fork, to allow some of the juice to exude, put them into a deep pan, sprinkle some salt between each layer, and let them remain for three days covered, then wash off the salt, and cover them with a pickle of *cold* vinegar, which has been boiled with the tomato juice, the mustard seed, cloves, and pepper. It will be ready for use in ten or twelve days, and is an excellent sauce for roast meat of any kind.

To Pickle Barberries.

1708. Take a quantity of barberries not over ripe, pick off the leaves and dead stalks, put them into jars with a large quantity of strong salt and water, and tie them down with a bladder. When you see a scum rise on the barberries put them into fresh salt and water, cover them close and set them by for use.

Or—

Time, half an hour.

1709. One quart of white wine vinegar;

one quart of water; one pound of coarse sugar; half a pound of salt. Take a quart of white wine vinegar and the same quantity of water, to which put one pound of coarse sugar, then take the worst of the barberries and put them into this liquor; boil the pickle carefully, taking off the scum until it assumes a fine colour, adding to every pound of sugar half a pound of salt. Let it stand until cold, then strain it through a coarse cloth, and let it settle, place your bunches of fresh barberries in glasses, pour the liquor clear over them, and tie them closely down with a bladder.

To Pickle Red Cabbage.

1710. To one quart of vinegar, one ounce of whole pepper.

Remove the coarse leaves from some red cabbage, and wipe them very clean; cut them in long thin slices or shreds, and put them on a large sieve, well covering them with salt, and let them drain all night; then put them into stone jars, and pour over them some boiling vinegar and whole peppers; cover them over, and set them by for use.

Herb Powder for Winter Use.

1711. Two ounces of sweet marjoram; two ounces of winter savory; two ounces of lemon thyme; four ounces of parsley; two ounces of lemon peel.

After the herbs are all thoroughly dry, pick off the leaves, pound them to a powder, and then sift them through a sieve. Mix all well together, adding the lemon peel dried and pounded as fine as the leaves. Keep it in glass bottles for use, tightly corked down. All other herbs dried and pounded are better kept in separate bottles, and added when required.

To Keep Parsley for Winter Use.

1712. Pick and tie some fresh parsley in bunches, and boil it for three or four minutes in boiling water in which a little salt has been melted and strained, drain it from the water on a sieve, and dry it very quickly before the fire; put it into bottles. When required for use, soak it in warm water for a few minutes.

BUTTER AND CHEESE.

To Make Butter.

1713. In order to make butter well, it is necessary that the vessels in which the milk is kept be sweet and clean, and the milk-room or cellar cool and airy in summer.

Large tin pans are mostly used for milk, the broadest are the best, allowing a greater surface for the cream to rise.

Vessels in which milk is kept, after being emptied, must first be washed in cold water to take off all the milk, and any remains of cream, then fill them with scalding hot water, which must be suffered to remain until nearly cold. One pan may be turned over another, which is filled with hot water, for a few minutes, then change their relative positions, pouring the water from one to the other. This will require less time and water than the other way. Lastly, wash them well in the water and turn them upside down in the sun. Tin milk pails are best, being most easily kept sweet. White, or hard wood pails are generally used, and must be washed well in cold water and then scalded the same as tin pans. Occasionally, scour both pails and pans with soft soap and sand, and afterwards scald them, rinse them in hot water, and dry them in the sun, or by a fire. Or, instead of scalding the milk tins, and other vessels, as above directed, have a large vessel of boiling water, and having first washed them in cold water (turning it round that every part may get its due), let it remain in for a few minutes, then wipe them dry, and set them by for use; their own heat will assist the drying.

Milk strainers are tin basins with a fine sieve at the bottom, or with a ring by which to fasten a linen cloth over a bottomless basin. The ring and cloth must be taken off every time it is used, and first washed in cold water. Allow it to remain in the water whilst washing the tins, then wash it out, pour scalding water in it, and lastly, rinse it in cold water, and hang it to dry.

A small frame or ladder is wanted to lay across the pan and support the strainer whilst the milk is poured through.

For taking the cream from the milk, a short handle tin skimmer or shell is used. A stone jar or pot is best for keeping cream. There should never be more than three days' gatherings for a churning; too long-keeping will make bitter butter. Wash the jar in cold water, and scald and dry as directed for the tins.

Wooden ware churns are mostly used. The old fashioned barrel churn is best for small churnings; a larger sort, in which the dasher is suspended and moved back and forth, instead of up and down, is less tiresome; the churn is to be kept sweet and clean in the same manner as the other vessels, exposing the inside to the heat of the sun until thoroughly dry, after each time washing.

A wooden tray and ladle are also necessary for receiving and working the butter after it is made.

Care is necessary that the churning is neither too fast nor too slowly performed. The dashes should be continued at intervals of about a second between them, and steadily, until the butter has come, when a slower and more gentle motion is desirable.

Scald the tray and ladle, then fill it with cold water until the butter is made.

After the butter is fairly gathered, take it from the buttermilk, with the ladle, pressing it against the sides of the churn, to free it from the milk; having thrown the water from the tray put the butter in, pour cold water over to cover it, and set it in a cool place for half an hour to harden it; then with the ladle work all the milk from it, changing the water until it is clear. It is best to have ice water in summer if possible.

To each pound of butter put a small tablespoonful of fine salt, and a small teaspoonful of fine white sugar; work it nicely into the butter and make it in rolls, or pack it in wooden or stone vessels; put a piece of muslin and a cover to keep the butter from the air.

Butter should be made and kept in a cool cellar or ice house; this direction is particularly for the summer, when it must be done in the coolest part of the day, and the coolest possible place. Cold water poured in occasionally, in small quantities, at the dasher, will make butter come better in summer.

In warm weather milk is generally ready for skimming after twenty-four hours' standing, when the cream is wanted for butter.

For cream for table or freezing, twelve hours' standing is sufficient. Take off the cream, let the milk remain until the next morning, then skim it and keep the cream for butter. When the weather is cold, let the milk become scalding hot without boiling before straining it. After twelve hours it is fit for skimming, and the milk which remains will be sweet and fit for common purposes. Another way to hasten cream is to dip the pans in boiling water before straining in the milk; by turning another pan scalded in the same manner over the pan with the milk, you may greatly facilitate the operation. Another way is to set the pans over vessels of boiling water; this will also cause the cream to rise quickly.

If you churn in winter pour boiling water into the churn, cover it, and let it remain until ready to put in the cream, at which time throw it out. Winter churning should be done in a moderately warm room.

The shelves and floor of a milk room should be washed and wiped twice a week in summer, and once each week in winter. The place should be sweet and cool, and free from any mustiness, which will affect the milk.

Buttermilk and sour milk are used to make cottage cheese, as it is sometimes called. Buttermilk is also a cooling summer drink, and very palatable, sweetened with sugar; a little grated nutmeg may also be added. Sour milk and buttermilk are kept for the pigs.

To Keep Milk and Cream in Hot Weather.

1714. In hot weather, when it is difficult to preserve milk from becoming sour and spoiling the cream, it may be kept perfectly sweet by scalding the new milk very gently, without boiling, and setting it by in the earthen dish or pan that it is done in. Cream already skimmed may be kept twenty-four hours if scalded without sugar; and by adding to it as much powdered lump sugar as shall make it pretty sweet will be good for two days, keeping it cool. Or milk may be preserved fresh in warm weather by placing the jug which contains it in ice, or very cold water.

Rolled Butter.

1715. Well wash the interior of the mould with cold water, and at all times the greatest care must be taken that they are kept delicately clean. Press the butter into the mould, after which it must be opened and the shape carefully taken out. Serve it in an ornamental glass butter dish, with a little water at the bottom; but if for luncheon or cheese course it must be placed on a flat glass dish, and garnished with a wreath of curled parsley.

To Freshen Salt Butter.

1716. Two or three pounds of salt butter; one small teaspoonful of fine white sugar; one large one of salt to each pound of butter.

Take two or three pounds of salt butter, put it into a wooden bowl, pour very cold water over it, and work it with a ladle, gently pressing it until the water is coloured; then drain it off, add more water, and continue to work it, changing the water until it is clear. Mix a small teaspoonful of fine white sugar, and a large one of fine salt together for each pound of butter, and after draining off the water for the last time, strew the mixture over, work it thoroughly in with a ladle by folding and gently pressing the butter; then make it into rolls, and wrap each piece in a separate piece of muslin; or pack it in stone jars, with muslin over it, and a cover to keep out the air. Keep it in a cold dry place.

Butter in Haste—From Winter Cream, or from the Milk of One Cow.

1717. Take the milk fresh from the cow; strain it into clean pans. Set it over a gentle fire until it is scalding hot; do not let it boil. Then set it aside. When it is cold, skim off the cream; the milk will still be fit for any ordinary use. When you have a sufficient quantity of cream, put it into a clean earthen basin; beat it with a wooden spoon until the butter is made, which will not be long; then take it from the milk and work it with a little cold water. Put a *small* tablespoonful of fine salt to each pound of butter and work it in; a small spoonful of fine white sugar worked in with the salt is also an improvement. Make the butter into a large roll, cover it with muslin, and keep it in a cool place.

To Scald Cream, as in the West of England.

Time, three-quarters of an hour over the fire.

1718. To stand in the winter twenty-four hours; twelve in the summer.
Strain the milk into large shallow pans about three or four inches deep, and let it stand twenty-four hours; then place the pan very carefully upon a hot plate, or *slow* fire, to heat gently, taking care it does *not boil*, or there will be a skim instead of a cream upon the milk. As soon as the cream forms a ring round the pan, and the undulations on the surface look thick, it is done: then remove it from the fire into the dairy, and let it remain for twenty-four hours, or if in cold weather, thirty-six; then skim it for use. The butter usually made in Devonshire of cream thus prepared is very firm and good.

To Prepare Rennet to Turn Milk.

1719. Take out the stomach of a calf as soon as killed, and scour it inside and out with salt. After it is cleared of the curds always found in it, let it drain a few hours; then sew it up with two handfuls of salt in it, or stretch it on a stick, well salted; or keep it in the salt wet, and soak a piece for use, which will do over and over again by washing it in fresh water.

To Make Cheese.

1720. Put the milk into a large tub, warming part of it to a degree of heat equal to new milk; if too hot the cheese will be tough. Put in as much rennet as will turn it, and cover it over. Let it stand till completely turned; then strike the curd down several times with the skimming-dish, and let it separate, still covering it. There are two modes of breaking the curd, and there will be a difference in the taste of the cheese according as either is observed; one is to gather it with the hands very gently towards the side of the tub, letting the whey pass through the fingers till it is cleared, and ladling it off as it collects; the other is to get the whey from it by early breaking the curd. The last method deprives it of many of its oily particles, and is therefore less proper.
Put the vat on a ladder over the tub and fill it with curd by a skimmer, press the curd close with your hand, and add more as it sinks, and it must be finally left two inches above the edge. Before the vat is filled, the cheese-cloth must be laid at the bottom, and when full, drawn smooth over on all sides.
There are two modes of salting cheese: one by mixing salt in the curd while in the tub after the whey is out; and the other by putting it into the vat and crumbling the curd all to pieces with it after the first squeezing with the hands has dried it. The first method appears best on some accounts, but not on all, and therefore the custom of the county must direct. Put a board under and over the vat, and place it in the press; in two hours turn it out, and put a fresh cheese-cloth, press it again for eight or nine hours, then salt it all over, and turn it again in the vat, and let it stand in the press fourteen or sixteen hours, observing to put the cheeses last made, undermost. Before putting them the last time into the vat pare the edges if they do not look smooth. The vat should have holes at the sides and at the bottom to let all the whey pass through. Put on clean boards, and change and scald them.

To Make Sage Cheese.

1721. Red sage leaves; leaves of spinach. Bruise the tops of some young red sage in a mortar with some leaves of spinach, and squeeze the juice; mix it with the rennet in the milk, more or less according as you like the colour and taste. When the curd has come, break it gently, and put it in with the skimmer till it is pressed two inches above the vat. Press it eight or ten hours, salt it, and turn it every day.

Imitation of Cheshire Cheese.

1722. The milk being set, and the curd come, do not break it with a dish as is customary in making other cheeses, but draw it together with your hands to one side of the vessel, breaking it gently and regularly, for if it is pressed roughly a great deal of the richness of the milk will go into the whey. Put the curd into the cheese vat as you thus gather it, and when it is full, press and turn it often, salting it at different times.

These cheeses must be made seven or eight inches in thickness, and they will be fit to cut in about twelve months.

You must turn and move them frequently upon the shelf, and rub them with a coarse cloth. At the year's end, bore a hole in the middle, and pour in a quarter of a pint of wine. Stop up the hole with some of the cheese, and set it in a wine cellar for six months to mellow. This cheese, if properly managed, will be exceedingly rich and fine.

An Excellent Cream Cheese.
Time, three days.

1723. One quart of good cream.

Put a quart of good cream aside to become sour and very thick, then lay a piece of thin calico inside a small hair sieve, taking care that the calico comes quite to the top, and rather above it, in order that you may be able to pull out the cheese without any difficulty; let the sieve stand upon a dish; pour the cream into the sieve and leave it to drain. Pour away the whey from the dish every morning. In about three days the cheese will be a proper consistency and fit to eat— as thick as butter, and very delicious. If the cream will not all go into the sieve *at once*, pour it in during the day, as the rest sinks from the whey leaving it.

At *Dieppe* little baskets are sold (heart-shape) for making cream cheeses, and answer the purpose exceedingly well, being very open, so that the whey drains quickly through the calico into the dish.

Cream Cheese.
Time, three or four days for the cream to drip; one hour to press.

1724. Three gills of thick cream; one tablespoonful of salt.

Take three gills of thick cream, and stir into it a tablespoonful of salt. Tie up the cream in a cloth, and let it drop for three or four days, changing the cloth every day. It must be hung upon a nail to drip, and when ready, on the third or fourth day, put it into a wooden mould, and press for one hour. It will then be ready for eating.

Napkin Cheese.
Time, three days.

1725. One pint of thick cream; one teaspoonful of salt.

Put a pint of thick cream and a teaspoonful of salt into a cloth, which should be placed in a sieve the size of a teasaucer. Let it stand for twenty-four hours, then turn it. Let it stand another whole day and turn it. The day following it will be ready to serve.

Artificial Cheese.
1726. One gallon of new milk; two quarts of cream; six or eight eggs; six or seven tablespoonfuls of vinegar; and a little salt.

Boil one gallon of milk with two quarts of cream, add six or eight eggs well beaten, and six or seven large spoonfuls of wine vinegar. Let it simmer until it comes to a tender curd, then tie it in a cheese-cloth, and hang it to drain for several hours, after which open the cloth, work some salt to the cheese, then lay a cloth in a colander or cheese-hoop, put the curd in, fold the cloth over, and lay a heavy weight upon it for one hour, or longer; then turn it on a dish and serve.

Milk Cheese.
Time, fourteen hours.

1727. Five quarts of new milk; two tablespoonfuls of rennet water.

Put five quarts of warm milk into a bowl with two large spoonfuls of rennet water. When the curd is formed break it gently with the hand, drawing it to the side of the basin or bowl. Let it stand for two hours. Spread a cheese-cloth over a sieve or round basket, put in the curd, let it drain until all the whey is off, and then salt it to your taste. Lay a cloth in a cheese-hoop, put in the curd, and lay a cloth over it. Put a wooden cover the size of the inside of the hoop over, place a two pounds weight upon it, and let it remain for twelve hours. Then take it out, put it in a frame, or tie a cloth tightly round it, and turn it from one side to the other every day until dry, then rub the outside with a little butter, and sprinkle pepper over to keep the flies from it. Put it to ripen between two pewter plates. If the weather is warm it will be ready in three weeks, if cold it will require a longer time.

WINES, SYRUPS, AND PUNCH.

Excellent English Sherry.
Time, half an hour to boil.

1728. Thirty pounds of good moist sugar; ten gallons of water; eight quarts of ale; six pounds of raisins; one quart of brandy; one pound of brown sugarcandy; two ounces of isinglass.

Put to thirty pounds of good moist sugar ten gallons of water. Boil it half an hour, skim it well, and then let it stand till quite cold. Add eight quarts of ale from the ale vat while fermenting, stir it well together, let it remain in the tub till the next day; then put it into the barrel with six pounds of raisins, one quart of brandy, one pound of brown sugarcandy, and two ounces of isinglass. Let it remain three weeks before the barrel is closed, and it must stand twelve months before it is put into bottles.

Very Superior Elder Wine.
Time, thirty-five minutes to boil.

1729. Five gallons of ripe elderberries; ten gallons of water; three pounds and a half of moist sugar to every gallon of water and juice; whites of five or six eggs; half a pound of ginger; six lemons.

Boil the five gallons of ripe elderberries in ten quarts of water for a quarter of an hour; then strain them through a hair sieve, not pressing the berries. Measure the liquor into the boiler, and to every gallon add three pounds and a half of moist sugar with the peels of five or six lemons and the strained juice, and let it boil twenty minutes. When scalding hot add the whites of five or six eggs well beaten, stirring the liquor well. When the whole is sufficiently cooled, put some yeast on the top of the cask, or a piece of toasted bread with yeast spread on it. When ready to be bunged up, hang half a pound of bruised ginger tied in a muslin bag in the middle of the cask. Let it remain for two months, and then it will be fit to bottle.

Raisin Wine.
Time to stand, twelve days.

1730. Half a hundred of Valencia raisins; ten gallons of soft water.

Take half a hundred of Valencia raisins pick them from the stalks, and chop them very small, then put them into a tub, and pour over them ten gallons of hot soft water. Let this be strained twice or thrice every day for twelve days successively, then pour the liquor into a cask, make a toast of bread, and while it is hot spread it on each side with yeast, and put it into the vessel. It will be fit to drink in four months.

Blackberry Wine.
Time, fifteen days to ferment.

1731. One pound of sugar to two pounds of blackberry juice; a quarter of a pint of gin or brandy.

Cover a quantity of blackberries with water, and put them into an oven to draw the juice out. Strain them through a sieve and leave them to ferment for fifteen days. Afterwards add a pound of sugar to two quarts of juice, with a quarter of a pint of gin or brandy. When bottled, do not cork it too close.

Clary Wine.
Time to boil, one hour; to make, five days; to stand, one year.

1732. Ten gallons of water; thirty-five pounds of loaf sugar; twelve eggs; two pecks of clary blossoms; one pint of new good yeast.

Put thirty-five pounds of loaf sugar to ten gallons of water, and the well-beaten whites of twelve eggs. Let it boil gently for nearly an hour, simmering and skimming it till it is quite clear. Let it stand till cold. Then put it into the cask with two pecks of clary blossoms stripped from the stalks (flowers and floral leaves together). Add a pint of new good yeast. Stir the wine three times a day for five days. Then stop it up, and let it stand for twelve months. It may be bottled at the end of six months if perfectly clear.

The clary plant is raised from seed sown in a hotbed, or warm border, and then planted out. It is generally two years before it blossoms.

Superior Ginger Wine.
Time, fit to bottle in three months.

1733. One pound of Jamaica ginger; fifty-six pounds of loaf sugar; six dozen lemons; two bottles of brandy; eighteen gallons of water; two tablespoonfuls of new yeast.

Take the best Jamaica ginger, slice it very thin, and tie it in a cloth. Boil it with the sugar and the water for three-quarters of an hour, skimming it all the time. Pare the lemons very thin, and pour the boiling liquor over the peels. Let it stand until the next day, then stir in the juice of the lemons, and put it into the cask with the ginger and the yeast. Stir all together, and let it stand until it has done working. Then add the brandy, and bung it up close. It will be fit to bottle in three months.

Black Currant Wine.

1734. To every gallon of currants—one gallon of water; three pounds and a half of moist sugar; to every six gallons, one quart of brandy.

To every gallon of juice, put the same quantity of cold water, and three pounds and a half of moist sugar. Put it into your cask, reserving some of the liquor for filling up. Put the cask in a warm dry place, and the liquor will ferment of itself. When the fermentation is over, skim off the refuse, and fill up the cask with the reserved liquor. When it has ceased working, pour one quart of brandy to six gallons of the wine. Bung it up close for eight or nine months, then bottle it off clear. Run the sediment through a jelly bag until it is clear, bottle, and keep it twelve months before it is used.

Cowslip Wine.

Time, half an hour to boil; thirty-six hours to ferment; to remain in the cask six weeks.

1735. To every gallon of water allow three pounds of loaf sugar, the juice of one lemon, the peel of two, and one Seville orange, one gallon of cowslip flowers, or pips; to every five gallons, a bottle of brandy, and a crust of toasted bread with three large spoonfuls of yeast.

Put the peel of the lemons and the oranges, with the strained juice, into a large pan. Boil the sugar and the water together for half an hour, and pour it over the juice and peel. When lukewarm, add the cowslip flowers, or pips picked from the stalks, and to every five gallons of wine put about three large spoonfuls of thick yeast spread on a crust of toasted bread. Let it ferment thirty-six hours; then put all together into a cask with the brandy, let the cask be close stopped, and stand six weeks before you bottle it off for use.

Orange Wine.

Time, to stand, four days.

1736. Seventy-five Seville oranges; thirty pounds of loaf sugar; one bottle of brandy; six eggs, and eight gallons of water.

Put the sugar, water, and the whites and shells of the eggs well beaten into a copper, and let the whole gently boil as long as any scum rises. Peel the oranges very thin, put the peels into a tub, and pour over them the boiling clarified sugar, cover it over, and let it stand for four days. On the third day, squeeze the oranges, and strain the juice through a hair sieve, letting it drain until the next day; then pour it into a cask, and fill it up with the clarified sugar, keeping back all the peels of the oranges. If not sufficient to fill the cask, boil some water, and when cold, add it; then pour in the brandy, and stop it down close. In twelve months, draw it off, and return it to the cask. If not fine, add a little isinglass.

Mock Champagne.

Time, to work, three weeks; to stand, six months.

1737. To every quart of grapes, one quart of water; to every gallon of juice, allow three pounds of loaf sugar; half an ounce of isinglass to every ten gallons of wine, and a quart of brandy to every five gallons.

Pick the grapes when full-grown and just beginning to change colour, bruise them in a tub, pour in the water, and let them stand for three days, stirring once each day; then press the fruit through a cloth, let it stand for three or four hours, pour it carefully from any sediment, and add to it the sugar. Barrel it, and put the bung slightly in; at the end of three weeks, or when it has done working, put in the isinglass, previously dissolved in some of the liquor. Stir it for three days once a day, and at the last stirring add the brandy. In three or four days bung it down close, and in six months it should be bottled, and the corks tied down, or wired.

Ginger Beer.

Time, one hour to boil.

1738. Five pounds of loaf sugar; three ounces of powdered ginger; three gallons of water; five lemons; a quarter of a teacupful of yeast; slice of toasted bread.

Boil the sugar and ginger in three gallons of water for one hour. When it is cold, add the juice and peels of five lemons, and a quarter of a teacupful of yeast on a slice of toasted bread. Let it stand in a tub covered with a thick cloth for two or three days. Then strain it through a thick cloth, and bottle it.

It will be ready to drink in four or five days after it is bottled.

If it is wished to be very strong of ginger, more may be added.

Lemonade.

Time, two hours.

1739. Six lemons; one quart of boiling water; one or two ounces of clarified sugar.

Grate the peel of six lemons, pour a quart of boiling water on it; let it stand some time; then add the juice of the lemons (take care not to let the lemon pips fall into the liquid), sweeten it with clarified sugar, and run it through a jelly bag.

Lemonade with Citric Acid.

1740. One pound and a half of loaf sugar; three-quarters of a pint of water; one ounce of citric acid, and twenty-two drops of essence of lemon.

Boil a pound and a half of loaf sugar in three-quarters of a pint of water for a few minutes, skim it, and when half cold mix the other ingredients with it, stir well together, and bottle it for use. Two tablespoonfuls is sufficient for a tumbler of water.

Milk Lemonade.

Time, twelve hours.

1741. Two dry lemons; two pounds of loaf sugar powdered; one quart of white wine; three quarts of *quite* fresh boiling milk.

Peel the lemons, taking care first to wash the peel quite clean. Let the peel be *very* thin. Squeeze the juice over it, and let it lay on the peel all night. In the morning add to it two pounds of powdered sugar, a quart of white wine, three quarts of fresh boiling milk. Strain it once or twice through a jelly bag till it is perfectly clear and nice. Let it get quite cold. This is a most delicious beverage in the summer.

Santa or Shrub.

Time, three days in the rum.

1742. Six lemons; two quarts of rum; and sufficient to fill the bottle; the peel of four or five Seville oranges; three pounds of moist sugar; three pints of water.

When you make orange marmalade save the gratings of four or five Seville oranges, and put them into a *very* large wide-mouthed bottle, with the peel of six lemons cut very thin, fill the vessel up with *rum*, and let it stand three days. Then boil the sugar and water, skim it well, and let it stand until cool. Squeeze and strain the juice of the six lemons into a large pan; add the two quarts of rum, the rum strained from the bottle, and the syrup. Mix all well together and bottle it for use.

Brandy or Rum Shrub.

1743. To one pint of Seville orange juice allow two pounds of loaf sugar, and three pints of brandy or rum.

Mix all thoroughly together, and when the sugar is dissolved, strain the whole through a jelly bag, and bottle it off for use.

Curaçoa.

Time, three weeks.

1744. Eighteen Seville oranges; one pound and a quarter of white sugar-candy; one ounce of cinnamon; six cloves, and a little powdered spice; three pints of French brandy.

Peel off *very* thin the outside rind of the Seville oranges, and bruise it in a mortar very fine. Pound fine a pound and a quarter of white sugar-candy, with an ounce of powdered cinnamon. Put this mixture into a half gallon stone bottle, pour on it three pints of very good French brandy, cork it down well, shake it every other day for three weeks, at the end of that time strain it off through a flannel bag into bottles.

Punch that will Keep for any Length of Time.

Time, to infuse, four days; to boil, a quarter of an hour; to bottle, in two months.

1745. Peel of ten lemons; the same of Seville oranges; three quarts of lemon juice; five quarts of orange juice; five gallons of the best rum; ten gallons of water; thirty pounds of sugar; whites of thirty eggs.

Put the peel of the lemons and Seville oranges into the rum, and let them stand four days. Then put the sugar and water into a copper, and when they boil add the whites of the eggs well beaten; let them all boil a quarter of an hour, and when cold strain it through a sieve, and pour the rum from the lemon and orange peels into the syrup. Then add the lemon and orange juice, which must also be strained through a sieve. Put all into a barrel, and it will be fit for bottling in two months.

This quantity will produce eighteen gallons of punch; the best cask to use for it is an old rum cask if to be had.

Whisky Punch.

Time, to infuse, one hour.

1746. Half a pint of whisky; one lemon; one glass of curaçoa; one pint of water; two bottles of iced soda-water; sugar to taste.

Pour half a pint of whisky on the peel of a lemon taken off very thin, and the lemon cut into very thin slices, after the whole of the white part has been carefully taken off;

Milk Punch.—Holmby, Claret, Champagne, Porter Cups, &c.

let it stand an hour. Then add a sufficient quantity of sugar, with a glass of curaçoa, about a pint of water, and two bottles of iced soda-water. Mix all well together.

To Make George IV. Milk Punch.
Time, to infuse, twelve hours; to stand, six hours.

1747. Two quarts of rum; peel of twelve lemons; peel of two Seville oranges; two quarts of cold spring water; one pound of loaf sugar; one pint of lemon juice; one nutmeg; one pint of strong green tea; a quarter of a pint of maraschino; one pint of Madeira; one pint of boiling milk.
Infuse the peels of the lemons and the oranges in the rum for twelve hours, then add the cold spring water, the loaf sugar, lemon juice, and the nutmeg grated, the green tea, maraschino and Madeira. Mix all together, and then stir in the new milk boiling hot. Let it stand six hours, then pour it through a jelly bag until it is perfectly clear, and bottle it off for use.

Holmby Cup.
1748. One bottle of claret; one of soda-water; one small glass of brandy; sugar to taste; one small lump of ice.

Cup from the "Blues."
1749. Four quarts of water; two bottles of cider; one bottle of perry; one pint of sherry; two large glasses of brandy; two of rum-shrub; sweeten to your taste.
Two bottles of champagne improve it very much, and borage put in it is also an improvement.

Christmas Bowl.
Time, three hours.

1750. Nine spongecakes; half a pound of macaroons; one pint of raisin wine; half a pint of sherry; two ounces of almonds; two ounces of powdered sugar-candy; one pint and a half of custard.
Break the spongecakes into small pieces, and place in a deep bowl with the macaroons; add the raisin wine and sherry, leaving them to soak thoroughly; sweeten with the sugar-candy, and pour over the top a very thick custard. Stick with sliced almonds. Place the bowl on a stand, ornamented with Christmas evergreens.

Claret Cup.
1751. One bottle of claret; one bottle of soda-water; one glass of brandy or sherry; one strip of cucumber; peel of half a lemon; sugar to your taste; a large lump of ice.

Put all the above ingredients into a silver cup, pass a napkin through one of the handles, that the edge of the cup may be wiped after the contents have been partaken of, and hand it round to each person.

Superior Claret Cup.
1752. Two bottles of claret; one of champagne; three glasses of sherry; one of noyau; half a pound of ice; one sprig of borage, or a few slices of cucumber; sugar, if required.
Mix and serve as above.

Champagne Cup.
1753. One bottle of champagne; two bottles of soda-water; one glass of brandy; one pound of ice; a sprig of green borage, or two or three slices of cucumber; two ounces of powdered loaf sugar.
Mix all together in a silver cup, and serve as Claret Cup.

Another Way.
1754. One bottle of champagne; three wineglasses of sherry; one wineglass of curaçoa; four slices of lemon; two slices of cucumber (or peel); one of pineapple; one bottle of soda-water; all mixed together, and iced.
Serve as Claret Cup.

Sherry Cobbler.
1755. Half a pint of sherry; a little mint; a tablespoonful of sugar; a *large* quantity of pounded ice; two slices of lemon; and a bottle of soda-water; all mixed together.

Porter Cup.
1756. One quart of porter; half a pint of sherry; four slices of lemons; and a little nutmeg; all well mixed together, and iced.

Capillaire.
Time, until a froth rises.

1757. Fourteen pounds of sugar; six eggs; three quarts of water; one gill of orange-flower water; with two or three drops of vanilla.
Take fourteen pounds of sugar, break six eggs in with the shells, stir into it gradually three quarts of water, set it over the fire, and boil it, and take off the scum until only a light froth rises; add to it a gill of orange-flower water, and two or three drops of vanilla, then strain it through a jelly bag, and when cold, bottle it; cork it tight to keep.
A wineglass of this put to a tumbler of ice-water is much liked, and very refreshing.
Slices of lemon, or pineapple, or crushed

strawberries, raspberries, or ripe currants may be added to it, also a glass of wine, brandy, or rum.

Cream Sherbet.

1758. Yolks of six eggs; one dessert-spoonful of orange-flower water; two quarts of cream; three-quarters of a pound of loaf sugar.

Put the yolks of six eggs and a dessert-spoonful of orange-flower water into two quarts of cream; boil it up *once* in a covered stewpan, then strain it; add to it three-quarters of a pound of fine loaf-sugar, and stir it until it is dissolved.

When cold, set it in ice, or freeze it the same as ice cream.

Lemon Sherbet.

1759. A pound and a half of loaf sugar; one quart of water; nine lemons.

Dissolve a pound and a half of loaf sugar in a quart of water; take nine large lemons, wipe them clean, and cut each in two; squeeze them, so as to extract the juice and the essence from the peel; stir into it the sugared water, then strain it, and freeze the same as ice cream.

Strawberry Sherbet.

Time, to stand, three or four hours.

1760. One pound of strawberries; three pints of water; juice of one lemon; one tablespoonful of orange-flower water; one pound of double-refined sugar.

Take one pound of picked strawberries, crush them to a smooth mass; then add three pints of water, the juice of a lemon, and a tablespoonful of orange-flower water; let it stand for three or four hours. Put a pound of double-refined sugar into another basin, stretch over it a large cloth or napkin, and strain the strawberries through it on the sugar, wring it, to extract as much of the juice as possible; stir until the sugar is dissolved, then strain again, and set it in ice for an hour before serving, in small tumblers.

Noyau.

Time, five days.

1761. To one quart of English gin, allow one pound of loaf sugar, and three ounces of bitter almonds.

Blanch and cut three ounces of bitter almonds into a quart of English gin; let it infuse three days by a fire, shaking the bottle often. Then add a pound of loaf sugar, just immersed in boiling water; let it stand two days longer, shaking it frequently.

Then filter it through blotting paper and it will be fit for use.

Honey Noyau.

Time, to make, ten days.

1762. Four ounces of bitter almonds; two ounces of sweet almonds; two pounds of loaf sugar; three lemons; two quarts of gin; two large spoonfuls of clarified honey; one pint of milk.

Blanch and pound the almonds, and mix them with the sugar, which should be rolled. Boil the milk, and when cold, mix all the ingredients together, and let them stand ten days, shaking them every day. Filter the mixture through blotting paper, bottle off for use, and seal the corks down.

Gingerette.

Time, to make, six days.

1763. One pound of currants; one pint of gin; the peel of one lemon; one pound of sugar; half an ounce of pulverized ginger.

Bruise one pound of currants, and put to them one pint of the best gin, and the peel of a lemon cut very thin; let it stand two days, then strain it, and add half an ounce of pulverized ginger, and one pound of loaf sugar to each pint. Let it stand a few days, stirring it occasionally. Strain it again and put it into bottles.

Ginger Cordial.

Time, three or four days.

1764. One ounce and a half of pounded ginger; one pound and a half of white or black currants; one quart of white brandy; one pound of loaf sugar.

Add to an ounce and a half of pounded ginger, a pound and a half of white or black currants picked and bruised; then pour in a quart of the best white brandy, and let it stand three or four days and strain it through a cloth. Dissolve a pound of double-refined loaf sugar in a little boiling water; when cold mix it all together, strain it through a flannel bag, and bottle it for use.

Orange Brandy.

Time, to steep, forty-eight hours.

1765. Eight lemons; eight Seville oranges; three pounds of loaf sugar; three pennyworth of saffron; one gallon of brandy.

Take the thin peel of the lemons and the oranges, put them into a pan or jar, with the sugar, saffron, and brandy. Let the whole steep for forty-eight hours, stirring it often. Then strain it off, and bottle for use. The dregs make orange cakes or marmalade.

Lemon Brandy.
Time, to steep, eight days.

1766. Three quarts of brandy; one pound and three-quarters of loaf sugar; peel of six lemons; juice of twelve; one quart of boiling milk.
Put three quarts of brandy into an earthen pan or jug, which has a cover; add to it a pound and three-quarters of loaf sugar, the peel of six lemons, cut very thin, the juice of twelve strained, and a quart of boiling milk. Let it steep for eight days, stirring it once a day; then strain it through a flannel bag and bottle it for use.

Morella Cherry Brandy.

1767. Four pounds of morella cherries; half a gallon of the best brandy; two pounds of loaf sugar.
Pick the cherries from the stalks, and put them into bottles with the loaf sugar; fill each bottle up with brandy; cover them first with bladder, over that paper, and set them by for use.

Raspberry Vinegar.
Time, to make, two days.

1768. Four quarts of raspberries; to every pint of juice allow a pound and a half of loaf sugar; one quart of vinegar.
Pour a quart of vinegar over *two* quarts of fresh raspberries, and let it stand twenty-four hours; then strain it through a sieve, without pressing the fruit; pour the liquor on another two quarts of fresh raspberries, and in twenty-four hours strain it off again. To every pint of juice allow a pound and a half of loaf sugar. Pour all into a deep jar, and set it in a pan of hot water till the sugar is all dissolved, then take off the scum and bottle it for use.

Blackberry Syrup.
Time, fifteen to twenty minutes.

1769. One pound of sugar to every pint of water; as many pints of blackberry juice as there are pounds of sugar; half a nutmeg; half a wineglass of brandy to each quart of syrup.
Make a syrup of a pound of sugar to each pint of water; boil it until it is rich and thick; then add to it as many pints of the juice of ripe blackberries as there are pounds of sugar; put half a nutmeg grated to each quart of syrup; let it boil fifteen or twenty minutes, then add to it half a wineglass of brandy for each quart of syrup.

Set it to become cold, and then bottle it for use.

Mulberry Syrup.
Time, twenty minutes.

1770. To each pint of mulberry juice allow one pound of loaf sugar.
Put some ripe mulberries into a jar, cover it over, and set it in a saucepan of water; let it boil, and as the liquor rises from the mulberries, drain it off. To each pint add a pound of loaf sugar. Set it over the fire and boil it to the consistency of cream, skim it well, and when cold, bottle and cork it down.

Mulled Wine.
Time, five minutes.

1771. One quart of new milk; one stick of cinnamon; nutmeg and sugar to taste; yolks of six eggs; a spoonful or two of cream.
Boil a quart of new milk five minutes with a stick of cinnamon, nutmeg, and sugar to your taste, then take it off the fire, and let it stand to cool. Beat the yolks of six eggs very well, and mix them with a large spoonful or two of cold cream, then mix it with the wine, and pour it backwards and forwards from the saucepan to the jug several times. Send it to table with biscuits.

Wine Whey.
Time, five minutes.

1772. Half a pint of milk; sugar to taste; one wineglass of white wine.
Put half a pint of milk over the fire, sweeten it to taste, and when boiling throw in a wineglass of sherry. As soon as the curd forms, strain the whey through muslin into a tumbler.

To Mull Ale.
Time, ten minutes.

1773. One pint of ale; three or four cloves; nutmeg and sugar to taste; yolks of four eggs; a little cold ale.
Take a pint of ale and put it into a saucepan with three or four cloves, nutmeg, and sugar to your taste, set it over the fire, and when it boils, take it off to cool. Beat the yolks of four eggs well, and mix them with a little cold ale, then put it to the warm ale, and pour it in and out of the saucepan several times, heat it again till quite hot, and serve it with dry toast.

Egg Wine.
Time, about five minutes.

1774. One glass of white wine; one spoonful of cold water; a few lumps of loaf sugar; a little grated nutmeg; one egg.

Put a glass of white wine with half a wineglass of cold water, a little sugar, and grated nutmeg, into a very clean saucepan; set it over the fire, and when it boils pour it by degrees over an egg well beaten with a spoonful of cold water, stir it one way for a minute, and serve it with dry toast in a plate.

Egg Flip.

1775. Three eggs; a quarter of a pound of good moist sugar; a pint and a half of beer.

Beat three whole eggs with a quarter of a pound of good moist sugar; make a pint and a half of beer very hot, but do not let it boil, then mix it gradually with the beaten eggs and sugar, toss it to and fro from the saucepan into a jug two or three times, grate a little nutmeg on the top, and serve it.

A wineglass of spirits may be added if liked.

Family Brewing.

Not many persons in the present day brew at home; but as some few might wish to do so, we give the following receipt supplied by a friend, and used in his family.

1776. Four bushels of malt; sixty gallons of water; (for small beer, after the first is drawn off, forty more gallons); three pounds of good Farnham hops; three-quarters of a pint of yeast.

The copper should hold forty gallons of water, which should, when boiling, be put into the mash vat. When it has stood until you can see your face in the water, then mash the malt in it, and stir it well till it is all wet. Cover it up with sacks to keep in the steam. To four bushels of malt put *forty* gallons of boiling water, let it stand one hour and a half, then add *twenty* gallons more water, let it stand two hours and a half longer, which will make in the whole four hours. When you add the water to the malt the second time, wet the hops with a bucket or two of boiling water. During this time the brewer should scald his barrel, and have forty gallons of boiling water ready to go on the malt when the first liquor is drawn off, which will make good small beer. Three pounds of good Farnham hops will be sufficient for this quantity, which we call ale and small beer. Be sure to boil your first wort with the hops at least three-quarters of an hour; keep it boiling all the time—galloping; (boil the small beer the same time). Then strain off the wort, in the shade if possible. When it is lukewarm, put it into the tun tub, and set it to work with half a pint of yeast. The next day draw it off into the barrel. When the beer has done fermenting, bung it down close; observe to paste brown paper over the vent hole with a little yeast, lest it should ferment, which is sometimes the case, but be sure to keep it stopped down as soon as the fermentation is over. The casks should hold thirty-three or thirty-six gallons. You will find a small barrel very useful to hold the overplus of ale which you will sometimes have, and which will be fit to drink sooner. Observe the same rules with strong beer, only with the addition of one and a half bushels of malt more, and two pounds of hops, and then your second tun will be very good table beer, and you may make twenty gallons of small beer for common use. Be sure to see the barrels are well cleaned with scalding (not boiling) water. A yard of small chain is a very good thing to put into the barrels, to clean them. Very much depends on the cleanliness of the vessels. As soon as the casks are empty be sure to cork them close, or they will get musty, which can never be remedied. You may add yeast to the small beer, and tun it as soon as it is cold. You must not stir the mash when you add the water to the first beer, but pour it milk-warm over the top of the malt.

Directions for Brewing in Cottages.

Time, three or four days.

1777. One peck of malt; two ounces of hops; six gallons of water; a few birch twigs, or a little wheat straw; one teacupful of yeast.

Boil three gallons of water; take it off as soon as it boils, and let it stand till you can see your face in it. While the water is heating, get ready a clean rinsing-tub with a small hole bored in the bottom, and stopped with a peg or cork. Cover it with a few birch twigs or some clean wheat straw, put a coarse bit of cloth over the bottom of the tub, then put in the malt. Pour the water on it, and stir it well for a few minutes. Cover it close with a sack, and let it stand for three days to keep warm near the fire; then pull out the peg or cork, and let the whole run into a bucket. Put the peg in again immediately, and having prepared another three gallons of water just as you did before, pour it on the malt, and set it by the fire as before, covered close, for two hours. As soon as you have emptied the second three gallons of water out of the boiler, put into it the first run from the malt, and boil it a quarter of an hour with the hops. Strain it through a sieve into a shallow vessel to cool as quickly as possible.

Run off the second three gallons, and boil

them with the same hops for half an hour; then strain and cool as for the first run. Mix both runs from the malt together, add a small teacupful of yeast, and let it ferment for two or three days, during which time it must be frequently skimmed.

Three pints of nice yeast will thus be obtained. When the fermentation is over, put the beer in a small cask, where it will probably ferment a little, after which stop it down close.

COOKERY FOR THE SICK.

A good nurse is frequently of as much importance as a skilful physician; and "kitchen physic," as it has been called, is often of the first importance. Every mother of a family ought to know how to cater for the fitful appetite and weak digestion of an invalid. A truly loving and tender woman would rather prepare the food of her beloved and suffering child, or of her husband, than trust it to the care of an ordinary cook. It has been our fate to be much thrown with sickness, and we have carefully garnered together many strengthening prescriptions in the way of food, which we can assure the reader have had the test of use and experience. We subjoin them, with some few commoner preparations for the sick-room.

Arrowroot.

1778. Half a pint of milk; one dessertspoonful of arrowroot; sugar to taste; lemon peel.

Take care to get the *very best* arrowroot, as many imitations are sold. Mix a dessertspoonful with a *little* cold water till it is quite smooth. Boil half a pint of milk; pour it on the arrowroot, *while boiling*, stirring it all the time. Add a lump or two of sugar, and a little lemon peel.

Water Arrowroot.

1779. One dessertspoonful of arrowroot; one gill of water; sugar; one tablespoonful of brandy, or one wineglass of wine.

Mix a dessertspoonful of arrowroot with a little water very smooth. Have ready water in a kettle *quite boiling*. Pour it on the arrowroot till it becomes clear, stirring it all the time. A few lumps of sugar and the wine or brandy can be mixed with it before pouring the boiling water on it, using the wine or brandy to mix the arrowroot with instead of the water.

Bread Jelly.

1780. One roll; one lemon; one quart of water; sugar to taste.

Take the crumb of a penny roll; cut it into thin slices, and toast them of a pale brown on both sides. Put them into a quart of spring water. Let it simmer over the fire till it has become a jelly. Strain it through a thin cloth, and flavour it immediately with a little lemon juice and sugar.

Broth—Chicken.

1781. Take an old fowl; stew it to pieces with a couple of onions. Season lightly with pepper and salt; skim and strain it.

Port Wine Jelly.

Time, fifteen or twenty minutes.

1782. One pint of port wine; one ounce of isinglass; one ounce of sugar; a quarter of a pint of water.

Put the isinglass and sugar into a quarter of a pint of water. Set it over the fire till the isinglass is dissolved; then add the wine. Strain it through a jelly bag or a clean piece of muslin into a jar or mould, and let it set. It is best to put it into a jar, to cover it till cold, and give a piece about the size of a walnut two or three times a day to the patient.

This jelly may be made to drink hot thus:—

Put a teaspoonful of melted isinglass to one wineglass of port wine, adding one clove and a lump of sugar. Make it hot over an etna.

Port Wine Jelly.

1783. One bottle of port wine; two ounces of gum arabic; two ounces of sugarcandy; two ounces of isinglass.

Put all these ingredients into a jar, stand it in a saucepan of water, and keep it simmering till all is dissolved.

Weaker Wine Jelly for Invalids.

Time, altogether, half an hour.

1784. The juice of two oranges; the peel of one; yolks of four eggs; half an ounce of isinglass; half a pint of sherry or white wine; half a pint of water; loaf sugar to taste.

Put the isinglass into hot water and gradually dissolve it, then stir in as much loaf sugar as is approved, with the juice of the oranges strained, and the peel cut very thin; well beat the yolks of the eggs with the

Broths.—Calf's Feet.—Isinglass.—Beef Tea.—Beef Essence

wine; put all into a saucepan and let it simmer for a minute or two, not boil; stirring it all the time, then let it stand a short time before putting it into a mould, which must be previously soaked in cold water. This quantity makes a pint, and if *good sherry* and new-laid eggs are used, it will be found excellent for invalids.

A Strong Broth.
Time, nearly four hours.

1785. One pound of veal; one pound of beef; one pound of the scrag end of a neck of mutton; a little salt; three quarts of water. Put the above quantities into three quarts of water, with a little salt, and a few whole peppers. Boil it until reduced to one quart.

Calf's Feet.
Time, four hours.

1786. Two calf's feet; two pints of water; one pint of new milk; a little lemon peel or mace.
Put the ingredients into a jar, cover it down, and keep it in the oven for four hours. When cold, remove the fat. Flavour it with lemon peel or mace, as preferred. This is very strengthening if taken the first thing in the morning and the last at night.

Isinglass.

1787. Isinglass should be put into the invalid's tea, morning and evening, a good pinchful for a teacup. It should be introduced as much as possible into the food of the weak, as it is most strengthening.

White Broth for Invalids.
Time, two hours.

1788. Two pounds of veal; a small fowl; a blade or two of mace; a slice or two of lemon peel; one tablespoonful of rice; two eggs.
Put the veal and a small fowl trussed into a stewpan, with sufficient water to cover it; add the mace, lemon peel, and the rice. Place the pan over a gentle fire, and let it simmer until the juice of the meat is thoroughly extracted. Well beat up two eggs, put them into a tureen, and pour the boiling broth very gradually on them, taking care to stir with a spoon the whole time. Serve it up with toasted sippets.

Ordinary Beef Tea.
Time, three or four hours.

1789. Two pounds of gravy beef; two pints and a half of water; a little salt.
Cut two pounds of gravy beef into slices, and put it into a jar with two pints and a half of water, and a pinch of salt. Cover it over. Set it in a *warm* oven for three or four hours. When done, strain it through a fine sieve, and set it in a cold place, warming a small portion when required.

Very Strong Beef Tea.
Time, four hours.

1790. Cut two pounds of lean beef into small square dice, put it into a jar or a basin without water, cover it over, stand it in the oven for three or four hours, till every drop of gravy is out of the meat. Then mix this rich stock with boiling water to the strength required.

Beef Essence.
Time, half an hour.

1791. One pound of lean beef; one pint of water; one clove; a lump of sugar, and a little salt.
Cut into thin slices a pound of beef from the rump; lay them on a trencher, and scrape them with a knife as quickly as possible until as fine as sausage meat. Put this into a saucepan, and stir it over the fire until thoroughly warmed through, which will take from five to ten minutes; then add one pint of water, one clove, a lump of sugar, and a little salt. Cover the saucepan as tightly as you can, and let it remain at the side of the fire for twenty minutes, press the meat with a spoon through a sieve to extract the essence, and it will be fit for use.

Mutton Broth.
Time, three hours

1792. Three pounds of scrag of mutton; three quarts of water; two turnips; one tablespoonful of pearl barley, or rice.
Boil in three quarts of water, three pounds of the scrag end of a neck of mutton, with two turnips sliced, and a tablespoonful of pearl barley, or rice. Let it boil gently for three hours, keeping it well skimmed. Serve it very hot with toasted bread.

Veal Broth.
Time, three hours.

1793. Four or five pounds of knuckle of veal; two blades of mace; a head of celery; a little parsley; pepper, salt, and two ounces of rice, with three quarts of water.
Stew four or five pounds of knuckle of veal in three quarts of water, with two blades of mace, an onion, a head of celery cut into slices, and a little parsley, pepper, and salt; let it simmer gently until reduced to two quarts, then take out the meat, and serve it

Soup for Invalids.—Groats, Gruels, Jellies, &c.

up with parsley and butter. Add to the broth two ounces of rice, separately boiled, or two ounces of vermicelli, put in only long enough to stew tender.

Nourishing Soup for Invalids.
Time, two hours.

1794. Two pounds of lean veal or beef; a quarter of a pound of pearl barley; a little fresh celery, or celery seed; a little salt.

Boil two pounds of lean veal, or beef, with a quarter of a pound of pearl barley in a quart of water very slowly, until it becomes the consistency of good cream; flavour it with a little fresh celery, or celery seed, and salt. Strain it when done through a fine hair sieve, and serve. This soup will only keep until the next day, therefore not more than the quantity required must be made.

Gloucester Jelly.
Time, two hours.

1795. One ounce of powdered rice; one ounce of sago; one ounce of pearl barley; one ounce of isinglass; one ounce of eringo root; one ounce of hartshorn shavings.

Simmer these ingredients in three pints of water till reduced to one pint; strain it. Pieces may be cut from this jelly and taken in tea or broth, or in a cup of new milk, as preferred, every morning.

Gruel of Patent Groats.
Time, ten minutes.

1796. Two dessertspoonfuls of patent groats; one pint of water; a wineglass of brandy or any other spirit, or of white wine.

Mix two dessertspoonfuls of patent groats in a basin with only sufficient water to work it into a cream; then pour over it a pint of boiling water, stirring it all the time; stir it over the fire until sufficiently thick. When done, sweeten it to taste, and add either a glass of white wine, brandy, or any other spirit, with a little grated ginger or nutmeg.

Gruel.
Time, a quarter of an hour.

1797. Two tablespoonfuls of oatmeal; half a blade of mace; a piece of lemon peel; three-quarters of a pint of water or milk; a little sugar; and white wine.

Mix two spoonfuls of oatmeal very smooth in a little water, and put it gradually to three-quarters of a pint; add a little lemon peel, and half a blade of mace; set it over the fire for a quarter of an hour, stirring it constantly. Then strain it, and add sugar to taste, and a little white wine.

Barberry Jelly.

1798. One pint of barberry juice; one pound of powdered white sugar.

Boil the barberry juice and sugar to a jelly; strain it, and pour it into a jam pot for use. It is excellent for colds and sore throats.

Silver Jelly.
Time, to boil the feet five hours and a half; to boil the jelly twenty minutes.

1799. One set of calf's feet; one ounce of isinglass; one pint of the best gin; one pound of loaf sugar; juice of six lemons; peel of two; whites of six eggs.

Boil the calf's feet in four quarts of water with the isinglass until the feet are done to rags, and the water wasted to half the quantity; strain it, and when cold remove the feet, and the jelly from the sediment very carefully. Put the jelly into a stewpan with the sugar, the juice of the lemons, and the peel of two; add the gin. When the flavour is thoroughly drawn from the lemon, put in the whites of the eggs well beaten, and their shells broken up, place the stewpan over the fire, and let it boil for twenty minutes; but do not stir it after the egg has been added. Dip a jelly bag into hot water and squeeze it dry; run the jelly through it several times until quite clear, and then pour it into the mould.

If calf's feet cannot be obtained, two ounces of gelatine and one ounce of isinglass will do as well.

Old-fashioned Caudle.
Time, twenty minutes.

1800. Six spoonfuls of oatmeal; one quart of water; one blade of old ginger, and a little grated; one quart of porter; sugar to taste.

Boil six spoonfuls of oatmeal groats in one quart of water with one blade of whole ginger and a little grated stirred in after, but not strained; then put in the fresh porter just before serving. Sweeten it to taste.

Or, if it is for a poor woman, it is better to send half a pound of brown sugar with it, as it does not keep so well if sweetened.

Old-fashioned Brown Caudle.
Time, a quarter of an hour.

1801. Three tablespoonfuls of oatmeal; half a blade of mace; a piece of lemon peel; one pint of water; one pint of ale; and sugar to taste.

Put two spoonfuls of oatmeal, half a blade of mace, and a piece of lemon peel into a pint and a half of water. Boil it about a quarter of an hour, taking care it does not boil over. Then strain it, and add a pint and a half of ale that is not bitter. Sweeten it to your taste, and warm it up for use.

Barley Cream—Light and Nourishing.

1802. Two pounds of lean veal; half a pound of pearl barley; two quarts of water; a little salt.

Take two pounds of veal free from fat or skin, cut it into pieces about the size of a nutmeg, and put it into a stewpan with half a pound of pearl barley and two quarts of water; let it simmer till reduced to half the quantity, then rub it through a sieve, add salt to your taste. It should be the consistency of thick cream.

Barley Gruel.

Time, twenty minutes.

1803. Two ounces of pearl barley; half a pint of water; then three pints and a half of boiling water.

Boil two ounces of pearl barley in half a pint of water to extract the colouring matter, throw this away, and put the barley into three pints and a half of boiling water, and let it boil till it is one half the quantity, then strain it for use.

Barley Water.

Time, twenty minutes.

1804. Two ounces of pearl barley; one lemon; sugar to taste.

First boil the barley in some water to extract the colouring, throw that water away, and put the barley into a jug; pour some boiling water over it, and let it stand for a short time. Peel a lemon very thin, pour some boiling water over it, with a little sugar, and mix it with the barley water, adding the lemon juice.

Artificial Ass's Milk.

Time, two hours or more, according to the strength of the fire.

1805. Two ounces of pearl barley; two quarts of water; half an ounce of hartshorn shavings; one ounce of candied eringo root.

Boil two ounces of pearl barley in two pints of water for a few minutes; strain it from this first water, and put the same quantity to it again; add half an ounce of hartshorn shavings, and one ounce of candied eringo root. Boil it gently *until half the liquor is consumed or boiled away.* Then strain it for use. Equal parts of this decoction and cow's milk to be mixed together, and taken in the same quantities, and at the same time that the real ass's milk would be drunk.

Tonic Drink.

Time, twenty-four hours.

1806. A quarter of an ounce of camomile flowers; a quarter of an ounce of sliced gentian root; a quarter of an ounce of bruised columba; a quarter of an ounce of dried orange peel; fifty cloves bruised; a pint and a quarter of cold spring water.

Put these ingredients into a jug, and pour on them rather more then a pint of cold spring water; let it stand twenty-four hours, then pour off the clear liquor. Take three tablespoonfuls for a dose, fasting every morning.

Blancmange for Invalids.

Time, fifteen minutes.

1807. One quart of milk; one ounce of isinglass; peel of one lemon; yolks of six eggs; a quarter of a pound of sugar.

Dissolve in a quart of warm milk an ounce of fine isinglass, and strain it through double muslin, put it into a delicately clean stewpan with the sugar pounded, and the peel of a lemon cut very thin. Let it warm gently, until the flavour is well extracted from the lemon, and then stir it *very* gradually to the yolks of the eggs; return it to the stewpan, and set it at the side of the fire until it thickens, stirring it all the time. Then pour it into a jug, and stir it until nearly cold; pour it into a mould dipped into cold water, or oiled, and set it in a very cold place for several hours, until perfectly cold and firm.

Chicken Cream.

Time, three-quarters of an hour.

1808. One chicken; a pint and a half of water; three or four spoonfuls of cream.

Mince and then pound in a mortar the breast of a cold roast chicken, stew the remainder with all the bones broken, in a pint and a half of water till reduced to half a pint; rub the breast through a sieve into the half pint of gravy strained off. Mix them together till of the consistency of cream; when taken, add three or four spoonfuls of cream, and warm it in a mug, in a saucepan of boiling water. Two or three spoonfuls may be taken by an invalid who cannot take animal food.

Arrowroot Jelly.

Time, eight minutes.

1809. Half a pint of water; a glass of sherry; or a tablespoonful of brandy; a little sugar; some grated nutmeg; one dessertspoonful of arrowroot.

Boil the water and sherry, or brandy, with a little sugar and nutmeg; rub the arrow-

Beaten Egg.—Brandy Mixture.—Sago Gruel, &c. 333

root down with two tablespoonfuls of cold water, then add the boiling wine and water gradually, stirring it all the time. Boil the whole three minutes, constantly stirring it.

Beaten Egg.

1810. One egg; one wineglass of sherry or one cup of tea; sugar to taste.
An egg beaten up in tea or wine will be found very strengthening for invalids. It is better to take the yolk only, as it is lighter.

Egg Wine.

1811. One egg; one glass of white wine; a little cold water, with sugar to taste.
Well beat a nice new-laid egg with a little water, and then pour over it a glass of white wine made very hot with half a tumbler of water, and a little pounded sugar. Stir it all the time until well mixed together. Then set it over the fire until it thickens and is very hot without coming to a boil. It must be stirred one way all the time, and when done, poured into a glass, and served with a slice of toasted bread cut into long thin slices, and placed on a plate crossed over each other. A little grated nutmeg may be added if the flavour is liked.

Brandy Mixture to be given in cases of Exhaustion.

1812. Two eggs; one gill of brandy; one gill of cinnamon water; half an ounce of sugar; two drops of oil of cinnamon.
Mix the brandy, cinnamon water, *the yolks* of two eggs, powdered white sugar, and two drops of oil of cinnamon well together. The doses should be given every quarter of an hour; three tablespoonfuls at a time, according to the state of the patient.

Sago Gruel.

Time, two hours and a quarter.

1813. One ounce of sago; one pint of water; one glass of sherry; sugar and ginger; lemon juice or nutmeg to taste.
Stand the sago in a pint of water on the hob to soften for two hours. Boil it for a quarter of an hour, keeping it well stirred. Sweeten and flavour as preferred, then add the wine.

Suet and Milk.

Time, ten to fifteen minutes.

1814. One tablespoonful of shredded beef-suet; half a pint of fresh milk.
Mix these ingredients and warm them sufficiently to melt the suet completely. Skim it. Warm the cup into which you pour it, and give it to the invalid to drink before it gets cool.

Milk and Rum.

1815. One tablespoonful of rum; half a pint of new milk.
Mix the rum *well* with the milk. Pour it from one cup into another twice before drinking it. It should be taken before breakfast.

Orange Jelly for Invalids.

Time, one hour.

1816. One dozen oranges; two lemons; quarter of a pound of sugar; one ounce and a half of isinglass; half a pint of water; peel of one orange.
Mix the juice of the oranges and lemons with the sugar. Boil the isinglass and peel of one orange in half a pint of water very gently. Strain the syrup, and add the dissolved isinglass to it while hot through a sieve; mix well together, and pour into the mould. Keep in a cool place.

Hartshorn Jelly.

1817. Ingredients: half a pound of hartshorn shavings; five pints of water; rinds of four China oranges, and four lemons; half a pound of sugar; the whites of six eggs.
Simmer the half pound of shavings in five pints of water until it is reduced to half the quantity; strain it, and boil it up with the rinds of the lemons pared very thin, and the oranges; when cold, add the juice, the loaf sugar, and the whites of the eggs beaten to a froth; let the jelly have four boils, without stirring, and strain it through a jelly-bag. Place it in the moulds in a cold place.

A Cooling Drink for Feverish Thirst.

1818. One tablespoonful of cream of tartar; juice of two large lemons; a pint of boiling water; sugar to taste; one wineglass of gin. Mix all together.

LUNCHEONS.

Luncheon differs from dinner in large households only in the general absence of soup and fish, and in the mode of serving; both meat, game, vegetables, puddings, fruit, &c., being placed on the table at the same time.

Luncheons in small families (not of large means) generally consist of the cold meat or poultry left from dinner; of cake, bread, cheese, &c.; but this slight repast ought to be properly served at all times, so that the servant may never feel awkward at the presence of unexpected guests. The butter should be sent up in summer in a glass dish with water; in winter garnished with parsley. The bread should be placed on the table on a wooden platter; the cheese on a nice cheese cloth. Everything must be as neat and nice as possible. We give two specimens of luncheons, such as are ordinarily sent up for guests. Home luncheons must be directed by the mistress of the family, according to her taste and means.

Luncheon for Ten Persons.

Roast Fowl.
(Hot.)

Potatoes.   Peas.

Chocolate Cakes.   Almond Gaufres.

Lemon Cake.

Cherries.   Strawberries.

Pickles.

Veal Cutlets.   Lobster.   Cruet Stand.   Salad.   Tongue.

Silver Sugar Dredge.

Apple Tart.   Neapolitan Cake.   Custard.

Cheese Fingers.   Biscuits.

Cold Lamb.

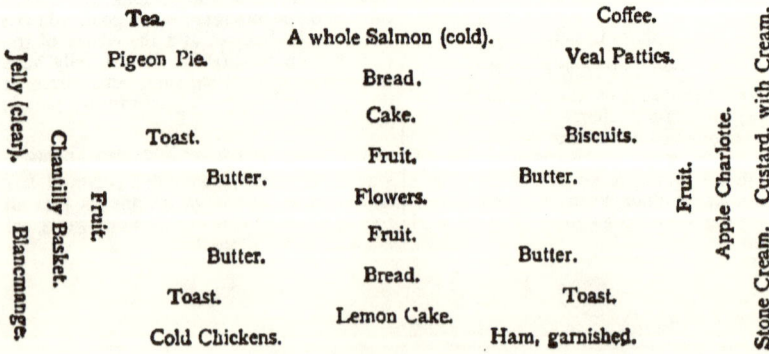

Croquet Tea for Twenty Persons.

Tea.   Coffee.

A whole Salmon (cold).

Pigeon Pie.   Veal Patties.

Bread.

Jelly (clear).   Chantilly Basket.   Fruit.   Cake.   Fruit.   Apple Charlotte.   Custard, with Cream.

Toast.   Biscuits.

Fruit.

Butter.   Butter.

Flowers.

Blancmange.   Fruit.   Stone Cream.

Butter.   Butter.

Bread.

Toast.   Toast.

Cold Chickens.   Lemon Cake.   Ham, garnished.

Cold Forequarter of Lamb.

Family Dinner for Six Persons.

Filleted Plaice.

Boiled Knuckle of Veal and Rice.

Potatoes.   Jerusalem Artichokes.

Rumpsteak and Oysters.

SECOND COURSE.

Tapioca Pudding.

Open Tart.

Dinner for Eight Persons.

Rice Soup.

Rolled Loin of Mutton.

Potatoes.   French Beans.

Curried Veal.

SECOND COURSE.

Plain Plum Pudding.   General Satisfaction.

Family Dinner for Six Persons.

SUMMER.

Spinach or Greenpea Soup.

Leg of Lamb.

Potatoes.   Green Peas.

Rumpsteak Stewed.

SECOND COURSE.

Currant and Raspberry Tart.

Jug of Cream.   Gooseberry Fool.

Spring Dinner for Party of Twelve Persons.

Filleted Soles.   Mock Turtle.   Stewed Eels.

Removes.

Entrées.   *Entrées.*

Saddle of Mutton.

Fricandel of Veal.   Broiled Ox-tail.

Roast Fowls and Tongue.

Asparagus.   Potatoes.

SECOND COURSE.

Nesselrode Pudding.

Orange Jelly.   Blancmange.

Ratafia Pudding.

Gooseberry Tart.

Spring Dinner for Party of Eight Persons.

Clear Gravy Soup.

Red Mullet.

Removes.

Entrées.   *Entrées.*

Leg of Lamb and Mint Sauce.

Fillets de Bœuf.   Tendons de Veau.

Boiled Chicken
and Tongue.

Potatoes.   Peas.

Asparagus.   Spring Cabbage.

SECOND COURSE.

Apple Tart.

Jersey Wonders.   Lemon Cheesecakes.

Boiled Custard.

Iced Venice Pudding.

Summer Dinner for a Party of Twelve Persons.
Julienne Soup.
Salmon and Lobster Sauce and Cucumber.

Removes.
Forequarter of Lamb.

Entrées.   *Entrées.*
Tongue.   Larded Sweetbreads.
Boiled Capon.
Kidneys Sautés au Vin.   Mutton Cutlets à la Financière.*
Asparagus.   Green Peas.   Cauliflowers.   Potatoes

SECOND COURSE.
Cherry Tart.

Chocolate Cakes.   Noyau Jelly.
Artichokes.
Vanilla Cream.   Iced Custards.

Summer Dinner For a Party of Sixteen Persons.
Asparagus Soup.
Soup Jardinière.
Salmon (Lobster Sauce and Cucumbers).
Tench Stewed.

Entrées.   *Removes.*   *Entrées.*
Tongue.   Spatchcock.
Turkey Poults.
Fricasseed Pigeons.   Turban of Rabbit
Lamb Cutlets and Peas.   Veal Patties.
Sirloin of Beef.

SECOND COURSE.
Plovers.

Iced Venice Pudding.   Sir Watkin's Pudding.
Crême à la Comtesse.   Maraschino Jelly.
Darioles.   Choux à la Comtesse.
Louis Philippe's Pudding.

* That is, dressed with Financière Sauce.

Autumn Dinner for a Party of Ten or Twelve Persons.

Mulligatawny Soup.

Salmon.

Spitchcock Eels.

Haunch of Venison.

Boiled Chickens and Celery Sauce.

Tongue, garnished with Brussels Sprouts.

Curried Eggs.

Kromeskies.

Fricandeau of Veal.

SECOND COURSE.

Milan Soufflé.

Pineapple Fritters.

Lemon Jelly.

Stone Cream.

College Puddings.

Partridges.

For Small Dinner Party.

Soupe Macaroni.

Fish: Boiled Cod and Oyster Sauce.

Removes.

Peahen larded.

Entrées.

Salmi of Wild Goose.

Entrées.

Escalloped Oysters.

Saddle of Mutton à la Portugaise.

Potatoes.

Brocoli.

SECOND COURSE.

Grouse.

Cheese Canapées.

Isinglass Jelly.

Custard with Cream.

Volunteer's Puddings.

Apricot Tart.

Autumn Dinner for Sixteen Persons.

Clear Gravy Soup.
Crecy Soupe à la Reine.
Salmon Trout.
Prawn Sauce.
Fillets of Soles.

Entrées.	*Removes.*	*Entrées.*
Cannelon de Bœuf.	Calf's Head.	Veal Cutlets.
Pigeon Pie.	Saddle of Mutton.	Oyster Patties.
Tongue.		Chicken à l'Estragon.

SECOND COURSE.

Sweet Vols-au-Vent.	Hare.	Maids of Honour.
Apple Hedgehog.	Chancellor's Pudding.	Open Jelly and Whipped Cream.
Soufflés in Cases.		Tartlets à la Crême.

Winter Dinner for Twelve or Sixteen Persons.

Brown Oyster Soup.
Very Rich White Soup.

Turbot à la Crême.		Fried Whitings.
Entrées.		*Entrées.*
Fricandeau of Ox Palates.		Chicken Cutlets.
	Boiled Turkey Stuffed with Chestnuts.	
	Chine of Pork.	
Croquettes of Beef.		Jugged Pigeons.
	Round of Beef à la Française.	
Roast Larks.		Vol-au-Vent.

SECOND COURSE.

Omelet Soufflé.	Palm Tree Pudding.	Jaunemange
Arrowroot Fritters.	Pheasants.	Lèche Créma.
Calf's Feet Jelly.		Ramakins.

Christmas Dinner for a Large Party.

Mock Turtle Soup.
Potage de Riz à la Piedmontaise.
Turbot and Lobster Sauce.
Carpe Farcie.

Fowls à la Milanaise.   Small Ham.
Roast Turkey and Sausages.
Pupton Pigeons.   Ragoût of Duck.
Baron of Beef.
Pork Cutlets with Tomato Sauce.   House Lamb Cutlets à la Royale.

SECOND COURSE.

Mince Pies.   Punch Jelly.
Christmas Pudding.
Meringue.   York Soufflé.
Gâteau de Pomme.   Charlotte Russe.
Guinea Fowl.

Desserts.

The dessert is placed on the table from the first in the dinners à la Russe; but sometimes the top and bottom dishes are added after the dinner is over. Even at family dinners this mode is the best. Between and amongst the dishes it is usual to put small glass dishes with preserved ginger, damson cheese, candied apricots, or any other of the sweet dishes given in our dessert receipts. Roasted chesnuts should be sent up *hot* on a folded table-napkin. We prefer almonds *blanched* for the raisins, but some people like them better in their skins. A few wine biscuits should be put round the centre cake, and olives are sometimes required for the gentlemen.

Suppers.

A lady has full space for exercising her taste at the supper table. A good eye for colour will give a great charm to the arrangement. With flowers, fruit, frothed whipped creams, coloured jellies, and all the elegance of sweet dishes, she can scarcely fail to offer a perfect picture of gastronomic beauty to the eye, if she will take a little care in the arrangement of the table herself. A plan drawn out on paper and given to an intelligent servant, will secure her from mistakes generally; if her footman is inexperienced, she should first glance at the table herself before her guests are invited to it. For two or three evening guests, a few sandwiches, a cake, fruit, and wine will suffice, as people now generally dine late. We offer the plan of two suppers, not so elaborate as those provided by Gunter would be, but sufficient for ordinary entertainments.

Supper.
SUMMER.

	Roast Turkey.	
Noyau Jelly.		Charlotte Russe.
	Ham with Aspic Jelly.	
Jelly and Whipped Cream.		Milan Soufflé.
Blancmange.		Flummery.
	Fruit. Fruit.	
	Vase of Flowers.	
	Gâteau de Chocolat.	
	Raised Game Pie.	
	Lobster Salad.	
	Trifle.	
	Veal Cake.	
	Fruit. Fruit.	
	Tipsy Cake.	
	Centre Vase.	
	Ferns, Grapes, &c.	
	Tipsy Cake.	
	Fruit. Fruit.	
	Crystallized Oranges.	
	Pigeon Pie.	
	Apple Trifle.	
	Mayonnaise de Saumon.	
	Raised Ham and Chicken Pie.	
	Gâteau Nourmahal.	
Lemon Sponge.		Custards.
	Vase of Flowers.	
Ribbon Jelly.		Rice Blancmange.
	Tongue Ornamented.	
Charlotte Russe.		Clear Jelly with Fruit in it.
	Fruit. Fruit.	

Left side (vertical): Cold Chickens cut up. Preserved Ginger. Meringues. Chantilly Basket. Cold Chickens cut up. Brandied Cherries. Cold Chickens cut up.

Right side (vertical): Cold Chickens cut up. Orange Chips. Meringues. Oranges with Jelly. Candied Apricots. Cold Chickens cut up.

Winter Supper.

Soup (White Soup).
Turkey.
Ham.
Raised Périgord Pie.
Christmas Cake.
Trifle.
Larded Pheasants.
Tipsy Cake.   Gâteau Nourmahal.
Grouse.
Mayonnaise de Poulet.
Oranges.   Oranges.
Custards.
Centre Ornament.
Custards.
Oranges.   Oranges.
Italian Salad.
Capon.
Partridges.
Trifle.
Twelfth Cake.
Vols-au-Vent of Chicken.
Ham.
Christmas Pie.
Partridges.
Pheasants.
Jardinière Soupe.

Left side (vertical labels, top to bottom): Pigeon Pie. Noyau Jelly. Tartlets à la Crême. Preserved Ginger. — Blancmange. Dominoes. Almond Gaufres. — Roasted Oysters. Open Jelly with Whipped Cream. Salmi of Game. — Custards. Neapolitan Pastry. Alexander Jelly. — Custards. Oranges with Jelly. Ribbon Blancmange. — Scalloped Oysters. Chickens. Maids of Honour. Orange Chips. — Mutton Cutlets à la Soubise. Orange Jelly.

Right side (vertical labels, top to bottom): Orange Chips. Ice Plum Pudding. — Flummery. Ribbon Jelly. — Scalloped Oysters. — Brunswick Jelly. Chocolate Cakes. Chickens. — Salmi of Game. Open Jelly with Whipped Cream. Roasted Oysters. — Almond Gaufres. Dominoes. Blancmange. — Candied Fruit. Vanilla Cream. Punch Jelly. Mutton Cutlets à la Soubise. — Lemon Jelly. Pigeon Pie.

USEFUL RECEIPTS FOR HOUSEKEEPERS AND SERVANTS.

To Clean Chimney Pieces.

1819. Equal quantities of soft soap and pearlash. Put the soap and pearl-ash on the chimney piece with a soft flannel, let it lay on the marble for a few minutes. Wash it off with warm water not too hot; wash it over a second time with cold spring water.

For Bright Polished Grates.

1820. Oil the bright part of the grate with good salad oil, dust over it some unslacked lime from a muslin bag. Let it remain one month, then rub it off with a fine rag. Polish it with a leather and a very little putty powder. If the grate is not in use put on the oil again.

To Take Stains out of Marble.

1821. Mixed unslacked lime in finest powder with the stronger soap-lye pretty thick, and instantly with a painter's brush lay it on the whole of the marble. In two months' time wash it off perfectly clean. Then have ready a fine thick lather of soft soap, boiled in soft water, dip a brush in it, and scour the marble with powder not as common cleaning. This will, by very good rubbing, give a beautiful polish. Clear off the soap, and finish with a smooth hard brush till the end be effected.

To Take Rust out of Steel.

1822. Cover the steel with sweet oil well rubbed in, and in forty-eight hours use unslacked lime finely powdered, and rub until all the rust disappears.

To Cement Broken China.

1823. Beat lime to a *very* fine almost invisible dust, sift it through book muslin. Then tie it up in a piece of thin muslin as powdered starch is sometimes used. Brush some white of egg over the edges of the china, dust the lime rapidly over them, put the edges together, and tie a string round the cup, &c., till it is firm.
Isinglass dissolved in spirits of wine, in the proportion of one ounce to two wine-glassfuls of the spirit, is also a good cement.

For Removing Paint from Wood.

1824. One pound of washing soda; two pounds of unslacked lime.
Mix one pound of washing soda with two pounds of unslacked lime, and if the paint is very strong on the wood add *half a pound of potash*. Mix these ingredients together, and dilute with water until the mixture becomes rather thicker than whitewash, and then rub it on the paint with a piece of *wood* folded up in rag. The person who uses this preparation must be careful not to touch it with the hands.

To Clean Paper-hangings.

1825. First blow the dust off with the bellows. Divide a white loaf of eight days old into eight parts. Take the crust into your hand, and, beginning at the top of the paper, wipe it downwards in the lightest manner with the crumb. Do not cross or go upwards. The dirt of the paper and the crumbs will fall together. Observe—you must not wipe above half a yard at a stroke, and after doing all the upper part go round again, beginning a little above were you left off. If you do not clean it very lightly you will make the dirt adhere to the paper.

To Clean Glazed Chintz Furniture when taken down for the Summer.

1826. Shake off the loose dust, then lightly brush with a small long-haired furniture brush; after which, wipe it closely with clean flannels, and rub it with dry bread. If properly done, the curtains will look nearly as well as at first, and if the colour be not light they will not require washing for years. Fold in large parcels and put carefully by.
While the furniture remains up, it should be preserved from the sun and air as much as possible, which injure delicate colours; and the dust may be blown off by bellows. By the above method, curtains may be kept sufficiently clean, to make up again with new linings.

To Remove Paint Stains from Glass Windows.

1827. It frequently happens that painters splash the plate or other glass windows when they are painting the sills. When this is the case, melt some soda in very hot water and wash them with it, using a soft flannel. It will entirely remove the paint.

Table Polish.

1828. Half a pint of spirits of wine; an ounce and a half of gum shellac; half an ounce of gum benzoin; half an ounce of gum sandrac.

Put the whole in a bottle for a day or two, and shake it a few times. When the gums are dissolved it is fit for use.

When the polish is laid on thick enough, take a clean wad and cloth; put a little clean spirits of wine on the wad, the same as you did with the polish, rub it the same way, but very lightly, and until quite dry. You must then put a little oil on the cloth, and rub as in laying on the polish.

Another Furniture Polish.

1829. Three gills of cold drawn oil : one gill of turpentine; one gill of varnish of turpentine; one of vinegar.

These quantities will fill a quart bottle. Pour a few drops in the middle of the table, add a teaspoonful of cold spring water, and rub with a soft cloth.

To Clean Covers and Tins.

1830. Half a pound of soap; a ball of pounded whitening; sufficient warm water to make it of the consistency of very thick cream.

Shred the soap into a jug, add a large ball of pounded whitening, and pour in sufficient warm water to make it of the consistency of a thick cream ; rub it well over the tins, and when dry, polish them with a clean leather and powdered whitening.

To Clean Plate.

1831. One ounce of prepared hartshorn-powder ; one quart of water.

Boil an ounce of prepared hartshorn-powder in a quart of water ; while on the fire, put into it as much plate as the vessel will hold ; let it boil a few minutes, take it out, drain it over the saucepan, and dry it near the fire. Then put into the water some pieces of linen, and let them remain to soak up all the water. When dry, put them aside to clean the plate, &c. When the plate is dry, rub it well with wash leather.

To Make Blacking.

1832. Four ounces of ivory black ; three ounces of treacle ; a tablespoonful of sweet oil; a pint and a half of small beer ; one ounce of sulphuric acid.

Mix with a spoonful of sweet oil the four ounces of ivory black, and the three ounces of treacle ; pour on it by degrees a pint and a half of small beer. Stir it well together, and then pour in an ounce of sulphuric acid, keeping it till the effervescence ceases ; bottle it, and it may be used immediately.

A Receipt for Blacking.

1833. Two ounces of sugarcandy ; one ounce of sulphuric acid ; half an ounce of gum arabic ; a quarter of an ounce of blue indigo ; half an ounce of turpentine ; four ounces of ivory black ; two tablespoonfuls of oil ; one quart of good vinegar. Mix all together.

To Bleach Linen.

1834. A quarter of a pound of chloride of lime ; one gallon of water.

Pour a gallon of boiling water over four ounces of chloride of lime ; let it stand two days, stirring it occasionally, then pour it clear off into bottles. To bleach linen take about half a pint, and mix it with a quart or three pints of cold spring water. Mix it well together, and after the linen is washed and rinsed from the soap, steep it in the lime water for a few hours.

To Take Stains out of Silk or Cloth.

1835. Pound some French chalk fine, and mix it with warm water to the thickness of mustard. Put it on the spots, rub it lightly with your finger, or the palm of your hand. Put a sheet of blotting, and of brown paper, over the spots, and press it with a warm iron.

To Take Grease out of Silk.

1836. Take a lump of magnesia, and rub it wet on the spot ; let it dry, then brush it off, and the spot will disappear.

To Take off Wax-Candle Grease.

1837. Have an iron made very hot; put a piece of clean blotting-paper over the spot, and hold the iron *close* to it, but do not let it touch the paper. The grease will be drawn into the paper.

To Wash Coloured Prints and Washing Silks.

1838. Put a little bran into lukewarm water, wash quickly through ; rinse in cold water also, quickly. Hang to dry in a room without fire or sunshine. Iron on wrong side with a coolish iron. No soap to be used.

To Clean an Old Silk Dress.

1839. Unpick the dress, and brush it with a velvet brush. Then grate two large potatoes into a quart of water ; let it stand to settle ; strain it off quite clear, and sponge the dress with it. Iron it on the wrong side, as the ironed side will be shiny.

Wash for the Hair.

1840. Half an ounce of glycerine; half an

Useful Receipts.

ounce of spirits of rosemary; five ounces of water.

To be well mixed together and shaken, and used night and morning.

Castor Oil Pomade for the Hair.

1841. Four ounces of castor oil; two ounces of prepared lard; two drachms of white wax; essence of jessamine, or otto of roses.

Melt the fat together, and when well mixed, and becoming cool, add whatever scent you prefer, and stir it constantly until cold; then put it into pots or bottles for use.

Another Pomade for the Hair.

1842. Half a pound of hog's lard; a wineglass of rose-water; a teaspoonful of ammonia; scented with jessamine or any other scent you prefer.

Mix all well together, and put it into pots or glass bottles.

French Pomatum.

1843. Four ounces of lard; four ounces of honey; two ounces of the best olive oil; a quarter of an ounce of essence of bitter almonds.

Melt all the above ingredients together, and let it stand till cool, when the honey will sink to the bottom; then melt it over again *without* the honey, and scent it with the essence of almonds, added after the second melting, and while liquid.

Cold Cream.

1844. Half a pint of rosewater; four ounces of oil of almonds; three drachms of white wax; three drachms of spermaceti.

Melt the white wax and spermaceti together with the oil of almonds. Then beat them all up, adding the rosewater slowly until it is cold. Put it in a pot, and pour some rosewater on the top.

A Winter Soap for Chapped or Rough Hands.

1845. Three pounds of common yellow soap; one ounce of camphor dissolved in one ounce of rose and one ounce of lavender water.

Beat three pounds of common yellow soap, and one ounce of camphor dissolved in one ounce of rose and one ounce of lavender water in a mortar until it becomes a paste. Make it into balls to dry, and set it in a cool place for the winter. The best time to make it is in the spring.

Tooth Powder.

1846. A quarter of an ounce of bole armoniac; a quarter of an ounce of bark; a quarter of an ounce of powdered camphor; a quarter of an ounce of powdered myrrh.

Mix the ingredients very thoroughly together. Tooth powders should be keep closely covered in wooden boxes.

The prescription is for *equal* quantities of the above ingredients, but one ounce of the whole mixed is enough at a time, unless a chemist is not of easy access.

To Cure Warts.

1847. Warts are very troublesome and disfiguring. The following is a perfect cure, even of the largest, without leaving any scar. It is a Frenchman's prescription, and has been tested in the author's family.

Take a small piece of raw beef, steep it all night in vinegar, cut as much from it as will cover the wart, tie it on it; or if the excressence is on the forehead, fasten it on with strips of sticking plaster. It may be removed in the day, and put on every night. In one fortnight the wart will die and peel off. The same prescription will cure corns.

Cartwright's Prescription for Toothache.

1848. A little ether and laudanum, mixed, and applied on wool to the tooth.

Embrocation for Chilblains not Broken.

Time, ten minutes.

1849. Half a pint of spirits of wine; two drachms of camphor; two drachms of laudanum.

Mix the ingredients, and rub the chilblains well with the embrocation for ten minutes at bed-time, and in the morning.

Marking Ink.

1850. One drachm and a half of lunar caustic; one scruple of sap green; six drachms of water; two drachms of mucilage. And—

Preparation Liquor.

1851. Half an ounce of salt of tartar or subcarbonate of potash; half an ounce of mucilage; half an ounce of water.

The preparation is to be put on with a small brush, and when it is nearly dry, smooth the surface by means of a spoon or a glass. After which use the marking ink.

Essence of Verbena—For the Toilet.

Time, one week.

1852. Half an ounce of oil of verbena; four ounces of spirits of wine; forty drops of essence of vanilla.

Put the oil of verbena, spirits of wine, and

essence of vanilla into a jar, and leave it, well covered over, for a week. Then, filter, and it will be ready for use.

Extract of Mareschal.
Time, three days.

1853. One ounce and a half of millefleur; one ounce of essence of jessamine; twenty drops of essence of citron; half an ounce of essence of ambergris; half a drachm of essence of orange-flower; half an ounce of essence of musk; one ounce of essence of violets; twenty drops of oil of rosemary; fifty drops of sweet spirits of nitre; forty-eight drops of oil of neroli; six ounces of spirits of wine.

Mix the whole well together, and keep in a closely-stoppered bottle or jar for three days, when it will be fit or use.

Bouquet de Victoria.
Time, one week.

1854. One ounce of essence of bergamot; half a drachm of oil of cloves; three drachms of oil of lavender; six grains of grain musk; half a drachm of aromatic vinegar; one pint and a half of spirits of wine.
Mix well, and distil.

Lavender Water.

1855. Half a pint of spirits of wine; a quarter of an ounce of oil of lavender; one drachm and a half of essence of bergamot; one drachm of essence of ambergris. All to be well mixed together.

Odor Delectabilis—For the Toilet.
Time, one week.

1856. Two ounces of rosewater; two ounces of orange-flower; half a drachm of oil of lavender; half a drachm of oil of cloves; one grain of grain musk; one drachm of bergamot; half a drachm of essence of musk; half a pint of rectified spirits of wine.
Mix all together, excepting the essence of musk, which must be added after the mixture has stood for one week closely stopped.

Eau-de-Cologne.

1857. One drachm of orange-flower; one drachm of essence of citron; four ounces of essence of mellisse; one ounce of cidret; one ounce of rosemary; three ounces of bergamot; one ounce of lavender; one ounce of musk; four pints of rectified spirits of wine.
When the chemist has mixed the essences, put them into two quart bottles of rectified spirits of wine, but care must be taken that potash is not used by the chemist to melt the essences, as it burns. Entire cost, 1*l*. 6*s*.

Pot Pourri.

1858. Half a pound of bay-salt; a quarter of a pound of saltpetre bruised with a little common salt. Then add to it threepennyworth of cloves pounded; the same of storax; one small nutmeg grated; two or three bay-leaves broken; lavender flowers freshly gathered; rose leaves *gathered* dry and added without drying to the above mixture,

DUTIES OF HOUSEHOLD SERVANTS.

Duties of the Maid of all Work.

The general servant must be an early riser.
Her first duty, of course, is to open the shutters, and in summer the windows of all the lower part of the house.
Then she must clean the kitchen range and hearth, sifting the cinders, clearing away the ashes, and polishing with a leather the bright parts of the stove, or range.
She must light the fire, fill the kettle, and as soon as the fire burns, set it on to boil.
She must then clean the room in which the family breakfast. She must roll up the rug, spread out a coarse piece of canvas before the fireplace, and (if it is winter) she must remove the fender, clean the grate, and light the fire. Then she must just lightly rub over the fire-irons with a leather, replace them, and the fender, and sweep the room over, first pinning up the curtains out of the dust.
She should let the dust settle for a few minutes, running meantime into the kitchen to get the breakfast things ready to bring in. In five minutes or so she must return, and thoroughly dust all the furniture, the ledges about the room, the mantelpiece, and all ornaments. Not a speck of dust should be left on any object in the room. Then she lays the breakfast cloth ready for breakfast, and shuts the dining, or breakfast-room door.
Her next duty is to sweep the hall, or passage, shake the door-mats, clean the door-step, and polish the brass knocker, if there is one. Then she cleans the boots, washes her hands and face, puts on a clean apron, and prepares the toast, eggs, bacon, kidneys, or whatever is required for breakfast.

Previously, however, she will carry in the urn that her mistress may make the tea.

She then has her own breakfast, goes up to the bedrooms, opens the windows, strips the bedclothes off, and leaves the mattresses or beds open.

By this time probably the bell will ring for her to clear away the breakfast things. She should do this quickly and carefully; bring a dustpan, and sweep up the crumbs, put back the chairs, make up the fire, and sweep up the hearth.

The china must be washed and put away, and the kitchen tidied a little. Her mistress will then give her orders about dinner.

As soon as these are settled, she will put on a large clean apron in which to make the beds, that she may not soil the bedclothes with her working dress. The mistress of the house generally assists a maid of all work in making the beds, but this is by no means *a right* of the servant's, and very frequently she has to do them alone.

In making beds, she should carefully turn the mattresses every day, shake the feather beds *well*, and rub out any lumps that may have gathered in them. The sheets should always be placed with the *marked* end towards the pillow.

When the beds are made and slops emptied, the rooms should be carefully dusted.

Then she sweeps down the stairs, and dusts the banisters. She sweeps the dust from each stair into a dustpan, and is careful that no dust flies about the passage, or hall which she has already dusted.

She now cleans the drawing-room grate (if a fire is burnt there), and dusts the room.

Dusting the ornaments is often done by the mistress, but cannot always be expected.

The maid of all work returns to the kitchen, puts on a large canvas apron which will tie all round her, and which has a bib, and proceeds to cook her dinner. While the meat is roasting or boiling, any little kitchen work which will not take her away from the neighbourhood of the fireplace, may be done.

Half an hour before taking up her dinner, she will lay her cloth nicely, according to the directions given in "Footman's Duties," and will set bread, &c., &c., ready on the sideboard.

She cannot, of course, be expected to wait at table, but she should remove her coarse apron, and be ready to bring in the pudding, or tart, or cheese when required.

When she has taken away the dinner (she will do wisely to place the joint to warm before the kitchen fire for her own dinner), she sweeps and folds up the tablecloth, sweeps up the crumbs under the dining-table, makes up the fire (if required), or if the room is left vacant, opens the windows.

Then she dines herself, spreading her own cloth nicely, and giving herself time for a comfortable meal.

After dinner, she has a kettle of boiling water ready, washes up the dishes and plates, cleans the knives (washing the grease off carefully before she rubs them on the knifeboard), washes the silver spoons and forks, and just rubs them over with the leather; cleans any boots and shoes required, and then cleans up her kitchen, sweeps up the hearth, and goes to wash and dress herself.

Her next duty is to bring in the tea, make the toast, &c.

After tea, she turns down the beds, sees that there is water in every jug and bottle, shuts the windows, and draws down the blinds. These are the ordinary daily duties; but in order that the house may be well cleaned, every bedroom should be swept *once* a week, and the tins and silver must have weekly attention beyond that of the daily washing.

A good servant will manage her work by division.

For example:—On Saturday she will thoroughly clean the hall, *i.e.*, wash the canvas, rub any mahogany, &c., and sweep the stairs very thoroughly, occasionally taking up the stair-carpets, and replacing them so that they may not wear out by the same part being always at the edge of the stairs. She must also rub and clean the brass rods.

She will seldom have more than four bedrooms to do. She can sweep two on Tuesday; the drawing-room may be thoroughly swept on Wednesday; two bedrooms may be swept on Thursday; mahogany furniture, &c., well polished in the dining-room on Friday. On Saturday she will clean the plate, and her tins—as covers, &c.—and clean up her kitchen for Sunday.

A good servant will generally wash up the glasses and plates after supper, and not leave them for the morning. She will carefully fasten up the house.

The general servant should ask her mistress for housemaid's gloves, and endeavour, as much as possible, to keep her hands clean, so as never to leave smutty marks of fingers on anything she touches. Her hair should be banded carefully back, and be kept smooth, and her face clean; and as she has to answer the door, she should wear her coarse apron as much as possible, and at a knock or ring exchange it for a clean white one, kept within reach—for instance, in the kitchen drawer.

She should be careful never to pour the water in which eggs have been boiled over her hands, as it will bring warts. If her hands get chapped in winter, she will do well to rub them with a little camphor-ball when she goes to bed at night.

We insist on this care for the hands, not to encourage fine ways or vanity, but because a general servant's hands are used both for *very dirty* and *very clean* work, and without care they will be unfit for the latter.

Recollect, my little general servant, that if your place is a hard one, it is also the best possible one for training you for a better. After all, too, you have not more to do, nor, in fact, so much as you would have as the mistress of your own home when married, when you would probably have to clean house, work for your family's support, and take care of children, besides enduring anxiety and the many cares of the mother and wife.

In your place you have no care for daily bread or clothes. Your food and raiment are sure, and you have every comfort.

If you rise early, bustle about, and waste no spare moments, you will get through your work very well—only do *think* about it. A little arrangement and thought will give you METHOD and HABIT, two fairies that will make the work disappear before a ready pair of hands. If, when you put your head on your pillow, you would just *plan* how best to get through next day's work, you would find it a great help.

Try not to *forget* orders. Do everything as well as possible *at once*. Remember, "Once well done is twice done;" "A place for everything, and everything in its place."

Be sure always to wash *china, i.e.*, cups, saucers, plates in very hot water, with a little soda occasionally (but not if they have gilt edges), and wipe them dry on a very clean dry cloth. A wet dirty cloth will make them smeary and sticky, than which nothing can be more nasty.

Find time for your own work of an evening, and take care to leave no holes in your stockings, or rents unmended. "A stitch in time saves nine;" and if every Saturday night you mend all fractures, both in the clothes that return and those that are going to the wash, you will keep your needlework nicely under.

Be personally clean. It is the great charm of ladies; and a good wash all over every night before going to bed will refresh you, make you healthy, prettier, and more

cheerful than if you fell asleep still dirty from your daily toil.

Be active, cheerful, good-tempered, and obliging, and you will find work easy and employers kind.

Do your daily duties "with all your might," remembering Whose eye is always on you; and believe that the Great King who gives us all our daily work to do, will not leave unmarked the efforts of even a little maid of all work.

Duties of the Housemaid.

The duties of the housemaid require order, method, and great cleanliness to be well fulfilled. If more than one is kept, the work will be fairly divided between them, but whether divided, or done by one, its nature is still the same.

A housemaid, if she wishes to get her work done easily and with comfort, should be an early riser. She should get up at six in summer, and half-past six or seven in winter; though, of course, much must depend (as to hours) on the rules of the service in which she is engaged.

Her first care on going downstairs from her bedroom will be to open the shutters of the sitting-rooms. If it is winter, she must take up the hearth-rugs, and move the fenders. She should then spread a piece of coarse wrapping canvas before the grates, and clean the latter, after which she lights the fire. She must have a tin cinder-pail, with a wire sifter to sift the cinders, a housemaid's box, with black-lead, and her stove-brushes. With a soft brush she will lay on the blacklead, and then polish it with a proper brush for that purpose. It is a great credit to a housemaid when her grates are nicely polished. She should regularly every morning rub with a dry leather all the polished parts of a grate, and also the fender and fire-irons. Generally there are two sets of bars to a drawing-room grate—bright steel, for summer use, and black for winter. If constantly well rubbed, no rust will ever appear on them. Should any be accidentally found, a receipt for removing rust-spots will be found in this book.

And now about lighting the fires. If this is done badly the room will be filled with smoke, which is very injurious to furniture. It is well when first winter fires are commenced to hold a blazing paper up the chimney for a few minutes before the first fire is lighted. This will dispel the cold air in the chimney, which may otherwise beat the smoke down into the room. The fire is laid by placing first cinders, rather apart, at the bottom of the grate; then a piece of

Duties of the Housemaid.

paper — *not* coarse brown, which will smoulder — and then a few crossbars of pieces of wood, which should be kept *well dried;* on the wood some rubbly coals—not too close together, for a draught is required to kindle the fuel. The coals must be well back in the grate. Light with a lucifer match—use Bryant and May's, because they will *not* ignite unless they are rubbed on their own box, and thus they are less dangerous than those which will kindle by stepping on.

If the grate smokes, light the fire from the top. In order to achieve this properly, cover the bottom of the grate with a piece of coarse thick paper; build a wall of rubbly coals round, *leaving a hole in the middle;* cover it *all* with a piece of dry paper; lay pieces of wood crossing each other on it; then put a piece more paper, and steady it with a few *good* cinders. Set light to the under paper. The sticks, &c., will kindle, and fall into the hollow centre. In about an hour there will be a good fire, which will not smoke, but must never be stirred. This is a very saving way of making a fire, as so lighted it consumes much less fuel.

Some persons light fires with wheels made with resin and other combustible materials. They are useful, and perhaps cheaper than wood, but not very safe things in a house, as they easily ignite. The housemaid should be careful not to waste wood. A clever girl will light two fires, if the grates are not very large, with one good-sized bundle. One wheel, value one farthing, will light a fire. The housemaid, when she has lighted the drawing-room fire, does those in the bedrooms, when required; but this will be the work generally of the *under* housemaid. Where only two servants are kept—cook and housemaid—the former is generally engaged to do the dining-room, as well as the hall.

The housemaid should wear proper housemaid's gloves for doing her grates; and have a good coarse apron to tie all round her, to preserve her dress clean.

If it is summer, all the labour of fire-making will be saved; but the housemaid must look jealously to the polishing of her bright bars, grates, and fire-irons, lest they rust. Her next business is to carry away her boxes, &c.; and then sweep the room. While the dust settles she carries hot water to the bedrooms, in any quantity that may be required. Dusting and polishing the furniture is the next duty, and this should be done very carefully with the dusting-brush and duster. Every ledge should be dusted — the window-panes, the legs of chairs, tables, &c., as well as their tops—books, pictures, &c. Cobwebs must be watched for; and the ceiling sometimes dusted with the long broom called a Turk's head. After her morning-room or drawing-room is finished, the housemaid sweeps down the stairs.

She then puts on a clean white apron, and making herself look as nice and fresh as possible, lays the breakfast-table, if no footman or parlourmaid is kept. She takes care to place everything that can possibly be required on the table—sees that there are enough spoons, plates, knives, forks, &c. (the mode of arranging the cups, &c., will be found at "Breakfast Dishes," page 65). She brings in the breakfast, which the cook prepares and gives to her.

As soon as all is brought in, she leaves the room, ties on a large clean apron, kept for the purpose, and goes up to make the beds (assisted by the cook, where only two servants are kept). She should open all the bedroom windows; strip the bedclothes off, placing them over the backs of two chairs; then, while the beds are airing, she empties the slops. She washes out *all* the bedroom china with *very* hot water, wipes it (taking care to keep a separate towel for the basin and jug), empties the bath, and then takes away the pail, and scalds it out.

It will now be time to shake the beds, turn the mattresses, and make them up again. Then she should take a hand-brush and dust-pan, and sweep over the carpet sufficiently to remove any dust. Her next act will be to dust and polish the furniture; then to do all window-ledges, windows, banister-rails, &c., &c.; after which she will bring up water, and fill the jugs and water-bottles.

She brings the bedroom candlesticks down, cleans them, and sets up the candles. The moderator lamps should then be carefully trimmed, *i.e.*, the wicks cut or renewed, oil poured in all ready for lighting at night.

The bedrooms must be thoroughly swept, each once a week. The drawing-room twice a week; but the little pieces of flue and dust should be swept up every day with the short brush into the dust-pan.

When the room is to be thoroughly swept, covers should be thrown over the sofas, ottomans, &c., and the window-curtains should be carefully raised and pinned up till the sweeping is finished, then they should be well shaken out again. Highly-glazed chintz curtains may be kept clean for years, if they are occasionally taken down and wiped all over with a very clean duster.

By one, or half-past one o'clock, the housemaid ought to be dressed for the afternoon, and ready to bring in the luncheon or early dinner. She must then lay the cloth for either meal, and be ready to bring in the dishes and wait table.

She does not wait luncheon; but leaving plates, &c., and all that may be required on the dumb-waiter or waggon, goes to her own dinner. Though, if it is an early dinner—not luncheon—the servants generally dine after the family.

She will then, when the dinner is removed, rub the mahogany table with a duster, to remove any marks of dishes, and sweep up the crumbs, leaving the window open for a time to remove the smell of dinner.

She washes up the glass and silver (the latter should be just rubbed with a leather when it is dried from the hot water), and sets everything to rights, and prepares for tea. She will, of course, have time in the afternoon for doing needlework, such as mending the stockings, &c., or the house-linen, if required.

She lays the tea, removes it, washes up the tea-things, turns down the beds, takes away all slops, shuts the windows, draws down the blinds, and places the bedroom candles in the hall ready for use.

Duties of the Cook.

When two servants only are kept, the cook is expected to clean the dining-room, as well as the hall, passage, steps, &c. Of course, everything relating to the cleaning of the kitchen, scullery, &c., will also belong to you.

When this dirty morning work is done, you should carefully wash your hands, and visit the larder. Here you should look to everything; see if the hanging meat or game requires cooking, change the soup to prevent its getting sour, and wipe out the bread-pan. The larder should be scrubbed and cleaned out twice a week.

Receive your mistress's orders attentively; and if your memory cannot be relied on, write them on a slate.

Don't "scatter" in the kitchen. Clear up as you go, and be sure to put scalding water into each saucepan or stewpan as you finish using it.

Weigh the joints the butcher brings you; and never omit asking him for the paper of weight. Examine the meat, and if it is not good do not receive it.

Keep a strict account of the milk, bread, &c., used weekly; and have an eye to your mistress's interest, not permitting waste of any kind in the kitchen.

A cook who is just and honest, and does as she would be done by, is worthy of the greatest respect, and may be sure of being successful and happy.

And now let us give our good inexperienced friend a few hints as to kitchen-work.

Keep your spice-box always replenished; and take care to let your mistress know if you are out of anything likely to be required, that its place may be supplied at once.

Be scrupulously careful not to use a knife that has cut onions for any other purpose. Put it carefully aside to be cleaned. Take care if you have copper utensils to use that the tin does not become worn off. If so, have it instantly replaced. *Dry* your saucepans before you put them away.

Pudding cloths and jelly bags require care. Wash the pudding cloths, scald them, and hang them to dry directly after using them, and keep them in a warm dry place, well airing them before you put them away, or they will smell musty. After washing up dishes used before you use the tubs used for the purpose with soap and water, and soda. Scrub them often. Stand them up sideways to dry. Keep the sink and sink brush very clean, and be careful never to throw anything but water down the former, lest you should choke it up; but never pour cabbage water down, as the smell is so unpleasant that it should always be carried outside the house, and thrown away where it is not likely to be perceived. Never have sticky, greasy plates and dishes. The way to avoid this is to use *very* hot water, and clean dry towels. Change the water when it is greasy. Perfectly clean plates and dishes are one proof of the cook being a good servant. Clean the coppers with turpentine and fine brick-dust, rubbed on with flannel, and polish them with a leather and a little dry brick-dust. Clean the tins with soap and whitening, rubbed on with a flannel. Wipe them with a dry soft cloth, and polish with a clean leather and powdered whitening, or use the excellent receipt in this volume.

Never scrub the inside of a frying-pan. Rub it with wet silver sand put on a leather, and wash it out with hot water afterwards. Be very particular in washing vegetables. Lay cauliflowers and cabbage in salt and water, to get out insects, &c., &c. If a dinner-party is in prospect, ask for the bill of fare, and get ready all you can the day before, to save worry and scrambling on the day fixed.

Whisk the white of eggs for soufflés, lemon and sponge-cakes, till they will bear the weight of an egg on them. This will assure the lightness of your cakes and soufflés; the latter ought to fly up like huge bubbles to

Duties of the Parlourmaid, Nurse and Laundrymaid. 351

be really excellent. Take notice of all orders that require *time* in the preparation of the dinner, and hurry nothing.

Wear large aprons and close dresses, so that you may avoid the risk of fire, and take especial care to bind back your hair so that there may be no chance of a loose one falling into your preparations. Exquisite cleanliness *tells* even on the taste of the dishes preferred.

Be careful of fuel. It is a great recommendation to a cook to use only the necessary amount of coals. If you cook by a grate, screw the sides nearer to each other when the fire has ceased to be required.

The Parlourmaid.

The parlourmaid takes the duties of an upper housemaid, and the waiting of a footman at meals, &c.

She cleans plate, lays the table, waits at meals, answers the drawing-room bell, and the door bell, trims the lamps, and performs the other minor duties of a footman. At her leisure she works at her needle, and keeps the linen in repair.

The Nurse and Nursemaid.

The nurse's duties are very responsible ones. She has to watch over the health, safety, and comfort of the little ones in the nursery. She should be a healthy woman, very clean in her person, of a bright, cheerful, good temper. With the assistance of a nursemaid, if the family is large, she must, at about seven o'clock, take up and dress the children, washing carefully and tenderly their faces, necks and arms; it is best, we think, to give them their bath *at night*. The water of the bath should be lukewarm (unless a cold bath is especially ordered). They may be *washed* in cold water in the morning. Brush the hair carefully and tenderly so as not to hurt the little heads. When the children are dressed, and have said their prayers, she should give them their breakfast, taking care that they are well and comfortably fed.

The nursemaid cleans the nursery, sets the breakfast, and helps the nurse to dress the children; after breakfast the nursemaid makes the little beds, and cleans the night nursery. The nurse, directly after breakfast, washes and dresses the baby, if there is one in the nursery.

Then the two servants take the children for a walk until it is time for the little ones to lie down for their morning nap. All children out of the schoolroom should lie down for an hour at least, to ease the spine of the weight of the head; they will grow stronger and straighter for it. While they lie down the nurse can work at her needle.

After dinner the children walk again. The nurse and nursemaid make and mend all the children's clothes. The nurse should try to get pretty patterns whenever she sees them for her task, and should take a pride in the neatness of her charges' wardrobes.

She should rule the nursery with a gentle but firm authority, making the children obedient and truthful, and taking care that she sets them a good example in all things. Her influence for good or evil is *very great*, and she should exercise great watchfulness, that no word may meet young ears in the nursery that is unfit for them to hear.

Whenever the children are sent for to the drawing-room, the nurse should take off their pinafores, smooth their hair, and make them look nice. The head nurse generally takes her meals with the children.

The Laundrymaid.

The laundrymaid should collect all the linen requiring washing on Monday morning, count it, and compare it with the list given to her. Then she must assort it, putting the sheets and body linen in one heap, the muslins and fine things in another, the cotton and woollen in a third. Ink spots, fruit stains, &c., should be removed. The heavy linen should be soaked in hot water all night. The washing begins next morning at five or six o'clock. In most large households where a laundrymaid is kept, there are now to be found washing and wringing machines, as well as mangles. Where these are not found, the old-fashioned labour of soaping with yellow soap in hot water, and rubbing well, must be resorted to.

The linen should be well washed in two waters, and the water should be hot and *plentiful*. Then it should be boiled in the copper for about an hour and a half, taken out, rinsed in clean hot water, then in cold water tinged with the blue bag, then wrung thoroughly, and hung out early in the sunshine and air to bleach and dry.

Coloured muslins should be washed in cold water to keep the colour, rubbed with yellow soap gently, and hung to dry in a shady place to save the colour from fading. A *little* soda added to the water will save mauve and lilac from washing out. New flannel should be washed in cold water before it is made up; that will prevent it from shrinking in the wash. Only *lukewarm* water should be used for them then, and yellow soap. It requires a good deal of rinsing to get the soap out of flannel before drying.

To Make Starch.—Mix the starch with cold water, using a wooden spoon. Make it quite smooth and free from lumps, then pour boiling water over it, stirring it all the time. When made, stir it round three times with a piece of wax candle, to prevent the iron from sticking.

When the washing is ended, scrub and put away the tubs, &c.

Thursday and Friday the laundrymaid irons and mangles. She should then air the clothes thoroughly, and fold them neatly before giving them to the housemaid or lady's-maid to sort.

Great care should be taken not to let wet clothes touch iron or a brick floor, for fear of iron moulds. Also, the laundress should be careful not to tear fine muslin or lace.

Handkerchiefs should be ironed *wet*, to stiffen and give them a gloss.

The Duties of a Lady's-Maid.

A lady's-maid is required to be a nice-mannered, respectable-looking young woman. She should be a tolerably good dressmaker, know how to make a cap or trim a bonnet, and she must be a good hairdresser. Her first morning duty will be to dress her lady, about which it is impossible to give directions, as ladies differ very much in their toilette arrangements. The housemaid generally takes up the warm water for the lady's bath, but occasionally she prefers her own maid doing so. After dressing her lady, the maid must examine her wardrobe, shake or iron out tumbled dresses, put away everything left about the room. She then sits down in the housekeeper's room to needlework, but must be ready to answer her lady's bell when it is rung, and to dress her for a walk, drive, or ride, having everything ready—boots, gloves, &c., in perfect order.

She must have everything prepared also for the lady's toilette for dinner, and as soon as that is over, and her mistress has left the room, she should examine the walking dress, brush it if it is a tweed or linsey, shake and wipe it, and remove mud stains if it is a silk or any light material. Silk dresses should be wiped with a soft piece of merino or very fine flannel. If anything wants mending it should be done *at once*. Everything should be carefully dusted and put away, either folded or hung in the wardrobe.

She must have the bedroom ready for her lady at the usual hour for retiring for the night. If it is winter she must have a bright fire, before which she should hang the night dress, &c. Hot water should be in a can or kettle ready for use, and the brushes put out on the toilette table. Her duty is then to undress the lady, and remain in attendance till she is dismissed. During the day, when not in actual attendance, she will have to mend, make, and probably to wash and iron lace and fine clothes, as handkerchiefs, collars, cuffs, &c. Very little instruction can be given verbally on this point. However, a few hints as to how best to wash Honiton lace, &c., may be of some service.

To Wash Honiton Lace.—Fold the lace evenly together, and tack it lightly on a piece of flannel; double the flannel over it. Squeeze it constantly (but do not rub it) in very hot soapsuds. When clean, let it dry, then open it, spread and pin it out on a cloth, and carefully pick up and raise all the threads. It should be pressed smooth, but not ironed.

To Stiffen Fine Cambric Handkerchiefs. —Wash them rather by squeezing them in hot soap and water than by rubbing them; blue them slightly, rinse them again in cold water, and *iron them wet with a box-heater.*

Tumbled muslin or thin dresses should be pressed out with an iron.

To Wash Brushes.—Brushes should be washed in *cold* soda and water, and not left to soak. Shake the water well out of the bristles, and dry in the open air if possible. Brush the comb and clean it with a piece of thread, but do not wash it. If it is greasy and you are compelled to wash it, dip it in cold soda and water. A receipt for an excellent wash for the hair will be found at the end of the book; also a tooth-powder and a valuable receipt for making Eau-de-Cologne. Skill in these matters is of great service to a maid.

Once a week the lady's-maid will have to send the linen to the wash and receive it back. She should look over the clothes, and mend everything that requires a stitch before sending it, making two lists—one in the book for the laundress, one in a book to be kept at home, comparing the clothes with the list when they are returned clean, looking at the marks to see that they have not been changed at the wash, sewing on any buttons, and not permitting bad washing, but returning any ill-washed article to the laundress.

Wax spots may be removed from silk or woollen dresses by placing a piece of blotting paper over them and holding a very hot iron in the air a little distance above the paper: the heat draws out the grease. As soon as seen through the paper, the latter should be removed to a cleaner part, the iron held over the spot again till it is out.

To Clean a Turned Silk.—Wash the breadths with spirits of wine, and press them with a hot iron the wrong side, or rather the worn side of the silk. Black silk is best washed with gin. Spirits of turpentine will remove paint spots if freshly done. The pile of velvet when crushed by sitting on it may be raised by holding the wrong side above the steam of hot water.

A respectful manner is required from a lady's-maid. She is not to keep her seat while her mistress is speaking to her, unless desired, and she is to rise when the lady enters the room.

She has breakfast and tea in the housekeeper's room, dines in the servants'-hall, but retires for her cheese, &c., with the housekeeper. A good deal of sitting up at night is sometimes required from a lady's-maid during the London season; she must strive to get what rest she can, and good-temperedly support any inevitable fatigue.

A cheerful, kindly performance of her duties, deference, obedience, industry, and strict honesty will secure for her a friend in her lady, and a happy home under all ordinary circumstances.

The Housekeeper.

The housekeeper in modern families (except in those of the highest nobility) is generally also the cook; but she has a kitchen-maid under her, who is about the same as an ordinary plain cook.

Her duties as housekeeper require early rising, both to get business over well, and as an example to the servants. She has her breakfast with the butler, lady's-maid, and valet, in her own private apartment. After breakfast she will make out on a slate her bill of fare for the day's luncheon and dinner, to be submitted to her lady's approval. After receiving her orders for the day, she will go over the house to see that the housemaids have done their duty well; that the furniture is rubbed, carpets swept, &c., &c. Then she has to market, give orders to the tradesmen, &c., &c. Afterwards her culinary preparations will engage her attention.

She heads the dinner table in the servants' hall, but retires to her own room with the butler and lady's-maid and valet, for her after-dinner cheese, &c. She has her tea with the upper servants in the same manner.

The still-room maid cleans the housekeeper's room, and waits on her. Where there is no still-room maid the scullery-maid or under housemaid generally has to do so.

It is the housekeeper's duty to look over the house linen and see that it is kept in good repair, and that it returns right from the wash. She also directs all cleaning, annual or otherwise. Once a week she should submit her books to her lady to be inspected and paid.

A housekeeper ought to be perfectly trustworthy. She has much committed to her, and will be respected, and will prosper in exact proportion to her fulfilment of the important duties devolving on her.

She should show a tender, motherly care towards the younger female servants, and endeavour as much as possible to rule them wisely and well. Many opportunities of doing good will be open to her. Her influence in a large household may be great. She should think for all, and endeavour to do good to all. Especially should she consider the interests of her employers, and endeavour to spend for them as she would wish other persons to do for her.

Directions given to lady housekeepers at the beginning of this volume will also be of use to the professional housekeeper in many ways, especially if she is young and inexperienced.

The Footman.

The footman is required to make himself generally useful, though, of course, the number of men kept will diminish or increase his work.

He has to clean knives and shoes, rub the furniture, clean the plate, trim the lamps, brush his master's clothes, carry up coals, attend to fires, open the door, go on errands or messages, and go out with the carriage. The footman must get over his dirty work before breakfast—*i.e.*, he must clean boots, shoes, knives, and lamps, and rub tables, &c.; then he must make himself fit to go in to prayers, and carry in the breakfast which he lays. He brushes his master's clothes, and carries them up with his boots and hot water to the gentleman's dressing-room. When there is no butler kept, he brings in the breakfast urn, and afterwards removes the breakfast things. The footman lays the luncheon cloth and dinner cloth, and waits table.

To Lay the Table for Luncheon and Dinner.—He lays the cloth; puts a water bottle (or caraffe) with a tumbler on it at each corner of the table, a salt-cellar and two tablespoons at each corner; a small knife and two small silver forks and one dessertspoon for each person round the table, a carving knife and fork at the top and bottom of the table, and a tablespoon near every side-dish; the cruet-stand in the

23

centre of the table, the silver sugar dredger on one side of it (towards the foot of the table), near it two decanters of wine; a tumbler and wineglass to each person. At luncheon the meat or chickens, tarts, biscuits, cake, &c., are all put on the table at the same time, but if a hot pudding is served the footman brings it in afterwards when required. The footman should be ready to push in the chair on which a lady seats herself as she sits down. He carries round the luncheon plates once, and then goes to early dinner (unless there should be a luncheon party). He takes the luncheon away. He lays the dinner either à la Russe or in the English fashion. On the sideboard before dinner he must arrange the plate, glass, &c., so that he may have everything ready to his hand. The dessert (unless it is a dinner à la Russe) must be put ready on the sideboard, and the wine decanted; the butler (if there is one) will look to the plate and wine. On each dessert-plate he must put a doyley and fingerglass (some people, East Indians especially, like a bayleaf put at the bottom of the water), and the silver knife and fork, or if the fingerglasses or wine coolers are left from dinner on the table, he puts the wineglasses on the plate. Then he must put the butler's tray ready. The tablecloth should be laid very evenly (slips are laid down each side for company). At each end of the table he should place a carving knife and fork and their rests; the same before any side-dish requiring it (such as bacon or tongue), a tablespoon at each dish's destined place. A large knife, two large forks, and a dessert-spoon by each plate, the spoon for soup, the extra fork for fish, where fish knives and forks are not used. At each corner of the table he puts salt-cellars, with a tablespoon on each side, the bowls in opposite directions; places a water-bottle and glass at each corner; a plate to each person with a nicely folded table-napkin on it, holding a dinner roll. If laying for a large party he puts a salt-cellar and a water bottle and glass between every two persons; the lamp in the centre of the table, or the épergne as required. The footman receives the dishes at the dining-room door; the butler puts the first dish upon the table; the footman stands behind the lady. He carries round plates of soup, offering one to each person; he must hand it on the *left hand* of the diner, and with *his own left hand*. Next he hands the soup, then the fish, next the entrées or side-dishes, then the removes or chief joints, &c. Wine is offered directly after soup, and frequently during dinner; sherry is used at the ordinary table. Sherry after soup and fish at a dinner party, then *immediately* afterwards Champagne or Hock, or any light wine. The footman must stand watching the table very attentively, so that he may change every plate as soon as required. On every clean plate handed, thus, he lays a clean silver fork. The soup ladle is always removed and put into the basket for the used silver, before the tureen is taken away. The carving knife and fork are also removed separately. The second course is brought in; the game is handed first; afterwards the sweets, changing the plates as required. He must be careful to learn from the cook which are the right sauces to hand with the different dishes.

Cheese, butter, &c., are next served, and handed round.

When dinner is over he removes the slips if it is a dinner party, or the cloth only if the family are alone. He brushes off the crumbs into a small waiter; puts the dessert and wine on the table, and to each person a dessert-plate (already prepared) and two wineglasses. The fruit is handed round; then the footman makes up the fire and leaves the room.

He then (where no butler is kept) proceeds to the drawing-room and attends to the fire and lamps; then, in the butler's pantry, he washes up the plate ready for cleaning the next day. After the ladies have left the dining-room he carries in coffee to them; and some time after he takes it into the dining-room to the gentlemen.

When the gentlemen go into the drawing-room, he carries in the tea. At the usual hour he brings the bedroom candles. These minor arrangements, however, differ in different families.

The footman brings in letters and notes; he must always hand them on a waiter. He must answer bells readily, especially the door bell, and he should speak civilly to visitors. He shows them in, asks the name if he does not know it, and takes care to announce them properly.

The footman should endeavour by careful observation and pains to fit himself for the place of under-butler.

Mode of Folding Table Napkins.

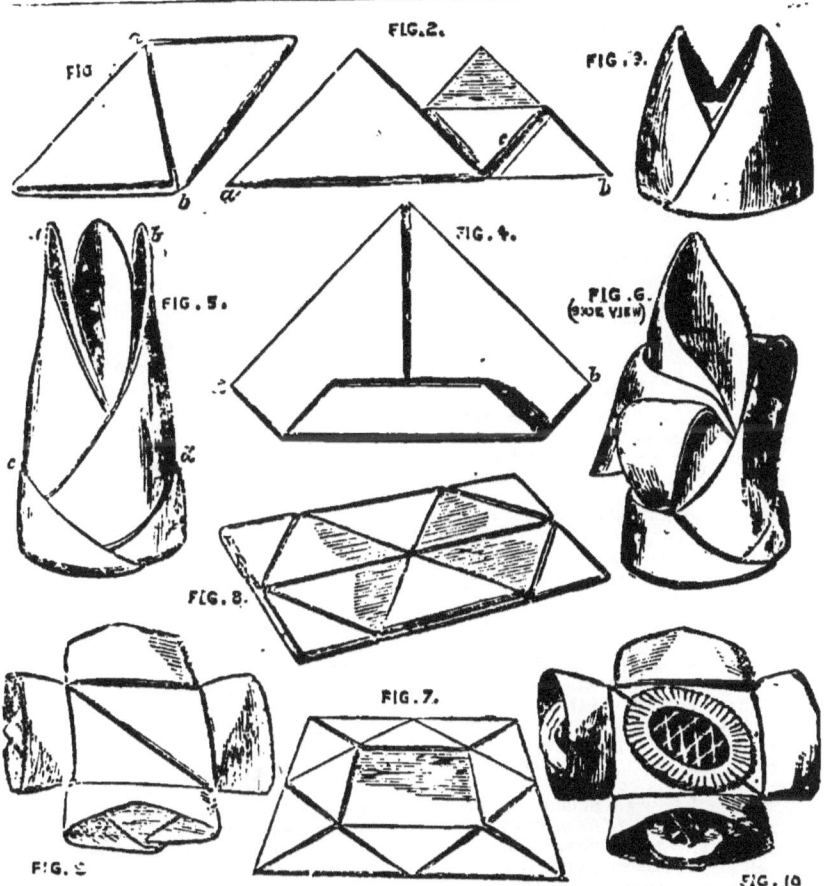

To Fold the Mitre.—The napkin must be folded in three, thus :—Fold one third over, turn it *backwards*, and thus make the three folds. Fold both ends to meet in the middle. Take the left-hand corner, *a*, and fold it across in a right angle. Take the opposite corner, *b*, on the left hand at the top, and fold it in the same manner; you will thus form figure 1. Turn over and fold in halves lengthwise; open the points, and you will have figure 2. Bend the point, *a*, towards the right, and tuck it in the groove, *c*; turn the point, *b*, backwards towards the right hand, and tuck it in as at *a*; you will then have figure 3—The Mitre.

The Water Lily.—Have a square napkin and fold it like a half handkerchief. Then take the two opposite points, and make them meet on the centre one, which forms a square. Take the bottom corner, opposite the points, and roll it up as at figure 4. Turn the napkin over, and roll point *a* to about the centre. Take point *b*, and tuck it in the groove; raise it, and you have figure 5—the Water Lily. Turn the corners over, and tuck them in at *c* and *d*. Turn back the second fold at the top—figure 6.

Napkin Folded for small Tarts at the side and a Cake in the middle.—Have a perfectly square napkin; turn the corners over so that they meet at the centre. Turn the four corners back to the edge, and you will have figure 7; carefully turn the napkin without unfolding it; turn it over from two opposite sides into the centre at figure 8; turn it over again and make the other two ends meet in the middle; you have then figure 9.

The Valet.

The valet's duty is to wait on his master. He sees that the gentleman's dressing-room fire is lighted in the morning; arranges the clothes, which he has brushed, on a table or chair, and places the linen before the fire. Then he fills the bath, &c. Sometimes the valet shaves his master; he brushes his hair, and should be able to cut it every fortnight. He hands the garments required to the gentleman.

The valet then receives his orders for the day, puts the dressing-room straight, brushes clothes, and cleans combs and brushes; he takes messages, posts letters, and is at his master's orders whenever required.

The Butler.

The butler is at the head of the men servants; he has care of the plate and wine.

He sees that the breakfast-table is well laid by the footman; and that he brings in the urn, &c.

He looks to the laying of luncheon, and waits at it till the family are helped; he offers wine or ale, and then leaves the dining-room and goes to dinner. If desired, he waits when there is company; but few persons like to have the servants waiting at luncheon.

He gives out and arranges the silver for dinner, announces dinner, and stands respectfully at the door till the family go into the dining-room; sets the first dish on the table; then he takes his place behind his master on the left hand, near the sideboard, after removing the cover and handing it to the footman. He waits at table with general supervision over the other servants. When the soup and fish are done with, he rings the bell for the removes, gives the dishes to the footman, receives the removes and places them on the table. He removes the covers, and again stands near the sideboard, unless he is required to assist in handing the entrées, which he must do if there is only a second man to wait.

He places the dessert also on the table and hands it round. If it is winter he takes care to have the fire made up; then he leaves the room with the footman.

He visits the drawing-room, sees that the upper-housemaid has set it to rights while the family were dressing, makes up the fire, sees to the lamps, &c.

He brings in the tea. At bed-time he appears with the candles. He secures the house, and sees that the fires and lights are out.

Brewing, racking, and bottling malt liquors —fining down and bottling wine, are duties which belong to him. In families where no groom of the chambers is kept, he should look occasionally into the drawing-room to see that the blinds are down if the sun pours in, &c. &c., and to pay any little attention to the comfort of the lady.

The butler also, when only a footman is kept, answers the hall door with the latter, and announces visitors. He is also ready when the carriage drives round to assist the lady of the house into it, and he is at hand when she returns.

The duties of a butler single-handed are of course heavy; if an under-butler is kept they are lighter.

SERVANTS' CHARACTERS.

A master or mistress is *not bound* to give a servant a character. If a character is given it must be a true one, but if not a good one, care should be exercised in the wording, particularly if it is a written one, because it may be actionable.* If any master or mistress give a false character of a servant in writing, knowing the same to be false, and the servant unfit for a situation from dishonesty, drunkenness, &c., they render themselves liable to a penalty of 20*l*. and 10*s*. costs.

If any person personates a master or mistress, and gives the character of a servant, they are liable to be fined 20*l*. and 10*s*. costs.

A servant altering a written character or bringing a false one—from a person representing the master or mistress—is liable to forfeit 20*l*. and 10*s*. costs upon being convicted of such offence.

* If a bad character is given *through malice* the person giving it becomes actionable, but not otherwise.

INDEX TO RECIPES.

NOTE.—*The figures within the brackets are the numbers of the recipes.*

ACID PUDDING (972), 206.
Adelaide pudding, the (973), 206.
Agnew pudding (983), 207.
Albert pudding, the (990), 208.
Ale, to mull (1773), 327.
Alexandra pudding. the (989), 208.
Almack preserve (1640), 305.
Almond sauce (320), 99 ; frase (1233), 244 ; pudding (986), 208 ; small (985), 208 ; and raisin pudding (986), 208 ; a rich boiled (987), 208 ; baked (988), 208.
Amber pudding (980), 207 ; sauce for (981), 207.
American pudding white (1202), 239.
Anchovy sauce for fish (291), 94; toast (47), 49 ; Madras (48), 49.
Anna's pudding (991). 209.
Apple and crumb pudding (982). 207 ; custard pudding (1036), 215 ; dumplings, boiled (978), 207 ; baked (979), 207 ; hedgehog (1366), 265 ; and rice (1367), 265; de par (1368), 265 ; jam (1670), 310 ; marmalade (1671), 310 ; jelly, for garnishing (317), 98 ; pudding (974), 206 ; pudding. boiled (975), 207 ; baked (976), 207 ; rich (977), 207 ; sauce (305), 96 ; snow (1373), 266 ; to prepare for dessert (1591), 298 ; tart, plain, to make (933), 199 ; open (934), 199 ; and custard (935), 200 ; with quince (936), 200.
Apricot chips (1602), 300 ; compote of (1599), 299 ; tart, to make (938), 200 ; (1629), 304 ; to dry (1630), 304 ; brandy (1631), 304 ; marmalade (1632), 304.
Artichokes, to boil (769), 174 ; to stew, in gravy (770), 174 ; Jerusalem (771), 174 ; to boil Jerusalem (772), 174.
Arrowroot jelly (1809), 332 ; sauce (318), 98 ; steamed, pudding (992), 209 ; baked (993), 209 ; (1778), 329 ; water (1779), 329.
Asparagus, to boil (773), 174 ; in French rolls (774), 175 ; pudding (994), 209.
Ass's milk, artificial (1805), 332.

BACKINGS (1234), 244.
Bacon, methods of curing (878), 190 ; to cure (869), 189 ; West Country way to cure (870), 189; to choose (505), 130; to boil (506), 130 ; and eggs (507), 130 ; to steam (508), 131; to salt larding (509), 131.
Bakewell pudding (1000), 210 ; with almonds (1002), 210.
Ballachony (701), 162.
Banbury cakes (1418), 273.
Barley cream (1802), 332 ; gruel (1803), 331 ; water (1804), 332.
Barberry jelly (1798), 331 ; jam (1645), 306 ; to preserve, in bunches (1646), 306.
Basse, dressed en Casserole (109), 61.
Bath pudding (1013), 212.
Bean (green) pudding (1015), 212.
Beans, to boil, French (792), 177 ; à la creme (793), 177 ; to boil broad (794), 178 ; white kidney, fricasseed (795), 178 ; to boil haricot (796), 178 ; haricot, à la Maitre d'Hôtel (797), 178 ; haricot, with white sauce (798), 178.
Beef, a pickle for (414), 114 ; au Miroton (628), 150 ; croquettes of (629), 150 ; fricassees of cold roast (630), 151 ; cuende (633), 151 ; fritters of (402), 112 ; fritters (385), 109 ; rechauffé of salt (635), 151 ; rissoles (644), 153 ; to dress, 104 ; to make tough, tender (360), 105 ; sirloin (361), 105 ; roast ribs (362), 105 ; ribs rolled (363), 105 ; to boil (364), 105 ; aitchbone of (365), 105 ; silverside, boiled (366), 106 ; Tom Thumb round of (367), 106 ; bouilli (368), 105; a. stew (369), 106 ; stewed shin of (370), 106 ; to dress the inside of a sirloin of (371), 107 ; à la mode (372), 107 ; olives (373), 107 ; breslau of (374), 107 ; fillets de (375) 107 ; fillets, à la St. Aubyn (376), 108 ; cakes (377), 108 ; palates (376), 108 ; to stew, palates (379), 103 ; to broil palates (380), 108 ; to eat cold (391), 110 ; collared (392), 110 ; spiced (393), 111 ; liver for gravy (394), 111 ; potted, like venison (888), 192 ; soup (214), 80 ; steak pie, plain (719), 165; pudding (740), 170 ; and kidney pudding (741), 170 ; to collar (906), 195 ; to pot (886), 191 ; teas, ordinary (1789), 330 ; very strong (1790), 330 ; essence (1791), 330.
Beetroot, to boil (799), 178.
Biscuits, devilled (24), 46 ; pudding (1008), 211 ; orange, for dessert (1604), 300 ; brown bread (1572), 295 ; caraway (1573), 295 ; French (1574), 296 ; Naples (1575), 296 ; Nun's (1576), 296 ; lemon (1577), 296 ; orange (1578), 296 ; Damascus (1579), 296 ; German (1580), 296 : American (1581), 297 ; sponge (1582), 297 ; Spanish (1583), 297 ; ginger (1584), 297 ; almond spice (1585), 297 ; arrowroot (1586), 297 ; spoon (1587), 297 ; pistachio (1588), 298 ; cocoa nut (1589), 298 ; plain (1590), 298.
Bishop's pudding (1003), 210.
Birds, a very cheap way of potting (882), 191 ; nests (37), 48.
Blackberry jam (1644), 306 ; syrup (1769), 327 ; wine (1731), 322.
Blackcap pudding (1009), 211 ; currant, black or red, pudding (1010), 211.
Blackcock, to truss (613), 148 ; to roast (614), 148.
Blacking, to make (1832), 344 ; a receipt for (1833), 344.
Black and red currant tarts, to make (929), 199.
Blancmange, for invalids (1807), 332 ; lemon (1251), 246 ; (1252), 247 ; isinglass (1253), 247 ; arrowroot (1254), 247 ; strawberry (1255), 247 ; quince (1256), 247 ; ribbon (1257), 247 ; raspberry (1258), 248 ; cheap (1259), 248 ; ground rice (1260), 248.
Bobotee (702), 162.
Boiled batter pudding (1004), 211 ; rich (1005), 211 ; cheap (1006), 211.
Bologna sausages (524), 132.

Index.

Bombay pudding (1000), 210.
Boston pudding (1007), 211.
Bouquet de Victoria (1854), 346.
Boulettes au foie de Veau (657). 155.
Brandy pudding (1011), 212; orange (1765), 326; lemon (1766), 327; Morrella cherry (1767), 327; mixture, to be given in cases of exhaustion (1812), 333.
Brasenose College pudding (1012), 212.
Brawn (33), 47; to make (518), 132.
Bread 42, 44; and milk (7), 43; to make (¿¹), 44; American mode of making (13), 45; German yeast (14), 45; potato (15), 45; brown, to make (16), 45; rice (17), 45; light breakfast, American recipe for (18), 45; panada, for forcemeats, quenelles, &c, (326), 100; crumbs, fried (342), 102; fried for borders (341), 102; brown, pudding (995), 209; plain (996), 209; (997), 210; and butter (998), 210; an economical, (999), 211; and marmalade pudding (1100), 224; pulled (1433), 275; real Scotch short (1499), 284; plain (1500) 284; sauce (301), 96; jelly (1780), 329.
Brewing, family (1776), 328; directions for, in cottages (1777), 328.
Brill (68), 54.
Brocoli, to boil (780), 176; and buttered eggs (781), 176.
Broth, mutton (1792), 330; veal (1793), 330; chicken (1781), 329; port wine jelly (1782, 1783), 329; Scotch barley (232), 83; veal (240), 85; a strong (1785), 330; white, for invalids (1788), 330.
Brown Charlotte pudding (1016), 212.
Brunswick tart, to make (941), 201.
Brussels sprouts, to boil (783) 176.
Bubble and Squeak (403), 112.
Bullock's heart, stewed, American receipt (381), 109; English receipt (382), 109; marrowbones, boiled (383), 109.
Buns, to make (1565). 294; light (1566), 294; Bath (1567), 294; cross (1568), 295.
Butter, melting, the author's way (274), 92; another way (275), 92; French (276), 92; clarified (323), 99; fairy (1414), 272; orange (1415), 272; Spanish (1416), 273; to make (1713), 318; milk, to keep, and cream in hot weather (1714), 319; rolled (1715), 319; to freshen salt (1716), 319; in haste for winter cream (1717), 329.

CABBAGE, to boil (782), 176; or Savoys, to boil (785) 176; with forcemeat à la Francaise (786), 176.
Cabinet pudding, a plain (1019), 213; (1020), 213; sauce (1021), 213.
Cake, beaulieu (1501), 284; Adelaide (1502). 284; to clean currants for (1503), 284; plain plum (1504), 284; small (1505), 284; a rich plum (1506), 285; raisin (1507), 285; Neapolitan (1508), 285; small Venetian (1509), 285; Vienna (1510), 285; a delicate (1511). 285; Portugal (1512), 286; a rich pound (1480), 281; cocoa-nut (1481), 281; plain almond (1482), 281; rice (1483). 282; Lady Freakes' (1484), 282; small rice (1485), 281; rice (1486), 282; Manx (1487). 282; Josephine (1488), 282; rich seed (1489), 282; a common seed (1490), 282; a light (1491), 282; sponge (1492), 283; Lafayette (1493), 283; lemon (1494), 283; a very rich (1495), 283; Savoy (1496). 283; soda (1497). 283; plain (1498), 283; chocolate (1532), 289; (1535), 290; rich spice (1536), 290; wine (1537), 290; snow (1538), 290; honey (1539), 290; Madeline (1540), 290; Webster (1541), 291; Dover (1542), 291; Maderia (1543), 291; cream (1544), 291; a la Polonaise (1545), 291; queen (1546), 291; small queen (1547), 291; Derby short (1548), 292; bread (1549), 292; Sally Lunn (1569), 295; icing for (1473), 280; to ice or frost a (1474), 280; almond icing for bride (1475), 280; sugar icing to the top (1476), 281; apricot (1601), 299; damson (1604), 300; ginger (1519), 287; cheap gingerbread (1520), 287; Rutland (1515), 286; Canadian (1516), 286; yeast (1517). 286; strawberry short (1552), 292; Shrewsbury (1553), 292; citron (1554), 292; rock (1555), 293; cocoa-nut (1556), 293; Irish luncheon (1528). 288; Sydenham (1529), 288; twelfth (1530), 289; rich bride (1531), 289.
Calf's head, to collar a (909), 195; to collar a, with oysters (910), 195; roasted (649), 154; boiled (469), 124; a savoury (470), 124; brains and tongue (471), 124; hashed (472), 124; fricassee of (473), 125; cheese (474), 125; a la Maitre d'Hotel (475), 125; collared (476), 125; in a shape (660), 156; brains a la Maitre d'Hotel. (661), 156; croquettes of, brains (662), 156; boiled, feet (663), 156; feet roasted (664) 156; head soup (224), 82; feet soup (225), 82; feet (1786), 330.
Calf's liver and bacon (487), 127.
Capon, to truss a roast (568), 141; to roast (569), 141; to truss a, for boiling (570) 141; to boil a (571), 142; a la Francaise (572), 142; Abd-el-Kader's, stewed (573), 142.
Cambridge pudding (1048), 217.
Cambridge sausage, the (522), 132.
Caudle, old fashioned (1800), 331; old-fashioned brown (1801), 331.
Canellons (947), 202; glacés (948), 202.
Caper Sauce, French white (282), 93.
Capillaire (1757). 325.
Cardoons, to stew (839), 184; to boil (840), 184; fried (841), 184; a la fromage (842), 184.
Carp, baked (112), 61; fried (113), 62; au bleu (114), 62; Fute (115), 62; to boil (116), 62; stewed (117), 62.
Carrack (353), 104.
Carrot pudding (1042), 216; rich (1043), 216.
Carrots, to boil (765). 173; Flemish way (766), 173; to stew (767), 173; mashed (768), 174; to preserve (1678), 312; common, soup (259), 88; purée of (260), 89; purée of red (849), 185.
Cassel pudding (1044), 216.
Cauliflowers, to boil (775), 175; in sauce (776), 175; moulded with sauce (777), 175; au gratin (778), (779), 175.
Celery, purée of (848), 185; soup, (261), 89; to serve (815), 180; à la creme (816), 181; with cream (817), 181; stewed (818), 181; fried (819), 181; white, sauce (304), 96.
Champagne cup (1753, 54), 325.
Champagne, mock (1737), 323.
Chancellor's pudding (1041) 216.
Charlotte de pomme, a (1380) 267; Swiss (1381), 267; a la Parisienne (1382), 267; Russe (1383), 269.
Char, potted (900), 194.
Cheese, to make (1720), 320; to make sage (1721), 320; imitation of Cheshire (1722), 320; an excellent cream (1723). 321; cream (1724), 321; napkin (1725), 321; artificial (1726), 321; milk (1727), 321.
Cheesecakes, curd for, Yorkshire, receipt (1400, 1401), 270; (1402), 271; apple (1403), 271; lemon (1404), 271; potato (1405), 271; almond (1406), 271; citron (1407), 271; cheap ratafia (1408), 271; bread (1409) 272; rice

Index.

(1410), 272 ; lemon (1412), 272 ; lemon, to keep several years (1413), 272.
Cheese fingers (1430), 275; canapees (1431), 275; puddings (1017-1018), 212, 213; snow (1417), 273; toasted (1440), 276.
Cherries, to preserve (1662), 309 ; to bottle (1663), 309; to dry (1664), 309 ; to candy (1665), 310; to dry with their leaves and stalks (1666), 310.
Cherry pudding (1023), 213 ; tart, to make (928), 199.
Chestnut, purée of (850), 185; sauce (303). 96.
Chester pudding (1029), 214.
Chicken broth (223), 81 ; cutlets, an entrée (675), 158; to fricasee (676), 158; cream (1808), 332 ; devilled (52), 50; and ham pie (725), 166 ; soufflé of (672), 158.
Chilblains, embrocation for, not broken (1849), 345.
Chimney pieces, to clean (1819), 343.
China, to cement broken (1823), 343.
Chintz furniture, to clean, when taken down for the summer (1826), 344.
Chocolate (4), 43 ; pudding, baked (1026), 214 ; tarts (965), 204.
Choux à la comtesse (963), 204.
Christmas bowl (1750), 375 ; pudding (1128), 229.
Citron puddings (1024), 213 ; and almond (1025), 213.
Clarence's, Duke of, pudding (1028), 214.
Claret cup (1751), 325 ; superior (1752), 325 ; (1457), 278.
Clary wine (1732), 322.
Coburg pudding, the (1050), 217.
Cock-a-leekie (228), 82.
Cockle sauce (287), 93.
Cockles and periwinkles, to boil, (191), 74 ; to pickle (192), 74.
Cocoa nibs (Dr. Todd) (5), 43 ; paste or powder (6), 43.
Cocoa-nut soup (222), 81 ; pudding (1035), 215 ; puddings, small (1032), 214; grated (1033); 215.
Cod, head and shoulders of (79), 56 ; browned head (80), 56 ; crimped (81), 56; piked (82), 56; salt (83), 56 ; salt, the second day (84), 57; sounds, boiled (85), 57 ; a recherche dish of (86), 57 ; broiled sounds (87), 57 ; to broil sounds (88), 57 ; to bake a (89), 57 ; cold 57; curried (691), 161.
Coffee, Soyer's mode of making (3), 42; to roast (1), 42; excellent for three breakfast cups (2), 42.
Cold pudding (1045-1047), 216 ; (1201), 239.

College pudding (1022), 213.
Collops, savoury minced (404), 112.
Conger, boiled (140), 67 ; stewed (141), 67 ; baked (142), 67 ; fried (143), 67 ; soup (268), 90.
Cooling drink for feverish thirst (1818), 333.
Corn, to boil green or maize (865), 188.
Cottage soup (218), 81; baked (219), 81.
Covers and tins, to clean (1830), 344.
Cow heel (384), 109.
Cowslip wine (1735), 323.
Crabs, to choose (173), 72; to dress boiled (174), 72; buttered (175), 72; to stew (176), 72; mock (1443), 576; sailor fashion (1444), 276.
Crabs, to preserve Siberian (1677), 312.
Cranberry tart, to make (931), 199.
Crayfish, potted (905), 194; to boil and serve (177), 72.
Cream, apple (1290), 253 ; apricot (1291), 253 ; superior apricot, iced (1292), 253 ; brulee (1293), 253 ; ground rice (1294), 254 ; stone (1295), 254; velvet (1296), 254; chocolate (1297), 254 ; iced chocolate (1298), 254 ; coffee (1299), 254 ; custard ice (1446), 277; strawberry ice (1447), 277; raspberry ice (1448), 277; lemon ice (1449), 277 ; Vanilla ice (1450), 277; plain (1451), 277 ; noyeau ice (1452), 277; coffee ice (1453), 277 ; tea ice (1454), 278 ; chocolate ice (1455), 278 ; custard pudding (1036), 215 ; boiled (1037), 215; baked (1038), 215; for puddings (1039), 215; tea (1300) 255; marachine (1301) 255 ; lemon (1302), 255 ; lemon, without cream (1303), 255 ; ratafia (1304), 255 ; iced ratafia (1305), 255 ; raspberry in a mould (1306), 255; raspberry, without cream (1307), 256; orange (1308), 256; Seville orange (1309), 256 ; preserved ginger (1310), 256; Bohemian (1311), 256; brandy (1312), 256; Italian (1313), 256; Spanish (1314), 257. Spanish, to ornament preserves (1315), 257 ; burnt (1316), 257 ; imperial (1317), 257 ; Rhenish (1318), 257 ; pistachio (1319), 257; noyeau (1320), 257 ; Chester (1321), 257 ; à la Vanilla (1322), 258; Vanilla or lemon ice (1323). 258; pineapple ice (1324), 258 ; spring (1325), 258; barley (1326), 258 ; German (1327), 258 ; almond (1328), 258 ; sponge cake (1329), 259; à la comtesse (1330), 259 ; Scicilian (1331), 259 ; housewife's (1333), 259 ; fruit

ice (1334). 259 ; Holwell (1335), 259 ; apple cheese and (1336), 260 ; peach ice (1337), 260 ; spinach (1338), 260 ; pudding (1030), 214 ; rich (1031), 214 ; to scald, as in the West of England (1718), 320.
Chantilly basket (1339), 260.
Cochineal, to prepare, to colour red or pink jelly (1340), 260.
Croutons (336), 101.
Crumpets (23), 46 ; (10), 43.
Crusades (949), 202.
Crust, common, for raised pies (713), 164; very rich short (917), 197.
Cucumbers, to stew (820), 181 ; to stuff and stew (821), 181 ; to roast (822), 181 ; to dress (823), 182 ; à la poulette (824), 182 ; to preserve (1667), 310.
Cup from the "Blues" (1749), 325.
Cup puddings (1049), 217.
Curaçoa (1744), 324.
Curd puddings (1027), 214.
Currant, black, jam (1647), 307 ; jelly (1648), 307 ; red, jelly (1649), 307 ; red, jam (1650), 307 ; white, jelly (1651), 307 ; dumplings (1052), 217 ; puddings (974), 206 ; iced, for dessert (1595), 299 ; wine, black (1734), 323.
Curate's pudding (1040), 216.
Currie; a Bengal mutton (699). 162 ; Lord Clive's (700), 162 ; hard egg (692), 161 ; powder (694-693), 161 ; lobster (688), 160 ; prawn (689), 160; soup (226), 82; (239), 85 ; Maylay (683), 160; kebobbed (684), 160 ; dry (685), 160 ; Madras (686), 160.
Custard, with jelly (1364), 265 ; iced, with preserved or dried fruit (1242), 245; orange (1243), 245; lemon (1244), 245; almond (1245), 245 ; cheese (1246), 246; mould (1247), 246 ; plain boiled (1248), 246 ; with cream (1249), 246.

DAMSON PUDDING (1052), 217 ; tart, to make (937), 200 ; to preserve (1610), 301; cheese (1611), 301; cheese, to clear (1612), 301.
Darioles (950), 202; almond (951), 202.
Date pudding (1053), 218.
Devil hot (346), 103.
Devilled biscuits (1426), 274 ; oysters (1425), 274.
Devonshire junket (1265), 249 ; pudding (1054), 218 ; squab pie (724), 166.
Dominoes (1363), 264.
Dripping to clarify beef (703) 163; to make a short crust with (704), 163 ; for children (705), 163 ; crust (706), 163 ; hard, to make plain crust with (707), 163.

Duck, to truss and roast a (545), 138; to roast a (546), 138; stewed (547), 138; cold, stewed with green peas (548), 138; ragout of (549), 138; to truss wild (599), 146; to roast (600), 146; hashed (601), 146; salmi of (602), 146.
Dutch pudding (1055), 218; sauce for fish (289), 94.

E AU DE COLOGNE (1857), 346.
Eel soup (273), 91; spitchcocked (132), 65; stewed (133), 65; baked (134), 65; boiled (135), 65; fried (136), 65; baked, stuffed (137), 66; collared (912), 196.
Egg and artichoke (1438), 276; frothed (1439), 276; balls (330), 100; beaten (1810), 333; wine (1811), 333; flip (1775), 328; sauce, common (277) 92; toast (39), 48; plovers' (34), 47; to boil (27), 46; poached (28) 46; and bacon (29), 47; baked (30), 47; devilled (31), 47; h la bonne femme (32), 47.
Elder wine, very superior (1729), 322.
Endive, stewed, with cream (825), 182.
Epicure's sauce, the (352), 104.
Evergreens. to ice, (1608), 301.
Eve's pudding (1056), 218.

F ADGE, Irish receipt (25), 46.
Fanchonettes (946), 201.
Fennel sauce (278), 92.
Feutillage (915), 197.
Fig pudding (1057), 218.
Figs, to preserve green (1660), 309.
Fish, cold, fish cake of (203). 76; to dress (204), 76; cooked, rissoles of (205), 76; dressed (206), 76; la boubillaise (207), 76; sauces, 91, 92; to fry (59), 52; to broil (60), 52; batter for frying (61), 52.
Floating island, lemon (1369), 265; Vanilla (1370), 265.
Flour, to brown (293), 95.
Flummery (1236), 244; Dutch (1237), 244; French (1238), 245; rice (1239), 245; almond (1240), 245; green melon, in (1241), 245.
Forcemeat, for savoury pies (329), 100; oyster (330), 100; for haddock or carp (331), 100; balls (333), 100.
Fowl, croquettes of cold (673), 158; minced (674), 158; to truss a roast (551), 139; to roast a, or chicken (552), 139; to roast a, family receipt (553), 139; roast with forcemeat (554), 139; to truss broiled (555), 139; to boil, or chickens (556), 139; boiled, and tongue (557), 140; la remonlade (559), 140; to stew a (558), 140; scallops of (560), 140; fricassee of cold roast (561), 140;

minced (562), 140; grilled (563), 140; and ham, potted (890), 192.
French marmalade (281), 93; pie (715), 165.
Fritters, raspberry (1235), 244; batter for (1217), 241; arrowroot (1218), 241; apple (1219), 242; potato (1220), 242; German (1221), 242; royal (1222), 242; Danish (1223), 242; cake (1224), 242; rice, or Portuguese (1225), 243; bread (1226), 243; custard (1227), 243; Spanish (1228), 243, orange (1229), 243; pineapple (1230), 243; strawberry (1231), 243; beetroot or pink-coloured (1232), 244.
Fruit, iced, for dessert or garnish (1593), 298; vols au vent of (940), 200; stewed (1597), 300.
Fun pudding (1058), 218.

G ALETTAS (1514), 286.
Game, to keep from tainting (624), 149.
Garfish (139), 66.
Gateau (1533), 289; de Nourmahl (1534), 289; de riz (1070), 220; de pommes (1365), 265.
Gaufrée (1361), 264; almond (1362), 264.
General satisfaction (1059), 218.
George pudding, a (1061), 219.
German paste (914), 196; pastry (954), 283; pudding (1063), 219; baked (1064), 219; (1065), 219; rich (1066), 219; puffs, with almonds (1067), 220.
Giblet pie (726), 167; stewed duck (550), 138; to stew (544), 137; soup (253). 87.
Ginger beer (1738), 323; bread loaf (1521), 287; honeycomb (1522), 287; cocoa nut or almond (1523), 287; orange (1524), 288; bread nuts (1526), 288; pudding (1062), 219.
Ginger cordial (1764), 326; puffs (1067), 220; snaps (1527), 288; to make wine, superior (1733), 322; pudding (1072), 220; dry (1073), 220; golden (1074), 221.
Gingerette (1763), 326.
Glaze (292), 95; (340), 102; how to use (327), 99.
Gloucester jelly (1793), 333; puddings (1069), 220.
Golden pippins (1673), 311; plovers (609), 147.
Goose, to truss a, for roasting (542), 137; to roast a (543), 137.
Gooseberry fool (1370), 266; green sauce for boiled mackerel (280), 92; pudding (974), 206; red, jam (1613), 301; green, jam (1614), 302; to preserve green whole (1615), 302; green, jelly (1616), 302; preserved as hops (1617), 302; tart, to make (930), 199.

Grapes, to preserve in brandy for winter dessert (1686), 313.
Grates, bright polished (1820), 343.
Graylings, to fry (111), 61.
Gravy, a cheap (294), 95; kidney (295), 95; for hashes (296), 95; jugged (297), 95; for a goose or ducks (298), 96; for a hare or goose (299), 96; to improve the flavour of (315), 98.
Grease, to take off wax candle (1837), 344.
Green caps (1376), 266.
Greengage jam (1687), 313; pudding (1071), 220; to preserve and dry (1624), 303; to brandy (1626), 303.
Green pea garnish (335), 101; soup maigre (255), 88; without meat (256) 88; simple (257) 88; winter, plain for family use (258), 88.
Greens, fregastied (787), 177.
Grouse pie (733), 168; to roast (605-606), 147; to roast white (607), 147; a Scotch recipe for dressing (608), 147.
Gruel of patent groats (1796), 331; (1797), 331.
Guinea fowl, roast larded (619), 148.
Gurnets, baked (201), 76; boiled (202), 76.

H ADDOCK SOUP (272), 91; Finnan (56), 50; to boil (155), 69; fried (156), 69; baked (157), 70; to broil (158-159), 70; to dry (160), 70.
Haggis (444), 119.
Hair, wash for (1840), 344; castor oil, pomade for (1841), 345; another pomade for the (1842), 345; French pomatum (1843), 345; cream cold (1844), 345.
Hake, baked (90), 58; cutlets (91), 58.
Halibut, stewed, head (107), 60; collops (108), 61.
Hallidays (1076), 221.
Ham, to salt a, of twelve pounds (871), 189; to cure (872-873), 189; pickle for Westphalia (874), 189; tongues and beef, Yorkshire fashion (875), 190; to cure, with hot pickle (876), 190; Berkshire way of curing (877), 190; to steam a (500), 129; to boil a (501), 130; to serve a, hot (502), 130; to bake a (503), 130; toast (35), 47; plain boiled and toast (38), 48; to cure, by the American mode (879). 190.
Hannah More's pudding (1077), 221.
Hard dumplings (1199), 239.
Hare, to truss a (582), 143; to roast (583), 143; jugged (584), 143; hashed (585), 144; to roast a leveret (586), 144; potted, a luncheon dish (894), 193. pie (727), 167; soup (259), 87.

Index.   361

Hartshorn jelly (1817), 333.
Hasty puddings, to make (1078), 221; oatmeal (1079), 221.
Herb powder for winter use (1711), 318.
Herbs, season for drying for flavouring (337), 101.
Herrings, red and bloaters (57), 51; potted (896), 193; to pot (897), 193; (194), 75; to boil (195), 75; to bake (196), 75; to smoke (197), 75; fried (198), 75; broiled (199), 75; home salted (200), 75.
Holmby cup (1749), 325.
Horseradish (843), 184; sauce for boiled mutton or roast beef (309). 97; sauce for fish (291), 94.
Hotch potch (228). 82.
Huitres au lit (38), 48.
Hunting nuts (1525), 288.

ICE PUDDINGS (1080), 221; to mould unfrozen dessert (1459). 273; directions for its use (1460). 278.
Indian devil mixture, Admiral Rous's (1423), 274; nabob (1427), 274; puddings, cheap (1081), 221.
Irish stew (442), 113.
Isinglass, to clarify (1341), 260; (1786), 330.
Italian griddle (1561), 293.

JARDINIERE Soup (265), 89
Jaunemange (1250), 246.
Jelly savoury. to put into cold pies (316), 98; the foundation of all (1343) 261; calf's feet, stock for (1244), 261; calf's feet (1345), 261; from cowheel (1346), 261; isinglass (1347), 262; strawberry (1348) 262; lemon (1349), 262; orange (1350), 262; open, with whipped cream (1351), 262; apple, in a mould (1352), 262; clear apple (1353), 262; riband or two coloured (1354), 263; noyeau, with almonds (1355), 263; French (1356), 263; rice (1357), 263; punch (1358), 264; Italian (1359), 264; orange filled with (1360), 264.
Jenny Lind pudding (1083), 222.
Jersey wonders (964), 204.
Jipper's sauce (350), 103.
John Dory, to boil the (69), 54; to bake the (70), 54.
Josephine puddings (1084), 222.
Jumbles (1550), 292; almond (1551), 292.

KEGEREE (40), 48.
Kennet, to prepare, to turn milk (1719), 320.
Kensington pudding. (1092), 223.
Kidney soup (230), 83; to fry beef (405), 112; stewed (406), 112; rissoles of (407). 112: minced (408), 113; hashed plain (409), 113; hashed rich (410), 113; cold, stewed with green peas (411), 113
Kromeskies aux huitres, an entrée (627), 150.

LADY FINGERS (1513), 286.
Lamb, house, steaks brown (637)152; sweetbreads, an entrée (638), 152; roast forequarter of (449), 120; boned quarter of (450), 120; roast target of (451), 120; roast leg of (452), 120; roast shou'der of (453), 120; roast loin of (454), 120 saddle of (455), 120; to broil a breast of (456), 121; breast of, a la Milanaise (457), 121; stewed with peas(458), 121; to prepare the brains of a head for serving under it (459), 121; head and pluck (460), 121: head, liver. and heart (461) 121; fry (462). 122; cutlet and green peas (463), 122; cutlets a la royal (464), 122; chops (465), 122.
Lampreys, to stew, as at Worcester (138), 66; Worcester receipt for potting (898), 193.
Landrail, to truss (615), 148; to roast (616), 148
Lark pie an entrée (730), 167; or sparrow pie (731), 168.
Larks, to roast (617), 148; the Dunstable way (618), 148.
Lavender water (1855), 346.
Leamington pudding (1090), 223.
Leek soup (Scotch receipt), (266), 90.
Leicester pudding (1086), 222.
Lemonade (1739), 323: with citric acid (1740), 324; milk (1741) 324
Lemon dumplings (1087), 222; puddings (1088), 222; plain boiled, suet pudding (1089), 223; flavouring (357), 104; store (1652), 307; to preserve, white (1653), 308; marmalade (1654), 308; turnovers (959), 283; puffs (960), 204; tartlets (961), 204; patties (960), 204.
Lettuce stalks, to preserve (1641), 306.
Lime preserves (1609), 304.
Linen, to bleach (1834), 344.
Lobster patties (737), 169; rissoles of (625), 150: sauce (283), 93; soup (American) (269), 90; to pot (901), 194; to choose (164), 70: to boil (165), 70; to dress a (166), 71; scalloped (167), 71; broiled (an American receipt) (168), 71: buttered (also American) (169), 71; to stew (170), 71; cutlets (171), 71; balls (172), 72.
Loche creme (1085), 222.
Louisa's, aunt, pudding (1091), 223.
Louis Phillipe's pudding (1075), 221.

MAB'S, QUEEN, PUDDING (1093), 223.
Macaroni pudding (1101), 225; baked, with almonds (1102), 225; as usually served (1419), 273; (1420), 273; fish (1421), 273; tembalade (1422), 273; soup (248), 86.
Macaroons, or meringues, to make a pyramid of (1384). 268; trifle, a cake (1385), 268; or Italian (1535), 293.
Mackerel, boiled (154), 69; à la Maitre d'Hotel (155), 69; fillets of, stewed (156), 69; collared (911), 196.
Madeira pudding (1106), 226.
Madonna pudding (1108), 226.
Maids of Honour (1411), 272.
Mareschal, extract of (1853). 346.
Maitre d'Hotel sauce (307-308), 97
Maizena blanc pudding (1186), 237; pudding, baked (1096), 224
Malvern pudding (1097), 224; apple (1099), 224.
Marble, to take stains out of (1821), 343.
Marking ink (1850), 345.
Marlborough pudding (1105), 226.
Marmalade pudding, baked (1095), 224; transparent (1657), 308; grated (1658), 308; with chips (1659) 309.
Marrow pudding (1108), 226.
Meal pudding, boiled (1105). 225.
Melons, to preserve (1679), 312.
Meringues (1393). 269; apple (1394), 269; almond (1395), 269; apple and apricot (1396), 270; rice (1307), 270; tart, to make (944), 201.
Michael Angelo (1103), 225.
Milk and rum (1815), 333.
Mince meat (966), 205; apple (967), 205; lemon (968), 205; (971) 206; Banbury (969), 205; egg (970), 205; pies (945), 201.
Mint sauce (311), 97.
Mock turtle soup (234), 83.
Monmouth pudding (1097). 224.
Montreal pudding (1104), 225.
Moor game or pheasants (893), 92.
Moselle cup (1458), 278.
Muffin pudding, with dried cherries (1094), 224; American (22), 46; potato (1571), 295; to toast (9), 43.
Mulberries, to preserve (1661), 309 · syrup (1770), 327.
Mullett, red, in papers (95), 58; to dress (96), 59; to stew red (97), 59; grey (98), 59.
Mulligatawny soup (236), 84; vegetable (253), 88.
Mushroom ketchup (344), 102; sauce (312), 97; broiled (51). 50; to choose (826), 182; stewed (827), 182; grilled (828), 182; baked (829), 182; to use dried (324), 99.
Mussels, to stew (193), 74.
Mutton, haricot (634), 151; pie (721), 166; pudding (742), 170; soup (230), 83; broth, Scotch (231). 83; to collar a breast of (907), 195; roast haunch of (417), 114; saddle of (418), 114; leg of, roasted (419), 114; roast shoulder of (420), 115; roast loin of (421), 115; to roll a loin of (422), 115; a mode of dress-

362 Index.

ing fillet of (423), 115; to roast a neck of (424), 115; kebbobed (425), 115; boiled leg of (426), 115; to boil a shoulder, with oysters (427), 116; boiled neck of (428), 116; boiled breast of, and caper sauce (429), 116; shoulder of, baked, 116; breast of, grilled (430), 116; stewed loin of (431), 116; to stew a neck of (432), 117; breast of, and green peas (433), 117; cutlets, with tomato sauce (434), 117; cutlets (435-436), 117; cutlets, à la Maintenon (437), 118; chops, broiled (438), 118; chops, to stew (439), 118; haricot of (440), 118; minced (441), 118; hashed (443), 119.

NASTURTIUMS used as capers (351), 104.
Neapolitan pudding, boiled (1115), 227; pastry (1398), 270.
Neats' tongues, potted (884), 191; to cure (881), 190.
Nectarines, to preserve (1633), 304; to candy (1634), 304.
Nesselrode (1445), 277.
Newcastle pudding (1113), 226.
Newmarket pudding (1112), 226.
Norfolk dumplings (1114), 227.
Normandy pippins (1674), 311.
Northumberland pudding (1110), 226.
Nottingham pudding (1111), 226.
Nougat (924), 198.
Noyeau (1761), 326; honey (1762), 326.

OATMEAL Porridge (8), 43. Odor delectabilia (1856), 346
Omelet (41), 48; ham or tongue (42), 48; soufflé, without vanilla (1284), 252; soufflé, in a mould (1285), 252; glacé (1286), 252; with sweetmeats (1287), 252; sweet (1288), 253; soufflé (1289), 253.
Omnibus pudding (1121), 227.
Onion, brown, soup (263), 89; common, sauce (306), 97; baked Spanish (811), 180; to stew, brown (812), 180; à la creme (813), 180; to stuff (814), 180; for garnishing (333), 101.
Orange chips (1603), 301; jelly, for invalids (1815), 333; pudding, (1116), 228; small (1117), 227; and batter (1118), 227; wafers (1600), 300; wine (1736), 323; compote of (1598), 300; to ice (1594), 298; to prepare, for dessert (1592), 298; to preserve, whole (1655), 308; marmalade (1656), 308.
Ormers, pickled (208), 77.
Ornamental frosting (1477), 281.
Ox-cheek cheese (389), 110.
Oxford pudding (1120), 227; sausages (520), 132; without skins (521), 132.
Ox-head, potted (891), 192; soup (237), 84; tail soup (238), 84; heart, roasted (658), 155; tails,

stewed (631), 151; haricot of (632), 151; tongue (386), 109; potted (885), 191.
Oyster fritters, American recipe (626), 150; loaves, American (53), 50; patties (736), 169; salsify of vegetable (832), 183; sauce (284), 93; for a large party (285), 93; soup (270), 90, for keeping and opening (178), 72; to feed (179), 73; stewed (180), 73; scalloped (181), 73; French scalloped (182), 73; to stew, plain (183), 73; fried, to garnish without ears (184), 73; fritters (185), 73; in marinade (186), 73.

PALESTINE SOUP (264),89.
Palm-tree pudding (1136),230
Pancake cream (1202), 239; French (1203), 240; French, with preserves (1204), 240; ground rice (1205), 240; ginger (1208), 240; Prussian (1209), 240; Irish (1210), 240; New England (1211), 241; with marmalade (1212), 241; American, plain (1213), 241; without lard or butter (1214), 241; common (1215), 241; snow (1216), 241.
Paper-hangings, to clean (1825), 343.
Parsley, crisped (338), 101; sauce (279), 92; to keep for winter use (1712), 318.
Parsnips, boiled (805), 179; fried (806), 179; fritters (807), 179; boiled and browned, under roast beef (808), 180; mashed (809), 180; stewed (810), 180.
Partridge, to truss a (574), 142; to roast a (575), 142; salmi of (576), 142; to pot (898), 192.
Paste for custards (918), 197; light, for tartlets (919), 197; croquante (920), 197; frangipane (921), 197; brioche (922), 197; pyramids of (953), 203; Pastry, to ice or, glaze (925), 198; icing, another way (926), 198; for currant or raspberry tart, to make (927), 198.
Pate aux choux (923), 198.
Peach preserves (1635), 305 to preserve (1636), 305; marmalade (1637), 305.
Peahen, to truss a (603), 146; larded and glazed (604), 146.
Pears, to bake (1606), 301; stewed (1607), 301; to preserve (1668), 310; to preserve Jargonelle (1669), 310.
Peas to boil, green (762), 173; pudding (1137), 230; purée of green, for lamb cutlets (847), 185; to stew (763), 173; stewed, with mint and lettuces (764), 173.
Pepper pot (250), 87.
Perch, to boil (144), 68; fried (145), 68; fish scallop (146), 68; to fry, plain (147), 68.
Pheasant, to truss a (577), 143;

roasted (578), 143; broiled (579), 143; hashed (580), 143; boiled (581), 143.
Pickle, a, for hams, beef, or pork (868), 188; Indian (1690), 314; piccalilly (1691), 314; melon mangoes (1692), 314; cucumber mangoes (1693), 315; cucumber (1694), 315; plums, like olive (1695), 315; peach (1696), 315; walnut, black (1697), 316; mushroom (1698), 316; brown mushroom (1699), 316; radish pod (1700), 316; French bean (1701), 316; cauliflower (1702), 317; beetroot (1703), 317; onion (1704), 317; capsicum (1705), 317; gherkin (1706), 317; tomato (1707), 317; barberry (1708-1709), 317; red cabbage (1710), 318.
Pickling, rules to be observed in (1688), 313.
Pigeon compote (677), 159; to fricassee a (678), 159; pie, a plain (740), 168; to truss (564), 141; to roast (565), 141; stuffed (566), 141; jugged, a simple recipe for (567), 141; to stew (680), 159.
Pie, à la Don Pedro (716), 165.
Pigs' liver (670), 157; fry (671), 157; kidneys (43), 49; feet and ears (44-45), 49; feet, soused (46), 49; tongues (512), 131; pettitoes (513), 131; head, to roast a (514), 131; head, boiled (515), 131; cheek (516), 131; Soyer's method of dressing a cheek (517), 131.
Pike, potted (899), 194; to boil (148), 68; to bake (149), 68; stewed (150),68; roasted (151),69
Pillau (697), 162.
Pineapple preserve (1680), 312; to preserve, without cooking (1681), 312; in brandy (1682),313
Pippins, frosted (1377), 266.
Pish pash (698), 162.
Plaice, the filletted (121), 63; to boil (122), 63; to fry (123), 63.
Plain pudding, a (1122), 228.
Plate, to clean (1831), 344.
Plum pudding, rich, without flour (1129), 229; cottage (1130), 229; plain (1131-1132), 229; a good plain, without eggs (1133), 229; pudding, Christmas (1127), 228.
Plums, stewed, French (1546), 300; to preserve (1638), 305; to preserve, for dessert (1639), 305
Polka pudding (1123-1124), 228.
Poor man's soup (220), 81.
Porcupine pudding (1138), 230.
Pork, to scald a sucking pig (488), 128; to make sage and onion stuffing for roast (489), 128; to roast (490), 128; to bake (491), 128; chine of, roasted (492), 128; to boil a chine of (493), 129; how to stuff a chine of (494), 129; to roast a leg of

(495), 189; to roast a leg of, the old-fashioned way, with stuffing (496), 129; to roast a loin of (497), 129; to roast a spare-rib of (498), 129; griskin (499), 129; sausages (519), 132; cutlets, broiled (668), 157; fried (669), 157; pickled (510), 131; a hand of (511), 131; to boil a leg of (504), 130; to pickle (866-867), 188; (880), 190.
Porter cup (1755), 325.
Portland's, Duke of, pudding (1134), 229.
Portugal pudding (1127), 228.
Portuguese tart, to make (939), 200
Pot au feu (221), 81.
Potato pasty (717), 165; pie (718), 165; purée of (846), 185; to prepare for garnishing (439), 102; to steam (745), 171; to boil (746), 171; to boil, with their skins on (747), 171; to mash (748), 171; to boil new (749), 171; baked (750), 171; fried (751), 171; ribbons (752), 171; croquettes (753), 172; to broil (754), 172; à la Maitre d'Hotel (755) 172; Kolcannon, as dressed in Ireland (756), 172; puffs (757), 172; to brown, under meat (758), 172; cones or loaves (759), 172; rolled, with sweet sauce (760), 172; with Parmesan cheese (761), 173; pudding (1162), 234.
Prawns, to boil and serve (190), 74
Preparation liquor (1851), 345.
Preserved ginger pudding (1060), 219.
Pressed beef (390), 110.
Prime pudding (1135), 230.
Puddings, black (527), 133; white (528), 133; black, to broil (58), 51
Puff paste, a light (708), 164; common (709), 164; benton (710), 164; very good (711), 164; a light (916), 197.
Puffs (944), 201.
Pumpkin pudding (1126), 228; preserved (1643), 306.
Punch that will keep for any length of time (1745), 324; whisky (1746), 324; to make George IV.'s, milk (1747), 325.

Q UAIL, to truss a (610), 147; to roast a (611, 612), 147.
Quaking pudding (1139), 230.
Quince pudding (1141), 231; to preserve whole (1683), 313; marmalade (1684), 313; cheese (1685), 313.
Queen's pudding (1140), 230.

R ABBITS, to fricassee, white (594), 145; to fricassee, brown (595), 145; pie, a plain (728), 167; to pot (883), 191; pudding (743), 170; brown, soup (251), 87; to truss roast (587), 144; roast (588, 589), 144; ragout of (590), 144; to truss boiled (591), 145; boiled (593), 145; to blanch rabbits, fowls, &c., (592), 145.
Radishes (844), 184.
Raisin pudding, boiled (1157), 233; economical (1158), 233; baked (1159), 233; wine (1730), 322.
Ramskins, Dutch (1435), 275; with ale (1436), 275; bread (1437), 275.
Rusk, egg (1570), 295.
Raspberry vinegar (1768), 326; jam (1630), 303; jelly (1623), 303
Reading sauce (349), 103.
Reindeer tongue, to boil (388) 110
Rhubarb marmalade (1627), 304; and orange preserve (1628), 304; pudding boiled (1119), 227; tart, to make (932), 199.
Riband wafers (1558), 293.
Rice, to boil, for currie (696), 161; croquettes of (1399), 270; and pears (1378), 267; pudding, plain (1142), 231; and apple (1143), 231; plain boiled, for children (1144), 231; without eggs (1145), 231; with preserve (1146), 231; small (1147), 231; meringue (1148), 232; iced (1149), 232; lemon (1150), 232; croquettes of (1151), 232; snow balls (1372), 266; whole, in a mould (1261), 248.
Roseberry pudding (1152), 233.
Ratafia pudding (1153), 232; boiled (1154), 233; plain (1155), 233; very rich (1156), 233.
Rolls, iced (1563), 294; Cheshire (1564), 294; French (19), 45.
Roly-poly pudding, jam (1082), 222.
Rook pie (734), 168.
Ruffs and Reeves, to roast (620), 148.
Rumpsteak and oyster pie (720) 165.

S AGE AND ONION (317), 100.
Sago gruel (1813), 333; pudding boiled (1162), 254; baked (1163), 234.
Salad mixture (851) (852), 185; another dressing (853), 186; Italian sauce for (854), 186; sauce (855), 186; Bohemia (856), 186; chicken (857), 186; of chicken and celery (858), 186; endive as a winter (859), 187; to make a, ascribed to the Rev. Sydney Smith (860). 187; lobster (861-863), 187, 188; Canadian (864), 188.
Salmagundy (1426), 274.
Salmon, Mayonnaise (1450), 276; boiled (71), 55; middle slice of (72), 55; pudding (73), 55; broiled (74), 55; grilled, cutlets (75), 55; fillets of (76), 55; fried (77), 55; cold, 55; home made pickled (78), 56; pie (714). 164; kippered for breakfast (54), 50; toasted (55), 50; grilled kippered (1432), 275.

Sandwiches, chicken and ham (1428), 274; plain (1429), 275.
Sauce for cabinet or souffle puddings (319), 98; for polka pudding (322), 99; tartare (314), 98; for any freshwater fish (289), 94.
Sausages, 51; to fry (526), 133; meat (523), 133.
Saveloys (525), 132.
Scallop fish, or St. James's cockle (187), 74; scalloped (188), 74; baked (189), 74.
Scotch collops, white (650), 154; brown (651), 154.
Souffle pudding (1175), 235; vanilla (1176), 235; baked (1177), 236; plain (1178), 236; ginger (1179), 236; cream (1180), 236.
Seakale (828), 183; stewed (829), 183.
Semolina pudding (1164), 234.
Sheep's kidneys (49-50), 50; kidney a la Tartar (639), 152; a la brochette (640), 152; tongue stewed (636), 152; head (445), 119; trotters (446-448), 119, 120.
Sherbert cream (1758), 326; lemon 1759), 326; strawberry (1760), 326.
Sherry cobler (1754), 325; excellent English (1728), 322.
Shrimp sauce (287), 93.
Shrub (1742), 324; brandy or rum (1743), 324.
Silk or cloth, to take stains out of (1835), 344; to take grease out of (1836), 344; silk washing, or coloured prints, to wash (1838), 344; to clean an old, dress (1839), 344.
Silver jelly (1793) 331.
Skates, to crimp (161), 70; to boil crimped (162), 70; to fry (163), 70.
Sledmere gingerbread (1518), 287.
Smelts, to fry (124) 64; the French way (125), 64; potted (903), 194.
Snipes, ragout of (679), 159.
Snow (1374), 266; eggs (1375), 266.
Snowball for children (1160), 233.
Snowdon pudding (1168), 234; sauce for (1169), 235.
Soap, a winter, for chapped or rough hands (1845), 345.
Sole, curried (690), 161; filleted (127), 64; cutlets of (128), 64; boiled (129), 64; fried (130), 64; fillets de, en gratin (131), 64
Souffle, Milan (1266), 249; York (1267), 249; omelet (1268), 249; apple (1269), 249; apple, in paste (1270), 250; orange (1271), 250; lemon (1272), 250; strawberry (1273), 250; apricot or strawberry (1274), 250; French (1275), 250; punch (1276), 251. rice (1277), 251; in cases (1278) 251; a plain (1279), 251; omelet aux comfitures (1280), 251; friar's (1281), 251; cream (1282), 252, (1283), 252.
Soups, how to make, 77; to

364   Index.

colour. 77 ; summary of directions for making, 78 ; stock, 78 ; general stock pot (208), 79 ; cheap stock (209), 79; bone stock for (210), 79 ; browning for (212), 79 ; to clarify (213), 80 ; best manner of making clear (226), 82 ; nourishing, for invalids (1794), 331 ; stock for white or brown fish (267), 90 ; Liebig (248), 86; et bouilli (215), 80 ; plain (216), 80 ; the young fisherman's. (271), 91 ; flavouring to make, taste like turtle (235), 84 ; cheap white (241), 85 ; an excellent white (242), 85 ; in haste (244). 86 ; baked (245), 86 ; vegetable (253) 87 ; very cheap (217), 80.
Soupon, or corn meal pudding (1203), 239.
Spanish pudding (1167), 234 ; puffs (952), 202.
Spatchcock, English fashion (681). 159 ; Indian mode and sea fashion (682), 159.
Spinach, to boil (788), 177 ; a la creme (789), 177.
Spongecake (1478), 281 ; cocoanut (1479). 281 ; pudding, cheap (1171), 235 ; 1172, 235 ; baked (1173), 235 ; boiled (1174), 235.
Sponge, orange (1391), 269 ; lemon (1392), 269.
Sprats (126), 64 ; preserved, like anchovies (913), 196.
Sprouts or young greens, to boil (784), 176.
Steak, broiled (395), 111 ; an Indian mode of dressing (396), 111 ; rump, fried (397), 111 ; with onions (398), 111 ; stewed in a plain way (399), 111 ; and oyster stewed (400), 112 ; broiled with oyster sauce (401), 112.
Steel, to take rust out of (1822), 343
Strasburgh potted meat (887), 191
Strawberry acid for jelly (1342), 261 ; and crumb pudding (1166), 234 ; to preserve whole (1618), 302 ; jam (1619). 302 ; jelly (1620), 302 ; stewed for tarts (1621), 303.
Sturgeon, to roast (103), 60 ; cutlets (104), 61 ; Russian sauce for (105), 60 ; stewed (106), 60.
Suet and milk (1814), 333 ; pudding (744), 170 ; pudding, plain (1181), 236 ; crust for puddings (712), 164.
Sugar, preparation of, (1461), 279 ; to boil to caramel (1468), 280 ; for compotes (1460), 280 ; to colour, red (1470), 280 ; clarified, or syrup (1471), 280 ; spun (1472), 280 ; to clarify, for ices (1456), 278.
Swansea pudding (1166), 234.
Sweetbreads curried (687), 160 ; rissoles of (645), 153 ; stewed, an American receipt (655), 155; roast (656), 155.

Swiss cream (1386), 268 ; gooseberry (1387), 268 ; apple (1388), 268 ; to make a rich (1389), 268; pudding, a plain (1170). 235
Syllabub, London (1262), 248 ; Somerset (1263), 248 ; whipped (1264), 248.

TABLE POLISH, (1828), 343; another kind of (1829), 344.
Tapioca pudding (1182), 236 ; plain (1183), 237.
Tartlets (955), 203 ; orange (956), 203 ; green apricots (957), 203 ; Paganini (958), 203.
Teacake pudding (1186), 237 ; or loaves (20), 46 ; tea cakes (1562), 294.
Teal, to truss (621), 149 ; to roast (622), 149.
Tench, fried (118). 62 ; to stew, brown (119). 63 ; sur le gril, aux fines herbes (120), 63.
Thatched pudding (1085), 237.
Tipsy cake (1390), 269
Toad in a hole (641, 642), 152 ; of cold meat (643), 153.
Tomato sauce, No. 1 (313), 97.
Tomatoes preserved (1675), 311 ; to candy (1676), 311 ; stewed (833), 183 ; baked (834), 183 ; scalloped (835), 183.
Tongue, to roast a fresh (387), 110 ; to pickle (415), 114.
Tonic drink (1806), 332.
Toothache, Cartwright's prescription for (1848). 345.
Tooth powder (1846), 345.
Transparent pudding (1185), 237.
Tripe (412), 113; roasted (413), 114
Trout, boiled (100). 59 ; to fry (101), 59 ; to broil (102), 59.
Truffles, to boil, green (836), 183; stewed (837), 184 ; morels, green, stewed (838), 184 ; to prepare, au naturel (337). 101.
Turbot, boiled (62), 53 ; twicelaid (63), 53 ; fillets of (64), 53 ; to dress a very small (65), 53 ; cold (66), 54.
Turkey, roast (534), 135 ; with chesnuts (535), 136 ; boiled (536), 136 ; stewed, with celery (537), 136 ; hashed (538), 136 ; poults (539), 137 ; to broil the leg of a (540), 137 ; pulled (541), 138
Turnips, boiled (790), 177 ; in white sauce (791), 177 ; purée of (845), 184.

VEAL and HAM PATTIES (738), 169 ; moulded (739), 169 ; and ham pie (722), 166 ; and potato rissoles (646), 153 ; rissoles of (647), 153 ; minced (648), 153 ; collops (652), 154 ; ragout of cold (653), 155 ; a fricandelle (654), 155 ; haricot of (659). 156 ; marble (895), 193 ; olives, an entrée (665), 156 ; with oysters (666), 156 ; cutlets, an entrée (667), 157 ; roast loin of (477), 125 ; roast loin of,

stuffed (478), 125 ; to roast a breast of (479), 126 ; stewed knuckle of, and rice (480), 126 ; knuckle of, boiled (481), 126; stewed, and green peas (482), 126 ; cutlets (483). 126 ; a savoury dish of, baked (484), 126; cold (485), 127; scallops of (486), 127 ; to collar a breast of (908), 195 ; to roast a fillet of (466), 123 ; fricandeau of (467), 123 ; fricandeaux of (468). 123.
Vegetables, a list of, and their season for pickling (1689), 314 ; marrow preserve (1642). 306; boiled (800). 179 ; stewed (801), 179 ; fried (802-803), 179 ; rissoles (804), 179 ; soup (:54), 89.
Venice pudding, ice (1187), 237.
Venison, haunch of (529), 134; neck of (530), 34, to hash (531), 134 ; to broil, steaks (532), 134; cutlets of (533), 135 ; pasty (729), 167 ; to pot (889), 192.
Verbena, essence of (1852) 345.
Vermicelli soup (246), 86 ; pudding (1190), 238.
Victoria pudding, in a mould (1188), 237.
Vinegar. Cayenne (358), 104 ; hot (345), 102 ; lemon (347), 103 ; walnut, for sauce (354). 104 ; horseradish (355), 104 ; Chili (356 , 104 ; eschalot (359), 104.
Vol-au-vent, a (735), 169.
Volunteer pudding (1189), 238.

WAFER Pudding (1193), 238.
Walnut ketchup (343) 102.
Warwickshire pudding (1076) 221
Warts, to cure (1847). 343.
Water cakes (21), 46 ; Sir Tatton Sykes's (26), 46 ; souchy (67), 54
Watkin's pudding (1194), 238.
Welsh rabbit (1441), 276.
Whitebait (110), 61.
White sauce (300), 96 ; for fowls (309), 97.
Whiting, fried (92), 58 ; filletted (93), 58 ; to boil (94), 58.
Widgeons, to roast (623), 149.
Wigs, to make light (1559), 293.
Windows, to remove paint stains from, (1827), 343.
Windsor pudding (1191), 238.
Wine, egg (1774), 327 ; mulled (1771), 327 ; whey (1772), 327 ; white, sauce (321) 99.
Wood, for removing paint from (1824), 343.
Woodcocks, snipes, and wheatears, to truss (596), 145 ; to cook (597-598), 145-146.
Wrexham pudding (1192), 238 ; soup (243), 86.
Wyvern puddings (1014), 212.

YEAST DUMPLINGS (1195) 238 ; or with homemade dough (1198), 239 ; how to make your own (11), 44.
Yorkshire pork pie, small raised (723), 166 ; pudding (1200), 239.

BILLING AND SONS, PRINTERS, GUILDFORD, SURREY.

Frederick Warne & Co., Publishers.

𝔚arne's 3s. 6d. Series of Gift-Books.

WITH ORIGINAL ILLUSTRATIONS.

THE WOODLEIGH STORIES; or, Tales for Sunday Reading. By Rev. H. C. ADAMS, M.A., Author of "The Encombe Stories."
TALES OF OLD OCEAN. By Lieutenant C. R. LOW.
HEROISM AND ADVENTURE. A Book for Boys. Selected and Edited by Mrs. VALENTINE.
THE HENRYS:—FRANCONIA STORIES.
THE SCHOOL-BOY BARONET. By the Hon. Mrs. R. J. GREENE.
THE ENCOMBE STORIES; or, Tales for Sunday Reading. By the Rev. H. C. ADAMS.
STORIES OF OLD. BIBLE NARRATIVES—Old and New Testament. By CAROLINE HADLEY.
ZENOBIA, QUEEN OF PALMYRA. By Rev. WILLIAM. WARE.
JULIAN; or, Scenes in Judea. Ditto.
THE JUVENILE GIFT-BOOK.
THE BIRTHDAY PRESENT.
RALPH LUTTREL'S FORTUNES. By H. ST. JOHN CORBET.
THE MILESTONES OF LIFE. By the Rev. A. F. THOMPSON.

By CATHERINE D. BELL (COUSIN KATE).

In small crown 8vo, with Original Illustrations, cloth, New Style, gilt.

HOPE CAMPBELL; or, Know Thyself.
HORACE AND MAY; or, Unconscious Influence.
ELLA AND MARIAN; or, Rest and Unrest.
HOME SUNSHINE; or, The Gordons.
KENNETH AND HUGH; or, Self-Mastery.
ROSA'S WISH; and How She Attained It.
MARGARET CECIL; or, I Can, because I Ought.
THE GRAHAMS; or, Home Life.
AUNT AILIE; or, Patience and its Reward.

Uniform with the above.

SYLVIA AND JANET; or, Too Quickly Judged. By A. C. D.
BAPTISTA. By the Author of "Eildon Manor," &c., &c.

Bedford Street, Covent Garden.

Frederick Warne & Co., Publishers.

WARNE'S
2s. 6d. "Golden Links" Series of Gift-Books.

Large fcap. 8vo, with Original Illustrations, cloth gilt.

MADELEINE'S TRIAL; and other Stories. By MADAME PRESSENSE.
A LIFE'S VOYAGE; or, With the Tide. By SIDNEY DARYL.
HESTER'S FORTUNE; or, Pride and Humility.
CAMPANELLA; or, The Teachings of Life. By Mrs. MERCIER.
PICCIOLA; or, The Prison Flower. By X. B. SAINTINE.
CHRISTABEL HOPE; or, The Beginnings of Life. By Mrs. MERCIER.
SYDNEY STUART; or, Love Seeketh Not Her Own. By C. D. BELL.
TALES FOR BOYS AND GIRLS. } Coloured
HOME RECREATIONS AND FOREIGN TRAVEL. } Plates.
TWO YEARS OF SCHOOL LIFE. By Madame DE PRESSENSE.
    Edited by the Author of "The Heir of Redclyffe."
EILDON MANOR: A Tale for Girls.
MARIAN AND HER PUPILS. By CHARLOTTE LANKESTER.
LILY GORDON, the Young Housekeeper. By C. D. BELL
THE HUGUENOT FAMILY; or, Help in Time of Need.
LAURA AND LUCY: A Tale for Girls. By CHARLOTTE ADAMS.
FIRST STEPS IN THE BETTER PATH. By AUNT FRIENDLY.
GOLDEN LINKS. By AUNT FRIENDLY.
FILLING UP THE CHINKS. By Hon. Mrs. GREENE.
WEARYFOOT COMMON. By LEITCH RITCHIE.
MY DOG MATCH. By HOLME LEE.

FAIRY TALES BY HOLME LEE.
LEGENDS FROM FAIRYLAND.
TUFLONGBO'S LIFE AND ADVENTURES, and How his Shoes got Worn Out.
TUFLONGBO AND LITTLE CONTENT: Their Wonderful Adventure in the Enchanted Forest.

Warne's 2s. 6d. "Daring Deeds" Library.

With Original Illustrations, Col. or Plain, Fcap. 8vo, gilt, New Style.

WARS OF THE ROSES. By J. G. EDGAR.
SEA FIGHTS, FROM SLUYS TO NAVARINO.
LAND BATTLES, FROM HASTINGS TO INKERMAN.
DARING DEEDS OF ADVENTURE. By J. S. BORLASE.
TRUE STORIES OF BRAVE DEEDS. Edited by Rev. G. T. HOARE.

WALTER'S ESCAPE; OR, THE CAPTURE OF BREDA. By DE LIEFDE.
THE BOY'S BOOK OF HEROES. By HELENA PEAKE.
LIFE OF NAPOLEON BUONAPARTE; A Soldier—A Ruler—A Prisoner of State. By H. BOYLE LEE.

Bedford Street, Covent Garden.

Frederick Warne & Co., Publishers,

COMPENDIUMS OF ENGLISH LITERATURE.

In Four Vols., each Volume Complete in itself, with Index, crown 8vo, price 5s. each, cloth gilt, with Steel Illustrations.

HALF-HOURS WITH THE BEST AUTHORS.

Remodelled by its Original Editor, CHARLES KNIGHT, with Selections from Authors added whose works have placed them amongst the "Best Authors" since the publication of the First Edition.

⁂ This book contains 320 Extracts of the best efforts of our great Standard Authors, wheth r they be Poets or Historians, Essayists or Divines, Travellers or Philosophers, arranged so as to form half an hour's reading for every day of the year. The student finds a taste of every quality, and a specimen of every style. Should he grow weary of one author, he can turn to another; and if inclined to be critical, he can weigh the merits of one writer against those of his fellow. It gives us a glimpse of the celebrities assembled within its portals. At a glance the student can obtain some idea of the subject. *Such books are the true foundations of that knowledge which renders men celebrated and famous.*

Ditto, THE LIBRARY EDITION, 4 vols., Complete Index, price 21s.; or half calf, 35s.

In Two Vols., demy 8vo, price 10s., cloth; 12s. with gilt edges; or half-calf extra, 17s.

THE PEOPLE'S EDITION OF
HALF-HOURS WITH THE BEST AUTHORS.

Selected and Edited by CHARLES KNIGHT. With 16 Steel Portraits.

In this Edition the Biographies are revised to 1866, the Pagination of the Volumes completed, and the Serial Nature of the Original Work entirely done away with; it now forms a Handsome Library Book.

In One Vol., demy 8vo, cloth, 5s.; with gilt edges, 6s.; or half-calf extra, 8s. 6d.

HALF-HOURS of ENGLISH HISTORY.

Selected and Arranged by CHARLES KNIGHT.

A Companion Volume to the " Half-Hours with the Best Authors."

Contains the Choicest Historical Extracts from upwards of Fifty Standard Authors, including Burke, Palgrave, Guizot, Sheridan Knowles, Thierry, H. Taylor, Rev. James White, Charles Knight, G. L. Craik, Landor, Hume, Keats, Hallam, Southey, Shakspeare, Froissart, Sir Walter Scott Hall, Barante, Lord Bacon, Cavendish, Bishop Burnet, Rev. H. H. Milman, Wordsworth, Lord Macaulay; with a General Index.

The articles are chiefly selected so as to afford a succession of graphic parts of English History, chronologically arranged, from the consideration that the portions of history upon which general readers delight to dwell are those which tell some story which is complete in itself, or furnish some illustration which has a separate as well as a general interest.

Bedford Street, Strand.

Frederick Warne and Co., Publishers,

A NEW AND ORIGINAL NOVEL

By BRET HARTE.

In 3 vols., crown 8vo, price £1 11s. 6d., cloth,

GABRIEL CONROY.

BY BRET HARTE.

"'Gabriel Conroy' is undoubtedly destined to take rank among Bret Harte's masterpieces."—*Lloyd's News.*

WARNE'S USEFUL BOOKS.—NEW VOLUME.

Price One Shilling. Picture Cover.

MODERN SPIRITUALISM

WITH AN

EXPOSURE OF THE HAND OF THE SO-CALLED SPIRIT MEDIA.

By JOHN NEVIL MASKELYNE

(OF MASKELYNE AND COOKE, EGYPTIAN HALL, LONDON).

Bedford Street, Strand.

Frederick Warne & Co., Publishers,

In large crown 8vo, price 7s. 6d., elegantly and strongly bound, 736 pp.;
or half morocco, 10s. 6d.

WARNE'S MODEL COOKERY
AND HOUSEKEEPING BOOK:
Containing Complete Instructions in Household Management,
AND RECEIPTS FOR

BREAKFAST DISHES.
BREAD, BISCUITS, &c.
FISH AND SOUP.
SAUCES AND GRAVIES.
BEEF, MUTTON.
LAMB, VENISON.
VEAL, PORK.
POULTRY AND GAME.
MADE DISHES, AND ENTREES.
MEAT AND FISH PIES, &c.
VEGETABLES.
POTTING AND COLLARING.

PASTRY AND PUDDINGS.
CREAMS AND JELLIES.
CUSTARDS, ICES, AND CAKES.
PRESERVES AND PICKLES.
SOUFFLES AND OMELETS.
WINES, DRINKS, AND ALE.
DESSERTS.
BUTTER AND CHEESE.
RELISHES.
COOKERY FOR THE SICK.
BILLS OF FARE.
DUTIES OF SERVANTS.

Compiled and Edited by MARY JEWRY.

With 3,000 Receipts, numerous Woodcuts, and Original Illustrations, printed in Colours by KRONHEIM, embodying nearly Two Hundred distinct Subjects.

A COMPANION VOLUME TO WARNE'S MODEL COOKERY BOOK.

In large crown 8vo, price 7s. 6d., elegantly and strongly bound, 736 pp.;
or half morocco, 10s. 6d.

THE MODERN HOUSEHOLDER.
A Manual of Domestic Economy
IN ALL ITS BRANCHES.

COMPILED AND EDITED BY ROSS MURRAY;
Assisted by a Committee of Ladies.

The Medical Portion by a Member of the Royal College of Surgeons.

With 16 pages of Original Illustrations, printed in Colours by
KRONHEIM, and numerous Woodcuts.

Bedford Street, Strand.

Frederick Warne & Co., Publishers,

POPULAR COOKERY BOOKS.

In crown 8vo, price 2s. 6d., cloth gilt.

Warne's Every Day Cookery Book. With nearly 2,000 Receipts, and Coloured Illustrations by KRONHEIM. 3s. 6d. Edition, with Additional Coloured Illustrations, half-bound, gilt lettering.

In large crown 8vo, price 1s., cloth boards; or half-bound, gilt lettering, 1s. 6d.

Warne's Model Cookery and Housekeeping Book. Eight Hundred Receipts, and Coloured Illustrations of Fifty Dishes.

In square 16mo, price 2d. cloth cover, 64 pp.

Warne's Cookery Book for the Million. With upwards of 200 Useful and Practical Receipts.

Ditto, One Penny Edition, sewed.

In royal 48mo, price 1s. cloth, gilt edges.

My Market Table. Showing the Value of any Article, at per Pound and Ounce, from Sixpence to Eighteenpence. *Invaluable to all Housekeepers who appreciate economical expenditure.*

In large crown 8vo, price 2s. 6d., cloth gilt.

Best of Everything. By the Author of "Enquire Within." Containing 1,800 Useful Articles on how to obtain "The Best of Everything," with a Special Calendar for the Cook and Gardener for each Month.

WARNE'S ILLUSTRATED BIJOU BOOKS.

In 48mo, price Sixpence each, cloth, gilt edges.

VENTRILOQUISM MADE EASY.
FUN AND FLIRTATION, FORFEITS.
ETIQUETTE FOR LADIES.
ETIQUETTE FOR GENTLEMEN.
THE BALL-ROOM GUIDE.
ETIQUETTE OF THE TOILET.
LANGUAGE OF FLOWERS.
ARCHERY. By J. B. HANCOCK.
BILLIARDS (THE A B C OF).
SWIMMING (THE A B C OF).
ELEMENTARY GYMNASTICS.
CRICKET. By Rev. J. G. WOOD.
CROQUET. By Rev. J. G. WOOD.
COURTSHIP AND MARRIAGE.

CHESS. By F. HARDY.
BIJOU LETTER WRITER.
CRIBBAGE AND DOMINOES.
DINNER-TABLE ETIQUETTE.
PARLOUR MAGIC. By F. HARDY.
DRAUGHTS AND BACKGAMMON.
WHIST. With Illustrations.
PEDESTRIANISM, HEALTH, TRAINING, &c.
LA CROSSE. By M. H. ROBINSON.
BESIQUE. (A COMPLETE GUIDE.)
BEAUTY: What it is, and How to Retain it.
LONDON IN MINIATURE.

WARNE'S BIJOU BOOKS are handy for the waistcoat pocket, neat in style, well illustrated and compiled by Competent Authors.

Bedford Street, Strand.

Frederick Warne and Co., Publishers,

WARNE'S STAR SERIES.

PUBLISHERS' PREFACE.

In this Series, from time to time will be issued a very popular edition of well-known Books, many of them copyright, and published at prices, united with style and completeness, hitherto unequalled.

ONE SHILLING VOLUMES,
STIFF PICTURE WRAPPERS.

1 **Daisy.**
 ELIZABETH WETHERELL.
2 **Daisy in the Field.**
 ELIZABETH WETHERELL.
3 **Nettie's Mission.**
 ALICE GRAY.
4 **Stepping Heavenward.**
 E. PRENTISS.
5 **Willow Brook.**
 ELIZABETH WETHERELL.
6 **Sceptres and Crowns, and the Flag of Truce.**
 ELIZABETH WETHERELL.
7 **Dunallan.**
 GRACE KENNEDY.
8 **Father Clement.**
 GRACE KENNEDY.
14 **From Jest to Earnest.**
 REV. E. P. ROE.
15 **Mary Elliot.**
 CATHERINE D. BELL.

16 **Sydney Stuart.**
 CATHERINE D. BELL.
17 **Picciola.**
 X. B. SAINTINE.
18 **Hope Campbell.**
 CATHERINE D. BELL.
19 **Horace and May.**
 CATHERINE D. BELL.
20 **Ella and Marion.**
 CATHERINE D. BELL.
21 **Kenneth and Hugh.**
 CATHERINE D. BELL.
22 **Rosa's Wish.**
 CATHERINE D. BELL.
23 **Margaret Cecil.**
 CATHERINE D. BELL.
24 **The Grahams.**
 CATHERINE D. BELL.
25 **Home Sunshine.**
 CATHERINE D. BELL.

EIGHTEENPENNY VOLUMES.

9 **Wide, Wide World.**
 ELIZABETH WETHERELL.
10 **Queechy.**
 ELIZABETH WETHERELL.
11 **Melbourne House.**
 ELIZABETH WETHERELL.

12 **Drayton Hall.**
 ALICE GRAY.
13 **Say and Seal.**
 ELIZABETH WETHERELL.

Cloth Gilt, price 1s. 6d. each.

Picciola.
Father Clement.
Willow Brook.
Dunallan.

From Jest to Earnest.
Stepping Heavenward.
Sceptres and Crowns; and
 The Flag of Truce.

Cloth Gilt, price 2s. each.

Wide, Wide World.
Melbourne House.

Queechy.
Say and Seal.

Bedford Street, Strand.

Frederick Warne and Co., Publishers,

THE COMPANION LIBRARY.

TWO SHILLING VOLUMES.

00 **Sylvester Sound.**
    H. COCKTON.
26 **The Love Match.**
    H. COCKTON.
29 **Walter Goring.**
    ANNIE THOMAS.
30 **On Guard.**
    ANNIE THOMAS.
36 **Love's Conflict.**
    FLORENCE MARRYAT.
37 **Woman against Woman.**
    FLORENCE MARRYAT.
38 **Gerald Estcourt.**
    FLORENCE MARRYAT.
39 **Too Good for Him.**
    FLORENCE MARRYAT.
41 **Nelly Brooke.**
    FLORENCE MARRYAT.
43 **The Sutherlands.**
    SIDNEY S. HARRIS.
44 **Rutledge.**
    SIDNEY S. HARRIS.
45 **Christine.**
    SIDNEY S. HARRIS.
46 **Lord Lynn's Wife.**
    SYDNEY S. HARRIS.
47 **Petronel.**
    FLORENCE MARRYAT.
48 **Veronique.**
    FLORENCE MARRYAT.
49 **Her Lord and Master.**
    FLORENCE MARRYAT.
50 **Prey of the Gods.**
    FLORENCE MARRYAT.
51 **The Girls of Faversham.**
    FLORENCE MARRYAT.
52 **The Season Ticket.**
    SAM SLICK.
53 **The Mummy.**
    MRS. LOUDON.
54 **The Chasseur d'Afrique.**
    COL. WALMSLEY.
55 **The Life Guardsman.**
    COL. WALMSLEY.
56 **Branksome Dene**
    COL. WALMSLEY.
57 **George Geith.**
    MRS. J. H. RIDDELL.
58 **Austin Friars.**
    MRS. J. H. RIDDELL.
59 **Too Much Alone.**
    MRS. J. H. RIDDELL.
60 **The Rich Husband.**
    MRS. J. H. RIDDELL.
61 **Maxwell Drewitt.**
    MRS. J. H. RIDDELL.
62 **Far above Rubies.**
    MRS. J. H. RIDDELL.
63 **A Life's Assize.**
    MRS. J. H. RIDDELL.
64 **The World and the Church.**
    MRS. J. H. RIDDELL.
65 **City and Suburb.**
    MRS. J. H. RIDDELL.
66 **Phemie Keller.**
    MRS. J. H. RIDDELL.
67 **Race for Wealth.**
    MRS. J. H. RIDDELL.
68 **Mad Dumaresq.**
    FLORENCE MARRYAT.
69 **No Intentions.**
    FLORENCE MARRYAT.
70 **Bright Morning.**
    MARIA M. GRANT.
71 **Victor Lescar.**
    MARIA M. GRANT.
72 **Artiste.**
    MARIA M. GRANT.
73 **Aunt Prue's Railway Journey.**
    MRS. GASCOIGNE.
74 **Home, Sweet Home.**
    MRS. J. H. RIDDELL.
75 **Joy after Sorrow.**
    MRS. J. H. RIDDELL.
76 **The Earl's Promise.**
    MRS. J. H. RIDDELL.
77 **Mortomley's Estate.**
    MRS. J. H. RIDDELL.
78 **Frank Sinclair's Wife.**
    MRS. J. H. RIDDELL.
79 **The Ruling Passion.**
    MRS. J. H. RIDDELL.
80 **My First Love and My Last Love.**
    MRS. J. H. RIDDELL.

Bedford Street, Strand.

Frederick Warne and Co., Publishers,

CHEAP, POPULAR, AND ORIGINAL.

WARNE'S USEFUL BOOKS
For the Country or the Fireside.

In fcap. 8vo, boards, price 1s. each, with Practical Illustrations.

Poultry: An Original Guide to their Breeding, Rearing, Feeding, and Exhibiting. By E. WATTS.
NOTICE.—This completely New Poultry Book is the only one the Author has fully written: all others bearing her name being only edited by her, and much anterior to this volume.

Vegetables; and How to Grow Them. A Guide to the Kitchen Garden. By E. WATTS.
"This manual will be found extremely useful by those who have gardens which they cultivate themselves."—*Dispatch.*

Flowers and the Flower Garden. With Instructions on the Culture of Ornamental Trees, Shrubs, &c. By E. WATTS.
"The book contains just the information necessary for those persons who wish to become growers of flowers."—*Weekly Times.*

The Orchard and Fruit Garden. Its Culture and Produce. By E. WATTS.
"Readable and instructive books of practical teaching."—*Church Standard.*

A Fern Book for Everybody. Containing all the British Ferns, with the Foreign Species suitable for a Fernery. With numerous Illustrations and Tinted Plates. By M. C. COOKE.
"The cheapest and most excellent little work on the subject we have met with."—*The Rock.*

English Wild Flowers, to be found by the Wayside, Fields, Hedgerows, Rivers, Moorlands, Meadows, Mountains, and Sea-shore. By J. T. BURGESS. With Practical Illustrations.
"This seasonable little book will be welcomed by the thousands of summer tourists who take delight in contemplating the beauties of country fields and lanes where wild flowers abound."—*News of the World.*

One Thousand Objects for the Microscope. By M. C. COOKE. With 500 Figures Illustrated.
"A valuable and entertaining companion."—*Sunday Times.*
"The thousand objects are all clearly described."—*Public Opinion.*

The Gentleman's Art of Dressing with Economy. By a Lounger at the Clubs.

Bedford Street, Strand.

Frederick Warne and Co., Publishers,

WARNE'S USEFUL BOOKS,—*continued.*
Fcap. 8vo, 1s. *each, boards, with Practical Illustrations.*

The Common Shells of the Sea-Shore. By the Rev. J. G. WOOD.
"The book is so copiously illustrated, that it is impossible to find a shell which cannot be identified by reference to the engravings."—*Vide* PREFACE.
"It would be difficult to select a more pleasant sea-side companion than this."—*Observer.*

The Common Sea-Weeds of the British Coast and Channel Islands. With some Insight into the Microscopic Beauties of their Structure and Fructification. By Mrs. L. LANE CLARKE. With Original Plates printed in Tinted Litho.
"This portable, cheap little manual will serve as an admirable introduction to the study of sea-weeds."—*Field.*

Angling, and How to Angle. A Practical Guide to Bottom-Fishing, Trolling, Spinning, Fly-Fishing, and Sea-Fishing. By J. T. BURGESS. Illustrated.
"An excellent little volume, and full of advice the angler will treasure."—*Sunday Times.*
"A practical and handy guide."—*Spectator.*

Bird-Keeping. A Practical Guide for the Management of Cage Birds. By the Author of "Home Pets." Illustrated and containing general Descriptions of Birds of Prey, Owls, Crow Tribe, Thrush Tribe, Warblers, Titmice, Wagtails, Pipits, Larks, Finches, Parrots, Coves, &c.
"We have tested the directions given for the treatment of canaries, linnets, &c., and having found them most useful, can heartily recommend the book to others."—*Illustrated Times.*

The Money Market. What it Is, What it Does, and How it is Managed.

The Companion Letter Writer. A Guide to Correspondence, with Commercial Forms, &c.

Modern Spiritualism. By JOHN H. MASKELYNE.

The Modern Gymnast. By CHARLES SPENCER.

Ladies' and Gentlemen's Model Letter Writer. With Household and Commercial Forms.

The Pig: Its Origin and Varieties. By H. D. RICHARDSON.

The Dog: Its Varieties, and Management in Health and Disease.

The Sheep: Ditto   ditto.
Cattle: Ditto   ditto.
Uniform with the above, price 1s. 6d.

The Horse: Its Varieties, and Management in Health and Disease.

Bedford Street, Strand.

Frederick Warne & Co., Publishers,

THE CHANDOS CLASSICS.
A SERIES OF STANDARD WORKS IN POETRY, BIOGRAPHY, &c.

In large crown 8vo, price 1s. 6d. each, stiff wrapper, or cloth gilt, 2s.

Hood's Poetical Works. With Life, &c.
Mrs. Hemans' Poetical Works. With Memoir, &c.
Longfellow's Poetical Works. Including Original Poems.
Byron's Poetical Works. With Explanatory Notes.
Scott's Poetical Works. With Notes.
Arabian Nights (The) Entertainments. New Edition.
Burns' Poetical Works. With Memoir, &c.
Moore's Poetical Works. With Explanatory Notes, &c.
Wordsworth's Poetical Works.
Milton's Poetical Works. With Memoir, &c.
Cowper's Poetical Works. Complete Edition.
Eliza Cook's Poems. Complete Edition.
Legendary Ballads of England and Scotland.
Johnson's Lives of the Poets.
Dante: Vision. Translated by CARY.
Dr. Syntax's Three Tours. With Coloured Portrait.
Butler's Hudibras. With Notes by ZACHARY GREY.
Shakspeare, Complete. Including Life, Glossary, &c.
Lockhart's Spanish Ballads (Historical and Romantic), and Southey's Romance of the Cid.
Hallam's Constitutional History of England, Edward I. to Henry VII.; and De Lolme's Constitution of England.
Twice Told Tales. By NATHANIEL HAWTHORNE.
History of the Saracens. By GIBBON and OCKLEY.
Robinson Crusoe. Unabridged. Many Woodcuts by GRISET.
Swiss Family Robinson. Including Sequel. With Illustrations.
Pope's Iliad. With FLAXMAN's Illustrations.
Pope's Odyssey. With FLAXMAN's Illustrations.
Keats' Poetical Works.
Coleridge's Poetical Works.
Scott's Lives of Eminent Novelists and Dramatists.
Scott's Essays on Chivalry, Romance, and the Drama
Shelley's Poetical Works.
Campbell's Poetical Works.
Andersen's (Hans) Fairy Tales.
Grimm's Fairy Tales.

Bedford Street, Strand.

Frederick Warne & Co., Publishers,

WARNE'S NOTABLE NOVELS.
COMPLETE EDITIONS.

In large crown 8vo., price 6d. each, picture covers.

1. Scottish Chiefs. By JANE PORTER.
2. Uncle Tom. By Mrs. H. BEECHER STOWE.
3. St. Clair of the Isles. By ELIZABETH HELME.
4. Children of the Abbey. By E. M. ROCHE.
5. The Lamplighter. By MISS CUMMINS.
6. Mabel Vaughan. ,, ,,
7. Thaddeus of Warsaw. By JANE PORTER.
8. Howards of Glen Luna.
9. The Old English Baron. The Castle of Otranto.
10. The Hungarian Brothers. By Miss PORTER.
11. Marriage. By Miss FERRIER.
12. Inheritance. ,,
13. Destiny. ,,
14. The King's Own. By CAPT. MARRYAT.
15. The Naval Officer. ,,
16. Newton Forster. ,,
17. Richelieu. By G. P. R. JAMES.
18. Darnley. ,,
19. Philip Augustus. ,,
20. Tom Cringle's Log. By MICHAEL SCOTT.

WARNE'S "NOVELISTS'" LIBRARY.

In large 8vo., picture boards, price 1s. 6d. each; or cloth gilt, 2s. each.

Vol. 1. Captain Marryatt, containing—"The King's Own," "The Naval Officer," and "Newton Forster."
,, 2. Miss Porter, &c., containing—"The Scottish Chiefs," "St. Clair of the Isles," and "Hungarian Brothers."
,, 3. E. M. Roche, &c., containing—"Children of the Abbey," "Thaddeus of Warsaw," and "Old English Baron."
,, 4. Miss Cummins, &c., containing—"The Lamplighter," "Mabel Vaughan," and "Howards of Glen Luna."
,, 5. Miss Ferrier, containing—"Marriage," "Inheritance," and "Destiny."
,, 6. G. P. R. James, containing—"Richelieu," "Darnley," and "Philip Augustus."

Bedford Street, Strand.

ROWLANDS' MACASSAR OIL possesses extraordinary properties for promoting the growth, restoring, preserving, and beautifying the Human Hair. Price 3s. 6d.—7s.—10s. 6d. and 21s. per bottle.

ROWLANDS' KALYDOR realizes a healthy and clear Complexion, and a softness and delicacy of Skin. Price 4s. 6d. and 8s. 6d. per bottle.

ROWLANDS' ODONTO imparts a Pearl like Whiteness to the Teeth, eradicates Tartar and Spots of Incipient Decay, strengthens the Gums, and gives a pleasing fragrance to the Breath. Price 2s. 9d. per box.

Sold by *Chemists and Perfumers.* *** *Ask for "Rowlands'" Articles.*

KEATING'S COUGH LOZENGES.

Medical Testimony states that unquestionably no remedy exists which is so certain in its effects.

ASTHMA, WINTER COUGH, DIFFICULTY OF BREATHING,

Alike yield to its influence. One Lozenge alone gives the sufferer relief. Many remedies are sold that contain Morphia, Opium, or violent drugs, but KEATING'S COUGH LOZENGES are composed only of the purest simple drugs, and the most delicate in health may use them with perfect confidence. KEATING'S COUGH LOZENGES are prepared by THOMAS KEATING, St. Paul's Churchyard, and sold by all Chemists, in Boxes, 1s. 1½d. and 2s. 9d. each.

WILLIAM CHURTON & SON,
HOSIERS,
SHIRT MAKERS,
LADIES' UNDERCLOTHING,
AND
GENERAL OUTFITTERS,
91 & 92, OXFORD STREET, LONDON, W.

DISCOUNT FOR READY MONEY.

J. ALLISON & CO.

SILK MERCERS, LINEN DRAPERS, &c.

REGENT HOUSE,

238, 240 & 242, REGENT STREET,

AND, CARRIAGE ENTRANCE,

26 & 27, ARGYLL STREET, LONDON, W.

DEPARTMENTS.

Silks, Irish Poplins, and Velvets.

Fancy Dresses.—*Grenadines, Chambray Gauzes, Muslins, Cambrics, Camlets and Mixed Fabrics.*

Ribbons *in every variety, for Bonnets, Trimming, Sashes, and Belts.*

Lace.—*Honiton, Brussels, Cluny, Maltese, British, and Irish, and every article of taste for the completeness of Ladies' attire, in accordance with the caprice of fashion.*

Ball and Evening Dresses, *in Tulle, Tarlatan, and Grenadine.*

Gloves and Hosiery *of every description.*

Shawls.—*Cashmere, Paisley, and Scotch Plaids.*

Mantles.—*Velvet, Cloth, Cashmere, Silk, Trimmed and Embroidered, Waterproof, Opera, and Evening.*

Ready-made Linen.—*Underclothing, Children's Dresses, Baby Linen, Petticoats, Dressing Gowns, and Jackets.*

Dress Trimmings *in all the Novelties as produced.*

Haberdashery *in the greatest variety and only the best make. Flowers, Head Dresses, Wreaths, Feathers, Fancy Handkerchiefs, Neck Ties, Fans, Bags, Jet Ornaments, and Articles of Paris. Parasols, Umbrellas, Fancy Aprons, and Furs.*

HOUSEHOLD AND FAMILY LINEN, FLANNELS, COUNTER-PANES, BLANKETS, QUILTS, AND LONG CLOTHS.

| **FAMILY MOURNING IN ALL ITS BRANCHES.** |

An Efficient Staff of Dressmakers and Milliners to execute all orders with punctuality and despatch.

*** Close at Two o'clock on Saturdays all the year round.

BANKERS: SIR SAMUEL SCOTT AND COMPANY.

www.ingramcontent.com/pod-product-compliance
Lightning Source LLC
Chambersburg PA
CBHW020106010526
44115CB00008B/716